HCSB New Testament VBS Edition

This Book Belongs to

Printed in the United States of America

ISBN: 1-4158-6865-4
Item Number: 005266467

The Bible is not like any other book.

The Bible is special because it is God's Word. Many years ago, God told Bible writers what He wanted us to know, and they wrote down God's words for us to read, learn from, and obey. The words you read in the Bible today are the same ones that God told people to write thousands of years ago. Every word in the Bible is absolutely true because it comes from God.

The Bible can help you . . .

- know God better
- know Jesus as your Savior and Lord
- learn how God wants you to live
- find answers to your questions
- find encouragement
- and much, much more!

Reading the Bible can be an exciting adventure!

Turn to page vi and find the "Day 1" devotion. This is a great place to start reading and learning from the Bible!

"Devotions" is a word that many people use when they talk about reading and studying the Bible. Devotions make it easy to read the Bible and pray every day. They can help you understand and learn from what you read in the Bible. The devotions in this Bible will help you connect more deeply with faith, love, trust, others, and life. So what are you waiting for? Jump in there and make a connection with God's words!

Here's how it works.

Start with Day 1. Even though there are two devotions on each page, read only one per day. Read the verse first. Think about what the verse means. Then read the rest of the devotion. Did it help you better understand what God wants you to learn from that verse? Is there anything you need to change about yourself after reading God's words in the Bible? There are journal pages at the end of each week of devotions. Write down your thoughts or even a prayer as you work through the devotion each day.

Take a few moments to pray.

Prayer is both talking and listening to God. You won't be able to hear God's voice with your ears, but the Holy Spirit will help you know what God wants to tell you. Each day, tell God what you learned from the Bible. Ask God to forgive you for the ways you sinned today. Ask for His help to do things differently tomorrow. Be still and quiet for a moment. God may help you to think of some other things to talk to Him about.

Once you make it a habit, reading your Bible and praying every day will be easy.

DAY 1

Now faith is the reality of what is hoped for, the proof of what is not seen.
Hebrews 11:1

What is Faith?

Maybe you've heard the word *faith*, but you don't really know what it means. Think about it this way … faith is what allows you to plop down in a chair without thinking about whether the legs might break and send you tumbling to the ground. Because of faith you don't worry about whether gravity will continue to work and keep you from floating into outer space.

Hebrews 11:1 gives a good definition of faith. God wants you to believe in Him and His Son Jesus, even though you can't see them. Faith is being sure of something you cannot see, hear, or feel.

Challenge: Make a case file of proof that Jesus exists. List your proof (Bible verses, things that have happened in your life, and so forth) so that you will be reminded of your faith in Jesus and can share that proof with others.

DAY 2

So faith comes from what is heard, and what is heard comes through the message about Christ.
Romans 10:17

An Important Message

The area between 40th and 53rd Streets and 6th and 9th Avenues in New York City is known as Times Square, named for The New York Times® newspaper whose headquarters were once located there. Times Square has become a famous tourist attraction, mostly because of the hundreds of lighted and digitally animated billboards displayed on every building. The signs capture the attention of everyone who walks by. Billboards advertise new Broadway musicals, the latest electronics, new television shows, and a variety of other products.

God doesn't need animated billboards to share His message with people. You can find God's important message anytime in His Word, the Bible.

Challenge: Make a billboard to share an important message about Jesus with people in your family. Post it in a place where others will see it.

DAY 3

As Big As a Mustard Seed

> He told them, "For I assure you: If you have faith the size of a mustard seed, you will tell this mountain, 'Move from here to there,' and it will move. Nothing will be impossible for you."
> *Matthew 17:20*

I once spent an hour looking for a doll that was as small as the top of a pin for my daughter. I needed a flashlight and a magnifying glass to find it in the bottom of her toy box. I had never seen anything so small. What is the smallest thing you can think of? A mustard seed is only about $1/20$ of an inch big. It was something small that people in Bible times were familiar with.

Jesus told people that if they had even a tiny bit of faith, God would do incredible things. Nothing is impossible for God. So, how's your faith? Do you trust God to take care of you? To help you? To work things out? He will!

Challenge: It can be difficult to believe in something you cannot see. Sing the song "By Faith" that you learned in VBS. Ask God to help you trust Him more.

DAY 4

Is Your Faith Showing?

> I assure you: The one who believes in Me will also do the works that I do. And he will do even greater works than these, because I am going to the Father.
> *John 14:12*

"I'll be right back. I am going over to ask Kendra to come to church with me Wednesday night," Jess told her friend.

"Why would you want to hang out with Kendra?" asked Kate. "She's always acting so weird."

"Because I don't think she knows about Jesus," replied Jess. "I want her to know who Jesus is and what He did for her."

When you believe in Jesus you will want to show it. You'll want to do the things He did. The Holy Spirit can help you treat people the way Jesus would. Just follow Jesus' example and ask for His help.

Challenge: Think about these words from a song you learned in VBS: "Live it out, shout it loud. Show the world what love's about." What is one way you can show someone this week what you believe about Jesus?

DAY 5

I testified to both Jews and Greeks about repentance toward God and faith in our Lord Jesus.
Acts 20:21

If You Know It, Show It

Paul had studied hard all of his life so that he could be an important Jewish leader. Paul knew what he believed and was willing to do whatever it took to defend what he believed. When he heard that Jesus' followers were telling people that Jesus was the Messiah, Paul set out to stop them. Paul *persecuted* Christians, helping to arrest or hurt them.

But everything changed the day Paul met Jesus. Paul began preaching about Jesus. Even when he was arrested, beaten, shipwrecked, and bitten by a snake, Paul took every opportunity to tell people what he believed about Jesus. Does your life show what you believe?

Challenge: Paul shared what he knew about Jesus with everyone he met. What do you know about Jesus? Write down five things you could tell someone about Jesus.

DAY 6

But now, apart from the law, God's righteousness has been revealed—attested by the Law and the Prophets—that is, God's righteousness through faith in Jesus Christ, to all who believe.
Romans 3:21-22

The Faith of Four Friends

There was a man who couldn't walk. He was paralyzed, but his friends knew that if they could get him to Jesus, he would be healed. The men carried their friend on a mat to the house where Jesus was staying. But the house was so crowded with people, they couldn't get anywhere near Jesus. So the men carried their friend to the roof of the house. They cut a hole in the roof and lowered their friend down until he was lying in front of Jesus. Jesus told the paralyzed man that he would be healed because of the faith of his friends.

Do you have faith (believe) that Jesus can do anything? Do you believe that Jesus is the Son of God?

Challenge: You can read more of this story by looking up Mark 2:1-12 in your Bible. Underline the verse that tells about the faith of the four friends.

DAY 7

We love because He first loved us. *1 John 4:19*

Love Makes the World Go Round

It seems that everyone has something to say on the subject of love. Benjamin Franklin said that if you want to be loved, you should love and be lovable. William Shakespeare said, "They do not love that do not show their love." In other words, if you don't show love to others, you won't get any in return. Someone once said, "No three words have greater power than 'I love you.'"

What do you think about love? John summed it up in one sentence. We wouldn't know anything about love if God hadn't loved us first.

Challenge: Choose one way to show love to someone in your family today. Explain to your family member that you love him or her because God loved you first.

DAY 8

If you love Me, you will keep My commandments. *John 14:15*

What Will You Do for Love?

"Let's stop at the Mini Mart for candy on our way to baseball practice," Mike suggested.

"I can't," replied Nick. "My parents don't want me to go there without an adult."

"But they won't know. You don't have to do what they say when they're not around," said Mike.

"I love my parents," said Nick. "I want to do what they tell me."

Your parents set rules because they love you. You obey your parents' rules because you love them. If you love Jesus, you will want to follow His commandments, too. That means you'll want to do the things He says are right and good.

Challenge: Can you list any of Jesus' commandments? Look up these verses for help: Matthew 5:43-44; Matthew 7:1; Matthew 22:37-39.

N.Y.
NEW YORK PIZZA
PIZZA

DAY 9

But God proves His own love for us in that while we were still sinners Christ died for us!
Romans 5:8

Just the Way You Are

Jackie grew up in an orphanage, but was still a happy child with lots of friends. But there was one thing Jackie wanted more than anything—a family of her own. When one friend after another got adopted, Jackie decided she would have to work harder to earn the love of a family. She dressed up and tried to impress people with her good behavior, but still wasn't adopted. "Don't try so hard," said her counselor. "Just be yourself." Jackie followed the advice and she was soon adopted by a wonderful family.

You can never be good enough to earn God's love. But God loves you just the way you are! He loves you so much that He sent Jesus to pay the penalty for your sin.

Challenge: Write a thank-you note to God. Tell Him how much His love means to you.

DAY 10

We know that all things work together for the good of those who love God: those who are called according to His purpose.
Romans 8:28

It's All Good!

Ever have one of those days when nothing seems to go right? You stub your toe getting out of bed, burn your toast, get toothpaste down the front of your new shirt, and things just get worse from there. Those are the days you feel like crawling back into bed and pulling the covers over your head. Everybody has bad days from time to time. Did you know that God cares about your bad days? He loves you and He wants the best for you. Romans 8:28 can remind you that God works out even the worst situations to bring glory to Himself.

The next time you are having a bad day, pray about it. Ask God to make something good out of even the worst day and then thank Him for doing it!

Challenge: Write a story about the worst day ever. Read the story and Romans 8:28 to a friend.

DAY 11

He said to him, "Love the Lord your God with all your heart, with all your soul, and with all your mind." *Matthew 22:37*

Don't Hold Back

What does it mean to love someone with all your heart, all your soul, and all your mind? The heart is the center, or most important part, of your body. Some people also talk about the heart when they're talking about feelings. The soul is your spiritual side. The mind is what causes you to think and understand. To love someone with your whole heart, soul, and mind means putting all your focus and attention on that person. It means loving that person with everything you've got and not holding back anything for yourself.

Do you love God with all your heart, soul, and mind? Don't hold back! He deserves all your love.

Challenge: Write the words *heart*, *soul*, and *mind* on a wide rubber band. Wear it as a wristband to remember to love God completely.

DAY 12

But whoever keeps His word, truly in him the love of God is perfected. This is how we know we are in Him. *1 John 2:5*

Prove It

I have several ways that I let my family members know how much I love them. Sometimes I tell them in words how much they mean to me. Sometimes I tell other people about the wonderful things my family members do. Sometimes I do nice things for the people in my family. When you love God you want Him to know it. You want to do what pleases Him.

1 John 2:5 says that a person who keeps the commandments in the Bible proves His love for God. Do you prove your love for God by obeying Him? When you do what the Bible says, you please God. You can find many things Jesus said to do in the first four books of the New Testament.

Challenge: Some Bibles print the words Jesus spoke in red letters. If you have a red-letter Bible at home ask a parent to look at it with you. Together read some of the words Jesus spoke.

DAY 13

"For God loved the world in this way: He gave His One and Only Son, so that everyone who believes in Him will not perish but have eternal life."
John 3:16

Symbol of Love

Tiffany & Co.® in New York City is one of the world's most famous jewelry stores. Every piece of jewelry from Tiffany's comes in a turquoise package tied with a white ribbon. Some women think that a diamond ring in a Tiffany's box is the best way for someone to say, "I love you." But Jesus showed how much He loved us in a different way. He did it by dying on a cross to pay the penalty for our sins.

When you see a cross are you reminded of what Jesus did to pay for your sins? He died for you so that you could live forever in heaven with God. Now that is real love!

Challenge: Draw the outline of a cross on a sheet of paper. On the cross list things that God has done to show His love for you.

DAY 14

For the wages of sin is death, but the gift of God is eternal life in Christ Jesus our Lord.
Romans 6:23

How Much?

In 1626, Peter Minuet of the Dutch West Indies Company bought Manhattan Island from the Manhattan Indians. The island was purchased for the New Amsterdam Fort and settlement. Minuet bought the island for the price of 60 guilders. That's about one thousand American dollars—not a very high price for what we know as New York City today.

The Bible says that the price we should pay because of our sin is death. That is a high price! But Jesus paid the price for us when He died on the cross. Receiving God's free gift is as easy as A, B, C. (See page 380 to read more about the ABCs of Becoming a Christian.)

Challenge: Use the word *SOLD* to make an acrostic of actions you can do to show Jesus your gratitude. Thank Jesus for the high price He was willing to pay for your life.

DAY 15

Jesus told him, "I am the way, the truth, and the life. No one comes to the Father except through Me." *John 14:6*

One Way

The Borough of Manhattan in New York City is an island surrounded by the Hudson, East, and Harlem rivers. If you want to drive into Manhattan you will have to take one of the eight bridges that go over the water or one of the four tunnels that go under the water. That can get a little confusing, so many people use a map or a GPS to find the best route. And, when one route is clogged with traffic, travelers have other choices.

There may be many ways to get to and from New York City, but there is only one way to spend eternity with God—it's by trusting in His Son, Jesus, as your Savior.

Challenge: Make a map showing how to get to your church. Give the map and an invitation to church to a friend.

DAY 16

This [Jesus] is the stone despised by you builders, who has become the cornerstone. There is salvation in no one else, for there is no other name under heaven given to people by which we must be saved. *Acts 4:11-12*

A Firm Foundation

For years, the Empire State Building in New York City was the world's tallest building. It is a very famous building. It has 102 floors; 73 elevators; 1,860 steps; and 6,500 windows! The skyscraper took 1 year and 45 days to build and cost over $40 million! The cornerstone was laid on September 17, 1930 and the building was completed on May 1, 1931.

A cornerstone is the first stone that is set in place for a building. It is the foundation for the outside walls and determines how all the other bricks will be laid. That makes it the most important. Acts 4:11-12 calls Jesus *the cornerstone*. His death on the cross paid the penalty for everyone's sin and His resurrection gives us something to celebrate. Doing what He taught in the Bible will help you make Him the most important person in your life. That's what having a strong foundation means.

Challenge: Use markers or paint to write *Jesus* on a smooth stone. Keep it in a place where you will be reminded that Jesus is the most important thing in life.

N.Y.
NEW YORK PIZZA
PIZZA

DAY 17

But to all who did receive Him, He gave them the right to be children of God, to those who believe in His name.
John 1:12

A New Beginning

During the years 1892-1954 about 16 million people came to America looking for freedom and a better life. For 12 million of those immigrants, the first stop was Ellis Island in New York Bay. As the steamships chugged into the harbor, the first thing people saw was a symbol of their new beginning and new hope for the future—the Statue of Liberty. The immigrants were interviewed at Ellis Island and then given the right to be American citizens.

Sometimes Christians are called "children of God" because they love and obey God like children with their parents. When you believe in God's Son, Jesus, you can have a new beginning and new hope for the future. Then you will have the right to be called a child of God, too.

Challenge: Ask a parent to help you take a virtual tour of Ellis Island by visiting *www.history.com/interactives/ellis-island*. Write your own definition of "freedom."

DAY 18

"Your heart must not be troubled. Believe in God; believe also in Me.
John 14:1

You Better Believe It!

Ripley's Believe It or Not® is located in Times Square, New York City. Ripley's is known for unbelievable exhibits and all kinds of amazing things. You can see attractions there such as Angelica the fire eater; Jellyboy the sword-swallowing clown; the world's largest collection of shrunken heads; a Mercedes carved out of wood; and a two-headed calf.

You can't believe everything you see or hear, but you can absolutely believe what you read in the Bible about God's Son, Jesus. What would you tell a friend about Him?

Challenge: Make your own "Believe It or Not" exhibit. Draw pictures and write captions that tell about the unbelievable things Jesus has done.

DAY 19

> Go, therefore, and make disciples of all nations, baptizing them in the name of the Father and of the Son and of the Holy Spirit, teaching them to observe everything I have commanded you.
> *Matthew 28:19-20a*

Commissioned

The USS Intrepid is a US Navy aircraft carrier that was built during World War II. The ship was commissioned in August 1943. She fought in several battles and eventually became an antisubmarine carrier. After a long military career, the Intrepid was decommissioned in March 1974, but she hasn't stopped working. Today the famous ship sits on the Hudson River in New York, as the home of the Intrepid Sea, Air & Space Museum.

To be *commissioned* means to be sent out for a special purpose. Matthew 28:19-20 is sometimes called the Great Commission because Jesus spoke these words to His disciples and sent them out for a special assignment. What job did He give them? This is your assignment, too!

Challenge: Print the words of the Great Commission on a poster for your room. It will help you remember the special job God has given you.

DAY 20

> As it is written: How welcome are the feet of those who announce the gospel of good things!
> *Romans 10:15*

A Living Example

Annie Armstrong loved Jesus and wanted others to love Him, too. Annie decided that the best way to help people know who Jesus is and what He had done was to support missionaries who served throughout the world. Annie began writing letters. In 1893 alone she typed or handwrote close to 18,000 letters. Annie also prayed for missionaries, collected offerings for missionaries, and gathered food and clothing to distribute to the needy. Today Southern Baptists collect a special missions offering each spring that is named after Annie Armstrong.

Because of her love for Jesus, Annie Armstrong spent a lifetime supporting missions around the world. How can you help people know about Jesus?

Challenge: Write a letter or send an e-mail to a missionary who works in your city or state. Ask a leader in your church to help you find contact information for missionaries.

DAY 21

"But you will receive power when the Holy Spirit has come upon you, and you will be My witnesses in Jerusalem, in all Judea and Samaria, and to the ends of the earth."
Acts 1:8

Tell It Everywhere

Jesus' words in Acts 1:8 are the last recorded words He spoke to His disciples before going to heaven. That makes this verse an important message not only for the disciples, but for all people. Jesus told the disciples to tell people everywhere about Him—the people in the city of Jerusalem; the people in the region surrounding the city, known as Judea; and the people in Samaria, which was the unfriendly next-door neighbor of Judea. In other words, Jesus commanded Christians to go to EVERY area of the world to tell people about Him.

Read the verse again. This time replace "Jerusalem" with the name of your city. Instead of "Judea," fill in the name of your state, and replace "Samaria" with the name of another state or country.

Challenge: Ask a parent to help you send an e-mail to a friend. Tell your friend what you know about Jesus.

DAY 22

He commanded us to preach to the people, and to solemnly testify that He is the One appointed by God to be the Judge of the living and the dead.
Acts 10:42

Tell What You Know

Wall Street is a famous street in lower Manhattan. Its most famous building is the New York Stock Exchange. There, brokers buy and sell stocks to make money for customers. A giant digital sign shows stock brokers and investors how much the stocks are worth. The values are always changing, so stock brokers have to pay attention to the board.

There is no giant digital sign to tell people about Jesus. That's our job! People can learn about Jesus when you tell them what you know. In fact, that's what Jesus told us to do. He commanded us to tell others about the things Jesus did and that Jesus is God's Son.

Challenge: Make a list of the things you can tell someone about Jesus. Pray and ask God to help you say the right words.

DAY 23

But Peter and John answered them, "Whether it's right in the sight of God [for us] to listen to you rather than to God, you decide; for we are unable to stop speaking about what we have seen and heard."
Acts 4:19-20

Gotta Talk About It

On June 13, 1927 four million people lined the streets of New York City for the wildest ticker tape parade in the city's history. The parade was held in honor of Charles Lindbergh who had just made the first solo airplane trip across the Atlantic Ocean. Lindbergh's New York to Paris flight was big news. For the first time, people saw what was possible with air travel. Until this point most people still thought the idea of traveling by plane was crazy!

Peter and John saw Jesus perform miracles, teach thousands, and even saw Him after He had risen from the dead. That's a bigger deal than the first flight across the ocean! They couldn't stop talking about the things they had witnessed. And their news is still exciting for people today.

Challenge: Make a "good news flier." Write a message about Jesus on a sheet of paper, fold the paper into an airplane, and fly it to a friend.

DAY 24

Then He said to His disciples, "The harvest is abundant, but the workers are few. Therefore, pray to the Lord of the harvest to send out workers into His harvest.
Matthew 9:37-38

Share the Good News

When Taylor Field moved to New York in 1986 to work at Graffiti Church, he knew God had placed him there to tell people about Jesus. Graffiti Church is located in one of the most underprivileged, drug-riddled communities in New York's lower east side. Over the years Taylor has found creative ways to share the good news about Jesus. Sometimes he gives sandwiches to hungry people. Other times he gives clothing to the homeless. No matter how he does it, Taylor Field tells people the good news of Jesus.

Will you be one of God's workers? Will you help others to know the things you know about Jesus? There are so many people who are ready to hear that Jesus loves them and died to pay the penalty for their sin.

Challenge: Make cookies and take them to a neighbor who needs to know about Jesus.

N.Y.
NEW YORK PIZZA
PIZZA

DAY 25

Be alert, stand firm in the faith, be brave and strong. Your every [action] must be done with love. *1 Corinthians 16:13-14*

Follow the Directions

Most people who live in New York City use public transportation to get around. The subway is a great way to explore the city. Traveling on the subway is easy if you remember a few things: 1) Read the subway map. Each subway line is marked in a different color. 2) Sit or stand near other people for safety. 3) Don't be afraid to ask for help. 4) Stay alert and listen for the announcement of your stop.

The Bible gives tips for traveling safely through life, too. This verse lists some of them. Read your Bible and know what you believe and why (stay alert). People may try to convince you it isn't true, but be strong (stand firm in the faith). Ask questions when you need help or don't understand something. Always show love to people, even when they don't believe the same as you.

Challenge: Write the words *Live it out!* on a strip of paper and place it in your Bible at this verse. Ask God to help you live out what the verse says to do.

DAY 26

"I give you a new commandment: love one another. Just as I have loved you, you must also love one another." *John 13:34*

The Perfect Model

John Roebling wanted to build a bridge across the East River to connect New York and Brooklyn. His design was unlike any suspension bridge of that day and many wondered if it would even work. It took years of drawing designs and making plans before the bridge was built. John Roebling died in an accident just as the building began. His son, Washington Roebling, took over as chief engineer of the project. Washington knew what to do because his father had taught him everything he needed to know about building bridges.

Jesus is the best teacher. By example He taught people everything they need to know about showing love to others. How are you following Jesus' example?

Challenge: Write down as many ways as you can think of that Jesus showed love to others. Circle the ones that you can do. Then choose one to do today.

DAY 27

Even a young man is known by his actions – by whether his behavior is pure and upright.
Proverbs 20:11

The Right Reputation

Three times a year citizens of the Charlotte-Mecklenburg area of North Carolina are invited to nominate kids for a special award. "Do the Right Thing" awards recently went to 12 outstanding kids including: SaVion, a 9-year-old, who volunteered to help a classmate in a wheelchair; Lily, an 11-year-old who helped keep fellow classmates safe when she bravely told a teacher about a student hiding a knife; and 9-year-old Logan who started a race team to raise money to fight breast cancer.

What you do affects what people think about you. Do you have a reputation for doing the right thing? Choosing to do what is right shows God and other people that you love Him.

Challenge: Tell your parent about one right choice you made today.

DAY 28

"Do not judge, and you will not be judged. Do not condemn, and you will not be condemned. Forgive, and you will be forgiven.
Luke 6:37

Follow the Leader

To *judge* someone is to form an opinion about him or make a conclusion about him. To *condemn* means to show strong disapproval towards someone or declare that the person is guilty of a crime. Jesus taught us not to judge or condemn others, but instead to treat others the way we want to be treated.

According to Luke 6:37, we should forgive people for the wrong things they have done to us. That isn't always easy to do. But Jesus did it. He even forgave the people who nailed Him on a cross to die. Will you follow His example? Will you forgive others, even when it's hard?

Challenge: Is there someone you need to forgive or ask for their forgiveness? Don't wait another minute. Go and talk to that person today.

DAY 29

I am able to do all things through Him who strengthens me. *Philippians 4:13*

Take My Life

Frances Havergal was an English poet who lived in the 1800s. Throughout her life Frances had poor health, but she didn't let that stop her from serving God. In her poem "Take My Life and Let It Be," which later became a hymn, Frances asked God to use her hands, her feet, her voice, her money, and her lips for His service. And she meant it! She even gave her entire jewelry collection as an offering to her church's missionary organization.

Frances relied on God for strength so she could serve Him in any way she could. Philippians 4:13 promises that God will give you strength to do the things He wants you to do. Can you think of some ways to use your hands, feet, voice, and lips to serve God?

Challenge: Find the words to "Take My Life and Let It Be" online or in a hymnal. Read it together with your parent.

DAY 30

Now this is His command: that we believe in the name of His Son Jesus Christ, and love one another as He commanded us. *1 John 3:23*

It Isn't Always Easy

Ryan came into the house and plopped down in a chair.

"What's wrong?" Ryan's mom asked.

"I hate Logan Wallace!" Ryan said angrily.

"But the Bible says you should love everyone," replied his mother.

Ryan signed, "How can I love someone who says he's going to beat me up everyday?"

"I know it isn't easy," said Ryan's mom, "But Jesus did it. He was treated very badly by some people and He still loved them enough to die for them."

Challenge: Think of someone who is difficult for you to love. Ask God to help you show love to that person, beginning this week.

N.Y.
NEW YORK PIZZA
PIZZA

The New Testament

Matthew

The Genealogy of Jesus Christ

1 The historical record[a] of Jesus Christ, the Son of David, the Son of Abraham:

From Abraham to David

2 Abraham fathered[b] Isaac,
Isaac fathered Jacob,
Jacob fathered Judah and his brothers,
3 Judah fathered Perez and Zerah
by Tamar,
Perez fathered Hezron,
Hezron fathered Aram,
4 Aram fathered Aminadab,
Aminadab fathered Nahshon,
Nahshon fathered Salmon,
5 Salmon fathered Boaz by Rahab,
Boaz fathered Obed by Ruth,
Obed fathered Jesse,
6 and Jesse fathered King David.

From David to the Babylonian Exile

Then[c] David fathered Solomon by Uriah's wife,

7 Solomon fathered Rehoboam,
Rehoboam fathered Abijah,
Abijah fathered Asa,[d]
8 Asa[d] fathered Jehoshaphat,
Jehoshaphat fathered Joram,
Joram fathered Uzziah,
9 Uzziah fathered Jotham,
Jotham fathered Ahaz,
Ahaz fathered Hezekiah,
10 Hezekiah fathered Manasseh,
Manasseh fathered Amon,[e]
Amon[e] fathered Josiah,
11 and Josiah fathered Jechoniah
and his brothers
at the time of the exile to Babylon.

From the Exile to the Messiah

12 Then after the exile to Babylon
Jechoniah fathered Salathiel,
Salathiel fathered Zerubbabel,
13 Zerubbabel fathered Abiud,
Abiud fathered Eliakim,
Eliakim fathered Azor,
14 Azor fathered Zadok,
Zadok fathered Achim,
Achim fathered Eliud,
15 Eliud fathered Eleazar,
Eleazar fathered Matthan,
Matthan fathered Jacob,
16 and Jacob fathered Joseph the husband
of Mary,
who gave birth to[f] Jesus who is called
the •Messiah.

17 So all the generations from Abraham to David were 14 generations; and from David until the exile to Babylon, 14 generations; and from the exile to Babylon until the Messiah, 14 generations.

The Nativity of the Messiah

18 The birth of Jesus Christ came about this way: After His mother Mary had been •engaged to Joseph, it was discovered before they came together that she was pregnant by the Holy Spirit.
19 So her husband Joseph, being a righteous man, and not wanting to disgrace her publicly, decided to divorce her secretly.

20 But after he had considered these things, an angel of the Lord suddenly appeared to him in a dream, saying, "Joseph, son of David, don't be afraid to take Mary as your wife, because what has been conceived in her is by the Holy Spirit.
21 She will give birth to a son, and you are to name Him Jesus,[g] because He will save His people from their sins."

22 Now all this took place to fulfill what was spoken by the Lord through the prophet:

23 **See, the virgin will become pregnant**
and give birth to a son,
and they will
name Him Immanuel,[h]

which is translated "God is with us."

24 When Joseph got up from sleeping, he did as the Lord's angel had commanded him. He married her
25 but did not know her intimately until she gave birth to a son.[i] And he named Him Jesus.

[a]**1:1** Or *The book of the genealogy* [b]**1:2** In vv. 2–16 either a son, as here, or a later descendant, as in v. 8 [c]**1:6** Other mss add *King* [d]**1:7,8** Other mss read *Asaph* [e]**1:10** Other mss read *Amos* [f]**1:16** Lit *Mary, from whom was born* [g]**1:21** *Jesus* is the Gk form of the Hb name "Joshua," which = "The Lord saves" or "Yahweh saves." [h]**1:23** Is 7:14 [i]**1:25** Other mss read *to her firstborn son*

Wise Men Seek the King

2 After Jesus was born in Bethlehem of Judea in the days of King •Herod, •wise men from the east arrived unexpectedly in Jerusalem, 2 saying, "Where is He who has been born King of the Jews? For we saw His star in the east[a] and have come to worship Him."[b]

3 When King Herod heard this, he was deeply disturbed, and all Jerusalem with him. 4 So he assembled all the •chief priests and •scribes of the people and asked them where the •Messiah would be born.

5 "In Bethlehem of Judea," they told him, "because this is what was written by the prophet:

> 6 **And you, Bethlehem,** in the land
> **of Judah,**
> are by no means **least**
> **among the leaders of Judah:**
> **because out of you will come**
> **a leader**
> **who will shepherd My people**
> **Israel.**"[c]

7 Then Herod secretly summoned the wise men and asked them the exact time the star appeared. 8 He sent them to Bethlehem and said, "Go and search carefully for the child. When you find Him, report back to me so that I too can go and worship Him."[d]

9 After hearing the king, they went on their way. And there it was—the star they had seen in the east![e] It led them until it came and stopped above the place where the child was. 10 When they saw the star, they were overjoyed beyond measure. 11 Entering the house, they saw the child with Mary His mother, and falling to their knees, they worshiped Him.[f] Then they opened their treasures and presented Him with gifts: gold, frankincense, and myrrh. 12 And being warned in a dream not to go back to Herod, they returned to their own country by another route.

The Flight into Egypt

13 After they were gone, an angel of the Lord suddenly appeared to Joseph in a dream, saying, "Get up! Take the child and His mother, flee to Egypt, and stay there until I tell you. For Herod is about to search for the child to destroy Him." 14 So he got up, took the child and His mother during the night, and escaped to Egypt. 15 He stayed there until Herod's death, so that what was spoken by the Lord through the prophet might be fulfilled: **Out of Egypt I called My Son.**[g]

The Massacre of the Innocents

16 Then Herod, when he saw that he had been outwitted by the wise men, flew into a rage. He gave orders to massacre all the male children in and around Bethlehem who were two years[h] old and under, in keeping with the time he had learned from the wise men. 17 Then what was spoken through Jeremiah the prophet was fulfilled:

> 18 **A voice was heard in Ramah,**
> **weeping,[i] and great mourning,**
> **Rachel weeping for her children;**
> **and she refused to be consoled,**
> **because they were no more.**[j]

The Holy Family in Nazareth

19 After Herod died, an angel of the Lord suddenly appeared in a dream to Joseph in Egypt, 20 saying, "Get up! Take the child and His mother and go to the land of Israel, because those who sought the child's life are dead." 21 So he got up, took the child and His mother, and entered the land of Israel. 22 But when he heard that Archelaus[k] was ruling over Judea in place of his father Herod, he was afraid to go there. And being warned in a dream, he withdrew to the region of Galilee. 23 Then he went and settled in a town called Nazareth to fulfill what was spoken through the prophets, that He will be called a •Nazarene.

The Messiah's Herald

3 In those days John the Baptist came, preaching in the Wilderness of Judea 2 and saying, "Repent, because the kingdom of heaven has come near!" 3 For he is the one spoken of through the prophet Isaiah, who said:

> **A voice of one crying out**
> **in the wilderness:**
> **"Prepare the way for the Lord;**
> **make His paths straight!"**[l]

4 John himself had a camel-hair garment with a leather belt around his waist, and his

[a]**2:2** Or *star at its rising* [b]**2:2** Or *to pay Him homage* [c]**2:6** Mc 5:2 [d]**2:8** Or *and pay Him homage* [e]**2:9** Or *star . . . at its rising* [f]**2:11** Or *they paid Him homage* [g]**2:15** Hs 11:1 [h]**2:16** Lit *were from two years* [i]**2:18** Other mss read *Ramah, lamentation, and weeping,* [j]**2:18** Jr 31:15 [k]**2:22** A son of Herod the Great who ruled a portion of his father's kingdom 4 B.C.–A.D. 6 [l]**3:3** Is 40:3

food was locusts and wild honey. 5 Then ⌊people from⌋ Jerusalem, all Judea, and all the vicinity of the Jordan were flocking to him, 6 and they were baptized by him in the Jordan River as they confessed their sins.

7 When he saw many of the •Pharisees and •Sadducees coming to the place of his baptism,[a] he said to them, "Brood of vipers! Who warned you to flee from the coming wrath? 8 Therefore produce fruit consistent with[b] repentance. 9 And don't presume to say to yourselves, 'We have Abraham as our father.' For I tell you that God is able to raise up children for Abraham from these stones! 10 Even now the ax is ready to strike the root of the trees! Therefore every tree that doesn't produce good fruit will be cut down and thrown into the fire.

11 "I baptize you with[c] water for repentance,[d] but the One who is coming after me is more powerful than I. I am not worthy to take off[e] His sandals. He Himself will baptize you with[c] the Holy Spirit and fire. 12 His winnowing shovel[f] is in His hand, and He will clear His threshing floor and gather His wheat into the barn. But the chaff He will burn up with fire that never goes out."

The Baptism of Jesus

13 Then Jesus came from Galilee to John at the Jordan, to be baptized by him. 14 But John tried to stop Him, saying, "I need to be baptized by You, and yet You come to me?"

15 Jesus answered him, "Allow it for now, because this is the way for us to fulfill all righteousness." Then he allowed Him ⌊to be baptized⌋.

16 After Jesus was baptized, He went up immediately from the water. The heavens suddenly opened for Him,[g] and He saw the Spirit of God descending like a dove and coming down on Him. 17 And there came a voice from heaven:

> This is My beloved Son.
> I take delight in Him!

The Temptation of Jesus

4 Then Jesus was led up by the Spirit into the wilderness to be tempted by the Devil. 2 After He had fasted 40 days and 40 nights, He was hungry. 3 Then the tempter approached Him and said, "If You are the Son of God, tell these stones to become bread."

4 But He answered, "It is written:

> **Man must not live on bread alone**
> **but on every word that comes**
> **from the mouth of God."**[h]

5 Then the Devil took Him to the holy city,[i] had Him stand on the pinnacle of the temple, 6 and said to Him, "If You are the Son of God, throw Yourself down. For it is written:

> **He will give His angels orders**
> **concerning you, and**
> **they will support you**
> **with their hands**
> **so that you will not strike**
> **your foot against a stone."**[j]

7 Jesus told him, "It is also written: **Do not test the Lord your God."**[k]

8 Again, the Devil took Him to a very high mountain and showed Him all the kingdoms of the world and their splendor. 9 And he said to Him, "I will give You all these things if You will fall down and worship me."[l]

10 Then Jesus told him, "Go away,[m] Satan! For it is written:

> **Worship the Lord your God,**
> **and serve only Him."**[n]

11 Then the Devil left Him, and immediately angels came and began to serve Him.

Ministry in Galilee

12 When He heard that John had been arrested, He withdrew into Galilee. 13 He left Nazareth behind and went to live in Capernaum by the sea, in the region of Zebulun and Naphtali. 14 This was to fulfill what was spoken through the prophet Isaiah:

> 15 **Land of Zebulun and land**
> **of Naphtali,**
> **along the sea road,**
> **beyond the Jordan,**
> **Galilee of the Gentiles!**
> 16 **The people who live in darkness**
> **have seen a great light,**
> **and for those living**
> **in the shadowland of death,**
> **light has dawned.**[o] [p]

[a]**3:7** Lit *to his baptism* [b]**3:8** Lit *fruit worthy of* [c]**3:11** Or *in* [d]**3:11** Baptism was the means by which repentance was expressed publicly. [e]**3:11** Or *to carry* [f]**3:12** A wooden farm implement used to toss threshed grain into the wind so the lighter chaff would blow away and separate from the heavier grain [g]**3:16** Other mss omit *for Him* [h]**4:4** Dt 8:3 [i]**4:5** Jerusalem [j]**4:6** Ps 91:11–12 [k]**4:7** Dt 6:16 [l]**4:9** Or *and pay me homage* [m]**4:10** Other mss read *Get behind Me* [n]**4:10** Dt 6:13 [o]**4:16** Lit *dawned on them* [p]**4:15–16** Is 9:1–2

17 From then on Jesus began to preach, "Repent, because the kingdom of heaven has come near!"

The First Disciples

18 As He was walking along the Sea of Galilee, He saw two brothers, Simon, who was called Peter, and his brother Andrew. They were casting a net into the sea, since they were fishermen. 19 "Follow Me," He told them, "and I will make you fish for[a] people!" 20 Immediately they left their nets and followed Him.

21 Going on from there, He saw two other brothers, James the son of Zebedee, and his brother John. They were in a boat with Zebedee their father, mending their nets, and He called them. 22 Immediately they left the boat and their father and followed Him.

Teaching, Preaching, and Healing

23 Jesus was going all over Galilee, teaching in their •synagogues, preaching the good news of the kingdom, and healing every[b] disease and sickness among the people. 24 Then the news about Him spread throughout Syria. So they brought to Him all those who were afflicted, those suffering from various diseases and intense pains, the demon-possessed, the epileptics, and the paralytics. And He healed them. 25 Large crowds followed Him from Galilee, •Decapolis, Jerusalem, Judea, and beyond the Jordan.

The Sermon on the Mount

5 When He saw the crowds, He went up on the mountain, and after He sat down, His disciples came to Him. 2 Then[c] He began to teach them, saying:

The Beatitudes

3 "Blessed are the poor in spirit,
because the kingdom of heaven
is theirs.
4 Blessed are those who mourn,
because they will be comforted.
5 Blessed are the gentle,
because they will inherit the earth.
6 Blessed are those who hunger
and thirst for righteousness,
because they will be filled.
7 Blessed are the merciful,
because they will be shown mercy.
8 Blessed are the pure in heart,
because they will see God.
9 Blessed are the peacemakers,
because they will be called
sons of God.
10 Blessed are those who are persecuted
for righteousness,
because the kingdom of heaven
is theirs.

11 "Blessed are you when they insult you and persecute you and falsely say every kind of evil against you because of Me. 12 Be glad and rejoice, because your reward is great in heaven. For that is how they persecuted the prophets who were before you.

Believers Are Salt and Light

13 "You are the salt of the earth. But if the salt should lose its taste, how can it be made salty? It's no longer good for anything but to be thrown out and trampled on by men.

14 "You are the light of the world. A city situated on a hill cannot be hidden. 15 No one lights a lamp and puts it under a basket,[d] but rather on a lampstand, and it gives light for all who are in the house. 16 In the same way, let your light shine[e] before men, so that they may see your good works and give glory to your Father in heaven.

Christ Fulfills the Law

17 "Don't assume that I came to destroy the Law or the Prophets. I did not come to destroy but to fulfill. 18 For •I assure you: Until heaven and earth pass away, not the smallest letter[f] or one stroke of a letter will pass from the law until all things are accomplished. 19 Therefore, whoever breaks one of the least of these commandments and teaches people to do so will be called least in the kingdom of heaven. But whoever practices and teaches ⌊these commandments⌋ will be called great in the kingdom of heaven. 20 For I tell you, unless your righteousness surpasses that of the •scribes and •Pharisees, you will never enter the kingdom of heaven.

Murder Begins in the Heart

21 "You have heard that it was said to our ancestors,[g] **Do not murder**,[h] and whoever murders will be subject to judgment. 22 But I

[a] **4:19** Lit *you fishers of* [b] **4:23** Or *every kind of* [c] **5:2** Lit *Then opening His mouth* [d] **5:15** A large basket used to measure grain [e] **5:16** Or *way, your light must shine* [f] **5:18** Or *not one iota*; *iota* is the *smallest letter* of the Gk alphabet. [g] **5:21** Lit *to the ancients* [h] **5:21** Ex 20:13; Dt 5:17

tell you, everyone who is angry with his
brother[a] will be subject to judgment. And whoever says to his brother, 'Fool!'[b] will be subject
to the •Sanhedrin. But whoever says, 'You
moron!' will be subject to •hellfire.[c] 23 So if you
are offering your gift on the altar, and there you
remember that your brother has something
against you, 24 leave your gift there in front of
the altar. First go and be reconciled with your
brother, and then come and offer your gift.
25 Reach a settlement quickly with your adversary while you're on the way with him, or your
adversary will hand you over to the judge, the
judge to[d] the officer, and you will be thrown
into prison. 26 I assure you: You will never get
out of there until you have paid the last
penny![e]

Adultery in the Heart

27 "You have heard that it was said, **Do not
commit adultery.**[f] 28 But I tell you, everyone
who looks at a woman to lust for her has
already committed adultery with her in his
heart. 29 If your right eye •causes you to sin,
gouge it out and throw it away. For it is better
that you lose one of the parts of your body than
for your whole body to be thrown into hell.
30 And if your right hand causes you to sin, cut
it off and throw it away. For it is better that you
lose one of the parts of your body than for your
whole body to go into hell!

Divorce Practices Censured

31 "It was also said, **Whoever divorces his
wife must give her a written notice of
divorce.**[g] 32 But I tell you, everyone who
divorces his wife, except in a case of sexual
immorality,[h] causes her to commit adultery.
And whoever marries a divorced woman commits adultery.

Tell the Truth

33 "Again, you have heard that it was said to
our ancestors,[i] **You must not break your oath,
but you must keep your oaths to the Lord.**[j]
34 But I tell you, don't take an oath at all: either
by heaven, because it is God's throne; 35 or by
the earth, because it is His footstool; or by
Jerusalem, because it is the city of the great
King. 36 Neither should you swear by your
head, because you cannot make a single hair
white or black. 37 But let your word 'yes' be
'yes,' and your 'no' be 'no.'[k] Anything more
than this is from the evil one.

Go the Second Mile

38 "You have heard that it was said, **An eye
for an eye and a tooth for a tooth.**[l] 39 But I tell
you, don't resist[m] an evildoer. On the contrary,
if anyone slaps you on your right cheek, turn
the other to him also. 40 As for the one who
wants to sue you and take away your shirt,[n] let
him have your coat[o] as well. 41 And if anyone
forces[p] you to go one mile, go with him two.
42 Give to the one who asks you, and don't turn
away from the one who wants to borrow from
you.

Love Your Enemies

43 "You have heard that it was said, **Love
your neighbor**[q] and hate your enemy. 44 But I
tell you, love your enemies[r] and pray for those
who[s] persecute you, 45 so that you may be[t]
sons of your Father in heaven. For He causes
His sun to rise on the evil and the good, and
sends rain on the righteous and the unrighteous. 46 For if you love those who love you,
what reward will you have? Don't even the tax
collectors do the same? 47 And if you greet only
your brothers, what are you doing out of the
ordinary?[u] Don't even the Gentiles[v] do the
same? 48 Be perfect, therefore, as your heavenly Father is perfect.

How to Give

6 "Be careful not to practice your righteousness[w] in front of people, to be seen
by them. Otherwise, you will have no reward
from your Father in heaven. 2 So whenever
you give to the poor, don't sound a trumpet
before you, as the hypocrites do in the •syna-
gogues and on the streets, to be applauded by
people. •I assure you: They've got their
reward! 3 But when you give to the poor, don't

[a]**5:22** Other mss add *without a cause* [b]**5:22** Lit *Raca*, an Aram term of abuse similar to "airhead" [c]**5:22** Lit *the gehenna of fire* [d]**5:25** Other mss read *judge will hand you over to* [e]**5:26** Lit *quadrans*, the smallest and least valuable Roman coin, worth 1/64 of a daily wage [f]**5:27** Ex 20:14; Dt 5:18 [g]**5:31** Dt 24:1 [h]**5:32** Gk *porneia* = fornication, or possibly a violation of Jewish marriage laws [i]**5:33** Lit *to the ancients* [j]**5:33** Lv 19:12; Nm 30:2; Dt 23:21 [k]**5:37** Say what you mean and mean what you say [l]**5:38** Ex 21:24; Lv 24:20; Dt 19:21 [m]**5:39** Or *don't set yourself against*, or *don't retaliate against* [n]**5:40** Lit *tunic* = inner garment [o]**5:40** Lit *robe*, or *garment* = outer garment [p]**5:41** Roman soldiers could require people to carry loads for them. [q]**5:43** Lv 19:18 [r]**5:44** Other mss add *bless those who curse you, do good to those who hate you,* [s]**5:44** Other mss add *mistreat you and* [t]**5:45** Or *may become*, or *may show yourselves to be* [u]**5:47** Lit *doing more*, or *doing that is superior* [v]**5:47** Other mss read *tax collectors* [w]**6:1** Other mss read *charitable giving*

let your left hand know what your right hand
is doing, 4 so that your giving may be in secret.
And your Father who sees in secret will
reward you.[a]

How to Pray

5 "Whenever you pray, you must not be
like the hypocrites, because they love to pray
standing in the synagogues and on the street
corners to be seen by people. I assure you:
They've got their reward! 6 But when you
pray, go into your private room, shut your
door, and pray to your Father who is in secret.
And your Father who sees in secret will
reward you.[b] 7 When you pray, don't babble
like the idolaters,[c] since they imagine they'll
be heard for their many words. 8 Don't be like
them, because your Father knows the things
you need before you ask Him.

The Model Prayer

9 "Therefore, you should pray like this:

Our Father in heaven,
Your name be honored as holy.
10 Your kingdom come.
Your will be done
on earth as it is in heaven.
11 Give us today our daily bread.[d]
12 And forgive us our debts,
as we also have forgiven
our debtors.
13 And do not bring us
into[e] temptation,
but deliver us from the evil one.[f]
[For Yours is the kingdom
and the power
and the glory forever. •Amen.][g]

14 "For if you forgive people their wrongdoing,[h] your heavenly Father will forgive you as
well. 15 But if you don't forgive people,[i] your
Father will not forgive your wrong- doing.[h]

How to Fast

16 "Whenever you fast, don't be sad-faced
like the hypocrites. For they make their faces
unattractive[j] so their fasting is obvious to people. I assure you: They've got their reward!
17 But when you fast, put oil on your head, and
wash your face, 18 so that you don't show your
fasting to people but to your Father who is in
secret. And your Father who sees in secret will
reward you.[b]

God and Possessions

19 "Don't collect for yourselves treasures[k]
on earth, where moth and rust destroy and
where thieves break in and steal. 20 But collect
for yourselves treasures in heaven, where neither moth nor rust destroys, and where thieves
don't break in and steal. 21 For where your treasure is, there your heart will be also.
22 "The eye is the lamp of the body. If your
eye is good, your whole body will be full of
light. 23 But if your eye is bad, your whole
body will be full of darkness. So if the light
within you is darkness—how deep is that
darkness!
24 "No one can be a slave of two masters,
since either he will hate one and love the other,
or be devoted to one and despise the other. You
cannot be slaves of God and of money.

The Cure for Anxiety

25 "This is why I tell you: Don't worry
about your life, what you will eat or what you
will drink; or about your body, what you will
wear. Isn't life more than food and the body
more than clothing? 26 Look at the birds of the
sky: they don't sow or reap or gather into
barns, yet your heavenly Father feeds them.
Aren't you worth more than they? 27 Can any
of you add a single •cubit to his height[l] by
worrying? 28 And why do you worry about
clothes? Learn how the wildflowers of the
field grow: they don't labor or spin thread.
29 Yet I tell you that not even Solomon in all
his splendor was adorned like one of these!
30 If that's how God clothes the grass of the
field, which is here today and thrown into the
furnace tomorrow, won't He do much more
for you—you of little faith? 31 So don't worry,
saying, 'What will we eat?' or 'What will we
drink?' or 'What will we wear?' 32 For the
idolaters[c] eagerly seek all these things, and
your heavenly Father knows that you need
them. 33 But seek first the kingdom of God[m]
and His righteousness, and all these things
will be provided for you. 34 Therefore don't
worry about tomorrow, because tomorrow
will worry about itself. Each day has enough
trouble of its own.

[a]**6:4** Other mss read *will Himself reward you openly* [b]**6:6,18** Other mss add *openly* [c]**6:7,32** Or *Gentiles*, or *nations*, or *heathen*, or *pagans* [d]**6:11** Or *our necessary bread*, or *our bread for tomorrow* [e]**6:13** Or *do not cause us to come into* [f]**6:13** Or *from evil* [g]**6:13** Other mss omit bracketed text [h]**6:14,15** Or *trespasses* [i]**6:15** Other mss add *their wrongdoing* [j]**6:16** Or *unrecognizable*, or *disfigured* [k]**6:19** Or *valuables* [l]**6:27** Or *add one moment to his life-span* [m]**6:33** Other mss omit *of God*

Do Not Judge

7 "Do not judge, so that you won't be judged. 2 For with the judgment you use,[a] you will be judged, and with the measure you use,[b] it will be measured to you. 3 Why do you look at the speck in your brother's eye but don't notice the log in your own eye? 4 Or how can you say to your brother, 'Let me take the speck out of your eye,' and look, there's a log in your eye? 5 Hypocrite! First take the log out of your eye, and then you will see clearly to take the speck out of your brother's eye. 6 Don't give what is holy to dogs or toss your pearls before pigs, or they will trample them with their feet, turn, and tear you to pieces.

Keep Asking, Searching, Knocking

7 "Keep asking,[c] and it will be given to you. Keep searching,[d] and you will find. Keep knocking,[e] and the door[f] will be opened to you. 8 For everyone who asks receives, and the one who searches finds, and to the one who knocks, the door[g] will be opened. 9 What man among you, if his son asks him for bread, will give him a stone? 10 Or if he asks for a fish, will give him a snake? 11 If you then, who are evil, know how to give good gifts to your children, how much more will your Father in heaven give good things to those who ask Him! 12 Therefore, whatever you want others to do for you, do also the same for them—this is the Law and the Prophets.[h]

Entering the Kingdom

13 "Enter through the narrow gate. For the gate is wide and the road is broad that leads to destruction, and there are many who go through it. 14 How narrow is the gate and difficult the road that leads to life, and few find it.

15 "Beware of false prophets who come to you in sheep's clothing but inwardly are ravaging wolves. 16 You'll recognize them by their fruit. Are grapes gathered from thornbushes or figs from thistles? 17 In the same way, every good tree produces good fruit, but a bad tree produces bad fruit. 18 A good tree can't produce bad fruit; neither can a bad tree produce good fruit. 19 Every tree that doesn't produce good fruit is cut down and thrown into the fire. 20 So you'll recognize them by their fruit.

21 "Not everyone who says to Me, 'Lord, Lord!' will enter the kingdom of heaven, but ⌊only⌋ the one who does the will of My Father in heaven. 22 On that day many will say to Me, 'Lord, Lord, didn't we prophesy in Your name, drive out demons in Your name, and do many miracles in Your name?' 23 Then I will announce to them, 'I never knew you! **Depart from Me, you lawbreakers!**'[i] [j]

The Two Foundations

24 "Therefore, everyone who hears these words of Mine and acts on them will be like a sensible man who built his house on the rock. 25 The rain fell, the rivers rose, and the winds blew and pounded that house. Yet it didn't collapse, because its foundation was on the rock. 26 But everyone who hears these words of Mine and doesn't act on them will be like a foolish man who built his house on the sand. 27 The rain fell, the rivers rose, the winds blew and pounded that house, and it collapsed. And its collapse was great!"

28 When Jesus had finished this sermon,[k] the crowds were astonished at His teaching, 29 because He was teaching them like one who had authority, and not like their •scribes.

Cleansing a Leper

8 When He came down from the mountain, large crowds followed Him. 2 Right away a man with a serious skin disease came up and knelt before Him, saying, "Lord, if You are willing, You can make me clean."[l]

3 Reaching out His hand He touched him, saying, "I am willing; be made clean." Immediately his disease was healed.[m] 4 Then Jesus told him, "See that you don't tell anyone; but go, show yourself to the priest, and offer the gift that Moses prescribed, as a testimony to them."

A Centurion's Faith

5 When He entered Capernaum, a •centurion came to Him, pleading with Him, 6 "Lord, my servant is lying at home paralyzed, in terrible agony!"

7 "I will come and heal him," He told him.

8 "Lord," the centurion replied, "I am not worthy to have You come under my roof. But only say the word, and my servant will be cured. 9 For I too am a man under authority, having soldiers under my command.[n] I say to

[a]**7:2** Lit *you judge* [b]**7:2** Lit *you measure* [c]**7:7** Or *Ask* [d]**7:7** Or *Search* [e]**7:7** Or *Knock* [f]**7:7** Lit *and it* [g]**7:8** Lit *knocks, it* [h]**7:12** When capitalized, *the Law and the Prophets* = the OT [i]**7:23** Lit *you who work lawlessness* [j]**7:23** Ps 6:8 [k]**7:28** Lit *had ended these words* [l]**8:2** In these vv. 2–3, *clean* includes healing, ceremonial purification, return to fellowship with people, and worship in the temple; Lv 14:1–32. [m]**8:3** Lit *cleansed* [n]**8:9** Lit *under me*

this one, 'Go!' and he goes; and to another,
'Come!' and he comes; and to my slave, 'Do
this!' and he does it."
10 Hearing this, Jesus was amazed and said
to those following Him, "•I assure you: I have
not found anyone in Israel with so great a faith!
11 I tell you that many will come from east and
west, and recline at the table with Abraham,
Isaac, and Jacob in the kingdom of heaven.
12 But the sons of the kingdom will be thrown
into the outer darkness. In that place there will
be weeping and gnashing of teeth." 13 Then
Jesus told the centurion, "Go. As you have
believed, let it be done for you." And his servant was cured that very moment.[a]

Healings at Capernaum

14 When Jesus went into Peter's house, He
saw his mother-in-law lying in bed with a fever.
15 So He touched her hand, and the fever left
her. Then she got up and began to serve Him.
16 When evening came, they brought to Him
many who were demon-possessed. He drove
out the spirits with a word and healed all who
were sick, 17 so that what was spoken through
the prophet Isaiah might be fulfilled:

> **He Himself took our weaknesses**
> **and carried our diseases.**[b]

Following Jesus

18 When Jesus saw large crowds[c] around
Him, He gave the order to go to the other side
⌊of the sea⌋.[d] 19 A •scribe approached Him and
said, "Teacher, I will follow You wherever You
go!"
20 Jesus told him, "Foxes have dens and
birds of the sky have nests, but the Son of Man
has no place to lay His head."
21 "Lord," another of His disciples said,
"first let me go bury my father."[e]
22 But Jesus told him, "Follow Me, and let
the dead bury their own dead."

Wind and Wave Obey the Master

23 As He got into the[f] boat, His disciples followed Him. 24 Suddenly, a violent storm arose
on the sea, so that the boat was being swamped
by the waves. But He was sleeping. 25 So the
disciples came and woke Him up, saying,
"Lord, save ⌊us⌋! We're going to die!"
26 But He said to them, "Why are you fearful, you of little faith?" Then He got up and
rebuked the winds and the sea. And there was
a great calm.
27 The men were amazed and asked, "What
kind of man is this?—even the winds and the
sea obey Him!"

Demons Driven Out by the Master

28 When He had come to the other side, to
the region of the Gadarenes,[g] two demon-possessed men met Him as they came out of the
tombs. They were so violent that no one could
pass that way. 29 Suddenly they shouted, "What
do You have to do with us,[h] [i] Son of God? Have
You come here to torment us before the time?"
30 Now a long way off from them, a large
herd of pigs was feeding. 31 "If You drive us
out," the demons begged Him, "send us into
the herd of pigs."
32 "Go!" He told them. So when they had
come out, they entered the pigs. And suddenly the whole herd rushed down the steep
bank into the sea and perished in the water.
33 Then the men who tended them fled.
They went into the city and reported everything—especially what had happened to
those who were demon-possessed. 34 At
that, the whole town went out to meet Jesus.
When they saw Him, they begged Him to
leave their region.

The Son of Man Forgives and Heals

9 So He got into a boat, crossed over, and
came to His own town. 2 Just then some
men[j] brought to Him a paralytic lying on a
stretcher. Seeing their faith, Jesus told the paralytic, "Have courage, son, your sins are forgiven."
3 At this, some of the •scribes said among
themselves, "He's blaspheming!"
4 But perceiving their thoughts, Jesus said,
"Why are you thinking evil things in your
hearts?[k] 5 For which is easier: to say, 'Your sins
are forgiven,' or to say, 'Get up and walk'? 6 But
so you may know that the •Son of Man has
authority on earth to forgive sins"—then He
told the paralytic, "Get up, pick up your
stretcher, and go home." 7 And he got up and
went home. 8 When the crowds saw this, they
were awestruck[l] [m] and gave glory to God who
had given such authority to men.

[a]**8:13** Or *that hour*; lit *very hour* [b]**8:17** Is 53:4 [c]**8:18** Other mss read *saw a crowd* [d]**8:18** Sea of Galilee [e]**8:21** Not necessarily meaning his father was already dead [f]**8:23** Other mss read *to a* [g]**8:28** Other mss read *Gergesenes* [h]**8:29** Other mss add *Jesus* [i]**8:29** Lit *What to us and to You* [j]**9:2** Lit *then they* [k]**9:4** Or *minds* [l]**9:8** Other mss read *amazed* [m]**9:8** Lit *afraid*

The Call of Matthew

9 As Jesus went on from there, He saw a man named Matthew sitting at the tax office, and He said to him, "Follow Me!" So he got up and followed Him.

10 While He was reclining at the table in the house, many tax collectors and sinners came as guests to eat[a] with Jesus and His disciples. 11 When the •Pharisees saw this, they asked His disciples, "Why does your Teacher eat with tax collectors and sinners?"

12 But when He heard this, He said, "Those who are well don't need a doctor, but the sick do. 13 Go and learn what this means: **I desire mercy and not sacrifice.**[b] For I didn't come to call the righteous, but sinners."[c]

A Question about Fasting

14 Then John's disciples came to Him, saying, "Why do we and the Pharisees fast often, but Your disciples do not fast?"

15 Jesus said to them, "Can the wedding guests[d] be sad while the groom is with them? The days will come when the groom will be taken away from them, and then they will fast. 16 No one patches an old garment with unshrunk cloth, because the patch pulls away from the garment and makes the tear worse. 17 And no one puts[e] new wine into old wineskins. Otherwise, the skins burst, the wine spills out, and the skins are ruined. But they put new wine into fresh wineskins, and both are preserved."

A Girl Restored and a Woman Healed

18 As He was telling them these things, suddenly one of the leaders[f] came and knelt down before Him, saying, "My daughter is near death,[g] but come and lay Your hand on her, and she will live." 19 So Jesus and His disciples got up and followed him.

20 Just then, a woman who had suffered from bleeding for 12 years approached from behind and touched the •tassel on His robe, 21 for she said to herself, "If I can just touch His robe, I'll be made well!"[h]

22 But Jesus turned and saw her. "Have courage, daughter," He said. "Your faith has made you well."[i] And the woman was made well from that moment.[j]

23 When Jesus came to the leader's house, He saw the flute players and a crowd lamenting loudly. 24 "Leave," He said, "because the girl isn't dead, but sleeping." And they started laughing at Him. 25 But when the crowd had been put outside, He went in and took her by the hand, and the girl got up. 26 And this news spread throughout that whole area.

Healing the Blind

27 As Jesus went on from there, two blind men followed Him, shouting, "Have mercy on us, Son of David!"

28 When He entered the house, the blind men approached Him, and Jesus said to them, "Do you believe that I can do this?"

"Yes, Lord," they answered Him.

29 Then He touched their eyes, saying, "Let it be done for you according to your faith!" 30 And their eyes were opened. Then Jesus warned them sternly, "Be sure that no one finds out!"[k] 31 But they went out and spread the news about Him throughout that whole area.

Driving Out a Demon

32 Just as they were going out, a demon-possessed man who was unable to speak was brought to Him. 33 When the demon had been driven out, the man[l] spoke. And the crowds were amazed, saying, "Nothing like this has ever been seen in Israel!"

34 But the Pharisees said, "He drives out demons by the ruler of the demons!"

The Lord of the Harvest

35 Then Jesus went to all the towns and villages, teaching in their •synagogues, preaching the good news of the kingdom, and healing every[m] disease and every sickness.[n] 36 When He saw the crowds, He felt compassion for them, because they were weary and worn out, like sheep without a shepherd. 37 Then He said to His disciples, "The harvest is abundant, but the workers are few. 38 Therefore, pray to the Lord of the harvest to send out workers into His harvest."

Commissioning the Twelve

10 Summoning His 12 disciples, He gave them authority over unclean[o] spirits, to

[a]**9:10** Lit *came, they were reclining* (at the table); at important meals the custom was to recline on a mat at a low table and lean on the left elbow. [b]**9:13** Hs 6:6 [c]**9:13** Other mss add *to repentance* [d]**9:15** Lit *the sons of the bridal chamber* [e]**9:17** Lit *And they do not put* [f]**9:18** A leader of a synagogue; Mk 5:22 [g]**9:18** Lit *daughter has now come to the end* [h]**9:21** Or *be delivered* [i]**9:22** Or *has saved you* [j]**9:22** Lit *hour* [k]**9:30** Lit *no one knows* [l]**9:33** Lit *the man who was unable to speak* [m]**9:35** Or *every kind of* [n]**9:35** Other mss add *among the people* [o]**10:1** Morally or ceremonially impure

drive them out and to heal every[a] disease and
sickness. 2 These are the names of the 12 apostles:

First, Simon, who is called Peter,
and Andrew his brother;
James the son of Zebedee,
and John his brother;
3 Philip and Bartholomew;[b]
Thomas and Matthew
the tax collector;
James the son of Alphaeus,
and Thaddaeus;[c]
4 Simon the Zealot,[d] and Judas Iscariot,[e]
who also betrayed Him.

5 Jesus sent out these 12 after giving them
instructions: "Don't take the road leading to
other nations, and don't enter any •Samaritan
town. 6 Instead, go to the lost sheep of the
house of Israel. 7 As you go, announce this:
'The kingdom of heaven has come near.' 8 Heal
the sick, raise the dead, cleanse those with skin
diseases, drive out demons. You have received
free of charge; give free of charge. 9 Don't take
along gold, silver, or copper for your money-
belts. 10 Don't take a traveling bag for the road,
or an extra shirt, sandals, or a walking stick, for
the worker is worthy of his food.

11 "When you enter any town or village,
find out who is worthy, and stay there until you
leave. 12 Greet a household when you enter it,
13 and if the household is worthy, let your
peace be on it. But if it is unworthy, let your
peace return to you. 14 If anyone will not welcome you or listen to your words, shake the
dust off your feet when you leave that house or
town. 15 •I assure you: It will be more tolerable
on the day of judgment for the land of Sodom
and Gomorrah than for that town.

Persecutions Predicted

16 "Look, I'm sending you out like sheep
among wolves. Therefore be as shrewd as ser-
pents and as harmless as doves. 17 Because people will hand you over to sanhedrins[f] and flog
you in their •synagogues, beware of them.
18 You will even be brought before governors
and kings because of Me, to bear witness to
them and to the nations. 19 But when they
hand you over, don't worry about how or what
you should speak. For you will be given what to
say at that hour, 20 because you are not speaking, but the Spirit of your Father is speaking
through you.

21 "Brother will betray brother to death, and
a father his child. Children will even rise up
against their parents and have them put to
death. 22 You will be hated by everyone because
of My name. But the one who endures to the
end will be delivered.[g] 23 When they persecute
you in one town, escape to another. For I assure
you: You will not have covered the towns of
Israel before the •Son of Man comes. 24 A disciple[h] is not above his teacher, or a slave above his
master. 25 It is enough for a disciple to become
like his teacher and a slave like his master. If
they called the head of the house '•Beelzebul,'
how much more the members of his household!

Fear God

26 "Therefore, don't be afraid of them, since
there is nothing covered that won't be uncovered, and nothing hidden that won't be made
known. 27 What I tell you in the dark, speak in
the light. What you hear in a whisper,[i] proclaim
on the housetops. 28 Don't fear those who kill
the body but are not able to kill the soul; rather,
fear Him who is able to destroy both soul and
body in •hell. 29 Aren't two sparrows sold for a
penny?[j] Yet not one of them falls to the ground
without your Father's consent.[k] 30 But even the
hairs of your head have all been counted.
31 Don't be afraid therefore; you are worth
more than many sparrows.

Acknowledging Christ

32 "Therefore, everyone who will acknowledge Me before men, I will also acknowledge
him before My Father in heaven. 33 But whoever denies Me before men, I will also deny
him before My Father in heaven. 34 Don't
assume that I came to bring peace on the earth.
I did not come to bring peace, but a sword.
35 For I came to turn

a man against his father,
a daughter against her mother,
a daughter-in-law against
her mother-in-law;
36 **and a man's enemies will be**
the members of his household.[l]

37 The person who loves father or mother

a10:1 Or *every kind of* b10:3 Probably the Nathanael of Jn 1:45–51 c10:3 Other mss read *and Lebbaeus, whose surname was Thaddaeus* d10:4 Lit *the Cananaean* e10:4 *Iscariot* probably = "a man of Kerioth," a town in Judea. f10:17 Local Jewish courts or local councils g10:22 Or *saved* h10:24 Or *student* i10:27 Lit *in the ear* j10:29 Gk *assarion*, a small copper coin k10:29 Lit *ground apart from your Father* l10:35–36 Mc 7:6

more than Me is not worthy of Me; the person who loves son or daughter more than Me is not worthy of Me. 38 And whoever doesn't take up his cross and follow[a] Me is not worthy of Me. 39 Anyone finding[b] his life will lose it, and anyone losing[c] his life because of Me will find it.

A Cup of Cold Water

40 "The one who welcomes you welcomes Me, and the one who welcomes Me welcomes Him who sent Me. 41 Anyone who[d] welcomes a prophet because he is a prophet[e] will receive a prophet's reward. And anyone who[f] welcomes a righteous person because he's righteous[g] will receive a righteous person's reward. 42 And whoever gives just a cup of cold water to one of these little ones because he is a disciple[h] —I assure you: He will never lose his reward!"

In Praise of John the Baptist

11 When Jesus had finished giving orders to His 12 disciples, He moved on from there to teach and preach in their towns. 2 When John heard in prison what the •Messiah was doing, he sent ⌊a message⌋ by his disciples 3 and asked Him, "Are You the One who is to come, or should we expect someone else?"

4 Jesus replied to them, "Go and report to John what you hear and see: 5 the blind see, the lame walk, those with skin diseases are healed,[i] the deaf hear, the dead are raised, and the poor are told the good news. 6 And if anyone is not offended because of Me, he is blessed."

7 As these men went away, Jesus began to speak to the crowds about John: "What did you go out into the wilderness to see? A reed swaying in the wind? 8 What then did you go out to see? A man dressed in soft clothes? Look, those who wear soft clothes are in kings' palaces. 9 But what did you go out to see? A prophet? Yes, I tell you, and far more than a prophet. 10 This is the one it is written about:

> **Look, I am sending My messenger**
> **ahead of You;**[j]
> **he will prepare Your way**
> **before You.**[k]

11 "•I assure you: Among those born of women no one greater than John the Baptist has appeared,[l] but the least in the kingdom of heaven is greater than he. 12 From the days of John the Baptist until now, the kingdom of heaven has been suffering violence,[m] and the violent have been seizing it by force. 13 For all the prophets and the law prophesied until John; 14 if you're willing to accept it, he is the Elijah who is to come. 15 Anyone who has ears[n] should listen!

An Unresponsive Generation

16 "To what should I compare this generation? It's like children sitting in the marketplaces who call out to each other:

> 17 We played the flute for you,
> but you didn't dance;
> we sang a lament,
> but you didn't mourn![o]

18 For John did not come eating or drinking, and they say, 'He has a demon!' 19 The •Son of Man came eating and drinking, and they say, 'Look, a glutton and a drunkard, a friend of tax collectors and sinners!' Yet wisdom is vindicated[p] by her deeds."[q]

20 Then He proceeded to denounce the towns where most of His miracles were done, because they did not repent: 21 "Woe to you, Chorazin! Woe to you, Bethsaida! For if the miracles that were done in you had been done in Tyre and Sidon, they would have repented in sackcloth and ashes long ago! 22 But I tell you, it will be more tolerable for Tyre and Sidon on the day of judgment than for you. 23 And you, Capernaum, will you be exalted to heaven? You will go down to •Hades. For if the miracles that were done in you had been done in Sodom, it would have remained until today. 24 But I tell you, it will be more tolerable for the land of Sodom on the day of judgment than for you."

The Son Gives Knowledge and Rest

25 At that time Jesus said, "I praise[r] You, Father, Lord of heaven and earth, because You have hidden these things from the wise and learned and revealed them to infants. 26 Yes,

[a] **10:38** Lit *follow after* [b] **10:39** Or *The one who finds* [c] **10:39** Or *and the one who loses* [d] **10:41** Or *The one who* [e] **10:41** Lit *prophet in the name of a prophet* [f] **10:41** Or *And the one who* [g] **10:41** Lit *person in the name of a righteous person* [h] **10:42** Lit *little ones in the name of a disciple* [i] **11:5** Lit *cleansed* [j] **11:10** Lit *messenger before Your face* [k] **11:10** Mal 3:1 [l] **11:11** Lit *arisen* [m] **11:12** Or *has been forcefully advancing* [n] **11:15** Other mss add *to hear* [o] **11:17** Or *beat your breasts* [p] **11:19** Or *declared right* [q] **11:19** Other mss read *children* [r] **11:25** Or *thank*

Father, because this was Your good pleasure.[a]
27 All things have been entrusted to Me by My
Father. No one knows[b] the Son except the
Father, and no one knows the Father except
the Son and anyone to whom the Son desires[c]
to reveal Him.
28 "Come to Me, all of you who are weary
and burdened, and I will give you rest. 29 All of
you, take up My yoke and learn from Me,
because I am gentle and humble in heart, and
you will find rest for yourselves. 30 For My yoke
is easy and My burden is light."

Lord of the Sabbath

12 At that time Jesus passed through the
grainfields on the Sabbath. His disciples were hungry and began to pick and eat
some heads of grain. 2 But when the •Phari-
sees saw it, they said to Him, "Look, Your disciples are doing what is not lawful to do on the
Sabbath!"
3 He said to them, "Haven't you read what
David did when he and those who were with
him were hungry— 4 how he entered the
house of God, and they ate[d] the •sacred bread,
which is not lawful for him or for those with
him to eat, but only for the priests? 5 Or haven't
you read in the Law[e] that on Sabbath days the
priests in the temple violate the Sabbath and
are innocent? 6 But I tell you that something
greater than the temple is here! 7 If you had
known what this means: **I desire mercy and
not sacrifice,**[f] you would not have condemned
the innocent. 8 For the •Son of Man is Lord of
the Sabbath."

The Man with the Paralyzed Hand

9 Moving on from there, He entered their
•synagogue. 10 There He saw a man who had a
paralyzed hand. And in order to accuse Him
they asked Him, "Is it lawful to heal on the Sabbath?"
11 But He said to them, "What man among
you, if he had a sheep[g] that fell into a pit on the
Sabbath, wouldn't take hold of it and lift it out?
12 A man is worth far more than a sheep, so it
is lawful to do good on the Sabbath."
13 Then He told the man, "Stretch out your
hand." So he stretched it out, and it was
restored, as good as the other. 14 But the Pharisees went out and plotted against Him, how
they might destroy Him.

The Servant of the Lord

15 When Jesus became aware of this, He
withdrew from there. Huge crowds[h] followed
Him, and He healed them all. 16 He warned
them not to make Him known, 17 so that what
was spoken through the prophet Isaiah might
be fulfilled:

18 **Here is My Servant**
whom I have chosen,
My beloved in whom
My soul delights;
I will put My Spirit on Him,
and He will proclaim justice
to the nations.
19 **He will not argue or shout,**
and no one will hear His voice
in the streets.
20 **He will not break a bruised reed,**
and He will not put out
a smoldering wick,
until He has led justice to victory.[i]
21 **The nations will put their hope**
in His name.[j]

A House Divided

22 Then a demon-possessed man who was
blind and unable to speak was brought to Him.
He healed him, so that the man[k] could both
speak and see. 23 And all the crowds were
astounded and said, "Perhaps this is the Son of
David!"
24 When the Pharisees heard this, they said,
"The man drives out demons only by •Beelze-
bul, the ruler of the demons."
25 Knowing their thoughts, He told them:
"Every kingdom divided against itself is headed
for destruction, and no city or house divided
against itself will stand. 26 If Satan drives out
Satan, he is divided against himself. How then
will his kingdom stand? 27 And if I drive out
demons by Beelzebul, who is it your sons drive
them out by? For this reason they will be your
judges. 28 If I drive out demons by the Spirit of
God, then the kingdom of God has come to you.
29 How can someone enter a strong man's
house and steal his possessions unless he first
ties up the strong man? Then he can rob his
house. 30 Anyone who is not with Me is against
Me, and anyone who does not gather with Me
scatters. 31 Because of this, I tell you, people
will be forgiven every sin and blasphemy, but

[a] **11:26** Lit *was well-pleasing in Your sight* [b] **11:27** Or *knows exactly* [c] **11:27** Or *wills*, or *chooses* [d] **12:4** Other mss read *he ate* [e] **12:5** The Torah (the Pentateuch) [f] **12:7** Hs 6:6 [g] **12:11** Or *had one sheep* [h] **12:15** Other mss read *Many* [i] **12:20** Or *until He has successfully put forth justice* [j] **12:18–21** Is 42:1–4 [k] **12:22** Lit *mute*

the blasphemy against[a] the Spirit will not be forgiven.[b] 32 Whoever speaks a word against the Son of Man, it will be forgiven him. But whoever speaks against the Holy Spirit, it will not be forgiven him, either in this age or in the one to come.

A Tree and Its Fruit

33 "Either make the tree good and its fruit good, or make the tree bad[c] and its fruit bad; for a tree is known by its fruit. 34 Brood of vipers! How can you speak good things when you are evil? For the mouth speaks from the overflow of the heart. 35 A good man produces good things from his storeroom of good,[d] and an evil man produces evil things from his storeroom of evil. 36 I tell you that on the day of judgment people will have to account for every careless word they speak.[e] 37 For by your words you will be acquitted, and by your words you will be condemned."

The Sign of Jonah

38 Then some of the •scribes and Pharisees said to Him, "Teacher, we want to see a sign from You."

39 But He answered them, "An evil and adulterous generation demands a sign, but no sign will be given to it except the sign of the prophet Jonah. 40 For as Jonah was in the belly of the great fish three days and three nights, so the Son of Man will be in the heart of the earth three days and three nights. 41 The men of Nineveh will stand up at the judgment with this generation and condemn it, because they repented at Jonah's proclamation; and look—something greater than Jonah is here! 42 The queen of the south will rise up at the judgment with this generation and condemn it, because she came from the ends of the earth to hear the wisdom of Solomon; and look—something greater than Solomon is here!

An Unclean Spirit's Return

43 "When an unclean[f] spirit comes out of a man, it roams through waterless places looking for rest but doesn't find any. 44 Then it says, 'I'll go back to my house that I came from.' And when it arrives, it finds ⌊the house⌋ vacant, swept, and put in order. 45 Then off it goes and brings with it seven other spirits more evil than itself, and they enter and settle down there. As a result, that man's last condition is worse than the first. That's how it will also be with this evil generation."

True Relationships

46 He was still speaking to the crowds when suddenly His mother and brothers were standing outside wanting to speak to Him. 47 Someone told Him, "Look, Your mother and Your brothers are standing outside, wanting to speak to You."[g]

48 But He replied to the one who told Him, "Who is My mother and who are My brothers?" 49 And stretching out His hand toward His disciples, He said, "Here are My mother and My brothers! 50 For whoever does the will of My Father in heaven, that person is My brother and sister and mother."

The Parable of the Sower

13 On that day Jesus went out of the house and was sitting by the sea. 2 Such large crowds gathered around Him that He got into a boat and sat down, while the whole crowd stood on the shore.

3 Then He told them many things in parables, saying: "Consider the sower who went out to sow. 4 As he was sowing, some seeds fell along the path, and the birds came and ate them up. 5 Others fell on rocky ground, where there wasn't much soil, and they sprang up quickly since the soil wasn't deep. 6 But when the sun came up they were scorched, and since they had no root, they withered. 7 Others fell among thorns, and the thorns came up and choked them. 8 Still others fell on good ground, and produced a crop: some 100, some 60, and some 30 times ⌊what was sown⌋. 9 Anyone who has ears[h] should listen!"

Why Jesus Used Parables

10 Then the disciples came up and asked Him, "Why do You speak to them in parables?"

11 He answered them, "Because the secrets[i] of the kingdom of heaven have been given for you to know, but it has not been given to them. 12 For whoever has, ⌊more⌋ will be given to him, and he will have more than enough. But whoever does not have, even what he has will be taken away from him. 13 For this reason I speak to them in parables, because looking they

[a] **12:31** Or *of* [b] **12:31** Other mss add *people* [c] **12:33** Lit *rotten,* or *decayed* [d] **12:35** Other mss read *from the storehouse of his heart* [e] **12:36** Lit *will speak* [f] **12:43** Morally or ceremonially impure [g] **12:47** Other mss omit this v. [h] **13:9** Other mss add *to hear*
[i] **13:11** The Gk word *mysteria* does not mean "mysteries" in the Eng sense; it means what we can know only by divine revelation.

do not see, and hearing they do not listen or understand. 14 Isaiah's prophecy is fulfilled in them, which says:

> **You will listen and listen,**
> **yet never understand;**
> **and you will look and look,**
> **yet never perceive.**
> 15 **For this people's heart**
> **has grown callous;**
> **their ears are hard of hearing,**
> **and they have shut their eyes;**
> **otherwise they might see**
> **with their eyes**
> **and hear with their ears,**
> **understand with their hearts**
> **and turn back—**
> **and I would cure them.**[a]

16 "But your eyes are blessed because they do see, and your ears because they do hear! 17 For •I assure you: Many prophets and righteous people longed to see the things you see yet didn't see them; to hear the things you hear yet didn't hear them.

The Parable of the Sower Explained

18 "You, then, listen to the parable of the sower: 19 When anyone hears the word[b] about the kingdom and doesn't understand it, the evil one comes and snatches away what was sown in his heart. This is the one sown along the path. 20 And the one sown on rocky ground—this is one who hears the word and immediately receives it with joy. 21 Yet he has no root in himself, but is short-lived. When pressure or persecution comes because of the word, immediately he stumbles. 22 Now the one sown among the thorns—this is one who hears the word, but the worries of this age and the seduction[c] of wealth choke the word, and it becomes unfruitful. 23 But the one sown on the good ground—this is one who hears and understands the word, who does bear fruit and yields: some 100, some 60, some 30 times ⌊what was sown⌋."

The Parable of the Wheat and the Weeds

24 He presented another parable to them: "The kingdom of heaven may be compared to a man who sowed good seed in his field. 25 But while people were sleeping, his enemy came, sowed weeds[d] among the wheat, and left. 26 When the plants sprouted and produced grain, then the weeds also appeared. 27 The landowner's slaves came to him and said, 'Master, didn't you sow good seed in your field? Then where did the weeds come from?'

28 " 'An enemy did this!' he told them.

" 'So, do you want us to go and gather them up?' the slaves asked him.

29 " 'No,' he said. 'When you gather up the weeds, you might also uproot the wheat with them. 30 Let both grow together until the harvest. At harvest time I'll tell the reapers: Gather the weeds first and tie them in bundles to burn them, but store the wheat in my barn.' "

The Parables of the Mustard Seed and of the Yeast

31 He presented another parable to them: "The kingdom of heaven is like a mustard seed that a man took and sowed in his field. 32 It's the smallest of all the seeds, but when grown, it's taller than the vegetables and becomes a tree, so that the birds of the sky come and nest in its branches."

33 He told them another parable: "The kingdom of heaven is like yeast that a woman took and mixed into 50 pounds[e] of flour until it spread through all of it."[f]

Using Parables Fulfills Prophecy

34 Jesus told the crowds all these things in parables, and He would not speak anything to them without a parable, 35 so that what was spoken through the prophet might be fulfilled:

> **I will open My mouth in parables;**
> **I will declare things kept secret**
> **from the foundation of the world.**[g]

Jesus Interprets the Wheat and the Weeds

36 Then He dismissed the crowds and went into the house. His disciples approached Him and said, "Explain the parable of the weeds in the field to us."

37 He replied: "The One who sows the good seed is the •Son of Man; 38 the field is the world; and the good seed—these are the sons of the kingdom. The weeds are the sons of the evil one, and 39 the enemy who sowed them is the Devil. The harvest is the end of the age, and the harvesters are angels. 40 Therefore just as the weeds are gathered

[a] **13:14–15** Is 6:9–10 [b] **13:19** Gk *logos* = *word*, or *message*, or *saying*, or *thing* [c] **13:22** Or *pleasure*, or *deceitfulness* [d] **13:25** Or *darnel*, a weed similar in appearance to wheat in the early stages [e] **13:33** Lit *3 sata*; about 40 quarts [f] **13:33** Or *until all of it was leavened* [g] **13:35** Ps 78:2

and burned in the fire, so it will be at the end of the age. 41 The Son of Man will send out His angels, and they will gather from His kingdom everything that causes sin[a] and those guilty of lawlessness.[b] 42 They will throw them into the blazing furnace where there will be weeping and gnashing of teeth. 43 Then the righteous will shine like the sun in their Father's kingdom. Anyone who has ears[c] should listen!

The Parables of the Hidden Treasure and of the Priceless Pearl

44 "The kingdom of heaven is like treasure, buried in a field, that a man found and reburied. Then in his joy he goes and sells everything he has and buys that field.

45 "Again, the kingdom of heaven is like a merchant in search of fine pearls. 46 When he found one priceless[d] pearl, he went and sold everything he had, and bought it.

The Parable of the Net

47 "Again, the kingdom of heaven is like a large net thrown into the sea. It collected every kind ⌊of fish⌋, 48 and when it was full, they dragged it ashore, sat down, and gathered the good ⌊fish⌋ into containers, but threw out the worthless ones. 49 So it will be at the end of the age. The angels will go out, separate the evil people from the righteous, 50 and throw them into the blazing furnace. In that place there will be weeping and gnashing of teeth.

The Storehouse of Truth

51 "Have you understood all these things?"[e]

"Yes," they told Him.

52 "Therefore," He said to them, "every student of Scripture[f] instructed in the kingdom of heaven is like a landowner who brings out of his storeroom what is new and what is old." 53 When Jesus had finished these parables, He left there.

Rejection at Nazareth

54 He went to His hometown and began to teach them in their •synagogue, so that they were astonished and said, "How did this wisdom and these miracles come to Him? 55 Isn't this the carpenter's son? Isn't His mother called Mary, and His brothers James, Joseph,[g] Simon, and Judas? 56 And His sisters, aren't they all with us? So where does He get all these things?" 57 And they were offended by Him.

But Jesus said to them, "A prophet is not without honor except in his hometown and in his household." 58 And He did not do many miracles there because of their unbelief.

John the Baptist Beheaded

14 At that time •Herod the tetrarch heard the report about Jesus. 2 "This is John the Baptist!" he told his servants. "He has been raised from the dead, and that's why supernatural powers are at work in him."

3 For Herod had arrested John, chained[h] him, and put him in prison on account of Herodias, his brother Philip's wife, 4 since John had been telling him, "It's not lawful for you to have her!" 5 Though he wanted to kill him, he feared the crowd, since they regarded him as a prophet.

6 But when Herod's birthday celebration came, Herodias' daughter danced before them[i] and pleased Herod. 7 So he promised with an oath to give her whatever she might ask. 8 And prompted by her mother, she answered, "Give me John the Baptist's head here on a platter!" 9 Although the king regretted it, he commanded that it be granted because of his oaths and his guests. 10 So he sent orders and had John beheaded in the prison. 11 His head was brought on a platter and given to the girl, who carried it to her mother. 12 Then his disciples came, removed the corpse,[j] buried it, and went and reported to Jesus.

Feeding 5,000

13 When Jesus heard about it, He withdrew from there by boat to a remote place to be alone. When the crowds heard this, they followed Him on foot from the towns. 14 As He stepped ashore,[k] He saw a huge crowd, felt compassion for them, and healed their sick.

15 When evening came, the disciples approached Him and said, "This place is a wilderness, and it is already late.[l] Send the crowds away so they can go into the villages and buy food for themselves."

[a] **13:41** Or *stumbling* [b] **13:41** Or *those who do lawlessness* [c] **13:43** Other mss add *to hear* [d] **13:46** Or *very precious* [e] **13:51** Other mss add *Jesus asked them* [f] **13:52** Or *every scribe* [g] **13:55** Other mss read *Joses*; Mk 6:3 [h] **14:3** Or *bound* [i] **14:6** Lit *danced in the middle* [j] **14:12** Other mss read *body* [k] **14:14** Lit *Coming out* (of the boat) [l] **14:15** Lit *and the time* (for the evening meal) *has already passed*

16 "They don't need to go away," Jesus told them. "You give them something to eat."

17 "But we only have five loaves and two fish here," they said to Him.

18 "Bring them here to Me," He said. 19 Then He commanded the crowds to sit down[a] on the grass. He took the five loaves and the two fish, and looking up to heaven, He blessed them. He broke the loaves and gave them to the disciples, and the disciples ⌊gave them⌋ to the crowds. 20 Everyone ate and was filled. Then they picked up 12 baskets full of leftover pieces! 21 Now those who ate were about 5,000 men, besides women and children.

Walking on the Water

22 Immediately He[b] made the disciples get into the boat and go ahead of Him to the other side, while He dismissed the crowds. 23 After dismissing the crowds, He went up on the mountain by Himself to pray. When evening came, He was there alone. 24 But the boat was already over a mile[c] from land,[d] battered by the waves, because the wind was against them. 25 Around three in the morning,[e] He came toward them walking on the sea. 26 When the disciples saw Him walking on the sea, they were terrified. "It's a ghost!" they said, and cried out in fear.

27 Immediately Jesus spoke to them. "Have courage! It is I. Don't be afraid."

28 "Lord, if it's You," Peter answered Him, "command me to come to You on the water."

29 "Come!" He said.

And climbing out of the boat, Peter started walking on the water and came toward Jesus. 30 But when he saw the strength of the wind,[f] he was afraid. And beginning to sink he cried out, "Lord, save me!"

31 Immediately Jesus reached out His hand, caught hold of him, and said to him, "You of little faith, why did you doubt?" 32 When they got into the boat, the wind ceased. 33 Then those in the boat worshiped Him and said, "Truly You are the Son of God!"

Miraculous Healings

34 Once they crossed over, they came to land at Gennesaret. 35 When the men of that place recognized Him, they alerted[g] the whole vicinity and brought to Him all who were sick. 36 They were begging Him that they might only touch the •tassel on His robe. And as many as touched it were made perfectly well.

The Tradition of the Elders

15 Then •Pharisees and •scribes came from Jerusalem to Jesus and asked, 2 "Why do Your disciples break the tradition of the elders? For they don't wash their hands when they eat!"[h]

3 He answered them, "And why do you break God's commandment because of your tradition? 4 For God said:[i]

Honor your father
and your mother;[j] **and,**
The one who speaks evil of father
or mother
must be put to death.[k]

5 But you say, 'Whoever tells his father or mother, "Whatever benefit you might have received from me is a gift ⌊committed to the temple⌋"— 6 he does not have to honor his father.'[l] In this way, you have revoked God's word[m] because of your tradition. 7 Hypocrites! Isaiah prophesied correctly about you when he said:

8 **These people**[n] **honor Me**
with their lips,
but their heart is far from Me.
9 **They worship Me in vain,**
teaching as doctrines
the commands of men."[o]

Defilement Is from Within

10 Summoning the crowd, He told them, "Listen and understand: 11 It's not what goes into the mouth that defiles a man, but what comes out of the mouth, this defiles a man."

12 Then the disciples came up and told Him, "Do You know that the Pharisees took offense when they heard this statement?"

13 He replied, "Every plant that My heavenly Father didn't plant will be uprooted.

[a]**14:19** Lit *to recline* [b]**14:22** Other mss read *Jesus* [c]**14:24** Lit *already many stadia*; 1 *stadion* = 600 feet [d]**14:24** Other mss read *already in the middle of the sea* [e]**14:25** Lit *fourth watch of the night* = 3 to 6 a.m. [f]**14:30** Other mss read *saw the wind* [g]**14:35** Lit *sent into* [h]**15:2** Lit *eat bread* = eat a meal [i]**15:4** Other mss read *commanded, saying* [j]**15:4** Ex 20:12; Dt 5:16 [k]**15:4** Ex 21:17; Lv 20:9 [l]**15:6** Other mss read *then he does not have to honor his father or mother* [m]**15:6** Other mss read *commandment* [n]**15:8** Other mss add *draws near to Me with their mouths, and* [o]**15:8–9** Is 29:13 LXX

14 Leave them alone! They are blind guides.[a] And if the blind guide the blind, both will fall into a pit."

15 Then Peter replied to Him, "Explain this parable to us."

16 "Are even you still lacking in understanding?" He[b] asked. 17 "Don't you realize[c] that whatever goes into the mouth passes into the stomach and is eliminated?[d] 18 But what comes out of the mouth comes from the heart, and this defiles a man. 19 For from the heart come evil thoughts, murders, adulteries, sexual immoralities, thefts, false testimonies, blasphemies. 20 These are the things that defile a man, but eating with unwashed hands does not defile a man."

A Gentile Mother's Faith

21 When Jesus left there, He withdrew to the area of Tyre and Sidon. 22 Just then a Canaanite woman from that region came and kept crying out,[e] "Have mercy on me, Lord, Son of David! My daughter is cruelly tormented by a demon."

23 Yet He did not say a word to her. So His disciples approached Him and urged Him, "Send her away because she cries out after us."[f]

24 He replied, "I was sent only to the lost sheep of the house of Israel."

25 But she came, knelt before Him, and said, "Lord, help me!"

26 He answered, "It isn't right to take the children's bread and throw it to their dogs."

27 "Yes, Lord," she said, "yet even the dogs eat the crumbs that fall from their masters' table!"

28 Then Jesus replied to her, "Woman, your faith is great. Let it be done for you as you want." And from that moment[g] her daughter was cured.

Healing Many People

29 Moving on from there, Jesus passed along the Sea of Galilee. He went up on a mountain and sat there, 30 and large crowds came to Him, having with them the lame, the blind, the deformed, those unable to speak, and many others. They put them at His feet, and He healed them. 31 So the crowd was amazed when they saw those unable to speak talking, the deformed restored, the lame walking, and the blind seeing. And they gave glory to the God of Israel.

Feeding 4,000

32 Now Jesus summoned His disciples and said, "I have compassion on the crowd, because they've already stayed with Me three days and have nothing to eat. I don't want to send them away hungry; otherwise they might collapse on the way."

33 The disciples said to Him, "Where could we get enough bread in this desolate place to fill such a crowd?"

34 "How many loaves do you have?" Jesus asked them.

"Seven," they said, "and a few small fish."

35 After commanding the crowd to sit down on the ground, 36 He took the seven loaves and the fish, and He gave thanks, broke them, and kept on giving them to the disciples, and the disciples ⌊gave them⌋ to the crowds. 37 They all ate and were filled. Then they collected the leftover pieces—seven large baskets full. 38 Now those who ate were 4,000 men, besides women and children. 39 After dismissing the crowds, He got into the boat and went to the region of Magadan.[h]

The Yeast of the Pharisees and the Sadducees

16 The •Pharisees and •Sadducees approached, and as a test, asked Him to show them a sign from heaven.

2 He answered them: "When evening comes you say, 'It will be good weather because the sky is red.' 3 And in the morning, 'Today will be stormy because the sky is red and threatening.' You[i] know how to read the appearance of the sky, but you can't read the signs of the times.[j] 4 An evil and adulterous generation wants a sign, but no sign will be given to it except the sign of[k] Jonah." Then He left them and went away.

5 The disciples reached the other shore,[l] and they had forgotten to take bread.

6 Then Jesus told them, "Watch out and beware of the yeast[m] of the Pharisees and Sadducees."

7 And they discussed among themselves, "We didn't bring any bread."

8 Aware of this, Jesus said, "You of little

[a]**15:14** Other mss add *for the blind* [b]**15:16** Other mss read *Jesus* [c]**15:17** Other mss add *yet* [d]**15:17** Lit *and goes out into the toilet* [e]**15:22** Other mss read *and cried out to Him* [f]**15:23** Lit *she is yelling behind us* or *after us* [g]**15:28** Lit *hour* [h]**15:39** Other mss read *Magdala* [i]**16:3** Other mss read *Hypocrites! You* [j]**16:2–3** Other mss omit *When* (v. 2) through end of v. 3 [k]**16:4** Other mss add *the prophet* [l]**16:5** Lit *disciples went to the other side* [m]**16:6** Or *leaven*

faith! Why are you discussing among yourselves
that you do not have bread? 9 Don't you understand yet? Don't you remember the five loaves
for the 5,000 and how many baskets you collected? 10 Or the seven loaves for the 4,000 and
how many large baskets you collected? 11 Why
is it you don't understand that when I told you,
'Beware of the yeast of the Pharisees and Sadducees,' it wasn't about bread?" 12 Then they
understood that He did not tell them to beware
of the yeast in bread, but of the teaching of the
Pharisees and Sadducees.

Peter's Confession of the Messiah

13 When Jesus came to the region of Caesarea Philippi,[a] He asked His disciples, "Who
do people say that the •Son of Man is?"[b]
14 And they said, "Some say John the Baptist; others, Elijah; still others, Jeremiah or one
of the prophets."
15 "But you," He asked them, "who do you
say that I am?"
16 Simon Peter answered, "You are the
•Messiah, the Son of the living God!"
17 And Jesus responded, "Simon son of
Jonah,[c] you are blessed because flesh and blood
did not reveal this to you, but My Father in
heaven. 18 And I also say to you that you are
Peter,[d] and on this rock[e] I will build My
church, and the forces[f] of •Hades will not over-
power it. 19 I will give you the keys of the kingdom of heaven, and whatever you bind on
earth is already bound[g] in heaven, and whatever you loose on earth is already loosed[h] in
heaven."
20 And He gave the disciples orders to tell
no one that He was[i] the Messiah.

His Death and Resurrection Predicted

21 From then on Jesus began to point out to
His disciples that He must go to Jerusalem and
suffer many things from the elders, •chief
priests, and •scribes, be killed, and be raised
the third day. 22 Then Peter took Him aside and
began to rebuke Him, "Oh no,[j] Lord! This will
never happen to You!"
23 But He turned and told Peter, "Get
behind Me, Satan! You are an offense to Me
because you're not thinking about God's concerns,[k] but man's."

Take Up Your Cross

24 Then Jesus said to His disciples, "If anyone wants to come with Me, he must deny
himself, take up his cross, and follow Me.
25 For whoever wants to save his •life will
lose it, but whoever loses his life because of
Me will find it. 26 What will it benefit a man
if he gains the whole world yet loses his life?
Or what will a man give in exchange for his
life? 27 For the Son of Man is going to come
with His angels in the glory of His Father, and
then He will reward each according to what
he has done. 28 •I assure you: There are some
standing here who will not taste death until
they see the Son of Man coming in His kingdom."

The Transfiguration

17 After six days Jesus took Peter, James,
and his brother John, and led them up
on a high mountain by themselves. 2 He was
transformed[l] in front of them, and His face
shone like the sun. Even His clothes became as
white as the light. 3 Suddenly, Moses and Elijah appeared to them, talking with Him.
4 Then Peter said to Jesus, "Lord, it's good
for us to be here! If You want, I will make[m]
three •tabernacles here: one for You, one for
Moses, and one for Elijah."
5 While he was still speaking, suddenly a
bright cloud covered[n] them, and a voice from
the cloud said:

> This is My beloved Son.
> I take delight in Him.
> Listen to Him!

6 When the disciples heard it, they fell facedown and were terrified.
7 Then Jesus came up, touched them, and
said, "Get up; don't be afraid." 8 When they
looked up they saw no one except Him[o]—
Jesus alone. 9 As they were coming down from
the mountain, Jesus commanded them, "Don't
tell anyone about the vision until the •Son of
Man is raised[p] from the dead."
10 So the disciples questioned Him, "Why
then do the •scribes say that Elijah must come
first?"
11 "Elijah is coming[q] and will restore everything," He replied.[r] 12 "But I tell you: Elijah has

[a]**16:13** A town north of Galilee at the base of Mount Hermon [b]**16:13** Other mss read *that I, the Son of Man, am* [c]**16:17** Or *son of John* [d]**16:18** *Peter* (Gk *Petros*) = a specific stone or rock [e]**16:18** *Rock* (Gk *petra*) = a rocky crag or bedrock [f]**16:18** Lit *gates* [g]**16:19** Or *earth will be bound* [h]**16:19** Or *earth will be loosed* [i]**16:20** Other mss add *Jesus* [j]**16:22** Lit *Mercy to You = May God have mercy on You* [k]**16:23** Lit *about the things of God* [l]**17:2** Or *transfigured* [m]**17:4** Other mss read *wish, let's make* [n]**17:5** Or *enveloped*; Ex 40:34–35 [o]**17:8** Other mss omit *Him* [p]**17:9** Other mss read *Man has risen* [q]**17:11** Other mss add *first* [r]**17:11** Other mss read *Jesus said to them*

already come, and they didn't recognize him. On the contrary, they did whatever they pleased to him. In the same way the Son of Man is going to suffer at their hands."[a] 13 Then the disciples understood that He spoke to them about John the Baptist.

The Power of Faith over a Demon

14 When they reached the crowd, a man approached and knelt down before Him. 15 "Lord," he said, "have mercy on my son, because he has seizures[b] and suffers severely. He often falls into the fire and often into the water. 16 I brought him to Your disciples, but they couldn't heal him."

17 Jesus replied, "You unbelieving and rebellious[c] generation! How long will I be with you? How long must I put up with you? Bring him here to Me." 18 Then Jesus rebuked the demon,[d] and it[e] came out of him, and from that moment[f] the boy was healed.

19 Then the disciples approached Jesus privately and said, "Why couldn't we drive it out?"

20 "Because of your little faith," He[g] told them. "For •I assure you: If you have faith the size of[h] a mustard seed, you will tell this mountain, 'Move from here to there,' and it will move. Nothing will be impossible for you. [21 However, this kind does not come out except by prayer and fasting.]"[i]

The Second Prediction of His Death

22 As they were meeting[j] in Galilee, Jesus told them, "The Son of Man is about to be betrayed into the hands of men. 23 They will kill Him, and on the third day He will be raised up." And they were deeply distressed.

Paying the Temple Tax

24 When they came to Capernaum, those who collected the double-drachma tax[k] approached Peter and said, "Doesn't your Teacher pay the double-drachma tax?"

25 "Yes," he said.

When he went into the house, Jesus spoke to him first,[l] "What do you think, Simon? Who do earthly kings collect tariffs or taxes from? From their sons or from strangers?"[m]

26 "From strangers," he said.[n]

"Then the sons are free," Jesus told him. 27 "But, so we won't offend them, go to the sea, cast in a fishhook, and catch the first fish that comes up. When you open its mouth you'll find a coin.[o] Take it and give it to them for Me and you."

Who Is the Greatest?

18 At that time[f] the disciples came to Jesus and said, "Who is greatest in the kingdom of heaven?"

2 Then He called a child to Him and had him stand among them. 3 "•I assure you," He said, "unless you are converted[p] and become like children, you will never enter the kingdom of heaven. 4 Therefore, whoever humbles himself like this child—this one is the greatest in the kingdom of heaven. 5 And whoever welcomes[q] one child like this in My name welcomes Me.

6 "But whoever •causes the downfall of one of these little ones who believe in Me—it would be better for him if a heavy millstone[r] were hung around his neck and he were drowned in the depths of the sea! 7 Woe to the world because of offenses.[s] For offenses must come, but woe to that man by whom the offense comes. 8 If your hand or your foot causes your downfall, cut it off and throw it away. It is better for you to enter life maimed or lame, than to have two hands or two feet and be thrown into the eternal fire. 9 And if your eye causes your downfall, gouge it out and throw it away. It is better for you to enter life with one eye, rather than to have two eyes and be thrown into •hellfire![t]

The Parable of the Lost Sheep

10 "See that you don't look down on one of these little ones, because I tell you that in heaven their angels continually view the face of My Father in heaven. [11 For the •Son of Man has come to save the lost.][u] 12 What do you think? If a man has 100 sheep, and one of them

[a] **17:12** Lit *suffer by them* [b] **17:15** Lit *he is moonstruck*; thought to be a form of epilepsy [c] **17:17** Or *corrupt*, or *perverted*, or *twisted*; Dt 32:5 [d] **17:18** Lit *rebuked him* or *it* [e] **17:18** Lit *the demon* [f] **17:18; 18:1** Lit *hour* [g] **17:20** Other mss read *your unbelief," Jesus* [h] **17:20** Lit *faith like* [i] **17:21** Other mss omit bracketed text; Mk 9:29 [j] **17:22** Other mss read *were staying* [k] **17:24** Jewish men paid this tax to support the temple; Ex 30:11–16. A double-drachma could purchase 2 sheep. [l] **17:25** Lit *Jesus anticipated him by saying* [m] **17:25** Or *foreigners* [n] **17:26** Other mss read *Peter said to Him* [o] **17:27** Gk *stater*, worth 2 double-drachmas [p] **18:3** Or *are turned around* [q] **18:5** Or *receives* [r] **18:6** A millstone turned by a donkey [s] **18:7** Or *causes of stumbling* [t] **18:9** Lit *gehenna of fire* [u] **18:11** Other mss omit bracketed text

goes astray, won't he leave the 99 on the hillside and go and search for the stray? 13 And if he finds it, I assure you: He rejoices over that sheep[a] more than over the 99 that did not go astray. 14 In the same way, it is not the will of your Father in heaven that one of these little ones perish.

Restoring a Brother

15 "If your brother sins against you,[b] go and rebuke him in private.[c] If he listens to you, you have won your brother. 16 But if he won't listen, take one or two more with you, so that **by the testimony[d] of two or three witnesses every fact may be established.**[e] 17 If he pays no attention to them, tell the church.[f] But if he doesn't pay attention even to the church, let him be like an unbeliever[g] and a tax collector to you. 18 I assure you: Whatever you bind on earth is already bound[h] in heaven, and whatever you loose on earth is already loosed[i] in heaven. 19 Again, I assure you: If two of you on earth agree about any matter that you[j] pray for, it will be done for you[k] by My Father in heaven. 20 For where two or three are gathered together in My name, I am there among them."

The Parable of the Unforgiving Slave

21 Then Peter came to Him and said, "Lord, how many times could my brother sin against me and I forgive him? As many as seven times?"

22 "I tell you, not as many as seven," Jesus said to him, "but 70 times seven.[l] 23 For this reason, the kingdom of heaven can be compared to a king who wanted to settle accounts with his •slaves. 24 When he began to settle accounts, one who owed 10,000 talents[m] was brought before him. 25 Since he had no way to pay it back, his master commanded that he, his wife, his children, and everything he had be sold to pay the debt.

26 "At this, the •slave fell facedown before him and said, 'Be patient with me, and I will pay you everything!' 27 Then the master of that •slave had compassion, released him, and forgave him the loan.

28 "But that •slave went out and found one of his fellow slaves who owed him 100 •denarii.[n] He grabbed him, started choking him, and said, 'Pay what you owe!'

29 "At this, his fellow •slave fell down[o] and began begging him, 'Be patient with me, and I will pay you back.' 30 But he wasn't willing. On the contrary, he went and threw him into prison until he could pay what was owed. 31 When the other slaves saw what had taken place, they were deeply distressed and went and reported to their master everything that had happened.

32 "Then, after he had summoned him, his master said to him, 'You wicked •slave! I forgave you all that debt because you begged me. 33 Shouldn't you also have had mercy on your fellow slave, as I had mercy on you?' 34 And his master got angry and handed him over to the jailers[p] until he could pay everything that was owed. 35 So My heavenly Father will also do to you if each of you does not forgive his brother[q] from his[r] heart."

The Question of Divorce

19 When Jesus had finished this instruction, He departed from Galilee and went to the region of Judea across the Jordan. 2 Large crowds followed Him, and He healed them there. 3 Some •Pharisees approached Him to test Him. They asked, "Is it lawful for a man to divorce his wife on any grounds?"

4 "Haven't you read," He replied, "that He who created[s] them in the beginning **made them male and female,**[t] 5 and He also said:

> **For this reason a man will leave**
> **his father and mother**
> **and be joined to his wife,**
> **and the two will become one flesh?**[u]

6 So they are no longer two, but one flesh. Therefore what God has joined together, man must not separate."

7 "Why then," they asked Him, "did Moses command ⌊us⌋ to give divorce papers and to send her away?"

8 He told them, "Moses permitted you to divorce your wives because of the hardness of your hearts. But it was not like that from the beginning. 9 And I tell you, whoever divorces

[a]**18:13** Lit *over it* [b]**18:15** Other mss omit *against you* [c]**18:15** Lit *him between you and him alone* [d]**18:16** Lit *mouth* [e]**18:16** Dt 19:15 [f]**18:17** Or *congregation* [g]**18:17** Or *like a Gentile* [h]**18:18** Or *earth will be bound* [i]**18:18** Or *earth will be loosed* [j]**18:19** Lit *they* [k]**18:19** Lit *for them* [l]**18:22** Or *but 77 times* [m]**18:24** A huge sum of money that could never be repaid by a slave; a talent = 6,000 denarii [n]**18:28** A small sum compared to 10,000 talents [o]**18:29** Other mss add *at his feet* [p]**18:34** Or *torturers* [q]**18:35** Other mss add *his trespasses* [r]**18:35** Lit *your* [s]**19:4** Other mss read *made* [t]**19:4** Gn 1:27; 5:2 [u]**19:5** Gn 2:24

his wife, except for sexual immorality, and marries another, commits adultery."[a]
10 His disciples said to Him, "If the relationship of a man with his wife is like this, it's better not to marry!"
11 But He told them, "Not everyone can
accept this saying, but only those it has been
given to. 12 For there are eunuchs who were
born that way from their mother's womb,
there are eunuchs who were made by men,
and there are eunuchs who have made themselves that way because of the kingdom of
heaven. Let anyone accept this who can."

Blessing the Children

13 Then children were brought to Him so
He might put His hands on them and pray. But
the disciples rebuked them. 14 Then Jesus said,
"Leave the children alone, and don't try to keep
them from coming to Me, because the kingdom
of heaven is made up of people like this."[b]
15 After putting His hands on them, He went
on from there.

The Rich Young Ruler

16 Just then someone came up and asked
Him, "Teacher, what good must I do to have
eternal life?"
17 "Why do you ask Me about what is
good?"[c] He said to him. "There is only One
who is good.[d] If you want to enter into life,
keep the commandments."
18 "Which ones?" he asked Him.
Jesus answered,

Do not murder;
do not commit adultery;
do not steal;
do not bear false witness;
19 **honor your father**
and your mother;
and love your neighbor
as yourself.[e]

20 "I have kept all these,"[f] the young man
told Him. "What do I still lack?"
21 "If you want to be perfect,"[g] Jesus said to
him, "go, sell your belongings and give to the
poor, and you will have treasure in heaven.
Then come, follow Me."
22 When the young man heard that command, he went away grieving, because he had
many possessions.

Possessions and the Kingdom

23 Then Jesus said to His disciples, "•I
assure you: It will be hard for a rich person to
enter the kingdom of heaven! 24 Again I tell
you, it is easier for a camel to go through the
eye of a needle than for a rich person to enter
the kingdom of God."
25 When the disciples heard this, they were
utterly astonished and asked, "Then who can
be saved?"
26 But Jesus looked at them and said, "With
men this is impossible, but with God all things
are possible."
27 Then Peter responded to Him, "Look, we
have left everything and followed You. So what
will there be for us?"
28 Jesus said to them, "I assure you: In the
Messianic Age,[h] when the •Son of Man sits on
His glorious throne, you who have followed
Me will also sit on 12 thrones, judging the 12
tribes of Israel. 29 And everyone who has left
houses, brothers or sisters, father or mother,[i]
children, or fields because of My name will
receive 100 times more and will inherit eternal life. 30 But many who are first will be last,
and the last first.

The Parable of the Vineyard Workers

20 "For the kingdom of heaven is like a
landowner who went out early in
the morning to hire workers for his vineyard. 2 After agreeing with the workers on
one •denarius for the day, he sent them into
his vineyard. 3 When he went out about
nine in the morning,[j] he saw others standing
in the marketplace doing nothing. 4 To those
men he said, 'You also go to my vineyard,
and I'll give you whatever is right.' So off
they went. 5 About noon and at three,[k] he
went out again and did the same thing.
6 Then about five[l] he went and found others
standing around,[m] and said to them, 'Why
have you been standing here all day doing
nothing?'
7 "'Because no one hired us,' they said to
him.
"'You also go to my vineyard,' he told

[a]**19:9** Other mss add *Also whoever marries a divorced woman commits adultery*; Mt 5:32 [b]**19:14** Lit *heaven is of such ones* [c]**19:17** Other mss read *Why do you call Me good?* [d]**19:17** Other mss read *No one is good but One—God* [e]**19:18–19** Ex 20:12–16; Dt 5:16–20; Lv 19:18 [f]**19:20** Other mss add *from my youth* [g]**19:21** Or *complete* [h]**19:28** Lit *the regeneration* [i]**19:29** Other mss add *or wife* [j]**20:3** Lit *about the third hour* [k]**20:5** Lit *about the sixth hour and the ninth hour* [l]**20:6** Lit *about the eleventh hour* [m]**20:6** Other mss add *doing nothing*

them.[a] 8 When evening came, the owner of the vineyard told his foreman, 'Call the workers and give them their pay, starting with the last and ending with the first.'[b]

9 "When those who were hired about five[c] came, they each received one denarius. 10 So when the first ones came, they assumed they would get more, but they also received a denarius each. 11 When they received it, they began to complain to the landowner: 12 'These last men put in one hour, and you made them equal to us who bore the burden of the day and the burning heat!'

13 "He replied to one of them, 'Friend, I'm doing you no wrong. Didn't you agree with me on a denarius? 14 Take what's yours and go. I want to give this last man the same as I gave you. 15 Don't I have the right to do what I want with my business?[d] Are you jealous[e] because I'm generous?'[f]

16 "So the last will be first, and the first last."[g]

The Third Prediction of His Death

17 While going up to Jerusalem, Jesus took the 12 disciples aside privately and said to them on the way: 18 "Listen! We are going up to Jerusalem. The •Son of Man will be handed over to the •chief priests and •scribes, and they will condemn Him to death. 19 Then they will hand Him over to the Gentiles to be mocked, flogged,[h] and crucified, and He will be resurrected[i] on the third day."

Suffering and Service

20 Then the mother of Zebedee's sons approached Him with her sons. She knelt down to ask Him for something. 21 "What do you want?" He asked her.

"Promise,"[j] she said to Him, "that these two sons of mine may sit, one on Your right and the other on Your left, in Your kingdom."

22 But Jesus answered, "You don't know what you're asking. Are you able to drink the cup[k] that I am about to drink?"[l]

"We are able," they said to Him.

23 He told them, "You will indeed drink My cup.[m] But to sit at My right and left is not Mine to give; instead, it belongs to those for whom it has been prepared by My Father." 24 When the 10 ⌊disciples⌋ heard this, they became indignant with the two brothers. 25 But Jesus called them over and said, "You know that the rulers of the Gentiles dominate them, and the men of high position exercise power over them. 26 It must not be like that among you. On the contrary, whoever wants to become great among you must be your servant, 27 and whoever wants to be first among you must be your slave; 28 just as the Son of Man did not come to be served, but to serve, and to give His life—a ransom for many."

Two Blind Men Healed

29 As they were leaving Jericho, a large crowd followed Him. 30 There were two blind men sitting by the road. When they heard that Jesus was passing by, they cried out, "Lord, have mercy on us, Son of David!" 31 The crowd told them to keep quiet, but they cried out all the more, "Lord, have mercy on us, Son of David!"

32 Jesus stopped, called them, and said, "What do you want Me to do for you?"

33 "Lord," they said to Him, "open our eyes!" 34 Moved with compassion, Jesus touched their eyes. Immediately they could see, and they followed Him.

The Triumphal Entry

21 When they approached Jerusalem and came to Bethphage at the •Mount of Olives, Jesus then sent two disciples, 2 telling them, "Go into the village ahead of you. At once you will find a donkey tied there, and a colt with her. Untie them and bring them to Me. 3 If anyone says anything to you, you should say that the Lord needs them, and immediately he will send them."

4 This took place so that what was spoken through the prophet might be fulfilled:

5 **Tell Daughter Zion,**
"See, your King is coming to you,
gentle, and mounted on a donkey,
even on a colt,
the foal of a beast
of burden."[n]

6 The disciples went and did just as Jesus directed them. 7 They brought the donkey and

[a]**20:7** Other mss add *'and you'll get whatever is right.'* [b]**20:8** Lit starting from the last until the first [c]**20:9** Lit *about the eleventh hour* [d]**20:15** Lit *with what is mine* [e]**20:15** Lit *Is your eye evil*; an idiom for jealousy or stinginess [f]**20:15** Lit *good* [g]**20:16** Other mss add *For many are called, but few are chosen.* [h]**20:19** Or *scourged* [i]**20:19** Other mss read *will rise again* [j]**20:21** Lit *Say* [k]**20:22** Figurative language referring to His coming suffering; Mt 26:39; Jn 18:11 [l]**20:22** Other mss add *and (or) to be baptized with the baptism that I am baptized with* [m]**20:23** Other mss add *and be baptized with the baptism that I am baptized with* [n]**21:5** Is 62:11; Zch 9:9

the colt; then they laid their robes on them, and
He sat on them. 8 A very large crowd spread
their robes on the road; others were cutting
branches from the trees and spreading them on
the road. 9 Then the crowds who went ahead of
Him and those who followed kept shouting:

> •*Hosanna* to the Son of David!
> **Blessed is He who comes**
> **in the name of the Lord!**[a]
> *Hosanna* in the highest heaven!

10 When He entered Jerusalem, the whole city
was shaken, saying, "Who is this?" 11 And the
crowds kept saying, "This is the prophet Jesus
from Nazareth in Galilee!"

Cleansing the Temple Complex

12 Jesus went into the •temple complex and
drove out all those buying and selling in the
temple. He overturned the money changers'
tables and the chairs of those selling doves.
13 And He said to them, "It is written, **My
house will be called a house of prayer.**[c] But
you are making it a **den of thieves!**"[d]

Children Cheer Jesus

14 The blind and the lame came to Him in
the temple complex, and He healed them.
15 When the •chief priests and the •scribes
saw the wonders that He did and the children
in the temple complex cheering, "*Hosanna* to
the Son of David!" they were indignant 16 and
said to Him, "Do You hear what these ⌊chil-
dren⌋ are saying?"

"Yes," Jesus told them. "Have you never
read:

> **You have prepared**[e] **praise**
> **from the mouths of children**
> **and nursing infants"?**[f]

17 Then He left them, went out of the city to
Bethany, and spent the night there.

The Barren Fig Tree

18 Early in the morning, as He was returning to the city, He was hungry. 19 Seeing a lone
fig tree by the road, He went up to it and found
nothing on it except leaves. And He said to it,
"May no fruit ever come from you again!" At
once the fig tree withered.

20 When the disciples saw it, they were
amazed and said, "How did the fig tree wither
so quickly?"

21 Jesus answered them, "•I assure you: If
you have faith and do not doubt, you will not
only do what was done to the fig tree, but even
if you tell this mountain, 'Be lifted up and
thrown into the sea,' it will be done. 22 And if
you believe, you will receive whatever you ask
for in prayer."

Messiah's Authority Challenged

23 When He entered the temple complex,
the chief priests and the elders of the people
came up to Him as He was teaching and said,
"By what authority are You doing these things?
Who gave You this authority?"

24 Jesus answered them, "I will also ask you
one question, and if you answer it for Me, then
I will tell you by what authority I do these
things. 25 Where did John's baptism come
from? From heaven or from men?"

They began to argue among themselves, "If
we say, 'From heaven,' He will say to us, 'Then
why didn't you believe him?' 26 But if we say,
'From men,' we're afraid of the crowd, because
everyone thought John was a prophet." 27 So
they answered Jesus, "We don't know."

And He said to them, "Neither will I tell you
by what authority I do these things.

The Parable of the Two Sons

28 "But what do you think? A man had two
sons. He went to the first and said, 'My son, go,
work in the vineyard today.'

29 "He answered, 'I don't want to!' Yet later
he changed his mind and went. 30 Then the
man went to the other and said the same thing.

" 'I will, sir,' he answered. But he didn't go.
31 "Which of the two did his father's will?"

"The first," they said.

Jesus said to them, "I assure you: Tax collectors and prostitutes are entering the kingdom of God before you! 32 For John came to
you in the way of righteousness,[g] and you
didn't believe him. Tax collectors and prostitutes did believe him, but you, when you saw
it, didn't even change your minds then and
believe him.

The Parable of the Vineyard Owner

33 "Listen to another parable: There was a
man, a landowner, who planted a vineyard, put
a fence around it, dug a winepress in it, and
built a watchtower. He leased it to tenant farmers and went away. 34 When the grape harvest[h]

[a]**21:9** Ps 118:25–26 [b]**21:12** Other mss add *of God* [c]**21:13** Is 56:7 [d]**21:13** Jr 7:11 [e]**21:16** Or *restored* [f]**21:16** Ps 8:3 LXX [g]**21:32** John came preaching and practicing righteousness [h]**21:34** Lit *the season of fruits*

drew near, he sent his slaves to the farmers to
collect his fruit. 35 But the farmers took his
slaves, beat one, killed another, and stoned a
third. 36 Again, he sent other slaves, more than
the first group, and they did the same to them.
37 Finally, he sent his son to them. 'They will
respect my son,' he said.

38 "But when the tenant farmers saw the
son, they said among themselves, 'This is the
heir. Come, let's kill him and take his inheritance!' 39 So they seized him and threw him out
of the vineyard, and killed him. 40 Therefore,
when the owner of the vineyard comes, what
will he do to those farmers?"

41 "He will completely destroy those terrible men," they told Him, "and lease his vineyard to other farmers who will give him his
produce at the harvest."[a]

42 Jesus said to them, "Have you never read
in the Scriptures:

> **The stone that the builders**
> **rejected**
> **has become the cornerstone.**[b]
> **This came from the Lord**
> **and is wonderful in our eyes?**[c]

43 Therefore I tell you, the kingdom of God
will be taken away from you and given to a
nation producing its[d] fruit. [44 Whoever falls
on this stone will be broken to pieces; but on
whomever it falls, it will grind him to
powder!"][e]

45 When the chief priests and the •Phari-
sees heard His parables, they knew He was
speaking about them. 46 Although they were
looking for a way to arrest Him, they feared
the crowds, because they[f] regarded Him as a
prophet.

The Parable of the Wedding Banquet

22 Once more Jesus spoke to them in parables: 2 "The kingdom of heaven may
be compared to a king who gave a wedding
banquet for his son. 3 He sent out his •slaves
to summon those invited to the banquet, but
they didn't want to come. 4 Again, he sent out
other slaves, and said, 'Tell those who are
invited: Look, I've prepared my dinner; my
oxen and fattened cattle have been slaughtered, and everything is ready. Come to the
wedding banquet.'

5 "But they paid no attention and went
away, one to his own farm, another to his business. 6 And the others seized his •slaves,
treated them outrageously and killed them.
7 The king[g] was enraged, so he sent out his
troops, destroyed those murderers, and burned
down their city.

8 "Then he told his •slaves, 'The banquet is
ready, but those who were invited were not
worthy. 9 Therefore, go to where the roads exit
the city and invite everyone you find to the banquet.' 10 So those slaves went out on the roads
and gathered everyone they found, both evil
and good. The wedding banquet was filled with
guests.[h] 11 But when the king came in to view
the guests, he saw a man there who was not
dressed for a wedding. 12 So he said to him,
'Friend, how did you get in here without wedding clothes?' The man was speechless.

13 "Then the king told the attendants, 'Tie
him up hand and foot,[i] and throw him into the
outer darkness, where there will be weeping
and gnashing of teeth.'

14 "For many are invited, but few are chosen."

God and Caesar

15 Then the •Pharisees went and plotted
how to trap Him by what He said.[j] 16 They sent
their disciples to Him, with the •Herodians.
"Teacher," they said, "we know that You are
truthful and teach truthfully the way of God.
You defer to no one, for You don't show partiality.[k] 17 Tell us, therefore, what You think. Is it
lawful to pay taxes to Caesar or not?"

18 But perceiving their malice, Jesus said,
"Why are you testing Me, hypocrites? 19 Show
Me the coin used for the tax." So they brought
Him a •denarius. 20 "Whose image and inscrip-
tion is this?" He asked them.

21 "Caesar's," they said to Him.

Then He said to them, "Therefore, give
back to Caesar the things that are Caesar's, and
to God the things that are God's." 22 When
they heard this, they were amazed. So they left
Him and went away.

The Sadducees and the Resurrection

23 The same day some •Sadducees, who
say there is no resurrection, came up to Him
and questioned Him: 24 "Teacher, Moses said,

[a] **21:41** Lit *him the fruits in their seasons* [b] **21:42** Lit *the head of the corner* [c] **21:42** Ps 118:22–23 [d] **21:43** The word *its* refers back to *kingdom*. [e] **21:44** Other mss omit this v. [f] **21:46** The crowds [g] **22:7** Other mss read *But when the (that) king heard about it he* [h] **22:10** Lit *those reclining* (to eat) [i] **22:13** Other mss add *take him away* [j] **22:15** Lit *trap Him in [a] word* [k] **22:16** Lit *don't look on the face of men*; that is, on the outward appearance

**if a man dies, having no children, his brother
is to marry his wife and raise up offspring for
his brother.**[a] 25 Now there were seven brothers among us. The first got married and died.
Having no offspring, he left his wife to his
brother. 26 The same happened to the second
also, and the third, and so to all seven.[b]
27 Then last of all the woman died.
28 Therefore, in the resurrection, whose wife
will she be of the seven? For they all had married her."[c]
29 Jesus answered them, "You are deceived,
because you don't know the Scriptures or the
power of God. 30 For in the resurrection they
neither marry nor are given in marriage but are
like[d] angels in heaven. 31 Now concerning the
resurrection of the dead, haven't you read what
was spoken to you by God: 32 **I am the God of
Abraham and the God of Isaac and the God of
Jacob?**[e] He[f] is not the God of the dead, but of
the living."
33 And when the crowds heard this, they
were astonished at His teaching.

The Primary Commandments

34 When the Pharisees heard that He had
silenced the Sadducees, they came together in
the same place. 35 And one of them, an expert
in the law, asked a question to test Him:
36 "Teacher, which commandment in the law
is the greatest?"[g]
37 He said to him, "**Love the Lord your
God with all your heart, with all your soul,
and with all your mind.**[h] 38 This is the
greatest and most important[i] commandment. 39 The second is like it: **Love your
neighbor as yourself.**[j] 40 All the Law and
the Prophets depend[k] on these two commandments."

The Question about the Messiah

41 While the Pharisees were together, Jesus
questioned them, 42 "What do you think about
the •Messiah? Whose Son is He?"
"David's," they told Him.
43 He asked them, "How is it then that
David, inspired by the Spirit,[l] calls Him 'Lord':

44 **The Lord declared to my Lord,
'Sit at My right hand
until I put Your enemies
under Your feet'?**[m n]

45 "If David calls Him 'Lord,' how then can
the Messiah be his Son?" 46 No one was able to
answer Him at all,[o] and from that day no one
dared to question Him any more.

Religious Hypocrites Denounced

23 Then Jesus spoke to the crowds and to
His disciples: 2 "The •scribes and the
•Pharisees are seated in the chair of Moses.[p]
3 Therefore do whatever they tell you and
observe ⌊it⌋. But don't do what they do,[q]
because they don't practice what they teach.
4 They tie up heavy loads that are hard to carry[r]
and put them on people's shoulders, but they
themselves aren't willing to lift a finger[s] to
move them. 5 They do everything[t] to be
observed by others: They enlarge their phylac-
teries[u] and lengthen their •tassels.[v] 6 They love
the place of honor at banquets, the front seats
in the •synagogues, 7 greetings in the marketplaces, and to be called '•Rabbi' by people.
8 "But as for you, do not be called 'Rabbi,'
because you have one Teacher,[w] and you are all
brothers. 9 Do not call anyone on earth your
father, because you have one Father, who is in
heaven. 10 And do not be called masters either,
because you have one Master,[x] the •Messiah.
11 The greatest among you will be your servant.
12 Whoever exalts himself will be humbled,
and whoever humbles himself will be exalted.
13 "But woe to you, scribes and Pharisees,
hypocrites! You lock up the kingdom of heaven
from people. For you don't go in, and you don't
allow those entering to go in.
[14 "Woe to you, scribes and Pharisees, hypocrites! You devour widows' houses and make
long prayers just for show.[y] This is why you will
receive a harsher punishment.][z]
15 "Woe to you, scribes and Pharisees, hypocrites! You travel over land and sea to make
one •proselyte, and when he becomes one, you
make him twice as fit for •hell[aa] as you are!
16 "Woe to you, blind guides, who say,

[a] **22:24** Dt 25:5 [b] **22:26** Lit *so until the seven* [c] **22:28** Lit *all had her* [d] **22:30** Other mss add *God's* [e] **22:32** Ex 3:6,15–16 [f] **22:32** Other mss read *God* [g] **22:36** Lit *is great* [h] **22:37** Dt 6:5 [i] **22:38** Lit *and first* [j] **22:39** Lv 19:18 [k] **22:40** Or *hang* [l] **22:43** Lit *David in Spirit* [m] **22:44** Other mss read *until I make Your enemies Your footstool* [n] **22:44** Ps 110:1 [o] **22:46** Lit *answer Him a word* [p] **23:2** Perhaps a special chair for teaching in synagogues, or a metaphorical phrase for teaching with Moses' authority [q] **23:3** Lit *do according to their works* [r] **23:4** Other mss omit *that are hard to carry* [s] **23:4** Lit *lift with their finger* [t] **23:5** Lit *do all their works* [u] **23:5** Small leather boxes containing OT texts, worn by Jews on their arms and foreheads [v] **23:5** Other mss add *on their robes* [w] **23:8** Other mss add *the Messiah* [x] **23:10** Or *Teacher* [y] **23:14** Or *prayers with false motivation* [z] **23:14** Other mss omit bracketed text [aa] **23:15** Lit *twice the son of gehenna*

'Whoever takes an oath by the sanctuary, it
means nothing. But whoever takes an oath by
the gold of the sanctuary is bound by his oath.'[a]
17 Blind fools![b] For which is greater, the gold or
the sanctuary that sanctified the gold? 18 Also,
'Whoever takes an oath by the altar, it means
nothing. But whoever takes an oath by the gift
that is on it is bound by his oath.'[a] 19 Blind people![c] For which is greater, the gift or the altar
that sanctifies the gift? 20 Therefore the one
who takes an oath by the altar takes an oath by
it and by everything on it. 21 The one who
takes an oath by the sanctuary takes an oath by
it and by Him who dwells in it. 22 And the one
who takes an oath by heaven takes an oath by
God's throne and by Him who sits on it.
23 "Woe to you, scribes and Pharisees, hypocrites! You pay a tenth of[d] mint, dill, and
cumin,[e] yet you have neglected the more
important matters of the law—justice, mercy,
and faith. These things should have been done
without neglecting the others. 24 Blind guides!
You strain out a gnat, yet gulp down a camel!
25 "Woe to you, scribes and Pharisees, hypocrites! You clean the outside of the cup and
dish, but inside they are full of greed[f] and self-
indulgence! 26 Blind Pharisee! First clean the
inside of the cup,[g] so the outside of it[h] may also
become clean.
27 "Woe to you, scribes and Pharisees, hypocrites! You are like whitewashed tombs,
which appear beautiful on the outside, but
inside are full of dead men's bones and every
impurity. 28 In the same way, on the outside
you seem righteous to people, but inside you
are full of hypocrisy and lawlessness.
29 "Woe to you, scribes and Pharisees, hypocrites! You build the tombs of the prophets
and decorate the monuments of the righteous,
30 and you say, 'If we had lived in the days of
our fathers, we wouldn't have taken part with
them in shedding the prophets' blood.'[i] 31 You
therefore testify against yourselves that you are
sons of those who murdered the prophets.
32 Fill up, then, the measure of your fathers'
sins![j]
33 "Snakes! Brood of vipers! How can you
escape being condemned to hell?[k] 34 This is
why I am sending you prophets, sages, and
scribes. Some of them you will kill and crucify, and some of them you will flog in your
synagogues and hound from town to town.
35 So all the righteous blood shed on the
earth will be charged to you,[l] from the blood
of righteous Abel to the blood of Zechariah,
son of Berechiah, whom you murdered
between the sanctuary and the altar. 36 •I
assure you: All these things will come on this
generation!

Jesus' Lamentation over Jerusalem

37 "Jerusalem, Jerusalem! The city who kills
the prophets and stones those who are sent to
her. How often I wanted to gather your children together, as a hen gathers her chicks[m]
under her wings, yet you were not willing!
38 See, your house is left to you desolate. 39 For
I tell you, you will never see Me again until you
say, **Blessed is He who comes in the name of
the Lord!**"[n]

Destruction of the Temple Predicted

24 As Jesus left and was going out of the
•temple complex, His disciples came
up and called His attention to the temple buildings. 2 Then He replied to them, "Don't you
see all these things? •I assure you: Not one
stone will be left here on another that will not
be thrown down!"

Signs of the End of the Age

3 While He was sitting on the •Mount of
Olives, the disciples approached Him privately
and said, "Tell us, when will these things happen? And what is the sign of Your coming and
of the end of the age?"
4 Then Jesus replied to them: "Watch out
that no one deceives you. 5 For many will come
in My name, saying, 'I am the •Messiah,' and
they will deceive many. 6 You are going to hear
of wars and rumors of wars. See that you are
not alarmed, because these things must take
place, but the end is not yet. 7 For nation will
rise up against nation, and kingdom against
kingdom. There will be famines[o] and earthquakes in various places. 8 All these events are
the beginning of birth pains.

Persecutions Predicted

9 "Then they will hand you over for persecution,[p] and they will kill you. You will be

[a]**23:16,18** Lit *is obligated* [b]**23:17** Lit *Fools and blind* [c]**23:19** Other mss read *Fools and blind* [d]**23:23** Or *You tithe* [e]**23:23** A plant whose seeds are used as a seasoning [f]**23:25** Or *full of violence* [g]**23:26** Other mss add *and dish* [h]**23:26** Other mss read *of them* [i]**23:30** Lit *have been partakers with them in the blood of the prophets* [j]**23:32** Lit *the measure of your fathers* [k]**23:33** Lit *escape from the judgment of gehenna* [l]**23:35** Lit *will come on you* [m]**23:37** Or *as a mother bird gathers her young* [n]**23:39** Ps 118:26 [o]**24:7** Other mss add *epidemics* [p]**24:9** Or *tribulation, or distress*

hated by all nations because of My name.
10 Then many will take offense, betray one
another and hate one another. 11 Many false
prophets will rise up and deceive many.
12 Because lawlessness will multiply, the love
of many will grow cold. 13 But the one who
endures to the end will be delivered.[a] 14 This
good news of the kingdom will be proclaimed
in all the world[b] as a testimony to all nations.
And then the end will come.

The Great Tribulation

15 "So when you see **the abomination that**
causes desolation,[c d] spoken of by the
prophet Daniel, standing in the holy place"
(let the reader understand[e]), 16 "then those
in Judea must flee to the mountains! 17 A man
on the housetop[f] must not come down to get
things out of his house. 18 And a man in the
field must not go back to get his clothes.
19 Woe to pregnant women and nursing mothers in those days! 20 Pray that your escape may
not be in winter or on a Sabbath. 21 For at that
time there will be great tribulation, the kind
that hasn't taken place from the beginning of
the world until now and never will again!
22 Unless those days were limited, no one
would[g] survive.[h] But those days will be limited because of the elect.

23 "If anyone tells you then, 'Look, here is
the Messiah!' or, 'Over here!' do not believe
it! 24 False messiahs[i] and false prophets will
arise and perform great signs and wonders to
lead astray, if possible, even the elect. 25 Take
note: I have told you in advance. 26 So if they
tell you, 'Look, he's in the wilderness!' don't
go out; 'Look, he's in the inner rooms!' do not
believe it. 27 For as the lightning comes from
the east and flashes as far as the west, so will
be the coming of the •Son of Man. 28 Wherever the carcass is, there the vultures[j] will
gather.

The Coming of the Son of Man

29 "Immediately after the tribulation of
those days:

> The sun will be darkened,
> and the moon will not shed its light;
> the stars will fall from the sky,
> and the celestial powers
> will be shaken.

30 "Then the sign of the Son of Man will
appear in the sky, and then all the peoples of
the earth[k] will mourn;[l] and they will see the
Son of Man coming on the clouds of heaven
with power and great glory. 31 He will send
out His angels with a loud trumpet, and they
will gather His elect from the four winds, from
one end of the sky to the other.

The Parable of the Fig Tree

32 "Now learn this parable from the fig tree:
As soon as its branch becomes tender and
sprouts leaves, you know that summer is near.
33 In the same way, when you see all these
things, recognize[m] that He[n] is near—at the
door! 34 I assure you: This generation will certainly not pass away until all these things take
place. 35 Heaven and earth will pass away, but
My words will never pass away.

No One Knows the Day or Hour

36 "Now concerning that day and hour no
one knows—neither the angels in heaven, nor
the Son[o] —except the Father only. 37 As the
days of Noah were, so the coming of the Son of
Man will be. 38 For in those days before the
flood they were eating and drinking, marrying
and giving in marriage, until the day Noah
boarded the ark. 39 They didn't know[p] until the
flood came and swept them all away. So this is
the way the coming of the Son of Man will be:
40 Then two men will be in the field: one will
be taken and one left. 41 Two women will be
grinding at the mill: one will be taken and one
left. 42 Therefore be alert, since you don't
know what day[q] your Lord is coming. 43 But
know this: If the homeowner had known what
time[r] the thief was coming, he would have
stayed alert and not let his house be broken
into. 44 This is why you also must be ready,
because the Son of Man is coming at an hour
you do not expect.

Faithful Service to the Messiah

45 "Who then is a faithful and sensible slave,
whom his master has put in charge of his household, to give them food at the proper time?

[a]**24:13** Or *be saved* [b]**24:14** Or *in all the inhabited earth* [c]**24:15** Or *abomination of desolation*, or *desolating sacrilege* [d]**24:15** Dn 9:27 [e]**24:15** These are, most likely, Matthew's words to his readers. [f]**24:17** Or *roof* [g]**24:22** Lit *short, all flesh would not* [h]**24:22** Or *be saved* or *delivered* [i]**24:24** Or *False christs* [j]**24:28** Or *eagles* [k]**24:30** Or *all the tribes of the land* [l]**24:30** Lit *will beat*; = beat their breasts [m]**24:33** Or *things, you know* [n]**24:33** Or *it*; = summer [o]**24:36** Other mss omit *nor the Son* [p]**24:39** *They didn't know* the day and hour of the coming judgment [q]**24:42** Other mss read *hour*; = time [r]**24:43** Lit *watch*; a division of the night in ancient times

46 That slave whose master finds him working
when he comes will be rewarded. 47 I assure
you: He will put him in charge of all his possessions. 48 But if that wicked slave says in his heart,
'My master is delayed,' 49 and starts to beat his
fellow slaves, and eats and drinks with drunkards, 50 that slave's master will come on a day he
does not expect and at an hour he does not
know. 51 He will cut him to pieces[a] and assign
him a place with the hypocrites. In that place
there will be weeping and gnashing of teeth.

The Parable of the 10 Virgins

25 "Then the kingdom of heaven will be
like 10 virgins[b] who took their lamps
and went out to meet the groom. 2 Five of
them were foolish and five were sensible.
3 When the foolish took their lamps, they
didn't take oil with them. 4 But the sensible
ones took oil in their flasks with their lamps.
5 Since the groom was delayed, they all
became drowsy and fell asleep.

6 "In the middle of the night there was a
shout: 'Here's the groom! Come out to meet
him.'

7 "Then all those virgins got up and
trimmed their lamps. 8 But the foolish ones said
to the sensible ones, 'Give us some of your oil,
because our lamps are going out.'

9 "The sensible ones answered, 'No, there
won't be enough for us and for you. Go instead
to those who sell, and buy oil for yourselves.'

10 "When they had gone to buy some, the
groom arrived. Then those who were ready
went in with him to the wedding banquet, and
the door was shut.

11 "Later the rest of the virgins also came
and said, 'Master, master, open up for us!'

12 "But he replied, '•I assure you: I do not
know you!'

13 "Therefore be alert, because you don't
know either the day or the hour.[c]

The Parable of the Talents

14 "For it is just like a man going on a journey. He called his own •slaves and turned over
his possessions to them. 15 To one he gave five
talents;[d] to another, two; and to another, one—
to each according to his own ability. Then he
went on a journey. Immediately 16 the man
who had received five talents went, put them
to work, and earned five more. 17 In the same
way the man with two earned two more. 18 But
the man who had received one talent went off,
dug a hole in the ground, and hid his master's
money.

19 "After a long time the master of those
•slaves came and settled accounts with them.
20 The man who had received five talents
approached, presented five more talents, and
said, 'Master, you gave me five talents. Look,
I've earned five more talents.'

21 "His master said to him, 'Well done, good
and faithful •slave! You were faithful over a few
things; I will put you in charge of many things.
Share your master's joy!'

22 "Then the man with two talents also
approached. He said, 'Master, you gave me two
talents. Look, I've earned two more talents.'

23 "His master said to him, 'Well done, good
and faithful •slave! You were faithful over a few
things; I will put you in charge of many things.
Share your master's joy!'

24 "Then the man who had received one talent also approached and said, 'Master, I know
you. You're a difficult man, reaping where you
haven't sown and gathering where you haven't
scattered seed. 25 So I was afraid and went off
and hid your talent in the ground. Look, you
have what is yours.'

26 "But his master replied to him, 'You evil,
lazy •slave! If you knew that I reap where I
haven't sown and gather where I haven't scattered, 27 then[e] you should have deposited my
money with the bankers. And when I returned
I would have received my money[f] back with
interest.

28 " 'So take the talent from him and give it
to the one who has 10 talents. 29 For to everyone who has, more will be given, and he will
have more than enough. But from the one who
does not have, even what he has will be taken
away from him. 30 And throw this good-for-
nothing •slave into the outer darkness. In that
place there will be weeping and gnashing of
teeth.'

The Sheep and the Goats

31 "When the •Son of Man comes in His
glory, and all the angels[g] with Him, then He
will sit on the throne of His glory. 32 All the
nations[h] will be gathered before Him, and He
will separate them one from another, just as a
shepherd separates the sheep from the goats.

[a]**24:51** Lit *him in two* [b]**25:1** Or *bridesmaids* [c]**25:13** Other mss add *in which the Son of Man is coming.* [d]**25:15** Worth a very large sum of money; a talent = 6,000 •denarii [e]**25:26–27** Or *So you knew . . . scattered? Then* (as a question)
[f]**25:27** Lit *received what is mine* [g]**25:31** Other mss read *holy angels* [h]**25:32** Or *the Gentiles*

33 He will put the sheep on His right, and the
goats on the left. 34 Then the King will say to
those on His right, 'Come, you who are blessed
by My Father, inherit the kingdom prepared for
you from the foundation of the world.

35 For I was hungry
and you gave Me something to eat;
I was thirsty
and you gave Me something to drink;
I was a stranger and you took Me in;
36 I was naked and you clothed Me;
I was sick and you took care of Me;
I was in prison and you visited Me.'

37 "Then the righteous will answer Him,
'Lord, when did we see You hungry and feed
You, or thirsty and give You something to
drink? 38 When did we see You a stranger and
take You in, or without clothes and clothe You?
39 When did we see You sick, or in prison, and
visit You?'

40 "And the King will answer them, 'I
assure you: Whatever you did for one of the
least of these brothers of Mine, you did for Me.'
41 Then He will also say to those on the left,
'Depart from Me, you who are cursed, into the
eternal fire prepared for the Devil and his
angels!

42 For I was hungry
and you gave Me nothing to eat;
I was thirsty
and you gave Me nothing to drink;
43 I was a stranger
and you didn't take Me in;
I was naked
and you didn't clothe Me,
sick and in prison
and you didn't take care of Me.'

44 "Then they too will answer, 'Lord, when
did we see You hungry, or thirsty, or a stranger,
or without clothes, or sick, or in prison, and not
help You?'

45 "Then He will answer them, 'I assure
you: Whatever you did not do for one of the
least of these, you did not do for Me either.'

46 "And they will go away into eternal punishment, but the righteous into eternal life."

The Plot to Kill Jesus

26 When Jesus had finished saying all
this, He told His disciples, 2 "You
know[a] that the •Passover takes place after two
days, and the •Son of Man will be handed over
to be crucified."

3 Then the •chief priests[b] and the elders of
the people assembled in the palace of the high
priest, who was called Caiaphas, 4 and they conspired to arrest Jesus in a treacherous way and
kill Him. 5 "Not during the festival," they said,
"so there won't be rioting among the people."

The Anointing at Bethany

6 While Jesus was in Bethany at the house of
Simon, a man who had a serious skin disease,
7 a woman approached Him with an alabaster
jar of very expensive fragrant oil. She poured it
on His head as He was reclining at the table.
8 When the disciples saw it, they were indignant. "Why this waste?" they asked. 9 "This
might have been sold for a great deal and given
to the poor."

10 But Jesus, aware of this, said to them,
"Why are you bothering this woman? She has
done a noble thing for Me. 11 You always have
the poor with you, but you do not always have
Me. 12 By pouring this fragrant oil on My body,
she has prepared Me for burial. 13 •I assure
you: Wherever this gospel is proclaimed in the
whole world, what this woman has done will
also be told in memory of her."

14 Then one of the Twelve—the man called
Judas Iscariot—went to the chief priests 15 and
said, "What are you willing to give me if I hand
Him over to you?" So they weighed out 30
pieces of silver for him. 16 And from that time
he started looking for a good opportunity to
betray Him.

Betrayal at the Passover

17 On the first day of •Unleavened Bread
the disciples came to Jesus and asked, "Where
do You want us to prepare the Passover so You
may eat it?"

18 "Go into the city to a certain man," He
said, "and tell him, 'The Teacher says: My time
is near; I am celebrating the Passover at your
place[c] with My disciples.' " 19 So the disciples
did as Jesus had directed them and prepared
the Passover. 20 When evening came, He was
reclining at the table with the Twelve. 21 While
they were eating, He said, "I assure you: One of
you will betray Me."

22 Deeply distressed, each one began to say
to Him, "Surely not I, Lord?"

23 He replied, "The one who dipped his

[a]**26:2** Or *Know* (as a command) [b]**26:3** Other mss add *and the scribes* [c]**26:18** Lit *Passover with you*

hand with Me in the bowl—he will betray Me. 24 The Son of Man will go just as it is written about Him, but woe to that man by whom the Son of Man is betrayed! It would have been better for that man if he had not been born."

25 Then Judas, His betrayer, replied, "Surely not I, •Rabbi?"

"You have said it," He told him.

The First Lord's Supper

26 As they were eating, Jesus took bread, blessed and broke it, gave it to the disciples, and said, "Take and eat it; this is My body." 27 Then He took a cup, and after giving thanks, He gave it to them and said, "Drink from it, all of you. 28 For this is My blood ⌊that establishes⌋ the covenant;[a] it is shed for many for the forgiveness of sins. 29 But I tell you, from this moment I will not drink of this fruit of the vine until that day when I drink it in a new way[b] in My Father's kingdom with you." 30 After singing psalms,[c] they went out to the •Mount of Olives.

Peter's Denial Predicted

31 Then Jesus said to them, "Tonight all of you will run away[d] because of Me, for it is written:

> **I will strike the shepherd,**
> **and the sheep of the flock**
> **will be scattered.**[e]

32 But after I have been resurrected, I will go ahead of you to Galilee."

33 Peter told Him, "Even if everyone runs away because of You, I will never run away!"

34 "I assure you," Jesus said to him, "tonight—before the rooster crows, you will deny Me three times!"

35 "Even if I have to die with You," Peter told Him, "I will never deny You!" And all the disciples said the same thing.

The Prayer in the Garden

36 Then Jesus came with them to a place called Gethsemane,[f] and He told the disciples, "Sit here while I go over there and pray." 37 Taking along Peter and the two sons of Zebedee, He began to be sorrowful and deeply distressed. 38 Then He said to them, "My soul is swallowed up in sorrow[g]—to the point of death.[h] Remain here and stay awake with Me." 39 Going a little farther,[i] He fell facedown and prayed, "My Father! If it is possible, let this cup pass from Me. Yet not as I will, but as You will."

40 Then He came to the disciples and found them sleeping. He asked Peter, "So, couldn't you[j] stay awake with Me one hour? 41 Stay awake and pray, so that you won't enter into temptation. The spirit is willing, but the flesh is weak."

42 Again, a second time, He went away and prayed, "My Father, if this[k] cannot pass[l] unless I drink it, Your will be done." 43 And He came again and found them sleeping, because they could not keep their eyes open.[m]

44 After leaving them, He went away again and prayed a third time, saying the same thing once more. 45 Then He came to the disciples and said to them, "Are you still sleeping and resting?[n] Look, the time is near. The Son of Man is being betrayed into the hands of sinners. 46 Get up; let's go! See—My betrayer is near."

The Judas Kiss

47 While He was still speaking, Judas, one of the Twelve, suddenly arrived. A large mob, with swords and clubs, was with him from the chief priests and elders of the people. 48 His betrayer had given them a sign: "The One I kiss, He's the One; arrest Him!" 49 So he went right up to Jesus and said, "Greetings, Rabbi!"—and kissed Him.

50 "Friend," Jesus asked him, "why have you come?"[o]

Then they came up, took hold of Jesus, and arrested Him. 51 At that moment one of those with Jesus reached out his hand and drew his sword. He struck the high priest's slave and cut off his ear.

52 Then Jesus told him, "Put your sword back in place because all who take up a sword will perish by a sword. 53 Or do you think that I cannot call on My Father, and He will provide Me at once with more than 12 legions[p] of angels? 54 How, then, would the Scriptures be fulfilled that say it must happen this way?"

55 At that time Jesus said to the crowds,

[a]**26:28** Other mss read *new covenant* [b]**26:29** Or *drink new wine*; lit *drink it new* [c]**26:30** Pss 113–118 were sung during and after the Passover meal. [d]**26:31** Or •*stumble* [e]**26:31** Zch 13:7 [f]**26:36** A garden east of Jerusalem at the base of the Mount of Olives; *Gethsemane* = olive oil press [g]**26:38** Or *I am deeply grieved*, or *I am overwhelmed by sorrow*; Ps 42:6,11; 43:5 [h]**26:38** Lit *unto death* [i]**26:39** Other mss read *Drawing nearer* [j]**26:40** *You* = all 3 disciples because the verb in Gk is pl [k]**26:42** Other mss add *cup* [l]**26:42** Other mss add *from Me* [m]**26:43** Lit *because their eyes were weighed down* [n]**26:45** Or *Sleep on now and take your rest.* [o]**26:50** Or *Jesus told him, "do what you have come for."* (as a statement) [p]**26:53** A Roman legion contained up to 6,000 soldiers.

"Have you come out with swords and clubs, as if I were a criminal,[a] to capture Me? Every day I used to sit, teaching in the •temple complex, and you didn't arrest Me. 56 But all this has happened so that the prophetic Scriptures[b] would be fulfilled." Then all the disciples deserted Him and ran away.

Jesus Faces the Sanhedrin

57 Those who had arrested Jesus led Him away to Caiaphas the high priest, where the •scribes and the elders had convened. 58 Meanwhile, Peter was following Him at a distance right to the high priest's courtyard.[c] He went in and was sitting with the temple police[d] to see the outcome.[e]

59 The chief priests and the whole •Sanhedrin were looking for false testimony against Jesus so they could put Him to death. 60 But they could not find any, even though many false witnesses came forward.[f] Finally, two[g] who came forward 61 stated, "This man said, 'I can demolish God's sanctuary and rebuild it in three days.' "

62 The high priest then stood up and said to Him, "Don't You have an answer to what these men are testifying against You?" 63 But Jesus kept silent. Then the high priest said to Him, "By the living God I place You under oath: tell us if You are the •Messiah, the Son of God!"

64 "You have said it,"[h] Jesus told him. "But I tell you, in the future[i] you will see **the Son of Man seated at the right hand** of the Power and **coming on the clouds of heaven.**"[j]

65 Then the high priest tore his robes and said, "He has blasphemed! Why do we still need witnesses? Look, now you've heard the blasphemy! 66 What is your decision?"[k]

They answered, "He deserves death!" 67 Then they spit in His face and beat Him; others slapped Him 68 and said, "Prophesy to us, Messiah! Who hit You?"

Peter Denies His Lord

69 Now Peter was sitting outside in the courtyard. A servant approached him and she said, "You were with Jesus the Galilean too."

70 But he denied it in front of everyone: "I don't know what you're talking about!"

71 When he had gone out to the gateway, another woman saw him and told those who were there, "This man was with Jesus the •Nazarene!"

72 And again he denied it with an oath, "I don't know the man!"

73 After a little while those standing there approached and said to Peter, "You certainly are one of them, since even your accent[l] gives you away."

74 Then he started to curse[m] and to swear with an oath, "I do not know the man!" Immediately a rooster crowed, 75 and Peter remembered the words Jesus had spoken, "Before the rooster crows, you will deny Me three times." And he went outside and wept bitterly.

Jesus Handed Over to Pilate

27 When daybreak came, all the •chief priests and the elders of the people plotted against Jesus to put Him to death. 2 After tying Him up, they led Him away and handed Him over to •Pilate,[n] the governor.

Judas Hangs Himself

3 Then Judas, His betrayer, seeing that He had been condemned, was full of remorse and returned the 30 pieces of silver to the chief priests and elders. 4 "I have sinned by betraying innocent blood," he said.

"What's that to us?" they said. "See to it yourself!"

5 So he threw the silver into the sanctuary and departed. Then he went and hanged himself.

6 The chief priests took the silver and said, "It's not lawful to put it into the temple treasury,[o] since it is blood money."[p] 7 So they conferred together and bought the potter's field with it as a burial place for foreigners. 8 Therefore that field has been called "Blood Field" to this day. 9 Then what was spoken through the prophet Jeremiah was fulfilled:

> **They took the 30 pieces of silver, the price of Him whose price was set by the sons of Israel, 10 and they gave them for the potter's field, as the Lord directed me.**[q]

Jesus Faces the Governor

11 Now Jesus stood before the governor.

[a]**26:55** Lit *as against a criminal* [b]**26:56** Or *the Scriptures of the prophets* [c]**26:58** Or *high priest's palace* [d]**26:58** Or *the officers*, or *the servants* [e]**26:58** Lit *end* [f]**26:60** Other mss add *they found none* [g]**26:60** Other mss add *false witnesses* [h]**26:64** Or *That is true*, an affirmative oath; Mt 27:11; Mk 15:2 [i]**26:64** Lit *you, from now* [j]**26:64** Ps 110:1; Dn 7:13 [k]**26:66** Lit *What does it seem to you?* [l]**26:73** Or *speech* [m]**26:74** To call down curses on himself if what he said weren't true [n]**27:2** Other mss read *Pontius Pilate* [o]**27:6** See Mk 7:11 where the same Gk word used here (*Corban*) means a gift (pledged to the temple). [p]**27:6** Lit *the price of blood* [q]**27:9–10** Jr 32:6–9; Zch 11:12–13

"Are You the King of the Jews?" the governor asked Him.

Jesus answered, "You have said it."[a] 12 And while He was being accused by the chief priests and elders, He didn't answer.

13 Then Pilate said to Him, "Don't You hear how much they are testifying against You?" 14 But He didn't answer him on even one charge, so that the governor was greatly amazed.

Jesus or Barabbas

15 At the festival the governor's custom was to release to the crowd a prisoner they wanted. 16 At that time they had a notorious prisoner called Barabbas.[b] 17 So when they had gathered together, Pilate said to them, "Who is it you want me to release for you—Barabbas,[b] or Jesus who is called •Messiah?" 18 For he knew they had handed Him over because of envy.

19 While he was sitting on the judge's bench, his wife sent word to him, "Have nothing to do with that righteous man, for today I've suffered terribly in a dream because of Him!"

20 The chief priests and the elders, however, persuaded the crowds to ask for Barabbas and to execute Jesus. 21 The governor asked them, "Which of the two do you want me to release for you?"

"Barabbas!" they answered.

22 Pilate asked them, "What should I do then with Jesus, who is called Messiah?"

They all answered, "Crucify Him!"[c]

23 Then he said, "Why? What has He done wrong?"

But they kept shouting, "Crucify Him!" all the more.

24 When Pilate saw that he was getting nowhere,[d] but that a riot was starting instead, he took some water, washed his hands in front of the crowd, and said, "I am innocent of this man's blood.[e] See to it yourselves!"

25 All the people answered, "His blood be on us and on our children!" 26 Then he released Barabbas to them. But after having Jesus flogged,[f] he handed Him over to be crucified.

Mocked by the Military

27 Then the governor's soldiers took Jesus into •headquarters and gathered the whole •company around Him. 28 They stripped Him and dressed Him in a scarlet robe. 29 They twisted together a crown of thorns, put it on His head, and placed a reed in His right hand. And they knelt down before Him and mocked Him: "Hail, King of the Jews!" 30 Then they spit at Him, took the reed, and kept hitting Him on the head. 31 When they had mocked Him, they stripped Him of the robe, put His clothes on Him, and led Him away to crucify Him.

Crucified Between Two Criminals

32 As they were going out, they found a Cyrenian man named Simon. They forced this man to carry His cross. 33 When they came to a place called *Golgotha* (which means Skull Place), 34 they gave Him wine[g] mixed with gall to drink. But when He tasted it, He would not drink it. 35 After crucifying Him they divided His clothes by casting lots.[h] 36 Then they sat down and were guarding Him there. 37 Above His head they put up the charge against Him in writing:

THIS IS JESUS
THE KING OF THE JEWS

38 Then two criminals[i] were crucified with Him, one on the right and one on the left. 39 Those who passed by were yelling insults at[j] Him, shaking their heads 40 and saying, "The One who would demolish the sanctuary and rebuild it in three days, save Yourself! If You are the Son of God, come down from the cross!" 41 In the same way the chief priests, with the •scribes and elders,[k] mocked Him and said, 42 "He saved others, but He cannot save Himself! He is the King of Israel! Let Him[l] come down now from the cross, and we will believe in Him. 43 He has put His trust in God; let God rescue Him now—if He wants Him![m] For He said, 'I am God's Son.' " 44 In the same way even the criminals who were crucified with Him kept taunting Him.

The Death of Jesus

45 From noon until three in the afternoon[n]

[a]**27:11** Or *That is true*, an affirmative oath; Mt 26:64; Mk 15:2 [b]**27:16,17** Other mss read *Jesus Barabbas* [c]**27:22** Lit *"Him—be crucified!"* [d]**27:24** Lit *that it availed nothing* [e]**27:24** Other mss read *this righteous man's blood* [f]**27:26** Roman flogging was done with a whip made of leather strips embedded with pieces of bone or metal that brutally tore the flesh. [g]**27:34** Other mss read *sour wine* [h]**27:35** Other mss add *that what was spoken by the prophet might be fulfilled: "They divided My clothes among them, and for My clothing they cast lots."* [i]**27:38** Or *revolutionaries* [j]**27:39** Lit *passed by blasphemed* or *were blaspheming* [k]**27:41** Other mss add *and Pharisees* [l]**27:42** Other mss read *If He . . . Israel, let Him* [m]**27:43** Or *if He takes pleasure in Him*; Ps 22:8 [n]**27:45** Lit *From the sixth hour to the ninth hour*

darkness came over the whole land.[a] 46 At about
three in the afternoon Jesus cried out with a loud
voice, ***"Elí, Elí, lemá sabachtháni?"*** that is,
**"My God, My God, why have You forsaken[b]
Me?"**[c]
47 When some of those standing there
heard this, they said, "He's calling for Elijah!"
48 Immediately one of them ran and got a
sponge, filled it with sour wine, fixed it on a
reed, and offered Him a drink. 49 But the rest
said, "Let's see if Elijah comes to save Him!"
50 Jesus shouted again with a loud voice and
gave up His spirit. 51 Suddenly, the curtain of
the sanctuary[d] was split in two from top to bottom; the earth quaked and the rocks were split.
52 The tombs also were opened and many bodies of the saints who had gone to their rest[e]
were raised. 53 And they came out of the tombs
after His resurrection, entered the holy city,
and appeared to many.
54 When the •centurion and those with
him, who were guarding Jesus, saw the earthquake and the things that had happened, they
were terrified and said, "This man really was
God's Son!"[f]
55 Many women who had followed Jesus
from Galilee and ministered to Him were there,
looking on from a distance. 56 Among them
were •Mary Magdalene, Mary the mother of
James and Joseph, and the mother of Zebedee's
sons.

The Burial of Jesus

57 When it was evening, a rich man from
Arimathea named Joseph came, who himself
had also become a disciple of Jesus. 58 He
approached Pilate and asked for Jesus' body.
Then Pilate ordered that it[g] be released. 59 So
Joseph took the body, wrapped it in clean, fine
linen, 60 and placed it in his new tomb, which
he had cut into the rock. He left after rolling a
great stone against the entrance of the tomb.
61 Mary Magdalene and the other Mary were
seated there, facing the tomb.

The Closely Guarded Tomb

62 The next day, which followed the preparation day, the chief priests and the •Pharisees
gathered before Pilate 63 and said, "Sir, we
remember that while this deceiver was still
alive, He said, 'After three days I will rise again.'
64 Therefore give orders that the tomb be made
secure until the third day. Otherwise, His disciples may come, steal Him, and tell the people,
'He has been raised from the dead.' Then the
last deception will be worse than the first."
65 "You have[h] a guard ⌊of soldiers⌋,"[i] Pilate
told them. "Go and make it as secure as you
know how." 66 Then they went and made the
tomb secure by sealing the stone and setting
the guard.[j]

Resurrection Morning

28 After the Sabbath, as the first day of
the week was dawning, •Mary
Magdalene and the other Mary went to view
the tomb. 2 Suddenly there was a violent
earthquake, because an angel of the Lord
descended from heaven and approached ⌊the
tomb⌋. He rolled back the stone and was sitting
on it. 3 His appearance was like lightning, and
his robe was as white as snow. 4 The guards
were so shaken from fear of him that they
became like dead men.
5 But the angel told the women, "Don't be
afraid, because I know you are looking for Jesus
who was crucified. 6 He is not here! For He has
been resurrected, just as He said. Come and see
the place where He lay. 7 Then go quickly and
tell His disciples, 'He has been raised from the
dead. In fact, He is going ahead of you to Galilee;
you will see Him there.' Listen, I have told you."
8 So, departing quickly from the tomb with
fear and great joy, they ran to tell His disciples
the news. 9 Just then[k] Jesus met them and said,
"Good morning!" They came up, took hold of
His feet, and worshiped Him. 10 Then Jesus
told them, "Do not be afraid. Go and tell My
brothers to leave for Galilee, and they will see
Me there."

The Soldiers Are Bribed to Lie

11 As they were on their way, some of the
guard came into the city and reported to the
•chief priests everything that had happened.
12 After the priests[l] had assembled with the
elders and agreed on a plan, they gave the soldiers a large sum of money 13 and told them,
"Say this, 'His disciples came during the night
and stole Him while we were sleeping.' 14 If

[a]**27:45** Or *whole earth* [b]**27:46** Or *abandoned* [c]**27:46** Ps 22:1 [d]**27:51** A heavy curtain separated the inner room of the temple from the outer. [e]**27:52** Lit *saints having fallen asleep*; that is, they had died [f]**27:54** Or *the Son of God* [g]**27:58** Other mss read *that the body* [h]**27:65** Or *"Take* [i]**27:65** It is uncertain whether this guard consisted of temple police or Roman soldiers. [j]**27:66** Lit *stone with the guard* [k]**28:9** Other mss add *as they were on their way to tell the news to His disciples* [l]**28:12** Lit *After they*

this reaches the governor's ears,[a] we will deal with[b] him and keep you out of trouble." 15 So they took the money and did as they were instructed. And this story has been spread among Jewish people to this day.

The Great Commission

16 The 11 disciples traveled to Galilee, to the mountain where Jesus had directed them. 17 When they saw Him, they worshiped,[c] but some doubted. 18 Then Jesus came near and said to them, "All authority has been given to Me in heaven and on earth. 19 Go, therefore, and make disciples of[d] all nations, baptizing them in the name of the Father and of the Son and of the Holy Spirit, 20 teaching them to observe everything I have commanded you. And remember,[e] I am with you always,[f] to the end of the age."

Mark

The Messiah's Herald

1 The beginning of the gospel of Jesus Christ, the Son of God. 2 As it is written in Isaiah the prophet:[g]

> **Look, I am sending My messenger**
> **ahead of You,**
> **who will prepare Your way.**[h]
> 3 **A voice of one crying out**
> **in the wilderness:**
> **"Prepare the way for the Lord;**
> **make His paths straight!"**[i]

4 John came baptizing[j] in the wilderness and preaching a baptism of repentance[k] for the forgiveness of sins. 5 The whole Judean countryside and all the people of Jerusalem were flocking to him, and they were baptized by him in the Jordan River as they confessed their sins. 6 John wore a camel-hair garment with a leather belt around his waist and ate locusts and wild honey. 7 He was preaching: "Someone more powerful than I will come after me. I am not worthy to stoop down and untie the strap of His sandals. 8 I have baptized you with[l] water, but He will baptize you with[l] the Holy Spirit."

The Baptism of Jesus

9 In those days Jesus came from Nazareth in Galilee and was baptized in the Jordan by John. 10 As soon as He came up out of the water, He saw the heavens being torn open and the Spirit descending to Him like a dove. 11 And a voice came from heaven:

> You are My beloved Son;
> I take delight in You![m]

The Temptation of Jesus

12 Immediately the Spirit drove Him into the wilderness. 13 He was in the wilderness 40 days, being tempted by Satan. He was with the wild animals, and the angels began to serve Him.

Ministry in Galilee

14 After John was arrested, Jesus went to Galilee, preaching the good news[n] [o] of God:[p] 15 "The time is fulfilled, and the kingdom of God has come near. Repent and believe in the good news!"

The First Disciples

16 As He was passing along by the Sea of Galilee, He saw Simon and Andrew, Simon's brother. They were casting a net into the sea, since they were fishermen.

17 "Follow Me," Jesus told them, "and I will make you fish for[q] people!" 18 Immediately they left their nets and followed Him. 19 Going on a little farther, He saw James the son of Zebedee and his brother John. They were in their boat mending their nets. 20 Immediately He called them, and they left their father Zebedee in the boat with the hired men and followed Him.

[a]**28:14** Lit *this is heard by the governor* [b]**28:14** Lit *will persuade* [c]**28:17** Other mss add *Him* [d]**28:19** Lit *and instruct*, or *and disciple* (as a verb) [e]**28:20** Lit *look* [f]**28:20** Lit *all the days* [g]**1:2** Other mss read *in the prophets* [h]**1:2** Other mss add *before You* [i]**1:2–3** Mal 3:1; Is 40:3 [j]**1:4** Or *John the Baptist came*, or *John the Baptizer came* [k]**1:4** Or *a baptism based on repentance* [l]**1:8** Or *in* [m]**1:11** Or *In You I am well pleased* [n]**1:14** Other mss add *of the kingdom* [o]**1:14** Or *gospel* [p]**1:14** Either *from God* or *about God* [q]**1:17** Lit *you to become fishers of*

Driving Out an Unclean Spirit

21 Then they went into Capernaum, and right away He entered the •synagogue on the Sabbath and began to teach. 22 They were astonished at His teaching because, unlike the •scribes, He was teaching them as one having authority.

23 Just then a man with an unclean spirit was in their synagogue. He cried out,[a] 24 "What do You have to do with us,[b] Jesus—Nazarene? Have You come to destroy us? I know who You are—the Holy One of God!"

25 But Jesus rebuked him and said, "Be quiet,[c] and come out of him!" 26 And the unclean spirit convulsed him, shouted with a loud voice, and came out of him.

27 Then they were all amazed, so they began to argue with one another, saying, "What is this? A new teaching with authority![d] He commands even the unclean spirits, and they obey Him." 28 His fame then spread throughout the entire vicinity of Galilee.

Healings at Capernaum

29 As soon as they left the synagogue, they went into Simon and Andrew's house with James and John. 30 Simon's mother-in-law was lying in bed with a fever, and they told Him about her at once. 31 So He went to her, took her by the hand, and raised her up. The fever left her,[e] and she began to serve them.

32 When evening came, after the sun had set, they began bringing to Him all those who were sick and those who were demon-possessed. 33 The whole town was assembled at the door, 34 and He healed many who were sick with various diseases and drove out many demons. But He would not permit the demons to speak, because they knew Him.

Preaching in Galilee

35 Very early in the morning, while it was still dark, He got up, went out, and made His way to a deserted place. And He was praying there. 36 Simon and his companions went searching for Him. 37 They found Him and said, "Everyone's looking for You!"

38 And He said to them, "Let's go on to the neighboring villages so that I may preach there too. This is why I have come." 39 So He went into all of Galilee, preaching in their synagogues and driving out demons.

Cleansing a Leper

40 Then a man with a serious skin disease came to Him and, on his knees,[f] begged Him: "If You are willing, You can make me clean."[g]

41 Moved with compassion, Jesus reached out His hand and touched him. "I am willing," He told him. "Be made clean." 42 Immediately the disease left him, and he was healed.[h] 43 Then He sternly warned him and sent him away at once, 44 telling him, "See that you say nothing to anyone; but go and show yourself to the priest, and offer what Moses prescribed for your cleansing, as a testimony to them." 45 Yet he went out and began to proclaim it widely and to spread the news, with the result that Jesus could no longer enter a town openly. But He was out in deserted places, and they would come to Him from everywhere.

The Son of Man Forgives and Heals

2 When He entered Capernaum again after some days, it was reported that He was at home. 2 So many people gathered together that there was no more room, not even in the doorway, and He was speaking the message to them. 3 Then they came to Him bringing a paralytic, carried by four men. 4 Since they were not able to bring him to[i] Jesus because of the crowd, they removed the roof above where He was. And when they had broken through, they lowered the stretcher on which the paralytic was lying.

5 Seeing their faith, Jesus told the paralytic, "Son, your sins are forgiven."

6 But some of the •scribes were sitting there, thinking to themselves:[j] 7 "Why does He speak like this? He's blaspheming! Who can forgive sins but God alone?"

8 Right away Jesus understood in His spirit that they were reasoning like this within themselves and said to them, "Why are you reasoning these things in your hearts?[k] 9 Which is easier: to say to the paralytic, 'Your sins are forgiven,' or to say, 'Get up, pick up your stretcher, and walk'? 10 But so you may know that the •Son of Man has authority on earth to forgive sins," He told the paralytic, 11 "I tell

[a]**1:23** Other mss add to the beginning of v. 24: *"Leave us alone.* [b]**1:24** Lit *What to us and to You* [c]**1:25** Or *Be muzzled* [d]**1:27** Other mss read *What is this? What is this new teaching? For with authority* [e]**1:31** Other mss add *at once* [f]**1:40** Other mss omit *on his knees* [g]**1:40** In these vv., *clean* includes healing, ceremonial purification, return to fellowship with people, and worship in the temple; Lv 14:1–32. [h]**1:42** Lit *made clean* [i]**2:4** Other mss read *able to get near* [j]**2:6** Or *there, reasoning in their hearts* [k]**2:8** Or *minds*

you: get up, pick up your stretcher, and go home."

12 Immediately he got up, picked up the stretcher, and went out in front of everyone. As a result, they were all astounded and gave glory to God, saying, "We have never seen anything like this!"

The Call of Matthew

13 Then Jesus went out again beside the sea. The whole crowd was coming to Him, and He taught them. 14 Then, moving on, He saw Levi the son of Alphaeus sitting at the tax office, and He said to him, "Follow Me!" So he got up and followed Him.

Dining with Sinners

15 While He was reclining at the table in Levi's house, many tax collectors and sinners were also guests[a] with Jesus and His disciples, because there were many who were following Him. 16 When the scribes of the •Pharisees[b] saw that He was eating with sinners and tax collectors, they asked His disciples, "Why does He eat[c] with tax collectors and sinners?"

17 When Jesus heard this, He told them, "Those who are well don't need a doctor, but the sick ⌊do need one⌋. I didn't come to call the righteous, but sinners."

A Question about Fasting

18 Now John's disciples and the Pharisees[d] were fasting. People came and asked Him, "Why do John's disciples and the Pharisees' disciples fast, but Your disciples do not fast?"

19 Jesus said to them, "The wedding guests[e] cannot fast while the groom is with them, can they? As long as they have the groom with them, they cannot fast. 20 But the time[f] will come when the groom is taken away from them, and then they will fast in that day. 21 No one sews a patch of unshrunk cloth on an old garment. Otherwise, the new patch pulls away from the old cloth, and a worse tear is made. 22 And no one puts new wine into old wineskins. Otherwise, the wine will burst the skins, and the wine is lost as well as the skins.[g] But new wine is for fresh wineskins."

Lord of the Sabbath

23 On the Sabbath He was going through the grainfields, and His disciples began to make their way picking some heads of grain. 24 The Pharisees said to Him, "Look, why are they doing what is not lawful on the Sabbath?"

25 He said to them, "Have you never read what David and those who were with him did when he was in need and hungry— 26 how he entered the house of God in the time of Abiathar the high priest and ate the •sacred bread—which is not lawful for anyone to eat except the priests—and also gave some to his companions?" 27 Then He told them, "The Sabbath was made for[h] man and not man for[h] the Sabbath. 28 Therefore the Son of Man is Lord even of the Sabbath."

The Man with the Paralyzed Hand

3 Now He entered the •synagogue again, and a man was there who had a paralyzed hand. 2 In order to accuse Him, they were watching Him closely to see whether He would heal him on the Sabbath. 3 He told the man with the paralyzed hand, "Stand before us."[i] 4 Then He said to them, "Is it lawful on the Sabbath to do good or to do evil, to save life or to kill?" But they were silent. 5 After looking around at them with anger and sorrow at the hardness of their hearts, He told the man, "Stretch out your hand." So he stretched it out, and his hand was restored. 6 Immediately the •Pharisees went out and started plotting with the •Herodians against Him, how they might destroy Him.

Ministering to the Multitude

7 Jesus departed with His disciples to the sea, and a great multitude followed from Galilee, Judea, 8 Jerusalem, Idumea, beyond the Jordan, and around Tyre and Sidon. The great multitude came to Him because they heard about everything He was doing. 9 Then He told His disciples to have a small boat ready for Him, so the crowd would not crush Him. 10 Since He had healed many, all who had diseases were pressing toward Him to touch Him. 11 Whenever the unclean spirits saw Him, those possessed fell down before Him and cried out, "You are the Son of God!" 12 And He would strongly warn them not to make Him known.

[a] **2:15** Lit *reclining* (at the table); at important meals the custom was to recline on a mat at a low table and lean on the left elbow. [b] **2:16** Other mss read *scribes and Pharisees* [c] **2:16** Other mss add *and drink* [d] **2:18** Other mss read *the disciples of John and of the Pharisees* [e] **2:19** Lit *The sons of the bridal chamber* [f] **2:20** Lit *the days* [g] **2:22** Other mss read *the wine spills out and the skins will be ruined* [h] **2:27** Or *because of* [i] **3:3** Lit *Rise up in the middle*

The 12 Apostles

13 Then He went up the mountain and summoned those He wanted, and they came to
Him. 14 He also appointed 12—He also named
them apostles[a] —to be with Him, to send them
out to preach, 15 and to have authority to[b] drive
out demons.
16 He appointed the Twelve:[c]

To Simon, He gave the name Peter;
17 and to James the son of Zebedee,
and to his brother John,
He gave the name "Boanerges"
(that is, "Sons of Thunder");
18 Andrew;
Philip and Bartholomew;
Matthew and Thomas;
James the son of Alphaeus,
and Thaddaeus;
Simon the Zealot,[d]
19 and Judas Iscariot,[e]
who also betrayed Him.

A House Divided

20 Then He went home, and the crowd
gathered again so that they were not even able
to eat.[f] 21 When His family heard this, they set
out to restrain Him, because they said, "He's
out of His mind."
22 The •scribes who had come down from
Jerusalem said, "He has •Beelzebul in Him!"
and, "He drives out demons by the ruler of the
demons!"
23 So He summoned them and spoke to
them in parables: "How can Satan drive out
Satan? 24 If a kingdom is divided against itself,
that kingdom cannot stand. 25 If a house is
divided against itself, that house cannot stand.
26 And if Satan rebels against himself and is
divided, he cannot stand but is finished![g]
27 "On the other hand, no one can enter a
strong man's house and rob his possessions
unless he first ties up the strong man. Then he
will rob his house. 28 •I assure you: People will
be forgiven for all sins[h] and whatever blasphemies they may blaspheme. 29 But whoever
blasphemes against the Holy Spirit never has
forgiveness, but is guilty of an eternal sin"[i] —
30 because they were saying, "He has an
unclean spirit."

True Relationships

31 Then His mother and His brothers came,
and standing outside, they sent ⌊word⌋ to Him
and called Him. 32 A crowd was sitting around
Him and told Him, "Look, Your mother, Your
brothers, and Your sisters[j] are outside asking
for You."
33 He replied to them, "Who are My mother
and My brothers?" 34 And looking about at
those who were sitting in a circle around Him,
He said, "Here are My mother and My brothers! 35 Whoever does the will of God is My
brother and sister and mother."

The Parable of the Sower

4 Again He began to teach by the sea, and
a very large crowd gathered around Him.
So He got into a boat on the sea and sat down,
while the whole crowd was on the shore facing the sea. 2 He taught them many things in
parables, and in His teaching He said to them:
3 "Listen! Consider the sower who went out to
sow. 4 As he sowed, this occurred: Some seed
fell along the path, and the birds came and ate
it up. 5 Other seed fell on rocky ground where
it didn't have much soil, and it sprang up right
away, since it didn't have deep soil. 6 When
the sun came up, it was scorched, and since it
didn't have a root, it withered. 7 Other seed
fell among thorns, and the thorns came up and
choked it, and it didn't produce a crop. 8 Still
others fell on good ground and produced a
crop that increased 30, 60, and 100 times
⌊what was sown⌋." 9 Then He said, "Anyone
who has ears to hear should listen!"

Why Jesus Used Parables

10 When He was alone with the Twelve,
those who were around Him asked Him about
the parables. 11 He answered them, "The
secret[k] of the kingdom of God has been granted
to you, but to those outside, everything comes
in parables 12 so that

they may look and look,
yet not perceive;
they may listen and listen,
yet not understand;
otherwise, they might turn back—
and be forgiven."[l m]

[a]**3:14** Other mss omit *He also named them apostles* [b]**3:15** Other mss add *heal diseases, and to* [c]**3:16** Other mss omit *He appointed the Twelve* [d]**3:18** Lit *the Cananaean* [e]**3:19** *Iscariot* probably = "a man of Kerioth," a town in Judea. [f]**3:20** Lit *eat bread*, or *eat a meal* [g]**3:26** Lit *but he has an end* [h]**3:28** Lit *All things will be forgiven the sons of men* [i]**3:29** Other mss read *is subject to eternal judgment* [j]**3:32** Other mss omit *and Your sisters* [k]**4:11** The Gk word *mysterion* does not mean "mystery" in the Eng sense; it means what we can know only by divine revelation. [l]**4:12** Other mss read *and their sins be forgiven them* [m]**4:12** Is 6:9–10

The Parable of the Sower Explained

13 Then He said to them: "Do you not understand this parable? How then will you understand any of the parables? 14 The sower sows the word. 15 These[a] are the ones along the path where the word is sown: when they hear, immediately Satan comes and takes away the word sown in them.[b] 16 And these are[c] the ones sown on rocky ground: when they hear the word, immediately they receive it with joy. 17 But they have no root in themselves; they are short-lived. When affliction or persecution comes because of the word, they immediately stumble. 18 Others are sown among thorns; these are the ones who hear the word, 19 but the worries of this age, the seduction[d] of wealth, and the desires for other things enter in and choke the word, and it becomes unfruitful. 20 But the ones sown on good ground are those who hear the word, welcome it, and produce a crop: 30, 60, and 100 times ⌊what was sown⌋."

Using Your Light

21 He also said to them, "Is a lamp brought in to be put under a basket or under a bed? Isn't it to be put on a lampstand? 22 For nothing is concealed except to be revealed, and nothing hidden except to come to light. 23 If anyone has ears to hear, he should listen!" 24 Then He said to them, "Pay attention to what you hear. By the measure you use,[e] it will be measured and added to you. 25 For to the one who has, it will be given, and from the one who does not have, even what he has will be taken away."

The Parable of the Growing Seed

26 "The kingdom of God is like this," He said. "A man scatters seed on the ground; 27 he sleeps and rises—night and day, and the seed sprouts and grows—he doesn't know how. 28 The soil produces a crop by itself—first the blade, then the head, and then the ripe grain on the head. 29 But as soon as the crop is ready, he sends for the sickle, because harvest has come."

The Parable of the Mustard Seed

30 And He said: "How can we illustrate the kingdom of God, or what parable can we use to describe it? 31 It's like a mustard seed that, when sown in the soil, is smaller than all the seeds on the ground. 32 And when sown, it comes up and grows taller than all the vegetables, and produces large branches, so that the birds of the sky can nest in its shade."

Using Parables

33 He would speak the word to them with many parables like these, as they were able to understand. 34 And He did not speak to them without a parable. Privately, however, He would explain everything to His own disciples.

Wind and Wave Obey the Master

35 On that day, when evening had come, He told them, "Let's cross over to the other side ⌊of the lake⌋." 36 So they left the crowd and took Him along since He was ⌊already⌋ in the boat. And other boats were with Him. 37 A fierce windstorm arose, and the waves were breaking over the boat, so that the boat was already being swamped. 38 But He was in the stern, sleeping on the cushion. So they woke Him up and said to Him, "Teacher! Don't you care that we're going to die?"

39 He got up, rebuked the wind, and said to the sea, "Silence! Be still!" The wind ceased, and there was a great calm. 40 Then He said to them, "Why are you fearful? Do you still have no faith?"

41 And they were terrified and asked one another, "Who then is this? Even the wind and the sea obey Him!"

Demons Driven Out by the Master

5 Then they came to the other side of the sea, to the region of the Gerasenes.[f] 2 As soon as He got out of the boat, a man with an unclean spirit came out of the tombs and met Him. 3 He lived in the tombs. No one was able to restrain him any more—even with chains— 4 because he often had been bound with shackles and chains, but had snapped off the chains and smashed the shackles. No one was strong enough to subdue him. 5 And always, night and day, he was crying out among the tombs and in the mountains and cutting himself with stones.

6 When he saw Jesus from a distance, he ran and knelt down before Him. 7 And he cried out with a loud voice, "What do You have to do

[a]4:15 Some people [b]4:15 Other mss read *in their hearts* [c]4:16 Other mss read *are like* [d]4:19 Or *pleasure, or deceitfulness* [e]4:24 Lit *you measure* [f]5:1 Other mss read *Gadarenes*; other mss read *Gergesenes*

with me,[a] Jesus, Son of the Most High God? I beg[b] You before God, don't torment me!" 8 For He had told him, "Come out of the man, you unclean spirit!"

9 "What is your name?" He asked him.

"My name is Legion,"[c] he answered Him, "because we are many." 10 And he kept begging Him not to send them out of the region.

11 Now a large herd of pigs was there, feeding on the hillside. 12 The demons[d] begged Him, "Send us to the pigs, so we may enter them." 13 And He gave them permission. Then the unclean spirits came out and entered the pigs, and the herd of about 2,000 rushed down the steep bank into the sea and drowned there. 14 The men who tended them[e] ran off and reported it in the town and the countryside, and people went to see what had happened. 15 They came to Jesus and saw the man who had been demon-possessed by the legion, sitting there, dressed and in his right mind; and they were afraid. 16 The eyewitnesses described to them what had happened to the demon-possessed man and ⌊told⌋ about the pigs. 17 Then they began to beg Him to leave their region.

18 As He was getting into the boat, the man who had been demon-possessed kept begging Him to be with Him. 19 But He would not let him; instead, He told him, "Go back home to your own people, and report to them how much the Lord has done for you and how He has had mercy on you." 20 So he went out and began to proclaim in the •Decapolis how much Jesus had done for him, and they were all amazed.

A Girl Restored and a Woman Healed

21 When Jesus had crossed over again by boat to the other side, a large crowd gathered around Him while He was by the sea. 22 One of the •synagogue leaders, named Jairus, came, and when he saw Jesus, he fell at His feet 23 and kept begging Him, "My little daughter is at death's door.[f] Come and lay Your hands on her so she can get well and live."

24 So Jesus went with him, and a large crowd was following and pressing against Him. 25 A woman suffering from bleeding for 12 years 26 had endured much under many doctors. She had spent everything she had and was not helped at all. On the contrary, she became worse. 27 Having heard about Jesus, she came behind Him in the crowd and touched His robe. 28 For she said, "If I can just touch His robes, I'll be made well!" 29 Instantly her flow of blood ceased, and she sensed in her body that she was cured of her affliction.

30 At once Jesus realized in Himself that power had gone out from Him. He turned around in the crowd and said, "Who touched My robes?"

31 His disciples said to Him, "You see the crowd pressing against You, and You say, 'Who touched Me?' "

32 So He was looking around to see who had done this. 33 Then the woman, knowing what had happened to her, came with fear and trembling, fell down before Him, and told Him the whole truth. 34 "Daughter," He said to her, "your faith has made you well.[g] Go in peace and be free[h] from your affliction."

35 While He was still speaking, people came from the synagogue leader's house and said, "Your daughter is dead. Why bother the Teacher any more?"

36 But when Jesus overheard what was said, He told the synagogue leader, "Don't be afraid. Only believe." 37 He did not let anyone accompany Him except Peter, James, and John, James' brother. 38 They came to the leader's house, and He saw a commotion—people weeping and wailing loudly. 39 He went in and said to them, "Why are you making a commotion and weeping? The child is not dead but •asleep."

40 They started laughing at Him, but He put them all outside. He took the child's father, mother, and those who were with Him, and entered the place where the child was. 41 Then He took the child by the hand and said to her, *"Talitha koum!"*[i] (which is translated, "Little girl, I say to you, get up!"). 42 Immediately the girl got up and began to walk. (She was 12 years old.) At this they were utterly astounded. 43 Then He gave them strict orders that no one should know about this and said that she should be given something to eat.

Rejection at Nazareth

6 He went away from there and came to His hometown, and His disciples followed Him. 2 When the Sabbath came, He

[a]**5:7** Lit *What to me and to You* [b]**5:7** Or *adjure* [c]**5:9** A Roman legion contained up to 6,000 soldiers; here *legion* indicates a large number. [d]**5:12** Other mss read *All the demons* [e]**5:14** Other mss read *tended the pigs* [f]**5:23** Lit *My little daughter has it finally*; = to be at the end of life [g]**5:34** Or *has saved you* [h]**5:34** Lit *healthy* [i]**5:41** An Aram expression

began to teach in the •synagogue, and many
who heard Him were astonished. "Where did
this man get these things?" they said. "What is
this wisdom given to Him, and how are these
miracles performed by His hands? 3 Isn't this
the carpenter, the son of Mary, and the brother
of James, Joses, Judas, and Simon? And aren't
His sisters here with us?" So they were
offended by Him.
4 Then Jesus said to them, "A prophet is not
without honor except in his hometown, among
his relatives, and in his household." 5 So He
was not able to do any miracles[a] there, except
that He laid His hands on a few sick people and
healed them. 6 And He was amazed at their
unbelief.

Commissioning the Twelve

Now He was going around the villages in a
circuit, teaching. 7 He summoned the Twelve
and began to send them out in pairs and gave
them authority over unclean spirits. 8 He
instructed them to take nothing for the road
except a walking stick: no bread, no traveling
bag, no money in their belts. 9 They were to
wear sandals, but not put on an extra shirt.
10 Then He said to them, "Whenever you enter
a house, stay there until you leave that place.
11 If any place does not welcome you and people refuse to listen to you, when you leave
there, shake the dust off your feet as a testimony against them."[b]
12 So they went out and preached that people should repent. 13 And they were driving out
many demons, anointing many sick people
with oil, and healing.

John the Baptist Beheaded

14 King •Herod heard of this, because Jesus'
name had become well known. Some[c] said,
"John the Baptist has been raised from the
dead, and that's why supernatural powers are
at work in him." 15 But others said, "He's Elijah." Still others said, "He's a prophet[d] —like
one of the prophets."
16 When Herod heard of it, he said, "John,
the one I beheaded, has been raised!" 17 For
Herod himself had given orders to arrest John
and to chain him in prison on account of
Herodias, his brother Philip's wife, whom he
had married. 18 John had been telling Herod,
"It is not lawful for you to have your brother's
wife!" 19 So Herodias held a grudge against him
and wanted to kill him. But she could not,
20 because Herod was in awe of[e] John and was
protecting him, knowing he was a righteous
and holy man. When Herod heard him he
would be very disturbed,[f] yet would hear him
gladly.
21 Now an opportune time came on his
birthday, when Herod gave a banquet for his
nobles, military commanders, and the leading
men of Galilee. 22 When Herodias' own
daughter[g] came in and danced, she pleased
Herod and his guests. The king said to the girl,
"Ask me whatever you want, and I'll give it to
you." 23 So he swore oaths to her: "Whatever
you ask me I will give you, up to half my kingdom."
24 Then she went out and said to her
mother, "What should I ask for?"
"John the Baptist's head!" she said.
25 Immediately she hurried to the king and
said, "I want you to give me John the Baptist's
head on a platter—right now!"
26 Though the king was deeply distressed, because of his oaths and the guests[h]
he did not want to refuse her. 27 The king
immediately sent for an executioner and
commanded him to bring John's head. So he
went and beheaded him in prison,
28 brought his head on a platter, and gave it
to the girl. Then the girl gave it to her
mother. 29 When his disciples[i] heard about
it, they came and removed his corpse and
placed it in a tomb.

Feeding 5,000

30 The apostles gathered around Jesus and
reported to Him all that they had done and
taught. 31 He said to them, "Come away by
yourselves to a remote place and rest a while."
For many people were coming and going, and
they did not even have time to eat. 32 So they
went away in the boat by themselves to a
remote place, 33 but many saw them leaving
and recognized them. People ran there by
land from all the towns and arrived ahead of
them.[j] 34 So as He stepped ashore, He saw a
huge crowd and had compassion on them,
because they were like sheep without a shep-

[a]**6:5** Lit *miracle* [b]**6:11** Other mss add *I assure you, it will be more tolerable for Sodom or Gomorrah on judgment day than for that town.* [c]**6:14** Other mss read *He* [d]**6:15** Lit *Others said, "A prophet* [e]**6:20** Or *Herod feared* [f]**6:20** Other mss read *When he heard him, he did many things* [g]**6:22** Other mss read *When his daughter Herodias* [h]**6:26** Lit *and those reclining at the table* [i]**6:29** John's disciples [j]**6:33** Other mss add *and gathered around Him*

herd. Then He began to teach them many
things.
35 When it was already late, His disciples
approached Him and said, "This place is a wilderness, and it is already late! 36 Send them
away, so they can go into the surrounding
countryside and villages to buy themselves
something to eat."
37 "You give them something to eat," He
responded.
They said to Him, "Should we go and buy
200 •denarii worth of bread and give them
something to eat?"
38 And He asked them, "How many loaves
do you have? Go look."
When they found out they said, "Five, and
two fish."
39 Then He instructed them to have all the
people sit down[a] in groups on the green grass.
40 So they sat down in ranks of hundreds and
fifties. 41 Then He took the five loaves and the
two fish, and looking up to heaven, He blessed
and broke the loaves. He kept giving them to
His disciples to set before the people. He also
divided the two fish among them all.
42 Everyone ate and was filled. 43 Then they
picked up 12 baskets full of pieces of bread and
fish. 44 Now those who ate the loaves were
5,000 men.

Walking on the Water

45 Immediately He made His disciples get
into the boat and go ahead of Him to the other
side, to Bethsaida, while He dismissed the
crowd. 46 After He said good-bye to them, He
went away to the mountain to pray. 47 When
evening came, the boat was in the middle of
the sea, and He was alone on the land. 48 He
saw them being battered as they rowed,[b]
because the wind was against them. Around
three in the morning[c] He came toward them
walking on the sea and wanted to pass by them.
49 When they saw Him walking on the sea,
they thought it was a ghost and cried out; 50 for
they all saw Him and were terrified. Immediately He spoke with them and said, "Have courage! It is I. Don't be afraid." 51 Then He got into
the boat with them, and the wind ceased. They
were completely astounded,[d] 52 because they
had not understood about the loaves. Instead,
their hearts were hardened.

Miraculous Healings

53 When they had crossed over, they came
to land at Gennesaret and beached the boat.
54 As they got out of the boat, people immediately recognized Him. 55 They hurried throughout that vicinity and began to carry the sick on
stretchers to wherever they heard He was.
56 Wherever He would go, into villages, towns,
or the country, they laid the sick in the marketplaces and begged Him that they might touch
just the •tassel of His robe. And everyone who
touched it was made well.

The Traditions of the Elders

7 The •Pharisees and some of the •scribes
who had come from Jerusalem gathered
around Him. 2 They observed that some of His
disciples were eating their bread with
unclean—that is, unwashed—hands. 3 (For
the Pharisees, in fact all the Jews, will not eat
unless they wash their hands ritually, keeping
the tradition of the elders. 4 When they come
from the marketplace, they do not eat unless
they have washed. And there are many other
customs they have received and keep, like the
washing of cups, jugs, copper utensils, and dining couches.[e]) 5 Then the Pharisees and the
scribes asked Him, "Why don't Your disciples
live according to the tradition of the elders,
instead of eating bread with ritually unclean[f]
hands?"
6 He answered them, "Isaiah prophesied
correctly about you hypocrites, as it is written:

These people honor Me
with their lips,
but their heart is far from Me.
7 **They worship Me in vain,**
teaching as doctrines the commands
of men.[g]

8 Disregarding the command of God, you keep
the tradition of men."[h] 9 He also said to them,
"You completely invalidate God's command in
order to maintain[i] your tradition! 10 For Moses
said:

Honor your father and your mother;[j]
and,
Whoever speaks evil of father
or mother
must be put to death.[k]

[a]**6:39** Lit *people recline* [b]**6:48** Or *them struggling as they rowed* [c]**6:48** Lit *Around the fourth watch of the night* = 3 to 6 a.m.
[d]**6:51** Lit *were astounded in themselves* [e]**7:4** Other mss omit *and dining couches* [f]**7:5** Other mss read *with unwashed*
[g]**7:6–7** Is 29:13 [h]**7:8** Other mss add *The washing of jugs, and cups, and many other similar things you practice.* [i]**7:9** Other mss read *to establish* [j]**7:10** Ex 20:12; Dt 5:16 [k]**7:10** Ex 21:17; Lv 20:9

11 But you say, 'If a man tells his father or
mother: Whatever benefit you might have
received from me is Corban' " (that is, a gift
⌊committed to the temple⌋), 12 "you no longer
let him do anything for his father or mother.
13 You revoke God's word by your tradition
that you have handed down. And you do many
other similar things." 14 Summoning the
crowd again, He told them, "Listen to Me, all
of you, and understand: 15 Nothing that goes
into a person from outside can defile him, but
the things that come out of a person are what
defile him. 16 If anyone has ears to hear, he
should listen!"[a]

17 When He went into the house away
from the crowd, the disciples asked Him about
the parable. 18 And He said to them, "Are you
also as lacking in understanding? Don't you
realize that nothing going into a man from the
outside can defile him? 19 For it doesn't go
into his heart but into the stomach and is eliminated."[b] (As a result, He made all foods
clean.[c]) 20 Then He said, "What comes out of
a person—that defiles him. 21 For from
within, out of people's hearts, come evil
thoughts, sexual immoralities, thefts, murders, 22 adulteries, greed, evil actions, deceit,
lewdness, stinginess,[d] blasphemy, pride, and
foolishness. 23 All these evil things come from
within and defile a person."

A Gentile Mother's Faith

24 He got up and departed from there to the
region of Tyre and Sidon.[e] He entered a house
and did not want anyone to know it, but He
could not escape notice. 25 Instead, immediately after hearing about Him, a woman whose
little daughter had an unclean spirit came and
fell at His feet. 26 Now the woman was Greek,
a Syrophoenician by birth, and she kept asking
Him to drive the demon out of her daughter.
27 He said to her, "Allow the children to be satisfied first, because it isn't right to take the children's bread and throw it to the dogs."

28 But she replied to Him, "Lord, even the
dogs under the table eat the children's
crumbs."

29 Then He told her, "Because of this reply,
you may go. The demon has gone out of your
daughter." 30 When she went back to her
home, she found her child lying on the bed,
and the demon was gone.

Jesus Does Everything Well

31 Again, leaving the region of Tyre, He
went by way of Sidon to the Sea of Galilee,
through[f] the region of the •Decapolis. 32 They
brought to Him a deaf man who also had a
speech difficulty, and begged Jesus to lay His
hand on him. 33 So He took him away from the
crowd privately. After putting His fingers in the
man's ears and spitting, He touched his tongue.
34 Then, looking up to heaven, He sighed
deeply and said to him, *"Ephphatha!"*[g] (that is,
"Be opened!"). 35 Immediately his ears were
opened, his speech difficulty was removed,[h]
and he began to speak clearly. 36 Then He
ordered them to tell no one, but the more He
would order them, the more they would proclaim it.

37 They were extremely astonished and
said, "He has done everything well! He even
makes deaf people hear, and people unable to
speak, talk!"

Feeding 4,000

8 In those days there was again a large
crowd, and they had nothing to eat. He
summoned the disciples and said to them, 2 "I
have compassion on the crowd, because
they've already stayed with Me three days and
have nothing to eat. 3 If I send them home
famished,[i] they will collapse on the way, and
some of them have come a long distance."

4 His disciples answered Him, "Where can
anyone get enough bread here in this desolate
place to fill these people?"

5 "How many loaves do you have?" He
asked them.

"Seven," they said. 6 Then He commanded
the crowd to sit down on the ground. Taking
the seven loaves, He gave thanks, broke the
⌊loaves⌋, and kept on giving ⌊them⌋ to His disciples to set before ⌊the people⌋. So they served
the ⌊loaves⌋ to the crowd. 7 They also had a few
small fish, and when He had blessed them, He
said these were to be served as well. 8 They ate
and were filled. Then they collected seven large
baskets of leftover pieces. 9 About 4,000 ⌊men⌋
were there. He dismissed them 10 and immediately got into the boat with His disciples and
went to the district of Dalmanutha.[j]

The Yeast of the Pharisees and Herod

11 The •Pharisees came out and began to

[a]**7:16** Other mss omit this verse [b]**7:19** Lit *goes out into the toilet* [c]**7:19** Other mss read *is eliminated, making all foods clean.*" [d]**7:22** Lit *evil eye* [e]**7:24** Other mss omit *and Sidon* [f]**7:31** Or *into* [g]**7:34** An Aram expression [h]**7:35** Lit *opened, the bond of his tongue was untied* [i]**8:3** Or *fasting* [j]**8:10** Probably on the western shore of the Sea of Galilee

argue with Him, demanding of Him a sign from heaven to test Him. 12 But sighing deeply in His spirit, He said, "Why does this generation demand a sign? •I assure you: No sign will be given to this generation!" 13 Then He left them, got on board ⌊the boat⌋ again, and went to the other side.

14 They had forgotten to take bread and had only one loaf with them in the boat. 15 Then He commanded them: "Watch out! Beware of the yeast of the Pharisees and the yeast of •Herod."

16 They were discussing among themselves that they did not have any bread. 17 Aware of this, He said to them, "Why are you discussing that you do not have any bread? Do you not yet understand or comprehend? Is your heart hardened? 18 **Do you have eyes, and not see, and do you have ears, and not hear?**[a] And do you not remember? 19 When I broke the five loaves for the 5,000, how many baskets full of pieces of bread did you collect?"

"Twelve," they told Him.

20 "When I broke the seven loaves for the 4,000, how many large baskets full of pieces of bread did you collect?"

"Seven," they said.

21 And He said to them, "Don't you understand yet?"

Healing a Blind Man

22 Then they came to Bethsaida. They brought a blind man to Him and begged Him to touch him. 23 He took the blind man by the hand and brought him out of the village. Spitting on his eyes and laying His hands on him, He asked him, "Do you see anything?"

24 He looked up and said, "I see people—they look to me like trees walking."

25 Again Jesus placed His hands on the man's eyes, and he saw distinctly. He was cured and could see everything clearly. 26 Then He sent him home, saying, "Don't even go into the village."[b]

Peter's Confession of the Messiah

27 Jesus went out with His disciples to the villages of Caesarea Philippi. And on the road He asked His disciples, "Who do people say that I am?"

28 They answered Him, "John the Baptist; others, Elijah; still others, one of the prophets."

29 "But you," He asked them again, "who do you say that I am?"

Peter answered Him, "You are the •Messiah!"

30 And He strictly warned them to tell no one about Him.

His Death and Resurrection Predicted

31 Then He began to teach them that the •Son of Man must suffer many things, and be rejected by the elders, the •chief priests, and the •scribes, be killed, and rise after three days. 32 He was openly talking about this. So Peter took Him aside and began to rebuke Him.

33 But turning around and looking at His disciples, He rebuked Peter and said, "Get behind Me, Satan, because you're not thinking about God's concerns,[c] but man's!"

Take Up Your Cross

34 Summoning the crowd along with His disciples, He said to them, "If anyone wants to be My follower, he must deny himself, take up his cross, and follow Me. 35 For whoever wants to save his •life will lose it, but whoever loses his life because of Me and the gospel will save it. 36 For what does it benefit a man to gain the whole world yet lose his life? 37 What can a man give in exchange for his life? 38 For whoever is ashamed of Me and of My words in this adulterous and sinful generation, the Son of Man will also be ashamed of him when He comes in the glory of His Father with the holy angels."

9 Then He said to them, "•I assure you: There are some standing here who will not taste death until they see the kingdom of God come in power."

The Transfiguration

2 After six days Jesus took Peter, James, and John and led them up on a high mountain by themselves to be alone. He was transformed[d] in front of them, 3 and His clothes became dazzling—extremely white as no launderer on earth could whiten them. 4 Elijah appeared to them with Moses, and they were talking with Jesus.

5 Then Peter said to Jesus, "•Rabbi, it is good for us to be here! Let us make three •tabernacles: one for You, one for Moses, and one

[a] **8:18** Jr 5:21; Ezk 12:2 [b] **8:26** Other mss add *or tell anyone in the village* [c] **8:33** Lit *about the things of God* [d] **9:2** Or *transfigured*

for Elijah"— 6 because he did not know what
he should say, since they were terrified.
7 A cloud appeared, overshadowing them,
and a voice came from the cloud:

> This is My beloved Son;
> listen to Him!

8 Then suddenly, looking around, they no
longer saw anyone with them except Jesus
alone.
9 As they were coming down from the
mountain, He ordered them to tell no one what
they had seen until the •Son of Man had risen
from the dead. 10 They kept this word to themselves, discussing what "rising from the dead"
meant.
11 Then they began to question Him, "Why
do the •scribes say that Elijah must come first?"
12 "Elijah does come first and restores
everything," He replied. "How then is it written about the Son of Man that He must suffer
many things and be treated with contempt?
13 But I tell you that Elijah really has come, and
they did to him whatever they wanted, just as
it is written about him."

The Power of Faith over a Demon

14 When they came to the disciples, they
saw a large crowd around them and scribes disputing with them. 15 All of a sudden, when the
whole crowd saw Him, they were amazed[a] and
ran to greet Him. 16 Then He asked them,
"What are you arguing with them about?"
17 Out of the crowd, one man answered
Him, "Teacher, I brought my son to You. He
has a spirit that makes him unable to speak.
18 Wherever it seizes him, it throws him down,
and he foams at the mouth, grinds his teeth,
and becomes rigid. So I asked Your disciples to
drive it out, but they couldn't."
19 He replied to them, "You unbelieving
generation! How long will I be with you? How
long must I put up with you? Bring him to Me."
20 So they brought him to Him. When the spirit
saw Him, it immediately convulsed the boy. He
fell to the ground and rolled around, foaming at
the mouth. 21 "How long has this been happening to him?" Jesus asked his father.
"From childhood," he said. 22 "And many
times it has thrown him into fire or water to
destroy him. But if You can do anything, have
compassion on us and help us."
23 Then Jesus said to him, " 'If You can?'[b c]
Everything is possible to the one who
believes."
24 Immediately the father of the boy cried
out, "I do believe! Help my unbelief."
25 When Jesus saw that a crowd was rapidly
coming together, He rebuked the unclean
spirit, saying to it, "You mute and deaf spirit,[d] I
command you: come out of him and never
enter him again!"
26 Then it came out, shrieking and convuls-
ing him[e] violently. The boy became like a
corpse, so that many said, "He's dead." 27 But
Jesus, taking him by the hand, raised him, and
he stood up.
28 After He went into a house, His disciples
asked Him privately, "Why couldn't we drive it
out?"
29 And He told them, "This kind can come
out by nothing but prayer [and fasting]."[f]

The Second Prediction of His Death

30 Then they left that place and made their
way through Galilee, but He did not want anyone to know it. 31 For He was teaching His disciples and telling them, "The Son of Man is being
betrayed[g] into the hands of men. They will kill
Him, and after He is killed, He will rise three
days later." 32 But they did not understand this
statement, and they were afraid to ask Him.

Who is the Greatest?

33 Then they came to Capernaum. When
He was in the house, He asked them, "What
were you arguing about on the way?" 34 But
they were silent, because on the way they had
been arguing with one another about who was
the greatest. 35 Sitting down, He called the
Twelve and said to them, "If anyone wants to
be first, he must be last of all and servant of all."
36 Then He took a child, had him stand among
them, and taking him in His arms, He said to
them, 37 "Whoever welcomes[h] one little child
such as this in My name welcomes Me. And
whoever welcomes Me does not welcome Me,
but Him who sent Me."

In His Name

38 John said to Him, "Teacher, we saw
someone[i] driving out demons in Your name,
and we tried to stop him because he wasn't following us."

[a]**9:15** Or *surprised* [b]**9:23** Other mss add *believe* [c]**9:23** Jesus appears to quote the father's words in v. 22 and then comment on them. [d]**9:25** A spirit that caused the boy to be deaf and unable to speak [e]**9:26** Other mss omit *him* [f]**9:29** Other mss omit bracketed text [g]**9:31** Or *handed over* [h]**9:37** Or *Whoever receives* [i]**9:38** Other mss add *who didn't go along with us*

39 "Don't stop him," said Jesus, "because
there is no one who will perform a miracle in
My name who can soon afterwards speak evil of
Me. 40 For whoever is not against us is for us.
41 And whoever gives you a cup of water to
drink because of My name,[a] since you belong to
the •Messiah—I assure you: He will never lose
his reward.

Warnings from Jesus

42 "But whoever •causes the downfall of
one of these little ones who believe in Me—it
would be better for him if a heavy millstone[b]
were hung around his neck and he were
thrown into the sea. 43 And if your hand causes
your downfall, cut it off. It is better for you to
enter life maimed than to have two hands and
go to •hell—the unquenchable fire, [44 where

Their worm does not die,
and the fire is not quenched.][c d]

45 And if your foot causes your downfall, cut it
off. It is better for you to enter life lame than to
have two feet and be thrown into hell— [the
unquenchable fire, 46 where

Their worm does not die,
and the fire is not quenched.][c d]

47 And if your eye causes your downfall, gouge
it out. It is better for you to enter the kingdom
of God with one eye than to have two eyes and
be thrown into hell, 48 where

Their worm does not die,
and the fire is not quenched.[d]

49 For everyone will be salted with fire.[e f]
50 Salt is good, but if the salt should lose its fla-
vor, how can you make it salty? Have salt
among yourselves and be at peace with one
another."

The Question of Divorce

10 He set out from there and went to the
region of Judea and across the Jordan.
Then crowds converged on Him again and, as
He usually did, He began teaching them once
more. 2 Some •Pharisees approached Him to
test Him. They asked, "Is it lawful for a man to
divorce ⌊his⌋ wife?"
3 He replied to them, "What did Moses
command you?"
4 They said, "Moses permitted us to write
divorce papers and send her away."
5 But Jesus told them, "He wrote this commandment for you because of the hardness of
your hearts. 6 But from the beginning of creation God[g] **made them male and female.**[h]

7 **For this reason a man**
will leave
his father and mother
[and be joined to his wife,][c]
8 **and the two will become one flesh.**[i]

So they are no longer two, but one flesh.
9 Therefore what God has joined together,
man must not separate."
10 Now in the house the disciples questioned Him again about this matter. 11 And He
said to them, "Whoever divorces his wife and
marries another commits adultery against her.
12 Also, if she divorces her husband and marries another, she commits adultery."

Blessing the Children

13 Some people were bringing little children
to Him so He might touch them, but His disciples rebuked them. 14 When Jesus saw it, He
was indignant and said to them, "Let the little
children come to Me. Don't stop them, for the
kingdom of God belongs to such as these. 15 •I
assure you: Whoever does not welcome[j] the
kingdom of God like a little child will never
enter it." 16 After taking them in His arms, He
laid His hands on them and blessed them.

The Rich Young Ruler

17 As He was setting out on a journey, a man
ran up, knelt down before Him, and asked Him,
"Good Teacher, what must I do to inherit eternal life?"
18 "Why do you call Me good?" Jesus asked
him. "No one is good but One—God. 19 You
know the commandments:

Do not murder;
do not commit adultery;
do not steal;
do not bear false witness;
do not defraud;
honor your father and mother."[k]

20 He said to Him, "Teacher, I have kept all
these from my youth."

[a]**9:41** Lit *drink in the name;* =Messiah [b]**9:42** A millstone turned by a donkey [c]**9:44,46; 10:7** Other mss omit bracketed text [d]**9:44,46,48** Is 66:24 [e]**9:49** Other mss add *and every sacrifice will be salted with salt* [f]**9:49** Lv 2:16; Ezk 43:24 [g]**10:6** Other mss omit *God* [h]**10:6** Gn 1:27; 5:2 [i]**10:7–8** Gn 2:24 [j]**10:15** Or *not receive* [k]**10:19** Ex 20:12–16; Dt 5:16–20

21 Then, looking at him, Jesus loved him and said to him, "You lack one thing: Go, sell all you have and give to the poor, and you will have treasure in heaven. Then come,[a] follow Me." 22 But he was stunned[b] at this demand, and he went away grieving, because he had many possessions.

Possessions and the Kingdom

23 Jesus looked around and said to His disciples, "How hard it is for those who have wealth to enter the kingdom of God!" 24 But the disciples were astonished at His words. Again Jesus said to them, "Children, how hard it is[c] to enter the kingdom of God! 25 It is easier for a camel to go through the eye of a needle than for a rich person to enter the kingdom of God."

26 So they were even more astonished, saying to one another, "Then who can be saved?"

27 Looking at them, Jesus said, "With men it is impossible, but not with God, because all things are possible with God."

28 Peter began to tell Him, "Look, we have left everything and followed You."

29 "I assure you," Jesus said, "there is no one who has left house, brothers or sisters, mother or father,[d] children, or fields because of Me and the gospel, 30 who will not receive 100 times more, now at this time—houses, brothers and sisters, mothers and children, and fields, with persecutions—and eternal life in the age to come. 31 But many who are first will be last, and the last first."

The Third Prediction of His Death

32 They were on the road, going up to Jerusalem, and Jesus was walking ahead of them. They were astonished, but those who followed Him were afraid. Taking the Twelve aside again, He began to tell them the things that would happen to Him.

33 "Listen! We are going up to Jerusalem. The •Son of Man will be handed over to the •chief priests and the •scribes, and they will condemn Him to death. Then they will hand Him over to the Gentiles, 34 and they will mock Him, spit on Him, flog[e] Him, and kill Him, and He will rise after three days."

Suffering and Service

35 Then James and John, the sons of Zebedee, approached Him and said, "Teacher, we want You to do something for us if we ask You."

36 "What do you want Me to do for you?" He asked them.

37 They answered Him, "Allow us to sit at Your right and at Your left in Your glory."

38 But Jesus said to them, "You don't know what you're asking. Are you able to drink the cup I drink or to be baptized with the baptism I am baptized with?"

39 "We are able," they told Him.

Jesus said to them, "You will drink the cup I drink, and you will be baptized with the baptism I am baptized with. 40 But to sit at My right or left is not Mine to give; instead, it is for those it has been prepared for." 41 When the ⌊other⌋ 10 ⌊disciples⌋ heard this, they began to be indignant with James and John.

42 Jesus called them over and said to them, "You know that those who are regarded as rulers of the Gentiles dominate them, and their men of high positions exercise power over them. 43 But it must not be like that among you. On the contrary, whoever wants to become great among you must be your servant, 44 and whoever wants to be first among you must be a •slave to all. 45 For even the Son of Man did not come to be served, but to serve, and to give His life—a ransom for many."[f]

A Blind Man Healed

46 They came to Jericho. And as He was leaving Jericho with His disciples and a large crowd, Bartimaeus (the son of Timaeus), a blind beggar, was sitting by the road. 47 When he heard that it was Jesus the •Nazarene, he began to cry out, "Son of David, Jesus, have mercy on me!" 48 Many people told him to keep quiet, but he was crying out all the more, "Have mercy on me, Son of David!"

49 Jesus stopped and said, "Call him."

So they called the blind man and said to him, "Have courage! Get up; He's calling for you." 50 He threw off his coat, jumped up, and came to Jesus.

51 Then Jesus answered him, "What do you want Me to do for you?"

"Rabbouni,"[g] the blind man told Him, "I want to see!"

[a] **10:21** Other mss add *taking up the cross, and* [b] **10:22** Or *he became gloomy* [c] **10:24** Other mss add *for those trusting in wealth* [d] **10:29** Other mss add *or wife* [e] **10:34** Or *scourge* [f] **10:45** Or *in the place of many*; Is 53:10–12 [g] **10:51** Hb for *my teacher*; Jn 20:16

52 "Go your way," Jesus told him. "Your faith has healed you." Immediately he could see and began to follow Him on the road.

The Triumphal Entry

11 When they approached Jerusalem, at Bethphage and Bethany near the •Mount of Olives, He sent two of His disciples 2 and told them, "Go into the village ahead of you. As soon as you enter it, you will find a young donkey tied there, on which no one has ever sat. Untie it and bring it here. 3 If anyone says to you, 'Why are you doing this?' say, 'The Lord needs it and will send it back here right away.' "

4 So they went and found a young donkey outside in the street, tied by a door. They untied it, 5 and some of those standing there said to them, "What are you doing, untying the donkey?" 6 They answered them just as Jesus had said, so they let them go. 7 Then they brought the donkey to Jesus and threw their robes on it, and He sat on it.

8 Many people spread their robes on the road, and others spread leafy branches cut from the fields.[a] 9 Then those who went ahead and those who followed kept shouting:

> •*Hosanna!*
> **Blessed is He who comes**
> **in the name of the Lord!**[b]
> 10 Blessed is the coming kingdom
> of our father David!
> *Hosanna* in the highest heaven!

11 And He went into Jerusalem and into the •temple complex. After looking around at everything, since it was already late, He went out to Bethany with the Twelve.

The Barren Fig Tree Is Cursed

12 The next day when they came out from Bethany, He was hungry. 13 After seeing in the distance a fig tree with leaves, He went to find out if there was anything on it. When He came to it, He found nothing but leaves, because it was not the season for figs. 14 He said to it, "May no one ever eat fruit from you again!" And His disciples heard it.

Cleansing the Temple Complex

15 They came to Jerusalem, and He went into the temple complex and began to throw out those buying and selling in the temple. He overturned the money changers' tables and the chairs of those selling doves, 16 and would not permit anyone to carry goods through the temple complex.

17 Then He began to teach them: "Is it not written, **My house will be called a house of prayer for all nations?**[c] But you have made it **a den of thieves!**"[d] 18 Then the •chief priests and the •scribes heard it and started looking for a way to destroy Him. For they were afraid of Him, because the whole crowd was astonished by His teaching.

19 And whenever evening came, they would go out of the city.

The Barren Fig Tree Is Withered

20 Early in the morning, as they were passing by, they saw the fig tree withered from the roots up. 21 Then Peter remembered and said to Him, "•Rabbi, look! The fig tree that You cursed is withered."

22 Jesus replied to them, "Have faith in God. 23 •I assure you: If anyone says to this mountain, 'Be lifted up and thrown into the sea,' and does not doubt in his heart, but believes that what he says will happen, it will be done for him. 24 Therefore, I tell you, all the things you pray and ask for—believe that you have received[e] them, and you will have them. 25 And whenever you stand praying, if you have anything against anyone, forgive him, so that your Father in heaven will also forgive you your wrongdoing.[f] [26 But if you don't forgive, neither will your Father in heaven forgive your wrongdoing."][g]

Messiah's Authority Challenged

27 They came again to Jerusalem. As He was walking in the temple complex, the chief priests, the scribes, and the elders came and asked Him, 28 "By what authority are You doing these things? Who gave You this authority to do these things?"

29 Jesus said to them, "I will ask you one question; then answer Me, and I will tell you by what authority I am doing these things. 30 Was John's baptism from heaven or from men? Answer Me."

31 They began to argue among themselves:

[a]**11:8** Other mss read *others were cutting leafy branches from the trees and spreading them on the road* [b]**11:9** Ps 118:26 [c]**11:17** Is 56:7 [d]**11:17** Jr 7:11 [e]**11:24** Other mss read *you receive*; other mss read *you will receive* [f]**11:25** These are the only uses of this word in Mk. It means "the violation of the Law" or "stepping over a boundary" or "departing from the path" or "trespass." [g]**11:26** Other mss omit bracketed text

"If we say, 'From heaven,' He will say, 'Then
why didn't you believe him?' 32 But if we say,
'From men' "—they were afraid of the crowd,
because everyone thought that John was a genuine prophet. 33 So they answered Jesus, "We
don't know."

And Jesus said to them, "Neither will I tell
you by what authority I do these things."

The Parable of the Vineyard Owner

12 Then He began to speak to them in
parables: "A man planted a vineyard,
put a fence around it, dug out a pit for a winepress, and built a watchtower. Then he leased
it to tenant farmers and went away. 2 At harvest time he sent a •slave to the farmers to collect some of the fruit of the vineyard from the
farmers. 3 But they took him, beat him, and
sent him away empty-handed. 4 Again he sent
another slave to them, and they[a] hit him on
the head and treated him shamefully.[b] 5 Then
he sent another, and they killed that one. ⌊He⌋
also ⌊sent⌋ many others; they beat some and
they killed some.

6 "He still had one to send, a beloved son.
Finally he sent him to them, saying, 'They will
respect my son.'

7 "But those tenant farmers said among
themselves, 'This is the heir. Come, let's kill
him, and the inheritance will be ours!' 8 So
they seized him, killed him, and threw him out
of the vineyard.

9 "Therefore, what will the owner[c] of the
vineyard do? He will come and destroy the
farmers and give the vineyard to others.
10 Haven't you read this Scripture:

> **The stone that**
> **the builders rejected**
> **has become**
> **the cornerstone.**[d]
> 11 **This came from the Lord**
> **and is wonderful in our eyes?"**[e]

12 Because they knew He had said this parable against them, they were looking for a way
to arrest Him, but they were afraid of the
crowd. So they left Him and went away.

God and Caesar

13 Then they sent some of the •Pharisees
and the •Herodians to Him to trap Him by what
He said.[f] 14 When they came, they said to Him,
"Teacher, we know You are truthful and defer
to no one, for You don't show partiality[g] but
teach truthfully the way of God. Is it lawful to
pay taxes to Caesar or not? 15 Should we pay, or
should we not pay?"

But knowing their hypocrisy, He said to
them, "Why are you testing Me? Bring Me a
•denarius to look at." 16 So they brought one.
"Whose image and inscription is this?" He
asked them.

"Caesar's," they said.

17 Then Jesus told them, "Give back to Caesar the things that are Caesar's, and to God the
things that are God's." And they were amazed
at Him.

The Sadducees and the Resurrection

18 Some •Sadducees, who say there is no
resurrection, came to Him and questioned
Him: 19 "Teacher, Moses wrote for us that **if**
a man's brother dies, leaves his wife
behind, and **leaves no child, his brother**
should take the wife and produce •off-
spring for his brother.[h] 20 There were
seven brothers. The first took a wife, and
dying, left no offspring. 21 The second also
took her, and he died, leaving no offspring.
And the third likewise. 22 The seven also[i]
left no offspring. Last of all, the woman died
too. 23 In the resurrection, when they rise,[j]
whose wife will she be, since the seven had
married her?"[k]

24 Jesus told them, "Are you not deceived
because you don't know the Scriptures or the
power of God? 25 For when they rise from the
dead, they neither marry nor are given in marriage but are like angels in heaven. 26 Now
concerning the dead being raised—haven't
you read in the book of Moses, in the passage
about the burning bush, how God spoke to
him: **I am the God of Abraham and the God**
of Isaac and the God of Jacob?[l] 27 He is not
God of the dead but of the living. You are
badly deceived."

The Primary Commandments

28 One of the •scribes approached. When
he heard them debating and saw that Jesus
answered them well, he asked Him, "Which
commandment is the most important of all?"[m]

[a]**12:4** Other mss add *threw stones and* [b]**12:4** Other mss add *and sent him off* [c]**12:9** Or *lord* [d]**12:10** Lit *the head of the corner* [e]**12:10–11** Ps 118:22–23 [f]**12:13** Lit *trap Him in (a) word* [g]**12:14** Lit *don't look on the face of men*; that is, on the outward appearance [h]**12:19** Gn 38:8; Dt 25:5 [i]**12:22** Other mss add *had taken her and* [j]**12:23** Other mss omit *when they rise* [k]**12:23** Lit *the seven had her as a wife* [l]**12:26** Ex 3:6,15–16 [m]**12:28** Lit *Which commandment is first of all?*

29 "This is the most important,"[a] Jesus answered:

> **Listen, Israel! The Lord our God, the Lord is One.**[b] 30 **Love the Lord your God with all your heart, with all your soul, with all your mind, and with all your strength.**[c d]

31 "The second is: **Love your neighbor as yourself.**[e] There is no other commandment greater than these."

32 Then the scribe said to Him, "You are right, Teacher! You have correctly said that He is One, and there is no one else except Him. 33 And to love Him with all your heart, with all your understanding,[f] and with all your strength, and to love your neighbor as yourself, is far more ⌊important⌋ than all the burnt offerings and sacrifices."

34 When Jesus saw that he answered intelligently, He said to him, "You are not far from the kingdom of God." And no one dared to question Him any longer.

The Question about the Messiah

35 So Jesus asked this question as He taught in the •temple complex, "How can the scribes say that the •Messiah is the Son of David? 36 David himself says by the Holy Spirit:

> **The Lord declared to my Lord,**
> **'Sit at My right hand**
> **until I put Your enemies**
> **under Your feet.'**[g]

37 David himself calls Him 'Lord'; how then can the Messiah be his Son?" And the large crowd was listening to Him with delight.

Warning against the Scribes

38 He also said in His teaching, "Beware of the scribes, who want to go around in long robes, and who want greetings in the marketplaces, 39 the front seats in the •synagogues, and the places of honor at banquets. 40 They devour widows' houses and say long prayers just for show. These will receive harsher punishment."

The Widow's Gift

41 Sitting across from the temple treasury, He watched how the crowd dropped money into the treasury. Many rich people were putting in large sums. 42 And a poor widow came and dropped in two tiny coins worth very little.[h] 43 Summoning His disciples, He said to them, "•I assure you: This poor widow has put in more than all those giving to the temple treasury. 44 For they all gave out of their surplus, but she out of her poverty has put in everything she possessed—all she had to live on."

Destruction of the Temple Predicted

13 As He was going out of the •temple complex, one of His disciples said to Him, "Teacher, look! What massive stones! What impressive buildings!"

2 Jesus said to him, "Do you see these great buildings? Not one stone will be left here on another that will not be thrown down!"

Signs of the End of the Age

3 While He was sitting on the •Mount of Olives across from the temple complex, Peter, James, John, and Andrew asked Him privately, 4 "Tell us, when will these things happen? And what will be the sign when all these things are about to take place?"

5 Then Jesus began by telling them: "Watch out that no one deceives you. 6 Many will come in My name, saying, 'I am He,' and they will deceive many. 7 When you hear of wars and rumors of wars, don't be alarmed; these things must take place, but the end is not yet. 8 For nation will rise up against nation, and kingdom against kingdom. There will be earthquakes in various places, and famines.[i] These are the beginning of birth pains.

Persecutions Predicted

9 "But you, be on your guard! They will hand you over to sanhedrins,[j] and you will be flogged in the •synagogues. You will stand before governors and kings because of Me, as a witness to them. 10 And the good news[k] must first be proclaimed to all nations. 11 So when they arrest you and hand you over, don't worry beforehand what you will say. On the contrary, whatever is given to you in that hour—say it. For it isn't you speaking, but the Holy Spirit. 12 Then brother will betray brother to death, and a father his child. Children will rise up against parents and put them to death. 13 And

[a]**12:29** Other mss add *of all the commandments* [b]**12:29** Or *The Lord our God is one Lord.* [c]**12:30** Dt 6:4–5; Jos 22:5 [d]**12:30** Other mss add *This is the first commandment.* [e]**12:31** Lv 19:18 [f]**12:33** Other mss add *with all your soul* [g]**12:36** Ps 110:1 [h]**12:42** Lit *dropped in two lepta, which is a quadrans*; the *lepton* was the smallest and least valuable Gk coin in use. The *quadrans,* 1/64 of a daily wage, was the smallest Roman coin. [i]**13:8** Other mss add *and disturbances* [j]**13:9** Local Jewish courts or local councils [k]**13:10** Or *the gospel*

you will be hated by everyone because of My name. But the one who endures to the end will be delivered.[a]

The Great Tribulation

14 "When you see the **abomination that causes desolation**[b] standing where it should not" (let the reader understand),[c] "then those in Judea must flee to the mountains! 15 A man on the housetop must not come down or go in to get anything out of his house. 16 And a man in the field must not go back to get his clothes. 17 Woe to pregnant women and nursing mothers in those days! 18 Pray it[d] won't happen in winter. 19 For those will be days of tribulation, the kind that hasn't been from the beginning of the world,[e] which God created, until now and never will be again! 20 Unless the Lord limited those days, no one would survive.[f] But He limited those days because of the elect, whom He chose.

21 "Then if anyone tells you, 'Look, here is the •Messiah! Look—there!' do not believe it! 22 For false messiahs[g] and false prophets will rise up and will perform signs and wonders to lead astray, if possible, the elect. 23 And you must watch! I have told you everything in advance.

The Coming of the Son of Man

24 "But in those days, after that tribulation:

The sun will be darkened,
and the moon will not shed its light;
25 the stars will be falling from the sky,
and the celestial powers
will be shaken.

26 Then they will see the •Son of Man coming in clouds with great power and glory. 27 He will send out the angels and gather His elect from the four winds, from the end of the earth to the end of the sky.

The Parable of the Fig Tree

28 "Learn this parable from the fig tree: As soon as its branch becomes tender and sprouts leaves, you know that summer is near. 29 In the same way, when you see these things happening, know[h] that He[i] is near—at the door! 30 •I assure you: This generation will certainly not pass away until all these things take place. 31 Heaven and earth will pass away, but My words will never pass away.

No One Knows the Day or Hour

32 "Now concerning that day or hour no one knows—neither the angels in heaven nor the Son—except the Father. 33 Watch! Be alert![j] For you don't know when the time is ⌊coming⌋. 34 It is like a man on a journey, who left his house, gave authority to his •slaves, gave each one his work, and commanded the doorkeeper to be alert. 35 Therefore be alert, since you don't know when the master of the house is coming—whether in the evening or at midnight or at the crowing of the rooster or early in the morning. 36 Otherwise, he might come suddenly and find you sleeping. 37 And what I say to you, I say to everyone: Be alert!"

The Plot to Kill Jesus

14 After two days it was the •Passover and the Festival of •Unleavened Bread. The •chief priests and the •scribes were looking for a treacherous way to arrest and kill Him. 2 "Not during the festival," they said, "or there may be rioting among the people."

The Anointing at Bethany

3 While He was in Bethany at the house of Simon who had a serious skin disease, as He was reclining at the table, a woman came with an alabaster jar of pure and expensive fragrant oil of nard. She broke the jar and poured it on His head. 4 But some were expressing indignation to one another: "Why has this fragrant oil been wasted? 5 For this oil might have been sold for more than 300 •denarii and given to the poor." And they began to scold her.

6 Then Jesus said, "Leave her alone. Why are you bothering her? She has done a noble thing for Me. 7 You always have the poor with you, and you can do good for them whenever you want, but you do not always have Me. 8 She has done what she could; she has anointed My body in advance for burial. 9 •I assure you: Wherever the gospel is proclaimed in the whole world, what this woman has done will also be told in memory of her."

10 Then Judas Iscariot, one of the Twelve, went to the chief priests to hand Him over to them. 11 And when they heard this, they were glad and promised to give him silver.[k] So he started looking for a good opportunity to betray Him.

[a]**13:13** Or *saved* [b]**13:14** Dn 9:27 [c]**13:14** These are, most likely, Mark's words to his readers. [d]**13:18** Other mss read *pray that your escape* [e]**13:19** Lit *creation* [f]**13:20** Lit *days, all flesh would not survive* [g]**13:22** Or *false christs* [h]**13:29** Or *you know* [i]**13:29** Or *it;* = summer [j]**13:33** Other mss add *and pray* [k]**14:11** Or *money*; in Mt 26:15 it is specified as 30 pieces of silver; see Zch 11:12–13

Preparation for Passover

12 On the first day of Unleavened Bread,
when they sacrifice the Passover lamb, His disciples asked Him, "Where do You want us to go
and prepare the Passover so You may eat it?"
13 So He sent two of His disciples and told
them, "Go into the city, and a man carrying a
water jug will meet you. Follow him.
14 Wherever he enters, tell the owner of the
house, 'The Teacher says, "Where is the guest
room for Me to eat the Passover with My disciples?"' 15 He will show you a large room
upstairs, furnished and ready. Make the preparations for us there." 16 So the disciples went
out, entered the city, and found it just as He
had told them, and they prepared the Passover.

Betrayal at the Passover

17 When evening came, He arrived with the
Twelve. 18 While they were reclining and eating, Jesus said, "I assure you: One of you will
betray Me—one who is eating with Me!"
19 They began to be distressed and to say to
Him one by one, "Surely not I?"
20 He said to them, "⌊It is⌋ one of the
Twelve—the one who is dipping ⌊bread⌋ with
Me in the bowl. 21 For the •Son of Man will go
just as it is written about Him, but woe to that
man by whom the Son of Man is betrayed! It
would have been better for that man if he had
not been born."

The First Lord's Supper

22 As they were eating, He took bread,
blessed and broke it, gave it to them, and said,
"Take ⌊it⌋;[a] this is My body."
23 Then He took a cup, and after giving
thanks, He gave it to them, and so they all
drank from it. 24 He said to them, "This is My
blood ⌊that establishes⌋ the covenant;[b] it is shed
for many. 25 I assure you: I will no longer drink
of the fruit of the vine until that day when I
drink it in a new way[c] in the kingdom of God."
26 After singing psalms,[d] they went out to the
•Mount of Olives.

Peter's Denial Predicted

27 Then Jesus said to them, "All of you will
run away,[e] [f] because it is written:

> **I will strike the shepherd,**
> **and the sheep will be scattered.**[g]

28 But after I have been resurrected, I will go
ahead of you to Galilee."
29 Peter told Him, "Even if everyone runs
away, I will certainly not!"
30 "I assure you," Jesus said to him, "today,
this very night, before the rooster crows twice,
you will deny Me three times!"
31 But he kept insisting, "If I have to die
with You, I will never deny You!" And they all
said the same thing.

The Prayer in the Garden

32 Then they came to a place named Gethsemane, and He told His disciples, "Sit here
while I pray." 33 He took Peter, James, and
John with Him, and He began to be deeply distressed and horrified. 34 Then He said to
them, "My soul is swallowed up in sorrow[h] —
to the point of death. Remain here and stay
awake." 35 Then He went a little farther, fell
to the ground, and began to pray that if it were
possible, the hour might pass from Him.
36 And He said, "•*Abba*, Father! All things are
possible for You. Take this cup away from Me.
Nevertheless, not what I will, but what You
will."
37 Then He came and found them sleeping.
"Simon, are you sleeping?" He asked Peter.
"Couldn't you stay awake one hour? 38 Stay
awake and pray so that you won't enter into
temptation. The spirit is willing, but the flesh is
weak."
39 Once again He went away and prayed,
saying the same thing. 40 And He came again
and found them sleeping, because they could
not keep their eyes open.[i] They did not know
what to say to Him. 41 Then He came a third
time and said to them, "Are you still sleeping
and resting? Enough! The time has come. Look,
the Son of Man is being betrayed into the hands
of sinners. 42 Get up; let's go! See—My
betrayer is near."

The Judas Kiss

43 While He was still speaking, Judas, one of
the Twelve, suddenly arrived. With him was a
mob, with swords and clubs, from the chief
priests, the scribes, and the elders. 44 His
betrayer had given them a signal. "The One I
kiss," he said, "He's the One; arrest Him and
take Him away under guard." 45 So when he
came, he went right up to Him and said,

[a]**14:22** Other mss add *eat;* [b]**14:24** Other mss read *the new covenant* [c]**14:25** Or *drink new wine;* lit *drink it new* [d]**14:26** Pss 113–118 were sung during and after the Passover meal. [e]**14:27** Other mss add *because of Me this night* [f]**14:27** Or •*stumble* [g]**14:27** Zch 13:7 [h]**14:34** Or *I am deeply grieved* [i]**14:40** Lit *because their eyes were weighed down*

"•Rabbi!"—and kissed Him. 46 Then they took
hold of Him and arrested Him. 47 And one of
those who stood by drew his sword, struck the
high priest's •slave, and cut off his ear.
48 But Jesus said to them, "Have you come
out with swords and clubs, as though I were a
criminal,[a] to capture Me? 49 Every day I was
among you, teaching in the •temple complex,
and you didn't arrest Me. But the Scriptures
must be fulfilled." 50 Then they all deserted
Him and ran away.
51 Now a certain young man,[b] having a
linen cloth wrapped around his naked body,
was following Him. They caught hold of him,
52 but he left the linen cloth behind and ran
away naked.

Jesus Faces the Sanhedrin

53 They led Jesus away to the high priest,
and all the chief priests, the elders, and the
scribes convened. 54 Peter followed Him at a
distance, right into the high priest's courtyard.
He was sitting with the temple police,[c] warming himself by the fire.[d]
55 The chief priests and the whole •Sanhe-
drin were looking for testimony against Jesus to
put Him to death, but they could find none.
56 For many were giving false testimony against
Him, but the testimonies did not agree.
57 Some stood up and were giving false testimony against Him, stating, 58 "We heard Him
say, 'I will demolish this sanctuary made by
⌊human⌋ hands, and in three days I will build
another not made by hands.'" 59 Yet their testimony did not agree even on this.
60 Then the high priest stood up before
them all and questioned Jesus, "Don't You have
an answer to what these men are testifying
against You?" 61 But He kept silent and did not
answer anything. Again the high priest questioned Him, "Are You the •Messiah, the Son of
the Blessed One?"
62 "I am," said Jesus, "and all of you[e] will
see **the Son of Man seated at the right hand** of
the Power and **coming with the clouds of
heaven.**"[f]
63 Then the high priest tore his robes and
said, "Why do we still need witnesses? 64 You
have heard the blasphemy! What is your
decision?"[g]
And they all condemned Him to be deserving of death. 65 Then some began to spit on
Him, to blindfold Him, and to beat Him, saying,
"Prophesy!" Even the temple police took Him
and slapped Him.

Peter Denies His Lord

66 While Peter was in the courtyard below,
one of the high priest's servants came. 67 When
she saw Peter warming himself, she looked at
him and said, "You also were with that •Naza-
rene, Jesus."
68 But he denied it: "I don't know or understand what you're talking about!" Then he
went out to the entryway, and a rooster
crowed.[h]
69 When the servant saw him again she
began to tell those standing nearby, "This man
is one of them!"
70 But again he denied it. After a little while
those standing there said to Peter again, "You
certainly are one of them, since you're also a
Galilean!"[i]
71 Then he started to curse[j] and to swear
with an oath, "I don't know this man you're
talking about!"
72 Immediately a rooster crowed a second
time, and Peter remembered when Jesus had
spoken the word to him, "Before the rooster
crows twice, you will deny Me three times."
When he thought about it, he began to weep.[k]

Jesus Faces Pilate

15 As soon as it was morning, the •chief
priests had a meeting with the elders,
•scribes, and the whole •Sanhedrin. After
tying Jesus up, they led Him away and handed
Him over to •Pilate.
2 So Pilate asked Him, "Are You the King of
the Jews?"
He answered him, "You have said it."[l]
3 And the chief priests began to accuse Him
of many things. 4 Then Pilate questioned Him
again, "Are You not answering anything? Look
how many things they are accusing You of!"
5 But Jesus still did not answer anything, so
Pilate was amazed.

Jesus or Barabbas

6 At the festival it was Pilate's custom to
release for the people a prisoner they requested.
7 There was one named Barabbas, who was in

[a]**14:48** Lit *as against a criminal* [b]**14:51** Perhaps John Mark who later wrote this Gospel [c]**14:54** Or *the officers*; lit *the servants* [d]**14:54** Lit *light* [e]**14:62** Lit *and you* (pl in Gk) [f]**14:62** Ps 110:1; Dn 7:13 [g]**14:64** Lit *How does it appear to you?* [h]**14:68** Other mss omit *and a rooster crowed* [i]**14:70** Other mss add *and your speech shows it* [j]**14:71** To call down curses on himself if what he said weren't true [k]**14:72** Or *he burst into tears*, or *he broke down* [l]**15:2** Or *That is true*, an affirmative oath; Mt 26:64; 27:11

prison with rebels who had committed murder during the rebellion. 8 The crowd came up and began to ask ⌊Pilate⌋ to do for them as was his custom. 9 So Pilate answered them, "Do you want me to release the King of the Jews for you?" 10 For he knew it was because of envy that the chief priests had handed Him over. 11 But the chief priests stirred up the crowd so that he would release Barabbas to them instead.

12 Pilate asked them again, "Then what do you want me to do with the One you call the King of the Jews?"

13 Again they shouted, "Crucify Him!"

14 Then Pilate said to them, "Why? What has He done wrong?"

But they shouted, "Crucify Him!" all the more.

15 Then, willing to gratify the crowd, Pilate released Barabbas to them. And after having Jesus flogged,[a] he handed Him over to be crucified.

Mocked by the Military

16 Then the soldiers led Him away into the courtyard (that is, •headquarters) and called the whole •company together. 17 They dressed Him in a purple robe, twisted together a crown of thorns, and put it on Him. 18 And they began to salute Him, "Hail, King of the Jews!" 19 They kept hitting Him on the head with a reed and spitting on Him. Getting down on their knees, they were paying Him homage. 20 When they had mocked Him, they stripped Him of the purple robe, put His clothes on Him, and led Him out to crucify Him.

Crucified between Two Criminals

21 They forced a man coming in from the country, who was passing by, to carry Jesus' cross. He was Simon, a Cyrenian, the father of Alexander and Rufus. 22 And they brought Jesus to the place called *Golgotha* (which means Skull Place). 23 They tried to give Him wine mixed with myrrh, but He did not take it. 24 Then they crucified Him and divided His clothes, casting lots for them to decide what each would get. 25 Now it was nine in the morning[b] when they crucified Him. 26 The inscription of the charge written against Him was

THE KING OF THE JEWS

27 They crucified two criminals[c] with Him, one on His right and one on His left. [28 So the Scripture was fulfilled that says: **And He was counted among outlaws.**][d e] 29 Those who passed by were yelling insults at[f] Him, shaking their heads, and saying, "Ha! The One who would demolish the sanctuary and build it in three days, 30 save Yourself by coming down from the cross!" 31 In the same way, the chief priests with the scribes were mocking Him to one another and saying, "He saved others; He cannot save Himself! 32 Let the •Messiah, the King of Israel, come down now from the cross, so that we may see and believe." Even those who were crucified with Him were taunting Him.

The Death of Jesus

33 When it was noon,[g] darkness came over the whole land[h] until three in the afternoon.[i] 34 And at three[i] Jesus cried out with a loud voice, ***"Eloi, Eloi, lemá***[j] ***sabachtháni?"*** which is translated, **"My God, My God, why have You forsaken Me?"**[k]

35 When some of those standing there heard this, they said, "Look, He's calling for Elijah!" 36 Someone ran and filled a sponge with sour wine, fixed it on a reed, offered Him a drink, and said, "Let's see if Elijah comes to take Him down!"

37 But Jesus let out a loud cry and breathed His last. 38 Then the curtain of the sanctuary[l] was split in two from top to bottom. 39 When the •centurion, who was standing opposite Him, saw the way He[m] breathed His last, he said, "This man really was God's Son!"[n]

40 There were also women looking on from a distance. Among them were •Mary Magdalene, Mary the mother of James the younger and of Joses, and Salome. 41 When He was in Galilee, they would follow Him and help Him. Many other women had come up with Him to Jerusalem.

The Burial of Jesus

42 When it was already evening, because it was preparation day (that is, the day before the Sabbath), 43 Joseph of Arimathea, a prominent member of the Sanhedrin who was himself looking forward to the kingdom of God, came and boldly went in to Pilate and asked for Jesus'

[a]**15:15** Roman flogging was done with a whip made of leather strips embedded with pieces of bone or metal that brutally tore the flesh. [b]**15:25** Lit *was the third hour* [c]**15:27** Or *revolutionaries* [d]**15:28** Other mss omit bracketed text [e]**15:28** Is 53:12 [f]**15:29** Lit *passed by blasphemed* [g]**15:33** Lit *the sixth hour* [h]**15:33** Or *whole earth* [i]**15:33,34** Lit *the ninth hour* [j]**15:34** Other mss read *lama*; other mss read *lima* [k]**15:34** Ps 22:1 [l]**15:38** A heavy curtain separated the inner room of the temple from the outer. [m]**15:39** Other mss read *saw that He cried out like this and* [n]**15:39** Or *the Son of God*; Mk 1:1

body. 44 Pilate was surprised that He was already dead. Summoning the centurion, he asked him whether He had already died. 45 When he found out from the centurion, he gave the corpse to Joseph. 46 After he bought some fine linen, he took Him down and wrapped Him in the linen. Then he placed Him in a tomb cut out of the rock, and rolled a stone against the entrance to the tomb. 47 Now Mary Magdalene and Mary the mother of Joses were watching where He was placed.

Resurrection Morning

16 When the Sabbath was over, •Mary Magdalene, Mary the mother of James, and Salome bought spices, so they could go and anoint Him. 2 Very early in the morning, on the first day of the week, they went to the tomb at sunrise. 3 They were saying to one another, "Who will roll away the stone from the entrance to the tomb for us?" 4 Looking up, they observed that the stone—which was very large—had been rolled away. 5 When they entered the tomb, they saw a young man[a] dressed in a long white robe sitting on the right side; they were amazed and alarmed.[b]

6 "Don't be alarmed," he told them. "You are looking for Jesus the •Nazarene, who was crucified. He has been resurrected! He is not here! See the place where they put Him. 7 But go, tell His disciples and Peter, 'He is going ahead of you to Galilee; you will see Him there just as He told you.' "

8 So they went out and started running from the tomb, because trembling and astonishment overwhelmed them. And they said nothing to anyone, since they were afraid.

Appearances of the Risen Lord

[9 Early on the first day of the week, after He had risen, He appeared first to Mary Magdalene, out of whom He had driven seven demons. 10 She went and reported to those who had been with Him, as they were mourning and weeping. 11 Yet, when they heard that He was alive and had been seen by her, they did not believe it. 12 Then after this, He appeared in a different form to two of them walking on their way into the country. 13 And they went and reported it to the rest, who did not believe them either.

The Great Commission

14 Later, He appeared to the Eleven themselves as they were reclining at the table. He rebuked their unbelief and hardness of heart, because they did not believe those who saw Him after He had been resurrected. 15 Then He said to them, "Go into all the world and preach the gospel to the whole creation. 16 Whoever believes and is baptized will be saved, but whoever does not believe will be condemned. 17 And these signs will accompany those who believe: In My name they will drive out demons; they will speak in new languages; 18 they will pick up snakes;[c] if they should drink anything deadly, it will never harm them; they will lay hands on the sick, and they will get well."

The Ascension

19 Then after speaking to them, the Lord Jesus was taken up into heaven and sat down at the right hand of God. 20 And they went out and preached everywhere, the Lord working with them and confirming the word by the accompanying signs.][d]

Luke

The Dedication to Theophilus

1 Many have undertaken to compile a narrative about the events that have been fulfilled[e] among us, 2 just as the original eyewitnesses and servants of the word handed them down to us. 3 It also seemed good to me, since I have carefully investigated everything from the very first, to write to you in orderly sequence, most honorable Theophilus, 4 so that you may know the certainty of the things about which you have been instructed.[f]

[a]**16:5** In Mt 28:2, the young man = an angel [b]**16:5** *Amazed and alarmed* translate the idea of one Gk word. [c]**16:18** Other mss add *with their hands* [d]**16:9–20** Other mss omit bracketed text [e]**1:1** Or *events that have been accomplished*, or *events most surely believed* [f]**1:4** Or *informed*

Gabriel Predicts John's Birth

5 In the days of King •Herod of Judea, there
was a priest of Abijah's division[a] named Zechariah. His wife was from the daughters of Aaron,
and her name was Elizabeth. 6 Both were righteous in God's sight, living without blame
according to all the commandments and
requirements of the Lord. 7 But they had no
children[b] because Elizabeth could not conceive,[c] and both of them were well along in
years.[d]
8 When his division was on duty and he was
serving as priest before God, 9 it happened that
he was chosen by lot, according to the custom
of the priesthood, to enter the sanctuary of the
Lord and burn incense. 10 At the hour of
incense the whole assembly of the people was
praying outside. 11 An angel of the Lord
appeared to him, standing to the right of the
altar of incense. 12 When Zechariah saw him,
he was startled and overcome with fear.[e] 13 But
the angel said to him:

Do not be afraid, Zechariah,
because your prayer has been heard.
Your wife Elizabeth will bear you
a son,
and you will name him John.
14 There will be joy and delight for you,
and many will rejoice at his birth.
15 For he will be great in the sight
of the Lord
and will never drink wine or beer.
He will be filled with the Holy Spirit
while still in his mother's womb.
16 He will turn many of the sons of Israel
to the Lord their God.
17 And he will go before Him
in the spirit and power of Elijah,
to turn the hearts of fathers
to their children,
and the disobedient
to the understanding
of the righteous,
to make ready for the Lord
a prepared people.

18 "How can I know this?" Zechariah asked
the angel. "For I am an old man, and my wife is
well along in years."[f]
19 The angel answered him, "I am Gabriel,
who stands in the presence of God, and I was
sent to speak to you and tell you this good
news. 20 Now listen! You will become silent
and unable to speak until the day these things
take place, because you did not believe my
words, which will be fulfilled in their proper
time."
21 Meanwhile, the people were waiting for
Zechariah, amazed that he stayed so long in the
sanctuary. 22 When he did come out, he could
not speak to them. Then they realized that he
had seen a vision in the sanctuary. He kept
making signs to them and remained speechless.
23 When the days of his ministry were completed, he went back home.
24 After these days his wife Elizabeth conceived and kept herself in seclusion for five
months. She said, 25 "The Lord has done this
for me. He has looked with favor in these
days to take away my disgrace among the
people."

Gabriel Predicts Jesus' Birth

26 In the sixth month, the angel Gabriel
was sent by God to a town in Galilee called
Nazareth, 27 to a virgin •engaged to a man
named Joseph, of the house of David. The virgin's name was Mary. 28 And ⌊the angel⌋ came
to her and said, "Rejoice, favored woman! The
Lord is with you."[g] 29 But she was deeply troubled by this statement, wondering what kind
of greeting this could be. 30 Then the angel
told her:

Do not be afraid, Mary,
for you have found favor with God.
31 Now listen:
You will conceive and give birth to
a son,
and you will call His name JESUS.
32 He will be great
and will be called
the Son of the Most High,
and the Lord God will give Him
the throne of His father David.
33 He will reign over the house of Jacob
forever,
and His kingdom will have no end.

34 Mary asked the angel, "How can this be,
since I have not been intimate with a man?"[h]
35 The angel replied to her:

"The Holy Spirit will come upon you,

[a]**1:5** One of the 24 divisions of priests appointed by David for temple service; 1 Ch 24:10 [b]**1:7** Lit *child* [c]**1:7** Lit *Elizabeth was sterile* or *barren* [d]**1:7** Lit *in their days* [e]**1:12** Lit *and fear fell on him* [f]**1:18** Lit *in her days* [g]**1:28** Other mss add *blessed are you among women* [h]**1:34** Lit *since I do not know a man*

and the power of the Most High
will overshadow you.
Therefore the holy One to be born
will be called the Son of God.

36 And consider your relative Elizabeth—even
she has conceived a son in her old age, and
this is the sixth month for her who was called
barren. 37 For nothing will be impossible with
God."
38 "I am the Lord's •slave,"[a] said Mary.
"May it be done to me according to your
word." Then the angel left her.

Mary's Visit to Elizabeth

39 In those days Mary set out and hurried to
a town in the hill country of Judah 40 where she
entered Zechariah's house and greeted Elizabeth. 41 When Elizabeth heard Mary's greeting, the baby leaped inside her,[b] and Elizabeth
was filled with the Holy Spirit. 42 Then she
exclaimed with a loud cry:

You are the most blessed of women,
and your child will be blessed![c]

43 How could this happen to me, that the
mother of my Lord should come to me? 44 For
you see, when the sound of your greeting
reached my ears, the baby leaped for joy inside
me![d] 45 She who has believed is blessed
because what was spoken to her by the Lord
will be fulfilled!"

Mary's Praise

46 And Mary said:

My soul proclaims the greatness
of[e] the Lord,
47 and my spirit has rejoiced in God
my Savior,
48 because He has looked with favor
on the humble condition of His •slave.
Surely, from now on all generations
will call me blessed,
49 because the Mighty One
has done great things for me,
and His name is holy.
50 His mercy is from generation
to generation
on those who fear Him.
51 He has done a mighty deed
with His arm;
He has scattered the proud
because of the thoughts
of their hearts;
52 He has toppled the mighty
from their thrones
and exalted the lowly.
53 He has satisfied the hungry
with good things
and sent the rich away empty.
54 He has helped His servant Israel,
mindful of His mercy,[f]
55 just as He spoke to our ancestors,
to Abraham and his
descendants[g] forever.

56 And Mary stayed with her about three
months; then she returned to her home.

The Birth and Naming of John

57 Now the time had come for Elizabeth to
give birth, and she had a son. 58 Then her neighbors and relatives heard that the Lord had shown
her His great mercy,[h] and they rejoiced with her.
59 When they came to circumcise the child
on the eighth day, they were going to name him
Zechariah, after his father. 60 But his mother
responded, "No! He will be called John."
61 Then they said to her, "None of your relatives has that name." 62 So they motioned to his
father to find out what he wanted him to be
called. 63 He asked for a writing tablet and wrote:

HIS NAME IS JOHN

And they were all amazed. 64 Immediately his
mouth was opened and his tongue ⌊set free⌋,
and he began to speak, praising God. 65 Fear
came on all those who lived around them, and
all these things were being talked about
throughout the hill country of Judea. 66 All
who heard about ⌊him⌋ took ⌊it⌋ to heart, saying, "What then will this child become?" For,
indeed, the Lord's hand was with him.

Zechariah's Prophecy

67 Then his father Zechariah was filled with
the Holy Spirit and prophesied:

68 Praise the Lord, the God of Israel,
because He has visited
and provided redemption
for His people.
69 He has raised up a •horn of salvation[i]
for us

[a]**1:38** Lit *Look, the Lord's slave* [b]**1:41** Lit *leaped in her abdomen* or *womb* [c]**1:42** Lit *and the fruit of your abdomen* (or *womb*) *is blessed* [d]**1:44** Lit *in my abdomen* or *womb* [e]**1:46** Or *soul magnifies* [f]**1:54** Because He remembered His mercy; see Ps 98:3 [g]**1:55** Or *offspring;* lit *seed* [h]**1:58** Lit *the Lord magnified His mercy with her* [i]**1:69** A strong Savior

in the house of His servant David,
70 just as He spoke by the mouth
of His holy prophets in ancient times;
71 salvation from our enemies
and from the clutches[a] of those
who hate us.
72 He has dealt mercifully
with our fathers
and remembered
His holy covenant—
73 the oath that He swore to our father
Abraham.
He has given us the privilege,
74 since we have been rescued
from our enemies' clutches,[b]
to serve Him without fear
75 in holiness and righteousness
in His presence all our days.
76 And child, you will be called
a prophet of the Most High,
for you will go before the Lord
to prepare His ways,
77 to give His people knowledge
of salvation
through the forgiveness of their sins.
78 Because of our God's merciful
compassion,
the Dawn from on high will visit us
79 to shine on those who live in darkness
and the shadow of death,
to guide our feet into the way
of peace.

80 The child grew up and became spiritually
strong, and he was in the wilderness until the
day of his public appearance to Israel.

The Birth of Jesus

2 In those days a decree went out from
Caesar Augustus[c] that the whole empire[d]
should be registered. 2 This first registration
took place while[e] Quirinius was governing
Syria. 3 So everyone went to be registered,
each to his own town.
4 And Joseph also went up from the town of
Nazareth in Galilee, to Judea, to the city of
David, which is called Bethlehem, because he
was of the house and family line of David, 5 to
be registered along with Mary, who was
•engaged to him[f] and was pregnant. 6 While
they were there, the time came for her to give
birth. 7 Then she gave birth to her firstborn
Son, and she wrapped Him snugly in cloth and
laid Him in a feeding trough—because there
was no room for them at the inn.

The Shepherds and the Angels

8 In the same region, shepherds were staying out in the fields and keeping watch at
night over their flock. 9 Then an angel of the
Lord stood before[g] them, and the glory of the
Lord shone around them, and they were terrified.[h] 10 But the angel said to them, "Don't be
afraid, for look, I proclaim to you good news of
great joy that will be for all the people:
11 today a Savior, who is •Messiah the Lord,
was born for you in the city of David. 12 This
will be the sign for you: you will find a baby
wrapped snugly in cloth and lying in a feeding
trough."
13 Suddenly there was a multitude of the
heavenly host with the angel, praising God and
saying:

14 Glory to God
in the highest heaven,
and peace on earth to people
He favors![i] [j]

15 When the angels had left them and
returned to heaven, the shepherds said to one
another, "Let's go straight to Bethlehem and
see what has happened, which the Lord has
made known to us."
16 They hurried off and found both Mary
and Joseph, and the baby who was lying in the
feeding trough. 17 After seeing ⌊them⌋, they
reported the message they were told about this
child, 18 and all who heard it were amazed at
what the shepherds said to them. 19 But Mary
was treasuring up all these things[k] in her heart
and meditating on them. 20 The shepherds
returned, glorifying and praising God for all
they had seen and heard, just as they had been
told.

The Circumcision and Presentation of Jesus

21 When the eight days were completed for
His circumcision, He was named JESUS—the
name given by the angel before He was conceived.[l] 22 And when the days of their purification according to the law of Moses were

[a]**1:71** Lit *the hand* [b]**1:74** Lit *from the hand of enemies* [c]**2:1** Emperor who ruled the Roman Empire 27 B.C.–A.D. 14; also known as Octavian, he established the peaceful era known as the *Pax Romana*; Caesar was a title of Roman emperors. [d]**2:1** Or *the whole inhabited world* [e]**2:2** Or *This registration was the first while*, or *This registration was before* [f]**2:5** Other mss read *was his engaged wife* [g]**2:9** Or *Lord appeared to* [h]**2:9** Lit *they feared a great fear* [i]**2:14** Other mss read *earth good will to people* [j]**2:14** Or *earth to men of good will* [k]**2:19** Lit *these words* [l]**2:21** Or *conceived in the womb*

finished, they brought Him up to Jerusalem to
present Him to the Lord 23 (just as it is written
in the law of the Lord: **Every firstborn male**[a]
will be dedicated[b] **to the Lord**[c]) 24 and to offer
a sacrifice (according to what is stated in the
law of the Lord: **a pair of turtledoves or two**
young pigeons[d]).

Simeon's Prophetic Praise

25 There was a man in Jerusalem whose
name was Simeon. This man was righteous and
devout, looking forward to Israel's consolation,[e] and the Holy Spirit was on him. 26 It had
been revealed to him by the Holy Spirit that he
would not see death before he saw the Lord's
Messiah. 27 Guided by the Spirit, he entered[f]
the •temple complex. When the parents
brought in the child Jesus to perform for Him
what was customary under the law, 28 Simeon
took Him up in his arms, praised God, and said:

29 Now, Master,
You can dismiss Your •slave in peace,
according to Your word.
30 For my eyes have seen Your salvation.
31 You have prepared ⌊it⌋
in the presence of all peoples—
32 a light for revelation to the Gentiles[g]
and glory to Your people Israel.

33 His father and mother[h] were amazed at
what was being said about Him. 34 Then Simeon blessed them and told His mother Mary:
"Indeed, this child is destined to cause the fall
and rise of many in Israel and to be a sign that
will be opposed[i] — 35 and a sword will pierce
your own soul—that the thoughts[j] of many
hearts may be revealed."

Anna's Testimony

36 There was also a prophetess, Anna, a
daughter of Phanuel, of the tribe of Asher. She
was well along in years,[k] having lived with her
husband seven years after her marriage,[l] 37 and
was a widow for 84 years.[m] She did not leave the
temple complex, serving God night and day with
fastings and prayers. 38 At that very moment,[n]
she came up and began to thank God and to
speak about Him to all who were looking forward to the redemption of Jerusalem.[o]

The Family's Return to Nazareth

39 When they had completed everything
according to the law of the Lord, they
returned to Galilee, to their own town of Nazareth. 40 The boy grew up and became strong,
filled with wisdom, and God's grace was on
Him.

In His Father's House

41 Every year His parents traveled to Jerusalem for the •Passover Festival. 42 When He was
12 years old, they went up according to the custom of the festival. 43 After those days were
over, as they were returning, the boy Jesus
stayed behind in Jerusalem, but His parents[p]
did not know it. 44 Assuming He was in the
traveling party, they went a day's journey.
Then they began looking for Him among their
relatives and friends. 45 When they did not find
Him, they returned to Jerusalem to search for
Him. 46 After three days, they found Him in the
temple complex sitting among the teachers, listening to them and asking them questions.
47 And all those who heard Him were
astounded at His understanding and His
answers. 48 When His parents saw Him, they
were astonished, and His mother said to Him,
"Son, why have You treated us like this? Your
father and I have been anxiously searching for
You."

49 "Why were you searching for Me?" He
asked them. "Didn't you know that I had to be
in My Father's house?"[q] 50 But they did not
understand what He said to them.

In Favor with God and with People

51 Then He went down with them and
came to Nazareth and was obedient to them.
His mother kept all these things in her heart.
52 And Jesus increased in wisdom and stature,
and in favor with God and with people.

The Messiah's Herald

3 In the fifteenth year of the reign of Tibe-
rius Caesar,[r] while Pontius •Pilate was
governor of Judea, •Herod was tetrarch[s] of
Galilee, his brother Philip tetrarch of the
region of Iturea[t] and Trachonitis,[t] and Lysa-
nias tetrarch of Abilene,[u] 2 during the high

[a]**2:23** Lit *"Every male that opens a womb* [b]**2:23** Lit *be called holy* [c]**2:23** Ex 13:2,12 [d]**2:24** Lv 5:11; 12:8 [e]**2:25** The coming of the Messiah with His salvation for the nation; Lk 2:26,30; Is 40:1; 61:2 [f]**2:27** Lit *And in the Spirit, he came into the* [g]**2:32** Or *the nations* [h]**2:33** Other mss read *But Joseph and His mother* [i]**2:34** Or *spoken against* [j]**2:35** Or *schemes* [k]**2:36** Lit *in many days* [l]**2:36** Lit *years from her virginity* [m]**2:37** Or *she was a widow until the age of 84* [n]**2:38** Lit *very hour* [o]**2:38** Other mss read *in Jerusalem* [p]**2:43** Other mss read *but Joseph and His mother* [q]**2:49** Or *be involved in My Father's interests* (or *things*), or *be among My Father's people* [r]**3:1** Emperor who ruled the Roman Empire A.D. 14–37 [s]**3:1** Or *ruler* [t]**3:1** A small province northeast of Galilee [u]**3:1** A small Syrian province

priesthood of Annas and Caiaphas, God's
word came to John the son of Zechariah in
the wilderness. 3 He went into all the vicinity
of the Jordan, preaching a baptism of repentance[a] for the forgiveness of sins, 4 as it is
written in the book of the words of the
prophet Isaiah:

A voice of one crying out
in the wilderness:
"Prepare the way for the Lord;
make His paths straight!
5 **Every valley will be filled,**
and every mountain and hill will be
made low;[b]
the crooked will become straight,
the rough ways smooth,
6 **and everyone**[c] **will see**
the salvation of God."[d]

7 He then said to the crowds who came out
to be baptized by him, "Brood of vipers! Who
warned you to flee from the coming wrath?
8 Therefore produce fruit consistent with
repentance. And don't start saying to yourselves, 'We have Abraham as our father,' for I
tell you that God is able to raise up children for
Abraham from these stones! 9 Even now the ax
is ready to strike[e] the root of the trees! Therefore every tree that doesn't produce good fruit
will be cut down and thrown into the fire."

10 "What then should we do?" the crowds
were asking him.

11 He replied to them, "The one who has
two shirts[f] must share with someone who has
none, and the one who has food must do the
same."

12 Tax collectors also came to be baptized,
and they asked him, "Teacher, what should we
do?"

13 He told them, "Don't collect any more
than what you have been authorized."

14 Some soldiers also questioned him:
"What should we do?"

He said to them, "Don't take money from
anyone by force or false accusation; be satisfied
with your wages."

15 Now the people were waiting expectantly, and all of them were debating in their
minds[g] whether John might be the •Messiah.
16 John answered them all, "I baptize you
with[h] water, but One is coming who is more
powerful than I. I am not worthy to untie the
strap of His sandals. He will baptize you with[h]
the Holy Spirit and fire. 17 His winnowing
shovel[i] is in His hand to clear His threshing
floor and gather the wheat into His barn, but
the chaff He will burn up with a fire that never
goes out." 18 Then, along with many other
exhortations, he proclaimed good news to the
people. 19 But Herod the tetrarch, being
rebuked by him about Herodias, his brother's
wife, and about all the evil things Herod had
done, 20 added this to everything else—he
locked John up in prison.

The Baptism of Jesus

21 When all the people were baptized,
Jesus also was baptized. As He was praying,
heaven opened, 22 and the Holy Spirit
descended on Him in a physical appearance
like a dove. And a voice came from heaven:

You are My beloved Son.
I take delight in You!

The Genealogy of Jesus Christ

23 As He began ⌊His ministry⌋, Jesus was
about 30 years old and was thought to be[j] the

son of Joseph, ⌊son⌋[k] of Heli,
24 ⌊son⌋ of Matthat, ⌊son⌋ of Levi,
⌊son⌋ of Melchi, ⌊son⌋ of Jannai,
⌊son⌋ of Joseph, 25 ⌊son⌋ of Mattathias,
⌊son⌋ of Amos, ⌊son⌋ of Nahum,
⌊son⌋ of Esli, ⌊son⌋ of Naggai,
26 ⌊son⌋ of Maath, ⌊son⌋ of Mattathias,
⌊son⌋ of Semein, ⌊son⌋ of Josech,
⌊son⌋ of Joda, 27 ⌊son⌋ of Joanan,
⌊son⌋ of Rhesa, ⌊son⌋ of Zerubbabel,
⌊son⌋ of Shealtiel, ⌊son⌋ of Neri,
28 ⌊son⌋ of Melchi, ⌊son⌋ of Addi,
⌊son⌋ of Cosam, ⌊son⌋ of Elmadam,
⌊son⌋ of Er, 29 ⌊son⌋ of Joshua,
⌊son⌋ of Eliezer, ⌊son⌋ of Jorim,
⌊son⌋ of Matthat, ⌊son⌋ of Levi,
30 ⌊son⌋ of Simeon, ⌊son⌋ of Judah,
⌊son⌋ of Joseph, ⌊son⌋ of Jonam,
⌊son⌋ of Eliakim, 31 ⌊son⌋ of Melea,
⌊son⌋ of Menna, ⌊son⌋ of Mattatha,
⌊son⌋ of Nathan,
⌊son⌋ of David,

[a] **3:3** Or *baptism based on repentance* [b] **3:5** Lit *be humbled* [c] **3:6** Lit *all flesh* [d] **3:4–6** Is 40:3–5 [e] **3:9** Lit *the ax lies at* [f] **3:11** Lit *tunics* [g] **3:15** Or *hearts* [h] **3:16** Or *in* [i] **3:17** A wooden farm implement used to toss threshed grain into the wind so the lighter chaff would blow away and separate from the heavier grain [j] **3:23** People did not know about His virgin birth; Lk 1:26–38; Mt 1:18–25 [k] **3:23** The relationship in some cases may be more distant than a son.

32 ⌊son⌋ of Jesse, ⌊son⌋ of Obed,
⌊son⌋ of Boaz,
⌊son⌋ of Salmon,[a]
⌊son⌋ of Nahshon,
33 ⌊son⌋ of Amminadab,
⌊son⌋ of Ram,[b] ⌊son⌋ of Hezron,
⌊son⌋ of Perez, ⌊son⌋ of Judah,
34 ⌊son⌋ of Jacob,
⌊son⌋ of Isaac,
⌊son⌋ of Abraham,
⌊son⌋ of Terah,
⌊son⌋ of Nahor,
35 ⌊son⌋ of Serug,
⌊son⌋ of Reu, ⌊son⌋ of Peleg,
⌊son⌋ of Eber, ⌊son⌋ of Shelah,
36 ⌊son⌋ of Cainan,
⌊son⌋ of Arphaxad,
⌊son⌋ of Shem, ⌊son⌋ of Noah,
⌊son⌋ of Lamech,
37 ⌊son⌋ of Methuselah,
⌊son⌋ of Enoch, ⌊son⌋ of Jared,
⌊son⌋ of Mahalaleel,
⌊son⌋ of Cainan,
38 ⌊son⌋ of Enos, ⌊son⌋ of Seth,
⌊son⌋ of Adam,
⌊son⌋ of God.

The Temptation of Jesus

4 Then Jesus returned from the Jordan, full
of the Holy Spirit, and was led by the
Spirit in the wilderness 2 for 40 days to be
tempted by the Devil. He ate nothing during
those days, and when they were over,[c] He was
hungry. 3 The Devil said to Him, "If You are
the Son of God, tell this stone to become
bread."

4 But Jesus answered him, "It is written:
Man must not live on bread alone."[d e]

5 So he took Him up[f] and showed Him all
the kingdoms of the world in a moment of time.
6 The Devil said to Him, "I will give You their
splendor and all this authority, because it has
been given over to me, and I can give it to anyone I want. 7 If You, then, will worship me,[g] all
will be Yours."

8 And Jesus answered him,[h] "It is written:

Worship the Lord your God,
and serve Him only."[i]

9 So he took Him to Jerusalem, had Him
stand on the pinnacle of the temple, and said to
Him, "If You are the Son of God, throw Yourself
down from here. 10 For it is written:

He will give His angels orders
concerning you,
to protect you,[j] 11 and
they will support you
with their hands,
so that you will not strike
your foot against a stone."[k]

12 And Jesus answered him, "It is said: **Do
not test the Lord your God.**"[l]

13 After the Devil had finished every temptation, he departed from Him for a time.

Ministry in Galilee

14 Then Jesus returned to Galilee in the
power of the Spirit, and news about Him spread
throughout the entire vicinity. 15 He was teaching in their •synagogues, being acclaimed[m] by
everyone.

Rejection at Nazareth

16 He came to Nazareth, where He had
been brought up. As usual, He entered the synagogue on the Sabbath day and stood up to
read. 17 The scroll of the prophet Isaiah was
given to Him, and unrolling the scroll, He
found the place where it was written:

18 **The Spirit of the Lord is**
on Me,
because He has anointed
Me
to preach good news
to the poor.
He has sent Me[n]
to proclaim freedom[o]
to the captives
and recovery of sight
to the blind,
to set free the oppressed,
19 **to proclaim the year**
of the Lord's favor.[p q]

20 He then rolled up the scroll, gave it
back to the attendant, and sat down. And the
eyes of everyone in the synagogue were fixed
on Him. 21 He began by saying to them,
"Today as you listen, this Scripture has been
fulfilled."

[a]**3:32** Other mss read *Sala* [b]**3:33** Other mss read *Amminadab, son of Aram, son of Joram*; other mss read *Amminadab, son of Admin, son of Arni* [c]**4:2** Lit *were completed* [d]**4:4** Other mss add *but on every word of God* [e]**4:4** Dt 8:3 [f]**4:5** Other mss read *So the Devil took Him up on a high mountain* [g]**4:7** Lit *will fall down before me* [h]**4:8** Other mss add *"Get behind Me, Satan!* [i]**4:8** Dt 6:13 [j]**4:10** Ps 91:11 [k]**4:11** Ps 91:12 [l]**4:12** Dt 6:16 [m]**4:15** Or *glorified* [n]**4:18** Other mss add *to heal the brokenhearted,* [o]**4:18** Or *release*, or *forgiveness* [p]**4:19** The time of messianic grace [q]**4:18–19** Is 61:1–2

22 They were all speaking well of Him[a] and were amazed by the gracious words that came from His mouth, yet they said, "Isn't this Joseph's son?"

23 Then He said to them, "No doubt you will quote this proverb[b] to Me: 'Doctor, heal yourself.' 'All we've heard that took place in Capernaum, do here in Your hometown also.' "

24 He also said, "•I assure you: No prophet is accepted in his hometown. 25 But I say to you, there were certainly many widows in Israel in Elijah's days, when the sky was shut up for three years and six months while a great famine came over all the land. 26 Yet Elijah was not sent to any of them—but to a widow at Zarephath in Sidon. 27 And in the prophet Elisha's time, there were many in Israel who had serious skin diseases, yet not one of them was healed[c] —only Naaman the Syrian."

28 When they heard this, everyone in the synagogue was enraged. 29 They got up, drove Him out of town, and brought Him to the edge[d] of the hill their town was built on, intending to hurl Him over the cliff. 30 But He passed right through the crowd and went on His way.

Driving Out an Unclean Spirit

31 Then He went down to Capernaum, a town in Galilee, and was teaching them on the Sabbath. 32 They were astonished at His teaching because His message had authority. 33 In the synagogue there was a man with an unclean demonic spirit who cried out with a loud voice, 34 "Leave us alone![e] What do You have to do with us,[f] Jesus—•Nazarene? Have You come to destroy us? I know who You are—the Holy One of God!"

35 But Jesus rebuked him and said, "Be quiet and come out of him!"

And throwing him down before them, the demon came out of him without hurting him at all. 36 They were all struck with amazement and kept saying to one another, "What is this message? For He commands the unclean spirits with authority and power, and they come out!" 37 And news about Him began to go out to every place in the vicinity.

Healings at Capernaum

38 After He left the synagogue, He entered Simon's house. Simon's mother-in-law was suffering from a high fever, and they asked Him about her. 39 So He stood over her and rebuked the fever, and it left her. She got up immediately and began to serve them.

40 When the sun was setting, all those who had anyone sick with various diseases brought them to Him. As He laid His hands on each one of them, He would heal them. 41 Also, demons were coming out of many, shouting and saying, "You are the Son of God!" But He rebuked them and would not allow them to speak, because they knew He was the •Messiah.

Preaching in Galilee

42 When it was day, He went out and made His way to a deserted place. But the crowds were searching for Him. They came to Him and tried to keep Him from leaving them. 43 But He said to them, "I must proclaim the good news about the kingdom of God to the other towns also, because I was sent for this purpose." 44 And He was preaching in the synagogues of Galilee.[g]

The First Disciples

5 As the crowd was pressing in on Jesus to hear God's word, He was standing by Lake Gennesaret.[h] 2 He saw two boats at the edge of the lake;[i] the fishermen had left them and were washing their nets. 3 He got into one of the boats, which belonged to Simon, and asked him to put out a little from the land. Then He sat down and was teaching the crowds from the boat.

4 When He had finished speaking, He said to Simon, "Put out into deep water and let down[j] your nets for a catch."

5 "Master," Simon replied, "we've worked hard all night long and caught nothing! But at Your word, I'll let down the nets."[k]

6 When they did this, they caught a great number of fish, and their nets[k] began to tear. 7 So they signaled to their partners in the other boat to come and help them; they came and filled both boats so full that they began to sink.

8 When Simon Peter saw this, he fell at Jesus' knees and said, "Go away from me, because I'm a sinful man, Lord!" 9 For he and all those with him were amazed[l] at the catch of fish they took, 10 and so were James and John,

[a]4:22 Or *They were testifying against Him* [b]4:23 Or *parable* [c]4:27 Lit *cleansed* [d]4:29 Lit *brow* [e]4:34 Or *Ha!,* or *Ah!* [f]4:34 Lit *What to us and to You* [g]4:44 Other mss read *Judea* [h]5:1 = Sea of Galilee [i]5:2 Lit *boats standing by the lake* [j]5:4 Lit *and you* (Gk pl) *let down* [k]5:5,6 Other mss read *net* (Gk sg) [l]5:9 Or *For amazement had seized him and all those with him*

Zebedee's sons, who were Simon's partners.

"Don't be afraid," Jesus told Simon. "From now on you will be catching people!" 11 Then they brought the boats to land, left everything, and followed Him.

Cleansing a Leper

12 While He was in one of the towns, a man was there who had a serious skin disease all over him. He saw Jesus, fell facedown, and begged Him: "Lord, if You are willing, You can make me clean."[a]

13 Reaching out His hand, He touched him, saying, "I am willing; be made clean," and immediately the disease left him. 14 Then He ordered him to tell no one: "But go and show yourself to the priest, and offer what Moses prescribed for your cleansing as a testimony to them."

15 But the news[b] about Him spread even more, and large crowds would come together to hear Him and to be healed of their sicknesses. 16 Yet He often withdrew to deserted places and prayed.

The Son of Man Forgives and Heals

17 On one of those days while He was teaching, •Pharisees and teachers of the law were sitting there who had come from every village of Galilee and Judea, and also from Jerusalem. And the Lord's power to heal was in Him. 18 Just then some men came, carrying on a stretcher a man who was paralyzed. They tried to bring him in and set him down before Him. 19 Since they could not find a way to bring him in because of the crowd, they went up on the roof and lowered him on the stretcher through the roof tiles into the middle of the crowd before Jesus.

20 Seeing their faith He said, "Friend,[c] your sins are forgiven you."

21 Then the •scribes and the Pharisees began to reason: "Who is this man who speaks blasphemies? Who can forgive sins but God alone?"

22 But perceiving their thoughts, Jesus replied to them, "Why are you reasoning this in your hearts?[d] 23 Which is easier: to say, 'Your sins are forgiven you,' or to say, 'Get up and walk'? 24 But so you may know that the •Son of Man has authority on earth to forgive sins"—He told the paralyzed man, "I tell you: get up, pick up your stretcher, and go home."

25 Immediately he got up before them, picked up what he had been lying on, and went home glorifying God. 26 Then everyone was astounded, and they were giving glory to God. And they were filled with awe and said, "We have seen incredible things today!"

The Call of Levi

27 After this, Jesus went out and saw a tax collector named Levi sitting at the tax office, and He said to him, "Follow Me!" 28 So, leaving everything behind, he got up and began to follow Him.

Dining with Sinners

29 Then Levi hosted a grand banquet for Him at his house. Now there was a large crowd of tax collectors and others who were guests[e] with them. 30 But the Pharisees and their scribes were complaining to His disciples, "Why do you eat and drink with tax collectors and sinners?"

31 Jesus replied to them, "The healthy don't need a doctor, but the sick do. 32 I have not come to call the righteous, but sinners to repentance."

A Question about Fasting

33 Then they said to Him, "John's disciples fast often and say prayers, and those of the Pharisees do the same, but Yours eat and drink."[f]

34 Jesus said to them, "You can't make the wedding guests[g] fast while the groom is with them, can you? 35 But the days will come when the groom will be taken away from them—then they will fast in those days."

36 He also told them a parable: "No one tears a patch from a new garment and puts it on an old garment. Otherwise, not only will he tear the new, but also the piece from the new garment will not match the old. 37 And no one puts new wine into old wineskins. Otherwise, the new wine will burst the skins, it will spill, and the skins will be ruined. 38 But new wine should be put into fresh wineskins.[h] 39 And no

[a]**5:12** In these verses, *clean* includes healing, ceremonial purification, return to fellowship with people, and worship in the temple; Lv 14:1–32. [b]**5:15** Lit *the word* [c]**5:20** Lit *Man* [d]**5:22** Or *minds* [e]**5:29** Lit *were reclining* (at the table); at important meals the custom was to recline on a mat at a low table and lean on the left elbow. [f]**5:33** Other mss read *"Why do John's . . . drink?"* (as a question) [g]**5:34** Or *the friends of the groom*; lit *sons of the bridal chamber* [h]**5:38** Other mss add *And so both are preserved.*

one, after drinking old wine, wants new,
because he says, 'The old is better.' "[a]

Lord of the Sabbath

6 On a Sabbath,[b] He passed through the
grainfields. His disciples were picking
heads of grain, rubbing them in their hands,
and eating them. 2 But some of the •Pharisees
said, "Why are you doing what is not lawful on
the Sabbath?"

3 Jesus answered them, "Haven't you read
what David and those who were with him did
when he was hungry— 4 how he entered the
house of God, and took and ate the •sacred
bread, which is not lawful for any but the
priests to eat? He even gave some to those who
were with him." 5 Then He told them, "The
•Son of Man is Lord of the Sabbath."

The Man with the Paralyzed Hand

6 On another Sabbath He entered the •syn-
agogue and was teaching. A man was there
whose right hand was paralyzed. 7 The •scribes
and Pharisees were watching Him closely, to
see if He would heal on the Sabbath, so that
they could find a charge against Him. 8 But He
knew their thoughts and told the man with the
paralyzed hand, "Get up and stand here."[c] So
he got up and stood there. 9 Then Jesus said to
them, "I ask you: is it lawful on the Sabbath to
do good or to do evil, to save life or to destroy
it?" 10 After looking around at them all, He told
him, "Stretch out your hand." He did so, and
his hand was restored.[d] 11 They, however,
were filled with rage and started discussing
with one another what they might do to Jesus.

The 12 Apostles

12 During those days He went out to the
mountain to pray and spent all night in prayer
to God. 13 When daylight came, He summoned
His disciples, and He chose 12 of them—He
also named them apostles:

14 Simon, whom He also
named Peter,
and Andrew his brother;
James and John;
Philip and Bartholomew;
15 Matthew and Thomas;
James the son of Alphaeus,
and Simon called the Zealot;
16 Judas the son of James,
and Judas Iscariot, who became
a traitor.

Teaching and Healing

17 After coming down with them, He stood
on a level place with a large crowd of His disciples and a great multitude of people from all
Judea and Jerusalem and from the seacoast of
Tyre and Sidon. 18 They came to hear Him and
to be healed of their diseases; and those tormented by unclean spirits were made well.
19 The whole crowd was trying to touch Him,
because power was coming out from Him and
healing them all.

The Beatitudes

20 Then looking up at[e] His disciples, He
said:

Blessed are you who are poor,
because the kingdom of God
is yours.
21 Blessed are you who are hungry now,
because you will be filled.
Blessed are you who weep now,
because you will laugh.
22 Blessed are you when people hate you,
when they exclude you, insult you,
and slander your name as evil,
because of the Son of Man.

23 "Rejoice in that day and leap for joy! Take
note—your reward is great in heaven, because
this is the way their ancestors used to treat the
prophets.

Woe to the Self-Satisfied

24 But woe to you who are rich,
because you have received
your comfort.
25 Woe to you who are full now,
because you will be hungry.
Woe to you[f]
who are laughing now,
because you will mourn and weep.
26 Woe to you[f]
when all people speak well of you,
because this is the way
their ancestors
used to treat the false prophets.

Love Your Enemies

27 "But I say to you who listen: Love your
enemies, do good to those who hate you,

[a]**5:39** Other mss read *is good* [b]**6:1** Other mss read *a second-first Sabbath*; perhaps a special Sabbath [c]**6:8** Lit *stand in the middle* [d]**6:10** Other mss add *as sound as the other* [e]**6:20** Lit *Then lifting up His eyes to* [f]**6:25,26** Other mss omit *to you*

28 bless those who curse you, pray for those who mistreat you. 29 If anyone hits you on the cheek, offer the other also. And if anyone takes away your coat, don't hold back your shirt either. 30 Give to everyone who asks from you, and from one who takes away your things, don't ask for them back. 31 Just as you want others to do for you, do the same for them. 32 If you love those who love you, what credit is that to you? Even sinners love those who love them. 33 If you do what is good to those who are good to you, what credit is that to you? Even sinners do that. 34 And if you lend to those from whom you expect to receive, what credit is that to you? Even sinners lend to sinners to be repaid in full. 35 But love your enemies, do what is good, and lend, expecting nothing in return. Then your reward will be great, and you will be sons of the Most High. For He is gracious to the ungrateful and evil. 36 Be merciful, just as your Father also is merciful.

Do Not Judge

37 "Do not judge, and you will not be judged. Do not condemn, and you will not be condemned. Forgive, and you will be forgiven. 38 Give, and it will be given to you; a good measure—pressed down, shaken together, and running over—will be poured into your lap. For with the measure you use,[a] it will be measured back to you."

39 He also told them a parable: "Can the blind guide the blind? Won't they both fall into a pit? 40 A disciple is not above his teacher, but everyone who is fully trained will be like his teacher.

41 "Why do you look at the speck in your brother's eye, but don't notice the log in your own eye? 42 Or how can you say to your brother, 'Brother, let me take out the speck that is in your eye,' when you yourself don't see the log in your eye? Hypocrite! First take the log out of your eye, and then you will see clearly to take out the speck in your brother's eye.

A Tree and Its Fruit

43 "A good tree doesn't produce bad fruit; on the other hand, a bad tree doesn't produce good fruit. 44 For each tree is known by its own fruit. Figs aren't gathered from thornbushes, or grapes picked from a bramble bush. 45 A good man produces good out of the good storeroom of his heart. An evil man produces evil out of the evil storeroom, for his mouth speaks from the overflow of the heart.

The Two Foundations

46 "Why do you call Me 'Lord, Lord,' and don't do the things I say? 47 I will show you what someone is like who comes to Me, hears My words, and acts on them: 48 He is like a man building a house, who dug deep[b] and laid the foundation on the rock. When the flood came, the river crashed against that house and couldn't shake it, because it was well built. 49 But the one who hears and does not act is like a man who built a house on the ground without a foundation. The river crashed against it, and immediately it collapsed. And the destruction of that house was great!"

A Centurion's Faith

7 When He had concluded all His sayings in the hearing of the people, He entered Capernaum. 2 A •centurion's •slave, who was highly valued by him, was sick and about to die. 3 When the centurion heard about Jesus, he sent some Jewish elders to Him, requesting Him to come and save the life of his slave. 4 When they reached Jesus, they pleaded with Him earnestly, saying, "He is worthy for You to grant this, 5 because he loves our nation and has built us a •synagogue." 6 Jesus went with them, and when He was not far from[c] the house, the centurion sent friends to tell Him, "Lord, don't trouble Yourself, since I am not worthy to have You come under my roof. 7 That is why I didn't even consider myself worthy to come to You. But say the word, and my servant will be cured.[d] 8 For I too am a man placed under authority, having soldiers under my command.[e] I say to this one, 'Go!' and he goes; and to another, 'Come!' and he comes; and to my slave, 'Do this!' and he does it."

9 Jesus heard this and was amazed at him, and turning to the crowd following Him, He said, "I tell you, I have not found so great a faith even in Israel!" 10 When those who had been sent returned to the house, they found the •slave in good health.

A Widow's Son Raised to Life

11 Soon afterwards He was on His way to a town called Nain. His disciples and a large crowd were traveling with Him. 12 Just as He

[a]**6:38** Lit *you measure* [b]**6:48** Lit *dug and went deep* [c]**7:6** Lit *and He already was not far from* [d]**7:7** Other mss read *and let my servant be cured* [e]**7:8** Lit *under me*

neared the gate of the town, a dead man was being carried out. He was his mother's only son, and she was a widow. A large crowd from the city was also with her. 13 When the Lord saw her, He had compassion on her and said, "Don't cry." 14 Then He came up and touched the open coffin,[a] and the pallbearers stopped. And He said, "Young man, I tell you, get up!"

15 The dead man sat up and began to speak, and Jesus gave him to his mother. 16 Then fear[b] came over everyone, and they glorified God, saying, "A great prophet has risen among us," and "God has visited[c] His people." 17 This report about Him went throughout Judea and all the vicinity.

In Praise of John the Baptist

18 Then John's disciples told him about all these things. So John summoned two of his disciples 19 and sent them to the Lord, asking, "Are You the One who is to come, or should we look for someone else?"

20 When the men reached Him, they said, "John the Baptist sent us to ask You, 'Are You the One who is to come, or should we look for someone else?' "

21 At that time Jesus healed many people of diseases, plagues, and evil spirits, and He granted sight to many blind people. 22 He replied to them, "Go and report to John the things you have seen and heard: The blind receive their sight, the lame walk, those with skin diseases are healed,[d] the deaf hear, the dead are raised, and the poor have the good news preached to them. 23 And anyone who is not offended because of Me is blessed." 24 After John's messengers left, He began to speak to the crowds about John: "What did you go out into the wilderness to see? A reed swaying in the wind? 25 What then did you go out to see? A man dressed in soft robes? Look, those who are splendidly dressed[e] and live in luxury are in royal palaces. 26 What then did you go out to see? A prophet? Yes, I tell you, and far more than a prophet. 27 This is the one it is written about:

Look, I am sending My messenger
ahead of You;[f]
he will prepare Your way
before You.[g]

28 I tell you, among those born of women no one is greater than John,[h] but the least in the kingdom of God is greater than he."

29 (And when all the people, including the tax collectors, heard this, they acknowledged God's way of righteousness,[i] because they had been baptized with John's baptism. 30 But since the •Pharisees and experts in the law had not been baptized by him, they rejected the plan of God for themselves.)

An Unresponsive Generation

31 "To what then should I compare the people of this generation, and what are they like? 32 They are like children sitting in the marketplace and calling to each other:

We played the flute for you,
but you didn't dance;
we sang a lament,
but you didn't weep!

33 For John the Baptist did not come eating bread or drinking wine, and you say, 'He has a demon!' 34 The •Son of Man has come eating and drinking, and you say, 'Look, a glutton and a drunkard, a friend of tax collectors and sinners!' 35 Yet wisdom is vindicated[j] by all her children."

Much Forgiveness, Much Love

36 Then one of the Pharisees invited Him to eat with him. He entered the Pharisee's house and reclined at the table. 37 And a woman in the town who was a sinner found out that Jesus was reclining at the table in the Pharisee's house. She brought an alabaster flask of fragrant oil 38 and stood behind Him at His feet, weeping, and began to wash His feet with her tears. She wiped His feet with the hair of her head, kissing them and anointing them with the fragrant oil.

39 When the Pharisee who had invited Him saw this, he said to himself, "This man, if He were a prophet, would know who and what kind of woman this is who is touching Him—she's a sinner!"

40 Jesus replied to him, "Simon, I have something to say to you."

"Teacher," he said, "say it."

41 "A creditor had two debtors. One owed 500 •denarii, and the other 50. 42 Since they could not pay it back, he graciously forgave them both. So, which of them will love him more?"

[a]**7:14** Or *the bier* [b]**7:16** Or *awe* [c]**7:16** Or *come to help* [d]**7:22** Lit *cleansed* [e]**7:25** Or *who have glorious robes* [f]**7:27** Lit *messenger before Your face* [g]**7:27** Mal 3:1 [h]**7:28** Other mss read *women is not a greater prophet than John the Baptist* [i]**7:29** Lit *they justified God* [j]**7:35** Or *wisdom is declared right*

43 Simon answered, "I suppose the one he
forgave more."
"You have judged correctly," He told him.
44 Turning to the woman, He said to Simon,
"Do you see this woman? I entered your house;
you gave Me no water for My feet, but she,
with her tears, has washed My feet and wiped
them with her hair. 45 You gave Me no kiss, but
she hasn't stopped kissing My feet since I came
in. 46 You didn't anoint My head with oil, but
she has anointed My feet with fragrant oil.
47 Therefore I tell you, her many sins have
been forgiven; that's why[a] she loved much. But
the one who is forgiven little, loves little."
48 Then He said to her, "Your sins are forgiven."
49 Those who were at the table with Him
began to say among themselves, "Who is this
man who even forgives sins?"
50 And He said to the woman, "Your faith
has saved you. Go in peace."

Many Women Support Christ's Work

8 Soon afterwards He was traveling from
one town and village to another, preaching and telling the good news of the kingdom
of God. The Twelve were with Him, 2 and also
some women who had been healed of evil spirits and sicknesses: Mary, called •Magdalene
(seven demons had come out of her); 3 Joanna
the wife of Chuza, •Herod's steward; Susanna;
and many others who were supporting them
from their possessions.

The Parable of the Sower

4 As a large crowd was gathering, and people were flocking to Him from every town,
He said in a parable: 5 "A sower went out to
sow his seed. As he was sowing, some fell
along the path; it was trampled on, and the
birds of the sky ate it up. 6 Other seed fell on
the rock; when it sprang up, it withered,
since it lacked moisture. 7 Other seed fell
among thorns; the thorns sprang up with it
and choked it. 8 Still other seed fell on good
ground; when it sprang up, it produced a
crop: 100 times ⌊what was sown⌋." As He
said this, He called out, "Anyone who has
ears to hear should listen!"

Why Jesus Used Parables

9 Then His disciples asked Him, "What does
this parable mean?" 10 So He said, "The
secrets[b] of the kingdom of God have been given
for you to know, but to the rest it is in parables,
so that

Looking they may not see,
and hearing they may
not understand.[c]

The Parable of the Sower Explained

11 "This is the meaning of the parable:[d]
The seed is the word of God. 12 The seeds
along the path are those who have heard.
Then the Devil comes and takes away the
word from their hearts, so that they may not
believe and be saved. 13 And the seeds on the
rock are those who, when they hear, welcome the word with joy. Having no root,
these believe for a while and depart in a time
of testing. 14 As for the seed that fell among
thorns, these are the ones who, when they
have heard, go on their way and are choked
with worries, riches, and pleasures of life,
and produce no mature fruit. 15 But the seed
in the good ground—these are the ones
who,[e] having heard the word with an honest
and good heart, hold on to it and by enduring, bear fruit.

Using Your Light

16 "No one, after lighting a lamp, covers it
with a basket or puts it under a bed, but puts
it on a lampstand so that those who come in
may see the light. 17 For nothing is concealed
that won't be revealed, and nothing hidden
that won't be made known and come to light.
18 Therefore, take care how you listen. For
whoever has, more will be given to him; and
whoever does not have, even what he thinks
he has will be taken away from him."

True Relationships

19 Then His mother and brothers came to
Him, but they could not meet with Him
because of the crowd. 20 He was told, "Your
mother and Your brothers are standing outside,
wanting to see You."
21 But He replied to them, "My mother and
My brothers are those who hear and do the
word of God."

Wind and Wave Obey the Master

22 One day He and His disciples got into a

[a]**7:47** Her love shows that she has been forgiven [b]**8:10** The Gk word *mysteria* does not mean "mysteries" in the Eng sense; it means what we can know only by divine revelation. [c]**8:10** Is 6:9 [d]**8:11** Lit *But this is the parable:* [e]**8:15** Or *these are the kind who*

boat, and He told them, "Let's cross over to the
other side of the lake." So they set out, 23 and
as they were sailing He fell asleep. Then a fierce
windstorm came down on the lake; they were
being swamped and were in danger. 24 They
came and woke Him up, saying, "Master, Master, we're going to die!" Then He got up and
rebuked the wind and the raging waves. So
they ceased, and there was a calm. 25 He said
to them, "Where is your faith?"

They were fearful and amazed, asking one
another, "Who can this be?[a] He commands
even the winds and the waves, and they obey
Him!"

Demons Driven Out by the Master

26 Then they sailed to the region of the
Gerasenes,[b] which is opposite Galilee.
27 When He got out on land, a demon-possessed man from the town met Him. For a
long time he had worn no clothes and did not
stay in a house but in the tombs. 28 When he
saw Jesus, he cried out, fell down before Him,
and said in a loud voice, "What do You have to
do with me,[c] Jesus, You Son of the Most High
God? I beg You, don't torment me!" 29 For He
had commanded the unclean spirit to come
out of the man. Many times it had seized him,
and although he was guarded, bound by
chains and shackles, he would snap the
restraints and be driven by the demon into
deserted places.

30 "What is your name?" Jesus asked him.

"Legion," he said—because many demons
had entered him. 31 And they begged Him not
to banish them to the •abyss.

32 A large herd of pigs was there, feeding
on the hillside. The demons begged Him to
permit them to enter the pigs, and He gave
them permission. 33 The demons came out of
the man and entered the pigs, and the herd
rushed down the steep bank into the lake and
drowned. 34 When the men who tended them
saw what had happened, they ran off and
reported it in the town and in the countryside.
35 Then people went out to see what had happened. They came to Jesus and found the man
the demons had departed from, sitting at
Jesus' feet, dressed and in his right mind. And
they were afraid. 36 Meanwhile the eyewitnesses reported to them how the demon-possessed man was delivered. 37 Then all the
people of the Gerasene region[b] asked Him to
leave them, because they were gripped by
great fear. So getting into the boat, He
returned.

38 The man from whom the demons had
departed kept begging Him to be with Him. But
He sent him away and said, 39 "Go back to your
home, and tell all that God has done for you."
And off he went, proclaiming throughout the
town all that Jesus had done for him.

A Girl Restored and a Woman Healed

40 When Jesus returned, the crowd welcomed Him, for they were all expecting Him.
41 Just then, a man named Jairus came. He was
a leader of the •synagogue. He fell down at
Jesus' feet and pleaded with Him to come to his
house, 42 because he had an only daughter
about 12 years old, and she was at death's
door.[d]

While He was going, the crowds were
nearly crushing Him. 43 A woman suffering
from bleeding for 12 years, who had spent all
she had on doctors[e] yet could not be healed by
any, 44 approached from behind and touched
the •tassel of His robe. Instantly her bleeding
stopped.

45 "Who touched Me?" Jesus asked.

When they all denied it, Peter[f] said, "Master, the crowds are hemming You in and pressing against You."[g]

46 "Somebody did touch Me," said Jesus. "I
know that power has gone out from Me."
47 When the woman saw that she was discovered,[h] she came trembling and fell down before
Him. In the presence of all the people, she
declared the reason she had touched Him and
how she was instantly cured. 48 "Daughter,"
He said to her, "your faith has made you well.[i]
Go in peace."

49 While He was still speaking, someone
came from the synagogue leader's ⌊house⌋, saying, "Your daughter is dead. Don't bother the
Teacher anymore."

50 When Jesus heard it, He answered him,
"Don't be afraid. Only believe, and she will be
made well." 51 After He came to the house, He
let no one enter with Him except Peter, John,
James, and the child's father and mother.
52 Everyone was crying and mourning for her.
But He said, "Stop crying, for she is not dead
but asleep."

[a]**8:25** Lit *Who then is this?* [b]**8:26,37** Other mss read *the Gadarenes* [c]**8:28** Lit *What to me and to You* [d]**8:42** Lit *she was dying* [e]**8:43** Other mss omit *who had spent all she had on doctors* [f]**8:45** Other mss add *and those with him* [g]**8:45** Other mss add *and You say, 'Who touched Me?'* [h]**8:47** Lit *she had not escaped notice* [i]**8:48** Or *has saved you*

53 They started laughing at Him, because they knew she was dead. 54 So He[a] took her by the hand and called out, "Child, get up!" 55 Her spirit returned, and she got up at once. Then He gave orders that she be given something to eat. 56 Her parents were astounded, but He instructed them to tell no one what had happened.

Commissioning the Twelve

9 Summoning the Twelve, He gave them power and authority over all the demons, and ⌊power⌋ to heal[b] diseases. 2 Then He sent them to proclaim the kingdom of God and to heal the sick.

3 "Take nothing for the road," He told them, "no walking stick, no traveling bag, no bread, no money; and don't take an extra shirt. 4 Whatever house you enter, stay there and leave from there. 5 If they do not welcome you, when you leave that town, shake off the dust from your feet as a testimony against them." 6 So they went out and traveled from village to village, proclaiming the good news and healing everywhere.

Herod's Desire to See Jesus

7 •Herod the tetrarch heard about everything that was going on. He was perplexed, because some said that John had been raised from the dead, 8 some that Elijah had appeared, and others that one of the ancient prophets had risen. 9 "I beheaded John," Herod said, "but who is this I hear such things about?" And he wanted to see Him.

Feeding 5,000

10 When the apostles returned, they reported to Jesus all that they had done. He took them along and withdrew privately to a[c] town called Bethsaida. 11 When the crowds found out, they followed Him. He welcomed them, spoke to them about the kingdom of God, and cured[d] those who needed healing.

12 Late in the day,[e] the Twelve approached and said to Him, "Send the crowd away, so they can go into the surrounding villages and countryside to find food and lodging, because we are in a deserted place here."

13 "You give them something to eat," He told them.

"We have no more than five loaves and two fish," they said, "unless we go and buy food for all these people." 14 (For about 5,000 men were there.)

Then He told His disciples, "Have them sit down[f] in groups of about 50 each." 15 They did so, and had them all sit down. 16 Then He took the five loaves and the two fish, and looking up to heaven, He blessed and broke them. He kept giving them to the disciples to set before the crowd. 17 Everyone ate and was filled. Then they picked up[g] 12 baskets of leftover pieces.

Peter's Confession of the Messiah

18 While He was praying in private and His disciples were with Him, He asked them, "Who do the crowds say that I am?"

19 They answered, "John the Baptist; others, Elijah; still others, that one of the ancient prophets has come back."[h]

20 "But you," He asked them, "who do you say that I am?"

Peter answered, "God's •Messiah!"

His Death and Resurrection Predicted

21 But He strictly warned and instructed them to tell this to no one, 22 saying, "The •Son of Man must suffer many things and be rejected by the elders, •chief priests, and •scribes, be killed, and be raised the third day."

Take Up Your Cross

23 Then He said to ⌊them⌋ all, "If anyone wants to come with[i] Me, he must deny himself, take up his cross daily,[j] and follow Me. 24 For whoever wants to save his •life will lose it, but whoever loses his life because of Me will save it. 25 What is a man benefited if he gains the whole world, yet loses or forfeits himself? 26 For whoever is ashamed of Me and My words, the Son of Man will be ashamed of him when He comes in His glory and that of the Father and the holy angels. 27 I tell you the truth: there are some standing here who will not taste death until they see the kingdom of God."

The Transfiguration

28 About eight days after these words, He

[a]**8:54** Other mss add *having put them all outside* [b]**9:1** In this passage, different Gk words are translated as *heal.* In Eng, "to heal" or "to cure" are synonyms with little distinction in meaning. Technically, we do not heal or cure diseases. People are healed or cured from diseases. [c]**9:10** Other mss add *deserted place near a* [d]**9:11** Or *healed*; in this passage, different Gk words are translated as *heal.* In Eng, "to heal" or "to cure" are synonyms with little distinction in meaning. Technically, we do not heal or cure diseases. People are healed or cured from diseases. [e]**9:12** Lit *When the day began to decline* [f]**9:14** Lit *them recline* [g]**9:17** Lit *Then were picked up by them* [h]**9:19** Lit *has risen* [i]**9:23** Lit *come after* [j]**9:23** Other mss omit *daily*

took along Peter, John, and James, and went up
on the mountain to pray. 29 As He was praying,
the appearance of His face changed, and His
clothes became dazzling white. 30 Suddenly,
two men were talking with Him—Moses and
Elijah. 31 They appeared in glory and were
speaking of His death,[a] which He was about to
accomplish in Jerusalem.

32 Peter and those with him were in a deep
sleep,[b] and when they became fully awake,
they saw His glory and the two men who were
standing with Him. 33 As the two men were
departing from Him, Peter said to Jesus, "Master, it's good for us to be here! Let us make
three •tabernacles: one for You, one for
Moses, and one for Elijah"—not knowing
what he said.

34 While he was saying this, a cloud
appeared and overshadowed them. They
became afraid as they entered the cloud.
35 Then a voice came from the cloud, saying:

> This is My Son, the Chosen One;[c]
> listen to Him!

36 After the voice had spoken, only Jesus
was found. They kept silent, and in those days
told no one what they had seen.

The Power of Faith over a Demon

37 The next day, when they came down
from the mountain, a large crowd met Him.
38 Just then a man from the crowd cried out,
"Teacher, I beg You to look at my son, because
he's my only ⌊child⌋. 39 Often a spirit seizes
him; suddenly he shrieks, and it throws him
into convulsions until he foams at the mouth;[d]
wounding[e] him, it hardly ever leaves him. 40 I
begged Your disciples to drive it out, but they
couldn't."

41 Jesus replied, "You unbelieving and
rebellious[f] generation! How long will I be with
you and put up with you? Bring your son
here."

42 As the boy was still approaching, the
demon knocked him down and threw him into
severe convulsions. But Jesus rebuked the
unclean spirit, cured the boy, and gave him
back to his father. 43 And they were all astonished at the greatness of God.

The Second Prediction of His Death

While everyone was amazed at all the
things He was doing, He told His disciples,
44 "Let these words sink in:[g] the Son of Man
is about to be betrayed into the hands of
men."

45 But they did not understand this statement; it was concealed from them so that they
could not grasp it, and they were afraid to ask
Him about it.[h]

Who Is the Greatest?

46 Then an argument started among them
about who would be the greatest of them.
47 But Jesus, knowing the thoughts of their
hearts, took a little child and had him stand
next to Him. 48 He told them, "Whoever welcomes[i] this little child in My name welcomes
Me. And whoever welcomes Me welcomes
Him who sent Me. For whoever is least among
you—this one is great."

In His Name

49 John responded, "Master, we saw someone driving out demons in Your name, and we
tried to stop him because he does not follow
us."

50 "Don't stop him," Jesus told him,
"because whoever is not against you is for
you."[j]

The Journey to Jerusalem

51 When the days were coming to a close
for Him to be taken up,[k] He determined[l] to
journey to Jerusalem. 52 He sent messengers
ahead of Him, and on the way they entered a
village of the •Samaritans to make preparations for Him. 53 But they did not welcome
Him, because He determined to journey to
Jerusalem. 54 When the disciples James and
John saw this, they said, "Lord, do You want
us to call down fire from heaven to consume
them?"[m]

55 But He turned and rebuked them,[n]
56 and they went to another village.

Following Jesus

57 As they were traveling on the road someone said to Him, "I will follow You wherever
You go!"

[a] **9:31** Or *departure*; Gk *exodus* [b] **9:32** Lit *were weighed down with sleep* [c] **9:35** Other mss read *the Beloved* [d] **9:39** Lit *convulsions with foam* [e] **9:39** Or *bruising*, or *mauling* [f] **9:41** Or *corrupt*, or *perverted*, or *twisted*; Dt 32:5 [g] **9:44** Lit *Put these words in your ears* [h] **9:45** Lit *about this statement* [i] **9:48** Or *receives* throughout the verse [j] **9:50** Other mss read *against us is for us* [k] **9:51** His ascension [l] **9:51** Lit *He stiffened His face to go*; Is 50:7 [m] **9:54** Other mss add *as Elijah also did* [n] **9:55–56** Other mss add *and said, "You don't know what kind of spirit you belong to.* 56 *For the Son of Man did not come to destroy people's lives but to save them."*

58 Jesus told him, "Foxes have dens, and birds of the sky[a] have nests, but the Son of Man has no place to lay His head." 59 Then He said to another, "Follow Me."

"Lord," he said, "first let me go bury my father."[b]

60 But He told him, "Let the dead bury their own dead, but you go and spread the news of the kingdom of God."

61 Another also said, "I will follow You, Lord, but first let me go and say good-bye to those at my house."

62 But Jesus said to him, "No one who puts his hand to the plow and looks back is fit for the kingdom of God."

Sending Out the Seventy

10 After this, the Lord appointed 70[c] others, and He sent them ahead of Him in pairs to every town and place where He Himself was about to go. 2 He told them: "The harvest is abundant, but the workers are few. Therefore, pray to the Lord of the harvest to send out workers into His harvest. 3 Now go; I'm sending you out like lambs among wolves. 4 Don't carry a money-bag, traveling bag, or sandals; don't greet anyone along the road. 5 Whatever house you enter, first say, 'Peace to this household.' 6 If a son of peace[d] is there, your peace will rest on him; but if not, it will return to you. 7 Remain in the same house, eating and drinking what they offer, for the worker is worthy of his wages. Don't be moving from house to house. 8 When you enter any town, and they welcome you, eat the things set before you. 9 Heal the sick who are there, and tell them, 'The kingdom of God has come near you.' 10 When you enter any town, and they don't welcome you, go out into its streets and say, 11 'We are wiping off ⌊as a witness⌋ against you even the dust of your town that clings to our feet. Know this for certain: the kingdom of God has come near.' 12 I tell you, on that day it will be more tolerable for Sodom than for that town.

Unrepentant Towns

13 "Woe to you, Chorazin! Woe to you, Bethsaida! For if the miracles that were done in you had been done in Tyre and Sidon, they would have repented long ago, sitting in sackcloth and ashes! 14 But it will be more tolerable for Tyre and Sidon at the judgment than for you. 15 And you, Capernaum, will you be exalted to heaven? No, you will go down to •Hades! 16 Whoever listens to you listens to Me. Whoever rejects you rejects Me. And whoever rejects Me rejects the One who sent Me."

The Return of the Seventy

17 The Seventy[e] returned with joy, saying, "Lord, even the demons submit to us in Your name."

18 He said to them, "I watched Satan fall from heaven like a lightning flash. 19 Look, I have given you the authority to trample on snakes and scorpions and over all the power of the enemy; nothing will ever harm you. 20 However, don't rejoice that[f] the spirits submit to you, but rejoice that your names are written in heaven."

The Son Reveals the Father

21 In that same hour He[g] rejoiced in the Holy[h] Spirit and said, "I praise[i] You, Father, Lord of heaven and earth, because You have hidden these things from the wise and the learned and have revealed them to infants. Yes, Father, because this was Your good pleasure.[j] 22 All things have[k] been entrusted to Me by My Father. No one knows who the Son is except the Father, and who the Father is except the Son, and anyone to whom the Son desires[l] to reveal Him."

23 Then turning to His disciples He said privately, "The eyes that see the things you see are blessed! 24 For I tell you that many prophets and kings wanted to see the things you see yet didn't see them; to hear the things you hear yet didn't hear them."

The Parable of the Good Samaritan

25 Just then an expert in the law stood up to test Him, saying, "Teacher, what must I do to inherit eternal life?"

26 "What is written in the law?" He asked him. "How do you read it?"

27 He answered:

Love the Lord your God with all your heart, with all your soul, with all your

[a]**9:58** Wild birds, as opposed to domestic birds [b]**9:59** Not necessarily meaning his father was already dead [c]**10:1** Other mss read *72* [d]**10:6** A peaceful person; one open to the message of the kingdom [e]**10:17** Other mss read *The Seventy-two* [f]**10:20** Lit *don't rejoice in this, that* [g]**10:21** Other mss read *Jesus* [h]**10:21** Other mss omit *Holy* [i]**10:21** Or *thank*, or *confess* [j]**10:21** Lit *was well-pleasing in Your sight* [k]**10:22** Other mss read *And turning to the disciples, He said, "Everything has* [l]**10:22** Or *wills*, or *chooses*

strength, and with all your mind; and **your neighbor as yourself.**[a]

28 "You've answered correctly," He told him. "Do this and you will live."

29 But wanting to justify himself, he asked Jesus, "And who is my neighbor?"

30 Jesus took up ⌊the question⌋ and said: "A man was going down from Jerusalem to Jericho and fell into the hands of robbers. They stripped him, beat him up, and fled, leaving him half dead. 31 A priest happened to be going down that road. When he saw him, he passed by on the other side. 32 In the same way, a Levite, when he arrived at the place and saw him, passed by on the other side. 33 But a •Samaritan on his journey came up to him, and when he saw ⌊the man⌋, he had compassion. 34 He went over to him and bandaged his wounds, pouring on oil and wine. Then he put him on his own animal, brought him to an inn, and took care of him. 35 The next day[b] he took out two •denarii, gave them to the innkeeper, and said, 'Take care of him. When I come back I'll reimburse you for whatever extra you spend.'

36 "Which of these three do you think proved to be a neighbor to the man who fell into the hands of the robbers?"

37 "The one who showed mercy to him," he said.

Then Jesus told him, "Go and do the same."

Martha and Mary

38 While they were traveling, He entered a village, and a woman named Martha welcomed Him into her home.[c] 39 She had a sister named Mary, who also sat at the Lord's[d] feet and was listening to what He said.[e] 40 But Martha was distracted by her many tasks, and she came up and asked, "Lord, don't You care that my sister has left me to serve alone? So tell her to give me a hand."[f]

41 The Lord[g] answered her, "Martha, Martha, you are worried and upset about many things, 42 but one thing is necessary. Mary has made the right choice,[h] and it will not be taken away from her."

The Model Prayer

11 He was praying in a certain place, and when He finished, one of His disciples said to Him, "Lord, teach us to pray, just as John also taught his disciples."

2 He said to them, "Whenever you pray, say:

Father,[i]
Your name be honored as holy.
Your kingdom come.[j]
3 Give us each day our daily bread.[k]
4 And forgive us our sins,
for we ourselves also forgive everyone
in debt[l] to us.
And do not bring us
into temptation."[m]

Keep Asking, Searching, Knocking

5 He also said to them: "Suppose one of you[n] has a friend and goes to him at midnight and says to him, 'Friend, lend me three loaves of bread, 6 because a friend of mine on a journey has come to me, and I don't have anything to offer him.'[o] 7 Then he will answer from inside and say, 'Don't bother me! The door is already locked, and my children and I have gone to bed. I can't get up to give you anything.' 8 I tell you, even though he won't get up and give him anything because he is his friend, yet because of his persistence,[p] he will get up and give him as much as he needs.

9 "So I say to you, keep asking,[q] and it will be given to you. Keep searching,[r] and you will find. Keep knocking,[s] and the door will be opened to you. 10 For everyone who asks receives, and the one who searches finds, and to the one who knocks, the door will be opened. 11 What father among you, if his son[t] asks for a fish, will give him a snake instead of a fish? 12 Or if he asks for an egg, will give him a scorpion? 13 If you then, who are evil, know how to give good gifts to your children, how much more will the heavenly Father give[u] the Holy Spirit to those who ask Him?"

A House Divided

14 Now He was driving out a demon that

[a]**10:27** Dt 6:5; Lv 19:18 [b]**10:35** Other mss add *as he was leaving* [c]**10:38** Other mss omit *into her home* [d]**10:39** Other mss read *at Jesus'* [e]**10:39** Lit *to His word* or *message* [f]**10:40** Or *tell her to help me* [g]**10:41** Other mss read *Jesus* [h]**10:42** Lit *has chosen the good part* [i]**11:2** Other mss read *Our Father in heaven* [j]**11:2** Other mss add *Your will be done on earth as it is in heaven* [k]**11:3** Or *our bread for tomorrow* [l]**11:4** Or *everyone who wrongs us* [m]**11:4** Other mss add *But deliver us from the evil one* [n]**11:5** Lit *Who of you* [o]**11:6** Lit *I have nothing to set before him* [p]**11:8** Or *annoying persistence*, or *shamelessness* [q]**11:9** Or *you, ask* [r]**11:9** Or *Search* [s]**11:9** Or *Knock* [t]**11:11** Other mss read *son asks for bread, would give him a stone? Or if he* [u]**11:13** Lit *the Father from heaven will give*

was mute.[a] When the demon came out, the
man who had been mute, spoke, and the
crowds were amazed. 15 But some of them
said, "He drives out demons by •Beelzebul, the
ruler of the demons!" 16 And others, as a test,
were demanding of Him a sign from heaven.
17 Knowing their thoughts, He told them:
"Every kingdom divided against itself is headed
for destruction, and a house divided against
itself falls. 18 If Satan also is divided against
himself, how will his kingdom stand? For you
say I drive out demons by Beelzebul. 19 And if
I drive out demons by Beelzebul, who is it your
sons[b] drive them out by? For this reason they
will be your judges. 20 If I drive out demons by
the finger of God, then the kingdom of God has
come to you. 21 When a strong man, fully
armed, guards his estate, his possessions are
secure.[c] 22 But when one stronger than he
attacks and overpowers him, he takes from him
all his weapons[d] he trusted in, and divides up
his plunder. 23 Anyone who is not with Me is
against Me, and anyone who does not gather
with Me scatters.

An Unclean Spirit's Return

24 "When an unclean spirit comes out of a
man, it roams through waterless places looking
for rest, and not finding rest, it then[e] says, 'I'll
go back to my house where I came from.'
25 And returning, it finds ⌊the house⌋ swept and
put in order. 26 Then it goes and brings seven
other spirits more evil than itself, and they
enter and settle down there. As a result, that
man's last condition is worse than the first."

True Blessedness

27 As He was saying these things, a woman
from the crowd raised her voice and said to
Him, "The womb that bore You and the one
who nursed You are blessed!"
28 He said, "Even more, those who hear the
word of God and keep it are blessed!"

The Sign of Jonah

29 As the crowds were increasing, He
began saying: "This generation is an evil generation. It demands a sign, but no sign will be
given to it except the sign of Jonah.[f] 30 For
just as Jonah became a sign to the people of
Nineveh, so also the •Son of Man will be to
this generation. 31 The queen of the south
will rise up at the judgment with the men of
this generation and condemn them, because
she came from the ends of the earth to hear
the wisdom of Solomon, and look—something greater than Solomon is here! 32 The
men of Nineveh will rise up at the judgment
with this generation and condemn it,
because they repented at Jonah's proclamation, and look—something greater than
Jonah is here!

The Lamp of the Body

33 "No one lights a lamp and puts it in the
cellar or under a basket,[g] but on a lampstand, so
that those who come in may see its light.
34 Your eye is the lamp of the body. When your
eye is good, your whole body is also full of light.
But when it is bad, your body is also full of darkness. 35 Take care then, that the light in you is
not darkness. 36 If therefore your whole body is
full of light, with no part of it in darkness, the
whole body will be full of light, as when a lamp
shines its light on you."[h]

Religious Hypocrisy Denounced

37 As He was speaking, a •Pharisee asked
Him to dine with him. So He went in and
reclined at the table. 38 When the Pharisee saw
this, he was amazed that He did not first perform the ritual washing[i] before dinner. 39 But
the Lord said to him: "Now you Pharisees clean
the outside of the cup and dish, but inside you
are full of greed and evil. 40 Fools! Didn't He
who made the outside make the inside too?
41 But give to charity what is within,[j] and then
everything is clean for you.
42 "But woe to you Pharisees! You give a
tenth[k] of mint, rue, and every kind of herb, and
you bypass[l] justice and love for God.[m] These
things you should have done without neglecting the others.
43 "Woe to you Pharisees! You love the
front seat in the •synagogues and greetings in
the marketplaces.
44 "Woe to you![n] You are like unmarked
graves; the people who walk over them don't
know it."
45 One of the experts in the law answered
Him, "Teacher, when You say these things You
insult us too."

[a] **11:14** A demon that caused the man to be mute [b] **11:19** Your exorcists [c] **11:21** Lit *his possessions are in peace* [d] **11:22** Gk *panoplia*, the armor and weapons of a foot soldier; Eph 6:11,13 [e] **11:24** Other mss omit *then* [f] **11:29** Other mss add *the prophet* [g] **11:33** Other mss omit *or under a basket* [h] **11:36** Or *shines on you with its rays* [i] **11:38** Lit *He did not first wash* [j] **11:41** Or *But donate from the heart as charity* [k] **11:42** Or *a tithe* [l] **11:42** Or *neglect* [m] **11:42** Lit *the justice and the love of God* [n] **11:44** Other mss read *you scribes and Pharisees, hypocrites!*

46 Then He said: "Woe also to you experts
in the law! You load people with burdens that
are hard to carry, yet you yourselves don't
touch these burdens with one of your fingers.
47 "Woe to you! You build monuments[a] to
the prophets, and your fathers killed them.
48 Therefore you are witnesses that you
approve[b] the deeds of your fathers, for they
killed them, and you build their monuments.[c]
49 Because of this, the wisdom of God said, 'I
will send them prophets and apostles, and
some of them they will kill and persecute,'
50 so that this generation may be held responsible for the blood of all the prophets shed since
the foundation of the world[d] — 51 from the
blood of Abel to the blood of Zechariah, who
perished between the altar and the sanctuary.

"Yes, I tell you, this generation will be held
responsible.[e]

52 "Woe to you experts in the law! You have
taken away the key of knowledge! You didn't go
in yourselves, and you hindered those who
were going in."

53 When He left there,[f] the •scribes and the
Pharisees began to oppose Him fiercely and to
cross-examine Him about many things; 54 they
were lying in wait for Him to trap Him in something He said.[g]

Beware of Religious Hypocrisy

12 In these circumstances,[h] a crowd of
many thousands came together, so that
they were trampling on one another. He began
to say to His disciples first: "Be on your guard
against the yeast[i] of the •Pharisees, which is
hypocrisy. 2 There is nothing covered that
won't be uncovered, nothing hidden that
won't be made known. 3 Therefore whatever
you have said in the dark will be heard in the
light, and what you have whispered in an ear
in private rooms will be proclaimed on the
housetops.

Fear God

4 "And I say to you, My friends, don't fear
those who kill the body, and after that can do
nothing more. 5 But I will show you the One
to fear: Fear Him who has authority to throw
⌊people⌋ into •hell after death. Yes, I say to
you, this is the One to fear! 6 Aren't five sparrows sold for two pennies?[j] Yet not one of
them is forgotten in God's sight. 7 Indeed, the
hairs of your head are all counted. Don't be
afraid; you are worth more than many sparrows!

Acknowledging Christ

8 "And I say to you, anyone who acknowledges Me before men, the •Son of Man will
also acknowledge him before the angels of
God, 9 but whoever denies Me before men
will be denied before the angels of God.
10 Anyone who speaks a word against the Son
of Man will be forgiven, but the one who blasphemes against the Holy Spirit will not be forgiven. 11 Whenever they bring you before
•synagogues and rulers and authorities, don't
worry about how you should defend yourselves or what you should say. 12 For the Holy
Spirit will teach you at that very hour what
must be said."

The Parable of the Rich Fool

13 Someone from the crowd said to Him,
"Teacher, tell my brother to divide the inheritance with me."

14 "Friend,"[k] He said to him, "who
appointed Me a judge or arbitrator over
you?" 15 He then told them, "Watch out and
be on guard against all greed because one's
life is not in the abundance of his possessions."

16 Then He told them a parable: "A rich
man's land was very productive. 17 He
thought to himself, 'What should I do, since I
don't have anywhere to store my crops? 18 I
will do this,' he said. 'I'll tear down my barns
and build bigger ones and store all my grain
and my goods there. 19 Then I'll say to myself,
"You[l] have many goods stored up for many
years. Take it easy; eat, drink, and enjoy
yourself." '

20 "But God said to him, 'You fool! This very
night your •life is demanded of you. And the
things you have prepared—whose will they
be?'

21 "That's how it is with the one who stores
up treasure for himself and is not rich toward
God."

The Cure for Anxiety

22 Then He said to His disciples: "Therefore

[a]**11:47** Or *graves* [b]**11:48** Lit *witnesses and approve* [c]**11:48** Other mss omit *their monuments* [d]**11:50** Lit *so that the blood of all . . . world may be required of this generation,* [e]**11:51** Lit *you, it will be required of this generation* [f]**11:53** Other mss read *And as He was saying these things to them* [g]**11:54** Other mss add *so that they might bring charges against Him* [h]**12:1** Or *Meanwhile,* or *At this time,* or *During this period* [i]**12:1** Or *leaven* [j]**12:6** Lit *two assaria*; the *assarion* (sg) was a small copper coin [k]**12:14** Lit *Man* [l]**12:19** Lit *say to my soul, "Soul, you*

I tell you, don't worry about your life, what you
will eat; or about the body, what you will wear.
23 For life is more than food and the body more
than clothing. 24 Consider the ravens: they
don't sow or reap; they don't have a storeroom
or a barn; yet God feeds them. Aren't you
worth much more than the birds? 25 Can any of
you add a •cubit to his height[a] by worrying?
26 If then you're not able to do even a little
thing, why worry about the rest?
27 "Consider how the wildflowers grow:
they don't labor or spin thread. Yet I tell you,
not even Solomon in all his splendor was
adorned like one of these! 28 If that's how God
clothes the grass, which is in the field today and
is thrown into the furnace tomorrow, how
much more will He do for you—you of little
faith? 29 Don't keep striving for what you
should eat and what you should drink, and
don't be anxious. 30 For the Gentile world
eagerly seeks all these things, and your Father
knows that you need them.
31 "But seek His kingdom, and these
things will be provided for you. 32 Don't be
afraid, little flock, because your Father
delights to give you the kingdom. 33 Sell your
possessions and give to the poor. Make
money-bags for yourselves that won't grow
old, an inexhaustible treasure in heaven,
where no thief comes near and no moth
destroys. 34 For where your treasure is, there
your heart will be also.

Ready for the Master's Return

35 "Be ready for service[b] and have your
lamps lit. 36 You must be like people waiting
for their master to return[c] from the wedding
banquet so that when he comes and knocks,
they can open ⌊the door⌋ for him at once.
37 Those •slaves the master will find alert
when he comes will be blessed. •I assure you:
He will get ready,[d] have them recline at the
table, then come and serve them. 38 If he
comes in the middle of the night, or even near
dawn,[e] and finds them alert, those slaves are
blessed. 39 But know this: if the homeowner
had known at what hour the thief was coming,
he would not have let his house be broken
into. 40 You also be ready, because the Son of
Man is coming at an hour that you do not
expect."

Rewards and Punishment

41 "Lord," Peter asked, "are You telling this
parable to us or to everyone?"
42 The Lord said: "Who then is the faithful and sensible manager his master will put
in charge of his household servants to give
them their allotted food at the proper time?
43 That •slave whose master finds him working when he comes will be rewarded. 44 I tell
you the truth: he will put him in charge of all
his possessions. 45 But if that slave says in his
heart, 'My master is delaying his coming,'
and starts to beat the male and female slaves,
and to eat and drink and get drunk, 46 that
slave's master will come on a day he does not
expect him and at an hour he does not know.
He will cut him to pieces[f] and assign him a
place with the unbelievers.[g] 47 And that
slave who knew his master's will and didn't
prepare himself or do it[h] will be severely
beaten. 48 But the one who did not know and
did things deserving of blows will be beaten
lightly. Much will be required of everyone
who has been given much. And even more
will be expected of the one who has been
entrusted with more.[i]

Not Peace but Division

49 "I came to bring fire on the earth, and
how I wish it were already set ablaze! 50 But I
have a baptism to be baptized with, and how it
consumes Me until it is finished! 51 Do you
think that I came here to give peace to the
earth? No, I tell you, but rather division!
52 From now on, five in one household will be
divided: three against two, and two against
three.

53 **They will be divided,**
father against son,
son against father,
mother against daughter,
daughter against mother,
mother-in-law against
her daughter-in-law,
and daughter-in-law
against mother-in-law."[j]

Interpreting the Time

54 He also said to the crowds: "When you
see a cloud rising in the west, right away you

[a]**12:25** Or *add one moment to his life-span* [b]**12:35** Lit *Let your loins be girded*; an idiom for tying up loose outer clothing in preparation for action; Ex 12:11 [c]**12:36** Lit *master, when he should return* [d]**12:37** Lit *will gird himself* [e]**12:38** Lit *even in the second or third watch* [f]**12:46** Lit *him in two* [g]**12:46** Or *unfaithful, or untrustworthy* [h]**12:47** Lit *or do toward his will* [i]**12:48** Or *much* [j]**12:53** Mc 7:6

say, 'A storm is coming,' and so it does. 55 And when the south wind is blowing, you say, 'It's going to be a scorcher!' and it is. 56 Hypocrites! You know how to interpret the appearance of the earth and the sky, but why don't you know how to interpret this time?

Settling Accounts

57 "Why don't you judge for yourselves what is right? 58 As you are going with your adversary to the ruler, make an effort to settle with him on the way. Then he won't drag you before the judge, the judge hand you over to the bailiff, and the bailiff throw you into prison. 59 I tell you, you will never get out of there until you have paid the last cent."[a]

Repent or Perish

13 At that time, some people came and reported to Him about the Galileans whose blood •Pilate had mixed with their sacrifices. 2 And He[b] responded to them, "Do you think that these Galileans were more sinful than all Galileans because they suffered these things? 3 No, I tell you; but unless you repent, you will all perish as well! 4 Or those 18 that the tower in Siloam fell on and killed—do you think they were more sinful than all the people who live in Jerusalem? 5 No, I tell you; but unless you repent, you will all perish as well!"

The Parable of the Barren Fig Tree

6 And He told this parable: "A man had a fig tree that was planted in his vineyard. He came looking for fruit on it and found none. 7 He told the vineyard worker, 'Listen, for three years I have come looking for fruit on this fig tree and haven't found any. Cut it down! Why should it even waste the soil?'

8 "But he replied to him, 'Sir,[c] leave it this year also, until I dig around it and fertilize it. 9 Perhaps it will bear fruit next year, but if not, you can cut it down.' "

Healing a Daughter of Abraham

10 As He was teaching in one of the •synagogues on the Sabbath, 11 a woman was there who had been disabled by a spirit[d] for over 18 years. She was bent over and could not straighten up at all.[e] 12 When Jesus saw her, He called out to her,[f] "Woman, you are free of your disability." 13 Then He laid His hands on her, and instantly she was restored and began to glorify God.

14 But the leader of the synagogue, indignant because Jesus had healed on the Sabbath, responded by telling the crowd, "There are six days when work should be done; therefore come on those days and be healed and not on the Sabbath day."

15 But the Lord answered him and said, "Hypocrites! Doesn't each one of you untie his ox or donkey from the feeding trough on the Sabbath and lead it to water? 16 Satan has bound this woman, a daughter of Abraham, for 18 years—shouldn't she be untied from this bondage on the Sabbath day?"

17 When He had said these things, all His adversaries were humiliated, but the whole crowd was rejoicing over all the glorious things He was doing.

The Parables of the Mustard Seed and of the Yeast

18 He said therefore, "What is the kingdom of God like, and what can I compare it to? 19 It's like a mustard seed that a man took and sowed in his garden. It grew and became a tree, and the birds of the sky nested in its branches."

20 Again He said, "What can I compare the kingdom of God to? 21 It's like yeast that a woman took and mixed into 50 pounds[g] of flour until it spread through the entire mixture."[h]

The Narrow Way

22 He went through one town and village after another, teaching and making His way to Jerusalem. 23 "Lord," someone asked Him, "are there few being saved?"[i]

He said to them, 24 "Make every effort to enter through the narrow door, because I tell you, many will try to enter and won't be able 25 once the homeowner gets up and shuts the door. Then you will stand[j] outside and knock on the door, saying, 'Lord, open up for us!' He will answer you, 'I don't know you or where you're from.' 26 Then you will say,[k] 'We ate and drank in Your presence, and You taught in

[a] **12:59** Gk *lepton,* the smallest and least valuable copper coin in use [b] **13:2** Other mss read *Jesus* [c] **13:8** Or *Lord* [d] **13:11** Lit *had a spirit of disability* [e] **13:11** Or *straighten up completely* [f] **13:12** Or *He summoned her* [g] **13:21** Lit *3 sata;* about 40 quarts [h] **13:21** Or *until all of it was leavened* [i] **13:23** Or *are the saved few?* (in number); lit *are those being saved few?* [j] **13:25** Lit *you will begin to stand* [k] **13:26** Lit *you will begin to say*

our streets!' 27 But He will say, 'I tell you, I
don't know you or where you're from. Get
away from Me, all you workers of unrighteousness!' 28 There will be weeping and gnashing of
teeth in that place, when you see Abraham,
Isaac, Jacob, and all the prophets in the kingdom of God but yourselves thrown out. 29 They
will come from east and west, from north and
south, and recline at the table in the kingdom
of God. 30 Note this: some are last who will be
first, and some are first who will be last."

Jesus and Herod Antipas

31 At that time some •Pharisees came and
told Him, "Go, get out of here! •Herod wants to
kill You!"
32 He said to them, "Go tell that fox, 'Look!
I'm driving out demons and performing heal-
ings today and tomorrow, and on the third day[a]
I will complete My work.'[b] 33 Yet I must travel
today, tomorrow, and the next day, because it
is not possible for a prophet to perish outside of
Jerusalem!

Jesus' Lamentation over Jerusalem

34 "Jerusalem, Jerusalem! The city who kills
the prophets and stones those who are sent to
her. How often I wanted to gather your children together, as a hen gathers her chicks
under her wings, but you were not willing!
35 See, your house[c] is abandoned to you. And I
tell you, you will not see Me until the time
comes when you say, **Blessed is He who
comes in the name of the Lord!**"[d]

A Sabbath Controversy

14 One Sabbath, when He went to eat[e] at
the house of one of the leading •Phari-
sees, they were watching Him closely. 2 There
in front of Him was a man whose body was
swollen with fluid.[f] 3 In response, Jesus asked
the law experts and the Pharisees, "Is it lawful
to heal on the Sabbath or not?" 4 But they kept
silent. He took the man, healed him, and sent
him away. 5 And to them, He said, "Which of
you whose son or ox falls into a well, will not
immediately pull him out on the Sabbath day?"
6 To this they could find no answer.

Teachings on Humility

7 He told a parable to those who were
invited, when He noticed how they would
choose the best places for themselves: 8 "When
you are invited by someone to a wedding banquet, don't recline at the best place, because a
more distinguished person than you may have
been invited by your host.[g] 9 The one who
invited both of you may come and say to you,
'Give your place to this man,' and then in humiliation, you will proceed to take the lowest place.
10 "But when you are invited, go and
recline in the lowest place, so that when the
one who invited you comes, he will say to you,
'Friend, move up higher.' You will then be honored in the presence of all the other guests.
11 For everyone who exalts himself will be
humbled, and the one who humbles himself
will be exalted."
12 He also said to the one who had invited
Him, "When you give a lunch or a dinner, don't
invite your friends, your brothers, your relatives, or your rich neighbors, because they
might invite you back, and you would be
repaid. 13 On the contrary, when you host a
banquet, invite those who are poor, maimed,
lame, or blind. 14 And you will be blessed,
because they cannot repay you; for you will be
repaid at the resurrection of the righteous."

The Parable of the Large Banquet

15 When one of those who reclined at the
table with Him heard these things, he said to
Him, "The one who will eat bread in the kingdom of God is blessed!"
16 Then He told him: "A man was giving a
large banquet and invited many. 17 At the time
of the banquet, he sent his slave to tell those
who were invited, 'Come, because everything
is now ready.'
18 "But without exception[h] they all began to
make excuses. The first one said to him, 'I have
bought a field, and I must go out and see it. I ask
you to excuse me.'
19 "Another said, 'I have bought five yoke of
oxen, and I'm going to try them out. I ask you
to excuse me.'
20 "And another said, 'I just got married,[i]
and therefore I'm unable to come.'
21 "So the slave came back and reported
these things to his master. Then in anger, the
master of the house told his slave, 'Go out
quickly into the streets and alleys of the city,
and bring in here the poor, maimed, blind, and
lame!'

[a]**13:32** Very shortly [b]**13:32** Lit *I will be finished* [c]**13:35** Probably the temple; Jr 12:7; 22:5 [d]**13:35** Ps 118:26 [e]**14:1** Lit *eat bread*; = eat a meal [f]**14:2** Afflicted with dropsy or edema [g]**14:8** Lit *by him* [h]**14:18** Lit *And from one* (voice) [i]**14:20** Lit *I have married a woman*

22 " 'Master,' the slave said, 'what you
ordered has been done, and there's still room.'
23 "Then the master told the slave, 'Go out
into the highways and lanes and make them
come in, so that my house may be filled. 24 For
I tell you, not one of those men who were
invited will enjoy my banquet!' "

The Cost of Following Jesus

25 Now great crowds were traveling with
Him. So He turned and said to them: 26 "If anyone comes to Me and does not hate his own
father and mother, wife and children, brothers
and sisters—yes, and even his own life—he
cannot be My disciple. 27 Whoever does not
bear his own cross and come after Me cannot
be My disciple.
28 "For which of you, wanting to build a
tower, doesn't first sit down and calculate the
cost to see if he has enough to complete it?
29 Otherwise, after he has laid the foundation
and cannot finish it, all the onlookers will begin
to make fun of him, 30 saying, 'This man started
to build and wasn't able to finish.'
31 "Or what king, going to war against
another king, will not first sit down and decide
if he is able with 10,000 to oppose the one who
comes against him with 20,000? 32 If not,
while the other is still far off, he sends a delegation and asks for terms of peace. 33 In the same
way, therefore, every one of you who does not
say good-bye to[a] all his possessions cannot be
My disciple.
34 "Now, salt is good, but if salt should lose
its taste, how will it be made salty? 35 It isn't fit
for the soil or for the manure pile; they throw
it out. Anyone who has ears to hear should listen!"

The Parable of the Lost Sheep

15 All the tax collectors and sinners were
approaching to listen to Him. 2 And
the •Pharisees and •scribes were complaining,
"This man welcomes sinners and eats with
them!"
3 So He told them this parable: 4 "What man
among you, who has 100 sheep and loses one
of them, does not leave the 99 in the open
field[b] and go after the lost one until he finds it?
5 When he has found it, he joyfully puts it on
his shoulders, 6 and coming home, he calls his
friends and neighbors together, saying to them,
'Rejoice with me, because I have found my lost
sheep!' 7 I tell you, in the same way, there will
be more joy in heaven over one sinner who
repents than over 99 righteous people who
don't need repentance.

The Parable of the Lost Coin

8 "Or what woman who has 10 silver
coins,[c] if she loses one coin, does not light a
lamp, sweep the house, and search carefully
until she finds it? 9 When she finds it, she calls
her women friends and neighbors together,
saying, 'Rejoice with me, because I have found
the silver coin I lost!' 10 I tell you, in the same
way, there is joy in the presence of God's
angels over one sinner who repents."

The Parable of the Lost Son

11 He also said: "A man had two sons.
12 The younger of them said to his father,
'Father, give me the share of the estate I have
coming to me.' So he distributed the assets[d] to
them. 13 Not many days later, the younger son
gathered together all he had and traveled to a
distant country, where he squandered his
estate in foolish living. 14 After he had spent
everything, a severe famine struck that country, and he had nothing.[e] 15 Then he went to
work for[f] one of the citizens of that country,
who sent him into his fields to feed pigs. 16 He
longed to eat his fill from[g] the carob pods[h] the
pigs were eating, but no one would give him
any. 17 When he came to his senses,[i] he said,
'How many of my father's hired hands have
more than enough food, and here I am dying[j]
of hunger![k] 18 I'll get up, go to my father, and
say to him, Father, I have sinned against
heaven and in your sight. 19 I'm no longer
worthy to be called your son. Make me like
one of your hired hands.' 20 So he got up and
went to his father. But while the son was still
a long way off, his father saw him and was
filled with compassion. He ran, threw his
arms around his neck,[l] and kissed him. 21 The
son said to him, 'Father, I have sinned against
heaven and in your sight. I'm no longer worthy to be called your son.'
22 "But the father told his •slaves, 'Quick!

[a]**14:33** Or *does not renounce* or *leave* [b]**15:4** Or *the wilderness* [c]**15:8** Gk *10 drachmas*; a *drachma* was a silver coin = a •denarius. [d]**15:12** Lit *livelihood*, or *living* [e]**15:14** Lit *and he began to be in need* [f]**15:15** Lit *went and joined with* [g]**15:16** Other mss read *to fill his stomach with* [h]**15:16** Seed casings of a tree used as food for cattle, pigs, and sometimes the poor [i]**15:17** Lit *to himself* [j]**15:17** The word *dying* is translated *lost* in vv. 4–9 and vv. 24,32. [k]**15:17** Or *dying in the famine*; v. 14 [l]**15:20** Lit *He ran, fell on his neck*

Bring out the best robe and put it on him; put a
ring on his finger[a] and sandals on his feet.
23 Then bring the fattened calf and slaughter it,
and let's celebrate with a feast, 24 because this
son of mine was dead and is alive again; he was
lost and is found!' So they began to celebrate.

25 "Now his older son was in the field; as he
came near the house, he heard music and dancing. 26 So he summoned one of the servants
and asked what these things meant. 27 'Your
brother is here,' he told him, 'and your father
has slaughtered the fattened calf because he
has him back safe and sound.'[b]

28 "Then he became angry and didn't want
to go in. So his father came out and pleaded
with him. 29 But he replied to his father, 'Look,
I have been slaving many years for you, and I
have never disobeyed your orders, yet you
never gave me a young goat so I could celebrate
with my friends. 30 But when this son of yours
came, who has devoured your assets[c] with
prostitutes, you slaughtered the fattened calf for
him.'

31 " 'Son,'[d] he said to him, 'you are always
with me, and everything I have is yours. 32 But
we had to celebrate and rejoice, because this
brother of yours was dead and is alive again; he
was lost and is found.' "

The Parable of the Dishonest Manager

16 He also said to the disciples: "There
was a rich man who received an accusation that his manager was squandering his
possessions. 2 So he called the manager in and
asked, 'What is this I hear about you? Give an
account of your management, because you can
no longer be ⌊my⌋ manager.'

3 "Then the manager said to himself, 'What
should I do, since my master is taking the management away from me? I'm not strong enough
to dig; I'm ashamed to beg. 4 I know what I'll
do so that when I'm removed from management, people will welcome me into their
homes.'

5 "So he summoned each one of his master's debtors. 'How much do you owe my master?' he asked the first one.

6 " 'A hundred measures of oil,' he said.

" 'Take your invoice,' he told him, 'sit down
quickly, and write 50.'

7 "Next he asked another, 'How much do
you owe?'

" 'A hundred measures of wheat,' he said.

" 'Take your invoice,' he told him, 'and
write 80.'

8 "The master praised the unrighteous
manager because he had acted astutely. For
the sons of this age are more astute than the
sons of light ⌊in dealing⌋ with their own people.[e] 9 And I tell you, make friends for yourselves by means of the unrighteous money so
that when it fails,[f] they may welcome you into
eternal dwellings. 10 Whoever is faithful in
very little is also faithful in much, and whoever is unrighteous in very little is also unrighteous in much. 11 So if you have not been
faithful with the unrighteous money, who will
trust you with what is genuine? 12 And if you
have not been faithful with what belongs to
someone else, who will give you what is your
own? 13 No household slave can be the •slave
of two masters, since either he will hate one
and love the other, or he will be devoted to
one and despise the other. You can't be slaves
to both God and money."

Kingdom Values

14 The •Pharisees, who were lovers of
money, were listening to all these things and
scoffing at Him. 15 And He told them: "You are
the ones who justify yourselves in the sight of
others, but God knows your hearts. For what is
highly admired by people is revolting in God's
sight.

16 "The Law and the Prophets were[g] until
John; since then, the good news of the kingdom
of God has been proclaimed, and everyone is
strongly urged to enter it.[h] 17 But it is easier for
heaven and earth to pass away than for one
stroke of a letter in the law to drop out.

18 "Everyone who divorces his wife and
marries another woman commits adultery, and
everyone who marries a woman divorced from
her husband commits adultery.

The Rich Man and Lazarus

19 "There was a rich man who would dress
in purple and fine linen, feasting lavishly
every day. 20 But a poor man named Lazarus,
covered with sores, was left at his gate. 21 He
longed to be filled with what fell from the rich
man's table, but instead the dogs would come
and lick his sores. 22 One day the poor man
died and was carried away by the angels to

[a]**15:22** Lit *hand* [b]**15:27** Lit *him back healthy* [c]**15:30** Lit *livelihood,* or *living* [d]**15:31** Or *Child* [e]**16:8** Lit *own generation* [f]**16:9** Other mss read *when you fail* or *pass away* [g]**16:16** Perhaps *were proclaimed,* or *were in effect* [h]**16:16** Or *everyone is forcing his way into it*

Abraham's side.[a] The rich man also died and
was buried. 23 And being in torment in
•Hades, he looked up and saw Abraham a long
way off, with Lazarus at his side. 24 'Father
Abraham!' he called out, 'Have mercy on me
and send Lazarus to dip the tip of his finger in
water and cool my tongue, because I am in
agony in this flame!'

25 " 'Son,'[b] Abraham said, 'remember that
during your life you received your good things,
just as Lazarus received bad things, but now he
is comforted here, while you are in agony.
26 Besides all this, a great chasm has been fixed
between us and you, so that those who want to
pass over from here to you cannot; neither can
those from there cross over to us.'

27 " 'Father,' he said, 'then I beg you to send
him to my father's house— 28 because I have
five brothers—to warn them, so they won't
also come to this place of torment.'

29 "But Abraham said, 'They have Moses
and the prophets; they should listen to them.'

30 " 'No, father Abraham,' he said. 'But if
someone from the dead goes to them, they will
repent.'

31 "But he told him, 'If they don't listen to
Moses and the prophets, they will not be persuaded if someone rises from the dead.' "

Warnings from Jesus

17 He said to His disciples, "Offenses[c]
will certainly come,[d] but woe to the
one they come through! 2 It would be better
for him if a millstone[e] were hung around his
neck and he were thrown into the sea than for
him to cause one of these little ones to •stum-
ble. 3 Be on your guard. If your brother sins,[f]
rebuke him, and if he repents, forgive him.
4 And if he sins against you seven times in a
day, and comes back to you seven times, saying, 'I repent,' you must forgive him."

Faith and Duty

5 The apostles said to the Lord, "Increase
our faith."

6 "If you have faith the size of[g] a mustard
seed," the Lord said, "you can say to this mul-
berry tree, 'Be uprooted and planted in the sea,'
and it will obey you.

7 "Which one of you having a slave plowing
or tending sheep, will say to him when he
comes in from the field, 'Come at once and sit
down to eat'? 8 Instead, will he not tell him,
'Prepare something for me to eat, get ready,[h]
and serve me while I eat and drink; later you
can eat and drink'? 9 Does he thank that slave
because he did what was commanded?[i] 10 In
the same way, when you have done all that you
were commanded, you should say, 'We are
good-for-nothing slaves; we've only done our
duty.' "

The 10 Lepers

11 While traveling to Jerusalem, He passed
between[j] Samaria and Galilee. 12 As He
entered a village, 10 men with serious skin diseases met Him. They stood at a distance 13 and
raised their voices, saying, "Jesus, Master, have
mercy on us!"

14 When He saw them, He told them, "Go
and show yourselves to the priests." And while
they were going, they were healed.[k]

15 But one of them, seeing that he was
healed, returned and, with a loud voice, gave
glory to God. 16 He fell facedown at His feet,
thanking Him. And he was a •Samaritan.

17 Then Jesus said, "Were not 10 cleansed?
Where are the nine? 18 Didn't any return[l] to
give glory to God except this foreigner?"
19 And He told him, "Get up and go on your
way. Your faith has made you well."[m]

The Coming of the Kingdom

20 Being asked by the •Pharisees when the
kingdom of God will come, He answered them,
"The kingdom of God is not coming with something observable; 21 no one will say,[n] 'Look
here!' or 'There!' For you see, the kingdom of
God is among you."

22 Then He told the disciples: "The days
are coming when you will long to see one of
the days of the •Son of Man, but you won't see
it. 23 They will say to you, 'Look there!' or
'Look here!' Don't follow or run after them.
24 For as the lightning flashes from horizon to
horizon and lights up the sky, so the Son of
Man will be in His day. 25 But first He must
suffer many things and be rejected by this generation.

26 "Just as it was in the days of Noah, so it

[a]**16:22** Lit *to the fold of Abraham's robe*, or *to Abraham's bosom*; see Jn 13:23 [b]**16:25** Lit *Child* [c]**17:1** Or *Traps*, or *Bait-sticks*, or *Causes of stumbling*, or *Causes of sin* [d]**17:1** Lit *It is impossible for offenses not to come* [e]**17:2** Large stone used for grinding grains into flour [f]**17:3** Other mss add *against you* [g]**17:6** Lit *faith like* [h]**17:8** Lit *eat, tuck in your robe*, or *eat, gird yourself* [i]**17:9** Other mss add *I don't think so* [j]**17:11** Or *through the middle of* [k]**17:14** Lit *cleansed* [l]**17:18** Lit *Were they not found returning* [m]**17:19** Or *faith has saved you* [n]**17:21** Lit *they will not say*

will be in the days of the Son of Man: 27 people
went on eating, drinking, marrying and giving
in marriage until the day Noah boarded the ark,
and the flood came and destroyed them all. 28 It
will be the same as it was in the days of Lot:
people went on eating, drinking, buying, selling, planting, building. 29 But on the day Lot
left Sodom, fire and sulfur rained from heaven
and destroyed them all. 30 It will be like that on
the day the Son of Man is revealed. 31 On that
day, a man on the housetop, whose belongings
are in the house, must not come down to get
them. Likewise the man who is in the field
must not turn back. 32 Remember Lot's wife!
33 Whoever tries to make his •life secure[a b]
will lose it, and whoever loses his life will preserve it. 34 I tell you, on that night two will be
in one bed: one will be taken and the other will
be left. 35 Two women will be grinding grain
together: one will be taken and the other left.
[36 Two will be in a field: one will be taken, and
the other will be left."][c]

37 "Where, Lord?" they asked Him.

He said to them, "Where the corpse is,
there also the vultures will be gathered."

The Parable of the Persistent Widow

18 He then told them a parable on the
need for them to pray always and not
become discouraged: 2 "There was a judge in
one town who didn't fear God or respect man.
3 And a widow in that town kept coming to him,
saying, 'Give me justice against my adversary.'

4 "For a while he was unwilling, but later he
said to himself, 'Even though I don't fear God or
respect man, 5 yet because this widow keeps pes-
tering me,[d] I will give her justice, so she doesn't
wear me out[e] by her persistent coming.' "

6 Then the Lord said, "Listen to what the
unjust judge says. 7 Will not God grant justice
to His elect who cry out to Him day and night?
Will He delay ⌊to help⌋ them?[f] 8 I tell you that
He will swiftly grant them justice. Nevertheless, when the •Son of Man comes, will He find
that faith[g] on earth?"

The Parable of the Pharisee and the Tax Collector

9 He also told this parable to some who
trusted in themselves that they were righteous
and looked down on everyone else: 10 "Two
men went up to the •temple complex to pray,
one a •Pharisee and the other a tax collector.
11 The Pharisee took his stand[h] and was praying like this: 'God, I thank You that I'm not like
other people[i] —greedy, unrighteous, adulterers, or even like this tax collector. 12 I fast twice
a week; I give a tenth[j] of everything I get.'

13 "But the tax collector, standing far off,
would not even raise his eyes to heaven but
kept striking his chest[k] and saying, 'God, turn
Your wrath from me[l] —a sinner!' 14 I tell you,
this one went down to his house justified
rather than the other; because everyone who
exalts himself will be humbled, but the one
who humbles himself will be exalted."

Blessing the Children

15 Some people were even bringing infants to
Him so He might touch them, but when the disciples saw it, they rebuked them. 16 Jesus, however, invited them: "Let the little children come
to Me, and don't stop them, because the kingdom of God belongs to such as these. 17 •I assure
you: Whoever does not welcome the kingdom of
God like a little child will never enter it."

The Rich Young Ruler

18 A ruler asked Him, "Good Teacher, what
must I do to inherit eternal life?"

19 "Why do you call Me good?" Jesus asked
him. "No one is good but One—God. 20 You
know the commandments:

> **Do not commit adultery;**
> **do not murder;**
> **do not steal;**
> **do not bear false witness;**
> **honor your father and mother."**[m]

21 "I have kept all these from my youth," he
said.

22 When Jesus heard this, He told him,
"You still lack one thing: sell all that you have
and distribute it to the poor, and you will have
treasure in heaven. Then come, follow Me."

23 After he heard this, he became extremely
sad, because he was very rich.

Possessions and the Kingdom

24 Seeing that he became sad,[n] Jesus said,

[a]**17:33** Other mss read *to save his life* [b]**17:33** Or *tries to retain his life* [c]**17:36** Other mss omit bracketed text [d]**18:5** Lit *widow causes me trouble* [e]**18:5** Or *doesn't give me a black eye*, or *doesn't ruin my reputation* [f]**18:7** Or *Will He put up with them?* [g]**18:8** Or *faith*, or *that kind of faith*, or *any faith*, or *the faith*, or *faithfulness*; the faith that persists in prayer for God's vindication [h]**18:11** Or *Pharisee stood by himself* [i]**18:11** Or *like the rest of men* [j]**18:12** Or *give tithes* [k]**18:13** Mourning [l]**18:13** Lit *God, be propitious*; = May Your wrath be turned aside by the sacrifice [m]**18:20** Ex 20:12–16; Dt 5:16–20 [n]**18:24** Other mss omit *he became sad*

"How hard it is for those who have wealth to
enter the kingdom of God! 25 For it is easier for
a camel to go through the eye of a needle than
for a rich person to enter the kingdom of God."
26 Those who heard this asked, "Then who
can be saved?"
27 He replied, "What is impossible with
men is possible with God."
28 Then Peter said, "Look, we have left
what we had and followed You."
29 So He said to them, "I assure you: There
is no one who has left a house, wife or brothers,
parents or children because of the kingdom of
God, 30 who will not receive many times more
at this time, and eternal life in the age to come."

The Third Prediction of His Death

31 Then He took the Twelve aside and told
them, "Listen! We are going up to Jerusalem.
Everything that is written through the prophets
about the Son of Man will be accomplished.
32 For He will be handed over to the Gentiles,
and He will be mocked, insulted, spit on;
33 and after they flog Him, they will kill Him,
and He will rise on the third day."
34 They understood none of these things.
This saying[a] was hidden from them, and they
did not grasp what was said.

A Blind Man Receives His Sight

35 As He drew near Jericho, a blind man
was sitting by the road begging. 36 Hearing a
crowd passing by, he inquired what this meant.
37 "Jesus the •Nazarene is passing by," they
told him.
38 So he called out, "Jesus, Son of David,
have mercy on me!" 39 Then those in front told
him to keep quiet,[b] but he kept crying out all
the more, "Son of David, have mercy on me!"
40 Jesus stopped and commanded that he be
brought to Him. When he drew near, He asked
him, 41 "What do you want Me to do for you?"
"Lord," he said, "I want to see!"
42 "Receive your sight!" Jesus told him.
"Your faith has healed you."[c] 43 Instantly he
could see, and he began to follow Him, glorifying God. All the people, when they saw it, gave
praise to God.

Jesus Visits Zacchaeus

19 He entered Jericho and was passing
through. 2 There was a man named
Zacchaeus who was a chief tax collector, and
he was rich. 3 He was trying to see who Jesus
was, but he was not able because of the crowd,
since he was a short man. 4 So running ahead,
he climbed up a sycamore tree to see Jesus,
since He was about to pass that way. 5 When
Jesus came to the place, He looked up and said
to him, "Zacchaeus, hurry and come down,
because today I must stay at your house."
6 So he quickly came down and welcomed
Him joyfully. 7 All who saw it began to complain, "He's gone to lodge with a sinful man!"
8 But Zacchaeus stood there and said to the
Lord, "Look, I'll give[d] half of my possessions to
the poor, Lord! And if I have extorted anything
from anyone, I'll pay[e] back four times as much!"
9 "Today salvation has come to this house,"
Jesus told him, "because he too is a son of Abraham. 10 For the •Son of Man has come to seek
and to save the lost."[f]

The Parable of the 10 Minas

11 As they were listening to this, He went
on to tell a parable because He was near Jerusalem, and they thought the kingdom of God
was going to appear right away.
12 Therefore He said: "A nobleman traveled
to a far country to receive for himself authority
to be king[g] and then return. 13 He called 10 of
his •slaves, gave them 10 minas,[h] and told
them, 'Engage in business until I come back.'
14 "But his subjects hated him and sent a
delegation after him, saying, 'We don't want
this man to rule over us!'
15 "At his return, having received the
authority to be king,[g] he summoned those
•slaves he had given the money to so he could
find out how much they had made in business.
16 The first came forward and said, 'Master,
your mina has earned 10 more minas.'
17 " 'Well done, good[i] •slave!' he told him.
'Because you have been faithful in a very small
matter, have authority over 10 towns.'
18 "The second came and said, 'Master,
your mina has made five minas.'
19 "So he said to him, 'You will be over five
towns.'
20 "And another came and said, 'Master,
here is your mina. I have kept it hidden away
in a cloth 21 because I was afraid of you, for
you're a tough man: you collect what you didn't
deposit and reap what you didn't sow.'

[a]**18:34** The meaning of the saying [b]**18:39** Or *those in front rebuked him* [c]**18:42** Or *has saved you* [d]**19:8** Or *I give*
[e]**19:8** Or *I pay* [f]**19:10** Or *save what was lost* [g]**19:12,15** Lit *to receive for himself a kingdom* or *sovereignty* [h]**19:13** = Gk
coin worth 100 drachmas or about 100 days' wages [i]**19:17** Or *capable*

22 "He told him, 'I will judge you by what you have said,[a] you evil •slave! ⌊If⌋ you knew I was a tough man, collecting what I didn't deposit and reaping what I didn't sow, 23 why didn't you put my money in the bank? And when I returned, I would have collected it with interest!' 24 So he said to those standing there, 'Take the mina away from him and give it to the one who has 10 minas.'

25 "But they said to him, 'Master, he has 10 minas.'

26 "'I tell you, that to everyone who has, more will be given; and from the one who does not have, even what he does have will be taken away. 27 But bring here these enemies of mine, who did not want me to rule over them, and slaughter[b] them in my presence.'"

The Triumphal Entry

28 When He had said these things, He went on ahead, going up to Jerusalem. 29 As He approached Bethphage and Bethany, at the place called the •Mount of Olives, He sent two of the disciples 30 and said, "Go into the village ahead of you. As you enter it, you will find a young donkey tied there, on which no one has ever sat. Untie it and bring it here. 31 If anyone asks you, 'Why are you untying it?' say this: 'The Lord needs it.'"

32 So those who were sent left and found it just as He had told them. 33 As they were untying the young donkey, its owners said to them, "Why are you untying the donkey?"

34 "The Lord needs it," they said. 35 Then they brought it to Jesus, and after throwing their robes on the donkey, they helped Jesus get on it. 36 As He was going along, they were spreading their robes on the road. 37 Now He came near the path down the Mount of Olives, and the whole crowd of the disciples began to praise God joyfully with a loud voice for all the miracles they had seen:

38 **Blessed is the King**
who comes in the name
of the Lord.[c] [d]
Peace in heaven
and glory in the highest heaven!

39 Some of the •Pharisees from the crowd told Him, "Teacher, rebuke Your disciples."

40 He answered, "I tell you, if they were to keep silent, the stones would cry out!"

Jesus' Love for Jerusalem

41 As He approached and saw the city, He wept over it, 42 saying, "If you knew this day what ⌊would bring⌋ peace—but now it is hidden from your eyes. 43 For the days will come on you when your enemies will build an embankment against you, surround you, and hem you in on every side. 44 They will crush you and your children within you to the ground, and they will not leave one stone on another in you, because you did not recognize the time of your visitation."

Cleansing the Temple Complex

45 He went into the •temple complex and began to throw out those who were selling,[e] 46 and He said, "It is written, **My house will be a house of prayer,** but you have made it **a den of thieves!**"[f]

47 Every day He was teaching in the temple complex. The •chief priests, the •scribes, and the leaders of the people were looking for a way to destroy Him, 48 but they could not find a way to do it, because all the people were captivated by what they heard.[g]

The Authority of Jesus Challenged

20 One day[h] as He was teaching the people in the •temple complex and proclaiming the good news, the •chief priests and the •scribes, with the elders, came up 2 and said to Him: "Tell us, by what authority are You doing these things? Who is it who gave You this authority?"

3 He answered them, "I will also ask you a question. Tell Me, 4 was the baptism of John from heaven or from men?"

5 They discussed it among themselves: "If we say, 'From heaven,' He will say, 'Why didn't you believe him?' 6 But if we say, 'From men,' all the people will stone us, because they are convinced that John was a prophet."

7 So they answered that they did not know its origin.[i]

8 And Jesus said to them, "Neither will I tell you by what authority I do these things."

The Parable of the Vineyard Owner

9 Then He began to tell the people this parable: "A man planted a vineyard, leased it to tenant farmers, and went away for a long time. 10 At harvest time he sent a •slave to the farm-

[a]**19:22** Lit *you out of your mouth* [b]**19:27** Or *execute* [c]**19:38** The words *the King* are substituted for *He* in Ps 118:26. [d]**19:38** Ps 118:26 [e]**19:45** Other mss add *and buying in it* [f]**19:46** Is 56:7; Jr 7:11 [g]**19:48** Lit *people hung on what they heard* [h]**20:1** Lit *It happened on one of the days* [i]**20:7** Or *know where it was from*

ers so that they might give him some fruit from
the vineyard. But the farmers beat him and sent
him away empty-handed. 11 He sent yet
another slave, but they beat that one too,
treated him shamefully, and sent him away
empty-handed. 12 And he sent yet a third, but
they wounded this one too and threw him out.
13 "Then the owner of the vineyard said,
'What should I do? I will send my beloved son.
Perhaps[a] they will respect him.'
14 "But when the tenant farmers saw him,
they discussed it among themselves and said,
'This is the heir. Let's kill him, so the inheritance will be ours!' 15 So they threw him out of
the vineyard and killed him.
"Therefore, what will the owner of the vineyard do to them? 16 He will come and destroy
those farmers and give the vineyard to others."
But when they heard this they said, "No—
never!"
17 But He looked at them and said, "Then
what is the meaning of this Scripture:[b]

The stone that the builders
rejected—
this has become
the cornerstone?[c d]

18 Everyone who falls on that stone will be
broken to pieces, and if it falls on anyone, it
will grind him to powder!"
19 Then the scribes and the chief priests
looked for a way to get their hands on Him that
very hour, because they knew He had told this
parable against them, but they feared the people.

God and Caesar

20 They[e] watched closely and sent spies
who pretended to be righteous,[f] so they could
catch Him in what He said,[g] to hand Him over
to the governor's rule and authority. 21 They
questioned Him, "Teacher, we know that You
speak and teach correctly, and You don't show
partiality,[h] but teach truthfully the way of God.
22 Is it lawful for us to pay taxes to Caesar or
not?"
23 But detecting their craftiness, He said to
them,[i] 24 "Show Me a •denarius. Whose image
and inscription does it have?"
"Caesar's," they said.
25 "Well then," He told them, "give back to
Caesar the things that are Caesar's and to God
the things that are God's."
26 They were not able to catch Him in what
He said[g] in public,[j] and being amazed at His
answer, they became silent.

The Sadducees and the Resurrection

27 Some of the •Sadducees, who say there is
no resurrection, came up and questioned Him:
28 "Teacher, Moses wrote for us that **if a man's**
brother has a wife, and **dies childless, his**
brother should take the wife and produce
•offspring for his brother.[k] 29 Now there were
seven brothers. The first took a wife and died
without children. 30 Also the second[l] 31 and
the third took her. In the same way, all seven
died and left no children. 32 Finally, the woman
died too. 33 Therefore, in the resurrection,
whose wife will the woman be? For all seven
had married her."[m]
34 Jesus told them, "The sons of this age
marry and are given in marriage. 35 But those
who are counted worthy to take part in that
age and in the resurrection from the dead neither marry nor are given in marriage. 36 For
they cannot die anymore, because they are
like angels and are sons of God, since they are
sons of the resurrection. 37 Moses even indi-
cated ⌊in the passage⌋ about the burning bush
that the dead are raised, where he calls the
Lord **the God of Abraham and the God of**
Isaac and the God of Jacob.[n] 38 He is not God
of the dead but of the living, because all are
living to[o] Him."
39 Some of the scribes answered, "Teacher,
You have spoken well." 40 And they no longer
dared to ask Him anything.

The Question about the Messiah

41 Then He said to them, "How can they say
that the •Messiah is the Son of David? 42 For
David himself says in the Book of Psalms:

The Lord declared to my Lord,
'Sit at My right hand
43 **until I make Your enemies**
Your footstool.'[p]

44 David calls Him 'Lord'; how then can the
Messiah be his Son?"

[a]**20:13** Other mss add *when they see him* [b]**20:17** Lit *What then is this that is written* [c]**20:17** Lit *the head of the corner* [d]**20:17** Ps 118:22 [e]**20:20** The scribes and chief priests of v. 19 [f]**20:20** Or *upright*; that is, loyal to God's law [g]**20:20,26** Lit *catch Him in [a] word* [h]**20:21** Lit *You don't receive a face* [i]**20:23** Other mss add *"Why are you testing Me?* [j]**20:26** Lit *in front of the people* [k]**20:28** Dt 25:5 [l]**20:30** Other mss add *took her as wife, and he died without children* [m]**20:33** Lit *had her as wife* [n]**20:37** Ex 3:6,15 [o]**20:38** Or *with* [p]**20:42–43** Ps 110:1

Warning against the Scribes

45 While all the people were listening, He
said to His disciples, 46 "Beware of the scribes,
who want to go around in long robes and who
love greetings in the marketplaces, the front
seats in the •synagogues, and the places of
honor at banquets. 47 They devour widows'
houses and say long prayers just for show.
These will receive greater punishment."[a]

The Widow's Gift

21 He looked up and saw the rich dropping their offerings into the temple
treasury. 2 He also saw a poor widow dropping
in two tiny coins.[b] 3 "I tell you the truth," He
said. "This poor widow has put in more than
all of them. 4 For all these people have put in
gifts out of their surplus, but she out of her
poverty has put in all she had to live on."

Destruction of the Temple Predicted

5 As some were talking about the •temple
complex, how it was adorned with beautiful
stones and gifts dedicated to God,[c] He said,
6 "These things that you see—the days will
come when not one stone will be left on
another that will not be thrown down!"

Signs of the End of the Age

7 "Teacher," they asked Him, "so when will
these things be? And what will be the sign
when these things are about to take place?"
8 Then He said, "Watch out that you are not
deceived. For many will come in My name, saying, 'I am He,' and, 'The time is near.' Don't follow them. 9 When you hear of wars and
rebellions,[d] don't be alarmed. Indeed, these
things must take place first, but the end won't
come right away."
10 Then He told them: "Nation will be
raised up against nation, and kingdom
against kingdom. 11 There will be violent
earthquakes, and famines and plagues in various places, and there will be terrifying sights
and great signs from heaven. 12 But before all
these things, they will lay their hands on you
and persecute you. They will hand you over
to the •synagogues and prisons, and you will
be brought before kings and governors
because of My name. 13 It will lead to an
opportunity for you to witness.[e] 14 Therefore
make up your minds[f] not to prepare your
defense ahead of time, 15 for I will give you
such words[g] and a wisdom that none of your
adversaries will be able to resist or contradict. 16 You will even be betrayed by parents,
brothers, relatives, and friends. They will kill
some of you. 17 You will be hated by everyone because of My name, 18 but not a hair of
your head will be lost. 19 By your endurance
gain[h] your •lives.

The Destruction of Jerusalem

20 "When you see Jerusalem surrounded by
armies, then recognize that its desolation has
come near. 21 Then those in Judea must flee to
the mountains! Those inside the city[i] must
leave it, and those who are in the country must
not enter it, 22 because these are days of vengeance to fulfill all the things that are written.
23 Woe to pregnant women and nursing mothers in those days, for there will be great distress
in the land[j] and wrath against this people.
24 They will fall by the edge of the sword and
be led captive into all the nations, and Jerusalem will be trampled by the Gentiles[k] until the
times of the Gentiles are fulfilled.

The Coming of the Son of Man

25 "Then there will be signs in the sun,
moon, and stars; and there will be anguish on
the earth among nations bewildered by the
roaring sea and waves. 26 People will faint from
fear and expectation of the things that are coming on the world, because the celestial powers
will be shaken. 27 Then they will see the •Son
of Man coming in a cloud with power and great
glory. 28 But when these things begin to take
place, stand up and lift up your heads, because
your redemption is near!"

The Parable of the Fig Tree

29 Then He told them a parable: "Look at
the fig tree, and all the trees. 30 As soon as they
put out ⌊leaves⌋ you can see for yourselves and
recognize that summer is already near. 31 In
the same way, when you see these things happening, recognize[l] that the kingdom of God is
near. 32 •I assure you: This generation will certainly not pass away until all things take place.
33 Heaven and earth will pass away, but My
words will never pass away.

[a] **20:47** Or *judgment* [b] **21:2** Lit *two lepta*; the *lepton* was the smallest and least valuable Gk coin in use. [c] **21:5** Gifts given to the temple in fulfillment of vows to God [d] **21:9** Or *insurrections*, or *revolutions* [e] **21:13** Lit *lead to a testimony for you* [f] **21:14** Lit *Therefore place* (determine) *in your hearts* [g] **21:15** Lit *you a mouth* [h] **21:19** Other mss read *endurance you will gain* [i] **21:21** Lit *inside her* [j] **21:23** Or *the earth* [k] **21:24** Or *nations* [l] **21:31** Or *you know*

The Need for Watchfulness

34 "Be on your guard, so that your minds are not dulled[a] from carousing,[b] drunkenness, and worries of life, or that day will come on you unexpectedly 35 like a trap. For it will come on all who live on the face of the whole earth. 36 But be alert at all times, praying that you may have strength[c] to escape all these things that are going to take place and to stand before the Son of Man."

37 During the day, He was teaching in the temple complex, but in the evening He would go out and spend the night on what is called the •Mount of Olives. 38 Then all the people would come early in the morning to hear Him in the temple complex.

The Plot to Kill Jesus

22 The Festival of •Unleavened Bread, which is called •Passover, was drawing near. 2 The •chief priests and the •scribes were looking for a way to put Him to death, because they were afraid of the people.

3 Then Satan entered Judas, called Iscariot, who was numbered among the Twelve. 4 He went away and discussed with the chief priests and temple police how he could hand Him over to them. 5 They were glad and agreed to give him silver.[d] 6 So he accepted ⌊the offer⌋ and started looking for a good opportunity to betray Him to them when the crowd was not present.

Preparation for Passover

7 Then the Day of Unleavened Bread came when the Passover lamb had to be sacrificed. 8 Jesus sent Peter and John, saying, "Go and prepare the Passover meal for us, so we can eat it."

9 "Where do You want us to prepare it?" they asked Him.

10 "Listen," He said to them, "when you've entered the city, a man carrying a water jug will meet you. Follow him into the house he enters. 11 Tell the owner of the house, 'The Teacher asks you, "Where is the guest room where I can eat the Passover with My disciples?"' 12 Then he will show you a large, furnished room upstairs. Make the preparations there."

13 So they went and found it just as He had told them, and they prepared the Passover.

The First Lord's Supper

14 When the hour came, He reclined at the table, and the apostles with Him. 15 Then He said to them, "I have fervently desired to eat this Passover with you before I suffer. 16 For I tell you, I will not eat it again[e] until it is fulfilled in the kingdom of God." 17 Then He took a cup, and after giving thanks, He said, "Take this and share it among yourselves. 18 For I tell you, from now on I will not drink of the fruit of the vine until the kingdom of God comes."

19 And He took bread, gave thanks, broke it, gave it to them, and said, "This is My body, which is given for you. Do this in remembrance of Me."

20 In the same way He also took the cup after supper and said, "This cup is the new covenant ⌊established by⌋ My blood; it is shed for you.[f] 21 But look, the hand of the one betraying Me is at the table with Me! 22 For the •Son of Man will go away as it has been determined, but woe to that man by whom He is betrayed!"

23 So they began to argue among themselves which of them it could be who was going to do this thing.

The Dispute over Greatness

24 Then a dispute also arose among them about who should be considered the greatest. 25 But He said to them, "The kings of the Gentiles dominate them, and those who have authority over them are called[g] 'Benefactors.'[h] 26 But it must not be like that among you. On the contrary, whoever is greatest among you must become like the youngest, and whoever leads, like the one serving. 27 For who is greater, the one at the table or the one serving? Isn't it the one at the table? But I am among you as the One who serves. 28 You are the ones who stood by Me in My trials. 29 I bestow on you a kingdom, just as My Father bestowed one on Me, 30 so that you may eat and drink at My table in My kingdom. And you will sit on thrones judging the 12 tribes of Israel.

Peter's Denial Predicted

31 "Simon, Simon,[i] look out! Satan has asked to sift you[j] like wheat. 32 But I have prayed for you[k] that your faith may not fail. And you, when you have turned back, strengthen your brothers."

[a]**21:34** Lit *your hearts are not weighed down* [b]**21:34** Or *hangovers* [c]**21:36** Other mss read *you may be counted worthy* [d]**22:5** Or *money*; Mt 26:15 specifies 30 pieces of silver; Zch 11:12–13 [e]**22:16** Other mss omit *again* [f]**22:19–20** Other mss omit *which is given for you* (v. 19) through the end of v. 20 [g]**22:25** Or *them call themselves* [h]**22:25** Title of honor given to those who benefited the public good [i]**22:31** Other mss read *Then the Lord said, "Simon, Simon* [j]**22:31** *you* (pl in Gk) [k]**22:32** *you* (sg in Gk)

33 “Lord,” he told Him, “I’m ready to go
with You both to prison and to death!”
34 “I tell you, Peter,” He said, “the rooster
will not crow today until[a] you deny three times
that you know Me!”

Money-Bag, Backpack, and Sword

35 He also said to them, “When I sent you
out without money-bag, traveling bag, or sandals, did you lack anything?”
“Not a thing,” they said.
36 Then He said to them, “But now, whoever has a money-bag should take it, and also a
traveling bag. And whoever doesn’t have a
sword should sell his robe and buy one. 37 For
I tell you, what is written must be fulfilled in
Me: **And He was counted among the outlaws.**[b] Yes, what is written about Me is coming
to its fulfillment.”
38 “Lord,” they said, “look, here are two
swords.”
“Enough of that!”[c] He told them.

The Prayer in the Garden

39 He went out and made His way as usual
to the •Mount of Olives, and the disciples followed Him. 40 When He reached the place, He
told them, “Pray that you may not enter into
temptation.” 41 Then He withdrew from them
about a stone’s throw, knelt down, and began
to pray, 42 “Father, if You are willing, take this
cup away from Me—nevertheless, not My will,
but Yours, be done.”
[43 Then an angel from heaven appeared to
Him, strengthening Him. 44 Being in anguish,
He prayed more fervently, and His sweat
became like drops of blood falling to the
ground.][d] 45 When He got up from prayer and
came to the disciples, He found them sleeping,
exhausted from their grief.[e] 46 “Why are you
sleeping?” He asked them. “Get up and pray, so
that you won’t enter into temptation.”

The Judas Kiss

47 While He was still speaking, suddenly a
mob was there, and one of the Twelve named
Judas was leading them. He came near Jesus to
kiss Him, 48 but Jesus said to him, “Judas, are
you betraying the Son of Man with a kiss?”
49 When those around Him saw what was
going to happen, they asked, “Lord, should we
strike with the sword?” 50 Then one of them
struck the high priest’s slave and cut off his
right ear.
51 But Jesus responded, “No more of this!”[f]
And touching his ear, He healed him. 52 Then
Jesus said to the chief priests, temple police,
and the elders who had come for Him, “Have
you come out with swords and clubs as if I were
a criminal?[g] 53 Every day while I was with you
in the •temple complex, you never laid a hand
on Me. But this is your hour—and the dominion of darkness.”

Peter Denies His Lord

54 They seized Him, led Him away, and
brought Him into the high priest’s house.
Meanwhile Peter was following at a distance.
55 They lit a fire in the middle of the courtyard
and sat down together, and Peter sat among
them. 56 When a servant saw him sitting in the
firelight, and looked closely at him, she said,
“This man was with Him too.”
57 But he denied it: “Woman, I don’t know
Him!”
58 After a little while, someone else saw
him and said, “You’re one of them too!”
“Man, I am not!” Peter said.
59 About an hour later, another kept insisting, “This man was certainly with Him, since
he’s also a Galilean.”
60 But Peter said, “Man, I don’t know what
you’re talking about!” Immediately, while he
was still speaking, a rooster crowed. 61 Then
the Lord turned and looked at Peter. So Peter
remembered the word of the Lord, how He had
said to him, “Before the rooster crows today,
you will deny Me three times.” 62 And he went
outside and wept bitterly.

Jesus Mocked and Beaten

63 The men who were holding Jesus started
mocking and beating Him. 64 After blindfolding
Him, they kept[h] asking, “Prophesy! Who hit
You?” 65 And they were saying many other
blasphemous things against Him.

Jesus Faces the Sanhedrin

66 When daylight came, the elders[i] of the
people, both the chief priests and the scribes,
convened and brought Him before their •San-
hedrin. 67 They said, “If You are the •Messiah,
tell us.”
But He said to them, “If I do tell you, you

[a]**22:34** Other mss read *before* [b]**22:37** Is 53:12 [c]**22:38** Or *It is enough!* [d]**22:43–44** Other mss omit bracketed text [e]**22:45** Lit *sleeping from grief* [f]**22:51** Lit *Permit as far as this* [g]**22:52** Lit *as against a criminal* [h]**22:64** Other mss add *striking Him on the face and* [i]**22:66** Or *council of elders*

will not believe. 68 And if I ask you, you will not answer. 69 But from now on, the Son of Man will be seated at the right hand of the Power of God."

70 They all asked, "Are You, then, the Son of God?"

And He said to them, "You say that I am."

71 "Why do we need any more testimony," they said, "since we've heard it ourselves from His mouth?"

Jesus Faces Pilate

23 Then their whole assembly rose up and brought Him before •Pilate. 2 They began to accuse Him, saying, "We found this man subverting our nation, opposing payment of taxes to Caesar, and saying that He Himself is the •Messiah, a King."

3 So Pilate asked Him, "Are You the King of the Jews?"

He answered him, "You have said it."[a]

4 Pilate then told the •chief priests and the crowds, "I find no grounds for charging this man."

5 But they kept insisting, "He stirs up the people, teaching throughout all Judea, from Galilee where He started even to here."

Jesus Faces Herod Antipas

6 When Pilate heard this,[b] he asked if the man was a Galilean. 7 Finding that He was under •Herod's jurisdiction, he sent Him to Herod, who was also in Jerusalem during those days. 8 Herod was very glad to see Jesus; for a long time he had wanted to see Him, because he had heard about Him and was hoping to see some miracle[c] performed by Him. 9 So he kept asking Him questions, but Jesus did not answer him. 10 The chief priests and the •scribes stood by, vehemently accusing Him. 11 Then Herod, with his soldiers, treated Him with contempt, mocked Him, dressed Him in a brilliant robe, and sent Him back to Pilate. 12 That very day Herod and Pilate became friends.[d] Previously, they had been hostile toward each other.

Jesus or Barabbas

13 Pilate called together the chief priests, the leaders, and the people, 14 and said to them, "You have brought me this man as one who subverts the people. But in fact, after examining Him in your presence, I have found no grounds to charge this man with those things you accuse Him of. 15 Neither has Herod, because he sent Him back to us. Clearly, He has done nothing to deserve death. 16 Therefore I will have Him whipped[e] and ⌊then⌋ release Him." [17 For according to the festival he had to release someone to them.][f]

18 Then they all cried out together, "Take this man away! Release Barabbas to us!" 19 (He had been thrown into prison for a rebellion that had taken place in the city, and for murder.)

20 Pilate, wanting to release Jesus, addressed them again, 21 but they kept shouting, "Crucify! Crucify Him!"

22 A third time he said to them, "Why? What has this man done wrong? I have found in Him no grounds for the death penalty. Therefore I will have Him whipped and ⌊then⌋ release Him."

23 But they kept up the pressure, demanding with loud voices that He be crucified. And their voices[g] won out. 24 So Pilate decided to grant their demand 25 and released the one they were asking for, who had been thrown into prison for rebellion and murder. But he handed Jesus over to their will.

The Way to the Cross

26 As they led Him away, they seized Simon, a Cyrenian, who was coming in from the country, and laid the cross on him to carry behind Jesus. 27 A great multitude of the people followed Him, including women who were mourning and lamenting Him. 28 But turning to them, Jesus said, "Daughters of Jerusalem, do not weep for Me, but weep for yourselves and your children. 29 Look, the days are coming when they will say, 'Blessed are the barren, the wombs that never bore, and the breasts that never nursed!' 30 Then they will begin **to say to the mountains, 'Fall on us!' and to the hills, 'Cover us!'**[h] 31 For if they do these things when the wood is green, what will happen when it is dry?"

Crucified between Two Criminals

32 Two others—criminals—were also led

[a]**23:3** Or *That is true*; an affirmative oath [b]**23:6** Other mss read *heard "Galilee"* [c]**23:8** Or *sign* [d]**23:12** Lit *friends with one another* [e]**23:16** Gk *paideuo;* to discipline or "teach a lesson"; 1 Kg 12:11,14 LXX; 2 Ch 10:11,14; perhaps a way of referring to the Roman scourging; Lat *flagellatio* [f]**23:17** Other mss omit bracketed text [g]**23:23** Other mss add *and those of the chief priests* [h]**23:30** Hs 10:8

away to be executed with Him. 33 When they
arrived at the place called The Skull, they crucified Him there, along with the criminals, one
on the right and one on the left. [34 Then Jesus
said, "Father, forgive them, because they do
not know what they are doing."][a] And they
divided His clothes and cast lots.
35 The people stood watching, and even the
leaders kept scoffing: "He saved others; let Him
save Himself if this is God's Messiah, the Chosen One!" 36 The soldiers also mocked Him.
They came offering Him sour wine 37 and said,
"If You are the King of the Jews, save Yourself!"
38 An inscription was above Him:[b]

THIS IS
THE KING OF THE JEWS

39 Then one of the criminals hanging there
began to yell insults at[c] Him: "Aren't You the
Messiah? Save Yourself and us!"
40 But the other answered, rebuking him:
"Don't you even fear God, since you are undergoing the same punishment? 41 We are punished justly, because we're getting back what
we deserve for the things we did, but this man
has done nothing wrong." 42 Then he said,
"Jesus, remember me[d] when You come into
Your kingdom!"
43 And He said to him, "•I assure you:
Today you will be with Me in paradise."

The Death of Jesus

44 It was now about noon,[e] and darkness
came over the whole land[f] until three,[g]
45 because the sun's light failed.[h] The curtain of
the sanctuary was split down the middle.
46 And Jesus called out with a loud voice,
"Father, **into Your hands I entrust My spirit.**"[i]
Saying this, He breathed His last.
47 When the •centurion saw what happened, he began to glorify God, saying, "This
man really was righteous!" 48 All the crowds
that had gathered for this spectacle, when they
saw what had taken place, went home, striking
their chests.[j] 49 But all who knew Him, including the women who had followed Him from
Galilee, stood at a distance, watching these
things.

The Burial of Jesus

50 There was a good and righteous man
named Joseph, a member of the •Sanhedrin,
51 who had not agreed with their plan and
action. He was from Arimathea, a Judean
town, and was looking forward to the kingdom of God. 52 He approached Pilate and
asked for Jesus' body. 53 Taking it down, he
wrapped it in fine linen and placed it in a tomb
cut into the rock, where no one had ever been
placed.[k] 54 It was preparation day, and the
Sabbath was about to begin.[l] 55 The women
who had come with Him from Galilee followed along and observed the tomb and how
His body was placed. 56 Then they returned
and prepared spices and perfumes. And they
rested on the Sabbath according to the commandment.

Resurrection Morning

24 On the first day of the week, very
early in the morning, they[m] came to
the tomb, bringing the spices they had prepared. 2 They found the stone rolled away
from the tomb. 3 They went in but did not find
the body of the Lord Jesus. 4 While they were
perplexed about this, suddenly two men stood
by them in dazzling clothes. 5 So the women
were terrified and bowed down to the
ground.[n]
"Why are you looking for the living among
the dead?" asked the men. 6 "He is not here,
but He has been resurrected! Remember how
He spoke to you when He was still in Galilee,
7 saying, 'The •Son of Man must be betrayed
into the hands of sinful men, be crucified, and
rise on the third day'?" 8 And they remembered His words.
9 Returning from the tomb, they reported all
these things to the Eleven and to all the rest.
10 •Mary Magdalene, Joanna, Mary the mother
of James, and the other women with them
were telling the apostles these things. 11 But
these words seemed like nonsense to them,
and they did not believe the women. 12 Peter,
however, got up and ran to the tomb. When he
stooped to look in, he saw only the linen
cloths.[o] So he went home, amazed at what had
happened.

[a]**23:34** Other mss omit bracketed text [b]**23:38** Other mss add *written in Greek, Latin, and Hebrew letters* [c]**23:39** Or *began to blaspheme* [d]**23:42** Other mss add *Lord* [e]**23:44** Lit *about the sixth hour* [f]**23:44** Or *whole earth* [g]**23:44** Lit *the ninth hour* [h]**23:45** Other mss read *three, and the sun was darkened* [i]**23:46** Ps 31:5 [j]**23:48** Mourning [k]**23:53** Or *interred*, or *laid* [l]**23:54** Lit *was dawning*; not in the morning but at sundown Friday [m]**24:1** Other mss add *and other women with them* [n]**24:5** Lit *and inclined their faces to the ground* [o]**24:12** Other mss add *lying there*

The Emmaus Disciples

13 Now that same day two of them were on their way to a village called[a] Emmaus, which was about seven miles[b] from Jerusalem. 14 Together they were discussing everything that had taken place. 15 And while they were discussing and arguing, Jesus Himself came near and began to walk along with them. 16 But they[c] were prevented from recognizing Him. 17 Then He asked them, "What is this dispute that you're having[d] with each other as you are walking?" And they stopped ⌊walking and looked⌋ discouraged.

18 The one named Cleopas answered Him, "Are You the only visitor in Jerusalem who doesn't know the things that happened there in these days?"

19 "What things?" He asked them.

So they said to Him, "The things concerning Jesus the •Nazarene, who was a Prophet powerful in action and speech before God and all the people, 20 and how our •chief priests and leaders handed Him over to be sentenced to death, and they crucified Him. 21 But we were hoping that He was the One who was about to redeem Israel. Besides all this, it's the third day since these things happened. 22 Moreover, some women from our group astounded us. They arrived early at the tomb, 23 and when they didn't find His body, they came and reported that they had seen a vision of angels who said He was alive. 24 Some of those who were with us went to the tomb and found it just as the women had said, but they didn't see Him."

25 He said to them, "How unwise and slow you are to believe in your hearts all that the prophets have spoken! 26 Didn't the •Messiah have to suffer these things and enter into His glory?" 27 Then beginning with Moses and all the Prophets, He interpreted for them the things concerning Himself in all the Scriptures.

28 They came near the village where they were going, and He gave the impression that He was going farther. 29 But they urged Him: "Stay with us, because it's almost evening, and now the day is almost over." So He went in to stay with them.

30 It was as He reclined at the table with them that He took the bread, blessed and broke it, and gave it to them. 31 Then their eyes were opened, and they recognized Him, but He disappeared from their sight. 32 So they said to each other, "Weren't our hearts ablaze within us while He was talking with us on the road and explaining the Scriptures to us?" 33 That very hour they got up and returned to Jerusalem. They found the Eleven and those with them gathered together, 34 who said,[e] "The Lord has certainly been raised, and has appeared to Simon!" 35 Then they began to describe what had happened on the road and how He was made known to them in the breaking of the bread.

The Reality of the Risen Jesus

36 And as they were saying these things, He Himself stood among them. He said to them, "Peace to you!" 37 But they were startled and terrified and thought they were seeing a ghost. 38 "Why are you troubled?" He asked them. "And why do doubts arise in your hearts? 39 Look at My hands and My feet, that it is I Myself! Touch Me and see, because a ghost does not have flesh and bones as you can see I have." 40 Having said this, He showed them His hands and feet. 41 But while they still could not believe[f] because of ⌊their⌋ joy and were amazed, He asked them, "Do you have anything here to eat?" 42 So they gave Him a piece of a broiled fish,[g] 43 and He took it and ate in their presence.

44 Then He told them, "These are My words that I spoke to you while I was still with you—that everything written about Me in the Law of Moses, the Prophets, and the Psalms must be fulfilled." 45 Then He opened their minds to understand the Scriptures. 46 He also said to them, "This is what is written:[h] the Messiah would suffer and rise from the dead the third day, 47 and repentance for[i] forgiveness of sins would be proclaimed in His name to all the nations, beginning at Jerusalem. 48 You are witnesses of these things. 49 And look, I am sending you[j] what My Father promised. As for you, stay in the city[k] until you are empowered[l] from on high."

[a] **24:13** Lit *village, which name is* [b] **24:13** Lit *about 60 stadia*; 1 *stadion* = 600 feet [c] **24:16** Lit *their eyes* [d] **24:17** Lit *What are these words that you are exchanging* [e] **24:34** Gk is specific that this refers to the Eleven and those with them. [f] **24:41** Or *they still disbelieved* [g] **24:42** Other mss add *and some honeycomb* [h] **24:46** Other mss add *and thus it was necessary that* [i] **24:47** Other mss read *repentance and* [j] **24:49** Lit *upon you* [k] **24:49** Other mss add *of Jerusalem* [l] **24:49** Lit *clothed with power*

The Ascension of Jesus

50 Then He led them out as far as Bethany,
and lifting up His hands He blessed them.
51 And while He was blessing them, He left
them and was carried up into heaven. 52 After
worshiping Him, they returned to Jerusalem
with great joy. 53 And they were continually in
the •temple complex blessing God.[a]

John

Prologue

1 In the beginning was the Word,[b]
and the Word was with God,
and the Word was God.
2 He was with God in the beginning.
3 All things were created
through Him,
and apart from Him not one thing
was created
that has been created.
4 Life was in Him,[c]
and that life was the light of men.
5 That light shines in the darkness,
yet the darkness
did not overcome[d] it.

6 There was a man named John
who was sent from God.
7 He came as a witness
to testify about the light,
so that all might believe
through him.[e]
8 He was not the light,
but he came to testify
about the light.
9 The true light, who gives light
to everyone,
was coming into the world.[f]

10 He was in the world,
and the world was created
through Him,
yet the world did not recognize Him.
11 He came to His own,[g]
and His own people[g]
did not receive Him.
12 But to all who did receive Him,
He gave them the right to be[h]
children of God,
to those who believe
in His name,
13 who were born,
not of blood,[i]
or of the will of the flesh,
or of the will of man,[j]
but of God.

14 The Word became flesh[k]
and took up residence[l] among us.
We observed His glory,
the glory as
the •One and Only Son[m]
from the Father,
full of grace and truth.
15 (John testified concerning Him
and exclaimed,
"This was the One
of whom I said,
'The One coming after me
has surpassed me,
because He existed before me.'")
16 Indeed, we have all received grace
after grace
from His fullness,
17 for although the law was given
through Moses,
grace and truth came
through Jesus Christ.

[a]**24:53** Other mss read *praising and blessing God. Amen.* [b]**1:1** The *Word* (Gk *Logos*) is a title for Jesus as the communication and the revealer of God the Father; Jn 1:14,18; Rv 19:13. [c]**1:3–4** Other punctuation is possible: . . . *not one thing was created. What was created in Him was life* [d]**1:5** Or *grasp*, or *comprehend*, or *overtake*; Jn 12:35 [e]**1:7** Or *through it* (the light) [f]**1:9** Or *The true light who comes into the world gives light to everyone*, or *The true light enlightens everyone coming into the world.* [g]**1:11** The same Gk adjective is used twice in this verse: the first refers to all that Jesus owned as Creator (*to His own*); the second refers to the Jews (*His own people*). [h]**1:12** Or *become* [i]**1:13** Lit *bloods*; the pl form of *blood* occurs only here in the NT. It may refer either to lineal descent (that is, blood from one's father and mother) or to the OT sacrificial system (that is, the various blood sacrifices). Neither is the basis for birth into the family of God. [j]**1:13** Or *not of human lineage, or of human capacity, or of human volition* [k]**1:14** The eternally existent Word (vv. 1–2) took on full humanity, but without sin; Heb 4:15. [l]**1:14** Lit *and tabernacled*, or *and dwelt in a tent*; this word occurs only here in John. A related word, referring to the Festival of Tabernacles, occurs only in 7:2; Ex 40:34–38. [m]**1:14** *Son* is implied from the reference to the Father and from Gk usage.

Turn to page 159.

18 No one has ever seen God.[a]
The One and Only Son[b] —
the One who is at the Father's side[c] —
He has revealed Him.

John the Baptist's Testimony

19 This is John's testimony when the •Jews
from Jerusalem sent priests and Levites to ask
him, "Who are you?"

20 He did not refuse to answer, but he
declared: "I am not the •Messiah."

21 "What then?" they asked him. "Are you
Elijah?"

"I am not," he said.

"Are you the Prophet?"[d]

"No," he answered.

22 "Who are you, then?" they asked. "We
need to give an answer to those who sent us.
What can you tell us about yourself?"

23 He said, "I am a **voice of one crying out
in the wilderness: Make straight the way of
the Lord**[e] —just as Isaiah the prophet said."

24 Now they had been sent from the •Phar-
isees. 25 So they asked him, "Why then do you
baptize if you aren't the Messiah, or Elijah, or
the Prophet?"

26 "I baptize with[f] water," John answered
them. "Someone stands among you, but you
don't know ⌊Him⌋. 27 He is the One coming
after me,[g] whose sandal strap I'm not worthy to
untie."

28 All this happened in Bethany[h] across the
Jordan,[i] where John was baptizing.

The Lamb of God

29 The next day John saw Jesus coming
toward him and said, "Here is the Lamb of God,
who takes away the sin of the world! 30 This is
the One I told you about: 'After me comes a
man who has surpassed me, because He
existed before me.' 31 I didn't know Him, but I
came baptizing with[f] water so He might be
revealed to Israel."

32 And John testified, "I watched the Spirit
descending from heaven like a dove, and He
rested on Him. 33 I didn't know Him, but He[j]
who sent me to baptize with[f] water told me,
'The One you see the Spirit descending and
resting on—He is the One who baptizes with[f]
the Holy Spirit.' 34 I have seen and testified that
He is the Son of God!"[k]

35 Again the next day, John was standing
with two of his disciples. 36 When he saw Jesus
passing by, he said, "Look! The Lamb of God!"

37 The two disciples heard him say this and
followed Jesus. 38 When Jesus turned and
noticed them following Him, He asked them,
"What are you looking for?"

They said to Him, "•Rabbi" (which means
"Teacher"), "where are You staying?"

39 "Come and you'll see," He replied. So
they went and saw where He was staying, and
they stayed with Him that day. It was about 10
in the morning.[l]

40 Andrew, Simon Peter's brother, was one
of the two who heard John and followed Him.
41 He first found his own brother Simon and
told him, "We have found the Messiah!"[m]
(which means "Anointed One"), 42 and he
brought ⌊Simon⌋ to Jesus.

When Jesus saw him, He said, "You are
Simon, son of John.[n] You will be called
•Cephas" (which means "Rock").

Philip and Nathanael

43 The next day He[o] decided to leave for
Galilee. Jesus found Philip and told him, "Follow Me!"

44 Now Philip was from Bethsaida, the
hometown of Andrew and Peter. 45 Philip
found Nathanael[p] and told him, "We have
found the One Moses wrote about in the Law
(and so did the prophets): Jesus the son of
Joseph, from Nazareth!"

46 "Can anything good come out of Nazareth?" Nathanael asked him.

"Come and see," Philip answered.

47 Then Jesus saw Nathanael coming
toward Him and said about him, "Here is a true
Israelite; no deceit is in him."

48 "How do you know me?" Nathanael
asked.

"Before Philip called you, when you were

[a]**1:18** Since God is an infinite being, no one can see Him in His absolute essential nature; Ex 33:18–23. [b]**1:18** Other mss read *God* [c]**1:18** Lit *is in the bosom of the Father* [d]**1:21** Probably = the Prophet in Dt 18:15 [e]**1:23** Is 40:3 [f]**1:26,31,33** Or *in* [g]**1:27** Other mss add *who came before me* [h]**1:28** Other mss read *in Bethabara* [i]**1:28** Another Bethany, near Jerusalem, was the home of Lazarus, Martha, and Mary; Jn 11:1. [j]**1:33** *He* refers to God the Father, who gave John a sign to help him identify the Messiah. Vv. 32–34 indicate that John did not know that Jesus was the Messiah until the Spirit descended upon Him at His baptism. [k]**1:34** Other mss read *is the Chosen One of God* [l]**1:39** Lit *about the tenth hour.* Various methods of reckoning time were used in the ancient world. John probably used a different method from the other 3 Gospels. If John used the same method of time reckoning as the other 3 Gospels, the translation would be: *It was about four in the afternoon.* [m]**1:41** In the NT, the word Messiah translates the Gk word *Christos* ("Anointed One"), except here and in Jn 4:25 where it translates *Messias.* [n]**1:42** Other mss read *Simon, son of Jonah* [o]**1:43** Or *he,* referring either to Peter (v. 42) or Andrew (vv. 40–41) [p]**1:45** Probably the Bartholomew of the other Gospels and Acts

under the fig tree, I saw you," Jesus answered.
49 "Rabbi," Nathanael replied, "You are the
Son of God! You are the King of Israel!"
50 Jesus responded to him, "Do you believe
⌊only⌋ because I told you I saw you under the fig
tree? You[a] will see greater things than this."
51 Then He said, "•I assure you: You[b] will see
heaven opened and the angels of God ascending and descending on the •Son of Man."

The First Sign: Turning Water into Wine

2 On the third day a wedding took place in
Cana of Galilee. Jesus' mother was there,
and 2 Jesus and His disciples were invited to
the wedding as well. 3 When the wine ran out,
Jesus' mother told Him, "They don't have any
wine."
4 "What has this concern of yours to do with
Me,[c] •woman?" Jesus asked. "My hour[d] has
not yet come."
5 "Do whatever He tells you," His mother
told the servants.
6 Now six stone water jars had been set
there for Jewish purification. Each contained
20 or 30 gallons.[e]
7 "Fill the jars with water," Jesus told them.
So they filled them to the brim. 8 Then He said
to them, "Now draw some out and take it to the
chief servant."[f] And they did.
9 When the chief servant tasted the water
(after it had become wine), he did not know
where it came from—though the servants who
had drawn the water knew. He called the
groom 10 and told him, "Everybody sets out the
fine wine first, then, after people have drunk
freely, the inferior. But you have kept the fine
wine until now."
11 Jesus performed this first sign[g] in Cana of
Galilee. He displayed His glory, and His disciples believed in Him.
12 After this, He went down to Capernaum,
together with His mother, His brothers, and
His disciples, and they stayed there only a few
days.

Cleansing the Temple Complex

13 The Jewish •Passover was near, so Jesus
went up to Jerusalem. 14 In the •temple complex He found people selling oxen, sheep, and
doves, and ⌊He also found⌋ the money changers
sitting there. 15 After making a whip out of
cords, He drove everyone out of the temple
complex with their sheep and oxen. He also
poured out the money changers' coins and
overturned the tables. 16 He told those who
were selling doves, "Get these things out of
here! Stop turning My Father's house into a
marketplace!"[h]
17 And His disciples remembered that it is
written: **Zeal for Your house will consume
Me.**[i]
18 So the Jews replied to Him, "What sign
⌊of authority⌋ will You show us for doing these
things?"
19 Jesus answered, "Destroy this sanctuary,
and I will raise it up in three days."
20 Therefore the Jews said, "This sanctuary
took 46 years to build, and will You raise it up
in three days?"
21 But He was speaking about the sanctuary
of His body. 22 So when He was raised from the
dead, His disciples remembered that He had
said this. And they believed the Scripture and
the statement Jesus had made.
23 While He was in Jerusalem at the Passover Festival, many trusted in His name
when they saw the signs He was doing.
24 Jesus, however, would not entrust Himself
to them, since He knew them all 25 and
because He did not need anyone to testify
about man; for He Himself knew what was in
man.

Jesus and Nicodemus

3 There was a man from the •Pharisees
named Nicodemus, a ruler of the Jews.
2 This man came to Him at night and said,
"•Rabbi, we know that You have come from
God as a teacher, for no one could perform
these signs You do unless God were with
him."
3 Jesus replied, "•I assure you: Unless someone is born again,[j] he cannot see the kingdom
of God."
4 "But how can anyone be born when he is
old?" Nicodemus asked Him. "Can he enter
his mother's womb a second time and be
born?"

[a] **1:50** *You* (sg in Gk) refers to Nathanael. [b] **1:51** *You* is pl in Gk and refers to Nathanael and the other disciples. [c] **2:4** Or *You and I see things differently*; lit *What to Me and to you*; Mt 8:29; Mk 1:24; 5:7; Lk 8:28 [d] **2:4** The time of His sacrificial death and exaltation; Jn 7:30; 8:20; 12:23,27; 13:1; 17:1 [e] **2:6** Lit *2 or 3 measures* [f] **2:8** Lit *ruler of the table*; perhaps *master of the feast*, or *headwaiter* [g] **2:11** Lit *this beginning of the signs*; Jn 4:54; 20:30. Seven miraculous signs occur in John's Gospel and are so noted in the headings. [h] **2:16** Lit *a house of business* [i] **2:17** Ps 69:9 [j] **3:3** The same Gk word can mean *again* or *from above* (also in v. 7).

5 Jesus answered, "I assure you: Unless someone is born of water and the Spirit,[a] he cannot enter the kingdom of God. 6 Whatever is born of the flesh is flesh, and whatever is born of the Spirit is spirit. 7 Do not be amazed that I told you that you[b] must be born again. 8 The wind[c] blows where it pleases, and you hear its sound, but you don't know where it comes from or where it is going. So it is with everyone born of the Spirit."

9 "How can these things be?" asked Nicodemus.

10 "Are you a teacher[d] of Israel and don't know these things?" Jesus replied. 11 "I assure you: We speak what We know and We testify to what We have seen, but you[e] do not accept Our testimony.[f] 12 If I have told you about things that happen on earth and you don't believe, how will you believe if I tell you about things of heaven? 13 No one has ascended into heaven except the One who descended from heaven—the •Son of Man.[g] 14 Just as Moses lifted up the snake in the wilderness, so the Son of Man must be lifted up, 15 so that everyone who believes in Him will[h] have eternal life.

16 "For God loved the world in this way: He gave His •One and Only Son, so that everyone who believes in Him will not perish but have eternal life. 17 For God did not send His Son into the world that He might condemn the world, but that the world might be saved through Him. 18 Anyone who believes in Him is not condemned, but anyone who does not believe is already condemned, because he has not believed in the name of the One and Only Son of God.

19 "This, then, is the judgment: the light has come into the world, and people loved darkness rather than the light because their deeds were evil. 20 For everyone who practices wicked things hates the light and avoids it,[i] so that his deeds may not be exposed. 21 But anyone who lives by[j] the truth comes to the light, so that his works may be shown to be accomplished by God."[k]

Jesus and John the Baptist

22 After this, Jesus and His disciples went to the Judean countryside, where He spent time with them and baptized. 23 John also was baptizing in Aenon near Salim, because there was plenty of water there. People were coming and being baptized, 24 since John had not yet been thrown into prison.

25 Then a dispute arose between John's disciples and a •Jew[l] about purification. 26 So they came to John and told him, "Rabbi, the One you testified about, and who was with you across the Jordan, is baptizing—and everyone is flocking to Him."

27 John responded, "No one can receive a single thing unless it's given to him from heaven. 28 You yourselves can testify that I said, 'I am not the •Messiah, but I've been sent ahead of Him.' 29 He who has the bride is the groom. But the groom's friend, who stands by and listens for him, rejoices greatly[m] at the groom's voice. So this joy of mine is complete. 30 He must increase, but I must decrease."

The One from Heaven

31 The One who comes from above is above all. The one who is from the earth is earthly and speaks in earthly terms.[n] The One who comes from heaven is above all. 32 He testifies to what He has seen and heard, yet no one accepts His testimony. 33 The one who has accepted His testimony has affirmed that God is true. 34 For God sent Him, and He speaks God's words, since He[o] gives the Spirit without measure. 35 The Father loves the Son and has given all things into His hands. 36 The one who believes in the Son has eternal life, but the one who refuses to believe in the Son will not see life; instead, the wrath of God remains on him.

Jesus and the Samaritan Woman

4 When Jesus[p] knew that the •Pharisees heard He was making and baptizing more disciples than John 2 (though Jesus Himself was not baptizing, but His disciples were), 3 He left Judea and went again to Galilee. 4 He had to travel through Samaria, 5 so He came to a town of Samaria called Sychar near the property[q] that Jacob had given his son Joseph. 6 Jacob's well was there, and Jesus, worn out

[a]**3:5** Or *spirit*, or *wind*; the Gk word *pneuma* can mean *wind*, *spirit*, or *Spirit*, each of which occurs in this context. [b]**3:7** The pronoun is pl in Gk. [c]**3:8** The Gk word *pneuma* can mean *wind*, *spirit*, or *Spirit*, each of which occurs in this context. [d]**3:10** Or *the teacher* [e]**3:11** The word *you* in Gk is pl here and throughout v. 12. [f]**3:11** The pl forms (*We*, *Our*) refer to Jesus and His authority to speak for the Father. [g]**3:13** Other mss add *who is in heaven* [h]**3:15** Other mss add *not perish, but* [i]**3:20** Lit *and does not come to the light* [j]**3:21** Lit *who does* [k]**3:21** It is possible that Jesus' words end at v. 15. Ancient Gk did not have quotation marks. [l]**3:25** Other mss read *and the Jews* [m]**3:29** Lit *with joy rejoices* [n]**3:31** Or *of earthly things* [o]**3:34** Other mss read *since God* [p]**4:1** Other mss read *the Lord* [q]**4:5** Lit *piece of land*

Turn to page 110.

from His journey, sat down at the well. It was
about six in the evening.[a]
7 A woman of Samaria came to draw water.
"Give Me a drink," Jesus said to her, 8 for
His disciples had gone into town to buy food.
9 "How is it that You, a Jew, ask for a drink
from me, a •Samaritan woman?" she asked
Him. For Jews do not associate with[b] Samaritans.[c]
10 Jesus answered, "If you knew the gift of
God, and who is saying to you, 'Give Me a
drink,' you would ask Him, and He would give
you living water."
11 "Sir," said the woman, "You don't even
have a bucket, and the well is deep. So where
do you get this 'living water'? 12 You aren't
greater than our father Jacob, are you? He gave
us the well and drank from it himself, as did his
sons and livestock."
13 Jesus said, "Everyone who drinks from
this water will get thirsty again. 14 But whoever
drinks from the water that I will give him will
never get thirsty again—ever! In fact, the water
I will give him will become a well[d] of water
springing up within him for eternal life."
15 "Sir," the woman said to Him, "give me
this water so I won't get thirsty and come here
to draw water."
16 "Go call your husband," He told her,
"and come back here."
17 "I don't have a husband," she answered.
"You have correctly said, 'I don't have a
husband,'" Jesus said. 18 "For you've had five
husbands, and the man you now have is not
your husband. What you have said is true."
19 "Sir," the woman replied, "I see that You
are a prophet. 20 Our fathers worshiped on this
mountain,[e] yet you ⌊Jews⌋ say that the place to
worship is in Jerusalem."
21 Jesus told her, "Believe Me, •woman, an
hour is coming when you will worship the
Father neither on this mountain nor in Jerusalem.
22 You Samaritans[f] worship what you do
not know. We worship what we do know,
because salvation is from the Jews. 23 But an
hour is coming, and is now here, when the true
worshipers will worship the Father in spirit and
truth. Yes, the Father wants such people to
worship Him. 24 God is spirit, and those who
worship Him must worship in spirit and truth."
25 The woman said to Him, "I know that
•Messiah[g] is coming" (who is called Christ).
"When He comes, He will explain everything
to us."
26 "I am ⌊He⌋," Jesus told her, "the One
speaking to you."

The Ripened Harvest

27 Just then His disciples arrived, and they
were amazed that He was talking with a
woman. Yet no one said, "What do You want?"
or "Why are You talking with her?"
28 Then the woman left her water jar, went
into town, and told the men, 29 "Come, see a
man who told me everything I ever did! Could
this be the Messiah?" 30 They left the town and
made their way to Him.
31 In the meantime the disciples kept urging
Him, "•Rabbi, eat something."
32 But He said, "I have food to eat that you
don't know about."
33 The disciples said to one another, "Could
someone have brought Him something to eat?"
34 "My food is to do the will of Him who
sent Me and to finish His work," Jesus told
them. 35 "Don't you say, 'There are still four
more months, then comes the harvest'? Listen
⌊to what⌋ I'm telling you: Open[h] your eyes and
look at the fields, for they are ready[i] for harvest.
36 The reaper is already receiving pay and gathering
fruit for eternal life, so the sower and
reaper can rejoice together. 37 For in this case
the saying is true: 'One sows and another
reaps.' 38 I sent you to reap what you didn't
labor for; others have labored, and you have
benefited from[j] their labor."

The Savior of the World

39 Now many Samaritans from that town
believed in Him because of what the woman
said[k] when she testified, "He told me everything
I ever did." 40 Therefore, when the
Samaritans came to Him, they asked Him to
stay with them, and He stayed there two days.
41 Many more believed because of what He
said.[l] 42 And they told the woman, "We no
longer believe because of what you said, for

[a]**4:6** Lit *the sixth hour*; see note at Jn 1:39; an alternate time reckoning would be *noon* [b]**4:9** Or *do not share vessels with* [c]**4:9** Other mss omit *For Jews do not associate with Samaritans.* [d]**4:14** Or *spring* [e]**4:20** Mount Gerizim, where there had been a Samaritan temple that rivaled Jerusalem's [f]**4:22** *Samaritans* is implied since the Gk verb and pronoun are pl. [g]**4:25** In the NT, the word Messiah translates the Gk word *Christos* ("Anointed One"), except here and in Jn 1:41 where it translates *Messias.* [h]**4:35** Lit *Raise* [i]**4:35** Lit *white* [j]**4:38** Lit *you have entered into* [k]**4:39** Lit *because of the woman's word* [l]**4:41** Lit *because of His word*

we have heard for ourselves and know that
this really is the Savior of the world."[a]

A Galilean Welcome

43 After two days He left there for Galilee.
44 Jesus Himself testified that a prophet has no
honor in his own country. 45 When they
entered Galilee, the Galileans welcomed Him
because they had seen everything He did in
Jerusalem during the festival. For they also had
gone to the festival.

The Second Sign: Healing an Official's Son

46 Then He went again to Cana of Galilee,
where He had turned the water into wine.
There was a certain royal official whose son
was ill at Capernaum. 47 When this man
heard that Jesus had come from Judea into
Galilee, he went to Him and pleaded with
Him to come down and heal his son, for he
was about to die.
48 Jesus told him, "Unless you ⌊people⌋ see
signs and wonders, you will not believe."
49 "Sir," the official said to Him, "come
down before my boy dies!"
50 "Go," Jesus told him, "your son will
live." The man believed what[b] Jesus said to him
and departed.
51 While he was still going down, his
•slaves met him saying that his boy was
alive. 52 He asked them at what time he got
better. "Yesterday at seven in the morning[c]
the fever left him," they answered. 53 The
father realized this was the very hour at
which Jesus had told him, "Your son will
live." Then he himself believed, along with
his whole household.
54 This therefore was the second sign Jesus
performed after He came from Judea to Galilee.

The Third Sign: Healing the Sick

5 After this, a Jewish festival took place,
and Jesus went up to Jerusalem. 2 By the
Sheep Gate in Jerusalem there is a pool, called
Bethesda[d] in Hebrew, which has five colon-
nades.[e] 3 Within these lay a multitude of the
sick—blind, lame, and paralyzed [—waiting
for the moving of the water, 4 because an angel
would go down into the pool from time to time
and stir up the water. Then the first one who
got in after the water was stirred up recovered
from whatever ailment he had].[f]
5 One man was there who had been sick
for 38 years. 6 When Jesus saw him lying
there and knew he had already been there a
long time, He said to him, "Do you want to
get well?"
7 "Sir," the sick man answered, "I don't
have a man to put me into the pool when the
water is stirred up, but while I'm coming,
someone goes down ahead of me."
8 "Get up," Jesus told him, "pick up your
bedroll and walk!" 9 Instantly the man got
well, picked up his bedroll, and started to
walk.
Now that day was the Sabbath, 10 so the
•Jews said to the man who had been healed,
"This is the Sabbath! It's illegal for you to pick
up your bedroll."
11 He replied, "The man who made me well
told me, 'Pick up your bedroll and walk.' "
12 "Who is this man who told you, 'Pick up
⌊your bedroll⌋ and walk?' " they asked. 13 But
the man who was cured did not know who it
was, because Jesus had slipped away into the
crowd that was there.[g]
14 After this, Jesus found him in the •tem-
ple complex and said to him, "See, you are
well. Do not sin any more, so that something
worse doesn't happen to you." 15 The man
went and reported to the Jews that it was Jesus
who had made him well.

Honoring the Father and the Son

16 Therefore, the Jews began persecuting
Jesus[h] because He was doing these things on
the Sabbath. 17 But Jesus responded to them,
"My Father is still working, and I am working
also." 18 This is why the Jews began trying all
the more to kill Him: not only was He breaking the Sabbath, but He was even calling God
His own Father, making Himself equal with
God.
19 Then Jesus replied, "•I assure you: The
Son is not able to do anything on His own, but
only what He sees the Father doing. For whatever the Father[i] does, the Son also does these
things in the same way. 20 For the Father loves
the Son and shows Him everything He is doing,
and He will show Him greater works than these
so that you will be amazed. 21 And just as the

[a] **4:42** Other mss add *the Messiah* [b] **4:50** Lit *the word* [c] **4:52** Or *seven in the evening*; lit *at the seventh hour*; see note at Jn 1:39; an alternate time reckoning would be *at one in the afternoon* [d] **5:2** Other mss read *Bethzatha*; other mss read *Bethsaida* [e] **5:2** Rows of columns supporting a roof [f] **5:3–4** Other mss omit bracketed text [g] **5:13** Lit *slipped away, there being a crowd in that place* [h] **5:16** Other mss add *and trying to kill Him* [i] **5:19** Lit *whatever that One*

Father raises the dead and gives them life, so
the Son also gives life to anyone He wants to.
22 The Father, in fact, judges no one but has
given all judgment to the Son, 23 so that all people will honor the Son just as they honor the
Father. Anyone who does not honor the Son
does not honor the Father who sent Him.

Life and Judgment

24 "I assure you: Anyone who hears My
word and believes Him who sent Me has eternal life and will not come under judgment but
has passed from death to life.

25 "I assure you: An hour is coming, and is
now here, when the dead will hear the voice
of the Son of God, and those who hear will
live. 26 For just as the Father has life in Himself, so also He has granted to the Son to have
life in Himself. 27 And He has granted Him the
right to pass judgment, because He is the •Son
of Man. 28 Do not be amazed at this, because
a time is coming when all who are in the
graves will hear His voice 29 and come out—
those who have done good things, to the resurrection of life, but those who have done
wicked things, to the resurrection of judgment.

30 "I can do nothing on My own. I judge
only as I hear, and My judgment is righteous,
because I do not seek My own will, but the will
of Him who sent Me.

Four Witnesses to Jesus

31 "If I testify about Myself, My testimony
is not valid.[a] 32 There is Another who testifies
about Me, and I know that the testimony He
gives about Me is valid.[b] 33 You have sent
⌊messengers⌋ to John, and he has testified to
the truth. 34 I don't receive man's testimony,
but I say these things so that you may be
saved. 35 John[c] was a burning and shining
lamp, and for a time you were willing to enjoy
his light.

36 "But I have a greater testimony than
John's because of the works that the Father has
given Me to accomplish. These very works I am
doing testify about Me that the Father has sent
Me. 37 The Father who sent Me has Himself
testified about Me. You have not heard His
voice at any time, and you haven't seen His
form. 38 You don't have His word living in you,
because you don't believe the One He sent.
39 You pore over[d] the Scriptures because you
think you have eternal life in them, yet they testify about Me. 40 And you are not willing to
come to Me that you may have life.

41 "I do not accept glory from men, 42 but
I know you—that you have no love for God
within you. 43 I have come in My Father's
name, yet you don't accept Me. If someone
else comes in his own name, you will accept
him. 44 How can you believe? While accepting glory from one another, you don't seek
the glory that comes from the only God.
45 Do not think that I will accuse you to the
Father. Your accuser is Moses, on whom you
have set your hope. 46 For if you believed
Moses, you would believe Me, because he
wrote about Me. 47 But if you don't believe
his writings, how will you believe My
words?"

The Fourth Sign: Feeding 5,000

6 After this, Jesus crossed the Sea of Galilee (or Tiberias). 2 And a huge crowd
was following Him because they saw the signs
that He was performing on the sick. 3 So Jesus
went up a mountain and sat down there with
His disciples.

4 Now the •Passover, a Jewish festival, was
near. 5 Therefore, when Jesus looked up and
noticed a huge crowd coming toward Him, He
asked Philip, "Where will we buy bread so
these people can eat?" 6 He asked this to test
him, for He Himself knew what He was going
to do.

7 Philip answered, "Two hundred •denarii
worth of bread wouldn't be enough for each of
them to have a little."

8 One of His disciples, Andrew, Simon
Peter's brother, said to Him, 9 "There's a boy
here who has five barley loaves and two fish—
but what are they for so many?"

10 Then Jesus said, "Have the people sit
down."

There was plenty of grass in that place, so
they sat down. The men numbered about
5,000. 11 Then Jesus took the loaves, and after
giving thanks He distributed them to those who
were seated—so also with the fish, as much as
they wanted.

12 When they were full, He told His disciples, "Collect the leftovers so that nothing is
wasted." 13 So they collected them and filled
12 baskets with the pieces from the five barley
loaves that were left over by those who had
eaten.

[a]**5:31** Or *not true* [b]**5:32** Or *true* [c]**5:35** Lit *That man* [d]**5:39** In Gk this could be a command: *Pore over . . .*

14 When the people saw the sign[a] He had
done, they said, "This really is the Prophet
who was to come into the world!"
15 Therefore, when Jesus knew that they were
about to come and take Him by force to make
Him king, He withdrew again[b] to the mountain by Himself.

The Fifth Sign: Walking on Water

16 When evening came, His disciples went
down to the sea, 17 got into a boat, and started
across the sea to Capernaum. Darkness had
already set in, but Jesus had not yet come to
them. 18 Then a high wind arose, and the sea
began to churn. 19 After they had rowed about
three or four miles,[c] they saw Jesus walking on
the sea. He was coming near the boat, and they
were afraid.
20 But He said to them, "It is I.[d] Don't be
afraid!" 21 Then they were willing to take Him
on board, and at once the boat was at the shore
where they were heading.

The Bread of Life

22 The next day, the crowd that had stayed
on the other side of the sea knew there had
been only one boat.[e] ⌊They also knew⌋ that
Jesus had not boarded the boat with His disciples, but that His disciples had gone off alone.
23 Some boats from Tiberias came near the
place where they ate the bread after the Lord
gave thanks. 24 When the crowd saw that neither Jesus nor His disciples were there, they got
into the boats and went to Capernaum looking
for Jesus.
25 When they found Him on the other side
of the sea, they said to Him, "•Rabbi, when did
You get here?"
26 Jesus answered, "•I assure you: You are
looking for Me, not because you saw the signs,
but because you ate the loaves and were filled.
27 Don't work for the food that perishes but for
the food that lasts for eternal life, which the
•Son of Man will give you, because God the
Father has set His seal of approval on Him."
28 "What can we do to perform the works of
God?" they asked.
29 Jesus replied, "This is the work of God:
that you believe in the One He has sent."
30 "What sign then are You going to do so
we may see and believe You?" they asked.
"What are You going to perform? 31 Our fathers
ate the manna in the wilderness, just as it is
written: **He gave them bread from heaven to
eat.**"[f g]
32 Jesus said to them, "I assure you: Moses
didn't give you the bread from heaven, but My
Father gives you the real bread from heaven.
33 For the bread of God is the One who comes
down from heaven and gives life to the world."
34 Then they said, "Sir, give us this bread
always!"
35 "I am the bread of life," Jesus told them.
"No one who comes to Me will ever be hungry, and no one who believes in Me will ever
be thirsty again. 36 But as I told you, you've
seen Me,[h] and yet you do not believe.
37 Everyone the Father gives Me will come to
Me, and the one who comes to Me I will never
cast out. 38 For I have come down from
heaven, not to do My will, but the will of Him
who sent Me. 39 This is the will of Him who
sent Me: that I should lose none of those He
has given Me but should raise them up on the
last day. 40 For this is the will of My Father:
that everyone who sees the Son and believes
in Him may have eternal life, and I will raise
him up on the last day."
41 Therefore the Jews started complaining
about Him, because He said, "I am the bread
that came down from heaven." 42 They were
saying, "Isn't this Jesus the son of Joseph,
whose father and mother we know? How can
He now say, 'I have come down from
heaven'?"
43 Jesus answered them, "Stop complaining among yourselves. 44 No one can come to
Me unless the Father who sent Me draws[i]
him, and I will raise him up on the last day.
45 It is written in the Prophets: **And they will
all be taught by God.**[j] Everyone who has listened to and learned from the Father comes to
Me— 46 not that anyone has seen the Father
except the One who is from God. He has seen
the Father.
47 "I assure you: Anyone who believes[k] has
eternal life. 48 I am the bread of life. 49 Your
fathers ate the manna in the wilderness, and
they died. 50 This is the bread that comes down
from heaven so that anyone may eat of it and
not die. 51 I am the living bread that came
down from heaven. If anyone eats of this bread

[a]**6:14** Other mss read *signs* [b]**6:15** A previous withdrawal is mentioned in Mk 6:31–32, an event that occurred just before the feeding of the 5,000. [c]**6:19** Lit *25 or 30 stadia*; 1 *stadion* = 600 feet [d]**6:20** Lit *I am* [e]**6:22** Other mss add *into which His disciples had entered* [f]**6:31** Bread miraculously provided by God for the Israelites [g]**6:31** Ex 16:4; Ps 78:24 [h]**6:36** Other mss omit *Me* [i]**6:44** Or *brings*, or *leads*; see the use of this Gk verb in Jn 12:32; 21:6; Ac 16:19; Jms 2:6. [j]**6:45** Is 54:13 [k]**6:47** Other mss add *in Me*

he will live forever. The bread that I will give
for the life of the world is My flesh."
52 At that, the Jews argued among themselves, "How can this man give us His flesh to
eat?"
53 So Jesus said to them, "I assure you:
Unless you eat the flesh of the Son of Man
and drink His blood, you do not have life in
yourselves. 54 Anyone who eats My flesh
and drinks My blood has eternal life, and I
will raise him up on the last day, 55 because
My flesh is real food and My blood is real
drink. 56 The one who eats My flesh and
drinks My blood lives in Me, and I in him.
57 Just as the living Father sent Me and I live
because of the Father, so the one who feeds
on Me will live because of Me. 58 This is the
bread that came down from heaven; it is not
like the manna[a] your fathers ate—and they
died. The one who eats this bread will live
forever."
59 He said these things while teaching in
the •synagogue in Capernaum.

Many Disciples Desert Jesus

60 Therefore, when many of His disciples
heard this, they said, "This teaching is hard!
Who can accept[b] it?"
61 Jesus, knowing in Himself that His disciples were complaining about this, asked them,
"Does this offend you? 62 Then what if you
were to observe the Son of Man ascending to
where He was before? 63 The Spirit is the One
who gives life. The flesh doesn't help at all. The
words that I have spoken to you are spirit and
are life. 64 But there are some among you who
don't believe." (For Jesus knew from the beginning those who would not[c] believe and the one
who would betray Him.) 65 He said, "This is
why I told you that no one can come to Me
unless it is granted to him by the Father."
66 From that moment many of His disciples
turned back and no longer accompanied Him.
67 Therefore Jesus said to the Twelve, "You
don't want to go away too, do you?"
68 Simon Peter answered, "Lord, who will
we go to? You have the words of eternal life.
69 We have come to believe and know that You
are the Holy One of God!"[d]
70 Jesus replied to them, "Didn't I choose
you, the Twelve? Yet one of you is the Devil!"
71 He was referring to Judas, Simon Iscariot's
son,[e f] one of the Twelve, because he was going
to betray Him.

The Unbelief of Jesus' Brothers

7 After this, Jesus traveled in Galilee, since
He did not want to travel in Judea
because the •Jews were trying to kill Him.
2 The Jewish Festival of Tabernacles[g h] was
near, 3 so His brothers said to Him, "Leave
here and go to Judea so Your disciples can see
Your works that You are doing. 4 For no one
does anything in secret while he's seeking public recognition. If You do these things, show
Yourself to the world." 5 (For not even His
brothers believed in Him.)
6 Jesus told them, "My time has not yet
arrived, but your time is always at hand. 7 The
world cannot hate you, but it does hate Me
because I testify about it—that its deeds are
evil. 8 Go up to the festival yourselves. I'm not
going up to the festival yet,[i] because My time
has not yet fully come." 9 After He had said
these things, He stayed in Galilee.

Jesus at the Festival of Tabernacles

10 After His brothers had gone up to the festival, then He also went up, not openly but
secretly. 11 The Jews were looking for Him at
the festival and saying, "Where is He?" 12 And
there was a lot of discussion about Him among
the crowds. Some were saying, "He's a good
man." Others were saying, "No, on the contrary, He's deceiving the people." 13 Still,
nobody was talking publicly about Him because
they feared the Jews.
14 When the festival was already half over,
Jesus went up into the •temple complex and
began to teach. 15 Then the Jews were amazed
and said, "How does He know the Scriptures,
since He hasn't been trained?"
16 Jesus answered them, "My teaching isn't
Mine but is from the One who sent Me. 17 If
anyone wants to do His will, he will understand
whether the teaching is from God or if I am
speaking on My own. 18 The one who speaks for
himself seeks his own glory. But He who seeks
the glory of the One who sent Him is true, and
there is no unrighteousness in Him. 19 Didn't
Moses give you the law? Yet none of you keeps
the law! Why do you want to kill Me?"
20 "You have a demon!" the crowd
responded. "Who wants to kill You?"

[a] **6:58** Other mss omit *the manna* [b] **6:60** Lit *hear* [c] **6:64** Other mss omit *not* [d] **6:69** Other mss read *You are the Messiah, the Son of the Living God* [e] **6:71** Other mss read *Judas Iscariot, Simon's son* [f] **6:71** Lit *Judas, of Simon Iscariot* [g] **7:2** Or *Booths* [h] **7:2** One of 3 great Jewish religious festivals, along with Passover and Pentecost; Ex 23:14; Dt 16:16 [i] **7:8** Other mss omit *yet*

21 "I did one work, and you are all amazed,"
Jesus answered. 22 "Consider this: Moses has
given you circumcision—not that it comes
from Moses but from the fathers—and you circumcise a man on the Sabbath. 23 If a man
receives circumcision on the Sabbath so that
the law of Moses won't be broken, are you
angry at Me because I made a man entirely well
on the Sabbath? 24 Stop judging according to
outward appearances; rather judge according to
righteous judgment."

The Identity of the Messiah

25 Some of the people of Jerusalem were
saying, "Isn't this the man they want to kill?
26 Yet, look! He's speaking publicly and they're
saying nothing to Him. Can it be true that the
authorities know He is the •Messiah? 27 But
we know where this man is from. When the
Messiah comes, nobody will know where He is
from."
28 As He was teaching in the temple complex, Jesus cried out, "You know Me and you
know where I am from. Yet I have not come on
My own, but the One who sent Me is true. You
don't know Him; 29 I know Him because I am
from Him, and He sent Me."
30 Then they tried to seize Him. Yet no one
laid a hand on Him because His hour[a] had not
yet come. 31 However, many from the crowd
believed in Him and said, "When the Messiah
comes, He won't perform more signs than this
man has done, will He?"
32 The •Pharisees heard the crowd mutter-
ing these things about Him, so the •chief
priests and the Pharisees sent temple police to
arrest Him.
33 Then Jesus said, "I am only with you for a
short time. Then I'm going to the One who sent
Me. 34 You will look for Me, but you will not
find Me; and where I am, you cannot come."
35 Then the Jews said to one another,
"Where does He intend to go so we won't find
Him? He doesn't intend to go to the Dispersion[b] among the Greeks and teach the Greeks,
does He? 36 What is this remark He made: 'You
will look for Me, and you will not find Me; and
where I am, you cannot come'?"

The Promise of the Spirit

37 On the last and most important day of the
festival, Jesus stood up and cried out, "If anyone
is thirsty, he should come to Me[c] and drink!
38 The one who believes in Me, as the Scripture has said,[d] will have streams of living water
flow from deep within him." 39 He said this
about the Spirit, whom those who believed in
Him were going to receive, for the Spirit[e] had
not yet been received,[f g] because Jesus had not
yet been glorified.

The People Are Divided over Jesus

40 When some from the crowd heard these
words, they said, "This really is the Prophet!"[h]
41 Others said, "This is the Messiah!" But some
said, "Surely the Messiah doesn't come from
Galilee, does He? 42 Doesn't the Scripture say
that the Messiah comes from David's offspring[i]
and from the town of Bethlehem, where David
once lived?" 43 So a division occurred among
the crowd because of Him. 44 Some of them
wanted to seize Him, but no one laid hands on
Him.

Debate over Jesus' Claims

45 Then the temple police came to the chief
priests and Pharisees, who asked them, "Why
haven't you brought Him?"
46 The police answered, "No man ever
spoke like this!"[j]
47 Then the Pharisees responded to them:
"Are you fooled too? 48 Have any of the rulers
believed in Him? Or any of the Pharisees?
49 But this crowd, which doesn't know the law,
is accursed!"
50 Nicodemus—the one who came to Him
previously, being one of them—said to them,
51 "Our law doesn't judge a man before it hears
from him and knows what he's doing, does it?"
52 "You aren't from Galilee too, are you?"
they replied. "Investigate and you will see that
no prophet arises from Galilee."[k]
8 [53 So each one went to his house. 1 But
Jesus went to the •Mount of Olives.

An Adulteress Forgiven

2 At dawn He went to the •temple complex
again, and all the people were coming to Him.
He sat down and began to teach them.
3 Then the •scribes and the •Pharisees
brought a woman caught in adultery, making
her stand in the center. 4 "Teacher," they said

[a] **7:30** The time of His sacrificial death and exaltation; Jn 2:4; 8:20; 12:23,27; 13:1; 17:1 [b] **7:35** Jewish people scattered throughout Gentile lands who spoke Gk and were influenced by Gk culture [c] **7:37** Other mss omit *to Me* [d] **7:38** Jesus may have had several OT passages in mind; Is 58:11; Ezk 47:1–12; Zch 14:8 [e] **7:39** Other mss read *Holy Spirit* [f] **7:39** Other mss read *had not yet been given* [g] **7:39** Lit *the Spirit was not yet*; the word *received* is implied from the previous clause. [h] **7:40** Probably = the Prophet in Dt 18:15 [i] **7:42** Lit *seed* [j] **7:46** Other mss read *like this man* [k] **7:52** Jonah and probably other prophets did come from Galilee; 2 Kg 14:25

to Him, "this woman was caught in the act of
committing adultery. 5 In the law Moses commanded us to stone such women. So what do
You say?" 6 They asked this to trap Him, in
order that they might have evidence to accuse
Him.
Jesus stooped down and started writing on
the ground with His finger. 7 When they per-
sisted in questioning Him, He stood up and said
to them, "The one without sin among you
should be the first to throw a stone at her."
8 Then He stooped down again and continued writing on the ground. 9 When they heard
this, they left one by one, starting with the
older men. Only He was left, with the woman
in the center. 10 When Jesus stood up, He said
to her, "•Woman, where are they? Has no one
condemned you?"
11 "No one, Lord,"[a] she answered.
"Neither do I condemn you," said Jesus.
"Go, and from now on do not sin any more."][b]

The Light of the World

12 Then Jesus spoke to them again: "I am
the light of the world. Anyone who follows Me
will never walk in the darkness but will have
the light of life."
13 So the Pharisees said to Him, "You are
testifying about Yourself. Your testimony is not
valid."[c]
14 "Even if I testify about Myself," Jesus
replied, "My testimony is valid,[d] because I
know where I came from and where I'm going.
But you don't know where I come from or
where I'm going. 15 You judge by human stan-
dards.[e] I judge no one. 16 And if I do judge, My
judgment is true, because I am not alone, but I
and the Father who sent Me ⌊judge together⌋.
17 Even in your law it is written that the witness of two men is valid. 18 I am the One who
testifies about Myself, and the Father who sent
Me testifies about Me."
19 Then they asked Him, "Where is Your
Father?"
"You know neither Me nor My Father,"
Jesus answered. "If you knew Me, you would
also know My Father." 20 He spoke these
words by the treasury,[f] while teaching in the
temple complex. But no one seized Him,
because His hour[g] had not come.

Jesus Predicts His Departure

21 Then He said to them again, "I'm going
away; you will look for Me, and you will die in
your sin. Where I'm going, you cannot come."
22 So the Jews said again, "He won't kill
Himself, will He, since He says, 'Where I'm
going, you cannot come'?"
23 "You are from below," He told them, "I
am from above. You are of this world; I am not
of this world. 24 Therefore I told you that you
will die in your sins. For if you do not believe
that I am ⌊He⌋,[h] you will die in your sins."
25 "Who are You?" they questioned.
"Precisely what I've been telling you from
the very beginning," Jesus told them. 26 "I
have many things to say and to judge about
you, but the One who sent Me is true, and
what I have heard from Him—these things I
tell the world."
27 They did not know He was speaking to
them about the Father. 28 So Jesus said to
them, "When you lift up the •Son of Man,
then you will know that I am ⌊He⌋, and that I
do nothing on My own. But just as the Father
taught Me, I say these things. 29 The One
who sent Me is with Me. He has not left Me
alone, because I always do what pleases
Him."

Truth and Freedom

30 As He was saying these things, many
believed in Him. 31 So Jesus said to the Jews
who had believed Him, "If you continue in My
word,[i] you really are My disciples. 32 You will
know the truth, and the truth will set you free."
33 "We are descendants[j] of Abraham," they
answered Him, "and we have never been
enslaved to anyone. How can You say, 'You will
become free'?"
34 Jesus responded, "•I assure you: Everyone who commits sin is a slave of sin. 35 A slave
does not remain in the household forever, but
a son does remain forever. 36 Therefore if the
Son sets you free, you really will be free. 37 I
know you are descendants[j] of Abraham, but
you are trying to kill Me because My word[i] is
not welcome among you. 38 I speak what I have
seen in the presence of the Father,[k] and therefore you do what you have heard from your
father."

[a]**8:11** Or *Sir*; Jn 4:15,49; 5:7; 6:34; 9:36 [b]**8:11** Other mss omit bracketed text [c]**8:13** The law of Moses required at least 2 witnesses to make a claim legally valid (v. 17). [d]**8:14** Or *true* [e]**8:15** Lit *You judge according to the flesh* [f]**8:20** A place for offerings to be given, perhaps in the court of women [g]**8:20** The time of His sacrificial death and exaltation; Jn 2:4; 7:30; 12:23,27; 13:1; 17:1 [h]**8:24** Jesus claimed to be deity, but the Pharisees didn't understand His meaning. [i]**8:31,37** Or *My teaching*, or *My message* [j]**8:33,37** Or *offspring*; lit *seed*; Jn 7:42 [k]**8:38** Other mss read *of My Father*

39 "Our father is Abraham!" they replied.
"If you were Abraham's children," Jesus
told them, "you would do what Abraham did.
40 But now you are trying to kill Me, a man who
has told you the truth that I heard from God.
Abraham did not do this! 41 You're doing what
your father does."
"We weren't born of sexual immorality,"
they said. "We have one Father—God."
42 Jesus said to them, "If God were your
Father, you would love Me, because I came
from God and I am here. For I didn't come on
My own, but He sent Me. 43 Why don't you
understand what I say? Because you cannot listen to[a] My word. 44 You are of your father the
Devil, and you want to carry out your father's
desires. He was a murderer from the beginning
and has not stood in the truth, because there is
no truth in him. When he tells a lie, he speaks
from his own nature,[b] because he is a liar and
the father of liars.[c] 45 Yet because I tell the
truth, you do not believe Me. 46 Who among
you can convict Me of sin? If I tell the truth,
why don't you believe Me? 47 The one who is
from God listens to God's words. This is why
you don't listen, because you are not from
God."

Jesus and Abraham

48 The Jews responded to Him, "Aren't we
right in saying that You're a •Samaritan and
have a demon?"
49 "I do not have a demon," Jesus
answered. "On the contrary, I honor My Father
and you dishonor Me. 50 I do not seek My
glory; the One who seeks it also judges. 51 I
assure you: If anyone keeps My word, he will
never see death—ever!"
52 Then the Jews said, "Now we know You
have a demon. Abraham died and so did the
prophets. You say, 'If anyone keeps My word,
he will never taste death—ever!' 53 Are You
greater than our father Abraham who died?
Even the prophets died. Who do You pretend to
be?"[d]
54 "If I glorify Myself," Jesus answered, "My
glory is nothing. My Father—you say about
Him, 'He is our God'—He is the One who glo-
rifies Me. 55 You've never known Him, but I
know Him. If I were to say I don't know Him, I
would be a liar like you. But I do know Him,
and I keep His word. 56 Your father Abraham
was overjoyed that he would see My day; he
saw it and rejoiced."
57 The Jews replied, "You aren't 50 years
old yet, and You've seen Abraham?"[e]
58 Jesus said to them, "I assure you: Before
Abraham was, I am."[f]
59 At that, they picked up stones to throw at
Him. But Jesus was hidden[g] and went out of
the temple complex.[h]

The Sixth Sign: Healing a Man Born Blind

9 As He was passing by, He saw a man
blind from birth. 2 His disciples questioned Him: "•Rabbi, who sinned, this man or
his parents, that he was born blind?"
3 "Neither this man nor his parents
sinned," Jesus answered. "⌊This came about⌋ so
that God's works might be displayed in him.
4 We[i] must do the works of Him who sent Me[j]
while it is day. Night is coming when no one
can work. 5 As long as I am in the world, I am
the light of the world."
6 After He said these things He spit on the
ground, made some mud from the saliva, and
spread the mud on his eyes. 7 "Go," He told
him, "wash in the pool of Siloam" (which
means "Sent"). So he left, washed, and came
back seeing.
8 His neighbors and those who formerly had
seen him as a beggar said, "Isn't this the man
who sat begging?" 9 Some said, "He's the one."
"No," others were saying, "but he looks like
him."
He kept saying, "I'm the one!"
10 Therefore they asked him, "Then how
were your eyes opened?"
11 He answered, "The man called Jesus
made mud, spread it on my eyes, and told me,
'Go to Siloam and wash.' So when I went and
washed I received my sight."
12 "Where is He?" they asked.
"I don't know," he said.

The Healed Man's Testimony

13 They brought the man who used to be
blind to the •Pharisees. 14 The day that Jesus
made the mud and opened his eyes was a Sabbath. 15 So again the Pharisees asked him how
he received his sight.

[a]**8:43** Or *cannot hear* [b]**8:44** Lit *from his own things* [c]**8:44** Lit *of it* [d]**8:53** Lit *Who do You make Yourself?* [e]**8:57** Other mss read *and Abraham has seen You?* [f]**8:58** *I AM* is the name God gave Himself at the burning bush; Ex 3:13–14; see note at Jn 8:24. [g]**8:59** Or *Jesus hid Himself* [h]**8:59** Other mss add *and having gone through their midst, He passed by* [i]**9:4** Other mss read *I* [j]**9:4** Other mss read *sent us*

"He put mud on my eyes," he told them. "I
washed and I can see."
16 Therefore some of the Pharisees said,
"This man is not from God, for He doesn't keep
the Sabbath!" But others were saying, "How
can a sinful man perform such signs?" And
there was a division among them.
17 Again they asked the blind man,[a] "What
do you say about Him, since He opened your
eyes?"
"He's a prophet," he said.
18 The Jews did not believe this about
him—that he was blind and received sight—
until they summoned the parents of the one
who had received his sight.
19 They asked them, "Is this your son, ⌊the
one⌋ you say was born blind? How then does he
now see?"
20 "We know this is our son and that he was
born blind," his parents answered. 21 "But we
don't know how he now sees, and we don't
know who opened his eyes. Ask him; he's of
age. He will speak for himself." 22 His parents
said these things because they were afraid of
the Jews, since the Jews had already agreed that
if anyone confessed Him as •Messiah, he would
be banned from the •synagogue. 23 This is why
his parents said, "He's of age; ask him."
24 So a second time they summoned the
man who had been blind and told him, "Give
glory to God.[b] We know that this man is a sinner!"
25 He answered, "Whether or not He's a
sinner, I don't know. One thing I do know: I
was blind, and now I can see!"
26 Then they asked him, "What did He do to
you? How did He open your eyes?"
27 "I already told you," he said, "and you
didn't listen. Why do you want to hear it again?
You don't want to become His disciples too, do
you?"
28 They ridiculed him: "You're that man's
disciple, but we're Moses' disciples. 29 We
know that God has spoken to Moses. But this
man—we don't know where He's from!"
30 "This is an amazing thing," the man told
them. "You don't know where He is from, yet
He opened my eyes! 31 We know that God
doesn't listen to sinners, but if anyone is God-
fearing and does His will, He listens to him.
32 Throughout history[c] no one has ever heard
of someone opening the eyes of a person born
blind. 33 If this man were not from God, He
wouldn't be able to do anything."
34 "You were born entirely in sin," they
replied, "and are you trying to teach us?" Then
they threw him out.[d]

The Blind Man's Sight and the Pharisees' Blindness

35 When Jesus heard that they had thrown
the man out, He found him and asked, "Do you
believe in the •Son of Man?"[e]
36 "Who is He, Sir, that I may believe in
Him?" he asked.
37 Jesus answered, "You have seen Him; in
fact, He is the One speaking with you."
38 "I believe, Lord!" he said, and he worshiped Him.
39 Jesus said, "I came into this world for
judgment, in order that those who do not see
will see and those who do see will become
blind."
40 Some of the Pharisees who were with
Him heard these things and asked Him, "We
aren't blind too, are we?"
41 "If you were blind," Jesus told them,
"you wouldn't have sin.[f] But now that you say,
'We see'—your sin remains.

The Ideal Shepherd

10 "•I assure you: Anyone who doesn't
enter the sheep pen by the door but
climbs in some other way, is a thief and a
robber. 2 The one who enters by the door is
the shepherd of the sheep. 3 The doorkeeper
opens it for him, and the sheep hear his
voice. He calls his own sheep by name and
leads them out. 4 When he has brought all
his own outside, he goes ahead of them. The
sheep follow him because they recognize his
voice. 5 They will never follow a stranger;
instead they will run away from him,
because they don't recognize the voice of
strangers."
6 Jesus gave them this illustration, but they
did not understand what He was telling them.

The Good Shepherd

7 So Jesus said again, "I assure you: I am the
door of the sheep. 8 All who came before Me[g]
are thieves and robbers, but the sheep didn't
listen to them. 9 I am the door. If anyone enters
by Me, he will be saved and will come in and

[a]**9:17** = the man who had been blind [b]**9:24** *Give glory to God* was a solemn charge to tell the truth; Jos 7:19. [c]**9:32** Lit *From the age* [d]**9:34** = they banned him from the synagogue; v. 22 [e]**9:35** Other mss read *the Son of God* [f]**9:41** To *have sin* is an idiom that refers to guilt caused by sin. [g]**10:8** Other mss omit *before Me*

go out and find pasture. 10 A thief comes only
to steal and to kill and to destroy. I have come
that they may have life and have it in abundance.
11 "I am the good shepherd. The good shepherd lays down his life for the sheep. 12 The
hired man, since he is not the shepherd and
doesn't own the sheep, leaves them[a] and runs
away when he sees a wolf coming. The wolf
then snatches and scatters them. 13 ⌊This hap-
pens⌋ because he is a hired man and doesn't
care about the sheep.
14 "I am the good shepherd. I know My
own sheep, and they know Me, 15 as the Father
knows Me, and I know the Father. I lay down
My life for the sheep. 16 But I have other sheep
that are not of this fold; I must bring them also,
and they will listen to My voice. Then there
will be one flock, one shepherd. 17 This is why
the Father loves Me, because I am laying down
My life so I may take it up again. 18 No one
takes it from Me, but I lay it down on My own.
I have the right to lay it down, and I have the
right to take it up again. I have received this
command from My Father."
19 Again a division took place among the
Jews because of these words. 20 Many of them
were saying, "He has a demon and He's crazy!
Why do you listen to Him?" 21 Others were
saying, "These aren't the words of someone
demon-possessed. Can a demon open the eyes
of the blind?"

Jesus at the Festival of Dedication

22 Then the Festival of Dedication[b] took
place in Jerusalem, and it was winter. 23 Jesus
was walking in the •temple complex in
Solomon's Colonnade.[c] 24 Then the Jews surrounded Him and asked, "How long are You
going to keep us in suspense?[d] If You are the
•Messiah, tell us plainly."[e]
25 "I did tell you and you don't believe,"
Jesus answered them. "The works that I do in
My Father's name testify about Me. 26 But
you don't believe because you are not My
sheep.[f] 27 My sheep hear My voice, I know
them, and they follow Me. 28 I give them
eternal life, and they will never perish—
ever! No one will snatch them out of My
hand. 29 My Father, who has given them to
Me, is greater than all. No one is able to
snatch them out of the Father's hand. 30 The
Father and I are one."[g]

Renewed Efforts to Stone Jesus

31 Again the Jews picked up rocks to stone
Him.
32 Jesus replied, "I have shown you many
good works from the Father. Which of these
works are you stoning Me for?"
33 "We aren't stoning You for a good work,"
the Jews answered, "but for blasphemy,
because You—being a man—make Yourself
God."
34 Jesus answered them, "Isn't it written
in your law,[h] **I said, you are gods**?[i] 35 If He
called those whom the word of God came to
'gods'—and the Scripture cannot be broken—
36 do you say, 'You are blaspheming' to the
One the Father set apart and sent into the
world, because I said: I am the Son of God?
37 If I am not doing My Father's works, don't
believe Me. 38 But if I am doing them and you
don't believe Me, believe the works. This way
you will know and understand[j] that the Father
is in Me and I in the Father." 39 Then they
were trying again to seize Him, yet He eluded
their grasp.

Many beyond the Jordan Believe in Jesus

40 So He departed again across the Jordan to
the place where John had been baptizing earlier, and He remained there. 41 Many came to
Him and said, "John never did a sign, but everything John said about this man was true."
42 And many believed in Him there.

Lazarus Dies at Bethany

11 Now a man was sick, Lazarus, from
Bethany, the village of Mary and her
sister Martha. 2 Mary was the one who
anointed the Lord with fragrant oil and wiped
His feet with her hair, and it was her brother
Lazarus who was sick. 3 So the sisters sent a
message to Him: "Lord, the one You love is
sick."
4 When Jesus heard it, He said, "This sickness will not end in death but is for the glory of
God, so that the Son of God may be glorified
through it." 5 (Jesus loved Martha, her sister,
and Lazarus.) 6 So when He heard that he was
sick, He stayed two more days in the place

[a]**10:12** Lit *leaves the sheep* [b]**10:22** Or *Hanukkah*, also called *the Feast of Lights*; this festival commemorated the rededication of the temple in 164 B.C. [c]**10:23** Rows of columns supporting a roof [d]**10:24** Lit *How long are you taking away our life?* [e]**10:24** Or *openly*, or *publicly* [f]**10:26** Other mss add *just as I told you* [g]**10:30** Lit *I and the Father—We are one.* [h]**10:34** Other mss read *in the law* [i]**10:34** Ps 82:6 [j]**10:38** Other mss read *know and believe*

where He was. 7 Then after that, He said to the disciples, "Let's go to Judea again."

8 "•Rabbi," the disciples told Him, "just now the Jews tried to stone You, and You're going there again?"

9 "Aren't there 12 hours in a day?" Jesus answered. "If anyone walks during the day, he doesn't stumble, because he sees the light of this world. 10 If anyone walks during the night, he does stumble, because the light is not in him." 11 He said this, and then He told them, "Our friend Lazarus has fallen •asleep, but I'm on My way to wake him up."

12 Then the disciples said to Him, "Lord, if he has fallen asleep, he will get well."

13 Jesus, however, was speaking about his death, but they thought He was speaking about natural sleep. 14 So Jesus then told them plainly, "Lazarus has died. 15 I'm glad for you that I wasn't there so that you may believe. But let's go to him."

16 Then Thomas (called "Twin") said to his fellow disciples, "Let's go so that we may die with Him."

The Resurrection and the Life

17 When Jesus arrived, He found that Lazarus had already been in the tomb four days. 18 Bethany was near Jerusalem (about two miles[a] away). 19 Many of the Jews had come to Martha and Mary to comfort them about their brother. 20 As soon as Martha heard that Jesus was coming, she went to meet Him. But Mary remained seated in the house.

21 Then Martha said to Jesus, "Lord, if You had been here, my brother wouldn't have died. 22 Yet even now I know that whatever You ask from God, God will give You."

23 "Your brother will rise again," Jesus told her.

24 Martha said, "I know that he will rise again in the resurrection at the last day."

25 Jesus said to her, "I am the resurrection and the life. The one who believes in Me, even if he dies, will live. 26 Everyone who lives and believes in Me will never die—ever. Do you believe this?"

27 "Yes, Lord," she told Him, "I believe You are the •Messiah, the Son of God, who was to come into the world."

Jesus Shares the Sorrow of Death

28 Having said this, she went back and called her sister Mary, saying in private, "The Teacher is here and is calling for you."

29 As soon as she heard this, she got up quickly and went to Him. 30 Jesus had not yet come into the village but was still in the place where Martha had met Him. 31 The Jews who were with her in the house consoling her saw that Mary got up quickly and went out. So they followed her, supposing that she was going to the tomb to cry there.

32 When Mary came to where Jesus was and saw Him, she fell at His feet and told Him, "Lord, if You had been here, my brother would not have died!"

33 When Jesus saw her crying, and the Jews who had come with her crying, He was angry[b] in His spirit and deeply moved. 34 "Where have you put him?" He asked.

"Lord," they told Him, "come and see."

35 Jesus wept.

36 So the Jews said, "See how He loved him!" 37 But some of them said, "Couldn't He who opened the blind man's eyes also have kept this man from dying?"

The Seventh Sign: Raising Lazarus from the Dead

38 Then Jesus, angry in Himself again, came to the tomb. It was a cave, and a stone was lying against it. 39 "Remove the stone," Jesus said.

Martha, the dead man's sister, told Him, "Lord, he already stinks. It's been four days."

40 Jesus said to her, "Didn't I tell you that if you believed you would see the glory of God?"

41 So they removed the stone. Then Jesus raised His eyes and said, "Father, I thank You that You heard Me. 42 I know that You always hear Me, but because of the crowd standing here I said this, so they may believe You sent Me." 43 After He said this, He shouted with a loud voice, "Lazarus, come out!" 44 The dead man came out bound hand and foot with linen strips and with his face wrapped in a cloth. Jesus said to them, "Loose him and let him go."

The Plot to Kill Jesus

45 Therefore many of the Jews who came to Mary and saw what He did believed in Him. 46 But some of them went to the •Pharisees and told them what Jesus had done.

47 So the •chief priests and the Pharisees

[a]**11:18** Lit *15 stadia*; 1 *stadion* = 600 feet [b]**11:33** The Gk word is very strong and probably indicates Jesus' anger against sin's tyranny and death.

convened the •Sanhedrin and said, "What are we going to do since this man does many signs? 48 If we let Him continue in this way, everybody will believe in Him! Then the Romans will come and remove both our place[a] and our nation."

49 One of them, Caiaphas, who was high priest that year, said to them, "You know nothing at all! 50 You're not considering that it is to your[b] advantage that one man should die for the people rather than the whole nation perish." 51 He did not say this on his own, but being high priest that year he prophesied that Jesus was going to die for the nation, 52 and not for the nation only, but also to unite the scattered children of God. 53 So from that day on they plotted to kill Him. 54 Therefore Jesus no longer walked openly among the Jews but departed from there to the countryside near the wilderness, to a town called Ephraim. And He stayed there with the disciples.

55 The Jewish •Passover was near, and many went up to Jerusalem from the country to purify[c] themselves before the Passover. 56 They were looking for Jesus and asking one another as they stood in the •temple complex: "What do you think? He won't come to the festival, will He?" 57 The chief priests and the Pharisees had given orders that if anyone knew where He was, he should report it so they could arrest Him.

The Anointing at Bethany

12 Six days before the •Passover, Jesus came to Bethany where Lazarus[d] was, the one Jesus had raised from the dead. 2 So they gave a dinner for Him there; Martha was serving them, and Lazarus was one of those reclining at the table with Him. 3 Then Mary took a pound of fragrant oil—pure and expensive nard—anointed Jesus' feet, and wiped His feet with her hair. So the house was filled with the fragrance of the oil.

4 Then one of His disciples, Judas Iscariot (who was about to betray Him), said, 5 "Why wasn't this fragrant oil sold for 300 •denarii[e] and given to the poor?" 6 He didn't say this because he cared about the poor but because he was a thief. He was in charge of the money-bag and would steal part of what was put in it.

7 Jesus answered, "Leave her alone; she has kept it for the day of My burial. 8 For you always have the poor with you, but you do not always have Me."

The Decision to Kill Lazarus

9 Then a large crowd of the Jews learned He was there. They came not only because of Jesus, but also to see Lazarus the one He had raised from the dead. 10 Therefore the •chief priests decided to also kill Lazarus, 11 because he was the reason many of the Jews were deserting them[f] and believing in Jesus.

The Triumphal Entry

12 The next day, when the large crowd that had come to the festival heard that Jesus was coming to Jerusalem, 13 they took palm branches and went out to meet Him. They kept shouting: "•***Hosanna!*** **Blessed is He who comes in the name of the Lord**[g] —the King of Israel!"

14 Jesus found a young donkey and sat on it, just as it is written: 15 **Fear no more, Daughter Zion; look! your King is coming, sitting on a donkey's colt.**[h]

16 His disciples did not understand these things at first. However, when Jesus was glorified, then they remembered that these things had been written about Him and that they had done these things to Him. 17 Meanwhile the crowd, which had been with Him when He called Lazarus out of the tomb and raised him from the dead, continued to testify.[i] 18 This is also why the crowd met Him, because they heard He had done this sign.

19 Then the •Pharisees said to one another, "You see? You've accomplished nothing. Look—the world has gone after Him!"

Jesus Predicts His Crucifixion

20 Now some Greeks were among those who went up to worship at the festival. 21 So they came to Philip, who was from Bethsaida in Galilee, and requested of him, "Sir, we want to see Jesus."

22 Philip went and told Andrew; then Andrew and Philip went and told Jesus. 23 Jesus replied to them, "The hour has come for the •Son of Man to be glorified.

24 "•I assure you: Unless a grain of wheat falls into the ground and dies, it remains by itself. But if it dies, it produces a large crop.[j]

[a] **11:48** The temple or possibly all of Jerusalem [b] **11:50** Other mss read *to our* [c] **11:55** The law of Moses required God's people to purify or cleanse themselves so they could celebrate the Passover. Jews often came to Jerusalem a week early to do this; Nm 9:4–11. [d] **12:1** Other mss read *Lazarus who died* [e] **12:5** This amount was about a year's wages for a common worker. [f] **12:11** Lit *going away* [g] **12:13** Ps 118:25–26 [h] **12:15** Zch 9:9 [i] **12:17** Other mss read *Meanwhile the crowd, which had been with Him, continued to testify that He had called Lazarus out of the tomb and raised him from the dead.* [j] **12:24** Lit *produces much fruit*

25 The one who loves his life will lose it, and
the one who hates his life in this world will
keep it for eternal life. 26 If anyone serves Me,
he must follow Me. Where I am, there My servant also will be. If anyone serves Me, the
Father will honor him.
27 "Now My soul is troubled. What should I
say—Father, save Me from this hour? But that
is why I came to this hour. 28 Father, glorify
Your name!"[a]

Then a voice came from heaven: "I have glorified it, and I will glorify it again!"
29 The crowd standing there heard it and
said it was thunder. Others said, "An angel has
spoken to Him!"
30 Jesus responded, "This voice came, not
for Me, but for you. 31 Now is the judgment of
this world. Now the ruler of this world will be
cast out. 32 As for Me, if I am lifted up[b] from the
earth I will draw all ⌊people⌋ to Myself." 33 He
said this to signify what kind of death He was
about to die.
34 Then the crowd replied to Him, "We
have heard from the law that the •Messiah will
remain forever. So how can You say, 'The Son
of Man must be lifted up'?[b] Who is this Son of
Man?"
35 Jesus answered, "The light will be with
you only a little longer. Walk while you have
the light so that darkness doesn't overtake you.
The one who walks in darkness doesn't know
where he's going. 36 While you have the light,
believe in the light so that you may become
sons of light." Jesus said this, then went away
and hid from them.

Isaiah's Prophecies Fulfilled

37 Even though He had performed so many
signs in their presence, they did not believe in
Him. 38 But this was to fulfill the word of Isaiah
the prophet, who said:[c]

> **Lord, who has believed**
> **our message?**
> **And who has the arm**
> **of the Lord been**
> **revealed to?**[d]

39 This is why they were unable to believe,
because Isaiah also said:

> 40 **He has blinded their eyes**
> **and hardened**
> **their hearts,**
> **so that they would not see**
> **with their eyes**
> **or understand with their hearts,**
> **and be converted,**
> **and I would heal them.**[e]

41 Isaiah said these things because[f] he saw His
glory and spoke about Him.
42 Nevertheless, many did believe in Him
even among the rulers, but because of the Pharisees they did not confess Him, so they would
not be banned from the •synagogue. 43 For
they loved praise from men more than praise
from God.[g]

A Summary of Jesus' Mission

44 Then Jesus cried out, "The one who
believes in Me believes not in Me, but in Him
who sent Me. 45 And the one who sees Me sees
Him who sent Me. 46 I have come as a light into
the world, so that everyone who believes in Me
would not remain in darkness. 47 If anyone
hears My words and doesn't keep them, I do
not judge him; for I did not come to judge the
world but to save the world. 48 The one who
rejects Me and doesn't accept My sayings has
this as his judge:[h] the word I have spoken will
judge him on the last day. 49 For I have not spoken on My own, but the Father Himself who
sent Me has given Me a command as to what I
should say and what I should speak. 50 I know
that His command is eternal life. So the things
that I speak, I speak just as the Father has told
Me."

Jesus Washes His Disciples' Feet

13 Before the •Passover Festival, Jesus
knew that His hour had come to
depart from this world to the Father. Having
loved His own who were in the world, He
loved them to the end.[i]
2 Now by the time of supper, the Devil had
already put it into the heart of Judas, Simon
Iscariot's son, to betray Him. 3 Jesus knew that
the Father had given everything into His hands,
that He had come from God, and that He was
going back to God. 4 So He got up from supper,
laid aside His robe, took a towel, and tied it
around Himself. 5 Next, He poured water into
a basin and began to wash His disciples' feet
and to dry them with the towel tied around
Him.
6 He came to Simon Peter, who asked Him,

[a] **12:28** Other mss read *Your Son* [b] **12:32,34** Or *exalted* [c] **12:38** Lit *which he said* [d] **12:38** Is 53:1 [e] **12:40** Is 6:10
[f] **12:41** Other mss read *when* [g] **12:43** Lit *loved glory of men more than glory of God*; v. 41; Jn 5:41 [h] **12:48** Lit *has the one judging him* [i] **13:1** *to the end* = *completely* or *always*

"Lord, are You going to wash my feet?"
7 Jesus answered him, "What I'm doing you
don't understand now, but afterwards you will
know."
8 "You will never wash my feet—ever!"
Peter said.
Jesus replied, "If I don't wash you, you have
no part with Me."
9 Simon Peter said to Him, "Lord, not only
my feet, but also my hands and my head."
10 "One who has bathed," Jesus told him,
"doesn't need to wash anything except his feet,
but he is completely clean. You are clean, but
not all of you." 11 For He knew who would
betray Him. This is why He said, "You are not
all clean."

The Meaning of Footwashing

12 When Jesus had washed their feet and
put on His robe, He reclined[a] again and said to
them, "Do you know what I have done for you?
13 You call Me Teacher and Lord. This is well
said, for I am. 14 So if I, your Lord and Teacher,
have washed your feet, you also ought to wash
one another's feet. 15 For I have given you an
example that you also should do just as I have
done for you.
16 "•I assure you: A slave is not greater than
his master,[b] and a messenger is not greater
than the one who sent him. 17 If you know
these things, you are blessed if you do them.
18 I'm not speaking about all of you; I know
those I have chosen. But the Scripture must be
fulfilled: **The one who eats My bread[c] has
raised his heel against Me.**[d]
19 "I am telling you now before it happens,
so that when it does happen you will believe
that I am ⌊He⌋. 20 I assure you: The one who
receives whomever I send receives Me, and the
one who receives Me receives Him who sent
Me."

Judas' Betrayal Predicted

21 When Jesus had said this, He was troubled in His spirit and testified, "I assure you:
One of you will betray Me!"
22 The disciples started looking at one
another—uncertain which one He was speaking about. 23 One of His disciples, the one Jesus
loved, was reclining close beside Jesus.[e]
24 Simon Peter motioned to him to find out
who it was He was talking about. 25 So he
leaned back against Jesus and asked Him,
"Lord, who is it?"
26 Jesus replied, "He's the one I give the
piece of bread to after I have dipped it." When
He had dipped the bread, He gave it to Judas,
Simon Iscariot's son.[f] 27 After ⌊Judas ate⌋ the
piece of bread, Satan entered him. Therefore
Jesus told him, "What you're doing, do
quickly."
28 None of those reclining at the table
knew why He told him this. 29 Since Judas
kept the money-bag, some thought that Jesus
was telling him, "Buy what we need for the
festival," or that he should give something to
the poor. 30 After receiving the piece of
bread, he went out immediately. And it was
night.

The New Commandment

31 When he had gone out, Jesus said, "Now
the •Son of Man is glorified, and God is glorified in Him. 32 If God is glorified in Him,[g] God
will also glorify Him in Himself and will glorify
Him at once.
33 "Children, I am with you a little while
longer. You will look for Me, and just as I told
the Jews, 'Where I am going you cannot come,'
so now I tell you.
34 "I give you a new commandment: love
one another. Just as I have loved you, you must
also love one another. 35 By this all people will
know that you are My disciples, if you have
love for one another."

Peter's Denials Predicted

36 "Lord," Simon Peter said to Him, "where
are You going?"
Jesus answered, "Where I am going you
cannot follow Me now, but you will follow
later."
37 "Lord," Peter asked, "why can't I follow
You now? I will lay down my life for You!"
38 Jesus replied, "Will you lay down your
life for Me? I assure you: A rooster will not
crow until you have denied Me three times.

The Way to the Father

14 "Your heart must not be troubled.
Believe[h] in God; believe also in Me.
2 In My Father's house are many dwelling

[a]**13:12** At important meals the custom was to recline on a mat at a low table and lean on the left elbow. [b]**13:16** Or *lord*
[c]**13:18** Other mss read *eats bread with Me* [d]**13:18** Ps 41:9 [e]**13:23** Lit *reclining at Jesus' breast*; that is, on His right;
Jn 1:18 [f]**13:26** Other mss read *Judas Iscariot, Simon's son* [g]**13:32** Other mss omit *If God is glorified in Him* [h]**14:1** Or *You
believe*

B—Believe Read John 14:6.

places;[a] if not, I would have told you. I am going away to prepare a place for you. 3 If I go away and prepare a place for you, I will come back and receive you to Myself, so that where I am you may be also. 4 You know the way where I am going."[b]

5 "Lord," Thomas said, "we don't know where You're going. How can we know the way?"

6 Jesus told him, "I am the way, the truth, and the life. No one comes to the Father except through Me.

Jesus Reveals the Father

7 "If you know Me, you will also know[c] My Father. From now on you do know Him and have seen Him."

8 "Lord," said Philip, "show us the Father, and that's enough for us."

9 Jesus said to him, "Have I been among you all this time without your knowing Me, Philip? The one who has seen Me has seen the Father. How can you say, 'Show us the Father'? 10 Don't you believe that I am in the Father and the Father is in Me? The words I speak to you I do not speak on My own. The Father who lives in Me does His works. 11 Believe Me that I am in the Father and the Father is in Me. Otherwise, believe[d] because of the works themselves.

Praying in Jesus' Name

12 "•I assure you: The one who believes in Me will also do the works that I do. And he will do even greater works than these, because I am going to the Father. 13 Whatever you ask in My name, I will do it so that the Father may be glorified in the Son. 14 If you ask Me[e] anything in My name, I will do it.[f]

Another Counselor Promised

15 "If you love Me, you will keep[g] My commandments. 16 And I will ask the Father, and He will give you another •Counselor to be with you forever. 17 He is the Spirit of truth. The world is unable to receive Him because it doesn't see Him or know Him. But you do know Him, because He remains with you and will be[h] in you. 18 I will not leave you as orphans; I am coming to you.

The Father, the Son, and the Holy Spirit

19 "In a little while the world will see Me no longer, but you will see Me. Because I live, you will live too. 20 In that day you will know that I am in My Father, you are in Me, and I am in you. 21 The one who has My commands and keeps them is the one who loves Me. And the one who loves Me will be loved by My Father. I also will love him and will reveal Myself to him."

22 Judas (not Iscariot) said to Him, "Lord, how is it You're going to reveal Yourself to us and not to the world?"

23 Jesus answered, "If anyone loves Me, he will keep My word. My Father will love him, and We will come to him and make Our home with him. 24 The one who doesn't love Me will not keep My words. The word that you hear is not Mine but is from the Father who sent Me.

25 "I have spoken these things to you while I remain with you. 26 But the Counselor, the Holy Spirit—the Father will send Him in My name—will teach you all things and remind you of everything I have told you.

Jesus' Gift of Peace

27 "Peace I leave with you. My peace I give to you. I do not give to you as the world gives. Your heart must not be troubled or fearful. 28 You have heard Me tell you, 'I am going away and I am coming to you.' If you loved Me, you would have rejoiced that I am going to the Father, because the Father is greater than I. 29 I have told you now before it happens so that when it does happen you may believe. 30 I will not talk with you much longer, because the ruler of the world is coming. He has no power over Me.[i] 31 On the contrary, ⌊I am going away⌋[j] so that the world may know that I love the Father. Just as the Father commanded Me, so I do.

"Get up; let's leave this place.

The Vine and the Branches

15 "I am the true vine, and My Father is the vineyard keeper. 2 Every branch in Me that does not produce fruit He removes, and He prunes every branch that produces fruit so that it will produce more

[a] **14:2** The Vg used the Lat term *mansio*, a traveler's resting place. The Gk word is related to the verb *meno*, meaning *remain* or *stay*, which occurs 40 times in John. [b] **14:4** Other mss read this verse: *And you know where I am going, and you know the way* [c] **14:7** Other mss read *If you had known Me, you would have known* [d] **14:11** Other mss read *believe Me* [e] **14:14** Other mss omit *Me* [f] **14:14** Other mss omit all of v. 14 [g] **14:15** Other mss read *If you love Me, keep* (as a command) [h] **14:17** Other mss read *and is* [i] **14:30** Lit *He has nothing in Me* [j] **14:31** Probably refers to the cross

Turn to page 122.

fruit. 3 You are already clean because of the word I have spoken to you. 4 Remain in Me, and I in you. Just as a branch is unable to produce fruit by itself unless it remains on the vine, so neither can you unless you remain in Me.

5 "I am the vine; you are the branches. The one who remains in Me and I in him produces much fruit, because you can do nothing without Me. 6 If anyone does not remain in Me, he is thrown aside like a branch and he withers. They gather them, throw them into the fire, and they are burned. 7 If you remain in Me and My words remain in you, ask whatever you want and it will be done for you. 8 My Father is glorified by this: that you produce much fruit and prove to be[a] My disciples.

Christlike Love

9 "As the Father has loved Me, I have also loved you. Remain in My love. 10 If you keep My commands you will remain in My love, just as I have kept My Father's commands and remain in His love.

11 "I have spoken these things to you so that My joy may be in you and your joy may be complete. 12 This is My command: love one another as I have loved you. 13 No one has greater love than this, that someone would lay down his life for his friends. 14 You are My friends if you do what I command you. 15 I do not call you slaves anymore, because a slave doesn't know what his master[b] is doing. I have called you friends, because I have made known to you everything I have heard from My Father. 16 You did not choose Me, but I chose you. I appointed you that you should go out and produce fruit and that your fruit should remain, so that whatever you ask the Father in My name, He will give you. 17 This is what I command you: love one another.

Persecutions Predicted

18 "If the world hates you, understand that it hated Me before it hated you. 19 If you were of the world, the world would love ⌊you as⌋ its own. However, because you are not of the world, but I have chosen you out of it, the world hates you. 20 Remember the word I spoke to you: 'A slave is not greater than his master.' If they persecuted Me, they will also persecute you. If they kept My word, they will also keep yours. 21 But they will do all these things to you on account of My name, because they don't know the One who sent Me. 22 If I had not come and spoken to them, they would not have sin.[c] Now they have no excuse for their sin. 23 The one who hates Me also hates My Father. 24 If I had not done the works among them that no one else has done, they would not have sin. Now they have seen and hated both Me and My Father. 25 But ⌊this happened⌋ so that the statement written in their law might be fulfilled: **They hated Me for no reason.**[d]

Coming Testimony and Rejection

26 "When the •Counselor comes, the One I will send to you from the Father—the Spirit of truth who proceeds from the Father—He will testify about Me. 27 You also will testify, because you have been with Me from the beginning.

16 "I have told you these things to keep you from stumbling. 2 They will ban you from the •synagogues. In fact, a time is coming when anyone who kills you will think he is offering service to God. 3 They will do these things because they haven't known the Father or Me. 4 But I have told you these things so that when their time[e] comes you may remember I told them to you. I didn't tell you these things from the beginning, because I was with you.

The Counselor's Ministry

5 "But now I am going away to Him who sent Me, and not one of you asks Me, 'Where are You going?' 6 Yet, because I have spoken these things to you, sorrow has filled your heart. 7 Nevertheless, I am telling you the truth. It is for your benefit that I go away, because if I don't go away the •Counselor will not come to you. If I go, I will send Him to you. 8 When He comes, He will convict the world about sin, righteousness, and judgment: 9 about sin, because they do not believe in Me; 10 about righteousness, because I am going to the Father and you will no longer see Me; 11 and about judgment, because the ruler of this world has been judged.

12 "I still have many things to tell you, but you can't bear them now. 13 When the Spirit of

[a]**15:8** Or *and become* [b]**15:15** Or *lord* [c]**15:22** To *have sin* is an idiom that refers to guilt caused by sin. [d]**15:25** Ps 69:4
[e]**16:4** Other mss read *when the time*

truth comes, He will guide you into all the truth.
For He will not speak on His own, but He will
speak whatever He hears. He will also declare to
you what is to come. 14 He will glorify Me,
because He will take from what is Mine and
declare it to you. 15 Everything the Father has is
Mine. This is why I told you that He takes from
what is Mine and will declare it to you.

Sorrow Turned to Joy

16 "A little while and you will no longer see
Me; again a little while and you will see Me."[a]
17 Therefore some of His disciples said to
one another, "What is this He tells us: 'A little
while and you will not see Me; again a little
while and you will see Me'; and, 'because I am
going to the Father'?" 18 They said, "What is
this He is saying,[b] 'A little while'? We don't
know what He's talking about!"
19 Jesus knew they wanted to question Him,
so He said to them, "Are you asking one
another about what I said, 'A little while and
you will not see Me; again a little while and you
will see Me'?
20 "•I assure you: You will weep and wail, but
the world will rejoice. You will become sorrowful, but your sorrow will turn to joy. 21 When a
woman is in labor she has pain because her time
has come. But when she has given birth to a
child, she no longer remembers the suffering
because of the joy that a person has been born
into the world. 22 So you also have sorrow[c] now.
But I will see you again. Your hearts will rejoice,
and no one will rob you of your joy. 23 In that day
you will not ask Me anything.
"I assure you: Anything you ask the Father
in My name, He will give you. 24 Until now you
have asked for nothing in My name. Ask and
you will receive, that your joy may be complete.

Jesus the Victor

25 "I have spoken these things to you in figures of speech. A time is coming when I will no
longer speak to you in figures, but I will tell you
plainly about the Father. 26 In that day you will
ask in My name. I am not telling you that I will
make requests to the Father on your behalf.
27 For the Father Himself loves you, because
you have loved Me and have believed that I
came from God.[d] 28 I came from the Father and
have come into the world. Again, I am leaving
the world and going to the Father."
29 "Ah!" His disciples said. "Now You're
speaking plainly and not using any figurative language. 30 Now we know that You know everything and don't need anyone to question You. By
this we believe that You came from God."
31 Jesus responded to them, "Do you now
believe? 32 Look: An hour is coming, and has
come, when each of you will be scattered to his
own home, and you will leave Me alone. Yet I
am not alone, because the Father is with Me.
33 I have told you these things so that in Me
you may have peace. You will have suffering in
this world. Be courageous! I have conquered
the world."

Jesus Prays for Himself

17 Jesus spoke these things, looked up to
heaven, and said:

Father,
the hour has come.
Glorify Your Son
so that the Son may glorify You,
2 for You gave Him authority
over all flesh;[e]
so He may give eternal life
to all You have given Him.
3 This is eternal life:
that they may know You,
the only true God,
and the One You have sent—
Jesus Christ.
4 I have glorified You on the earth
by completing the work You gave Me
to do.
5 Now, Father, glorify Me
in Your presence
with that glory I had with You
before the world existed.

Jesus Prays for His Disciples

6 I have revealed Your name
to the men You gave Me
from the world.
They were Yours, You gave them
to Me,
and they have kept Your word.
7 Now they know that all things
You have given to Me are from You,
8 because the words that You gave Me,
I have given them.
They have received them
and have known for certain
that I came from You.

[a]**16:16** Other mss add *because I am going to the Father* [b]**16:18** Other mss omit *He is saying* [c]**16:22** Other mss read *will have sorrow* [d]**16:27** Other mss read *from the Father* [e]**17:2** Or *people*

They have believed that You sent Me.
9 I pray[a] for them.
I am not praying for the world
but for those You have given Me,
because they are Yours.
10 All My things are Yours,
and Yours are Mine,
and I have been glorified in them.
11 I am no longer in the world,
but they are in the world,
and I am coming to You.
Holy Father,
protect[b] them by Your name
that You have given Me,
so that they may be one
as We are one.
12 While I was with them,
I was protecting them by Your name
that You have given Me.
I guarded them and not one of them
is lost,
except the son of destruction,[c]
so that the Scripture may be fulfilled.
13 Now I am coming to You,
and I speak these things in the world
so that they may have My joy completed in them.
14 I have given them Your word.
The world hated them
because they are not of the world,
as I am not of the world.
15 I am not praying
that You take them out of the world
but that You protect them
from the evil one.
16 They are not of the world,
as I am not of the world.
17 Sanctify[d] them by the truth;
Your word is truth.
18 As You sent Me into the world,
I also have sent them into the world.
19 I sanctify Myself for them,
so they also may be sanctified
by the truth.

Jesus Prays for All Believers

20 I pray not only for these,
but also for those who believe in Me
through their message.
21 May they all be one,
as You, Father, are in Me and I am
in You.
May they also be one[e] in Us,
so the world may believe
You sent Me.
22 I have given them the glory
You have given Me.
May they be one as We are one.
23 I am in them and You are in Me.
May they be made completely one,
so the world may know You have
sent Me
and have loved them as
You have loved Me.
24 Father,
I desire those You have given Me
to be with Me where I am.
Then they will see My glory,
which You have given Me
because You loved Me
before the world's foundation.
25 Righteous Father!
The world has not known You.
However, I have known You,
and these have known
that You sent Me.
26 I made Your name known to them
and will make it known,
so the love You have loved Me with
may be in them and I may be
in them.

Jesus Betrayed

18 After Jesus had said these things, He
went out with His disciples across the
Kidron Valley, where there was a garden, and
He and His disciples went into it. 2 Judas, who
betrayed Him, also knew the place, because
Jesus often met there with His disciples. 3 So
Judas took a •company of soldiers and some
temple police from the •chief priests and the
•Pharisees and came there with lanterns,
torches, and weapons.
4 Then Jesus, knowing everything that was
about to happen to Him, went out and said to
them, "Who is it you're looking for?"
5 "Jesus the •Nazarene," they answered.
"I am He,"[f] Jesus told them.
Judas, who betrayed Him, was also standing
with them. 6 When He told them, "I am He,"
they stepped back and fell to the ground.
7 Then He asked them again, "Who is it
you're looking for?"
"Jesus the Nazarene," they said.
8 "I told you I am ⌊He⌋," Jesus replied. "So if

[a]**17:9** Lit *ask* (throughout this passage) [b]**17:11** Lit *keep* (throughout this passage) [c]**17:12** The one destined for destruction, loss, or perdition [d]**17:17** Set apart for special use [e]**17:21** Other mss omit *one* [f]**18:5** Lit *I am*; see note at Jn 8:58

you're looking for Me, let these men go." 9 This
was to fulfill the words He had said: "I have not
lost one of those You have given Me."
10 Then Simon Peter, who had a sword,
drew it, struck the high priest's slave, and cut
off his right ear. (The slave's name was Mal-
chus.)
11 At that, Jesus said to Peter, "Sheathe your
sword! Am I not to drink the cup the Father has
given Me?"

Jesus Arrested and Taken to Annas

12 Then the company of soldiers, the commander, and the Jewish temple police arrested
Jesus and tied Him up. 13 First they led Him to
Annas, for he was the father-in-law of Caiaphas,
who was high priest that year. 14 Caiaphas was
the one who had advised the Jews that it was
advantageous that one man should die for the
people.

Peter Denies Jesus

15 Meanwhile Simon Peter was following
Jesus, as was another disciple. That disciple
was an acquaintance of the high priest; so he
went with Jesus into the high priest's courtyard. 16 But Peter remained standing outside by
the door. So the other disciple, the one known
to the high priest, went out and spoke to the
girl who was the doorkeeper and brought Peter
in.
17 Then the slave girl who was the doorkeeper said to Peter, "You aren't one of this
man's disciples too, are you?"
"I am not!" he said. 18 Now the slaves and
the temple police had made a charcoal fire,
because it was cold. They were standing there
warming themselves, and Peter was standing
with them, warming himself.

Jesus before Annas

19 The high priest questioned Jesus about
His disciples and about His teaching.
20 "I have spoken openly to the world,"
Jesus answered him. "I have always taught in
the •synagogue and in the •temple complex,
where all the Jews congregate, and I haven't
spoken anything in secret. 21 Why do you
question Me? Question those who heard
what I told them. Look, they know what I
said."
22 When He had said these things, one of
the temple police standing by slapped Jesus,
saying, "Is this the way you answer the high
priest?"
23 "If I have spoken wrongly," Jesus
answered him, "give evidence[a] about the
wrong; but if rightly, why do you hit Me?"
24 Then Annas sent Him bound to Caiaphas
the high priest.

Peter Denies Jesus Twice More

25 Now Simon Peter was standing and
warming himself. They said to him, "You aren't
one of His disciples too, are you?"
He denied it and said, "I am not!"
26 One of the high priest's slaves, a relative
of the man whose ear Peter had cut off, said,
"Didn't I see you with Him in the garden?"
27 Peter then denied it again. Immediately a
rooster crowed.

Jesus before Pilate

28 Then they took Jesus from Caiaphas to
the governor's •headquarters. It was early
morning. They did not enter the headquarters
themselves; otherwise they would be defiled
and unable to eat the •Passover.
29 Then •Pilate came out to them and said,
"What charge do you bring against this man?"
30 They answered him, "If this man weren't
a criminal,[b] we wouldn't have handed Him
over to you."
31 So Pilate told them, "Take Him yourselves and judge Him according to your law."
"It's not legal[c] for us to put anyone to
death," the Jews declared. 32 They said this so
that Jesus' words might be fulfilled signifying
what sort of death He was going to die.
33 Then Pilate went back into the headquarters, summoned Jesus, and said to Him, "Are
You the King of the Jews?"
34 Jesus answered, "Are you asking this on
your own, or have others told you about Me?"
35 "I'm not a Jew, am I?" Pilate replied.
"Your own nation and the chief priests
handed You over to me. What have You
done?"
36 "My kingdom is not of this world," said
Jesus. "If My kingdom were of this world, My
servants[d] would fight, so that I wouldn't be
handed over to the Jews. As it is, My kingdom
does not have its origin here."[e]
37 "You are a king then?" Pilate asked.
"You say that I'm a king," Jesus replied. "I
was born for this, and I have come into the

[a]**18:23** Or *him, testify* [b]**18:30** Lit *an evil doer* [c]**18:31** According to Roman law [d]**18:36** Or *attendants*, or *helpers*
[e]**18:36** Lit *My kingdom is not from here*

world for this: to testify to the truth. Everyone who is of the truth listens to My voice."

38 "What is truth?" said Pilate.

Jesus or Barabbas

After he had said this, he went out to the Jews again and told them, "I find no grounds for charging Him. 39 You have a custom that I release one ⌊prisoner⌋ to you at the Passover. So, do you want me to release to you the King of the Jews?"

40 They shouted back, "Not this man, but Barabbas!" Now Barabbas was a revolutionary.[a]

Jesus Flogged and Mocked

19 Then •Pilate took Jesus and had Him flogged. 2 The soldiers also twisted together a crown of thorns, put it on His head, and threw a purple robe around Him. 3 And they repeatedly came up to Him and said, "Hail, King of the Jews!" and were slapping His face.

4 Pilate went outside again and said to them, "Look, I'm bringing Him outside to you to let you know I find no grounds for charging Him."

Pilate Sentences Jesus to Death

5 Then Jesus came out wearing the crown of thorns and the purple robe. Pilate said to them, "Here is the man!"

6 When the •chief priests and the temple police saw Him, they shouted, "Crucify! Crucify!"

Pilate responded, "Take Him and crucify Him yourselves, for I find no grounds for charging Him."

7 "We have a law," the Jews replied to him, "and according to that law He must die, because He made Himself[b] the Son of God."

8 When Pilate heard this statement, he was more afraid than ever. 9 He went back into the •headquarters and asked Jesus, "Where are You from?" But Jesus did not give him an answer. 10 So Pilate said to Him, "You're not talking to me? Don't You know that I have the authority to release You and the authority to crucify You?"

11 "You would have no authority over Me at all," Jesus answered him, "if it hadn't been given you from above. This is why the one who handed Me over to you has the greater sin."[c]

12 From that moment Pilate made every effort[d] to release Him. But the Jews shouted, "If you release this man, you are not Caesar's friend. Anyone who makes himself a king opposes Caesar!"

13 When Pilate heard these words, he brought Jesus outside. He sat down on the judge's bench in a place called the Stone Pavement (but in Hebrew *Gabbatha*). 14 It was the preparation day for the •Passover, and it was about six in the morning.[e] Then he told the Jews, "Here is your king!"

15 But they shouted, "Take Him away! Take Him away! Crucify Him!"

Pilate said to them, "Should I crucify your king?"

"We have no king but Caesar!" the chief priests answered.

16 So then, because of them, he handed Him over to be crucified.

The Crucifixion

Therefore they took Jesus away.[f] 17 Carrying His own cross, He went out to what is called Skull Place, which in Hebrew is called *Golgotha*. 18 There they crucified Him and two others with Him, one on either side, with Jesus in the middle. 19 Pilate also had a sign lettered and put on the cross. The inscription was:

JESUS THE NAZARENE THE KING OF THE JEWS

20 Many of the Jews read this sign, because the place where Jesus was crucified was near the city, and it was written in Hebrew,[g] Latin, and Greek. 21 So the chief priests of the Jews said to Pilate, "Don't write, 'The King of the Jews,' but that He said, 'I am the King of the Jews.' "

22 Pilate replied, "What I have written, I have written."

23 When the soldiers crucified Jesus, they took His clothes and divided them into four parts, a part for each soldier. They also took the tunic, which was seamless, woven in one piece from the top. 24 So they said to one another, "Let's not tear it, but toss for it, to see who gets it." ⌊They did this⌋ to fulfill the Scripture that says: **They divided My clothes among themselves, and they cast lots for My clothing.**[h] And this is what the soldiers did.

[a] **18:40** Or *robber*, see Jn 10:1,8 for the same Gk word used here [b] **19:7** He claimed to be [c] **19:11** To *have sin* is an idiom that refers to guilt caused by sin. [d] **19:12** Lit *Pilate was trying* [e] **19:14** Lit *the sixth hour*, see note at Jn 1:39; an alternate time reckoning would be *about noon* [f] **19:16** Other mss add *and led Him out* [g] **19:20** Or *Aramaic* [h] **19:24** Ps 22:18

Jesus' Provision for His Mother

25 Standing by the cross of Jesus were His
mother, His mother's sister, Mary the wife of
Clopas, and •Mary Magdalene. 26 When Jesus
saw His mother and the disciple He loved
standing there, He said to His mother,
"•Woman, here is your son." 27 Then He said
to the disciple, "Here is your mother." And
from that hour the disciple took her into his
home.

The Finished Work of Jesus

28 After this, when Jesus knew that everything was now accomplished that the Scripture
might be fulfilled, He said, "I'm thirsty!" 29 A
jar full of sour wine was sitting there; so they
fixed a sponge full of sour wine on hyssop[a] and
held it up to His mouth.

30 When Jesus had received the sour wine,
He said, "It is finished!" Then bowing His
head, He gave up His spirit.

Jesus' Side Pierced

31 Since it was the preparation day, the
Jews did not want the bodies to remain on
the cross on the Sabbath (for that Sabbath
was a special[b] day). They requested that
Pilate have the men's legs broken and that
⌊their bodies⌋ be taken away. 32 So the soldiers came and broke the legs of the first man
and of the other one who had been crucified
with Him. 33 When they came to Jesus, they
did not break His legs since they saw that He
was already dead. 34 But one of the soldiers
pierced His side with a spear, and at once
blood and water came out. 35 He who saw
this has testified so that you also may believe.
His testimony is true, and he knows he is telling the truth. 36 For these things happened
so that the Scripture would be fulfilled: **Not
one of His bones will be broken.**[c] 37 Also,
another Scripture says: **They will look at the
One they pierced.**[d]

Jesus' Burial

38 After this, Joseph of Arimathea, who was
a disciple of Jesus—but secretly because of his
fear of the Jews—asked Pilate that he might
remove Jesus' body. Pilate gave him permission, so he came and took His body away.
39 Nicodemus (who had previously come to
Him at night) also came, bringing a mixture of
about 75 pounds[e] of myrrh and aloes. 40 Then
they took Jesus' body and wrapped it in linen
cloths with the aromatic spices, according to
the burial custom of the Jews. 41 There was a
garden in the place where He was crucified. A
new tomb was in the garden; no one had yet
been placed in it. 42 They placed Jesus there
because of the Jewish preparation and since the
tomb was nearby.

The Empty Tomb

20 On the first day of the week •Mary
Magdalene came to the tomb early,
while it was still dark. She saw that the stone
had been removed[f] from the tomb. 2 So she
ran to Simon Peter and to the other disciple,
the one Jesus loved, and said to them, "They
have taken the Lord out of the tomb, and we
don't know where they have put Him!"

3 At that, Peter and the other disciple went
out, heading for the tomb. 4 The two were running together, but the other disciple outran
Peter and got to the tomb first. 5 Stooping
down, he saw the linen cloths lying there, yet
he did not go in. 6 Then, following him, Simon
Peter came also. He entered the tomb and saw
the linen cloths lying there. 7 The wrapping
that had been on His head was not lying with
the linen cloths but was folded up in a separate
place by itself. 8 The other disciple, who had
reached the tomb first, then entered the tomb,
saw, and believed. 9 For they still did not
understand the Scripture that He must rise
from the dead. 10 Then the disciples went
home again.

Mary Magdalene Sees the Risen Lord

11 But Mary stood outside facing the tomb,
crying. As she was crying, she stooped to look
into the tomb. 12 She saw two angels in white
sitting there, one at the head and one at the
feet, where Jesus' body had been lying. 13 They
said to her, "•Woman, why are you crying?"

"Because they've taken away my Lord," she
told them, "and I don't know where they've
put Him." 14 Having said this, she turned
around and saw Jesus standing there, though
she did not know it was Jesus.

15 "Woman," Jesus said to her, "why are
you crying? Who is it you are looking for?"

Supposing He was the gardener, she
replied, "Sir, if you've removed Him, tell me
where you've put Him, and I will take Him
away."

[a] **19:29** Or *with hyssop* [b] **19:31** Lit *great* [c] **19:36** Ex 12:46; Nm 9:12; Ps 34:20 [d] **19:37** Zch 12:10 [e] **19:39** Lit *100 litrai*; a Roman *litrai* = 12 ounces [f] **20:1** Lit *She saw the stone removed*

16 Jesus said, "Mary."
Turning around, she said to Him in Hebrew,
"Rabbouni!" [a] —which means "Teacher."
17 "Don't cling to Me," Jesus told her, "for I
have not yet ascended to the Father. But go to
My brothers and tell them that I am ascending
to My Father and your Father—to My God and
your God."
18 Mary Magdalene went and announced to
the disciples, "I have seen the Lord!" And she
told them what[b] He had said to her.

The Disciples Commissioned

19 In the evening of that first day of the
week, the disciples were ⌊gathered together⌋
with the doors locked because of their fear of
the Jews. Then Jesus came, stood among them,
and said to them, "Peace to you!"
20 Having said this, He showed them His
hands and His side. So the disciples rejoiced
when they saw the Lord.
21 Jesus said to them again, "Peace to you!
As the Father has sent Me, I also send you."
22 After saying this, He breathed on them
and said,[c] "Receive the Holy Spirit. 23 If you
forgive the sins of any, they are forgiven
them; if you retain ⌊the sins of⌋ any, they are
retained."

Thomas Sees and Believes

24 But one of the Twelve, Thomas (called
"Twin"), was not with them when Jesus came.
25 So the other disciples kept telling him, "We
have seen the Lord!"
But he said to them, "If I don't see the mark
of the nails in His hands, put my finger into the
mark of the nails, and put my hand into His
side, I will never believe!"
26 After eight days His disciples were
indoors again, and Thomas was with them.
Even though the doors were locked, Jesus came
and stood among them. He said, "Peace to
you!"
27 Then He said to Thomas, "Put your finger
here and observe My hands. Reach out your
hand and put it into My side. Don't be an unbeliever, but a believer."
28 Thomas responded to Him, "My Lord
and my God!"
29 Jesus said, "Because you have seen Me,
you have believed.[d] Those who believe without
seeing are blessed."

The Purpose of This Gospel

30 Jesus performed many other signs in the
presence of His disciples that are not written in
this book. 31 But these are written so that you
may believe Jesus is the •Messiah, the Son of
God,[e] and by believing you may have life in His
name.

Jesus' Third Appearance to the Disciples

21 After this, Jesus revealed Himself
again to His disciples by the Sea of
Tiberias.[f] He revealed Himself in this way:
2 Simon Peter, Thomas (called "Twin"),
Nathanael from Cana of Galilee, Zebedee's sons,
and two others of His disciples were together.
3 "I'm going fishing," Simon Peter said to
them.
"We're coming with you," they told him.
They went out and got into the boat, but that
night they caught nothing.
4 When daybreak came, Jesus stood on the
shore. However, the disciples did not know it
was Jesus.
5 "Men,"[g] Jesus called to them, "you don't
have any fish, do you?"
"No," they answered.
6 "Cast the net on the right side of the
boat," He told them, "and you'll find some." So
they did,[h] and they were unable to haul it in
because of the large number of fish. 7 Therefore
the disciple, the one Jesus loved, said to Peter,
"It is the Lord!"
When Simon Peter heard that it was the
Lord, he tied his outer garment around him[i]
(for he was stripped) and plunged into the sea.
8 But since they were not far from land (about
100 yards[j] away), the other disciples came in
the boat, dragging the net full of fish. 9 When
they got out on land, they saw a charcoal fire
there, with fish lying on it, and bread.
10 "Bring some of the fish you've just
caught," Jesus told them. 11 So Simon Peter got
up and hauled the net ashore, full of large
fish—153 of them. Even though there were so
many, the net was not torn.
12 "Come and have breakfast," Jesus told
them. None of the disciples dared ask Him,

[a]**20:16** *Rabbouni* is also used in Mk 10:51 [b]**20:18** Lit *these things* [c]**20:22** Lit *He breathed and said to them* [d]**20:29** Or *have you believed?* (as a question) [e]**20:31** Or *that the Messiah, the Son of God, is Jesus* [f]**21:1** The Sea of Galilee; *Sea of Tiberias* is used only in John; Jn 6:1,23 [g]**21:5** Lit *Children* [h]**21:6** Lit *they cast* [i]**21:7** Lit *he girded his garment* [j]**21:8** Lit *about 200 cubits*

"Who are You?" because they knew it was the
Lord. 13 Jesus came, took the bread, and gave it
to them. He did the same with the fish.
14 This was now the third time[a] Jesus
appeared[b] to the disciples after He was raised
from the dead.

Jesus' Threefold Restoration of Peter

15 When they had eaten breakfast, Jesus
asked Simon Peter, "Simon, son of John,[c] do
you love[d] Me more than these?"

"Yes, Lord," he said to Him, "You know that
I love You."

"Feed My lambs," He told him.
16 A second time He asked him, "Simon,
son of John, do you love Me?"

"Yes, Lord," he said to Him, "You know that
I love You."

"Shepherd My sheep," He told him.
17 He asked him the third time, "Simon, son
of John, do you love Me?"

Peter was grieved that He asked him the
third time, "Do you love Me?" He said, "Lord,
You know everything! You know that I love
You."

"Feed My sheep," Jesus said.
18 "•I assure
you: When you were young, you would tie your
belt and walk wherever you wanted. But when
you grow old, you will stretch out your hands
and someone else will tie you and carry you
where you don't want to go."
19 He said this to
signify by what kind of death he would glorify
God.[e] After saying this, He told him, "Follow
Me!"

Correcting a False Report

20 So Peter turned around and saw the disciple Jesus loved following them. ⌊That disciple⌋
was the one who had leaned back against Jesus
at the supper and asked, "Lord, who is the one
that's going to betray You?"
21 When Peter saw
him, he said to Jesus, "Lord—what about
him?"
22 "If I want him to remain until I come,"
Jesus answered, "what is that to you? As for
you, follow Me."
23 So this report[f] spread to the brothers[g]
that this disciple would not die. Yet Jesus did
not tell him that he would not die, but, "If I
want him to remain until I come, what is that
to you?"

Epilogue

24 This is the disciple who testifies to these
things and who wrote them down. We know
that his testimony is true.
25 And there are also many other things that
Jesus did, which, if they were written one by
one, I suppose not even the world itself could
contain the books[h] that would be written.

Acts

Prologue

1 I wrote the first narrative, Theophilus,
about all that Jesus began to do and teach
2 until the day He was taken up, after He had
given orders through the Holy Spirit to the
apostles whom He had chosen.
3 After He had
suffered, He also presented Himself alive to
them by many convincing proofs, appearing to
them during 40 days and speaking about the
kingdom of God.

The Holy Spirit Promised

4 While He was together with them,[i] He
commanded them not to leave Jerusalem, but
to wait for the Father's promise. "This," ⌊He
said, "is what⌋ you heard from Me;
5 for John

[a]**21:14** The other two are in Jn 20:19–29. [b]**21:14** Lit *was revealed* (see v. 1) [c]**21:15–17** Other mss read *Simon, son of Jonah*; Jn 1:42; Mt 16:17 [d]**21:15–17** Two synonyms are translated *love* in this conversation: *agapao*, the first 2 times by Jesus (vv. 15–16); and *phileo*, the last time by Jesus (v. 17) and all 3 times by Peter (vv. 15–17). Peter's threefold confession of love for Jesus corresponds to his earlier threefold denial of Jesus; Jn 18:15–18,25–27. [e]**21:19** Jesus predicts that Peter would be martyred. Church tradition says that Peter was crucified upside down. [f]**21:23** Lit *this word* [g]**21:23** The word *brothers* refers to the whole Christian community. [h]**21:25** Lit *scroll* [i]**1:4** Or *He was eating with them*, or *He was lodging with them*

baptized with water, but you will be baptized with the Holy Spirit not many days from now."

6 So when they had come together, they asked Him, "Lord, at this time are You restoring the kingdom to Israel?"

7 He said to them, "It is not for you to know times or periods that the Father has set by His own authority. 8 But you will receive power when the Holy Spirit has come upon you, and you will be My witnesses in Jerusalem, in all Judea and Samaria, and to the ends[a] of the earth."

The Ascension

9 After He had said this, He was taken up as they were watching, and a cloud received Him out of their sight. 10 While He was going, they were gazing into heaven, and suddenly two men in white clothes stood by them. 11 They said, "Men of Galilee, why do you stand looking up into heaven? This Jesus, who has been taken from you into heaven, will come in the same way that you have seen Him going into heaven."

United in Prayer

12 Then they returned to Jerusalem from the mount called Olive Grove, which is near Jerusalem—a Sabbath day's journey away. 13 When they arrived, they went to the room upstairs where they were staying:

> Peter, John,
> James, Andrew,
> Philip, Thomas,
> Bartholomew, Matthew,
> James the son of Alphaeus,
> Simon the Zealot, and Judas
> the son of James.

14 All these were continually united in prayer,[b] along with the women, including Mary[c] the mother of Jesus, and His brothers.

Matthias Chosen

15 During these days Peter stood up among the brothers[d] —the number of people who were together was about 120—and said: 16 "Brothers, the Scripture had to be fulfilled that the Holy Spirit through the mouth of David spoke in advance about Judas, who became a guide to those who arrested Jesus. 17 For he was one of our number and was allotted a share in this ministry." 18 Now this man acquired a field with his unrighteous wages; and falling headfirst, he burst open in the middle, and all his insides spilled out. 19 This became known to all the residents of Jerusalem, so that in their own language that field is called *Hakeldama*, that is, Field of Blood. 20 "For it is written in the Book of Psalms:

> **Let his dwelling become desolate;**
> **let no one live in it;[e] and**
> **Let someone else take his position.[f]**

21 "Therefore, from among the men who have accompanied us during the whole time the Lord Jesus went in and out among us— 22 beginning from the baptism of John until the day He was taken up from us—from among these, it is necessary that one become a witness with us of His resurrection."

23 So they proposed two: Joseph, called Barsabbas, who was also known as Justus, and Matthias. 24 Then they prayed, "You, Lord, know the hearts of all; show which of these two You have chosen 25 to take the place[g] in this apostolic service that Judas left to go to his own place." 26 Then they cast lots for them, and the lot fell to Matthias. So he was numbered with the 11 apostles.

Pentecost

2 When the day of Pentecost had arrived, they were all together in one place. 2 Suddenly a sound like that of a violent rushing wind came from heaven, and it filled the whole house where they were staying. 3 And tongues, like flames of fire that were divided, appeared to them and rested on each one of them. 4 Then they were all filled with the Holy Spirit and began to speak in different languages, as the Spirit gave them ability for speech.

5 There were Jews living in Jerusalem, devout men from every nation under heaven. 6 When this sound occurred, the multitude came together and was confused because each one heard them speaking in his own language. 7 And they were astounded and amazed, saying,[h] "Look, aren't all these who are speaking Galileans? 8 How is it that we hear, each of us, in our own native language? 9 Parthians, Medes, Elamites; those who live in Mesopotamia, in Judea and Cappadocia, Pontus and Asia, 10 Phrygia and Pamphylia, Egypt and the

[a]**1:8** Lit *the end* [b]**1:14** Other mss add *and petition* [c]**1:14** Or *prayer, with their wives and Mary* [d]**1:15** Other mss read *disciples* [e]**1:20** Ps 69:25 [f]**1:20** Ps 109:8 [g]**1:25** Other mss read *to share* [h]**2:7** Other mss add *to one another*

parts of Libya near Cyrene; visitors from
Rome, both Jews and •proselytes, 11 Cretans
and Arabs—we hear them speaking in our
own languages the magnificent acts of God."
12 And they were all astounded and perplexed, saying to one another, "What could
this be?" 13 But some sneered and said,
"They're full of new wine!"

Peter's Sermon

14 But Peter stood up with the Eleven,
raised his voice, and proclaimed to them: "Jewish men and all you residents of Jerusalem, let
this be known to you and pay attention to my
words. 15 For these people are not drunk, as
you suppose, since it's only nine in the morning.[a] 16 On the contrary, this is what was spoken through the prophet Joel:

17 **And it will be** in the last days,
says God,
**that I will pour out My Spirit
on all humanity;
then your sons
and your daughters
will prophesy,
your young men will see visions,
and your old men will dream
dreams.**
18 **I will even pour out My Spirit
on My male and female slaves
in those days,**
and they will prophesy.
19 **I will display wonders
in the heaven above
and signs on the earth below:
blood and fire and a cloud
of smoke.**
20 **The sun will be turned
to darkness,
and the moon to blood,
before the great and remarkable
day of the Lord comes;**
21 **then whoever calls on the name
of the Lord will be saved.**[b]

22 "Men of Israel, listen to these words:
This Jesus the •Nazarene was a man pointed
out to you by God with miracles, wonders, and
signs that God did among you through Him,
just as you yourselves know. 23 Though He was
delivered up according to God's determined
plan and foreknowledge, you used[c] lawless people[d] to nail Him to a cross and kill Him. 24 God
raised Him up, ending the pains of death,
because it was not possible for Him to be held
by it. 25 For David says of Him:

**I saw the Lord ever before me;
because He is at my right hand,
I will not be shaken.**
26 **Therefore my heart was glad,
and my tongue rejoiced.
Moreover my flesh will rest
in hope,**
27 **because You will not leave my soul
in •Hades,
or allow Your Holy One
to see decay.**
28 **You have revealed the paths of life
to me;
You will fill me with gladness
in Your presence.**[e]

29 "Brothers, I can confidently speak to you
about the patriarch David: he is both dead and
buried, and his tomb is with us to this day.
30 Since he was a prophet, he knew that God
had sworn an oath to him to seat one of his
descendants[f g] on his throne. 31 Seeing this in
advance, he spoke concerning the resurrection
of the •Messiah:

**He[h] was not left in Hades,
and His flesh** did **not experience
decay.**[i]

32 "God has resurrected this Jesus. We are
all witnesses of this. 33 Therefore, since He
has been exalted to the right hand of God and
has received from the Father the promised
Holy Spirit, He has poured out what you both
see and hear. 34 For it was not David who
ascended into the heavens, but he himself
says:

**The Lord said to my Lord,
'Sit at My right hand**
35 **until I make Your enemies
Your footstool.'**[j]

36 "Therefore let all the house of Israel
know with certainty that God has made this
Jesus, whom you crucified, both Lord and Messiah!"

Forgiveness through the Messiah

37 When they heard this, they were pierced

[a]**2:15** Lit *it's the third hour of the day* [b]**2:17–21** Jl 2:28–32 [c]**2:23** Other mss read *you have taken* [d]**2:23** Or *used the hand of lawless ones* [e]**2:25–28** Ps 16:8–11 [f]**2:30** Other mss add *according to the flesh to raise up the Messiah* [g]**2:30** Lit *one from the fruit of his loin* [h]**2:31** Other mss read *His soul* [i]**2:31** Ps 16:10 [j]**2:34–35** Ps 110:1

to the heart and said to Peter and the rest of the apostles: "Brothers, what must we do?"

38 "Repent," Peter said to them, "and be baptized, each of you, in the name of Jesus the Messiah for the forgiveness of your sins, and you will receive the gift of the Holy Spirit. 39 For the promise is for you and for your children, and for all who are far off,[a] as many as the Lord our God will call." 40 And with many other words he testified and strongly urged them, saying, "Be saved from this corrupt[b] generation!"

A Generous and Growing Church

41 So those who accepted his message were baptized, and that day about 3,000 people were added to them. 42 And they devoted themselves to the apostles' teaching, to fellowship, to the breaking of bread, and to prayers.

43 Then fear came over everyone, and many wonders and signs were being performed through the apostles. 44 Now all the believers were together and had everything in common. 45 So they sold their possessions and property and distributed the proceeds to all, as anyone had a need.[c] 46 And every day they devoted themselves ⌊to meeting⌋ together in the •temple complex, and broke bread from house to house. They ate their food with gladness and simplicity of heart, 47 praising God and having favor with all the people. And every day the Lord added to them[d] those who were being saved.

Healing of a Lame Man

3 Now Peter and John were going up together to the •temple complex at the hour of prayer at three in the afternoon.[e] 2 And a man who was lame from his mother's womb was carried there and placed every day at the temple gate called Beautiful, so he could beg from those entering the temple complex. 3 When he saw Peter and John about to enter the temple complex, he asked for help. 4 Peter, along with John, looked at him intently and said, "Look at us." 5 So he turned to them,[f] expecting to get something from them. 6 But Peter said, "I have neither silver nor gold, but what I have, I give to you: In the name of Jesus Christ the •Nazarene, get up and walk!" 7 Then, taking him by the right hand he raised him up, and at once his feet and ankles became strong. 8 So he jumped up, stood, and started to walk, and he entered the temple complex with them—walking, leaping, and praising God. 9 All the people saw him walking and praising God, 10 and they recognized that he was the one who used to sit and beg at the Beautiful Gate of the temple complex. So they were filled with awe and astonishment at what had happened to him.

Preaching in Solomon's Colonnade

11 While he[g] was holding on to Peter and John, all the people, greatly amazed, ran toward them in what is called Solomon's Colonnade. 12 When Peter saw this, he addressed the people: "Men of Israel, why are you amazed at this? Or why do you stare at us, as though by our own power or godliness we had made him walk? 13 The God of Abraham, Isaac, and Jacob, the God of our fathers, has glorified His Servant Jesus, whom you handed over and denied in the presence of •Pilate, when he had decided to release Him. 14 But you denied the Holy and Righteous One, and asked to have a murderer given to you. 15 And you killed the source[h] of life, whom God raised from the dead; we are witnesses of this. 16 By faith in His name, His name has made this man strong, whom you see and know. So the faith that comes through Him has given him this perfect health in front of all of you.

17 "And now, brothers, I know that you did it in ignorance, just as your leaders also did. 18 But what God predicted through the mouth of all the prophets—that His •Messiah would suffer—He has fulfilled in this way. 19 Therefore repent and turn back, that your sins may be wiped out so that seasons of refreshing may come from the presence of the Lord, 20 and He may send Jesus, who has been appointed Messiah for you. 21 Heaven must welcome[i] Him until the times of the restoration of all things, which God spoke about by the mouth of His holy prophets from the beginning. 22 Moses said:[j]

> **The Lord your God will raise up for you a Prophet like me from among your brothers. You must listen to Him in everything He will say to you. 23 And it will be that everyone who will not listen to that Prophet will be completely cut off from the people.[k]**

[a]**2:39** Remote in time or space [b]**2:40** Or *crooked*, or *twisted* [c]**2:45** Or *to all, according to one's needs* [d]**2:47** Other mss read *to the church* [e]**3:1** Lit *at the ninth hour* [f]**3:5** Or *he paid attention to them* [g]**3:11** Other mss read *the lame man who was healed* [h]**3:15** Or *the Prince*, or *the Ruler* [i]**3:21** Or *receive*, or *retain* [j]**3:22** Other mss add *to the fathers* [k]**3:22–23** Dt 18:15–19

Turn to page 233.

 B—Believe Read Acts 4:12.

24 "In addition, all the prophets who have spoken, from Samuel and those after him, have also announced these days. 25 You are the sons of the prophets and of the covenant that God made with your forefathers, saying to Abraham, **And in your seed all the families of the earth will be blessed.**[a] 26 God raised up His Servant[b] and sent Him first to you to bless you by turning each of you from your evil ways."

Peter and John Arrested

4 Now as they were speaking to the people, the priests, the commander of the temple guard, and the •Sadducees confronted them, 2 because they were provoked that they were teaching the people and proclaiming in the person of Jesus[c] the resurrection from the dead. 3 So they seized them and put them in custody until the next day, since it was already evening. 4 But many of those who heard the message believed, and the number of the men came to about 5,000.

Peter and John Face the Jewish Leadership

5 The next day, their rulers, elders, and •scribes assembled in Jerusalem 6 with Annas the high priest, Caiaphas, John and Alexander, and all the members of the high-priestly family.[d] 7 After they had Peter and John stand[e] before them, they asked the question: "By what power or in what name have you done this?"

8 Then Peter was filled with the Holy Spirit and said to them, "Rulers of the people and elders:[f] 9 If we are being examined today about a good deed done to a disabled man—by what means he was healed— 10 let it be known to all of you and to all the people of Israel, that by the name of Jesus Christ the •Nazarene—whom you crucified and whom God raised from the dead—by Him this man is standing here before you healthy. 11 This ⌊Jesus⌋ is

The stone despised by you
builders,
who has become
the cornerstone.[g]

12 There is salvation in no one else, for there is no other name under heaven given to people by which we must be saved."

The Name Forbidden

13 When they observed the boldness of Peter and John and realized that they were uneducated and untrained men, they were amazed and knew that they had been with Jesus. 14 And since they saw the man who had been healed standing with them, they had nothing to say in response. 15 After they had ordered them to leave the •Sanhedrin, they conferred among themselves, 16 saying, "What should we do with these men? For an obvious sign, evident to all who live in Jerusalem, has been done through them, and we cannot deny it! 17 But so this does not spread any further among the people, let's threaten them against speaking to anyone in this name again." 18 So they called for them and ordered them not to preach or teach at all in the name of Jesus.

19 But Peter and John answered them, "Whether it's right in the sight of God ⌊for us⌋ to listen to you rather than to God, you decide; 20 for we are unable to stop speaking about what we have seen and heard."

21 After threatening them further, they released them. They found no way to punish them, because the people were all giving glory to God over what had been done; 22 for the man was over 40 years old on whom this sign of healing had been performed.

Prayer for Boldness

23 After they were released, they went to their own fellowship[h] and reported all that the •chief priests and the elders had said to them. 24 When they heard this, they raised their voices to God unanimously and said, "Master, You are the One who made the heaven, the earth, and the sea, and everything in them. 25 You said through the Holy Spirit, by the mouth of our father David Your servant:[i]

Why did the Gentiles rage,
and the peoples plot futile things?
26 **The kings of the earth**
took their stand,
and the rulers assembled together
against the Lord and
against His •Messiah.[j]

27 "For, in fact, in this city both •Herod and Pontius •Pilate, with the Gentiles and the peoples of Israel, assembled together

[a] **3:25** Gn 12:3; 18:18; 22:18; 26:4 [b] **3:26** Other mss add *Jesus* [c] **4:2** Lit *proclaiming in Jesus* [d] **4:6** Or *high-priestly class*, or *high-priestly clan* [e] **4:7** Lit *had placed them* [f] **4:8** Other mss add *of Israel* [g] **4:11** Ps 118:22 [h] **4:23** Or *friends*, or *companions* [i] **4:25** Other mss read *through the mouth of David Your servant* [j] **4:25–26** Ps 2:1–2

Turn to page 155.

against Your holy Servant Jesus, whom You anointed, 28 to do whatever Your hand and Your plan had predestined to take place. 29 And now, Lord, consider their threats, and grant that Your slaves may speak Your message with complete boldness, 30 while You stretch out Your hand for healing, signs, and wonders to be performed through the name of Your holy Servant Jesus." 31 When they had prayed, the place where they were assembled was shaken, and they were all filled with the Holy Spirit and began to speak God's message with boldness.

Believers Sharing

32 Now the multitude of those who believed were of one heart and soul, and no one said that any of his possessions was his own, but instead they held everything in common. 33 And with great power the apostles were giving testimony to the resurrection of the Lord Jesus, and great grace was on all of them. 34 For there was not a needy person among them, because all those who owned lands or houses sold them, brought the proceeds of the things that were sold, 35 and laid them at the apostles' feet. This was then distributed to each person as anyone had a need.

36 Joseph, a Levite and a Cypriot by birth, whom the apostles named Barnabas, which is translated Son of Encouragement, 37 sold a field he owned, brought the money, and laid it at the apostles' feet.

Lying to the Holy Spirit

5 But a man named Ananias, with Sapphira his wife, sold a piece of property. 2 However, he kept back part of the proceeds with his wife's knowledge, and brought a portion of it and laid it at the apostles' feet.

3 Then Peter said, "Ananias, why has Satan filled your heart to lie to the Holy Spirit and keep back part of the proceeds from the field? 4 Wasn't it yours while you possessed it? And after it was sold, wasn't it at your disposal? Why is it that you planned this thing in your heart? You have not lied to men but to God!" 5 When he heard these words, Ananias dropped dead, and a great fear came on all who heard. 6 The young men got up, wrapped ⌊his body⌋, carried him out, and buried him.

7 There was an interval of about three hours; then his wife came in, not knowing what had happened. 8 "Tell me," Peter asked her, "did you sell the field for this price?"

"Yes," she said, "for that price."

9 Then Peter said to her, "Why did you agree to test the Spirit of the Lord? Look! The feet of those who have buried your husband are at the door, and they will carry you out!"

10 Instantly she dropped dead at his feet. When the young men came in, they found her dead, carried her out, and buried her beside her husband. 11 Then great fear came on the whole church and on all who heard these things.

Apostolic Signs and Wonders

12 Many signs and wonders were being done among the people through the hands of the apostles. By common consent they would all meet in Solomon's Colonnade. 13 None of the rest dared to join them, but the people praised them highly. 14 Believers were added to the Lord in increasing numbers—crowds of both men and women. 15 As a result, they would carry the sick out into the streets and lay them on beds and pallets so that when Peter came by, at least his shadow might fall on some of them. 16 In addition, a multitude came together from the towns surrounding Jerusalem, bringing sick people and those who were tormented by unclean spirits, and they were all healed.

In and Out of Prison

17 Then the high priest took action. He and all his colleagues, those who belonged to the party of the •Sadducees, were filled with jealousy. 18 So they arrested[a] the apostles and put them in the city jail. 19 But an angel of the Lord opened the doors of the jail during the night, brought them out, and said, 20 "Go and stand in the •temple complex, and tell the people all about this life." 21 In obedience to this, they entered the temple complex at daybreak and began to teach.

The Apostles on Trial Again

When the high priest and those who were with him arrived, they convened the •Sanhedrin—the full Senate of the sons of Israel—and sent ⌊orders⌋ to the jail to have them brought. 22 But when the temple police got there, they did not find them in the jail, so they returned and reported, 23 "We found the jail securely locked, with the guards standing in front of

[a]**5:18** Lit *laid hands on*

the doors; but when we opened them, we found no one inside!" 24 As[a] the captain of the temple police and the •chief priests heard these things, they were baffled about them, as to what could come of this.

25 Someone came and reported to them, "Look! The men you put in jail are standing in the temple complex and teaching the people." 26 Then the captain went with the temple police and brought them in without force, because they were afraid the people might stone them. 27 When they had brought them in, they had them stand before the Sanhedrin, and the high priest asked, 28 "Didn't we strictly order you not to teach in this name? And look, you have filled Jerusalem with your teaching and are determined to bring this man's blood on us!"

29 But Peter and the apostles replied, "We must obey God rather than men. 30 The God of our fathers raised up Jesus, whom you had murdered by hanging Him on a tree. 31 God exalted this man to His right hand as ruler and Savior, to grant repentance to Israel, and forgiveness of sins. 32 We are witnesses of these things, and so is the Holy Spirit whom God has given to those who obey Him."

Gamaliel's Advice

33 When they heard this, they were enraged and wanted to kill them. 34 A •Pharisee named Gamaliel, a teacher of the law who was respected by all the people, stood up in the Sanhedrin and ordered the men[b] to be taken outside for a little while. 35 He said to them, "Men of Israel, be careful about what you're going to do to these men. 36 Not long ago Theudas rose up, claiming to be somebody, and a group of about 400 men rallied to him. He was killed, and all his partisans were dispersed and came to nothing. 37 After this man, Judas the Galilean rose up in the days of the census and attracted a following.[c] That man also perished, and all his partisans were scattered. 38 And now, I tell you, stay away from these men and leave them alone. For if this plan or this work is of men, it will be overthrown; 39 but if it is of God, you will not be able to overthrow them. You may even be found fighting against God." So they were persuaded by him. 40 After they called in the apostles and had them flogged, they ordered them not to speak in the name of Jesus and released them. 41 Then they went out from the presence of the Sanhedrin, rejoicing that they were counted worthy to be dishonored on behalf of the name.[d] 42 Every day in the temple complex, and in various homes, they continued teaching and proclaiming the good news that the •Messiah is Jesus.[e]

Seven Chosen to Serve

6 In those days, as the number of the disciples was multiplying, there arose a complaint by the Hellenistic Jews[f] against the Hebraic Jews[g] that their widows were being overlooked in the daily distribution. 2 Then the Twelve summoned the whole company of the disciples and said, "It would not be right for us to give up preaching about God to wait on tables. 3 Therefore, brothers, select from among you seven men of good reputation, full of the Spirit and wisdom, whom we can appoint to this duty. 4 But we will devote ourselves to prayer and to the preaching ministry." 5 The proposal pleased the whole company. So they chose Stephen, a man full of faith and the Holy Spirit, and Philip, Prochorus, Nicanor, Timon, Parmenas, and Nicolaus, a •proselyte from Antioch. 6 They had them stand before the apostles, who prayed and laid their hands on them.[h]

7 So the preaching about God flourished, the number of the disciples in Jerusalem multiplied greatly, and a large group of priests became obedient to the faith.

Stephen Accused of Blasphemy

8 Stephen, full of grace and power, was performing great wonders and signs among the people. 9 Then some from what is called the Freedmen's •Synagogue, composed of both Cyrenians and Alexandrians, and some from Cilicia and Asia, came forward and disputed with Stephen. 10 But they were unable to stand up against the wisdom and the Spirit by whom he spoke.

11 Then they induced men to say, "We heard him speaking blasphemous words against Moses and God!" 12 They stirred up the people, the elders, and the •scribes; so they came up, dragged him off, and took him to the •Sanhedrin. 13 They also presented false witnesses who said, "This man does not stop

[a]**5:24** Other mss add *the high priest and* [b]**5:34** Other mss read *apostles* [c]**5:37** Lit *and drew people after him* [d]**5:41** Other mss add *of Jesus*, or *of Christ* [e]**5:42** Or *that Jesus is the Messiah* [f]**6:1** Jews of Gk language and culture [g]**6:1** Jews of Aram or Hb language and culture [h]**6:6** The laying on of hands signified the prayer of blessing for the beginning of a new ministry.

speaking blasphemous words against this holy place and the law. 14 For we heard him say that Jesus, this •Nazarene, will destroy this place and change the customs that Moses handed down to us." 15 And all who were sitting in the Sanhedrin looked intently at him and saw that his face was like the face of an angel.

Stephen's Address

7 "Is this true?"[a] the high priest asked. 2 "Brothers and fathers," he said, "listen: The God of glory appeared to our father Abraham when he was in Mesopotamia, before he settled in Haran, 3 and said to him:

> **Get out of your country**
> **and away from your relatives,**
> **and come to the land that I will show you.**[b]

4 "Then he came out of the land of the Chaldeans and settled in Haran. And from there, after his father died, God had him move to this land in which you now live. 5 He didn't give him an inheritance in it, not even a foot of ground, but He promised to give it to him as a possession, and to his descendants after him, even though he was childless. 6 God spoke in this way:

> **His descendants would be**
> **strangers in a foreign country,**
> **and they would enslave**
> **and oppress them for 400 years.**
> 7 **I will judge the nation**
> **that they will serve as slaves,**
> God said.
> **After this, they will come out**
> **and worship Me in this place.**[c]

8 Then He gave him the covenant of circumcision. This being so, he fathered Isaac and circumcised him on the eighth day; Isaac did the same with Jacob, and Jacob with the 12 patriarchs.

The Patriarchs in Egypt

9 "The patriarchs became jealous of Joseph and sold him into Egypt, but God was with him 10 and rescued him out of all his troubles. He gave him favor and wisdom in the sight of Pharaoh, king of Egypt, who appointed him governor over Egypt and over his whole household. 11 Then a famine came over all of Egypt and Canaan, with great suffering, and our forefathers could find no food. 12 When Jacob heard there was grain in Egypt, he sent our forefathers the first time. 13 The second time, Joseph was revealed to his brothers, and Joseph's family became known to Pharaoh. 14 Joseph then invited his father Jacob and all his relatives, 75 people in all, 15 and Jacob went down to Egypt. He and our forefathers died there, 16 were carried back to Shechem, and were placed in the tomb that Abraham had bought for a sum of silver from the sons of Hamor in Shechem.

Moses, a Rejected Savior

17 "As the time was drawing near to fulfill the promise that God had made to Abraham, the people flourished and multiplied in Egypt 18 until a different king ruled over Egypt[d] who did not know Joseph. 19 He dealt deceitfully with our race and oppressed our forefathers by making them leave their infants outside so they wouldn't survive.[e] 20 At this time Moses was born, and he was beautiful before God. He was nursed in his father's home three months, 21 and when he was left outside, Pharaoh's daughter adopted and raised him as her own son. 22 So Moses was educated in all the wisdom of the Egyptians, and was powerful in his speech and actions.

23 "As he was approaching the age of 40, he decided[f] to visit his brothers, the sons of Israel. 24 When he saw one of them being mistreated, he came to his rescue and avenged the oppressed man by striking down the Egyptian. 25 He assumed his brothers would understand that God would give them deliverance through him, but they did not understand. 26 The next day he showed up while they were fighting and tried to reconcile them peacefully, saying, 'Men, you are brothers. Why are you mistreating each other?'

27 "But the one who was mistreating his neighbor pushed him[g] away, saying:

> **Who appointed you a ruler and a judge over us? 28 Do you want to kill me, the same way you killed the Egyptian yesterday?**[h]

29 "At this disclosure, Moses fled and became an exile in the land of Midian, where he fathered two sons. 30 After 40 years had

[a]**7:1** Lit *"Are these things so?"* [b]**7:3** Gn 12:1 [c]**7:6–7** Gn 15:13–14 [d]**7:18** Other mss omit *over Egypt* [e]**7:19** A common pagan practice of population control by leaving infants outside to die [f]**7:23** Lit *40, it came into his heart* [g]**7:27** Moses [h]**7:27–28** Ex 2:14

passed, an angel[a] appeared to him in the
desert of Mount Sinai, in the flame of a burning bush. 31 When Moses saw it, he was
amazed at the sight. As he was approaching
to look at it, the voice of the Lord came: 32 **I**
am the God of your forefathers—the God of
Abraham, of Isaac, and of Jacob.[b] So Moses
began to tremble and did not dare to look.
33 "Then the Lord said to him:

Take the sandals off your feet,
because the place where you are
standing is holy ground. 34 **I have cer-**
tainly seen the oppression of My peo-
ple in Egypt; I have heard their
groaning and have come down to res-
cue them. And now, come, I will send
you to Egypt.[c]

35 "This Moses, whom they rejected when
they said, **Who appointed you a ruler and a**
judge?[d] —this one God sent as a ruler and a
redeemer by means of the angel who appeared
to him in the bush. 36 This man led them out
and performed wonders and signs in the land of
Egypt, at the Red Sea, and in the desert for 40
years.

Israel's Rebellion against God

37 "This is the Moses who said to the sons
of Israel, **God**[e] **will raise up for you a**
Prophet like me from among your broth-
ers.[f] 38 He is the one who was in the congregation in the desert together with the angel
who spoke to him on Mount Sinai, and with
our forefathers. He received living oracles to
give to us. 39 Our forefathers were unwilling
to obey him, but pushed him away, and in
their hearts turned back to Egypt. 40 They
told Aaron:

Make us gods who will go before us.
As for this Moses who brought us out
of the land of Egypt, we don't know
what's become of him.[g]

41 They even made a calf in those days, offered
sacrifice to the idol, and were celebrating what
their hands had made. 42 Then God turned
away and gave them up to worship the host of
heaven, as it is written in the book of the
prophets:

Did you bring Me offerings
and sacrifices
for 40 years in the desert,
O house of Israel?
43 **No, you took up the tent**
of Moloch[h]
and the star of your god Rephan,[i]
the images that you made
to worship.
So I will deport you
beyond Babylon![j]

God's Real Tabernacle

44 "Our forefathers had the tabernacle of
the testimony in the desert, just as He who
spoke to Moses commanded him to make it
according to the pattern he had seen. 45 Our
forefathers in turn received it and with Joshua
brought it in when they dispossessed the
nations that God drove out before our fathers,
until the days of David. 46 He found favor in
God's sight and asked that he might provide a
dwelling place for the God[k] of Jacob. 47 But it
was Solomon who built Him a house.
48 However, the Most High does not dwell in
sanctuaries made with hands, as the prophet
says:

49 **Heaven is My throne,**
and earth My footstool.
What sort of house will you build
for Me? says the Lord,
or what is My resting place?
50 **Did not My hand make all**
these things?[l]

Resisting the Holy Spirit

51 "You stiff-necked people with uncircumcised hearts and ears! You are always resisting
the Holy Spirit; as your forefathers did, so do
you. 52 Which of the prophets did your fathers
not persecute? They even killed those who
announced beforehand the coming of the Righteous One, whose betrayers and murderers you
have now become. 53 You received the law
under the direction of angels and yet have not
kept it."

The First Christian Martyr

54 When they heard these things, they were
enraged in their hearts[m] and gnashed their
teeth at him. 55 But Stephen, filled by the Holy

[a]**7:30** Other mss add *of the Lord* [b]**7:32** Ex 3:6,15 [c]**7:33–34** Ex 3:5,7–8,10 [d]**7:35** Ex 2:14 [e]**7:37** Other mss read *'The Lord your God* [f]**7:37** Dt 18:15 [g]**7:40** Ex 32:1,23 [h]**7:43** Canaanite or Phoenician sky or sun god [i]**7:43** Perhaps an Assyrian star god—the planet Saturn [j]**7:42–43** Am 5:25–27 [k]**7:46** Other mss read *house* [l]**7:49–50** Is 66:1–2 [m]**7:54** Or *were cut to the quick*

Spirit, gazed into heaven. He saw God's glory, with[a] Jesus standing at the right hand of God, and he said, 56 "Look! I see the heavens opened and the •Son of Man standing at the right hand of God!"

57 Then they screamed at the top of their voices, stopped their ears, and rushed together against him. 58 They threw him out of the city and began to stone him. And the witnesses laid their robes at the feet of a young man named Saul. 59 They were stoning Stephen as he called out: "Lord Jesus, receive my spirit!" 60 Then he knelt down and cried out with a loud voice, "Lord, do not charge them with this sin!" And saying this, he fell •asleep.[b]

Saul the Persecutor

8 Saul agreed with putting him to death. On that day a severe persecution broke out against the church in Jerusalem, and all except the apostles were scattered throughout the land of Judea and Samaria. 2 But devout men buried Stephen and mourned deeply over him. 3 Saul, however, was ravaging the church, and he would enter house after house, drag off men and women, and put them in prison.

Philip in Samaria

4 So those who were scattered went on their way proclaiming the message of good news. 5 Philip went down to a[c] city in Samaria and preached the •Messiah to them. 6 The crowds paid attention with one mind to what Philip said, as they heard and saw the signs he was performing. 7 For unclean spirits, crying out with a loud voice, came out of many who were possessed, and many who were paralyzed and lame were healed. 8 So there was great joy in that city.

The Response of Simon

9 A man named Simon had previously practiced sorcery in that city and astounded the •Samaritan people, while claiming to be somebody great. 10 They all paid attention to him, from the least of them to the greatest, and they said, "This man is called the Great Power of God!"[d] 11 They were attentive to him because he had astounded them with his sorceries for a long time. 12 But when they believed Philip, as he proclaimed the good news about the kingdom of God and the name of Jesus Christ, both men and women were baptized. 13 Then even Simon himself believed. And after he was baptized, he went around constantly with[e] Philip and was astounded as he observed the signs and great miracles that were being performed.

Simon's Sin

14 When the apostles who were at Jerusalem heard that Samaria had welcomed God's message, they sent Peter and John to them. 15 After they went down there, they prayed for them, that they might receive the Holy Spirit. 16 For He had not yet come down on[f] any of them; they had only been baptized in the name of the Lord Jesus. 17 Then Peter and John laid their hands on them, and they received the Holy Spirit.

18 When Simon saw that the Holy[g] Spirit was given through the laying on of the apostles' hands, he offered them money, 19 saying, "Give me this power too, so that anyone I lay hands on may receive the Holy Spirit."

20 But Peter told him, "May your silver be destroyed with you, because you thought the gift of God could be obtained with money! 21 You have no part or share in this matter, because your heart is not right before God. 22 Therefore repent of this wickedness of yours, and pray to the Lord that the intent of your heart may be forgiven you. 23 For I see you are poisoned by bitterness and bound by iniquity."

24 "Please pray[h] to the Lord for me," Simon replied, "so that nothing you[h] have said may happen to me."

25 Then, after they had testified and spoken the message of the Lord, they traveled back to Jerusalem, evangelizing many villages of the •Samaritans.

The Conversion of the Ethiopian Official

26 An angel of the Lord spoke to Philip: "Get up and go south to the road that goes down from Jerusalem to desert Gaza."[i] 27 So he got up and went. There was an Ethiopian man, a eunuch and high official of Candace, queen of the Ethiopians, who was in charge of her entire treasury. He had come to worship in Jerusalem 28 and was sitting in his chariot on his way home, reading the prophet Isaiah aloud.

29 The Spirit told Philip, "Go and join that chariot."

30 When Philip ran up to it, he heard him

[a]**7:55** Lit *and* [b]**7:60** He died; see Jn 11:11; 1 Co 11:30; 1 Th 4:13–15 [c]**8:5** Other mss read *the* [d]**8:10** Or *This is the power of God called Great* [e]**8:13** Or *he kept close company with* [f]**8:16** Or *yet fallen on* [g]**8:18** Other mss omit *Holy* [h]**8:24** Gk words *you* and *pray* are plural [i]**8:26** Perhaps old Gaza or the road near the desert

reading the prophet Isaiah, and said, "Do you
understand what you're reading?"
31 "How can I," he said, "unless someone
guides me?" So he invited Philip to come up
and sit with him. 32 Now the Scripture passage
he was reading was this:

He was led like a sheep
to the slaughter,
and as a lamb is silent
before its shearer,
so He does not open His mouth.
33 **In His humiliation justice was denied**
Him.
Who will describe His generation?
For His life is taken
from the earth.[a]

34 The eunuch replied to Philip, "I ask you,
who is the prophet saying this about—himself
or another person?" 35 So Philip proceeded[b] to
tell him the good news about Jesus, beginning
from that Scripture.
36 As they were traveling down the road,
they came to some water. The eunuch said,
"Look, there's water! What would keep me
from being baptized?" [37 And Philip said, "If
you believe with all your heart you may." And
he replied, "I believe that Jesus Christ is the
Son of God."][c] 38 Then he ordered the chariot
to stop, and both Philip and the eunuch went
down into the water, and he baptized him.
39 When they came up out of the water, the
Spirit of the Lord carried Philip away, and the
eunuch did not see him any longer. But he
went on his way rejoicing. 40 Philip appeared
in[d] Azotus,[e] and passing through, he was evangelizing all the towns until he came to Caesarea.

The Damascus Road

9 Meanwhile Saul, still breathing threats
and murder against the disciples of the
Lord, went to the high priest 2 and requested
letters from him to the •synagogues in Damascus, so that if he found any who belonged to
the Way, either men or women, he might
bring them as prisoners to Jerusalem. 3 As he
traveled and was nearing Damascus, a light
from heaven suddenly flashed around him.
4 Falling to the ground, he heard a voice saying
to him, "Saul, Saul, why are you persecuting
Me?"
5 "Who are You, Lord?" he said.
"I am Jesus, whom you are persecuting," He
replied. 6 "But get up and go into the city, and
you will be told what you must do."
7 The men who were traveling with him
stood speechless, hearing the sound but seeing no one. 8 Then Saul got up from the
ground, and though his eyes were open, he
could see nothing. So they took him by the
hand and led him into Damascus. 9 He was
unable to see for three days, and did not eat or
drink.

Saul's Baptism

10 Now in Damascus there was a disciple
named Ananias. And the Lord said to him in a
vision, "Ananias!"
"Here I am, Lord!" he said.
11 "Get up and go to the street called
Straight," the Lord said to him, "to the house of
Judas, and ask for a man from Tarsus named
Saul, since he is praying there. 12 In a vision[f] he
has seen a man named Ananias coming in and
placing his hands on him so he may regain his
sight."
13 "Lord," Ananias answered, "I have heard
from many people about this man, how much
harm he has done to Your saints in Jerusalem.
14 And he has authority here from the •chief
priests to arrest all who call on Your name."
15 But the Lord said to him, "Go! For this
man is My chosen instrument to carry My
name before Gentiles, kings, and the sons of
Israel. 16 I will certainly show him how much
he must suffer for My name!"
17 So Ananias left and entered the house.
Then he placed his hands on him and said,
"Brother Saul, the Lord Jesus, who appeared to
you on the road you were traveling, has sent
me so you may regain your sight and be filled
with the Holy Spirit."
18 At once something like scales fell from
his eyes, and he regained his sight. Then he got
up and was baptized. 19 And after taking some
food, he regained his strength.

Saul Proclaiming the Messiah

Saul[g] was with the disciples in Damascus for
some days. 20 Immediately he began proclaiming Jesus in the synagogues: "He is the Son of
God."
21 But all who heard him were astounded

[a]**8:32–33** Is 53:7–8 [b]**8:35** Lit *Philip opened his mouth* [c]**8:37** Other mss omit bracketed text [d]**8:40** Or *Philip was found at*, or *Philip found himself in* [e]**8:40** Or *Ashdod* [f]**9:12** Other mss omit *In a vision* [g]**9:19** Lit *He*

and said, "Isn't this the man who, in Jerusalem,
was destroying those who called on this name,
and then came here for the purpose of taking
them as prisoners to the chief priests?"
22 But Saul grew more capable, and kept
confounding the Jews who lived in Damascus
by proving that this One is the •Messiah.
23 After many days had passed, the Jews
conspired to kill him, 24 but their plot became
known to Saul. So they were watching the
gates day and night intending to kill him,
25 but his disciples took him by night and lowered him in a large basket through ⌊an opening
in⌋ the wall.

Saul in Jerusalem

26 When he arrived in Jerusalem, he tried to
associate with the disciples, but they were all
afraid of him, since they did not believe he was
a disciple. 27 Barnabas, however, took him and
brought him to the apostles and explained to
them how, on the road, Saul[a] had seen the
Lord, and that He had talked to him, and how
in Damascus he had spoken boldly in the name
of Jesus. 28 Saul[a] was coming and going with
them in Jerusalem, speaking boldly in the name
of the Lord. 29 He conversed and debated with
the Hellenistic Jews,[b] but they attempted to kill
him. 30 When the brothers found out, they took
him down to Caesarea and sent him off to Tarsus.
31 So the church throughout all Judea, Galilee, and Samaria had peace, being built up and
walking in the fear of the Lord and in the
encouragement of the Holy Spirit, and it
increased in numbers.

The Healing of Aeneas

32 As Peter was traveling from place to
place,[c] he also came down to the saints[d] who
lived in Lydda. 33 There he found a man named
Aeneas, who was paralyzed and had been bed-
ridden for eight years. 34 Peter said to him,
"Aeneas, Jesus Christ heals you. Get up and
make your own bed,"[e] and immediately he got
up. 35 So all who lived in Lydda and Sharon saw
him and turned to the Lord.

Dorcas Restored to Life

36 In Joppa there was a disciple named
Tabitha, which is translated Dorcas.[f] She was
always doing good works and acts of charity.
37 In those days she became sick and died.
After washing her, they placed her in a room
upstairs. 38 Since Lydda was near Joppa, the
disciples heard that Peter was there and sent
two men to him who begged him, "Don't delay
in coming with us." 39 So Peter got up and
went with them. When he arrived, they led
him to the room upstairs. And all the widows
approached him, weeping and showing him
the robes and clothes that Dorcas had made
while she was with them. 40 Then Peter sent
them all out of the room. He knelt down,
prayed, and turning toward the body said,
"Tabitha, get up!" She opened her eyes, saw
Peter, and sat up. 41 He gave her his hand and
helped her stand up. Then he called the saints
and widows and presented her alive. 42 This
became known throughout all Joppa, and many
believed in the Lord. 43 And Peter[a] stayed on
many days in Joppa with Simon, a leather
tanner.[g]

Cornelius' Vision

10 There was a man in Caesarea named
Cornelius, a •centurion of what was
called the Italian •Regiment. 2 He was a
devout man and feared God along with his
whole household. He did many charitable
deeds for the ⌊Jewish⌋ people and always
prayed to God. 3 At about three in the afternoon[h] he distinctly saw in a vision an angel of
God who came in and said to him, "Cornelius!"
4 Looking intently at him, he became afraid
and said, "What is it, Lord?"
And he told him, "Your prayers and your
acts of charity have come up as a memorial
offering before God. 5 Now send men to Joppa
and call for Simon, who is also named Peter.
6 He is lodging with Simon, a tanner, whose
house is by the sea."
7 When the angel who spoke to him had
gone, he called two of his household slaves and
a devout soldier, who was one of those who
attended him. 8 After explaining everything to
them, he sent them to Joppa.

Peter's Vision

9 The next day, as they were traveling and
nearing the city, Peter went up to pray on the
housetop at about noon.[i] 10 Then he became
hungry and wanted to eat, but while they were

[a] **9:27,28,43** Lit *he* [b] **9:29** Lit *Hellenists*; that is, Gk-speaking Jews [c] **9:32** Lit *Peter was passing through all* [d] **9:32** The believers [e] **9:34** Or *and get ready to eat* [f] **9:36** *Dorcas* = Gazelle [g] **9:43** Tanners were considered ritually unclean because of their occupation. [h] **10:3** Lit *about the ninth hour* [i] **10:9** Lit *about the sixth hour*

preparing something he went into a visionary
state. 11 He saw heaven opened and an object
coming down that resembled a large sheet
being lowered to the earth by its four corners.
12 In it were all the four-footed animals and reptiles of the earth, and the birds of the sky.
13 Then a voice said to him, "Get up, Peter; kill
and eat!"
14 "No, Lord!" Peter said. "For I have never
eaten anything common[a] and unclean!"
15 Again, a second time, a voice said to him,
"What God has made clean, you must not call
common." 16 This happened three times, and
then the object was taken up into heaven.

Peter Visits Cornelius

17 While Peter was deeply perplexed about
what the vision he had seen might mean, the
men who had been sent by Cornelius, having
asked directions to Simon's house, stood at the
gate. 18 They called out, asking if Simon, who
was also named Peter, was lodging there.
19 While Peter was thinking about the
vision, the Spirit told him, "Three men are here
looking for you. 20 Get up, go downstairs, and
accompany them with no doubts at all, because
I have sent them."
21 Then Peter went down to the men and
said, "Here I am, the one you're looking for.
What is the reason you're here?"
22 They said, "Cornelius, a centurion, an
upright and God-fearing man, who has a good
reputation with the whole Jewish nation, was
divinely directed by a holy angel to call you to
his house and to hear a message from you."
23 Peter[b] then invited them in and gave them
lodging.
The next day he got up and set out with
them, and some of the brothers from Joppa
went with him. 24 The following day he
entered Caesarea. Now Cornelius was expecting them and had called together his relatives
and close friends. 25 When Peter entered, Cornelius met him, fell at his feet, and worshiped
him.
26 But Peter helped him up and said, "Stand
up! I myself am also a man." 27 While talking
with him, he went on in and found that many
had come together there. 28 Peter[b] said to
them, "You know it's forbidden for a Jewish
man to associate with or visit a foreigner. But
God has shown me that I must not call any person common or unclean. 29 That's why I came
without any objection when I was sent for. So I
ask, 'Why did you send for me?' "
30 Cornelius replied, "Four days ago at this
hour, at three in the afternoon,[c] I was[d] praying
in my house. Just then a man in a dazzling robe
stood before me 31 and said, 'Cornelius, your
prayer has been heard, and your acts of charity
have been remembered in God's sight. 32
Therefore send someone to Joppa and invite
Simon here, who is also named Peter. He is
lodging in Simon the tanner's house by the
sea.'[e] 33 Therefore I immediately sent for you,
and you did the right thing in coming. So we
are all present before God, to hear everything
you have been commanded by the Lord."

Good News for Gentiles

34 Then Peter began to speak: "In truth, I
understand that God doesn't show favoritism,
35 but in every nation the person who fears
Him and does righteousness is acceptable to
Him. 36 He sent the message to the sons of
Israel, proclaiming the good news of peace
through Jesus Christ—He is Lord of all. 37 You
know the events[f] that took place throughout all
Judea, beginning from Galilee after the baptism
that John preached: 38 how God anointed Jesus
of Nazareth with the Holy Spirit and with
power, and how He went about doing good and
curing all who were under the tyranny of the
Devil, because God was with Him. 39 We ourselves are witnesses of everything He did in
both the Judean country and in Jerusalem; yet
they killed Him by hanging Him on a tree.
40 God raised up this man on the third day and
permitted Him to be seen, 41 not by all the people, but by us, witnesses appointed beforehand
by God, who ate and drank with Him after He
rose from the dead. 42 He commanded us to
preach to the people, and to solemnly testify
that He is the One appointed by God to be the
Judge of the living and the dead. 43 All the
prophets testify about Him that through His
name everyone who believes in Him will
receive forgiveness of sins."

Gentile Conversion and Baptism

44 While Peter was still speaking these
words, the Holy Spirit came down on all those
who heard the message. 45 The circumcised
believers[g] who had come with Peter were

[a] **10:14** Perhaps *profane*, or *non-sacred*; Jews ate distinctive food according to OT law and their traditions, similar to modern kosher or non-kosher foods. [b] **10:23,28** Lit *He* [c] **10:30** Lit *at the ninth hour* [d] **10:30** Other mss add *fasting and* [e] **10:32** Other mss add *When he arrives, he will speak to you.* [f] **10:37** Lit *thing*, or *word* [g] **10:45** Jewish Christians who stressed circumcision; Ac 11:2; 15:5; Gl 2:12; Col 4:11; Ti 1:10

astounded, because the gift of the Holy Spirit
had been poured out on the Gentiles also.
46 For they heard them speaking in ⌊other⌋ languages and declaring the greatness of[a] God.
Then Peter responded, 47 "Can anyone
withhold water and prevent these from being
baptized, who have received the Holy Spirit
just as we have?" 48 And he commanded them
to be baptized in the name of Jesus Christ.
Then they asked him to stay for a few days.

Gentile Salvation Defended

11 The apostles and the brothers who
were throughout Judea heard that the
Gentiles had welcomed God's message also.
2 When Peter went up to Jerusalem, those
who stressed circumcision[b] argued with him,
3 saying, "You visited uncircumcised men and
ate with them!"
4 Peter began to explain to them in an
orderly sequence, saying: 5 "I was in the town
of Joppa praying, and I saw, in a visionary state,
an object coming down that resembled a large
sheet being lowered from heaven by its four corners, and it came to me. 6 When I looked closely
and considered it, I saw the four-footed animals
of the earth, the wild beasts, the reptiles, and
the birds of the sky. 7 Then I also heard a voice
telling me, 'Get up, Peter; kill and eat!'
8 " 'No, Lord!' I said. 'For nothing common
or unclean has ever entered my mouth!' 9 But a
voice answered from heaven a second time,
'What God has made clean, you must not call
common.'
10 "Now this happened three times, and
then everything was drawn up again into
heaven. 11 At that very moment, three men
who had been sent to me from Caesarea
arrived at the house where we were. 12 Then
the Spirit told me to go with them with no
doubts at all. These six brothers accompanied
me, and we went into the man's house. 13 He
reported to us how he had seen the angel standing in his house and saying, 'Send[c] to Joppa,
and call for Simon, who is also named Peter.
14 He will speak words[d] to you by which you
and all your household will be saved.'
15 "As I began to speak, the Holy Spirit
came down on them, just as on us at the beginning. 16 Then I remembered the word of the
Lord, how He said, 'John baptized with water,
but you will be baptized with the Holy Spirit.'
17 Therefore, if God gave them the same gift
that He also gave to us when we believed on
the Lord Jesus Christ, how could I possibly
hinder God?"
18 When they heard this they became
silent. Then they glorified God, saying, "So God
has granted repentance resulting in life[e] to
even the Gentiles!"

The Church in Antioch

19 Those who had been scattered as a result
of the persecution that started because of
Stephen made their way as far as Phoenicia,
Cyprus, and Antioch, speaking the message to
no one except Jews. 20 But there were some of
them, Cypriot and Cyrenian men, who came to
Antioch and began speaking to the Hellenists,[f] [g]
proclaiming the good news about the Lord
Jesus. 21 The Lord's hand was with them, and a
large number who believed turned to the Lord.
22 Then the report about them reached the ears
of the church in Jerusalem, and they sent out
Barnabas to travel[h] as far as Antioch. 23 When
he arrived and saw the grace of God, he was
glad, and he encouraged all of them to remain
true to the Lord with a firm resolve of the
heart— 24 for he was a good man, full of the
Holy Spirit and of faith—and large numbers of
people were added to the Lord. 25 Then he[i]
went to Tarsus to search for Saul, 26 and when
he found him he brought him to Antioch. For a
whole year they met with the church and taught
large numbers, and the disciples were first
called Christians in Antioch.

Famine Relief

27 In those days some prophets came down
from Jerusalem to Antioch. 28 Then one of
them, named Agabus, stood up and predicted
by the Spirit that there would be a severe famine throughout the Roman world.[j] This took
place during the time of Claudius.[k] 29 So each
of the disciples, according to his ability, determined to send relief to the brothers who lived
in Judea. 30 This they did, sending it to the
elders by means of Barnabas and Saul.

James Martyred and Peter Jailed

12 About that time King •Herod cruelly
attacked some who belonged to the
church, 2 and he killed James, John's brother,

[a]**10:46** Or *and magnifying* [b]**11:2** Lit *those of the circumcision* [c]**11:13** Other mss add *men* [d]**11:14** Or *speak a message*
[e]**11:18** Or *repentance to life* [f]**11:20** Other mss read *Greeks* [g]**11:20** In this context, a non-Jewish person who spoke Gk
[h]**11:22** Other mss omit *to travel* [i]**11:25** Other mss read *Barnabas* [j]**11:28** Or *the whole world* [k]**11:28** Emperor A.D. 41–54;
there was a famine A.D. 47–48.

with the sword. 3 When he saw that it pleased the Jews, he proceeded to arrest Peter too, during the days of •Unleavened Bread. 4 After the arrest, he put him in prison and assigned four squads of four soldiers each to guard him, intending to bring him out to the people after the •Passover. 5 So Peter was kept in prison, but prayer was being made earnestly to God for him by the church.

Peter Rescued

6 On the night before Herod was to bring him out ⌊for execution⌋, Peter was sleeping between two soldiers, bound with two chains, while the sentries in front of the door guarded the prison. 7 Suddenly an angel of the Lord appeared, and a light shone in the cell. Striking Peter on the side, he woke him up and said, "Quick, get up!" Then the chains fell off his wrists. 8 "Get dressed," the angel told him, "and put on your sandals." And he did so. "Wrap your cloak around you," he told him, "and follow me." 9 So he went out and followed, and he did not know that what took place through the angel was real, but thought he was seeing a vision. 10 After they passed the first and second guard posts, they came to the iron gate that leads into the city, which opened to them by itself. They went outside and passed one street, and immediately the angel left him.

11 Then Peter came to himself and said, "Now I know for certain that the Lord has sent His angel and rescued me from Herod's grasp and from all that the Jewish people expected." 12 When he realized this, he went to the house of Mary, the mother of John Mark,[a] where many had assembled and were praying. 13 He knocked at the door in the gateway, and a servant named Rhoda came to answer. 14 She recognized Peter's voice, and because of her joy she did not open the gate, but ran in and announced that Peter was standing at the gateway.

15 "You're crazy!" they told her. But she kept insisting that it was true. Then they said, "It's his angel!" 16 Peter, however, kept on knocking, and when they opened the door and saw him, they were astounded.

17 Motioning to them with his hand to be silent, he explained to them how the Lord had brought him out of the prison. "Report these things to James[b] and the brothers," he said. Then he departed and went to a different place.

18 At daylight, there was a great commotion[c] among the soldiers as to what could have become of Peter. 19 After Herod had searched and did not find him, he interrogated the guards and ordered their execution. Then Herod went down from Judea to Caesarea and stayed there.

Herod's Death

20 He had been very angry with the Tyrians and Sidonians.[d] Together they presented themselves before him, and having won over Blastus, who was in charge of the king's bedroom, they asked for peace, because their country was supplied with food from the king's country. 21 So on an appointed day, dressed in royal robes and seated on the throne, Herod delivered a public address to them. 22 The populace began to shout, "It's the voice of a god and not of a man!" 23 At once an angel of the Lord struck him because he did not give the glory to God, and he became infected with worms and died. 24 Then God's message flourished and multiplied. 25 And Barnabas and Saul returned to[e] Jerusalem after they had completed their relief mission, on which they took John Mark.[a]

Preparing for the Mission Field

13 In the local church at Antioch there were prophets and teachers: Barnabas, Simeon who was called Niger, Lucius the Cyrenian, Manaen, a close friend of •Herod the tetrarch, and Saul.

2 As they were ministering to[f] the Lord and fasting, the Holy Spirit said, "Set apart for Me Barnabas and Saul for the work that I have called them to." 3 Then, after they had fasted, prayed, and laid hands on them,[g] they sent them off.

The Mission to Cyprus

4 Being sent out by the Holy Spirit, they came down to Seleucia, and from there they sailed to Cyprus. 5 Arriving in Salamis, they proclaimed God's message in the Jewish •synagogues. They also had John as their assistant. 6 When they had gone through the whole island as far as Paphos, they came across a sorcerer, a Jewish false prophet named Bar-Jesus.

[a]**12:12,25** Lit *John who was called Mark* [b]**12:17** This was James, the Lord's brother; see Mk 6:3. This was not James the apostle; see Ac 12:2. [c]**12:18** Or *was no small disturbance* [d]**12:20** The people of the area of modern Lebanon [e]**12:25** Other mss read *from* [f]**13:2** Or *were worshiping* [g]**13:3** See note at Ac 6:6

7 He was with the •proconsul, Sergius Paulus,
an intelligent man. This man summoned Barnabas and Saul and desired to hear God's message. 8 But Elymas, the sorcerer, which is how
his name is translated, opposed them and tried
to turn the proconsul away from the faith.

9 Then Saul—also called Paul—filled with
the Holy Spirit, stared straight at the sorcerer[a]
10 and said, "You son of the Devil, full of all
deceit and all fraud, enemy of all righteousness!
Won't you ever stop perverting the straight paths
of the Lord? 11 Now, look! The Lord's hand is
against you: you are going to be blind, and will
not see the sun for a time." Suddenly a mist and
darkness fell on him, and he went around seeking someone to lead him by the hand.

12 Then the proconsul, seeing what happened, believed and was astonished at the
teaching about the Lord.

Paul's Sermon in Antioch of Pisidia

13 Paul and his companions set sail from
Paphos and came to Perga in Pamphylia. John,
however, left them and went back to Jerusalem. 14 They continued their journey from
Perga and reached Antioch in Pisidia. On the
Sabbath day they went into the synagogue and
sat down. 15 After the reading of the Law and
the Prophets, the leaders of the synagogue sent
⌊word⌋ to them, saying, "Brothers, if you have
any message of encouragement for the people,
you can speak."

16 Then standing up, Paul motioned with
his hand and spoke: "Men of Israel, and you
who fear God, listen! 17 The God of this people Israel chose our forefathers, exalted the
people during their stay in the land of Egypt,
and led them out of it with a mighty[b] arm.
18 And for about 40 years He put up with
them[c] in the desert; 19 then after destroying
seven nations in the land of Canaan, He gave
their land to them as an inheritance. 20 This
all took about 450 years. After this, He gave
them judges until Samuel the prophet.
21 Then they asked for a king, so God gave
them Saul the son of Kish, a man of the tribe
of Benjamin, for 40 years. 22 After removing
him, He raised up David as their king, of
whom He testified: **'I have found David** the
son of Jesse, **a man after My heart,**[d] who will
carry out all My will.'

23 "From this man's descendants, according
to the promise, God brought the Savior, Jesus,[e]
to Israel. 24 Before He came to public attention,[f] John had previously proclaimed a baptism
of repentance to all the people of Israel.
25 Then as John was completing his life work,
he said, 'Who do you think I am? I am not the
One. But look! Someone is coming after me,
and I am not worthy to untie the sandals on His
feet.'

26 "Brothers, sons of Abraham's race, and
those among you who fear God, the message
of this salvation has been sent to us. 27 For the
residents of Jerusalem and their rulers, since
they did not recognize Him or the voices of
the prophets that are read every Sabbath, have
fulfilled their words[g] by condemning Him.
28 Though they found no grounds for the
death penalty, they asked •Pilate to have Him
killed. 29 When they had fulfilled all that had
been written about Him, they took Him down
from the tree and put Him in a tomb. 30 But
God raised Him from the dead, 31 and He
appeared for many days to those who came up
with Him from Galilee to Jerusalem, who are
now His witnesses to the people. 32 And we
ourselves proclaim to you the good news of
the promise that was made to our forefathers.
33 God has fulfilled this to us their children by
raising up Jesus, as it is written in the second
Psalm:

> **You are My Son;**
> **today I have become Your Father.**[h] [i]

34 Since He raised Him from the dead, never
to return to decay, He has spoken in this way, **I
will grant you the faithful covenant blessings**[j]
made to David.[k] 35 Therefore He also says in
another passage, **You will not allow Your Holy
One to see decay.**[l] 36 For David, after serving
his own generation in God's plan, fell •asleep,
was buried with his fathers, and decayed.
37 But the One whom God raised up did not
decay. 38 Therefore, let it be known to you,
brothers, that through this man forgiveness of
sins is being proclaimed to you, 39 and everyone who believes in Him is justified from
everything, which you could not be justified
from through the law of Moses. 40 So beware
that what is said in the prophets does not happen to you:

[a]**13:9** Lit *at him* [b]**13:17** Lit *with an uplifted* [c]**13:18** Other mss read *He cared for them* [d]**13:22** 1 Sm 13:14; Ps 89:20 [e]**13:23** Other mss read *brought salvation* [f]**13:24** Lit *Before the face of His entrance* [g]**13:27** Lit *fulfilled them* [h]**13:33** Or *I have begotten You* [i]**13:33** Ps 2:7 [j]**13:34** Lit *faithful holy things* [k]**13:34** Is 55:3 [l]**13:35** Ps 16:10

41 **Look, you scoffers,**
marvel and vanish away,
because I am doing a work
in your days,
a work that you will never believe,
even if someone were to explain it
to you."[a]

Paul and Barnabas in Antioch

42 As they[b] were leaving, they[c] [d] begged
that these matters be presented to them the following Sabbath. 43 After the synagogue had
been dismissed, many of the Jews and devout
•proselytes followed Paul and Barnabas, who
were speaking with them and persuading them
to continue in the grace of God.
44 The following Sabbath almost the whole
town assembled to hear the message of the
Lord.[e] 45 But when the Jews saw the crowds,
they were filled with jealousy and began to
oppose what Paul was saying by insulting him.
46 Then Paul and Barnabas boldly said: "It
was necessary that God's message be spoken to
you first. But since you reject it, and consider
yourselves unworthy of eternal life, we now
turn to the Gentiles! 47 For this is what the
Lord has commanded us:

I have appointed you as a light
for the Gentiles,
to bring salvation to the ends[f]
of the earth."[g]

48 When the Gentiles heard this, they rejoiced
and glorified the message of the Lord, and all
who had been appointed to eternal life
believed. 49 So the message of the Lord spread
through the whole region. 50 But the Jews
incited the religious women of high standing
and the leading men of the city. They stirred
up persecution against Paul and Barnabas and
expelled them from their district. 51 But shaking the dust off their feet against them, they
proceeded to Iconium. 52 And the disciples
were filled with joy and the Holy Spirit.

Growth and Persecution in Iconium

14 The same thing happened in Iconium;
they entered the Jewish •synagogue
and spoke in such a way that a great number of
both Jews and Greeks believed. 2 But the Jews
who refused to believe stirred up and poisoned
the minds[h] of the Gentiles against the brothers. 3 So they stayed there for some time and
spoke boldly, in reliance on the Lord, who testified to the message of His grace by granting
that signs and wonders be performed through
them. 4 But the people of the city were
divided, some siding with the Jews and some
with the apostles. 5 When an attempt was
made by both the Gentiles and Jews, with
their rulers, to assault and stone them, 6 they
found out about it and fled to the Lycaonian
towns called Lystra and Derbe, and to the surrounding countryside. 7 And there they kept
evangelizing.

Mistaken for Gods in Lystra

8 In Lystra a man without strength in his
feet, lame from birth,[i] and who had never
walked, sat 9 and heard Paul speaking. After
observing him closely and seeing that he had
faith to be healed, 10 ⌊Paul⌋ said in a loud voice,
"Stand up straight on your feet!" And he
jumped up and started to walk around.
11 When the crowds saw what Paul had
done, they raised their voices, saying in the
Lycaonian language, "The gods have come
down to us in the form of men!" 12 And they
started to call Barnabas, Zeus, and Paul, Hermes, because he was the main speaker.
13 Then the priest of Zeus, whose temple was
just outside the town, brought oxen and gar-
lands to the gates. He, with the crowds,
intended to offer sacrifice.
14 The apostles Barnabas and Paul tore
their robes when they heard this and rushed
into the crowd, shouting: 15 "Men! Why are
you doing these things? We are men also, with
the same nature as you, and we are proclaiming good news to you, that you should turn
from these worthless things to the living God,
who made the heaven, the earth, the sea,
and everything in them.[j] 16 In past generations He allowed all the nations to go their
own way, 17 although He did not leave Himself without a witness, since He did good: giving you rain from heaven and fruitful seasons,
and satisfying your[k] hearts with food and hap-
piness." 18 Even though they said these
things, they barely stopped the crowds from
sacrificing to them.
19 Then some Jews came from Antioch and
Iconium, and when they had won over the
crowds and stoned Paul, they dragged him out

[a] **13:41** Hab 1:5 [b] **13:42** Paul and Barnabas [c] **13:42** Other mss read *they were leaving the synagogue of the Jews, the Gentiles* [d] **13:42** The people [e] **13:44** Other mss read *of God* [f] **13:47** Lit *the end* [g] **13:47** Is 49:6 [h] **14:2** Lit *and harmed the souls* [i] **14:8** Lit *from his mother's womb* [j] **14:15** Ex 20:11; Ps 146:6 [k] **14:17** Other mss read *our*

of the city, thinking he was dead. 20 After the
disciples surrounded him, he got up and went
into the town. The next day he left with Barnabas for Derbe.

Church Planting

21 After they had evangelized that town and
made many disciples, they returned to Lystra,
to Iconium, and to Antioch, 22 strengthening
the hearts[a] of the disciples by encouraging
them to continue in the faith, and by telling
them, "It is necessary to pass through many
troubles on our way into the kingdom of God."
23 When they had appointed elders in every
church and prayed with fasting, they committed them to the Lord in whom they had
believed. 24 Then they passed through Pisidia
and came to Pamphylia. 25 After they spoke the
message in Perga, they went down to Attalia.
26 From there they sailed back to Antioch
where they had been entrusted to the grace of
God for the work they had completed. 27 After
they arrived and gathered the church together,
they reported everything God had done with
them, and that He had opened the door of faith
to the Gentiles. 28 And they spent a considerable time[b] with the disciples.

Dispute in Antioch

15 Some men came down from Judea and
began to teach the brothers: "Unless
you are circumcised according to the custom
prescribed by Moses, you cannot be saved!"
2 But after Paul and Barnabas had engaged
them in serious argument and debate, they
arranged for Paul and Barnabas and some others of them to go up to the apostles and elders
in Jerusalem concerning this controversy.
3 When they had been sent on their way by
the church, they passed through both Phoenicia and Samaria, explaining in detail the con-
version of the Gentiles, and they created great
joy among all the brothers.
4 When they arrived at Jerusalem, they
were welcomed by the church, the apostles,
and the elders, and they reported all that God
had done with them. 5 But some of the believers from the party of the •Pharisees stood up
and said, "It is necessary to circumcise them
and to command them to keep the law of
Moses!"

The Jerusalem Council

6 Then the apostles and the elders assembled to consider this matter. 7 After there had
been much debate, Peter stood up and said to
them: "Brothers, you are aware that in the
early days God made a choice among you,[c] that
by my mouth the Gentiles would hear the gospel message and believe. 8 And God, who
knows the heart, testified to them by giving[d]
the Holy Spirit, just as He also did to us. 9 He
made no distinction between us and them,
cleansing their hearts by faith. 10 Why, then,
are you now testing God by putting on the disciples' necks a yoke that neither our forefathers
nor we have been able to bear? 11 On the contrary, we believe we are saved through the
grace of the Lord Jesus, in the same way they
are."
12 Then the whole assembly fell silent and
listened to Barnabas and Paul describing all the
signs and wonders God had done through them
among the Gentiles. 13 After they stopped
speaking, James responded: "Brothers, listen to
me! 14 Simeon[e] has reported how God first
intervened to take from the Gentiles a people
for His name. 15 And the words of the prophets
agree with this, as it is written:

16 **After these things**
I will return
and will rebuild David's tent,
which has fallen down.
I will rebuild its ruins
and will set it up again,
17 **so that those who are left of mankind**
may seek the Lord—
even all the Gentiles who are called
by My name,
says the Lord who does these things,
18 **which have been known from long**
ago.[f g]

19 Therefore, in my judgment, we should not
cause difficulties for those who turn to God
from among the Gentiles, 20 but instead we
should write to them to abstain from things
polluted by idols, from sexual immorality, from
eating anything that has been strangled, and
from blood. 21 For since ancient times, Moses
has had in every city those who proclaim him,
and he is read aloud in the •synagogues every
Sabbath day."

[a]**14:22** Lit *souls* [b]**14:28** Or *spent no little time* [c]**15:7** Other mss read *us* [d]**15:8** Other mss add *them* [e]**15:14** Simon (Peter) [f]**15:17–18** Other mss read *says the Lord who does all these things. Known to God from long ago are all His works.* [g]**15:16–18** Am 9:11–12; Is 45:21

The Letter to the Gentile Believers

22 Then the apostles and the elders, with the whole church, decided to select men from among them and to send them to Antioch with Paul and Barnabas: Judas, called Barsabbas, and Silas, both leading men among the brothers. 23 They wrote this letter to be delivered by them:[a]

From the apostles and the elders, your brothers,

To the brothers from among the Gentiles in Antioch, Syria, and Cilicia:

Greetings.

24 Because we have heard that some to whom we gave no authorization went out from us and troubled you with their words and unsettled your hearts,[b] 25 we have unanimously decided to select men and send them to you along with our beloved Barnabas and Paul, 26 who have risked their lives for the name of our Lord Jesus Christ. 27 Therefore we have sent Judas and Silas, who will personally report the same things by word of mouth.[c] 28 For it was the Holy Spirit's decision—and ours—to put no greater burden on you than these necessary things: 29 that you abstain from food offered to idols, from blood, from eating anything that has been strangled, and from sexual immorality. If you keep yourselves from these things, you will do well.

Farewell.

The Outcome of the Jerusalem Letter

30 Then, being sent off, they went down to Antioch, and after gathering the assembly, they delivered the letter. 31 When they read it, they rejoiced because of its encouragement. 32 Both Judas and Silas, who were also prophets themselves, encouraged the brothers and strengthened them with a long message. 33 After spending some time there, they were sent back in peace by the brothers to those who had sent them.[d] [e] 35 But Paul and Barnabas, along with many others, remained in Antioch teaching and proclaiming the message of the Lord.

Paul and Barnabas Part Company

36 After some time had passed, Paul said to Barnabas, "Let's go back and visit the brothers in every town where we have preached the message of the Lord, and see how they're doing." 37 Barnabas wanted to take along John Mark.[f] 38 But Paul did not think it appropriate to take along this man who had deserted them in Pamphylia and had not gone on with them to the work. 39 There was such a sharp disagreement that they parted company, and Barnabas took Mark with him and sailed off to Cyprus. 40 Then Paul chose Silas and departed, after being commended to the grace of the Lord by the brothers. 41 He traveled through Syria and Cilicia, strengthening the churches.

Paul Selects Timothy

16 Then he went on to Derbe and Lystra, where there was a disciple named Timothy, the son of a believing Jewish woman, but his father was a Greek. 2 The brothers at Lystra and Iconium spoke highly of him. 3 Paul wanted Timothy[g] to go with him, so he took him and circumcised him because of the Jews who were in those places, since they all knew that his father was a Greek. 4 As they traveled through the towns, they delivered the decisions reached by the apostles and elders at Jerusalem for them to observe. 5 So the churches were strengthened in the faith and were increased in number daily.

Evangelization of Europe

6 They went through the region of Phrygia and Galatia and were prevented by the Holy Spirit from speaking the message in the province of Asia. 7 When they came to Mysia, they tried to go into Bithynia, but the Spirit of Jesus did not allow them. 8 So, bypassing Mysia, they came down to Troas. 9 During the night a vision appeared to Paul: a Macedonian man was standing and pleading with him, "Cross over to Macedonia and help us!" 10 After he had seen the vision, we[h] immediately made efforts to set out for Macedonia, concluding that God had called us to evangelize them.

Lydia's Conversion

11 Then, setting sail from Troas, we ran a straight course to Samothrace, the next day to

[a] **15:23** Lit *Writing by their hand:* [b] **15:24** Other mss add *by saying, "Be circumcised and keep the law,"* [c] **15:27** Lit *things through word* [d] **15:33** Other mss read *the brothers to the apostles* [e] **15:33** Other mss add v. 34: *But Silas decided to stay there.* [f] **15:37** Lit *John who was called Mark* [g] **16:3** Lit *wanted this one* [h] **16:10** The use of *we* in this passage probably indicates that the author Luke is joining Paul's missionary team here.

Neapolis, 12 and from there to Philippi, a
Roman colony, which is a leading city of that
district of Macedonia. We stayed in that city for
a number of days. 13 On the Sabbath day we
went outside the city gate by the river, where
we thought there was a place of prayer. We sat
down and spoke to the women gathered there.
14 A woman named Lydia, a dealer in purple
cloth from the city of Thyatira, who worshiped
God, was listening. The Lord opened her heart
to pay attention to what was spoken by Paul.
15 After she and her household were baptized,
she urged us, "If you consider me a believer in
the Lord, come and stay at my house." And she
persuaded us.

Paul and Silas in Prison

16 Once, as we were on our way to prayer,
a slave girl met us who had a spirit of prediction[a] and made a large profit for her owners by
fortune-telling. 17 As she followed Paul and us
she cried out, "These men are the slaves of the
•Most High God, who are proclaiming to you[b]
the way of salvation." 18 And she did this for
many days.

But Paul was greatly aggravated, and turning
to the spirit, said, "I command you in the name
of Jesus Christ to come out of her!" And it came
out right away.[c]

19 When her owners saw that their hope of
profit was gone, they seized Paul and Silas and
dragged them into the marketplace to the
authorities. 20 And bringing them before the
chief magistrates, they said, "These men are
seriously disturbing our city. They are Jews,
21 and are promoting customs that are not legal
for us as Romans to adopt or practice."

22 Then the mob joined in the attack against
them, and the chief magistrates stripped off
their clothes and ordered them to be beaten
with rods. 23 After they had inflicted many
blows on them, they threw them in jail, ordering the jailer to keep them securely guarded.
24 Receiving such an order, he put them into
the inner prison and secured their feet in the
stocks.

A Midnight Deliverance

25 About midnight Paul and Silas were praying and singing hymns to God, and the prisoners were listening to them. 26 Suddenly there
was such a violent earthquake that the foundations of the jail were shaken, and immediately
all the doors were opened, and everyone's
chains came loose. 27 When the jailer woke up
and saw the doors of the prison open, he drew
his sword and was going to kill himself, since
he thought the prisoners had escaped.

28 But Paul called out in a loud voice, "Don't
harm yourself, because all of us are here!"

29 Then the jailer[d] called for lights, rushed
in, and fell down trembling before Paul and
Silas. 30 Then he escorted them out and said,
"Sirs, what must I do to be saved?"

31 So they said, "Believe on the Lord Jesus,
and you will be saved—you and your household." 32 Then they spoke the message of the
Lord to him along with everyone in his house.
33 He took them the same hour of the night and
washed their wounds. Right away he and all his
family were baptized. 34 He brought them up
into his house, set a meal before them, and
rejoiced because he had believed God with his
entire household.

An Official Apology

35 When daylight came, the chief magistrates sent the police to say, "Release those
men!"

36 The jailer reported these words to Paul:
"The magistrates have sent orders for you to be
released. So come out now and go in peace."

37 But Paul said to them, "They beat us in
public without a trial, although we are Roman
citizens, and threw us in jail. And now are they
going to smuggle us out secretly? Certainly not!
On the contrary, let them come themselves and
escort us out!"

38 Then the police reported these words to
the magistrates. And they were afraid when
they heard that Paul and Silas[e] were Roman citizens. 39 So they came and apologized to them,
and escorting them out, they urged them to
leave town. 40 After leaving the jail, they came
to Lydia's house where they saw and encouraged the brothers, and departed.

A Short Ministry in Thessalonica

17 Then they traveled through Amphipo-
lis and Apollonia and came to Thessalonica, where there was a Jewish •synagogue.
2 As usual, Paul went to them, and on three
Sabbath days reasoned with them from the
Scriptures, 3 explaining and showing that the

[a]**16:16** Or *a spirit by which she predicted the future* [b]**16:17** Other mss read *us* [c]**16:18** Lit *out this hour* [d]**16:29** Lit *Then he* [e]**16:38** Lit *heard they*

•Messiah had to suffer and rise from the dead, and saying: "This is the Messiah, Jesus, whom I am proclaiming to you." 4 Then some of them were persuaded and joined Paul and Silas, including a great number of God-fearing Greeks, as well as a number[a] of the leading women.

The Assault on Jason's House

5 But the Jews became jealous, and when they had brought together some scoundrels from the marketplace and formed a mob, they set the city in an uproar. Attacking Jason's house, they searched for them to bring them out to the public assembly. 6 When they did not find them, they dragged Jason and some of the brothers before the city officials, shouting, "These men who have turned the world upside down have come here too, 7 and Jason has received them as guests! They are all acting contrary to Caesar's decrees, saying that there is another king—Jesus!" 8 The Jews[b] stirred up the crowd and the city officials who heard these things. 9 So taking a security bond from Jason and the others, they released them.

The Beroeans Search the Scriptures

10 As soon as it was night, the brothers sent Paul and Silas off to Beroea. On arrival, they went into the synagogue of the Jews. 11 The people here were more open-minded than those in Thessalonica, since they welcomed the message with eagerness and examined the Scriptures daily to see if these things were so. 12 Consequently, many of them believed, including a number of the prominent Greek women as well as men. 13 But when the Jews from Thessalonica found out that God's message had been proclaimed by Paul at Beroea, they came there too, agitating and disturbing[c] the crowds. 14 Then the brothers immediately sent Paul away to go to the sea, but Silas and Timothy stayed on there. 15 Those who escorted Paul brought him as far as Athens, and after receiving instructions for Silas and Timothy to come to him as quickly as possible, they departed.

Paul in Athens

16 While Paul was waiting for them in Athens, his spirit was troubled within him when he saw that the city was full of idols. 17 So he reasoned in the synagogue with the Jews and with those who worshiped God, and in the marketplace every day with those who happened to be there. 18 Then also, some of the Epicurean and Stoic philosophers argued with him. Some said, "What is this pseudo-intellectual[d] trying to say?"

Others replied, "He seems to be a preacher of foreign deities"—because he was telling the good news about Jesus and the resurrection.

19 They took him and brought him to the Areopagus,[e] and said, "May we learn about this new teaching you're speaking of? 20 For what you say sounds strange to us, and we want to know what these ideas mean." 21 Now all the Athenians and the foreigners residing there spent their time on nothing else but telling or hearing something new.

The Areopagus Address

22 Then Paul stood in the middle of the Areopagus and said: "Men of Athens! I see that you are extremely religious in every respect. 23 For as I was passing through and observing the objects of your worship, I even found an altar on which was inscribed:

TO AN UNKNOWN GOD

Therefore, what you worship in ignorance, this I proclaim to you. 24 The God who made the world and everything in it—He is Lord of heaven and earth and does not live in shrines made by hands. 25 Neither is He served by human hands, as though He needed anything, since He Himself gives everyone life and breath and all things. 26 From one man[f] He has made every nation of men to live all over the earth and has determined their appointed times and the boundaries of where they live, 27 so that they might seek God, and perhaps they might reach out and find Him, though He is not far from each one of us. 28 For in Him we live and move and exist, as even some of your own poets have said, 'For we are also His offspring.'[g] 29 Being God's offspring, then, we shouldn't think that the divine nature is like gold or silver or stone, an image fashioned by human art and imagination.

30 "Therefore, having overlooked the times of ignorance, God now commands all people

[a]**17:4** Lit *as well as not a few* [b]**17:8** Lit *They* [c]**17:13** Other mss omit *and disturbing* [d]**17:18** Lit *this seed picker*; that is, one who picks up scraps [e]**17:19** Or *Mars Hill*, the oldest and most famous court in Athens with jurisdiction in moral, religious, and civil matters [f]**17:26** Other mss read *one blood* [g]**17:28** This citation is from Aratus, a third-century B.C. Gk poet.

everywhere to repent, 31 because He has set a
day on which He is going to judge the world in
righteousness by the Man He has appointed.
He has provided proof of this to everyone by
raising Him from the dead."
32 When they heard about resurrection of
the dead, some began to ridicule him. But others said, "We will hear you about this again."
33 So Paul went out from their presence.
34 However, some men joined him and
believed, among whom were Dionysius the
Areopagite, a woman named Damaris, and others with them.

Founding the Corinthian Church

18 After this, he[a] left from Athens and
went to Corinth, 2 where he found a
Jewish man named Aquila, a native of Pontus,
who had recently come from Italy with his
wife Priscilla because Claudius[b] had ordered
all the Jews to leave Rome. Paul[c] came to
them, 3 and being of the same occupation,
stayed with them and worked, for they were
tentmakers by trade. 4 He reasoned in the
•synagogue every Sabbath and tried to persuade both Jews and Greeks.
5 When Silas and Timothy came down from
Macedonia, Paul was occupied with preaching
the message[d] and solemnly testified to the Jews
that the •Messiah is Jesus. 6 But when they
resisted and blasphemed, he shook out his
clothes[e] and told them, "Your blood is on your
own heads! I am clean. From now on I will go
to the Gentiles." 7 So he left there and went to
the house of a man named Titius Justus, a wor-
shiper of God, whose house was next door to
the synagogue. 8 Crispus, the leader of the synagogue, believed the Lord, along with his
whole household; and many of the Corinthians,
when they heard, believed and were baptized.
9 Then the Lord said to Paul in a night
vision, "Don't be afraid, but keep on speaking
and don't be silent. 10 For I am with you, and
no one will lay a hand on you to hurt you,
because I have many people in this city."
11 And he stayed there a year and six months,
teaching the word of God among them.
12 While Gallio was •proconsul of Achaia,
the Jews made a united attack against Paul and
brought him to the judge's bench. 13 "This
man," they said, "persuades people to worship
God contrary to the law!"
14 And as Paul was about to open his mouth,
Gallio said to the Jews, "If it were a matter of a
crime or of moral evil, it would be reasonable
for me to put up with you Jews. 15 But if these
are questions about words, names, and your
own law, see to it yourselves. I don't want to be
a judge of such things." 16 So he drove them
from the judge's bench. 17 Then they all[f] seized
Sosthenes, the leader of the synagogue, and
beat him in front of the judge's bench. But none
of these things concerned Gallio.

The Return Trip to Antioch

18 So Paul, having stayed on for many days,
said good-bye to the brothers and sailed away to
Syria. Priscilla and Aquila were with him. He
shaved his head at Cenchreae, because he had
taken a vow. 19 When they reached Ephesus he
left them there, but he himself entered the synagogue and engaged in discussion with[g] the
Jews. 20 And though they asked him to stay for
a longer time, he declined, 21 but said good-bye
and stated,[h] "I'll come back to you again, if God
wills." Then he set sail from Ephesus.
22 On landing at Caesarea, he went up and
greeted the church,[i] and went down to Antioch. 23 He set out, traveling through one place
after another in the Galatian territory and Phrygia, strengthening all the disciples.

The Eloquent Apollos

24 A Jew named Apollos, a native Alexandrian, an eloquent man who was powerful in
the Scriptures, arrived in Ephesus. 25 This man
had been instructed in the way of the Lord; and
being fervent in spirit,[j] he spoke and taught the
things about Jesus accurately, although he
knew only John's baptism. 26 He began to
speak boldly in the synagogue. After Priscilla
and Aquila heard him, they took him home[k]
and explained the way of God to him more
accurately. 27 When he wanted to cross over to
Achaia, the brothers wrote to the disciples urging them to welcome him. After he arrived, he
greatly helped those who had believed through
grace. 28 For he vigorously refuted the Jews in
public, demonstrating through the Scriptures
that Jesus is the Messiah.

[a]**18:1** Other mss read *Paul* [b]**18:2** Roman emperor A.D. 41–54; he expelled all Jews from Rome in A.D. 49. [c]**18:2** Lit *He* [d]**18:5** Other mss read *was urged by the Spirit* [e]**18:6** A symbolic display of protest; see Ac 13:51; Mt 10:14 [f]**18:17** Other mss read *Then all the Greeks* [g]**18:19** Or *and addressed* [h]**18:21** Other mss add *"By all means it is necessary to keep the coming festival in Jerusalem. But* [i]**18:22** The church in Jerusalem [j]**18:25** Or *in the Spirit* [k]**18:26** Lit *they received him*

Twelve Disciples of John the Baptist

19 While Apollos was in Corinth, Paul traveled through the interior regions and came to Ephesus. He found some disciples 2 and asked them, "Did you receive the Holy Spirit when you believed?"

"No," they told him, "we haven't even heard that there is a Holy Spirit."

3 "Then with what ⌊baptism⌋ were you baptized?" he asked them.

"With John's baptism," they replied.

4 Paul said, "John baptized with a baptism of repentance, telling the people that they should believe in the One who would come after him, that is, in Jesus."

5 On hearing this, they were baptized in the name of the Lord Jesus. 6 And when Paul had laid his hands on them, the Holy Spirit came on them, and they began to speak with ⌊other⌋ languages and to prophesy. 7 Now there were about 12 men in all.

In the Lecture Hall of Tyrannus

8 Then he entered the •synagogue and spoke boldly over a period of three months, engaging in discussion and trying to persuade them about the things related to the kingdom of God. 9 But when some became hardened and would not believe, slandering the Way in front of the crowd, he withdrew from them and met separately with the disciples, conducting discussions every day in the lecture hall of Tyrannus. 10 And this went on for two years, so that all the inhabitants of the province of Asia, both Jews and Greeks, heard the word of the Lord.

Demonism Defeated at Ephesus

11 God was performing extraordinary miracles by Paul's hands, 12 so that even facecloths or work aprons[a] that had touched his skin were brought to the sick, and the diseases left them, and the evil spirits came out of them.

13 Then some of the itinerant Jewish exorcists attempted to pronounce the name of the Lord Jesus over those who had evil spirits, saying, "I command you by the Jesus whom Paul preaches!" 14 Seven sons of Sceva, a Jewish •chief priest, were doing this. 15 The evil spirit answered them, "Jesus I know, and Paul I recognize—but who are you?" 16 Then the man who had the evil spirit leaped on them, overpowered them all, and prevailed against them, so that they ran out of that house naked and wounded. 17 This became known to everyone who lived in Ephesus, both Jews and Greeks. Then fear fell on all of them, and the name of the Lord Jesus was magnified. 18 And many who had become believers came confessing and disclosing their practices, 19 while many of those who had practiced magic collected their books and burned them in front of everyone. So they calculated their value, and found it to be 50,000 pieces of silver. 20 In this way the Lord's message flourished and prevailed.

The Riot in Ephesus

21 When these events were over, Paul resolved in the Spirit to pass through Macedonia and Achaia and go to Jerusalem. "After I've been there," he said, "I must see Rome as well!" 22 So after sending two of those who assisted him, Timothy and Erastus, to Macedonia, he himself stayed in the province of Asia for a while.

23 During that time there was a major[b] disturbance about the Way. 24 For a person named Demetrius, a silversmith who made silver shrines of Artemis,[c] provided a great deal of[d] business for the craftsmen. 25 When he had assembled them, as well as the workers engaged in this type of business, he said: "Men, you know that our prosperity is derived from this business. 26 You both see and hear that not only in Ephesus, but in almost the whole province of Asia, this man Paul has persuaded and misled a considerable number of people by saying that gods made by hand are not gods! 27 So not only do we run a risk that our business may be discredited, but also that the temple of the great goddess Artemis may be despised and her magnificence come to the verge of ruin—the very one whom the whole province of Asia and the world adore."

28 When they had heard this, they were filled with rage and began to cry out, "Great is Artemis of the Ephesians!" 29 So the city was filled with confusion; and they rushed all together into the amphitheater, dragging along Gaius and Aristarchus, Macedonians who were Paul's traveling companions. 30 Though Paul wanted to go in before the people, the disciples did not let him. 31 Even some of the provincial officials of Asia, who were his friends, sent word to him, pleading with him not to take a

[a] **19:12** Or *that also sweatbands and sweatcloths* or *handkerchiefs* [b] **19:23** Lit *was not a little* [c] **19:24** Artemis was the ancient Gk mother goddess believed to control all fertility. [d] **19:24** Lit *provided not a little*

chance by going[a] into the amphitheater.
32 Meanwhile, some were shouting one thing
and some another, because the assembly was in
confusion, and most of them did not know why
they had come together. 33 Then some of the
crowd gave Alexander advice when the Jews
pushed him to the front. So motioning with his
hand, Alexander wanted to make his defense to
the people. 34 But when they recognized that
he was a Jew, a united cry went up from all of
them for about two hours: "Great is Artemis of
the Ephesians!"
35 However, when the city clerk had
calmed the crowd down, he said, "Men of
Ephesus! What man is there who doesn't
know that the city of the Ephesians is the temple guardian of the great[b] Artemis, and of the
image that fell from heaven? 36 Therefore,
since these things are undeniable, you must
keep calm and not do anything rash. 37 For
you have brought these men here who are not
temple robbers or blasphemers of our[c] goddess. 38 So if Demetrius and the craftsmen
who are with him have a case against anyone,
the courts are in session, and there are •pro-
consuls. Let them bring charges against one
another. 39 But if you want something else, it
must be decided in a legal assembly. 40 In fact,
we run a risk of being charged with rioting for
what happened today, since there is no justification that we can give as a reason for this disorderly gathering." 41 After saying this, he
dismissed the assembly.

Paul in Macedonia

20 After the uproar was over, Paul sent
for the disciples, encouraged them,
and after saying good-bye, departed to go to
Macedonia. 2 And when he had passed
through those areas and exhorted them at
length, he came to Greece 3 and stayed
three months. When he was about to set sail
for Syria, a plot was devised against him by
the Jews, so a decision was made to go back
through Macedonia. 4 He was accompanied[d] by Sopater, son of Pyrrhus,[e] from
Beroea, Aristarchus and Secundus from
Thessalonica, Gaius from Derbe, Timothy,
and Tychicus and Trophimus from Asia.
5 These men went on ahead and waited for
us in Troas, 6 but we sailed away from Philippi after the days of •Unleavened Bread. In
five days we reached them at Troas, where
we spent seven days.

Eutychus Revived at Troas

7 On the first day of the week,[f] we[g] assembled to break bread. Paul spoke to them, and
since he was about to depart the next day, he
extended his message until midnight. 8 There
were many lamps in the room upstairs where
we were assembled, 9 and a young man named
Eutychus was sitting on a window sill and sank
into a deep sleep as Paul kept on speaking. When
he was overcome by sleep he fell down from the
third story, and was picked up dead. 10 But Paul
went down, threw himself on him, embraced
him, and said, "Don't be alarmed, for his •life is
in him!" 11 After going upstairs, breaking the
bread, and eating, he conversed a considerable
time until dawn. Then he left. 12 They brought
the boy home alive and were greatly comforted.

From Troas to Miletus

13 Then we went on ahead to the ship and
sailed for Assos, from there intending to take
Paul on board. For these were his instructions,
since he himself was going by land. 14 When he
met us at Assos, we took him on board and
came to Mitylene. 15 Sailing from there, the
next day we arrived off Chios. The following
day we crossed over to Samos, and[h] the day
after, we came to Miletus. 16 For Paul had
decided to sail past Ephesus so he would not
have to spend time in the province of Asia,
because he was hurrying to be in Jerusalem, if
possible, for the day of Pentecost.

Farewell Address to the Ephesian Elders

17 Now from Miletus, he sent to Ephesus
and called for the elders of the church. 18 And
when they came to him, he said to them: "You
know, from the first day I set foot in Asia, how
I was with you the whole time— 19 serving the
Lord with all humility, with tears, and with the
trials that came to me through the plots of the
Jews— 20 and that I did not shrink back from
proclaiming to you anything that was profitable, or from teaching it to you in public and
from house to house. 21 I testified to both Jews
and Greeks about repentance toward God and
faith in our Lord Jesus.
22 "And now I am on my way to Jerusalem,
bound in my spirit, not knowing what I will

[a] **19:31** Lit *not to give himself* [b] **19:35** Other mss add *goddess* [c] **19:37** Other mss read *your* [d] **20:4** Other mss add *to Asia*
[e] **20:4** Other mss omit *son of Pyrrhus* [f] **20:7** Lit *On one between the Sabbaths*; that is, Sunday [g] **20:7** Other mss read *the disciples* [h] **20:15** Other mss add *after staying at Trogyllium*

encounter there, 23 except that in town after
town the Holy Spirit testifies to me that chains
and afflictions are waiting for me. 24 But I count
my life of no value to myself, so that I may finish my course[a] and the ministry I received from
the Lord Jesus, to testify to the gospel of God's
grace.
25 "And now I know that none of you,
among whom I went about preaching the
kingdom, will ever see my face again.
26 Therefore I testify to you this day that I am
innocent[b] of everyone's blood, 27 for I did
not shrink back from declaring to you the
whole plan of God. 28 Be on guard for yourselves and for all the flock, among whom the
Holy Spirit has appointed you as •overseers,
to shepherd the church of God,[c] which He
purchased with His own blood. 29 I know
that after my departure savage wolves will
come in among you, not sparing the flock.
30 And men from among yourselves will rise
up with deviant doctrines to lure the disciples into following them. 31 Therefore be on
the alert, remembering that night and day for
three years I did not stop warning each one
of you with tears.
32 "And now[d] I commit you to God and to
the message of His grace, which is able to build
you up and to give you an inheritance among all
who are sanctified. 33 I have not coveted anyone's silver or gold or clothing. 34 You yourselves know that these hands have provided for
my needs, and for those who were with me.
35 In every way I've shown you that by laboring
like this, it is necessary to help the weak and to
keep in mind the words of the Lord Jesus, for
He said, 'It is more blessed to give than to
receive.' "
36 After he said this, he knelt down and
prayed with all of them. 37 There was a great
deal of weeping by everyone. And embracing
Paul, they kissed him, 38 grieving most of all
over his statement that they would never see
his face again. Then they escorted him to the
ship.

Warnings on the Journey to Jerusalem

21 After we tore ourselves away from
them and set sail, we came by a direct
route to Cos, the next day to Rhodes, and from
there to Patara. 2 Finding a ship crossing over
to Phoenicia, we boarded and set sail. 3 After
we sighted Cyprus, leaving it on the left, we
sailed on to Syria and arrived at Tyre, because
the ship was to unload its cargo there. 4 So we
found some disciples and stayed there seven
days. They said to Paul through the Spirit not
to go to Jerusalem. 5 When our days there
were over, we left to continue our journey,
while all of them, with their wives and children, escorted us out of the city. After kneeling
down on the beach to pray, 6 we said good-bye
to one another. Then we boarded the ship, and
they returned home.
7 When we completed our voyage from
Tyre, we reached Ptolemais, where we greeted
the brothers and stayed with them one day.
8 The next day we left and came to Caesarea,
where we entered the house of Philip the evangelist, who was one of the Seven, and stayed
with him. 9 This man had four virgin daughters
who prophesied.
10 While we were staying there many days,
a prophet named Agabus came down from
Judea. 11 He came to us, took Paul's belt, tied
his own feet and hands, and said, "This is
what the Holy Spirit says: 'In this way the
Jews in Jerusalem will bind the man who
owns this belt, and deliver him into Gentile
hands.' " 12 When we heard this, both we and
the local people begged him not to go up to
Jerusalem.
13 Then Paul replied, "What are you doing,
weeping and breaking my heart? For I am ready
not only to be bound, but also to die in Jerusalem for the name of the Lord Jesus."
14 Since he would not be persuaded, we
stopped talking and simply said, "The Lord's
will be done!"

Conflict over the Gentile Mission

15 After these days we got ready and went
up to Jerusalem. 16 Some of the disciples from
Caesarea also went with us and brought us to
Mnason, a Cypriot and an early disciple, with
whom we were to stay.
17 When we reached Jerusalem, the brothers welcomed us gladly. 18 The following day
Paul went in with us to James, and all the elders
were present. 19 After greeting them, he
related one by one what God did among the
Gentiles through his ministry.
20 When they heard it, they glorified God
and said, "You see, brother, how many thousands of Jews there are who have believed, and
they are all zealous for the law. 21 But they

[a]**20:24** Other mss add *with joy* [b]**20:26** Lit *clean* [c]**20:28** Other mss read *church of the Lord*; other mss read *church of the Lord and God* [d]**20:32** Other mss add *brothers,*

have been told about you that you teach all the
Jews who are among the Gentiles to abandon
Moses, by telling them not to circumcise their
children or to walk in our customs. 22 So what
is to be done?[a] They will certainly hear that
you've come. 23 Therefore do what we tell you:
We have four men who have obligated themselves with a vow. 24 Take these men, purify
yourself along with them, and pay for them to
get their heads shaved. Then everyone will
know that what they were told about you
amounts to nothing, but that you yourself are
also careful about observing the law. 25 With
regard to the Gentiles who have believed, we
have written a letter containing our decision
that[b] they should keep themselves from food
sacrificed to idols, from blood, from what is
strangled, and from sexual immorality."

The Riot in the Temple Complex

26 Then the next day, Paul took the men,
having purified himself along with them, and
entered the temple, announcing the completion of the purification days when the offering
for each of them would be made. 27 As the
seven days were about to end, the Jews from
the province of Asia saw him in the •temple
complex, stirred up the whole crowd, and
seized him, 28 shouting, "Men of Israel, help!
This is the man who teaches everyone everywhere against our people, our law, and this
place. What's more, he also brought Greeks
into the temple and has profaned this holy
place." 29 For they had previously seen Trophimus the Ephesian in the city with him, and
they supposed that Paul had brought him into
the temple complex.[c]

30 The whole city was stirred up, and the
people rushed together. They seized Paul,
dragged him out of the temple complex, and at
once the gates were shut. 31 As they were trying
to kill him, word went up to the commander of
the •regiment that all Jerusalem was in chaos.
32 Taking along soldiers and •centurions, he
immediately ran down to them. Seeing the commander and the soldiers, they stopped beating
Paul. 33 Then the commander came up, took
him into custody, and ordered him to be bound
with two chains. He asked who he was and
what he had done. 34 Some in the mob were
shouting one thing and some another. Since he
was not able to get reliable information because
of the uproar, he ordered him to be taken into
the barracks. 35 When Paul[d] got to the steps, he
had to be carried by the soldiers because of the
mob's violence, 36 for the mass of people were
following and yelling, "Kill him!"

Paul's Defense before the Jerusalem Mob

37 As he was about to be brought into the
barracks, Paul said to the commander, "Am I
allowed to say something to you?"

He replied, "Do you know Greek? 38 Aren't
you the Egyptian who raised a rebellion some
time ago and led 4,000 Assassins[e] into the
desert?"

39 Paul said, "I am a Jewish man from Tarsus of Cilicia, a citizen of an important city.[f]
Now I ask you, let me speak to the people."

40 After he had given permission, Paul stood
on the steps and motioned with his hand to the
people. When there was a great hush, he
addressed them in the Hebrew language:

22
1 "Brothers and fathers, listen now to
my defense before you." 2 When they
heard that he was addressing them in the
Hebrew language, they became even quieter.
3 He continued, "I am a Jewish man, born in
Tarsus of Cilicia, but brought up in this city[g] at
the feet of Gamaliel, and educated according to
the strict view of our patriarchal law. Being
zealous for God, just as all of you are today, 4 I
persecuted this Way to the death, binding and
putting both men and women in jail, 5 as both
the high priest and the whole council of elders
can testify about me. Having received letters
from them to the brothers, I was traveling to
Damascus to bring those who were prisoners
there to be punished in Jerusalem.

Paul's Testimony

6 "As I was traveling and near Damascus,
about noon an intense light from heaven suddenly flashed around me. 7 I fell to the ground
and heard a voice saying to me, 'Saul, Saul, why
are you persecuting Me?'
8 "I answered, 'Who are You, Lord?'

"He said to me, 'I am Jesus the •Nazarene,
whom you are persecuting!' 9 Now those who
were with me saw the light,[h] but they did not
hear the voice of the One who was speaking to
me.

[a]**21:22** Other mss add *A multitude has to come together, since* [b]**21:25** Other mss add *they should observe no such thing, except that* [c]**21:29** The inner temple court for Jewish men [d]**21:35** Lit *he* [e]**21:38** Lit *4,000 men of the Assassins*; that is, *Sicarii*, a Lat loanword from *sica*, dagger; compare "cut-throats" or daggermen. [f]**21:39** Lit *of no insignificant city*
[g]**22:3** Probably Jerusalem, but others think Tarsus [h]**22:9** Other mss add *and were afraid*

10 “Then I said, ‘What should I do, Lord?’
“And the Lord told me, ‘Get up and go into
Damascus, and there you will be told about
everything that is assigned for you to do.’
11 “Since I couldn’t see because of the
brightness of that light, I was led by the hand
by those who were with me, and came into
Damascus. 12 Someone named Ananias, a
devout man according to the law, having a good
reputation with all the Jews residing there,
13 came to me, stood by me, and said, ‘Brother
Saul, regain your sight.’ And in that very hour I
looked up and saw him. 14 Then he said, ‘The
God of our fathers has appointed you to know
His will, to see the Righteous One, and to hear
the sound of His voice.[a] 15 For you will be a witness for Him to all people of what you have
seen and heard. 16 And now, why delay? Get
up and be baptized, and wash away your sins by
calling on His name.’
17 “After I came back to Jerusalem and was
praying in the •temple complex, I went into a
visionary state 18 and saw Him telling me,
‘Hurry and get out of Jerusalem quickly,
because they will not accept your testimony
about Me!’
19 “But I said, ‘Lord, they know that in •syn-
agogue after synagogue I had those who
believed in You imprisoned and beaten. 20 And
when the blood of Your witness Stephen was
being shed, I myself was standing by and
approving,[b] and I guarded the clothes of those
who killed him.’
21 “Then He said to me, ‘Go, because I will
send you far away to the Gentiles.’ ”

Paul’s Roman Protection

22 They listened to him up to this word.
Then they raised their voices, shouting, “Wipe
this person off the earth—it’s a disgrace for him
to live!”
23 As they were yelling and flinging aside
their robes and throwing dust into the air,
24 the commander ordered him to be brought
into the barracks, directing that he be examined with the scourge, so he could discover the
reason they were shouting against him like
this. 25 As they stretched him out for the lash,
Paul said to the •centurion standing by, “Is it
legal for you to scourge a man who is a Roman
citizen and is uncondemned?”
26 When the centurion heard this, he went
and reported to the commander, saying, “What
are you going to do? For this man is a Roman
citizen.”
27 The commander came and said to him,
“Tell me—are you a Roman citizen?”
“Yes,” he said.
28 The commander replied, “I bought this
citizenship for a large amount of money.”
“But I myself was born a citizen,” Paul said.
29 Therefore, those who were about to
examine him withdrew from him at once. The
commander too was alarmed when he realized
Paul was a Roman citizen and he had bound
him.

Paul before the Sanhedrin

30 The next day, since he wanted to find out
exactly why Paul was being accused by the
Jews, he released him[c] and instructed the
•chief priests and all the •Sanhedrin to con-
vene. Then he brought Paul down and placed
23 him before them. 1 Paul looked
intently at the •Sanhedrin and said,
“Brothers, I have lived my life before God in all
good conscience until this day.” 2 But the high
priest Ananias ordered those who were standing next to him to strike him on the mouth.
3 Then Paul said to him, “God is going to strike
you, you whitewashed wall! You are sitting
there judging me according to the law, and in
violation of the law are you ordering me to be
struck?”
4 And those standing nearby said, “Do you
dare revile God’s high priest?”
5 “I did not know, brothers,” Paul said,
“that it was the high priest. For it is written,
**You must not speak evil of a ruler of your
people.**”[d] 6 When Paul realized that one part
of them were •Sadducees and the other part
were •Pharisees, he cried out in the Sanhedrin, “Brothers, I am a Pharisee, a son of
Pharisees! I am being judged because of the
hope of the resurrection of the dead!”
7 When he said this, a dispute broke out
between the Pharisees and the Sadducees,
and the assembly was divided. 8 For the Sadducees say there is no resurrection, and no
angel or spirit, but the Pharisees affirm them
all.
9 The shouting grew loud, and some of the
•scribes of the Pharisees’ party got up and
argued vehemently: “We find nothing evil in
this man. What if a spirit or an angel has spoken
to him?”[e] 10 When the dispute became violent,

[a]**22:14** Lit *to hear a voice from His mouth* [b]**22:20** Other mss add *of his murder* [c]**22:30** Other mss add *from his chains*
[d]**23:5** Ex 22:28 [e]**23:9** Other mss add *Let us not fight God.*

the commander feared that Paul might be torn
apart by them and ordered the troops to go
down, rescue him from them, and bring him
into the barracks.

The Plot against Paul

11 The following night, the Lord stood by
him and said, "Have courage! For as you have
testified about Me in Jerusalem, so you must
also testify in Rome."

12 When it was day, the Jews formed a
conspiracy and bound themselves under a
curse: neither to eat nor to drink until they
had killed Paul. 13 There were more than 40
who had formed this plot. 14 These men
went to the •chief priests and elders and
said, "We have bound ourselves under a solemn curse that we won't eat anything until
we have killed Paul. 15 So now you, along
with the Sanhedrin, make a request to the
commander that he bring him down to you[a]
as if you were going to investigate his case
more thoroughly. However, before he gets
near, we are ready to kill him."

16 But the son of Paul's sister, hearing about
their ambush, came and entered the barracks
and reported it to Paul. 17 Then Paul called one
of the •centurions and said, "Take this young
man to the commander, because he has something to report to him."

18 So he took him, brought him to the
commander, and said, "The prisoner Paul
called me and asked me to bring this young
man to you, because he has something to tell
you."

19 Then the commander took him by the
hand, led him aside, and inquired privately,
"What is it you have to report to me?"

20 "The Jews," he said, "have agreed to
ask you to bring Paul down to the Sanhedrin
tomorrow, as though they are going to hold a
somewhat more careful inquiry about him.
21 Don't let them persuade you, because
there are more than 40 of them arranging to
ambush him, men who have bound themselves under a curse not to eat or drink until
they kill him. Now they are ready, waiting for
a commitment from you."

22 So the commander dismissed the young
man and instructed him, "Don't tell anyone
that you have informed me about this."

To Caesarea by Night

23 He summoned two of his centurions and
said, "Get 200 soldiers ready with 70 cavalry
and 200 spearmen to go to Caesarea at nine
tonight.[b] 24 Also provide mounts so they can
put Paul on them and bring him safely to Felix
the governor."

25 He wrote a letter of this kind:

26 Claudius Lysias,

To the most excellent governor Felix:

Greetings.

27 When this man had been seized by
the Jews and was about to be killed by
them, I arrived with my troops and rescued him because I learned that he is a
Roman citizen. 28 Wanting to know the
charge for which they were accusing
him, I brought him down before their
Sanhedrin. 29 I found out that the accusa-
tions were about disputed matters in
their law, and that there was no charge
that merited death or chains. 30 When I
was informed that there was a plot
against the man,[c] I sent him to you right
away. I also ordered his accusers to state
their case against him in your presence.[d]

31 Therefore, during the night, the soldiers
took Paul and brought him to Antipatris as
they were ordered. 32 The next day, they
returned to the barracks, allowing the cavalry
to go on with him. 33 When these men
entered Caesarea and delivered the letter to
the governor, they also presented Paul to him.
34 After he[e] read it, he asked what province
he was from. So when he learned he was from
Cilicia, 35 he said, "I will give you a hearing
whenever your accusers get here too." And he
ordered that he be kept under guard in
•Herod's palace.[f]

The Accusation against Paul

24 After five days Ananias the high priest
came down with some elders and a
lawyer[g] named Tertullus. These men presented their case against Paul to the governor. 2 When he was called in, Tertullus
began to accuse him and said: "Since we
enjoy great peace because of you, and
reforms are taking place for the benefit of

[a]**23:15** Other mss add *tomorrow* [b]**23:23** Lit *at the third hour tonight* [c]**23:30** Other mss add *by the Jews* [d]**23:30** Other mss add *Farewell* [e]**23:34** Other mss read *the governor* [f]**23:35** Lit *praetorium,* a Lat word that can also refer to a military headquarters, to the governor's palace, or to the emperor's imperial guard [g]**24:1** Gk *rhetor*; compare the Eng "rhetoric," "rhetorician"—an orator skilled in public speaking. In this situation, skill in the Gk language was needed.

this nation by your foresight, 3 we gratefully
receive them always and in all places, most
excellent Felix, with all thankfulness. 4
However, so that I will not burden you any
further, I beg you in your graciousness to
give us a brief hearing. 5 For we have found
this man to be a plague, an agitator among
all the Jews throughout the Roman world,
and a ringleader of the sect of the •Nazare-
nes! 6 He even tried to desecrate the temple,
so we apprehended him [and wanted to
judge him according to our law. 7 But Lysias
the commander came and took him from our
hands, commanding his accusers to come to
you.][a] 8 By examining him yourself you will
be able to discern all these things of which
we accuse him." 9 The Jews also joined in
the attack, alleging that these things were
so.

Paul's Defense before Felix

10 When the governor motioned to him to
speak, Paul replied: "Because I know you
have been a judge of this nation for many
years, I am glad to offer my defense in what
concerns me. 11 You are able to determine
that it is no more than 12 days since I went
up to worship in Jerusalem. 12 And they
didn't find me disputing with anyone or causing a disturbance among the crowd, either in
the •temple complex or in the •synagogues,
or anywhere in the city. 13 Neither can they
provide evidence to you of what they now
bring against me. 14 But I confess this to you:
that according to the Way, which they call a
sect, so I worship my fathers' God, believing
all the things that are written in the Law and
in the Prophets. 15 And I have a hope in God,
which these men themselves also accept,
that there is going to be a resurrection,[b] both
of the righteous and the unrighteous. 16 I
always do my best to have a clear conscience
toward God and men. 17 After many years, I
came to bring charitable gifts and offerings to
my nation, 18 and while I was doing this,
some Jews from the province of Asia found
me ritually purified in the temple, without a
crowd and without any uproar. 19 It is they
who ought to be here before you to bring
charges, if they have anything against me.
20 Either let these men here state what
wrongdoing they found in me when I stood
before the •Sanhedrin, 21 or about this one
statement I cried out while standing among
them, 'Today I am being judged before you
concerning the resurrection of the dead.' "

The Verdict Postponed

22 Since Felix was accurately informed
about the Way, he adjourned the hearing, saying, "When Lysias the commander comes
down, I will decide your case." 23 He ordered
that the •centurion keep Paul[c] under guard,
though he could have some freedom, and that
he should not prevent any of his friends from
serving[d] him.

24 After some days, when Felix came with
his wife Drusilla, who was Jewish, he sent for
Paul and listened to him on the subject of faith
in Christ Jesus. 25 Now as he spoke about righteousness, self-control, and the judgment to
come, Felix became afraid and replied, "Leave
for now, but when I find time I'll call for you."
26 At the same time he was also hoping that
money would be given to him by Paul.[e] For this
reason he sent for him quite often and conversed with him.

27 After two years had passed, Felix
received a successor, Porcius Festus, and
because he wished to do a favor for the Jews,
Felix left Paul in prison.

Appeal to Caesar

25 Three days after Festus arrived in the
province, he went up to Jerusalem
from Caesarea. 2 Then the •chief priests and
the leaders of the Jews presented their case
against Paul to him; and they appealed,
3 asking him to do them a favor against Paul,[f]
that he might summon him to Jerusalem. They
were preparing an ambush along the road to
kill him. 4 However, Festus answered that Paul
should be kept at Caesarea, and that he himself was about to go there shortly.
5 "Therefore," he said, "let the men of authority among you go down with me and accuse
him, if there is any wrong in this man."

6 When he had spent not more than eight or
10 days among them, he went down to Caesarea. The next day, seated at the judge's
bench, he commanded Paul to be brought in.
7 When he arrived, the Jews who had come
down from Jerusalem stood around him and
brought many serious charges that they were
not able to prove, 8 while Paul made the
defense that, "Neither against the Jewish law,

[a]**24:6–7** Other mss omit bracketed text [b]**24:15** Other mss add *of the dead* [c]**24:23** Lit *him* [d]**24:23** Other mss add *or visiting* [e]**24:26** Other mss add *so that he might release him* [f]**25:3** Lit *asking a favor against him*

nor against the temple, nor against Caesar have I sinned at all."

9 Then Festus, wanting to do a favor for the Jews, replied to Paul, "Are you willing to go up to Jerusalem, there to be tried before me on these charges?"

10 But Paul said: "I am standing at Caesar's tribunal, where I ought to be tried. I have done no wrong to the Jews, as even you can see very well. 11 If then I am doing wrong, or have done anything deserving of death, I do not refuse to die, but if there is nothing to what these men accuse me of, no one can give me up to them. I appeal to Caesar!"

12 After Festus conferred with his council, he replied, "You have appealed to Caesar; to Caesar you will go!"

King Agrippa and Bernice Visit Festus

13 After some days had passed, King Agrippa[a] and Bernice arrived in Caesarea and paid a courtesy call on Festus. 14 Since they stayed there many days, Festus presented Paul's case to the king, saying, "There's a man who was left as a prisoner by Felix. 15 When I was in Jerusalem, the chief priests and the elders of the Jews presented their case and asked for a judgment against him. 16 I answered them that it's not the Romans' custom to give any man up[b] before the accused confronts the accusers face to face and has an opportunity to give a defense concerning the charge. 17 Therefore, when they had assembled here, I did not delay. The next day I sat at the judge's bench and ordered the man to be brought in. 18 Concerning him, the accusers stood up and brought no charge of the sort I was expecting. 19 Instead they had some disagreements with him about their own religion and about a certain Jesus, a dead man whom Paul claimed to be alive. 20 Since I was at a loss in a dispute over such things, I asked him if he wished to go to Jerusalem and be tried there concerning these matters. 21 But when Paul appealed to be held for trial by the Emperor, I ordered him to be kept in custody until I could send him to Caesar."

22 Then Agrippa said to Festus, "I would like to hear the man myself."

"Tomorrow," he said, "you will hear him."

Paul before Agrippa

23 So the next day, Agrippa and Bernice came with great pomp and entered the auditorium with the commanders and prominent men of the city. When Festus gave the command, Paul was brought in. 24 Then Festus said: "King Agrippa and all men present with us, you see this man about whom the whole Jewish community has appealed to me, both in Jerusalem and here, shouting that he should not live any longer. 25 Now I realized that he had not done anything deserving of death, but when he himself appealed to the Emperor, I decided to send him. 26 I have nothing definite to write to the Emperor about him. Therefore, I have brought him before all of you, and especially before you, King Agrippa, so that after this examination is over, I may have something to write. 27 For it seems unreasonable to me to send a prisoner and not to indicate the charges against him."

Paul's Defense before Agrippa

26 Agrippa said to Paul, "It is permitted for you to speak for yourself."

Then Paul stretched out his hand and began his defense: 2 "I consider myself fortunate, King Agrippa, that today I am going to make a defense before you about everything I am accused of by the Jews, 3 especially since you are an expert in all the Jewish customs and controversies. Therefore I beg you to listen to me patiently.

4 "All the Jews know my way of life from my youth, which was spent from the beginning among my own nation and in Jerusalem. 5 They had previously known me for quite some time, if they were willing to testify, that according to the strictest party of our religion I lived as a •Pharisee. 6 And now I stand on trial for the hope of the promise made by God to our fathers, 7 ⌊the promise⌋ our 12 tribes hope to attain as they earnestly serve Him night and day. Because of this hope I am being accused by the Jews, O king! 8 Why is it considered incredible by any of you that God raises the dead? 9 In fact, I myself supposed it was necessary to do many things in opposition to the name of Jesus the •Nazarene. 10 This I actually did in Jerusalem, and I locked up many of the saints in prison, since I had received authority for that from the •chief priests. When they were put to death, I cast my vote against them. 11 In all the •synagogues I often tried to make them blaspheme by punishing them. Being greatly

[a]**25:13** Herod Agrippa II ruled Palestine A.D. 52–92. [b]**25:16** Other mss add *to destruction*

enraged at them, I even pursued them to foreign cities.

Paul's Account of His Conversion and Commission

12 "Under these circumstances I was traveling to Damascus with authority and a commission from the chief priests. 13 At midday, while
on the road, O king, I saw a light from heaven
brighter than the sun, shining around me and
those traveling with me. 14 When we had all
fallen to the ground, I heard a voice speaking to
me in the Hebrew language, 'Saul, Saul, why
are you persecuting Me? It is hard for you to
kick against the goads.'[a]

15 "But I said, 'Who are You, Lord?'

"And the Lord replied: 'I am Jesus, whom
you are persecuting. 16 But get up and stand on
your feet. For I have appeared to you for this
purpose, to appoint you as a servant and a witness of things you have seen,[b] and of things in
which I will appear to you. 17 I will rescue you
from the people and from the Gentiles, to
whom I now send you, 18 to open their eyes
that they may turn from darkness to light and
from the power of Satan to God, that they may
receive forgiveness of sins and a share among
those who are sanctified by faith in Me.'

19 "Therefore, King Agrippa, I was not disobedient to the heavenly vision. 20 Instead, I
preached to those in Damascus first, and to
those in Jerusalem and in all the region of
Judea, and to the Gentiles, that they should
repent and turn to God, and do works worthy
of repentance. 21 For this reason the Jews
seized me in the •temple complex and were
trying to kill me. 22 Since I have obtained help
that comes from God, to this day I stand and
testify to both small and great, saying nothing
else than what the prophets and Moses said
would take place— 23 that the •Messiah must
suffer, and that as the first to rise from the dead,
He would proclaim light to our people and to
the Gentiles."

Not Quite Persuaded

24 As he was making his defense this way,
Festus exclaimed in a loud voice, "You're out of
your mind, Paul! Too much study is driving you
mad!"

25 But Paul replied, "I'm not out of my
mind, most excellent Festus. On the contrary,
I'm speaking words of truth and good judgment. 26 For the king knows about these matters. It is to him I am actually speaking boldly.
For I'm not convinced that any of these things
escapes his notice, since this was not done in a
corner! 27 King Agrippa, do you believe the
prophets? I know you believe."

28 Then Agrippa said to Paul, "Are you
going to persuade me to become a Christian so
easily?"

29 "I wish before God," replied Paul, "that
whether easily or with difficulty, not only you
but all who listen to me today might become as
I am—except for these chains."

30 So the king, the governor, Bernice, and
those sitting with them got up, 31 and when
they had left they talked with each other and
said, "This man is doing nothing that deserves
death or chains."

32 Then Agrippa said to Festus, "This man
could have been released if he had not appealed
to Caesar."

Sailing for Rome

27 When it was decided that we were to
sail to Italy, they handed over Paul and
some other prisoners to a •centurion named
Julius, of the Imperial •Regiment. 2 So when
we had boarded a ship of Adramyttium, we put
to sea, intending to sail to ports along the coast
of the province of Asia. Aristarchus, a Macedonian of Thessalonica, was with us. 3 The
next day we put in at Sidon, and Julius treated
Paul kindly and allowed him to go to his
friends to receive their care. 4 When we had
put out to sea from there, we sailed along the
northern coast[c] of Cyprus because the winds
were against us. 5 After sailing through the
open sea off Cilicia and Pamphylia, we reached
Myra in Lycia. 6 There the centurion found an
Alexandrian ship sailing for Italy and put us on
board. 7 Sailing slowly for many days, we came
with difficulty as far as Cnidus. But since the
wind did not allow us to approach it, we sailed
along the south side[c] of Crete off Salmone.
8 With yet more difficulty we sailed along the
coast, and came to a place called Fair Havens
near the city of Lasea.

Paul's Advice Ignored

9 By now much time had passed, and the
voyage was already dangerous. Since the Fast[d]
was already over, Paul gave his advice 10 and
told them, "Men, I can see that this voyage is

[a]**26:14** Sharp sticks used to prod animals, such as oxen in plowing [b]**26:16** Other mss read *things in which you have seen Me* [c]**27:4,7** Lit *sailed under the lee* [d]**27:9** The Day of Atonement

headed toward damage and heavy loss, not only of the cargo and the ship, but also of our lives." 11 But the centurion paid attention to the captain and the owner of the ship rather than to what Paul said. 12 Since the harbor was unsuitable to winter in, the majority decided to set sail from there, hoping somehow to reach Phoenix, a harbor on Crete open to the southwest and northwest, and to winter there.

Storm-Tossed Vessel

13 When a gentle south wind sprang up, they thought they had achieved their purpose; they weighed anchor and sailed along the shore of Crete. 14 But not long afterwards, a fierce wind called the "northeaster"[a] rushed down from the island.[b] 15 Since the ship was caught and was unable to head into the wind, we gave way to it and were driven along. 16 After running under the shelter of a little island called Cauda,[c] we were barely able to get control of the skiff. 17 After hoisting it up, they used ropes and tackle and girded the ship. Then, fearing they would run aground on the Syrtis,[d] they lowered the drift-anchor, and in this way they were driven along. 18 Because we were being severely battered by the storm, they began to jettison the cargo the next day. 19 On the third day, they threw the ship's gear overboard with their own hands.

20 For many days neither sun nor stars appeared, and the severe storm kept raging; finally all hope that we would be saved was disappearing. 21 Since many were going without food, Paul stood up among them and said, "You men should have followed my advice not to sail from Crete and sustain this damage and loss. 22 Now I urge you to take courage, because there will be no loss of any of your lives, but only of the ship. 23 For this night an angel of the God I belong to and serve stood by me, 24 saying, 'Don't be afraid, Paul. You must stand before Caesar. And, look! God has graciously given you all those who are sailing with you.' 25 Therefore, take courage, men, because I believe God that it will be just the way it was told to me. 26 However, we must run aground on a certain island."

27 When the fourteenth night came, we were drifting in the Adriatic Sea,[e] and in the middle of the night the sailors thought they were approaching land.[f] 28 They took a sounding and found it to be 120 feet[g] deep; when they had sailed a little farther and sounded again, they found it to be 90 feet[h] deep. 29 Then, fearing we might run aground in some rocky place, they dropped four anchors from the stern and prayed for daylight to come.

30 Some sailors tried to escape from the ship; they had let down the skiff into the sea, pretending that they were going to put out anchors from the bow. 31 Paul said to the centurion and the soldiers, "Unless these men stay in the ship, you cannot be saved." 32 Then the soldiers cut the ropes holding the skiff and let it drop away.

33 When it was just about daylight, Paul urged them all to take food, saying, "Today is the fourteenth day that you have been waiting and going without food, having eaten nothing. 34 Therefore I urge you to take some food. For this has to do with your survival, since not a hair will be lost from the head of any of you." 35 After he said these things and had taken some bread, he gave thanks to God in the presence of them all, and when he had broken it, he began to eat. 36 They all became encouraged and took food themselves. 37 In all there were 276 of us on the ship. 38 And having eaten enough food, they began to lighten the ship by throwing the grain overboard into the sea.

Shipwreck

39 When daylight came, they did not recognize the land, but sighted a bay with a beach. They planned to run the ship ashore if they could. 40 After casting off the anchors, they left them in the sea, at the same time loosening the ropes that held the rudders. Then they hoisted the foresail to the wind and headed for the beach. 41 But they struck a sandbar and ran the ship aground. The bow jammed fast and remained immovable, but the stern began to break up with the pounding of the waves.

42 The soldiers' plan was to kill the prisoners so that no one could swim off and escape. 43 But the centurion kept them from carrying out their plan because he wanted to save Paul, so he ordered those who could swim to jump overboard first and get to land. 44 The rest were to follow, some on planks and some on debris from the ship. In this way, all got safely to land.

[a]**27:14** Lit *Euraquilo*, a violent northeast wind [b]**27:14** Lit *from her* [c]**27:16** Or *Clauda* [d]**27:17** *Syrtis* = sand banks or bars near North Africa [e]**27:27** Part of the northern Mediterranean Sea; not the modern Adriatic Sea east of Italy [f]**27:27** Lit *thought there was land approaching them* [g]**27:28** Lit *20 fathoms* [h]**27:28** Lit *15 fathoms*

Malta's Hospitality

28 Safely ashore, we then learned that
the island was called Malta. 2 The
local people showed us extraordinary kindness, for they lit a fire and took us all in, since
rain was falling and it was cold. 3 As Paul gathered a bundle of brushwood and put it on the
fire, a viper came out because of the heat and
fastened itself to his hand. 4 When the local
people saw the creature hanging from his
hand, they said to one another, "This man is
probably a murderer, and though he has
escaped the sea, Justice[a] does not allow him to
live!" 5 However, he shook the creature off
into the fire and suffered no harm. 6 They
expected that he would swell up or suddenly
drop dead. But after they waited a long time
and saw nothing unusual happen to him, they
changed their minds and said he was a god.

Ministry in Malta

7 Now in the area around that place was an
estate belonging to the leading man of the island,
named Publius, who welcomed us and enter-
tained us hospitably for three days. 8 It happened
that Publius' father was in bed suffering from
fever and dysentery. Paul went to him, and praying and laying his hands on him, he healed him.
9 After this, the rest of those on the island who
had diseases also came and were cured. 10 So
they heaped many honors on us, and when we
sailed, they gave us what we needed.

Rome at Last

11 After three months we set sail in an Alexandrian ship that had wintered at the island,
with the Twin Brothers[b] as its figurehead.
12 Putting in at Syracuse, we stayed three days.
13 From there, after making a circuit along the
coast,[c] we reached Rhegium. After one day a
south wind sprang up, and the second day we
came to Puteoli. 14 There we found believers[d]
and were invited to stay with them for seven
days.

And so we came to Rome. 15 Now the
believers[d] from there had heard the news about
us and had come to meet us as far as Forum of
Appius and Three Taverns. When Paul saw
them, he thanked God and took courage.
16 And when we entered Rome,[e] Paul was permitted to stay by himself with the soldier who
guarded him.

Paul's First Interview with Roman Jews

17 After three days he called together the
leaders of the Jews. And when they had gathered he said to them: "Brothers, although I
have done nothing against our people or the
customs of our forefathers, I was delivered as
a prisoner from Jerusalem into the hands of
the Romans 18 who, after examining me,
wanted to release me, since I had not committed a capital offense. 19 Because the Jews
objected, I was compelled to appeal to Caesar; it was not as though I had any accusation
against my nation. 20 So, for this reason I've
asked to see you and speak to you. In fact, it
is for the hope of Israel that I'm wearing this
chain."

21 And they said to him, "We haven't
received any letters about you from Judea; none
of the brothers has come and reported or spoken anything evil about you. 22 But we consider it suitable to hear from you what you
think. For concerning this sect, we are aware
that it is spoken against everywhere."

The Response to Paul's Message

23 After arranging a day with him, many
came to him at his lodging. From dawn to dusk
he expounded and witnessed about the kingdom of God. He persuaded them concerning
Jesus from both the Law of Moses and the
Prophets. 24 Some were persuaded by what he
said, but others did not believe.

25 Disagreeing among themselves, they
began to leave after Paul made one statement:
"The Holy Spirit correctly spoke through the
prophet Isaiah to your[f] forefathers 26 when He
said,

Go to this people and say:
'You will listen and listen,
yet never understand;
and you will look and look,
yet never perceive.
27 **For this people's heart**
has grown callous,
their ears are hard
of hearing,
and they have shut their eyes;
otherwise
they might see with their eyes
and hear with their ears,
understand with their heart,

[a]**28:4** Gk *Dike*, a goddess of justice [b]**28:11** Gk *Dioscuri*, twin sons of Zeus [c]**28:13** Other mss read *From there, casting off,*
[d]**28:14,15** Lit *brothers* [e]**28:16** Other mss add *the centurion turned the prisoners over to the military commander; but*
[f]**28:25** Other mss read *our*

and be converted—
and I would heal them.'[a]

28 Therefore, let it be known to you that this saving work of God has been sent to the Gentiles; they will listen!" [29 After he said these things, the Jews departed, while engaging in a prolonged debate among themselves.][b]

Paul's Ministry Unhindered

30 Then he stayed two whole years in his own rented house. And he welcomed all who visited him, 31 proclaiming the kingdom of God and teaching the things concerning the Lord Jesus Christ with full boldness and without hindrance.

Romans

God's Good News for Rome

1 Paul, a slave of Christ Jesus, called as an apostle[c] and singled out for God's good news— 2 which He promised long ago through His prophets in the Holy Scriptures— 3 concerning His Son, Jesus Christ our Lord, who was a descendant of David[d] according to the flesh 4 and was established as the powerful Son of God by the resurrection from the dead according to the Spirit of holiness.[e] 5 We have received grace and apostleship through Him to bring about[f] the obedience of faith[g] among all the nations,[h] on behalf of His name, 6 including yourselves who are also Jesus Christ's by calling:

7 To all who are in Rome, loved by God, called as saints.

Grace to you and peace from God our Father and the Lord Jesus Christ.

The Apostle's Desire to Visit Rome

8 First, I thank my God through Jesus Christ for all of you because the news of your faith[i] is being reported in all the world. 9 For God, whom I serve with my spirit in ⌊telling⌋ the good news about His Son, is my witness that I constantly mention you, 10 always asking in my prayers that if it is somehow in God's will, I may now at last succeed in coming to you. 11 For I want very much to see you, that I may impart to you some spiritual gift to strengthen you, 12 that is, to be mutually encouraged by each other's faith, both yours and mine.

13 Now I want you to know,[j] brothers, that I often planned to come to you (but was prevented until now) in order that I might have a fruitful ministry[k] among you, just as among the rest of the Gentiles. 14 I am obligated both to Greeks and barbarians,[l] both to the wise and the foolish. 15 So I am eager to preach the good news to you also who are in Rome.

The Righteous Will Live by Faith

16 For I am not ashamed of the gospel,[m] because it is God's power for salvation to everyone who believes, first to the Jew, and also to the Greek. 17 For in it God's righteousness is revealed from faith to faith,[n] just as it is written: **The righteous will live by faith.**[o] [p]

The Guilt of the Gentile World

18 For God's wrath is revealed from heaven against all godlessness and unrighteousness of people who by their unrighteousness suppress the truth, 19 since what can be known[q] about God is evident among them, because God has shown it to them. 20 From the creation of the world His invisible attributes, that is, His eternal power and divine nature, have been clearly seen, being understood through what He has made. As a result, people[r] are without excuse. 21 For though they knew God, they did not glorify Him as God or show gratitude. Instead, their thinking became nonsense, and their senseless minds[s] were darkened. 22 Claiming to be wise, they became fools 23 and exchanged the glory of the immortal God for images resembling mortal man, birds, four-footed animals, and reptiles.

24 Therefore God delivered them over in

[a]**28:26–27** Is 6:9–10 [b]**28:29** Other mss omit bracketed text [c]**1:1** Or *Jesus, a called apostle* [d]**1:3** Lit *was of the seed of David* [e]**1:4** Or *the spirit of holiness*, or *the Holy Spirit* [f]**1:5** Lit *Him into*, or *Him for* [g]**1:5** Or *the obedience that is faith*, or *the faithful obedience*, or *the obedience that comes from faith* [h]**1:5** Or *Gentiles* [i]**1:8** Or *because your faith* [j]**1:13** Lit *I don't want you to be unaware* [k]**1:13** Lit *have some fruit* [l]**1:14** Or *non-Greeks* [m]**1:16** Other mss add *of Christ* [n]**1:17** Or *revealed out of faith into faith* [o]**1:17** Or *The one who is righteous by faith will live* [p]**1:17** Hab 2:4 [q]**1:19** Or *what is known* [r]**1:20** Lit *they* [s]**1:21** Lit *hearts*

the cravings of their hearts to sexual impurity,
so that their bodies were degraded among
themselves. 25 They exchanged the truth of
God for a lie, and worshiped and served something created instead of the Creator, who is
blessed forever. •Amen.

From Idolatry to Depravity

26 This is why God delivered them over to
degrading passions. For even their females
exchanged natural sexual intercourse[a] for what
is unnatural. 27 The males in the same way also
left natural sexual intercourse[a] with females
and were inflamed in their lust for one another.
Males committed shameless acts with males
and received in their own persons[b] the appropriate penalty for their perversion.[c]
28 And because they did not think it worth-
while to have God in their knowledge, God
delivered them over to a worthless mind to do
what is morally wrong. 29 They are filled with
all unrighteousness,[d] evil, greed, and wickedness. They are full of envy, murder, disputes,
deceit, and malice. They are gossips,
30 slanderers, God-haters, arrogant, proud,
boastful, inventors of evil, disobedient to parents, 31 undiscerning, untrustworthy, unloving,[e] and unmerciful. 32 Although they know
full well God's just sentence—that those who
practice such things deserve to die[f]—they not
only do them, but even applaud[g] others who
practice them.

God's Righteous Judgment

2 Therefore, anyone of you[h] who judges is
without excuse. For when you judge
another, you condemn yourself, since you,
the judge, do the same things. 2 We know
that God's judgment on those who do such
things is based on the truth. 3 Do you really
think—anyone of you who judges those who
do such things yet do the same—that you will
escape God's judgment? 4 Or do you despise
the riches of His kindness, restraint, and
patience, not recognizing[i] that God's kindness is intended to lead you to repentance?
5 But because of your hardness and unrepen-
tant heart you are storing up wrath for yourself in the day of wrath, when God's
righteous judgment is revealed. 6 He **will
repay each one according to his works:**[j]
7 eternal life to those who by patiently doing
good seek for glory, honor, and immortality;
8 but wrath and indignation to those who are
self-seeking and disobey the truth, but are
obeying unrighteousness; 9 affliction and distress for every human being who does evil,
first to the Jew, and also to the Greek; 10 but
glory, honor, and peace for everyone who
does good, first to the Jew, and also to the
Greek. 11 There is no favoritism with God.
12 All those who sinned without the law
will also perish without the law, and all those
who sinned under the law will be judged by the
law. 13 For the hearers of the law are not righteous before God, but the doers of the law will
be declared righteous.[k] 14 So, when Gentiles,
who do not have the law, instinctively do what
the law demands, they are a law to themselves
even though they do not have the law. 15 They
show that the work of the law[l] is written on
their hearts. Their consciences testify in support of this, and their competing thoughts
either accuse or excuse them[m] 16 on the day
when God judges what people have kept
secret, according to my gospel through Christ
Jesus.

Jewish Violation of the Law

17 Now if[n] you call yourself a Jew, and rest
in the law, and boast in God, 18 and know His
will, and approve the things that are superior,
being instructed from the law, 19 and are convinced that you are a guide for the blind, a
light to those in darkness, 20 an instructor of
the ignorant, a teacher of the immature, having in the law the full expression[o] of knowledge and truth— 21 you then, who teach
another, do you not teach yourself? You who
preach, "You must not steal"—do you steal?
22 You who say, "You must not commit adultery"—do you commit adultery? You who
detest idols, do you rob their temples? 23 You
who boast in the law, do you dishonor God by
breaking the law? 24 For, as it is written: **The
name of God is blasphemed among the Gentiles because of you.**[p]

Circumcision of the Heart

25 For circumcision benefits you if you
observe the law, but if you are a lawbreaker,
your circumcision has become uncircumcision.

[a]**1:26,27** Lit *natural use* [b]**1:27** Or *in themselves* [c]**1:27** Or *error* [d]**1:29** Other mss add *sexual immorality* [e]**1:31** Other mss add *unforgiving* [f]**1:32** Lit *things are worthy of death* [g]**1:32** Lit *even take pleasure in* [h]**2:1** Lit *Therefore, O man, every one* [i]**2:4** Or *patience, because you do not recognize* [j]**2:6** Ps 62:12; Pr 24:12 [k]**2:13** Or *will be justified* or *acquitted* [l]**2:15** The code of conduct required by the law [m]**2:15** Internal debate, either in a person or among the pagan moralists [n]**2:17** Other mss read *Look—* [o]**2:20** Or *the embodiment* [p]**2:24** Is 52:5

26 Therefore if an uncircumcised man keeps the law's requirements, will his uncircumcision not be counted as circumcision? 27 A man who is physically uncircumcised, but who fulfills the law, will judge you who are a lawbreaker in spite of having the letter ⌊of the law⌋ and circumcision. 28 For a person is not a Jew who is one outwardly, and ⌊true⌋ circumcision is not something visible in the flesh. 29 On the contrary, a person is a Jew who is one inwardly, and circumcision is of the heart—by the Spirit, not the letter.[a] His praise[b] is not from men but from God.

Paul Answers an Objection

3 So what advantage does the Jew have? Or what is the benefit of circumcision? 2 Considerable in every way. First, they were entrusted with the spoken words of God. 3 What then? If some did not believe, will their unbelief cancel God's faithfulness? 4 Absolutely not! God must be true, but everyone is a liar, as it is written:

That You may be justified
in Your words
and triumph when You judge.[c]

5 But if our unrighteousness highlights[d] God's righteousness, what are we to say? I use a human argument:[e] Is God unrighteous to inflict wrath? 6 Absolutely not! Otherwise, how will God judge the world? 7 But if by my lie God's truth is amplified to His glory, why am I also still judged as a sinner? 8 And why not say, just as some people slanderously claim we say, "Let us do evil so that good may come"? Their condemnation is deserved!

The Whole World Guilty before God

9 What then? Are we any better?[f] Not at all! For we have previously charged that both Jews and Gentiles[g] are all under sin,[h] 10 as it is written:[i]

There is no one righteous,
not even one;
11 **there is no one who understands,**
there is no one who seeks God.
12 **All have turned away,**
together they have become
useless;
there is no one who does good,
there is not even one.[j]
13 **Their throat is an open grave;**
they deceive with their tongues.[k]
Vipers' venom is under their lips.[l]
14 **Their mouth is full of cursing**
and bitterness.[m]
15 **Their feet are swift to shed blood;**
16 **ruin and wretchedness are**
in their paths,
17 **and the path of peace**
they have not known.[n]
18 **There is no fear of God**
before their eyes.[o]

19 Now we know that whatever the law says speaks to those who are subject to the law,[p] so that every mouth may be shut and the whole world may become subject to God's judgment.[q] 20 For no flesh will be justified[r] in His sight by the works of the law, for through the law ⌊comes⌋ the knowledge of sin.

God's Righteousness through Faith

21 But now, apart from the law, God's righteousness has been revealed—attested by the Law and the Prophets[s] 22 —that is, God's righteousness through faith in Jesus Christ,[t] to all who believe, since there is no distinction. 23 For all have sinned and fall short of the[u] glory of God. 24 They are justified freely by His grace through the redemption that is in Christ Jesus. 25 God presented Him as a propitiation[v] through faith in His blood, to demonstrate His righteousness, because in His restraint God passed over the sins previously committed. 26 He presented Him to demonstrate His righteousness at the present time, so that He would be righteous and declare righteous[w] the one who has faith in Jesus.

Boasting Excluded

27 Where then is boasting? It is excluded. By what kind of law?[x] By one of works? No, on the contrary, by a law[y] of faith. 28 For we

[a]**2:29** Or *heart—spiritually, not literally* [b]**2:29** In Hb, the words *Jew, Judah,* and *praise* are related. [c]**3:4** Ps 51:4 [d]**3:5** Or *shows,* or *demonstrates* [e]**3:5** Lit *I speak as a man* [f]**3:9** Are we Jews any better than the Gentiles? [g]**3:9** Lit *Greeks* [h]**3:9** Under sin's power or dominion [i]**3:10** Paul constructs this charge from a chain of OT quotations, mainly from the Psalms. [j]**3:10–12** Ps 14:1–3; 53:1–3; see Ec 7:20 [k]**3:13** Ps 5:9 [l]**3:13** Ps 140:3 [m]**3:14** Ps 10:7 [n]**3:15–17** Is 59:7–8 [o]**3:18** Ps 36:1 [p]**3:19** Lit *those in the law* [q]**3:19** Or *become guilty before God,* or *may be accountable to God* [r]**3:20** Or *will be declared righteous,* or *will be acquitted* [s]**3:21** When capitalized, *the Law and the Prophets* = OT [t]**3:22** Or *through the faithfulness of Jesus Christ* [u]**3:23** Or *and lack the* [v]**3:25** Or *as a propitiatory sacrifice,* or *as an offering of atonement,* or *as a mercy seat;* see Heb 9:5. The word *propitiation* has to do with the removal of divine wrath. Jesus' death is the means that turns God's wrath from the sinner; see 2 Co 5:21. [w]**3:26** Or *and justify,* or *and acquit* [x]**3:27** Or *what principle?* [y]**3:27** Or *a principle*

Turn to page 156.

conclude that a man is justified by faith apart
from works of law. 29 Or is God for Jews only?
Is He not also for Gentiles? Yes, for Gentiles
too, 30 since there is one God who will justify
the circumcised by faith and the uncircumcised
through faith. 31 Do we then cancel the law
through faith? Absolutely not! On the contrary,
we uphold the law.

Abraham Justified by Faith

4 What then can we say that Abraham,
our forefather according to the flesh, has
found? 2 If Abraham was justified[a] by works,
then he has something to brag about—but not
before God.[b] 3 For what does the Scripture
say?

> **Abraham believed God,**
> **and it was credited to him**
> **for righteousness.**[c]

4 Now to the one who works, pay is not considered as a gift, but as something owed. 5 But
to the one who does not work, but believes on
Him who declares righteous[d] the ungodly, his
faith is credited for righteousness.

David Celebrating the Same Truth

6 Likewise, David also speaks of the blessing
of the man to whom God credits righteousness
apart from works:

> 7 **How happy those whose lawless acts**
> **are forgiven**
> **and whose sins are covered!**
> 8 **How happy the man whom**
> **the Lord will never charge**
> **with sin!**[e]

Abraham Justified before Circumcision

9 Is this blessing only for the circumcised,
then? Or is it also for the uncircumcised? For
we say, **Faith was credited to Abraham for**
righteousness.[c] 10 How then was it credited—
while he was circumcised, or uncircumcised?
Not while he was circumcised, but uncircumcised. 11 And he received the sign of circumcision as a seal of the righteousness that he had
by faith[f] while still uncircumcised. This was to
make him the father of all who believe but are
not circumcised, so that righteousness may be
credited to them also. 12 And he became the
father of the circumcised, not only to those who
are circumcised, but also to those who follow in
the footsteps of the faith our father Abraham
had while still uncircumcised.

The Promise Granted through Faith

13 For the promise to Abraham or to his
descendants that he would inherit the world
was not through the law, but through the righteousness that comes by faith.[f] 14 If those who
are of the law are heirs, faith is made empty and
the promise is canceled. 15 For the law produces wrath; but where there is no law, there
is no transgression.

16 This is why the promise is by faith, so
that it may be according to grace, to guarantee
it to all the descendants—not only to those who
are of the law,[g] but also to those who are of
Abraham's faith. He is the father of us all 17 in
God's sight. As it is written: **I have made you**
the father of many nations.[h] He believed in
God, who gives life to the dead and calls things
into existence that do not exist. 18 Against
hope, with hope he believed, so that he
became **the father of many nations,**[h] according to what had been spoken: **So will your**
descendants be.[i] 19 He considered[j] his own
body to be already dead (since he was about a
hundred years old), and the deadness of Sarah's
womb, without weakening in the faith. 20 He
did not waver in unbelief at God's promise, but
was strengthened in his faith and gave glory to
God, 21 because he was fully convinced that
what He had promised He was also able to perform. 22 Therefore, **it was credited to him for**
righteousness.[c] 23 Now **it was credited to him**
was not written for Abraham alone, 24 but also
for us. It will be credited to us who believe in
Him who raised Jesus our Lord from the dead.
25 He was delivered up for[k] our trespasses and
raised for[k] our justification.[l]

Faith Triumphs

5 Therefore, since we have been declared
righteous by faith, we have peace[m] with
God through our Lord Jesus Christ. 2 Also
through Him, we have obtained access by
faith[n] into this grace in which we stand, and
we rejoice in the hope of the glory of God.
3 And not only that, but we also rejoice in our

[a]**4:2** Or *was declared righteous,* or *was acquitted* [b]**4:2** He has no reason for boasting in God's presence [c]**4:3,9,22** Gn 15:6 [d]**4:5** Or *who acquits,* or *who justifies* [e]**4:7–8** Ps 32:1–2 [f]**4:11,13** Lit *righteousness of faith* [g]**4:16** Or *not to those who are of the law only* [h]**4:17,18** Gn 17:5 [i]**4:18** Gn 15:5 [j]**4:19** Other mss read *He did not consider* [k]**4:25** Or *because of* [l]**4:25** Or *acquittal* [m]**5:1** Other mss read *faith, let us have peace,* which can also be translated *faith, let us grasp the fact that we have peace* [n]**5:2** Other mss omit *by faith*

afflictions, because we know that affliction produces endurance, 4 endurance produces proven character, and proven character produces hope. 5 This hope does not disappoint, because God's love has been poured out in our hearts through the Holy Spirit who was given to us.

Those Declared Righteous Are Reconciled

6 For while we were still helpless, at the appointed moment, Christ died for the ungodly. 7 For rarely will someone die for a just person—though for a good person perhaps someone might even dare to die. 8 But God proves His own love for us in that while we were still sinners Christ died for us! 9 Much more then, since we have now been declared righteous by His blood, we will be saved through Him from wrath. 10 For if, while we were enemies, we were reconciled to God through the death of His Son, ⌊then how⌋ much more, having been reconciled, will we be saved by His life! 11 And not only that, but we also rejoice in God through our Lord Jesus Christ, through whom we have now received reconciliation.

Death through Adam and Life through Christ

12 Therefore, just as sin entered the world through one man, and death through sin, in this way death spread to all men, because all sinned.[a] 13 In fact, sin was in the world before the law, but sin is not charged to one's account when there is no law. 14 Nevertheless, death reigned from Adam to Moses, even over those who did not sin in the likeness of Adam's transgression. He is a prototype of the Coming One.

15 But the gift is not like the trespass. For if by the one man's trespass the many died, how much more have the grace of God and the gift overflowed to the many by the grace of the one man, Jesus Christ. 16 And the gift is not like the one man's sin, because from one sin came the judgment, resulting in condemnation, but from many trespasses came the gift, resulting in justification.[b] 17 Since by the one man's trespass, death reigned through that one man, how much more will those who receive the overflow of grace and the gift of righteousness reign in life through the one man, Jesus Christ.

18 So then, as through one trespass there is condemnation for everyone, so also through one righteous act there is life-giving justification[c] for everyone. 19 For just as through one man's disobedience the many were made sinners, so also through the one man's obedience the many will be made righteous. 20 The law came along to multiply the trespass. But where sin multiplied, grace multiplied even more, 21 so that, just as sin reigned in death, so also grace will reign through righteousness, resulting in eternal life through Jesus Christ our Lord.

The New Life in Christ

6 What should we say then? Should we continue in sin in order that grace may multiply? 2 Absolutely not! How can we who died to sin still live in it? 3 Or are you unaware that all of us who were baptized into Christ Jesus were baptized into His death? 4 Therefore we were buried with Him by baptism into death, in order that, just as Christ was raised from the dead by the glory of the Father, so we too may •walk in a new way[d] of life. 5 For if we have been joined with Him in the likeness of His death, we will certainly also be[e] in the likeness of His resurrection. 6 For we know that our old self[f] was crucified with Him in order that sin's dominion over the body[g] may be abolished, so that we may no longer be enslaved to sin, 7 since a person who has died is freed[h] from sin's claims.[i] 8 Now if we died with Christ, we believe that we will also live with Him, 9 because we know that Christ, having been raised from the dead, no longer dies. Death no longer rules over Him. 10 For in that He died, He died to sin once for all; but in that He lives, He lives to God. 11 So, you too consider yourselves dead to sin, but alive to God in Christ Jesus.[j]

12 Therefore do not let sin reign in your mortal body, so that you obey[k] its desires. 13 And do not offer any parts[l] of it to sin as weapons for unrighteousness. But as those who are alive from the dead, offer yourselves to God, and all the parts[l] of yourselves to God as weapons for righteousness. 14 For sin will not rule over you, because you are not under law but under grace.

From Slaves of Sin to Slaves of God

15 What then? Should we sin because we

[a]**5:12** Or *have sinned* [b]**5:16** Or *acquittal* [c]**5:18** Lit *is justification of life* [d]**6:4** Or *in newness* [e]**6:5** Be joined with Him [f]**6:6** Lit *man*; that is, the person that one was in Adam [g]**6:6** Lit *that the body of sin* [h]**6:7** Lit *acquitted*, or *justified* [i]**6:7** Lit *from sin* [j]**6:11** Other mss add *our Lord* [k]**6:12** Other mss add *sin* (lit *it*) *in* [l]**6:13** Or *members*

Turn to page 191.

A—Admit Read Romans 6:23.

are not under law but under grace? Absolutely not! 16 Do you not know that if you offer yourselves to someone[a] as obedient slaves, you are slaves of that one you obey—either of sin leading to death or of obedience leading to righteousness? 17 But thank God that, although you used to be slaves of sin, you obeyed from the heart that pattern of teaching you were entrusted to, 18 and having been liberated from sin, you became enslaved to righteousness. 19 I am using a human analogy[b] because of the weakness of your flesh.[c] For just as you offered the parts[d] of yourselves as slaves to moral impurity, and to greater and greater lawlessness, so now offer them as slaves to righteousness, which results in sanctification. 20 For when you were slaves of sin, you were free from allegiance to righteousness.[e] 21 And what fruit was produced[f] then from the things you are now ashamed of? For the end of those things is death. 22 But now, since you have been liberated from sin and become enslaved to God, you have your fruit, which results in sanctification[g] —and the end is eternal life! 23 For the wages of sin is death, but the gift of God is eternal life in Christ Jesus our Lord.

An Illustration from Marriage

7 Since I am speaking to those who understand law, brothers, are you unaware that the law has authority over someone as long as he lives? 2 For example, a married woman is legally bound to her husband while he lives. But if her husband dies, she is released from the law regarding the husband. 3 So then, if she gives herself to another man while her husband is living, she will be called an adulteress. But if her husband dies, she is free from that law. Then, if she gives herself to another man, she is not an adulteress.

4 Therefore, my brothers, you also were put to death in relation to the law through the ⌊crucified⌋ body of the •Messiah, so that you may belong to another—to Him who was raised from the dead—that we may bear fruit for God. 5 For when we were in the flesh,[h] the sinful passions operated through the law in every part of us[i] and bore fruit for death. 6 But now we have been released from the law, since we have died to what held us, so that we may serve in the new way[j] of the Spirit and not in the old letter of the law.

Sin's Use of the Law

7 What should we say then? Is the law sin? Absolutely not! On the contrary, I would not have known sin if it were not for the law. For example, I would not have known what it is to covet if the law had not said, **Do not covet.**[k] 8 And sin, seizing an opportunity through the commandment, produced in me coveting of every kind. For apart from the law sin is dead. 9 Once I was alive apart from the law, but when the commandment came, sin sprang to life 10 and I died. The commandment that was meant for life resulted in death for me. 11 For sin, seizing an opportunity through the commandment, deceived me, and through it killed me. 12 So then, the law is holy, and the commandment is holy and just and good.

The Problem of Sin in Us

13 Therefore, did what is good cause my death?[l] Absolutely not! On the contrary, sin, in order to be recognized as sin, was producing death in me through what is good, so that through the commandment sin might become sinful beyond measure. 14 For we know that the law is spiritual; but I am made out of flesh,[m] sold into sin's power. 15 For I do not understand what I am doing, because I do not practice what I want to do, but I do what I hate. 16 And if I do what I do not want to do, I agree with the law that it is good. 17 So now I am no longer the one doing it, but it is sin living in me. 18 For I know that nothing good lives in me, that is, in my flesh. For the desire to do what is good is with me, but there is no ability to do it. 19 For I do not do the good that I want to do, but I practice the evil that I do not want to do. 20 Now if I do what I do not want, I am no longer the one doing it, but it is the sin that lives in me. 21 So I discover this principle:[n] when I want to do good, evil is with me. 22 For in my inner self[o] I joyfully agree with God's law. 23 But I see a different law in the parts of my body,[p] waging war against the law of my mind and taking me prisoner to the law of sin in the parts of my body.[p] 24 What a wretched

[a]**6:16** Lit *that to whom you offer yourselves* [b]**6:19** Lit *I speak humanly*; Paul is personifying sin and righteousness as slave masters. [c]**6:19** Or *your human nature* [d]**6:19** Or *members* [e]**6:20** Lit *free to righteousness* [f]**6:21** Lit *what fruit do you have* [g]**6:22** Or *holiness* [h]**7:5** *in the flesh* = a person's life before accepting Christ [i]**7:5** Lit *of our members* [j]**7:6** Lit *in newness* [k]**7:7** Ex 20:17 [l]**7:13** Lit *good become death to me?* [m]**7:14** Other mss read *I am carnal* [n]**7:21** Or *law* [o]**7:22** Lit *inner man* [p]**7:23** Lit *my members*

Turn to page 121.

man I am! Who will rescue me from this body of death? 25 I thank God through Jesus Christ our Lord![a] So then, with my mind I myself am a slave to the law of God, but with my flesh, to the law of sin.

The Life-Giving Spirit

8 Therefore, no condemnation now exists for those in Christ Jesus,[b] 2 because the Spirit's law of life in Christ Jesus has set you[c] free from the law of sin and of death. 3 What the law could not do since it was limited[d] by the flesh, God did. He condemned sin in the flesh by sending His own Son in flesh like ours under sin's domain,[e] and as a sin offering, 4 in order that the law's requirement would be accomplished in us who do not •walk according to the flesh but according to the Spirit. 5 For those whose lives are[f] according to the flesh think about the things of the flesh, but those whose lives are[f] according to the Spirit, about the things of the Spirit. 6 For the mind-set of the flesh is death, but the mind-set of the Spirit is life and peace. 7 For the mind-set of the flesh is hostile to God because it does not submit itself to God's law, for it is unable to do so. 8 Those whose lives are[g] in the flesh are unable to please God. 9 You, however, are not in the flesh, but in the Spirit, since[h] the Spirit of God lives in you. But if anyone does not have the Spirit of Christ, he does not belong to Him. 10 Now if Christ is in you, the body is dead[i] because of sin, but the Spirit[j] is life because of righteousness. 11 And if the Spirit of Him who raised Jesus from the dead lives in you, then He who raised Christ from the dead will also bring your mortal bodies to life through[k] His Spirit who lives in you.

The Holy Spirit's Ministries

12 So then, brothers, we are not obligated to the flesh to live according to the flesh, 13 for if you live according to the flesh, you are going to die. But if by the Spirit you put to death the deeds of the body, you will live. 14 All those led by God's Spirit are God's sons. 15 For you did not receive a spirit of slavery to fall back into fear, but you received the Spirit of adoption, by whom we cry out, "•*Abba*, Father!" 16 The Spirit Himself testifies together with our spirit that we are God's children, 17 and if children, also heirs—heirs of God and co-heirs with Christ—seeing that[h] we suffer with Him so that we may also be glorified with Him.

From Groans to Glory

18 For I consider that the sufferings of this present time are not worth comparing with the glory that is going to be revealed to us. 19 For the creation eagerly waits with anticipation for God's sons to be revealed. 20 For the creation was subjected to futility—not willingly, but because of Him who subjected it—in the hope 21 that the creation itself will also be set free from the bondage of corruption into the glorious freedom of God's children. 22 For we know that the whole creation has been groaning together with labor pains until now. 23 And not only that, but we ourselves who have the Spirit as the •firstfruits—we also groan within ourselves, eagerly waiting for adoption, the redemption of our bodies. 24 Now in this hope we were saved, yet hope that is seen is not hope, because who hopes for what he sees? 25 But if we hope for what we do not see, we eagerly wait for it with patience.

26 In the same way the Spirit also joins to help in our weakness, because we do not know what to pray for as we should, but the Spirit Himself intercedes for us[l] with unspoken groanings. 27 And He who searches the hearts knows the Spirit's mind-set, because He intercedes for the saints according to the will of God.

28 We know that all things work together[m] for the good[n] of those who love God: those who are called according to His purpose. 29 For those He foreknew[o] He also predestined to be conformed to the image of His Son, so that He would be the firstborn among many brothers. 30 And those He predestined, He also called; and those He called, He also justified; and those He justified, He also glorified.

The Believer's Triumph

31 What then are we to say
about these things?
If God is for us, who is against us?
32 He did not even spare His own Son,
but offered Him up for us all;

[a]**7:25** Or *Thanks be to God—*(it is done) *through Jesus Christ our Lord!* [b]**8:1** Other mss add *who do not walk according to the flesh but according to the Spirit* [c]**8:2** Other mss read *me* [d]**8:3** Or *weak* [e]**8:3** Lit *in the likeness of sinful flesh* [f]**8:5** Or *those who are* [g]**8:8** Or *Those who are* [h]**8:9,17** Or *provided that* [i]**8:10** Or *the body will die* [j]**8:10** Or *spirit* [k]**8:11** Other mss read *because of* [l]**8:26** Some mss omit *for us* [m]**8:28** Other mss read *that God works together in all things* [n]**8:28** The ultimate good [o]**8:29** From eternity God knew His people and entered into a personal relationship with them

how will He not also with Him
grant us everything?
33 Who can bring an accusation
against God's elect?
God is the One who justifies.
34 Who is the one who condemns?
Christ Jesus is the One who died,
but even more, has been raised;
He also is at the right hand of God
and intercedes for us.
35 Who can separate us
from the love of Christ?
Can affliction or anguish
or persecution
or famine or nakedness or danger
or sword?
36 As it is written:
Because of You we are being
put to death all day long;
we are counted as sheep
to be slaughtered.[a]
37 No, in all these things we are
more than victorious
through Him who loved us.
38 For I am persuaded that neither death
nor life,
nor angels nor rulers,
nor things present,
nor things to come, nor powers,
39 nor height, nor depth, nor any other
created thing
will have the power to separate us
from the love of God that is
in Christ Jesus our Lord!

Israel's Rejection of Christ

9 I speak the truth in Christ—I am not
lying; my conscience is testifying to me
with the Holy Spirit[b] — 2 that I have intense
sorrow and continual anguish in my heart. 3 For
I could wish that I myself were cursed and cut
off[c] from the •Messiah for the benefit of my
brothers, my countrymen by physical descent.[d]
4 They are Israelites, and to them belong the
adoption, the glory, the covenants, the giving of
the law, the temple service, and the promises.
5 The forefathers are theirs, and from them, by
physical descent,[e] came the Messiah, who is
God over all, blessed forever.[f] •Amen.

God's Gracious Election of Israel

6 But it is not as though the word of God has
failed. For not all who are descended from
Israel are Israel. 7 Neither are they all children
because they are Abraham's descendants.[g] On
the contrary, **in Isaac your seed will be**
called.[h] 8 That is, it is not the children by physical descent[i] who are God's children, but the
children of the promise are considered seed.
9 For this is the statement of the promise: **At**
this time I will come, and Sarah will have a
son.[j] 10 And not only that, but also when Rebekah became pregnant[k] by Isaac our forefather
11 (for though they had not been born yet or
done anything good or bad, so that God's purpose according to election might stand, 12 not
from works but from the One who calls) she
was told: **The older will serve the younger.**[l]
13 As it is written: **Jacob I have loved, but Esau**
I have hated.[m]

God's Selection Is Just

14 What should we say then? Is there injustice with God? Absolutely not! 15 For He tells
Moses:

I will show mercy to whom
I show mercy,
and I will have compassion on whom
I have compassion.[n]

16 So then it does not depend on human will
or effort,[o] but on God who shows mercy.
17 For the Scripture tells Pharaoh:

For this reason I raised you up:
so that I may display
My power in you,
and that My name
may be proclaimed
in all the earth.[p]

18 So then, He shows mercy to whom He wills,
and He hardens whom He wills.
19 You will say to me, therefore, "Why then
does He still find fault? For who can resist His
will?" 20 But who are you—anyone[q] who talks
back to God? Will what is formed say to the one
who formed it, "Why did you make me like
this?" 21 Or has the potter no right over His clay,
to make from the same lump one piece of pottery

[a]**8:36** Ps 44:22; see Is 53:7; Zch 11:4,7 [b]**9:1** Or *testifying with me by the Holy Spirit* [c]**9:3** Lit *were anathema* [d]**9:3** Lit *countrymen according to the flesh* [e]**9:5** Lit *them, according to the flesh* [f]**9:5** Or *the Messiah, the One who is over all, the God who is blessed forever,* or *Messiah. God, who is over all, be blessed forever* [g]**9:7** Lit *seed* [h]**9:7** Gn 21:12 [i]**9:8** Lit *children of the flesh* [j]**9:9** Gn 18:10,14 [k]**9:10** Or *Rebekah conceived by the one act of sexual intercourse* [l]**9:12** Gn 25:23 [m]**9:13** Mal 1:2–3 [n]**9:15** Ex 33:19 [o]**9:16** Lit *on the one willing,* or *on the one running* [p]**9:17** Ex 9:16 [q]**9:20** Lit *you, O man*

for honor and another for dishonor? 22 And what
if God, desiring to display His wrath and to make
His power known, endured with much patience
objects of wrath ready for destruction? 23 And
⌊what if⌋ He did this to make known the riches
of His glory on objects of mercy that He prepared
beforehand for glory— 24 on us whom He also
called, not only from the Jews but also from the
Gentiles? 25 As He also says in Hosea:

I will call "Not-My-People,"
"My-People,"
and she who is "Unloved,"
"Beloved."[a]
26 **And it will be in the place where**
they were told,
you are not My people,
there they will be called
sons of the living God.[b]

27 But Isaiah cries out concerning Israel:

Though the number
of Israel's sons is like
the sand of the sea,
only the remnant will be saved;
28 **for the Lord will execute**
His sentence
completely and decisively
on the earth.[c d]

29 And just as Isaiah predicted:

If the Lord of Hosts[e]
had not left us a seed,
we would have become
like Sodom,
and we would have been made
like Gomorrah.[f]

Israel's Present State

30 What should we say then? Gentiles, who
did not pursue righteousness, have obtained
righteousness—namely the righteousness that
comes from faith. 31 But Israel, pursuing the
law for righteousness, has not achieved the
law.[g] 32 Why is that? Because they did not pursue it by faith, but as if it were by works.[h] They
stumbled over the stumbling stone. 33 As it is
written:

Look! I am putting a stone in Zion
to stumble over,
and a rock to trip over,
yet the one who believes on Him
will not be put to shame.[i]

Righteousness by Faith Alone

10 Brothers, my heart's desire and
prayer to God concerning them[j] is for
their salvation! 2 I can testify about them
that they have zeal for God, but not according to knowledge. 3 Because they disregarded the righteousness from God and
attempted to establish their own righteousness, they have not submitted to God's righteousness. 4 For Christ is the end[k] of the law
for righteousness to everyone who believes.
5 For Moses writes about the righteousness
that is from the law: **The one who does
these things will live by them.**[l] 6 But the
righteousness that comes from faith speaks
like this: **Do not say in your heart, "Who
will go up to heaven?"**[m] that is, to bring
Christ down 7 or, **"Who will go down into
the •abyss?"**[n] that is, to bring Christ up
from the dead. 8 On the contrary, what does
it say? **The message is near you, in your
mouth and in your heart.**[o] This is the message of faith that we proclaim: 9 if you confess with your mouth, "Jesus is Lord," and
believe in your heart that God raised Him
from the dead, you will be saved. 10 With
the heart one believes, resulting in righteousness, and with the mouth one confesses, resulting in salvation. 11 Now the
Scripture says, **No one who believes on
Him will be put to shame,**[p] 12 for there is
no distinction between Jew and Greek, since
the same Lord of all is rich to all who call on
Him. 13 **For everyone who calls on the
name of the Lord will be saved.**[q]

Israel's Rejection of the Message

14 But how can they call on Him in whom
they have not believed? And how can they
believe without hearing about Him? And how
can they hear without a preacher? 15 And
how can they preach unless they are sent? As
it is written: **How welcome**[r] **are the feet of
those**[s] **who announce the gospel of good
things!**[t] 16 But all did not obey the gospel. For
Isaiah says, **Lord, who has believed our**

[a]**9:25** Hs 2:23 [b]**9:26** Hs 1:10 [c]**9:28** Or *land* [d]**9:27–28** Is 10:22–23; 28:22; Hs 1:10 [e]**9:29** Gk *Sabaoth*; this word is a transliteration of the Hb word for *Hosts*, or *Armies*. [f]**9:29** Is 1:9 [g]**9:31** Other mss read *the law for righteousness*
[h]**9:32** Other mss add *of the law* [i]**9:33** Is 8:14; 28:16 [j]**10:1** Other mss read *God for Israel* [k]**10:4** Or *goal* [l]**10:5** Lv 18:5
[m]**10:6** Dt 9:4; 30:12 [n]**10:7** Dt 30:13 [o]**10:8** Dt 30:14 [p]**10:11** Is 28:16 [q]**10:13** Jl 2:32 [r]**10:15** Or *timely*, or *beautiful*
[s]**10:15** Other mss read *feet of those who announce the gospel of peace, of those* [t]**10:15** Is 52:7; Nah 1:15

Turn to page 380.

message?[a] 17 So faith comes from what is
heard, and what is heard comes through the
message about Christ.[b] 18 But I ask, "Did they
not hear?" Yes, they did:

Their voice has gone out
to all the earth,
and their words to the ends
of the inhabited world.[c]

19 But I ask, "Did Israel not understand?" First,
Moses said:

I will make you jealous of those
who are not a nation;
I will make you angry by a nation
that lacks understanding.[d]

20 And Isaiah says boldly:

I was found by those who were not
looking for Me;
I revealed Myself to those
who were not asking
for Me.[e]

21 But to Israel he says: **All day long I have**
spread out My hands to a disobedient and
defiant people.[f]

Israel's Rejection Not Total

11 I ask, then, has God rejected His people? Absolutely not! For I too am an
Israelite, a descendant of Abraham, from the
tribe of Benjamin. 2 God has not rejected His
people whom He foreknew. Or do you not
know what the Scripture says in the Elijah sec-
tion—how he pleads with God against Israel?

3 **Lord, they have killed**
Your prophets, torn down
Your altars;
and I am the only one left,
and they are trying to take
my life![g]

4 But what was God's reply to him? **I have left**
7,000 men for Myself who have not bowed
down to Baal.[h] 5 In the same way, then, there
is also at the present time a remnant chosen by
grace. 6 Now if by grace, then it is not by
works; otherwise grace ceases to be grace.[i]
7 What then? Israel did not find what it was
looking for, but the elect did find it. The rest
were hardened, 8 as it is written:

God gave them a spirit of stupor,
eyes that cannot see and ears
that cannot hear, to this day.[j]

9 And David says:

Let their feasting[k] **become a snare**
and a trap,
a pitfall and a retribution to them.
10 **Let their eyes be darkened**
so they cannot see,
and their backs
be bent continually.[l]

Israel's Rejection Not Final

11 I ask, then, have they stumbled so as to
fall? Absolutely not! On the contrary, by their
stumbling,[m] salvation has come to the Gentiles
to make Israel[n] jealous. 12 Now if their stumbling[m] brings riches for the world, and their
failure riches for the Gentiles, how much more
will their full number bring!
13 Now I am speaking to you Gentiles. In
view of the fact that I am an apostle to the Gentiles, I magnify my ministry, 14 if I can somehow make my own people[o] jealous and save
some of them. 15 For if their being rejected is
world reconciliation, what will their acceptance mean but life from the dead? 16 Now if
the •firstfruits offered up are holy, so is the
whole batch. And if the root is holy, so are the
branches.
17 Now if some of the branches were broken off, and you, though a wild olive branch,
were grafted in among them, and have come to
share in the rich root[p] of the cultivated olive
tree, 18 do not brag that you are better than
those branches. But if you do brag—you do not
sustain the root, but the root sustains you.
19 Then you will say, "Branches were broken
off so that I might be grafted in." 20 True
enough; they were broken off by unbelief, but
you stand by faith. Do not be arrogant, but be
afraid. 21 For if God did not spare the natural
branches, He will not spare you either.
22 Therefore, consider God's kindness and
severity: severity toward those who have fallen,
but God's kindness toward you—if you remain
in His kindness. Otherwise you too will be cut
off. 23 And even they, if they do not remain in
unbelief, will be grafted in, because God has
the power to graft them in again. 24 For if you

[a] **10:16** Is 53:1 [b] **10:17** Other mss read *God* [c] **10:18** Ps 19:4 [d] **10:19** Dt 32:21 [e] **10:20** Is 65:1 [f] **10:21** Is 65:2 [g] **11:3** 1 Kg 19:10,14 [h] **11:4** 1 Kg 19:18 [i] **11:6** Other mss add *But if of works it is no longer grace; otherwise work is no longer work.* [j] **11:8** Dt 29:4; Is 29:10 [k] **11:9** Lit *table* [l] **11:9–10** Ps 69:22–23 [m] **11:11,12** Or *transgression* [n] **11:11** Lit *them* [o] **11:14** Lit *flesh* [p] **11:17** Other mss read *the root and the richness*

were cut off from your native wild olive, and against nature were grafted into a cultivated olive tree, how much more will these—the natural branches—be grafted into their own olive tree?

25 So that you will not be conceited, brothers, I do not want you to be unaware of this •mystery: a partial hardening has come to Israel until the full number of the Gentiles has come in. 26 And in this way all[a] Israel will be saved, as it is written:

The Liberator will come
from Zion;
He will turn away godlessness
from Jacob.
27 **And this will be My covenant**
with them,[b]
when I take away their sins.[c]

28 Regarding the gospel, they are enemies for your advantage, but regarding election, they are loved because of their forefathers, 29 since God's gracious gifts and calling are irrevocable.[d] 30 As you once disobeyed God, but now have received mercy through their disobedience, 31 so they too have now disobeyed, ⌊resulting⌋ in mercy to you, so that they also now[e] may receive mercy. 32 For God has imprisoned all in disobedience, so that He may have mercy on all.

A Hymn of Praise

33 Oh, the depth of the riches
both of the wisdom
and the knowledge of God!
How unsearchable His judgments
and untraceable His ways!
34 **For who has known the mind**
of the Lord?
Or who has been His counselor?
35 **Or who has ever first given to Him,**
and has to be repaid?[f]
36 For from Him and through Him
and to Him are all things.
To Him be the glory forever. •Amen.

A Living Sacrifice

12 Therefore, brothers, by the mercies of God, I urge you to present your bodies as a living sacrifice, holy and pleasing to God; this is your spiritual worship.[g] 2 Do not be conformed to this age, but be transformed by the renewing of your mind, so that you may discern what is the good, pleasing, and perfect will of God.

Many Gifts but One Body

3 For by the grace given to me, I tell everyone among you not to think of himself more highly than he should think. Instead, think sensibly, as God has distributed a measure of faith to each one. 4 Now as we have many parts in one body, and all the parts do not have the same function, 5 in the same way we who are many are one body in Christ and individually members of one another. 6 According to the grace given to us, we have different gifts:

If prophecy, use it according to
the standard of faith;
7 if service, in service; if teaching,
in teaching;
8 if exhorting, in exhortation; giving,
with generosity;
leading, with diligence;
showing mercy, with cheerfulness.

Christian Ethics

9 Love must be without hypocrisy. Detest evil; cling to what is good. 10 Show family affection to one another with brotherly love. Outdo one another in showing honor. 11 Do not lack diligence; be fervent in spirit; serve the Lord. 12 Rejoice in hope; be patient in affliction; be persistent in prayer. 13 Share with the saints in their needs; pursue hospitality. 14 Bless those who persecute you; bless and do not curse. 15 Rejoice with those who rejoice; weep with those who weep. 16 Be in agreement with one another. Do not be proud; instead, associate with the humble. Do not be wise in your own estimation. 17 Do not repay anyone evil for evil. Try to do what is honorable in everyone's eyes. 18 If possible, on your part, live at peace with everyone. 19 Friends, do not avenge yourselves; instead, leave room for His[h] wrath. For it is written: **Vengeance belongs to Me; I will repay,**[i] says the Lord. 20 But

If your enemy is hungry, feed him.
If he is thirsty, give him something
to drink.
For in so doing you will be
heaping fiery coals on his head.[j]

[a]**11:26** Or *And then all* [b]**11:26–27** Is 59:20–21 [c]**11:27** Jr 31:31–34 [d]**11:29** Or *are not taken back* [e]**11:31** Other mss omit *now* [f]**11:34–35** Is 40:13; Jb 41:11; Jr 23:18 [g]**12:1** Or *your reasonable service* [h]**12:19** Lit *the* [i]**12:19** Dt 32:35 [j]**12:20** Pr 25:21–22

21 Do not be conquered by evil, but conquer evil with good.

A Christian's Duties to the State

13 Everyone must submit to the governing authorities, for there is no authority except from God, and those that exist are instituted by God. 2 So then, the one who resists the authority is opposing God's command, and those who oppose it will bring judgment on themselves. 3 For rulers are not a terror to good conduct, but to bad. Do you want to be unafraid of the authority? Do good and you will have its approval. 4 For government is God's servant to you for good. But if you do wrong, be afraid, because it does not carry the sword for no reason. For government is God's servant, an avenger that brings wrath on the one who does wrong. 5 Therefore, you must submit, not only because of wrath, but also because of your conscience. 6 And for this reason you pay taxes, since the ⌊authorities⌋ are God's public servants, continually attending to these tasks.[a] 7 Pay your obligations to everyone: taxes to those you owe taxes, tolls to those you owe tolls, respect to those you owe respect, and honor to those you owe honor.

Love Our Primary Duty

8 Do not owe anyone anything,[b] except to love one another, for the one who loves another has fulfilled the law. 9 The commandments:

> **Do not commit adultery,**
> **do not murder,**
> **do not steal,**[c]
> **do not covet,**[d]

and if there is any other commandment—all are summed up by this: **Love your neighbor as yourself.**[e]

10 Love does no wrong to a neighbor. Love, therefore, is the fulfillment of the law.

Put On Christ

11 Besides this, knowing the time, it is already the hour for you[f] to wake up from sleep, for now our salvation is nearer than when we first believed. 12 The night is nearly over, and the daylight is near, so let us discard the deeds of darkness and put on the armor of light. 13 Let us •walk with decency, as in the daylight: not in carousing and drunkenness; not in sexual impurity and promiscuity; not in quarreling and jealousy. 14 But put on the Lord Jesus Christ, and make no plans to satisfy the fleshly desires.

The Law of Liberty

14 Accept anyone who is weak in faith,[g] but don't argue about doubtful issues. 2 One person believes he may eat anything, but one who is weak eats only vegetables. 3 One who eats must not look down on one who does not eat; and one who does not eat must not criticize one who does, because God has accepted him. 4 Who are you to criticize another's household slave? Before his own Lord he stands or falls. And stand he will! For the Lord is able[h] to make him stand.

5 One person considers one day to be above another day. Someone else considers every day to be the same. Each one must be fully convinced in his own mind. 6 Whoever observes the day, observes it to the Lord.[i] Whoever eats, eats to the Lord, since he gives thanks to God; and whoever does not eat, it is to the Lord that he does not eat, yet he thanks God. 7 For none of us lives to himself, and no one dies to himself. 8 If we live, we live to the Lord; and if we die, we die to the Lord. Therefore, whether we live or die, we belong to the Lord. 9 Christ died and came to life for this: that He might rule over both the dead and the living. 10 But you, why do you criticize your brother? Or you, why do you look down on your brother? For we will all stand before the judgment seat of God.[j] 11 For it is written:

> **As I live, says the Lord,**
> **every knee will bow to Me,**
> **and every tongue will give praise**
> **to God.**[k]

12 So then, each of us will give an account of himself to God.

The Law of Love

13 Therefore, let us no longer criticize one another, but instead decide not to put a stumbling block or pitfall in your brother's way. 14 (I know and am persuaded by the Lord Jesus that

[a] **13:6** Lit *to this very thing* [b] **13:8** Or *Leave no debt outstanding to anyone* [c] **13:9** Other mss add *you shall not bear false witness* [d] **13:9** Ex 20:13–17; Dt 5:17–21 [e] **13:9** Lv 19:18 [f] **13:11** Other mss read *for us* [g] **14:1** Or *weak in the Faith* [h] **14:4** Other mss read *For God has the power* [i] **14:6** Other mss add *but whoever does not observe the day, it is to the Lord that he does not observe it* [j] **14:10** Other mss read *of Christ* [k] **14:11** Is 45:23; 49:18

nothing is unclean in itself. Still, to someone who considers a thing to be unclean, to that one it is unclean.) 15 For if your brother is hurt by what you eat, you are no longer •walking according to love. By what you eat, do not destroy that one for whom Christ died. 16 Therefore, do not let your good be slandered, 17 for the kingdom of God is not eating and drinking, but righteousness, peace, and joy in the Holy Spirit. 18 Whoever serves the •Messiah in this way is acceptable to God and approved by men.

19 So then, we must pursue what promotes peace and what builds up one another. 20 Do not tear down God's work because of food. Everything is clean, but it is wrong for a man to cause stumbling by what he eats. 21 It is a noble thing not to eat meat, or drink wine, or do anything that makes your brother stumble.[a] 22 Do you have faith? Keep it to yourself before God. Blessed is the man who does not condemn himself by what he approves. 23 But whoever doubts stands condemned if he eats, because his eating is not from faith, and everything that is not from faith is sin.

Pleasing Others, Not Ourselves

15 Now we who are strong have an obligation to bear the weaknesses of those without strength, and not to please ourselves. 2 Each one of us must please his neighbor for his good, in order to build him up. 3 For even the •Messiah did not please Himself. On the contrary, as it is written, **The insults of those who insult You have fallen on Me.**[b] 4 For whatever was written before was written for our instruction, so that through our endurance and through the encouragement of the Scriptures we may have hope. 5 Now may the God of endurance and encouragement grant you agreement with one another, according to Christ Jesus, 6 so that you may glorify the God and Father of our Lord Jesus Christ with a united mind and voice.

Glorifying God Together

7 Therefore accept one another, just as the Messiah also accepted you, to the glory of God. 8 Now I say that Christ has become a servant of the circumcised[c] on behalf of the truth of God, to confirm the promises to the fathers, 9 and so that Gentiles may glorify God for His mercy. As it is written:

Therefore I will praise You
among the Gentiles,
and I will sing psalms
to Your name.[d]

10 Again it says: **Rejoice, you Gentiles, with His people!**[e] 11 And again:

Praise the Lord, all you Gentiles;
all the peoples should praise Him![f]

12 And again, Isaiah says:

The root of Jesse will appear,
the One who rises to rule
the Gentiles;
in Him the Gentiles will hope.[g]

13 Now may the God of hope fill you with all joy and peace in believing, so that you may overflow with hope by the power of the Holy Spirit.

From Jerusalem to Illyricum

14 Now, my brothers, I myself am convinced about you that you also are full of goodness, filled with all knowledge, and able to instruct one another. 15 Nevertheless, to remind you, I have written to you more boldly on some points[h] because of the grace given me by God 16 to be a minister of Christ Jesus to the Gentiles, serving as a priest of God's good news. My purpose is that the offering of the Gentiles may be acceptable, sanctified by the Holy Spirit. 17 Therefore I have reason to boast in Christ Jesus regarding what pertains to God. 18 For I would not dare say anything except what Christ has accomplished through me to make the Gentiles obedient by word and deed, 19 by the power of miraculous signs and wonders, and by the power of God's Spirit. As a result, I have fully proclaimed the good news about the Messiah from Jerusalem all the way around to Illyricum.[i] 20 So my aim is to evangelize where Christ has not been named, in order that I will not be building on someone else's foundation, 21 but, as it is written:

Those who had no report of Him
will see,
and those who have not heard
will understand.[j]

Paul's Travel Plans

22 That is why I have been prevented many

[a]**14:21** Other mss add *or offended or weakened* [b]**15:3** Ps 69:9 [c]**15:8** The Jews [d]**15:9** 2 Sm 22:50; Ps 18:49 [e]**15:10** Dt 32:43 [f]**15:11** Ps 117:1 [g]**15:12** Is 11:10 [h]**15:15** Other mss add *brothers* [i]**15:19** A Roman province northwest of Greece on the eastern shore of the Adriatic Sea [j]**15:21** Is 52:15

times from coming to you. 23 But now I no
longer have any work to do in these provinces,[a] and I have strongly desired for many
years to come to you 24 whenever I travel to
Spain.[b] For I do hope to see you when I pass
through, and to be sent on my way there by
you, once I have first enjoyed your company
for a while. 25 Now, however, I am traveling
to Jerusalem to serve the saints; 26 for Macedonia and Achaia[c] were pleased to make a
contribution to the poor among the saints in
Jerusalem. 27 Yes, they were pleased, and they
are indebted to them. For if the Gentiles have
shared in their spiritual benefits, then they are
obligated to minister to Jews[d] in material
needs. 28 So when I have finished this and
safely delivered the funds[e] to them, I will go
by way of you to Spain. 29 But I know that
when I come to you, I will come in the fullness
of the blessing[f] of Christ.

30 Now I implore you, brothers, through the
Lord Jesus Christ and through the love of the
Spirit, to agonize together with me in your
prayers to God on my behalf: 31 that I may be
rescued from the unbelievers in Judea, that my
service for Jerusalem may be acceptable to the
saints, 32 and that, by God's will, I may come to
you with joy and be refreshed together with
you.

33 The God of peace be with all of you.
•Amen.

Paul's Commendation of Phoebe

16 I commend to you our sister Phoebe,
who is a servant[g] of the church in
Cenchreae. 2 So you should welcome her in
the Lord in a manner worthy of the saints, and
assist her in whatever matter she may require
your help. For indeed she has been a benefac-
tor of many—and of me also.

Greeting to Roman Christians

3 Give my greetings to Prisca[h] and
Aquila, my co-workers in Christ
Jesus, 4 who risked their own
necks for my life. Not only do I
thank them, but so do all the Gentile churches.
5 Greet also the church that meets in
their home.
Greet my dear friend Epaenetus,
who is the first convert[i] to Christ
from Asia.[j]
6 Greet Mary,[k] who has worked very
hard for you.[l]
7 Greet Andronicus and Junia,[m] my
fellow countrymen and fellow
prisoners. They are outstanding
among the apostles, and they were
also in Christ before me.
8 Greet Ampliatus, my dear friend in
the Lord.
9 Greet Urbanus, our co-worker in
Christ, and my dear friend
Stachys.
10 Greet Apelles, who is approved in
Christ.
Greet those who belong to the
household of Aristobulus.
11 Greet Herodion, my fellow
countryman.
Greet those who belong to the
household of Narcissus who are
in the Lord.
12 Greet Tryphaena and Tryphosa, who
have worked hard in the Lord.
Greet my dear friend Persis, who has
worked very hard in the Lord.
13 Greet Rufus, chosen in the Lord; also
his mother—and mine.
14 Greet Asyncritus, Phlegon, Hermes,
Patrobas, Hermas, and the brothers who are with them.
15 Greet Philologus and Julia, Nereus
and his sister, and Olympas, and
all the saints who are with them.
16 Greet one another with a holy kiss.
All the churches of Christ send you
greetings.

Warning against Divisive People

17 Now I implore you, brothers, watch
out for those who cause dissensions and pit-
falls contrary to the doctrine you have
learned. Avoid them; 18 for such people do
not serve our Lord Christ but their own appe-
tites,[n] and by smooth talk and flattering
words they deceive the hearts of the unsus-
pecting.

[a]**15:23** Lit *now, having no longer a place in these parts* [b]**15:24** Other mss add *I will come to you.* [c]**15:26** The churches of these provinces [d]**15:27** Lit *to them* [e]**15:28** Lit *delivered this fruit* [f]**15:29** Other mss add *of the gospel* [g]**16:1** Others interpret this term in a technical sense: *deacon*, or *deaconess*, or *minister* [h]**16:3** Traditionally, *Priscilla*, as in Ac 18:2,18,26 [i]**16:5** Lit *the firstfruits* [j]**16:5** Other mss read *Achaia* [k]**16:6** Or *Maria* [l]**16:6** Other mss read *us* [m]**16:7** Either a feminine name or *Junias*, a masculine name [n]**16:18** Lit *belly*

Paul's Gracious Conclusion

19 The report of your obedience has reached
everyone. Therefore I rejoice over you. But I
want you to be wise about what is good, yet
innocent about what is evil. 20 The God of
peace will soon crush Satan under your feet.
The grace of our Lord Jesus be with you.
21 Timothy, my co-worker, and Lucius,
Jason, and Sosipater, my fellow countrymen,
greet you.
22 I Tertius, who penned this epistle in the
Lord, greet you.
23 Gaius, who is host to me and to the
whole church, greets you. Erastus, the city trea-
surer, and our brother Quartus greet you.
[24 The grace of our Lord Jesus Christ be
with you all.][a]

Glory to God

25 Now to Him who has power to
strengthen you according to my gospel and the
proclamation of Jesus Christ, according to the
revelation of the sacred secret kept silent for
long ages, 26 but now revealed and made
known through the prophetic Scriptures,
according to the command of the eternal God,
to advance the obedience of faith among all
nations— 27 to the only wise God, through
Jesus Christ—to Him be the glory forever![b]
•Amen.

1 Corinthians

Greeting

1 Paul, called as an apostle of Christ Jesus
by God's will, and our brother Sosthenes:
2 To God's church at Corinth, to those who
are sanctified in Christ Jesus and called as
saints, with all those in every place who call on
the name of Jesus Christ our Lord—theirs and
ours.
3 Grace to you and peace from God our
Father and the Lord Jesus Christ.

Thanksgiving

4 I always thank my God for you because of
God's grace given to you in Christ Jesus, 5 that
by Him you were made rich in everything—in
all speaking and all knowledge— 6 as the testimony about Christ was confirmed among
you, 7 so that you do not lack any spiritual gift
as you eagerly wait for the revelation of our
Lord Jesus Christ. 8 He will also confirm you
to the end, blameless in the day of our Lord
Jesus Christ. 9 God is faithful; by Him you
were called into fellowship with His Son,
Jesus Christ our Lord.

Divisions at Corinth

10 Now I urge you, brothers, in the name
of our Lord Jesus Christ, that you all say the
same thing, that there be no divisions among
you, and that you be united with the same
understanding and the same conviction.
11 For it has been reported to me about you,
my brothers, by members of Chloe's household, that there are quarrels among you.
12 What I am saying is this: each of you says,
"I'm with Paul," or "I'm with Apollos," or
"I'm with •Cephas," or "I'm with Christ."
13 Is Christ divided? Was it Paul who was crucified for you? Or were you baptized in Paul's
name? 14 I thank God[c] [d] that I baptized none
of you except Crispus and Gaius, 15 so that no
one can say you had been baptized in my
name. 16 I did, in fact, baptize the household
of Stephanas; beyond that, I don't know if I
baptized anyone else. 17 For Christ did not
send me to baptize, but to preach the gospel—
not with clever words, so that the cross of
Christ will not be emptied ⌊of its effect⌋.

Christ the Power and Wisdom of God

18 For to those who are perishing the message of the cross is foolishness, but to us who
are being saved it is God's power. 19 For it is
written:

> **I will destroy the wisdom**
> **of the wise,**
> **and I will set aside**
> **the understanding**
> **of the experts.**[e]

[a] **16:24** Other mss omit bracketed text; see v. 20 [b] **16:25–27** Other mss have these vv. at the end of chap 14 or 15.
[c] **1:14** Other mss omit *God* [d] **1:14** Or *I am thankful* [e] **1:19** Is 29:14

20 Where is the philosopher?[a] Where is the scholar? Where is the debater of this age? Hasn't God made the world's wisdom foolish? 21 For since, in God's wisdom, the world did not know God through wisdom, God was pleased to save those who believe through the foolishness of the message preached. 22 For the Jews ask for signs and the Greeks seek wisdom, 23 but we preach Christ crucified, a stumbling block to the Jews and foolishness to the Gentiles.[b] 24 Yet to those who are called, both Jews and Greeks, Christ is God's power and God's wisdom, 25 because God's foolishness is wiser than human wisdom, and God's weakness is stronger than human strength.

Boasting Only in the Lord

26 Brothers, consider your calling: not many are wise from a human perspective,[c] not many powerful, not many of noble birth. 27 Instead, God has chosen the world's foolish things to shame the wise, and God has chosen the world's weak things to shame the strong. 28 God has chosen the world's insignificant and despised things—the things viewed as nothing—so He might bring to nothing the things that are viewed as something, 29 so that no one[d] can boast in His presence. 30 But from Him you are in Christ Jesus, who for us became wisdom from God, as well as righteousness, sanctification, and redemption, 31 in order that, as it is written: **The one who boasts must boast in the Lord.**[e]

Paul's Proclamation

2 When I came to you, brothers, announcing the testimony[f] of God to you, I did not come with brilliance of speech or wisdom. 2 For I determined to know nothing among you except Jesus Christ and Him crucified. 3 And I was with you in weakness, in fear, and in much trembling. 4 My speech and my proclamation were not with persuasive words of wisdom,[g] but with a demonstration of the Spirit and power, 5 so that your faith might not be based on men's wisdom but on God's power.

Spiritual Wisdom

6 However, among the mature we do speak a wisdom, but not a wisdom of this age, or of the rulers of this age, who are coming to nothing. 7 On the contrary, we speak God's hidden wisdom in a •mystery, which God predestined before the ages for our glory. 8 None of the rulers of this age knew it, for if they had known it, they would not have crucified the Lord of glory. 9 But as it is written:

What no eye has seen and no ear
has heard,
and what has never come
into a man's heart,
is what God has prepared for those
who love Him.[h]

10 Now God has revealed them to us by the Spirit, for the Spirit searches everything, even the deep things of God. 11 For who among men knows the concerns[i] of a man except the spirit of the man that is in him? In the same way, no one knows the concerns[i] of God except the Spirit of God. 12 Now we have not received the spirit of the world, but the Spirit who is from God, in order to know what has been freely given to us by God. 13 We also speak these things, not in words taught by human wisdom, but in those taught by the Spirit, explaining spiritual things to spiritual people.[j] 14 But the natural man does not welcome what comes from God's Spirit, because it is foolishness to him; he is not able to know it since it is evaluated[k] spiritually. 15 The spiritual person, however, can evaluate[l] everything, yet he himself cannot be evaluated[k] by anyone. 16 For:

who has known
the Lord's mind,
that he may instruct Him?[m]

But we have the mind of Christ.

The Problem of Immaturity

3 Brothers, I was not able to speak to you as spiritual people but as people of the flesh, as babies in Christ. 2 I fed you milk, not solid food, because you were not yet able to receive it. In fact, you are still not able, 3 because you are still fleshly. For since there is envy and strife[n] among you, are you not fleshly and living like ordinary people?[o] 4 For whenever someone says, "I'm with Paul," and another, "I'm with Apollos," are you not ⌊typical⌋ men?[p]

[a]**1:20** Or *wise* [b]**1:23** Other mss read *Greeks* [c]**1:26** Lit *wise according to the flesh* [d]**1:29** Lit *that not all flesh* [e]**1:31** Jr 9:24 [f]**2:1** Other mss read *mystery* [g]**2:4** Other mss read *human wisdom* [h]**2:9** Is 52:15; 64:4 [i]**2:11** Lit *things* [j]**2:13** Or *things with spiritual words* [k]**2:14,15** Or *judged*, or *discerned* [l]**2:15** Or *judge*, or *discern* [m]**2:16** Is 40:13 [n]**3:3** Other mss add *and divisions* [o]**3:3** Lit *and walking according to man* [p]**3:4** Other mss read *are you not carnal*

The Role of God's Servants

5 So, what is Apollos? And what is Paul?
They are servants through whom you believed,
and each has the role the Lord has given. 6 I
planted, Apollos watered, but God gave the
growth. 7 So then neither the one who plants
nor the one who waters is anything, but only
God who gives the growth. 8 Now the one who
plants and the one who waters are equal, and
each will receive his own reward according to
his own labor. 9 For we are God's co-workers.
You are God's field, God's building.
10 According to God's grace that was given to
me, as a skilled master builder I have laid a foundation, and another builds on it. But each one
must be careful how he builds on it, 11 because
no one can lay any other foundation than what
has been laid—that is, Jesus Christ. 12 If anyone
builds on the foundation with gold, silver, costly
stones, wood, hay, or straw, 13 each one's work
will become obvious, for the day[a] will disclose
it, because it will be revealed by fire; the fire
will test the quality of each one's work. 14 If
anyone's work that he has built survives, he will
receive a reward. 15 If anyone's work is burned
up, it will be lost, but he will be saved; yet it will
be like an escape through fire.[b]

16 Don't you know that you are God's sanctuary and that the Spirit of God lives in you?
17 If anyone ruins God's sanctuary, God will
ruin him; for God's sanctuary is holy, and that
is what you are.

The Folly of Human Wisdom

18 No one should deceive himself. If anyone
among you thinks he is wise in this age, he
must become foolish so that he can become
wise. 19 For the wisdom of this world is foolishness with God, since it is written: **He catches
the wise in their craftiness**[c] — 20 and again,
**The Lord knows the reasonings of the wise,
that they are futile.**[d] 21 So no one should boast
in men, for all things are yours: 22 whether Paul
or Apollos or •Cephas or the world or life or
death or things present or things to come—all
are yours, 23 and you belong to Christ, and
Christ to God.

The Faithful Manager

4 A person should consider us in this way:
as servants of Christ and managers of
God's •mysteries. 2 In this regard, it is
expected of managers that each one be found
faithful. 3 It is of little importance that I should
be evaluated by you or by a human court.[e] In
fact, I don't even evaluate myself. 4 For I am
not conscious of anything against myself, but I
am not justified by this. The One who evaluates me is the Lord. 5 Therefore don't judge
anything prematurely, before the Lord comes,
who will both bring to light what is hidden in
darkness and reveal the intentions of the
hearts. And then praise will come to each one
from God.

The Apostles' Example of Humility

6 Now, brothers, I have applied these things
to myself and Apollos for your benefit, so that
you may learn from us the saying: "Nothing
beyond what is written."[f] The purpose is that
none of you will be inflated with pride in favor
of one person over another. 7 For who makes
you so superior? What do you have that you
didn't receive? If, in fact, you did receive it,
why do you boast as if you hadn't received it?
8 Already you are full! Already you are rich! You
have begun to reign as kings without us—and I
wish you did reign, so that we also could reign
with you! 9 For I think God has displayed us,
the apostles, in last place, like men condemned
to die: we have become a spectacle to the world
and to angels and to men. 10 We are fools for
Christ, but you are wise in Christ! We are
weak, but you are strong! You are distinguished, but we are dishonored! 11 Up to the
present hour we are both hungry and thirsty;
we are poorly clothed, roughly treated, homeless; 12 we labor, working with our own hands.
When we are reviled, we bless; when we are
persecuted, we endure it; 13 when we are slandered, we entreat. We are, even now, like the
world's garbage, like the filth of all things.

Paul's Fatherly Care

14 I'm not writing this to shame you, but to
warn you as my dear children. 15 For you can
have 10,000 instructors in Christ, but you can't
have many fathers. Now I have fathered you in
Christ Jesus through the gospel. 16 Therefore I
urge you, be imitators of me. 17 This is why I
have sent to you Timothy, who is my beloved
and faithful child in the Lord. He will remind
you about my ways in Christ Jesus, just as I
teach everywhere in every church. 18 Now
some are inflated with pride, as though I were
not coming to you. 19 But I will come to you

[a]**3:13** The Day of Christ's judgment of believers [b]**3:15** Lit *yet so as through fire* [c]**3:19** Jb 5:13 [d]**3:20** Ps 94:11 [e]**4:3** Lit *a human day* [f]**4:6** The words in quotation marks could refer to the OT, a Jewish maxim, or a popular proverb.

soon, if the Lord wills, and I will know not the
talk but the power of those who are inflated
with pride. 20 For the kingdom of God is not in
talk but in power. 21 What do you want? Should
I come to you with a rod, or in love and a spirit
of gentleness?

Immoral Church Members

5 It is widely reported that there is sexual
immorality among you, and the kind of
sexual immorality that is not even condoned[a]
among the Gentiles—a man is living with his
father's wife. 2 And you are inflated with pride,
instead of filled with grief so that he who has
committed this act might be removed from
among you. 3 For though absent in body but
present in spirit, I have already decided about
him who has done this thing as though I were
present. 4 In the name of our Lord Jesus, when
you are assembled, along with my spirit and
with the power of our Lord Jesus, 5 turn that
one over to Satan for the destruction of the
flesh, so that his spirit may be saved in the Day
of the Lord.
6 Your boasting is not good. Don't you know
that a little yeast permeates the whole batch of
dough? 7 Clean out the old yeast so that you
may be a new batch, since you are unleavened.
For Christ our •Passover has been sacrificed.[b]
8 Therefore, let us observe the feast, not with
old yeast, or with the yeast of malice and evil,
but with the unleavened bread of sincerity and
truth.

Church Discipline

9 I wrote to you in a letter not to associate
with sexually immoral people— 10 by no means
referring to this world's immoral people, or to
the greedy and swindlers, or to idolaters; otherwise you would have to leave the world. 11 But
now I am writing[c] you not to associate with anyone who bears the name of brother who is sexually immoral or greedy, an idolater or a reviler, a
drunkard or a swindler. Do not even eat with
such a person. 12 For what is it to me to judge
outsiders? Do you not judge those who are
inside? 13 But God judges outsiders. **Put away
the evil person from among yourselves.**[d]

Lawsuits among Believers

6 Does any of you who has a complaint
against someone dare go to law before
the unrighteous,[e] and not before the saints?
2 Or do you not know that the saints will judge
the world? And if the world is judged by you,
are you unworthy to judge the smallest cases?
3 Do you not know that we will judge angels—
not to speak of things pertaining to this life?
4 So if you have cases pertaining to this life, do
you select those[f] who have no standing in the
church to judge? 5 I say this to your shame! Can
it be that there is not one wise person among
you who will be able to arbitrate between his
brothers? 6 Instead, brother goes to law against
brother, and that before unbelievers!
7 Therefore, it is already a total defeat for
you that you have lawsuits against one another.
Why not rather put up with injustice? Why not
rather be cheated? 8 Instead, you act unjustly
and cheat—and this to brothers! 9 Do you not
know that the unjust will not inherit God's
kingdom? Do not be deceived: no sexually
immoral people, idolaters, adulterers, male
prostitutes, homosexuals, 10 thieves, greedy
people, drunkards, revilers, or swindlers will
inherit God's kingdom. 11 Some of you were
like this; but you were washed, you were sanctified, you were justified in the name of the
Lord Jesus Christ and by the Spirit of our God.

Glorifying God in Body and Spirit

12 "Everything is permissible for me,"[g] but
not everything is helpful. "Everything is permissible for me,"[g] but I will not be brought
under the control of anything. 13 "Foods for the
stomach and the stomach for foods,"[g] but God
will do away with both of them.[h] The body is
not for sexual immorality but for the Lord, and
the Lord for the body. 14 God raised up the
Lord and will also raise us up by His power.
15 Do you not know that your bodies are the
members of Christ? So should I take the members of Christ and make them members of a
prostitute? Absolutely not! 16 Do you not know
that anyone joined to a prostitute is one body
with her? For it says, **The two will become
one flesh.**[i] 17 But anyone joined to the Lord is
one spirit with Him.
18 Flee from sexual immorality! "Every sin a
person can commit is outside the body,"[j] but
the person who is sexually immoral sins against
his own body. 19 Do you not know that your
body is a sanctuary of the Holy Spirit who is in

[a] **5:1** Other mss read *named* [b] **5:7** Other mss add *for us* [c] **5:11** Or *now I wrote* [d] **5:13** Dt 17:7 [e] **6:1** Unbelievers; see v. 6
[f] **6:4** Or *life, appoint those* (as a command) [g] **6:12,13** The words in quotation marks are most likely slogans used by some Corinthian Christians. Paul evaluates and corrects these slogans. [h] **6:13** Lit *both it and them* [i] **6:16** Gn 2:24 [j] **6:18** See note at 1 Co 6:12

you, whom you have from God? You are not
your own, 20 for you were bought at a price;
therefore glorify God in your body.[a]

Principles of Marriage

7 About the things you wrote:[b] "It is good
for a man not to have relations with[c] a
woman."[d] 2 But because of sexual immorality,[e]
each man should have his own wife, and each
woman should have her own husband. 3 A
husband should fulfill his marital duty to his
wife, and likewise a wife to her husband. 4 A
wife does not have authority over her own
body, but her husband does. Equally, a husband does not have authority over his own
body, but his wife does. 5 Do not deprive one
another—except when you agree, for a time,
to devote yourselves to[f] prayer. Then come
together again; otherwise, Satan may tempt
you because of your lack of self-control. 6 I say
this as a concession, not as a command. 7 I
wish that all people were just like me. But
each has his own gift from God, one this and
another that.

A Word to the Unmarried

8 I say to the unmarried and to widows: It is
good for them if they remain as I am. 9 But if
they do not have self-control, they should
marry, for it is better to marry than to burn
with desire.

Advice to Married People

10 I command the married—not I, but the
Lord—a wife is not to leave[g] her husband. 11 But
if she does leave, she must remain unmarried or
be reconciled to her husband—and a husband is
not to leave his wife. 12 But to the rest I, not the
Lord, say: If any brother has an unbelieving wife,
and she is willing to live with him, he must not
leave her. 13 Also, if any woman has an unbelieving husband, and he is willing to live with her,
she must not leave her husband. 14 For the
unbelieving husband is sanctified by the wife,
and the unbelieving wife is sanctified by the
Christian husband. Otherwise your children
would be unclean, but now they are holy. 15 But
if the unbeliever leaves, let him leave.[g] A
brother or a sister is not bound in such cases.
God has called you[h] to peace. 16 For you, wife,
how do you know whether you will save your
husband? Or you, husband, how do you know
whether you will save your wife?

Various Situations of Life

17 However, each one must live his life in
the situation the Lord assigned when God
called him.[i] This is what I command in all the
churches. 18 Was anyone already circumcised
when he was called? He should not undo his
circumcision. Was anyone called while uncircumcised? He should not get circumcised.
19 Circumcision does not matter and uncircumcision does not matter, but keeping God's commandments does. 20 Each person should
remain in the life situation[j] in which he was
called. 21 Were you called while a slave? It
should not be a concern to you. But if you can
become free, by all means take the opportunity.[k] 22 For he who is called by the Lord as a
slave is the Lord's freedman.[l] Likewise he who
is called as a free man[m] is Christ's slave. 23 You
were bought at a price; do not become slaves of
men. 24 Brothers, each person should remain
with God in whatever situation he was called.

About the Unmarried and Widows

25 About virgins: I have no command from
the Lord, but I do give an opinion as one who
by the Lord's mercy is trustworthy. 26 Therefore I consider this to be good because of the
present distress: it is fine for a man to stay as he
is. 27 Are you bound to a wife? Do not seek to
be loosed. Are you loosed from a wife? Do not
seek a wife. 28 However, if you do get married,
you have not sinned, and if a virgin marries,
she has not sinned. But such people will have
trouble in this life,[n] and I am trying to spare
you. 29 And I say this, brothers: the time is limited, so from now on those who have wives
should be as though they had none, 30 those
who weep as though they did not weep, those
who rejoice as though they did not rejoice,
those who buy as though they did not possess,
31 and those who use the world as though they
did not make full use of it. For this world in its
current form is passing away.

32 I want you to be without concerns. An
unmarried man is concerned about the things
of the Lord—how he may please the Lord.

[a] **6:20** Other mss add *and in your spirit, which belong to God.* [b] **7:1** Other mss add *to me* [c] **7:1** Lit *not to touch* [d] **7:1** The words in quotation marks are a principle that the Corinthians wrote to Paul and asked for his view about. [e] **7:2** Lit *immoralities* [f] **7:5** Other mss add *fasting and to* [g] **7:10,15** Or *separate from*, or *divorce* [h] **7:15** Other mss read *us* [i] **7:17** Lit *called each* [j] **7:20** Lit *in the calling* [k] **7:21** Or *But even though you can become free, make the most of your position as a slave.* [l] **7:22** A former slave [m] **7:22** A man who was never a slave [n] **7:28** Lit *in the flesh*

33 But a married man is concerned about the things of the world—how he may please his wife— 34 and he is divided. An unmarried woman or a virgin is concerned about the things of the Lord, so that she may be holy both in body and in spirit. But a married woman is concerned about the things of the world—how she may please her husband. 35 Now I am saying this for your own benefit, not to put a restraint on you, but because of what is proper, and so that you may be devoted to the Lord without distraction.

36 But if any man thinks he is acting improperly toward his virgin,[a] if she is past marriageable age,[b] and so it must be, he can do what he wants. He is not sinning; they can get married. 37 But he who stands firm in his heart (who is under no compulsion, but has control over his own will) and has decided in his heart to keep his own virgin, will do well. 38 So then he who marries[c] his virgin does well, but he who does not marry[d] will do better.

39 A wife is bound[e] as long as her husband is living. But if her husband dies, she is free to be married to anyone she wants—only in the Lord.[f] 40 But she is happier if she remains as she is, in my opinion. And I think that I also have the Spirit of God.

Food Offered to Idols

8 About food offered to idols: We know that "we all have knowledge."[g] Knowledge inflates with pride, but love builds up. 2 If anyone thinks he knows anything, he does not yet know it as he ought to know it. 3 But if anyone loves God, he is known by Him.

4 About eating food offered to idols, then, we know that "an idol is nothing in the world,"[g] and that "there is no God but one."[g] 5 For even if there are so-called gods, whether in heaven or on earth—as there are many "gods" and many "lords"—

6 yet for us there is one God, the Father,
from whom are all things, and we
for Him;
and one Lord, Jesus Christ,
through whom are all things, and we
through Him.

7 However, not everyone has this knowledge. In fact, some have been so used to idolatry up until now, that when they eat food offered to an idol, their conscience, being weak, is defiled. 8 Food will not make us acceptable to God. We are not inferior if we don't eat, and we are not better if we do eat. 9 But be careful that this right of yours in no way becomes a stumbling block to the weak. 10 For if somebody sees you, the one who has this knowledge, dining in an idol's temple, won't his weak conscience be encouraged to eat food offered to idols? 11 Then the weak person, the brother for whom Christ died, is ruined by your knowledge. 12 Now when you sin like this against the brothers and wound their weak conscience, you are sinning against Christ. 13 Therefore, if food causes my brother to fall, I will never again eat meat, so that I won't cause my brother to fall.

Paul's Example as an Apostle

9 Am I not free? Am I not an apostle? Have I not seen Jesus our Lord? Are you not my work in the Lord? 2 If I am not an apostle to others, at least I am to you, for you are the seal of my apostleship in the Lord. 3 My defense to those who examine me is this: 4 Don't we have the right to eat and drink? 5 Don't we have the right to be accompanied by a Christian wife, like the other apostles, the Lord's brothers, and •Cephas? 6 Or is it only Barnabas and I who have no right to refrain from working? 7 Who ever goes to war at his own expense? Who plants a vineyard and does not eat its fruit? Or who shepherds a flock and does not drink the milk from the flock? 8 Am I saying this from a human perspective? Doesn't the law also say the same thing? 9 For it is written in the law of Moses, **Do not muzzle an ox while it treads out the grain.**[h] Is God really concerned with oxen? 10 Or isn't He really saying it for us? Yes, this is written for us, because he who plows ought to plow in hope, and he who threshes should do so in hope of sharing the crop. 11 If we have sown spiritual things for you, is it too much if we reap material things from you? 12 If others share this authority over you, don't we even more?

However, we have not used this authority; instead we endure everything so that we will not hinder the gospel of Christ. 13 Do you not know that those who perform the temple services eat the food from the temple, and those who serve at the altar share in the offerings of the altar? 14 In the same way, the Lord has

[a]**7:36** (1) a man's fiancée, or (2) his daughter, or (3) his Levirate wife, or (4) a celibate companion [b]**7:36** Or *virgin, if his passions are strong,* [c]**7:38** Or *marries off* [d]**7:38** Or *marry her off* [e]**7:39** Other mss add *by law* [f]**7:39** Only a believer [g]**8:1,4** See note at 1 Co 6:12 [h]**9:9** Dt 25:4

commanded that those who preach the gospel
should earn their living by the gospel.
15 But I have used none of these rights, and
I have not written this to make it happen that
way for me. For it would be better for me to die
than for anyone to deprive me of my boast!
16 For if I preach the gospel, I have no reason to
boast, because an obligation is placed on me.
And woe to me if I do not preach the gospel!
17 For if I do this willingly, I have a reward; but
if unwillingly, I am entrusted with a steward-
ship. 18 What then is my reward? To preach the
gospel and offer it free of charge, and not make
full use of my authority in the gospel.
19 For although I am free from all people, I
have made myself a slave to all, in order to win
more people. 20 To the Jews I became like a
Jew, to win Jews; to those under the law, like
one under the law—though I myself am not
under the law[a] —to win those under the law.
21 To those who are outside the law, like one
outside the law—not being outside God's law,
but under the law of Christ—to win those outside the law. 22 To the weak I became weak, in
order to win the weak. I have become all things
to all people, so that I may by all means save
some. 23 Now I do all this because of the gospel, that I may become a partner in its
benefits.[b]
24 Do you not know that the runners in a
stadium all race, but only one receives the
prize? Run in such a way that you may win.
25 Now everyone who competes exercises self-
control in everything. However, they do it to
receive a perishable crown, but we an imperishable one. 26 Therefore I do not run like one
who runs aimlessly, or box like one who beats
the air. 27 Instead, I discipline my body and
bring it under strict control, so that after
preaching to others, I myself will not be disqualified.

Warnings from Israel's Past

10 Now I want you to know, brothers,
that our fathers were all under the
cloud, all passed through the sea, 2 and all
were baptized into Moses in the cloud and in
the sea. 3 They all ate the same spiritual food,
4 and all drank the same spiritual drink. For
they drank from a spiritual rock that followed
them, and that rock was Christ. 5 But God was
not pleased with most of them, for they were
struck down in the desert.
6 Now these things became examples for us,
so that we will not desire evil as they did.[c]
7 Don't become idolaters as some of them
were; as it is written, **The people sat down to
eat and drink, and got up to play.**[d] [e] 8 Let us
not commit sexual immorality as some of them
did,[f] and in a single day 23,000 people fell
dead. 9 Let us not tempt Christ as some of them
did,[g] and were destroyed by snakes. 10 Nor
should we complain as some of them did,[h] and
were killed by the destroyer.[i] 11 Now these
things happened to them as examples, and they
were written as a warning to us, on whom the
ends of the ages have come. 12 Therefore, whoever thinks he stands must be careful not to fall!
13 No temptation has overtaken you except
what is common to humanity. God is faithful
and He will not allow you to be tempted
beyond what you are able, but with the temptation He will also provide a way of escape, so
that you are able to bear it.

Warning against Idolatry

14 Therefore, my dear friends, flee from
idolatry. 15 I am speaking as to wise people.
Judge for yourselves what I say. 16 The cup of
blessing that we bless, is it not a sharing in the
blood of Christ? The bread that we break, is it
not a sharing in the body of Christ? 17 Because
there is one bread, we who are many are one
body, for all of us share that one bread. 18 Look
at the people of Israel.[j] Are not those who eat
the sacrifices partners in the altar? 19 What am
I saying then? That food offered to idols is anything, or that an idol is anything? 20 No, but I
do say that what they[k] sacrifice, they sacrifice
to demons and not to God. I do not want you to
be partners with demons! 21 You cannot drink
the cup of the Lord and the cup of demons. You
cannot share in the Lord's table and the table of
demons. 22 Or are we provoking the Lord to
jealousy? Are we stronger than He?

Christian Liberty

23 "Everything is permissible,"[l] [m] but not
everything is helpful. "Everything is permissible," [l] [m] but not everything builds up. 24 No
one should seek his own ⌊good⌋, but ⌊the good⌋
of the other person.

[a]**9:20** Other mss omit *though I myself am not under law* [b]**9:23** Lit *partner of it* [c]**10:6** Lit *they desired* [d]**10:7** Or *to dance* [e]**10:7** Ex 32:6 [f]**10:8** Lit *them committed sexual immorality* [g]**10:9** Lit *them tempted* [h]**10:10** Lit *them complained* [i]**10:10** Or *the destroying angel* [j]**10:18** Lit *Look at Israel according to the flesh* [k]**10:20** Other mss read *Gentiles* [l]**10:23** Other mss add *for me* [m]**10:23** See note at 1 Co 6:12

25 Eat everything that is sold in the meat
market, asking no questions for conscience'
sake, for 26 **the earth is the Lord's, and all that
is in it.**[a] 27 If one of the unbelievers invites you
over and you want to go, eat everything that is
set before you, without raising questions of
conscience. 28 But if someone says to you,
"This is food offered to an idol," do not eat it,
out of consideration for the one who told you,
and for conscience' sake.[b] 29 I do not mean
your own conscience, but the other person's.
For why is my freedom judged by another person's conscience? 30 If I partake with thanks,
why am I slandered because of something for
which I give thanks?

31 Therefore, whether you eat or drink, or
whatever you do, do everything for God's
glory. 32 Give no offense to the Jews or the
Greeks or the church of God, 33 just as I also
try to please all people in all things, not seeking
my own profit, but the profit of many, that they
may be saved.
11 1 Be imitators of me, as I
also am of Christ.

Instructions about Head Coverings

2 Now I praise you[c] because you remember
me in all things and keep the traditions just as I
delivered them to you. 3 But I want you to know
that Christ is the head of every man, and the
man is the head of the woman,[d] and God is the
head of Christ. 4 Every man who prays or prophesies with something on his head dishonors his
head. 5 But every woman who prays or prophesies with her head uncovered dishonors her
head, since that is one and the same as having
her head shaved. 6 So if a woman's head[e] is not
covered, her hair should be cut off. But if it is
disgraceful for a woman to have her hair cut off
or her head shaved, she should be covered.

7 A man, in fact, should not cover his head,
because he is God's image and glory, but
woman is man's glory. 8 For man did not come
from woman, but woman came from man;
9 and man was not created for woman, but
woman for man. 10 This is why a woman
should have ⌊a symbol of⌋ authority on her
head: because of the angels. 11 However, in the
Lord, woman is not independent of man, and
man is not independent of woman. 12 For just
as woman came from man, so man comes
through woman, and all things come from God.
13 Judge for yourselves: Is it proper for a
woman to pray to God with her head uncovered? 14 Does not even nature itself teach you
that if a man has long hair it is a disgrace to
him, 15 but that if a woman has long hair, it is
her glory? For her hair is given to her[f] as a covering. 16 But if anyone wants to argue about
this, we have no other[g] custom, nor do the
churches of God.

The Lord's Supper

17 Now in giving the following instruction I
do not praise you, since you come together not
for the better but for the worse. 18 For, to begin
with, I hear that when you come together as a
church there are divisions among you, and in
part I believe it. 19 There must, indeed, be factions among you, so that the approved among
you may be recognized. 20 Therefore when you
come together in one place, it is not really to eat
the Lord's Supper. 21 For in eating, each one
takes his own supper ahead of others, and one
person is hungry while another is drunk!
22 Don't you have houses to eat and drink in?
Or do you look down on the church of God and
embarrass those who have nothing? What
should I say to you? Should I praise you? I do
not praise you for this!

23 For I received from the Lord what I also
passed on to you: on the night when He was
betrayed, the Lord Jesus took bread, 24 gave
thanks, broke it, and said,[h] "This is My body,
which is[i] for you. Do this in remembrance of
Me."

25 In the same way ⌊He⌋ also ⌊took⌋ the cup,
after supper, and said, "This cup is the new
covenant in My blood. Do this, as often as you
drink it, in remembrance of Me." 26 For as
often as you eat this bread and drink the cup,
you proclaim the Lord's death until He comes.

Self-Examination

27 Therefore, whoever eats the bread or
drinks the cup of the Lord in an unworthy way
will be guilty of sin against the body[j] and blood
of the Lord. 28 So a man should examine himself; in this way he should eat of the bread and
drink of the cup. 29 For whoever eats and
drinks without recognizing the body,[k] eats
and drinks judgment on himself. 30 This is why
many are sick and ill among you, and many

[a]**10:26** Ps 24:1 [b]**10:28** Other mss add *"For the earth is the Lord's and all that is in it."* [c]**11:2** Other mss add *brothers,* [d]**11:3** Or *the husband is the head of the wife* [e]**11:6** Lit *a woman* [f]**11:15** Other mss omit *to her* [g]**11:16** Or *no such* [h]**11:24** Other mss add *"Take, eat.* [i]**11:24** Other mss add *broken* [j]**11:27** Lit *be guilty of the body* [k]**11:29** Other mss read *drinks unworthily, not discerning the Lord's body*

have fallen •asleep. 31 If we were properly eval-
uating ourselves, we would not be judged,
32 but when we are judged, we are disciplined
by the Lord, so that we may not be condemned
with the world.
33 Therefore, my brothers, when you come
together to eat, wait for one another. 34 If anyone is hungry, he should eat at home, so that
you can come together and not cause judgment.
And I will give instructions about the other
matters whenever I come.

Diversity of Spiritual Gifts

12 About matters of the spirit:[a] brothers, I
do not want you to be unaware. 2 You
know how, when you were pagans, you were
led to dumb idols—being led astray.
3 Therefore I am informing you that no one
speaking by the Spirit of God says, "Jesus is
cursed," and no one can say, "Jesus is Lord,"
except by the Holy Spirit.
4 Now there are different gifts, but the same
Spirit. 5 There are different ministries, but the
same Lord. 6 And there are different activities,
but the same God is active in everyone and
everything.[b] 7 A manifestation of the Spirit is
given to each person to produce what is beneficial:

8 to one is given a message of wisdom
through the Spirit,
to another, a message of knowledge
by the same Spirit,
9 to another, faith by the same Spirit,
to another, gifts of healing
by the one Spirit,
10 to another, the performing
of miracles,
to another, prophecy,
to another, distinguishing
between spirits,
to another, different kinds
of languages,
to another, interpretation of languages.

11 But one and the same Spirit is active in all
these, distributing to each one as He wills.

Unity Yet Diversity in the Body

12 For as the body is one and has many parts,
and all the parts of that body, though many, are
one body—so also is Christ. 13 For we were all
baptized by one Spirit into one body—whether
Jews or Greeks, whether slaves or free—and we
were all made to drink of one Spirit. 14 So the
body is not one part but many. 15 If the foot
should say, "Because I'm not a hand, I don't
belong to the body," in spite of this it still
belongs to the body. 16 And if the ear should say,
"Because I'm not an eye, I don't belong to the
body," in spite of this it still belongs to the body.
17 If the whole body were an eye, where would
the hearing be? If the whole were an ear, where
would be the sense of smell? 18 But now God has
placed the parts, each one of them, in the body
just as He wanted. 19 And if they were all the
same part, where would the body be? 20 Now
there are many parts, yet one body.
21 So the eye cannot say to the hand, "I don't
need you!" nor again the head to the feet, "I
don't need you!" 22 On the contrary, all the
more, those parts of the body that seem to be
weaker are necessary. 23 And those parts of the
body that we think to be less honorable, we
clothe these with greater honor, and our unpre-
sentable parts have a better presentation. 24 But
our presentable parts have no need ⌊of clothing⌋.
Instead, God has put the body together, giving
greater honor to the less honorable, 25 so that
there would be no division in the body, but that
the members would have the same concern for
each other. 26 So if one member suffers, all the
members suffer with it; if one member is honored, all the members rejoice with it.
27 Now you are the body of Christ, and individual members of it. 28 And God has placed
these in the church:

first apostles, second prophets,
third teachers, next, miracles,
then gifts of healing, helping,
managing, various kinds
of languages.
29 Are all apostles? Are all prophets?
Are all teachers? Do all do miracles?
30 Do all have gifts of healing?
Do all speak in languages?
Do all interpret?

31 But desire the greater gifts. And I will show
you an even better way.

Love: The Superior Way

13 If I speak the languages of men
and of angels,
but do not have love,
I am a sounding gong
or a clanging cymbal.

[a]**12:1** Lit *About things spiritual* [b]**12:6** Lit *God acts all things in all*

2 If I have ⌊the gift of⌋ prophecy,
and understand all •mysteries
and all knowledge,
and if I have all faith,
so that I can move mountains,
but do not have love, I am nothing.
3 And if I donate all my goods to feed
the poor,
and if I give my body
to be burned,[a]
but do not have love,
I gain nothing.
4 Love is patient; love is kind.
Love does not envy;
is not boastful; is not conceited;
5 does not act improperly;
is not selfish;
is not provoked; does not keep
a record of wrongs;
6 finds no joy in unrighteousness,
but rejoices in the truth;
7 bears all things, believes all things,
hopes all things, endures all things.

8 Love never ends.
But as for prophecies, they will come
to an end;
as for languages, they will cease;
as for knowledge, it will come
to an end.
9 For we know in part, and we prophesy
in part.
10 But when the perfect comes,
the partial will come to an end.
11 When I was a child, I spoke
like a child,
I thought like a child,
I reasoned like a child.
When I became a man, I put aside
childish things.
12 For now we see indistinctly,
as in a mirror, but then
face to face.
Now I know in part, but then
I will know fully,
as I am fully known.
13 Now these three remain:
faith, hope, and love.
But the greatest of these is love.

Prophecy: A Superior Gift

14 Pursue love and desire spiritual gifts,
and above all that you may prophesy.
2 For the person who speaks in ⌊another⌋ language is not speaking to men but to God, since
no one understands him; however, he speaks
•mysteries in the Spirit.[b] 3 But the person who
prophesies speaks to people for edification,
encouragement, and consolation. 4 The person
who speaks in ⌊another⌋ language builds himself up, but he who prophesies builds up the
church. 5 I wish all of you spoke in other languages, but even more that you prophesied.
The person who prophesies is greater than the
person who speaks in languages, unless he
interprets so that the church may be built up.
6 But now, brothers, if I come to you speaking in ⌊other⌋ languages, how will I benefit you
unless I speak to you with a revelation or
knowledge or prophecy or teaching? 7 Even
inanimate things producing sounds—whether
flute or harp—if they don't make a distinction
in the notes, how will what is played on the
flute or harp be recognized? 8 In fact, if the
trumpet makes an unclear sound, who will prepare for battle? 9 In the same way, unless you
use your tongue for intelligible speech, how
will what is spoken be known? For you will be
speaking into the air. 10 There are doubtless
many different kinds of languages in the world,
and all have meaning.[c] 11 Therefore, if I do not
know the meaning of the language, I will be a
foreigner[d] to the speaker, and the speaker will
be a foreigner to me. 12 So also you—since you
are zealous in matters of the spirit,[e] seek to
excel in building up the church.
13 Therefore the person who speaks in ⌊an-
other⌋ language should pray that he can interpret. 14 For if I pray in ⌊another⌋ language, my
spirit prays, but my understanding is unfruitful.
15 What then? I will pray with the spirit, and I
will also pray with my understanding. I will
sing with the spirit, and I will also sing with my
understanding. 16 Otherwise, if you bless with
the spirit, how will the uninformed person[f] say
"•Amen" at your giving of thanks, since he
does not know what you are saying? 17 For you
may very well be giving thanks, but the other
person is not being built up. 18 I thank God that
I speak in ⌊other⌋ languages more than all of
you; 19 yet in the church I would rather speak
five words with my understanding, in order to
teach others also, than 10,000 words in ⌊an-
other⌋ language.
20 Brothers, don't be childish in your think-

[a] **13:3** Other mss read *to boast* [b] **14:2** Or *in spirit*, or *in his spirit* [c] **14:10** Lit *and none is without a sound* [d] **14:11** Gk *barbaros* = in Eng *a barbarian*. To a Gk, a *barbaros* was anyone who did not speak Gk. [e] **14:12** Lit *zealous of spirits*; *spirits* = human spirits, spiritual gifts or powers, or the Holy Spirit [f] **14:16** Lit *the one filling the place of the uninformed*

ing, but be infants in evil and adult in your thinking. 21 It is written in the law:

By people of other languages
and by the lips of foreigners,
I will speak to this people;
and even then, they will not listen
to Me,[a]

says the Lord. 22 It follows that speaking in other languages is intended as a sign,[b] not to believers but to unbelievers. But prophecy is not for unbelievers but for believers. 23 Therefore if the whole church assembles together, and all are speaking in ⌊other⌋ languages, and people who are uninformed or unbelievers come in, will they not say that you are out of your minds? 24 But if all are prophesying, and some unbeliever or uninformed person comes in, he is convicted by all and is judged by all. 25 The secrets of his heart will be revealed, and as a result he will fall down on his face and worship God, proclaiming, "God is really among you."

Order in Church Meetings

26 How is it then, brothers? Whenever you come together, each one[c] has a psalm, a teaching, a revelation, ⌊another⌋ language, or an interpretation. All things must be done for edification. 27 If any person speaks in ⌊another⌋ language, there should be only two, or at the most three, each in turn, and someone must interpret. 28 But if there is no interpreter, that person should keep silent in the church and speak to himself and to God. 29 Two or three prophets should speak, and the others should evaluate. 30 But if something has been revealed to another person sitting there, the first prophet should be silent. 31 For you can all prophesy one by one, so that everyone may learn and everyone may be encouraged. 32 And the prophets' spirits are under the control of the prophets, 33 since God is not a God of disorder but of peace.

As in all the churches of the saints, 34 the women[d] should be silent in the churches, for they are not permitted to speak, but should be submissive, as the law also says. 35 And if they want to learn something, they should ask their own husbands at home, for it is disgraceful for a woman to speak in the church meeting. 36 Did the word of God originate from you, or did it come to you only?

37 If anyone thinks he is a prophet or spiritual, he should recognize that what I write to you is the Lord's command. 38 But if anyone ignores this, he will be ignored.[e] 39 Therefore, my brothers, be eager to prophesy, and do not forbid speaking in ⌊other⌋ languages. 40 But everything must be done decently and in order.

Resurrection Essential to the Gospel

15 Now brothers, I want to clarify[f] for you the gospel I proclaimed to you; you received it and have taken your stand on it. 2 You are also saved by it, if you hold to the message I proclaimed to you—unless you believed to no purpose.[g] 3 For I passed on to you as most important what I also received:

that Christ died for our sins
according to the Scriptures,
4 that He was buried,
that He was raised on the third day
according to the Scriptures,
5 and that He appeared to •Cephas,
then to the Twelve.
6 Then He appeared to
over 500 brothers at one time,
most of whom remain to the present,
but some have fallen •asleep.
7 Then He appeared to James, then to all
the apostles.
8 Last of all, as to one abnormally born,
He also appeared to me.

9 For I am the least of the apostles, unworthy to be called an apostle, because I persecuted the church of God. 10 But by God's grace I am what I am, and His grace toward me was not ineffective. However, I worked more than any of them, yet not I, but God's grace that was with me. 11 Therefore, whether it is I or they, so we preach and so you have believed.

Resurrection Essential to the Faith

12 Now if Christ is preached as raised from the dead, how can some of you say, "There is no resurrection of the dead"? 13 But if there is no resurrection of the dead, then Christ has not been raised; 14 and if Christ has not been raised, then our preaching is without foundation, and so is your faith.[h] 15 In addition, we are

[a]**14:21** Is 28:11–12 [b]**14:22** Lit *that tongues are for a sign* [c]**14:26** Other mss add *of you* [d]**14:34** Other mss read *your women* [e]**14:38** Other mss read *he should be ignored* [f]**15:1** Or *I make known* [g]**15:2** Or *believed in vain* [h]**15:14** Or *preaching is useless, and your faith also is useless*, or *preaching is empty, and your faith also is empty*

found to be false witnesses about God, because
we have testified about God that He raised up
Christ—whom He did not raise up if in fact the
dead are not raised. 16 For if the dead are not
raised, Christ has not been raised. 17 And if
Christ has not been raised, your faith is worthless; you are still in your sins. 18 Therefore
those who have fallen asleep in Christ have also
perished. 19 If we have placed our hope in
Christ for this life only, we should be pitied
more than anyone.

Christ's Resurrection Guarantees Ours

20 But now Christ has been raised from
the dead, the •firstfruits of those who have
fallen asleep. 21 For since death came
through a man, the resurrection of the dead
also comes through a man. 22 For just as in
Adam all die, so also in Christ all will be
made alive. 23 But each in his own order:
Christ, the firstfruits; afterward, at His coming, the people of Christ. 24 Then comes the
end, when He hands over the kingdom to
God the Father, when He abolishes all rule
and all authority and power. 25 For He must
reign until He puts all His enemies under His
feet. 26 The last enemy to be abolished is
death. 27 For **He has put everything under
His feet.**[a] But when it says "everything" is
put under Him, it is obvious that He who
puts everything under Him is the exception.
28 And when everything is subject to Him,
then the Son Himself will also be subject to
Him who subjected everything to Him, so
that God may be all in all.

Resurrection Supported by Christian Experience

29 Otherwise what will they do who are
being baptized for the dead? If the dead are not
raised at all, then why are people[b] baptized for
them?[c] 30 Why are we in danger every hour?
31 I affirm by the pride in you that I have in
Christ Jesus our Lord: I die every day! 32 If I
fought wild animals in Ephesus with only
human hope,[d] what good does that do me?[e] If
the dead are not raised, **Let us eat and drink,
for tomorrow we die.**[f] 33 Do not be deceived:
"Bad company corrupts good morals."[g] 34
Become right-minded[h] and stop sinning,
because some people are ignorant about God. I
say this to your shame.

The Nature of the Resurrection Body

35 But someone will say, "How are the dead
raised? What kind of body will they have when
they come?" 36 Foolish one! What you sow
does not come to life unless it dies. 37 And as
for what you sow—you are not sowing the
future body, but only a seed,[i] perhaps of wheat
or another grain. 38 But God gives it a body as
He wants, and to each of the seeds its own
body. 39 Not all flesh is the same flesh; there is
one flesh for humans, another for animals,
another for birds, and another for fish. 40 There
are heavenly bodies and earthly bodies, but the
splendor of the heavenly bodies is different
from that of the earthly ones. 41 There is a
splendor of the sun, another of the moon, and
another of the stars; for star differs from star in
splendor. 42 So it is with the resurrection of the
dead:

Sown in corruption,
raised in incorruption;
43 sown in dishonor, raised in glory;
sown in weakness,
raised in power;
44 sown a natural body,
raised a spiritual body.

If there is a natural body, there is also a spiritual body. 45 So it is written: **The first man
Adam became a living being;**[j] the last Adam
became a life-giving Spirit. 46 However, the
spiritual is not first, but the natural; then the
spiritual.

47 The first man was from the earth
and made of dust;
the second man is[k] from heaven.
48 Like the man made of dust,
so are those who are made
of dust;
like the heavenly man, so are those
who are heavenly.
49 And just as we have borne the image
of the man made of dust,
we will also bear the image
of the heavenly man.

Victorious Resurrection

50 Brothers, I tell you this: flesh and blood
cannot inherit the kingdom of God, and corruption cannot inherit incorruption. 51 Listen! I
am telling you a •mystery:

[a]**15:27** Ps 8:6 [b]**15:29** Lit *they* [c]**15:29** Other mss read *for the dead* [d]**15:32** Lit *Ephesus according to man* [e]**15:32** Lit *what to me the profit?* [f]**15:32** Is 22:13 [g]**15:33** A quotation from the poet Menander, *Thais,* 218 [h]**15:34** Lit *Sober up righteously* [i]**15:37** Lit *but a naked seed* [j]**15:45** Gn 2:7 [k]**15:47** Other mss add *the Lord*

We will not all fall asleep,
but we will all be changed,
52 in a moment, in the twinkling
of an eye, at the last trumpet.
For the trumpet will sound,
and the dead will be raised
incorruptible,
and we will be changed.
53 Because this corruptible
must be clothed
with incorruptibility,
and this mortal must be clothed
with immortality.
54 Now when this corruptible is clothed
with incorruptibility,
and this mortal is clothed
with immortality,
then the saying that is written
will take place:
Death has been swallowed up
in victory.[a]
55 **O Death, where is your victory?**
O Death, where is your sting?[b]
56 Now the sting of death is sin, and
the power of sin is the law.
57 But thanks be to God, who gives us
the victory
through our Lord Jesus Christ!

58 Therefore, my dear brothers, be steadfast,
immovable, always excelling in the Lord's
work, knowing that your labor in the Lord is
not in vain.

Collection for the Jerusalem Church

16 Now about the collection for the saints:
you should do the same as I instructed
the Galatian churches. 2 On the first day of the
week, each of you is to set something aside and
save to the extent that he prospers, so that no
collections will need to be made when I come.
3 And when I arrive, I will send those whom
you recommend by letter to carry your gracious
gift to Jerusalem. 4 If it is also suitable for me to
go, they will travel with me.

Paul's Travel Plans

5 I will come to you after I pass through
Macedonia—for I will be traveling through
Macedonia— 6 and perhaps I will remain with
you, or even spend the winter, that you may
send me on my way wherever I go. 7 I don't
want to see you now just in passing, for I hope
to spend some time with you, if the Lord
allows. 8 But I will stay in Ephesus until Pentecost, 9 because a wide door for effective
ministry has opened for me[c] —yet many
oppose me. 10 If Timothy comes, see that he
has nothing to fear from you, because he is
doing the Lord's work, just as I am. 11 Therefore no one should look down on him; but you
should send him on his way in peace so he can
come to me, for I am expecting him with the
brothers.[d]
12 About our brother Apollos: I strongly
urged him to come to you with the brothers,
but he was not at all willing to come now. However, when he has time, he will come.

Final Exhortation

13 Be alert, stand firm in the faith, be brave
and strong. 14 Your every ⌊action⌋ must be done
with love.
15 Brothers, you know the household of
Stephanas: they are the •firstfruits of Achaia
and have devoted themselves to serving the
saints. I urge you 16 also to submit to such
people, and to everyone who works and
labors with them. 17 I am delighted over the
presence of Stephanas, Fortunatus, and Acha-
icus, because these men have made up for
your absence. 18 For they have refreshed my
spirit and yours. Therefore recognize such
people.

Conclusion

19 The churches of the Asian province greet
you. Aquila and Priscilla greet you heartily in
the Lord, along with the church that meets in
their home. 20 All the brothers greet you. Greet
one another with a holy kiss.
21 This greeting is in my own hand[e] —Paul.
22 If anyone does not love the Lord, a curse be
on him. *Maranatha!*[f] 23 The grace of our Lord
Jesus be with you. 24 My love be with all of you
in Christ Jesus.

[a]**15:54** Is 25:8 [b]**15:55** Hs 13:14 [c]**16:9** Lit *for a door has opened to me, great and effective* [d]**16:11** *With the brothers* may connect with Paul or Timothy. [e]**16:21** Paul normally dictated his letters to a secretary, but signed the end of each letter himself; see Rm 16:22; Gl 6:11; Col 4:18; 2 Th 3:17. [f]**16:22** Aram expression meaning *Our Lord come!*, or *Our Lord has come!*

2 Corinthians

Greeting

1 Paul, an apostle of Christ Jesus by God's will, and Timothy our[a] brother:

To God's church at Corinth, with all the saints who are throughout Achaia.

2 Grace to you and peace from God our Father and the Lord Jesus Christ.

The God of Comfort

3 Blessed be the God and Father of our Lord Jesus Christ, the Father of mercies and the God of all comfort. 4 He comforts us in all our affliction,[b] so that we may be able to comfort those who are in any kind of affliction, through the comfort we ourselves receive from God. 5 For as the sufferings of Christ overflow to us, so our comfort overflows through Christ. 6 If we are afflicted, it is for your comfort and salvation; if we are comforted, it is for your comfort, which is experienced in the endurance of the same sufferings that we suffer. 7 And our hope for you is firm, because we know that as you share in the sufferings, so you will share in the comfort.

8 For we don't want you to be unaware, brothers, of our affliction that took place in the province of Asia: we were completely overwhelmed—beyond our strength—so that we even despaired of life. 9 However, we personally had a death sentence within ourselves so that we would not trust in ourselves, but in God who raises the dead. 10 He has delivered us from such a terrible death, and He will deliver us; we have placed our hope in Him that He will deliver us again. 11 And you can join in helping with prayer for us, so that thanks may be given by many[c] on our[d] behalf for the gift that came to us through ⌊the prayers of⌋ many.

A Clear Conscience

12 For our boast is this: the testimony of our conscience that we have conducted ourselves in the world, and especially toward you, with God-given sincerity and purity, not by fleshly[e] wisdom but by God's grace. 13 Now we are writing you nothing other than what you can read and also understand. I hope you will understand completely— 14 as you have partially understood us—that we are your reason for pride, as you are ours, in the day of our[f] Lord Jesus.

A Visit Postponed

15 In this confidence, I planned to come to you first, so you could have a double benefit,[g] 16 and to go on to Macedonia with your help, then come to you again from Macedonia and be given a start by you on my journey to Judea. 17 So when I planned this, was I irresponsible? Or what I plan, do I plan in a purely human[h] way so that I say "Yes, yes" and "No, no" ⌊simultaneously⌋? 18 As God is faithful, our message to you is not "Yes and no." 19 For the Son of God, Jesus Christ, who was preached among you by us—by me and Silvanus[i] and Timothy—did not become "Yes and no"; on the contrary, "Yes" has come about in Him. 20 For every one of God's promises is "Yes" in Him. Therefore the "•Amen" is also through Him for God's glory through us. 21 Now the One who confirms us with you in Christ, and has anointed us, is God; 22 He has also sealed us and given us the Spirit as a down payment in our hearts.

23 I call on God as a witness against me:[j] it was to spare you that I did not come to Corinth. 24 Not that we have control of[k] your faith, but we are workers with you for your joy,

2 because you stand by faith. 1 In fact, I made up my mind about this:[l] not to come to you on another painful visit.[m] 2 For if I cause you pain, then who will cheer me other than the one hurt?[n] 3 I wrote this very thing so that when I came I wouldn't have pain from those who ought to give me joy, because I am confident about all of you that my joy is yours.[o] 4 For out of an extremely troubled and anguished heart I wrote to you with many tears—not that you should be hurt,

[a]**1:1** Lit *the* [b]**1:4** Or *trouble*, or *tribulation*, or *trials*, or *oppression*; the Gk word has a lit meaning of being under pressure. [c]**1:11** Lit *by many faces* [d]**1:11** Other mss read *your* [e]**1:12** The word *fleshly* (characterized by flesh) indicates that the wisdom is natural rather than spiritual. [f]**1:14** Other mss omit *our* [g]**1:15** Other mss read *a second joy* [h]**1:17** Or *a worldly*, or *a fleshly*, or *a selfish* [i]**1:19** Or *Silas*; see Ac 15:22–32; 16:19–40; 17:1–16 [j]**1:23** Lit *against my soul* [k]**1:24** Or *we lord it over*, or *we rule over* [l]**2:1** Lit *I decided this for myself* [m]**2:1** Lit *not again in sorrow to come to you* [n]**2:2** Lit *the one pained* [o]**2:3** Lit *is of you all*

but that you should know the abundant love I have for you.

A Sinner Forgiven

5 If anyone has caused pain, he has not caused pain to me, but in some degree—not to exaggerate—to all of you. 6 The punishment by the majority is sufficient for such a person, 7 so now you should forgive and comfort him instead; otherwise, this one may be overwhelmed by excessive grief. 8 Therefore I urge you to confirm your love to him. 9 It was for this purpose I wrote: so I may know your proven character, if you are obedient in everything. 10 Now to whom you forgive anything, I do too. For what I have forgiven, if I have forgiven anything, it is for you in the presence of Christ, 11 so that we may not be taken advantage of by Satan; for we are not ignorant of his intentions.[a]

A Trip to Macedonia

12 When I came to Troas for the gospel of Christ, a door was opened to me by the Lord. 13 I had no rest in my spirit because I did not find my brother Titus, but I said good-bye to them and left for Macedonia.

A Ministry of Life or Death

14 But thanks be to God, who always puts us on display[b] in Christ,[c] and spreads through us in every place the scent of knowing Him. 15 For to God we are the fragrance of Christ among those who are being saved and among those who are perishing. 16 To some we are a scent of death leading to death, but to others, a scent of life leading to life. And who is competent for this? 17 For we are not like the many[d] who make a trade in God's message ⌊for profit⌋, but as those with sincerity, we speak in Christ, as from God and before God.

Living Letters

3 Are we beginning to commend ourselves again? Or like some, do we need letters of recommendation to you or from you? 2 You yourselves are our letter, written on our hearts, recognized and read by everyone, 3 since it is plain that you are Christ's letter, produced[e] by us, not written with ink but with the Spirit of the living God; not on stone tablets but on tablets that are hearts of flesh.

Paul's Competence

4 We have this kind of confidence toward God through Christ: 5 not that we are competent in[f] ourselves to consider anything as coming from ourselves, but our competence is from God. 6 He has made us competent to be ministers of a new covenant, not of the letter, but of the Spirit; for the letter kills, but the Spirit produces life.

New Covenant Ministry

7 Now if the ministry of death, chiseled in letters on stones, came with glory, so that the sons of Israel were not able to look directly at Moses' face because of the glory from his face—a fading ⌊glory⌋— 8 how will the ministry of the Spirit not be more glorious? 9 For if the ministry of condemnation had glory, the ministry of righteousness overflows with even more glory. 10 In fact, what had been glorious is not glorious in this case because of the glory that surpasses it. 11 For if what was fading away was glorious, what endures will be even more glorious.

12 Therefore having such a hope, we use great boldness— 13 not like Moses, who used to put a veil over his face so that the sons of Israel could not look at the end of what was fading away. 14 But their minds were closed.[g] For to this day, at the reading of the old covenant, the same veil remains; it is not lifted, because it is set aside ⌊only⌋ in Christ. 15 However, to this day, whenever Moses is read, a veil lies over their hearts, 16 but whenever a person turns to the Lord, the veil is removed. 17 Now the Lord is the Spirit; and where the Spirit of the Lord is, there is freedom. 18 We all, with unveiled faces, are reflecting[h] the glory of the Lord and are being transformed into the same image from glory to glory;[i] this is from the Lord who is the Spirit.[j]

The Light of the Gospel

4 Therefore, since we have this ministry, as we have received mercy, we do not give up. 2 Instead, we have renounced shameful secret things, not •walking in deceit or distorting God's message, but in God's sight we

[a]**2:11** Or *thoughts* [b]**2:14** Or *always leads us in a triumphal procession*, or less likely, *always causes us to triumph* [c]**2:14** Lit *in the Christ*, or *in the Messiah*; see 1 Co 15:22; Eph 1:10,12,20; 3:11 [d]**2:17** Other mss read *the rest* [e]**3:3** Lit *ministered to* [f]**3:5** Lit *from* [g]**3:14** Lit *their thoughts were hardened* [h]**3:18** Or *are looking as in a mirror at* [i]**3:18** Progressive glorification or sanctification [j]**3:18** Or *from the Spirit of the Lord*, or *from the Lord, the Spirit*

commend ourselves to every person's
conscience by an open display of the truth.
3 But if, in fact, our gospel is veiled, it is veiled
to those who are perishing. 4 Regarding them:
the god of this age has blinded the minds
of the unbelievers so they cannot see the light
of the gospel of the glory of Christ,[a] who is the
image of God. 5 For we are not proclaiming
ourselves but Jesus Christ as Lord, and ourselves as your slaves because of Jesus. 6 For
God, who said, "Light shall shine out of darkness"—He has shone in our hearts to give the
light of the knowledge of God's glory in the
face of Jesus Christ.

Treasure in Clay Jars

7 Now we have this treasure in clay jars, so
that this extraordinary power may be from God
and not from us. 8 We are pressured in every
way but not crushed; we are perplexed but not
in despair; 9 we are persecuted but not abandoned; we are struck down but not destroyed.
10 We always carry the death of Jesus in our
body, so that the life of Jesus may also be
revealed in our body. 11 For we who live are
always given over to death because of Jesus, so
that Jesus' life may also be revealed in our mortal flesh. 12 So death works in us, but life in
you. 13 And since we have the same spirit of
faith in accordance with what is written, I
believed, therefore I spoke,[b] we also believe,
and therefore speak, 14 knowing that the One
who raised the Lord Jesus will raise us also with
Jesus, and present us with you. 15 For all this is
because of you, so that grace, extended through
more and more people, may cause thanksgiving
to overflow to God's glory.

16 Therefore we do not give up; even though
our outer person is being destroyed, our inner
person is being renewed day by day. 17 For our
momentary light affliction[c] is producing for us
an absolutely incomparable eternal weight of
glory. 18 So we do not focus on what is seen, but
on what is unseen; for what is seen is temporary, but what is unseen is eternal.

Our Future after Death

5 For we know that if our earthly house, a
tent,[d] is destroyed, we have a building
from God, a house[e] not made with hands, eternal in the heavens. 2 And, in fact, we groan in
this one, longing to put on our house from
heaven, 3 since, when we are clothed,[f] we will
not be found naked. 4 Indeed, we who are in
this tent groan, burdened as we are, because
we do not want to be unclothed but clothed,
so that mortality may be swallowed up by life.
5 And the One who prepared us for this very
thing is God, who gave us the Spirit as a down
payment.

6 Therefore, though we are always confident and know that while we are at home in
the body we are away from the Lord— 7 for we
•walk by faith, not by sight— 8 yet we are confident and satisfied to be out of the body and at
home with the Lord. 9 Therefore, whether we
are at home or away, we make it our aim to be
pleasing to Him. 10 For we must all appear
before the judgment seat of Christ, so that each
may be repaid for what he has done in the
body, whether good or bad.

11 Knowing, then, the fear of the Lord, we
persuade people. We are completely open
before God, and I hope we are completely open
to your consciences as well. 12 We are not com-
mending ourselves to you again, but giving you
an opportunity to be proud of us, so that you
may have a reply for those who take pride in the
outward appearance[g] rather than in the heart.
13 For if we are out of our mind, it is for God; if
we have a sound mind, it is for you. 14 For
Christ's love compels[h] us, since we have
reached this conclusion: if One died for all, then
all died. 15 And He died for all so that those who
live should no longer live for themselves, but for
the One who died for them and was raised.

The Ministry of Reconciliation

16 From now on, then, we do not know[i]
anyone in a purely human way.[j] Even if we
have known[k] Christ in a purely human way,[l]
yet now we no longer know[i] Him like that.
17 Therefore if anyone is in Christ, there is a
new creation; old things have passed away, and
look, new things[m] have come. 18 Now everything is from God, who reconciled us to Himself through Christ and gave us the ministry of
reconciliation: 19 that is, in Christ, God was
reconciling the world to Himself, not counting
their trespasses against them, and He has committed the message of reconciliation to us.
20 Therefore, we are ambassadors for Christ;

[a] **4:4** Or *the gospel of the glorious Christ*, or *the glorious gospel of Christ* [b] **4:13** Ps 116:10 LXX [c] **4:17** See note at 2 Co 1:4 [d] **5:1** Our present physical body [e] **5:1** *a building . . . a house* = our future body [f] **5:3** Other mss read *stripped* [g] **5:12** Lit *in face* [h] **5:14** Or *For the love of Christ impels*, or *For the love of Christ controls* [i] **5:16** Or *regard* [j] **5:16** Lit *anyone according to the flesh* [k] **5:16** Or *have regarded* [l] **5:16** Lit *Christ according to the flesh* [m] **5:17** Other mss read *look, all new things*

certain that God is appealing through us, we
plead on Christ's behalf, "Be reconciled to
God." 21 He made the One who did not know
sin to be sin for us, so that we might become
the righteousness of God in Him.

6 Working together[a] with Him, we also
appeal to you: "Don't receive God's
grace in vain." 2 For He says:

> **In an acceptable time,**
> **I heard you,**
> **and in the day of salvation,**
> **I helped you.**[b]

Look, now is the acceptable time; look, now is
the day of salvation.

The Character of Paul's Ministry

3 We give no opportunity for stumbling to
anyone, so that the ministry will not be blamed.
4 But in everything, as God's ministers, we
commend ourselves:

by great endurance, by afflictions,
by hardship, by pressures,
5 by beatings, by imprisonments,
by riots, by labors,
by sleepless nights,
by times of hunger,
6 by purity, by knowledge, by patience,
by kindness,
by the Holy Spirit, by sincere love,
7 by the message of truth, by the power
of God;
through weapons of righteousness
on the right hand and the left,
8 through glory and dishonor,
through slander and good report;
as deceivers yet true;
9 as unknown yet recognized; as dying
and look—we live;
as being chastened yet not killed;
10 as grieving yet always rejoicing;
as poor yet enriching many;
as having nothing
yet possessing everything.

11 We have spoken openly[c] to you, Corinthians; our heart has been opened wide.
12 You are not limited by us, but you are limited by your own affections. 13 Now in like
response—I speak as to children—you also
should be open to us.

Separation to God

14 Do not be mismatched with unbelievers. For what partnership is there between
righteousness and lawlessness? Or what fellowship does light have with darkness?
15 What agreement does Christ have with
Belial?[d] Or what does a believer have in common with an unbeliever? 16 And what agreement does God's sanctuary have with idols?
For we[e] are the sanctuary of the living God, as
God said:

> **I will dwell among them and walk**
> **among them,**
> **and I will be their God,**
> **and they will be My people.**[f]
> 17 **Therefore, come out**
> **from among them**
> **and be separate, says the Lord;**
> **do not touch any unclean thing,**
> **and I will welcome you.**[g]
> 18 **I will be a Father to you,**
> **and you will be sons and daughters**
> **to Me,**
> **says the Lord Almighty.**[h]

7 Therefore dear friends, since we have
such promises, we should wash ourselves clean from every impurity of the flesh
and spirit, making our sanctification complete[i]
in the fear of God.

Joy and Repentance

2 Take us into your hearts.[j] We have
wronged no one, corrupted no one, defrauded
no one. 3 I don't say this to condemn you, for I
have already said that you are in our hearts, to
die together and to live together. 4 I have great
confidence in you; I have great pride in you. I
am filled with encouragement; I am overcome
with joy in all our afflictions.
5 In fact, when we came into Macedonia,
we[k] had no rest. Instead, we were afflicted in
every way: struggles on the outside, fears
inside. 6 But God, who comforts the humble,
comforted us by the coming of Titus, 7 and not
only by his coming, but also by the comfort he
received from you. He announced to us your
deep longing, your sorrow,[l] your zeal for me, so
that I rejoiced even more. 8 For although I
grieved you with my letter, I do not regret it—
even though I did regret it since I saw that the

[a]**6:1** Or *As we work together* [b]**6:2** Is 49:8 [c]**6:11** Lit *Our mouths have been open* [d]**6:15** Or *Beliar*, a name for the Devil or antichrist in extra-biblical Jewish writings [e]**6:16** Other mss read *you* [f]**6:16** Lv 26:12; Jr 31:33; 32:38; Ezk 37:26 [g]**6:17** Is 52:11 [h]**6:18** 2 Sm 7:14; Is 43:6; 49:22; 60:4; Hs 1:10 [i]**7:1** Or *spirit, perfecting holiness* [j]**7:2** Lit *Make room for us.* [k]**7:5** Lit *our flesh* [l]**7:7** Or *lamentation*, or *mourning*

letter grieved you, though only for a little while.
9 Now I am rejoicing, not because you were
grieved, but because your grief led to repentance. For you were grieved as God willed, so
that you didn't experience any loss from us.
10 For godly grief produces a repentance not to
be regretted and leading to salvation, but
worldly grief produces death. 11 For consider
how much diligence this very thing—this
grieving as God wills—has produced in you:
what a desire to clear yourselves, what indignation, what fear, what deep longing, what zeal,
what justice! In every way you have commended yourselves to be pure in this matter.
12 So even though I wrote to you, it was not
because of the one who did wrong, or because
of the one who was wronged, but in order that
your diligence for us might be made plain to
you in the sight of God. 13 For this reason we
have been comforted.

In addition to our comfort, we were made to
rejoice even more over the joy Titus had,[a]
because his spirit was refreshed by all of you.
14 For if I have made any boast to him about
you, I have not been embarrassed; but as I have
spoken everything to you in truth, so our boasting to Titus has also turned out to be the truth.
15 And his affection toward you is even greater
as he remembers the obedience of all of you,
and how you received him with fear and trembling. 16 I rejoice that I have complete confidence in you.

Appeal to Complete the Collection

8 We want you to know, brothers, about
the grace of God granted to the churches
of Macedonia: 2 during a severe testing by
affliction, their abundance of joy and their
deep poverty overflowed into the wealth of
their generosity. 3 I testify that, on their own,
according to their ability and beyond their ability, 4 they begged us insistently for the privilege of sharing in the ministry to the saints,
5 and not just as we had hoped. Instead, they
gave themselves especially to the Lord, then to
us by God's will. 6 So we urged Titus that, just
as he had begun, so he should also complete
this grace to you. 7 Now as you excel in everything—in faith, in speech, in knowledge, in all
diligence, and in your love for us[b] —excel also
in this grace.

8 I am not saying this as a command.
Rather, by means of the diligence of others, I
am testing the genuineness of your love. 9 For
you know the grace of our Lord Jesus Christ:
although He was rich, for your sake He
became poor, so that by His poverty you might
become rich. 10 Now I am giving an opinion
on this because it is profitable for you, who a
year ago began not only to do something but
also to desire it.[c] 11 But now finish the task[d] as
well, that just as there was eagerness to desire
it, so there may also be a completion from
what you have. 12 For if the eagerness is
there, it is acceptable according to what one
has, not according to what he does not have.
13 It is not that there may be relief for others
and hardship for you, but it is a question of
equality[e] — 14 at the present time your surplus is ⌊available⌋ for their need, so that their
abundance may also become ⌊available⌋ for
your need, that there may be equality. 15 As it
has been written:

The person who gathered much
did not have too much,
and the person who gathered little
did not have too little.[f]

Administration of the Collection

16 Thanks be to God who put the same
diligence for you into the heart of Titus.
17 For he accepted our urging and, being very
diligent, went out to you by his own choice.
18 With him we have sent the brother who is
praised throughout the churches for his gospel ministry.[g] 19 And not only that, but he
was also appointed by the churches to accompany us with this gift[h] that is being administered by us for the glory of the Lord Himself
and to show our eagerness ⌊to help⌋. 20 We
are taking this precaution so no one can find
fault with us concerning this large sum
administered by us. 21 For we are making
provision for what is honorable, not only
before the Lord but also before men. 22 We
have also sent with them our brother whom
we have often tested, in many circumstances, and found diligent—and now even
more diligent because of his great confidence
in you. 23 As for Titus, he is my partner and
co-worker serving you; as for our brothers,
they are the messengers of the churches, the
glory of Christ. 24 Therefore, before the
churches, show them the proof of your love
and of our boasting about you.

[a]**7:13** Lit *the joy of Titus* [b]**8:7** Other mss read *in our love for you* [c]**8:10** Lit *to will* [d]**8:11** Lit *finish the doing* [e]**8:13** Lit *but from equality* [f]**8:15** Ex 16:18 [g]**8:18** Lit *churches, in the gospel* [h]**8:19** Or *grace*

Motivations for Giving

9 Now concerning the ministry to the
saints, it is unnecessary for me to write
to you. 2 For I know your eagerness, and I brag
about you to the Macedonians:[a] "Achaia[b] has
been prepared since last year," and your zeal
has stirred up most of them. 3 But I sent the
brothers so our boasting about you in the matter would not prove empty, and so you would
be prepared just as I said. 4 For if any Macedonians should come with me and find you
unprepared, we, not to mention you, would be
embarrassed in that situation.[c] 5 Therefore I
considered it necessary to urge the brothers to
go on ahead to you and arrange in advance the
generous gift you promised, so that it will be
ready as a gift and not an extortion.

6 Remember this:[d] the person who sows
sparingly will also reap sparingly, and the person who sows generously will also reap generously. 7 Each person should do as he has
decided in his heart—not out of regret or out of
necessity, for God loves a cheerful giver. 8 And
God is able to make every grace overflow to
you, so that in every way, always having everything you need, you may excel in every good
work. 9 As it is written:

> **He has scattered;**
> **He has given to the poor;**
> **His righteousness endures forever.**[e]

10 Now the One who provides seed for the
sower and bread for food will provide and multiply your seed and increase the harvest of your
righteousness, 11 as you are enriched in every
way for all generosity, which produces thanksgiving to God through us. 12 For the ministry of
this service is not only supplying the needs of
the saints, but is also overflowing in many acts
of thanksgiving to God. 13 Through the proof of
this service, they will glorify God for your obedience to the confession of[f] the gospel of Christ,
and for your generosity in sharing with them
and with others. 14 And in their prayers for you
they will have deep affection for[g] you because of
the surpassing grace of God on you. 15 Thanks
be to God for His indescribable gift.

Paul's Apostolic Authority

10 Now I, Paul, make a personal appeal
to you by the gentleness and graciousness of Christ—I who am humble among you
in person, but bold toward you when absent.
2 I beg you that when I am present I will not
need to be bold with the confidence by which
I plan to challenge certain people who think
we are •walking in a fleshly way.[h] 3 For
although we are walking in the flesh, we do
not wage war in a fleshly way,[i] 4 since the
weapons of our warfare are not fleshly, but are
powerful through God for the demolition of
strongholds. We demolish arguments 5 and
every high-minded thing that is raised up
against the knowledge of God, taking every
thought captive to the obedience of Christ.
6 And we are ready to punish any disobedience, once your obedience is complete.

7 Look at what is obvious.[j] If anyone is confident that he belongs to Christ, he should
remind himself of this: just as he belongs to
Christ, so do we. 8 For if I boast some more
about our authority, which the Lord gave for
building you up and not for tearing you down,
I am not ashamed. 9 I don't want to seem as
though I am trying to terrify you with my letters. 10 For it is said, "His letters are weighty
and powerful, but his physical presence is
weak, and his public speaking is despicable."
11 Such a person should consider this: what we
are in the words of our letters when absent, we
will be in actions when present.

12 For we don't dare classify or compare ourselves with some who commend themselves.
But in measuring themselves by themselves and
comparing themselves to themselves, they lack
understanding. 13 We, however, will not boast
beyond measure, but according to the measure
of the area ⌊of ministry⌋ that God has assigned to
us, ⌊which⌋ reaches even to you. 14 For we are
not overextending ourselves, as if we had not
reached you, since we have come to you with
the gospel of Christ. 15 We are not bragging
beyond measure about other people's labors. But
we have the hope that as your faith increases,
our area ⌊of ministry⌋ will be greatly enlarged,
16 so that we may preach the gospel to the
regions beyond you, not boasting about what has
already been done in someone else's area ⌊of
ministry⌋. 17 So **the one who boasts must boast
in the Lord.**[k] 18 For it is not the one commend-
ing himself who is approved, but the one the
Lord commends.

[a] **9:2** Macedonia was a Roman province in the northern area of modern Greece. [b] **9:2** Achaia was the Roman province, south of Macedonia, where Corinth was located. [c] **9:4** Or *in this confidence* [d] **9:6** Lit *And this* [e] **9:9** Ps 112:9 [f] **9:13** Or *your obedient confession to* [g] **9:14** Or *will long for* [h] **10:2** Lit *walking according to flesh* [i] **10:3** Lit *war according to flesh* [j] **10:7** Or *You are looking at things outwardly* [k] **10:17** Jr 9:24

Paul and the False Apostles

11 I wish you would put up with a little
foolishness from me. Yes, do put up
with me.[a] 2 For I am jealous over you with a
godly jealousy, because I have promised you in
marriage to one husband—to present a pure
virgin to Christ. 3 But I fear that, as the serpent
deceived Eve by his cunning, your minds may
be corrupted from a complete and pure[b] devotion to Christ. 4 For if a person comes and
preaches another Jesus, whom we did not
preach, or you receive a different spirit, which
you had not received, or a different gospel,
which you had not accepted, you put up with
it splendidly!
5 Now I consider myself in no way inferior
to the "super-apostles." 6 Though untrained in
public speaking, I am certainly not ⌊untrained⌋
in knowledge. Indeed, we have always made
that clear to you in everything. 7 Or did I commit a sin by humbling myself so that you might
be exalted, because I preached the gospel of
God to you free of charge? 8 I robbed other
churches by taking pay ⌊from them⌋ to minister to you. 9 When I was present with you and
in need, I did not burden anyone, for the
brothers who came from Macedonia supplied
my needs. I have kept myself, and will keep
myself, from burdening you in any way. 10 As
the truth of Christ is in me, this boasting of
mine will not be stopped[c] in the regions of
Achaia. 11 Why? Because I don't love you?
God knows I do!
12 But I will continue to do what I am doing,
in order to cut off the opportunity of those who
want an opportunity to be regarded just as we
are in what they are boasting about. 13 For such
people are false apostles, deceitful workers, dis-
guising themselves as apostles of Christ. 14 And
no wonder! For Satan himself is disguised as an
angel of light. 15 So it is no great thing if his servants also disguise themselves as servants of
righteousness. Their destiny[d] will be according
to their works.

Paul's Sufferings for Christ

16 I repeat: no one should consider me a
fool. But if ⌊you do⌋, at least accept me as a fool,
so I too may boast a little. 17 What I say in this
matter[e] of boasting, I don't speak as the Lord
would, but foolishly. 18 Since many boast from
a human perspective,[f] I will also boast. 19 For
you gladly put up with fools since you are so
smart![g] 20 In fact, you put up with it if someone
enslaves you, if someone devours you, if someone captures you, if someone dominates you, or
if someone hits you in the face. 21 I say this to
⌊our⌋ shame: we have been weak.
But in whatever anyone dares ⌊to boast⌋—I
am talking foolishly—I also dare:

22 Are they Hebrews? So am I.
Are they Israelites? So am I.
Are they the seed of Abraham?
So am I.
23 Are they servants of Christ?
I'm talking like a madman—
I'm a better one:
with far more labors,
many more imprisonments,
far worse beatings, near death[h]
many times.
24 Five times I received from the Jews
40 lashes minus one.
25 Three times I was beaten with rods.[i]
Once I was stoned.[j]
Three times I was shipwrecked.
I have spent a night and a day
in the depths of the sea.
26 On frequent journeys, ⌊I faced⌋
dangers from rivers,
dangers from robbers,
dangers from my own people,
dangers from the Gentiles,
dangers in the city,
dangers in the open country,
dangers on the sea, and dangers
among false brothers;
27 labor and hardship,
many sleepless nights,
hunger and thirst,
often without food, cold,
and lacking clothing.

28 Not to mention[k] other things, there is the
daily pressure on me: my care for all the
churches. 29 Who is weak, and I am not weak?
Who is made to stumble, and I do not burn with
indignation? 30 If boasting is necessary, I will
boast about my weaknesses. 31 The eternally
blessed One, the God and Father of the Lord
Jesus, knows I am not lying. 32 In Damascus,
the governor under King Aretas[l] guarded the

[a] **11:1** Or *Yes, you are putting up with me* [b] **11:3** Other mss omit *and pure* [c] **11:10** Or *silenced* [d] **11:15** Lit *end* [e] **11:17** Or *business,* or *confidence* [f] **11:18** Lit *boast according to the flesh* [g] **11:19** Or *are wise* [h] **11:23** Lit *and in deaths* [i] **11:25** A specifically Roman punishment; see Ac 16:22 [j] **11:25** A common Jewish method of capital punishment; see Ac 14:5 [k] **11:28** Lit *Apart from* [l] **11:32** Aretus IV (9 B.C.–A.D. 40), a Nabatean Arab king

city of the Damascenes in order to arrest me,
33 so I was let down in a basket through a window in the wall and escaped his hands.

Sufficient Grace

12 It is necessary to boast; it is not helpful, but I will move on to visions and
revelations of the Lord. 2 I know a man in
Christ who was caught up into the third
heaven 14 years ago. Whether he was in the
body or out of the body, I don't know; God
knows. 3 I know that this man—whether in
the body or out of the body I do not know, God
knows— 4 was caught up into paradise. He
heard inexpressible words, which a man is not
allowed to speak. 5 I will boast about this person, but not about myself, except of my weaknesses. 6 For if I want to boast, I will not be a
fool, because I will be telling the truth. But I
will spare you, so that no one can credit me
with something beyond what he sees in me or
hears from me, 7 especially because of the
extraordinary revelations. Therefore, so that I
would not exalt myself, a thorn in the flesh
was given to me, a messenger[a] of Satan to torment me so I would not exalt myself. 8 Concerning this, I pleaded with the Lord three
times to take it away from me. 9 But He said to
me, "My grace is sufficient for you, for power[b]
is perfected in weakness." Therefore, I will
most gladly boast all the more about my weaknesses, so that Christ's power may reside in
me. 10 So because of Christ, I am pleased in
weaknesses, in insults, in catastrophes, in persecutions, and in pressures. For when I am
weak, then I am strong.

Signs of an Apostle

11 I have become a fool; you forced it on me.
I ought to have been recommended by you,
since I am in no way inferior to the "super-apostles," even though I am nothing. 12 The
signs of an apostle were performed among you
in all endurance—not only signs but also wonders and miracles. 13 So in what way were you
treated worse than the other churches, except
that I personally did not burden you? Forgive
me this wrong!

Paul's Concern for the Corinthians

14 Look! I am ready to come to you this
third time. I will not burden you, for I am not
seeking what is yours, but you. For children
are not obligated to save up for their parents,
but parents for their children. 15 I will most
gladly spend and be spent for you.[c] If I love
you more, am I to be loved less? 16 Now
granted, I have not burdened you; yet sly as I
am, I took you in by deceit! 17 Did I take
advantage of you by anyone I sent you? 18 I
urged Titus ⌊to come⌋, and I sent the brother
with him. Did Titus take advantage of you?
Didn't we •walk in the same spirit and in the
same footsteps?

19 You have thought all along that we were
defending ourselves to you.[d] ⌊No⌋, in the sight
of God we are speaking in Christ, and everything, dear friends, is for building you up.
20 For I fear that perhaps when I come I will
not find you to be what I want, and I may not
be found by you to be what you want;[e] there
may be quarreling, jealousy, outbursts of
anger, selfish ambitions, slander, gossip, arrogance, and disorder. 21 I fear that when I
come my God will again[f] humiliate me in your
presence, and I will grieve for many who
sinned before and have not repented of the
uncleanness, sexual immorality, and promiscuity they practiced.

Final Warnings and Exhortations

13 This is the third time I am coming to
you. **On the testimony[g] of two or
three witnesses every word will be confirmed.**[h] 2 I gave warning, and I give warning—as when I was present the second time,
so now while I am absent—to those who
sinned before and to all the rest: if I come
again, I will not be lenient, 3 since you seek
proof of Christ speaking in me. He is not weak
toward you, but powerful among you. 4 In fact,
He was crucified in weakness, but He lives by
God's power. For we also are weak in Him, yet
toward you we will live with Him by God's
power.

5 Test yourselves ⌊to see⌋ if you are in the
faith. Examine yourselves. Or do you not recognize for yourselves that Jesus Christ is in
you?—unless you fail the test.[i] 6 And I hope
you will recognize that we are not failing the
test. 7 Now we pray to God that you do nothing
wrong, not that we may appear to pass the test,
but that you may do what is right, even though
we ⌊may appear⌋ to fail. 8 For we are not able to

[a]**12:7** Or *angel* [b]**12:9** Other mss read *My power* [c]**12:15** Lit *for your souls*, or *for your lives* [d]**12:19** Or *Have you thought . . . to you?* [e]**12:20** Lit *be as you want* [f]**12:21** Or *come again my God will* [g]**13:1** Lit *mouth* [h]**13:1** Dt 17:6; 19:15 [i]**13:5** Or *you are disqualified*, or *you are counterfeit*

do anything against the truth, but only for the
truth. 9 In fact, we rejoice when we are weak
and you are strong. We also pray for this: your
maturity.[a] 10 This is why I am writing these
things while absent, that when I am there I will
not use severity, in keeping with the authority
the Lord gave me for building up and not for
tearing down.

11 Finally, brothers, rejoice. Be restored, be
encouraged, be of the same mind, be at peace,
and the God of love and peace will be with you.
12 Greet one another with a holy kiss. All the
saints greet you.

13 The grace of the Lord Jesus Christ, and
the love of God, and the fellowship of the Holy
Spirit be with all of you.[b]

Galatians

Greeting

1 Paul, an apostle—not from men or by
man, but by Jesus Christ and God the
Father who raised Him from the dead— 2 and
all the brothers who are with me:

To the churches of Galatia.[c]

3 Grace to you and peace from God the
Father and our Lord[d] Jesus Christ, 4 who gave
Himself for our sins to rescue us from this
present evil age, according to the will of our
God and Father, 5 to whom be the glory forever
and ever. •Amen.

No Other Gospel

6 I am amazed that you are so quickly turning away from Him who called you by the grace
of Christ, ⌊and are turning⌋ to a different gospel— 7 not that there is another ⌊gospel⌋, but
there are some who are troubling you and want
to change the gospel of Christ. 8 But even if we
or an angel from heaven should preach to you a
gospel other than what we have preached to
you, a curse be on him![e] 9 As we have said
before, I now say again: if anyone preaches to
you a gospel contrary to what you received, a
curse be on him![f]

10 For am I now trying to win the favor of
people, or God? Or am I striving to please people? If I were still trying to please people, I
would not be a slave of Christ.

Paul Defends His Apostleship

11 Now I want you to know, brothers, that
the gospel preached by me is not based on a
human point of view.[g] 12 For I did not receive
it from a human source and I was not taught it,
but it came by a revelation from Jesus Christ.

13 For you have heard about my former way
of life in Judaism: I persecuted God's church to
an extreme degree and tried to destroy it;
14 and I advanced in Judaism beyond many con-
temporaries among my people, because I was
extremely zealous for the traditions of my
ancestors. 15 But when God, who from my
mother's womb set me apart and called me by
His grace, was pleased 16 to reveal His Son in
me, so that I could preach Him among the Gentiles, I did not immediately consult with anyone.[h] 17 I did not go up to Jerusalem to those
who had become apostles before me; instead I
went to Arabia and came back to Damascus.

18 Then after three years I did go up to
Jerusalem to get to know •Cephas,[i] and I stayed
with him 15 days. 19 But I didn't see any of the
other apostles except James, the Lord's
brother. 20 Now in what I write to you, I'm not
lying. God is my witness.[j]

21 Afterwards, I went to the regions of Syria
and Cilicia. 22 I remained personally unknown
to the Judean churches in Christ; 23 they simply kept hearing: "He who formerly persecuted
us now preaches the faith he once tried to
destroy." 24 And they glorified God because
of me.

Paul Defends His Gospel at Jerusalem

2 Then after 14 years I went up again to
Jerusalem with Barnabas, taking Titus

[a]**13:9** Or *completion*, or *restoration* [b]**13:12–13** Some translations divide these 2 vv. into 3 vv. so that v. 13 begins with *All the saints* . . . and v. 14 begins with *The grace of* . . . [c]**1:2** A Roman province in what is now Turkey [d]**1:3** Other mss read *God our Father and the Lord* [e]**1:8** Or *you, let him be condemned*, or *you, let him be condemned to hell*; Gk *anathema* [f]**1:9** Or *received, let him be condemned*, or *received, let him be condemned to hell*; Gk *anathema* [g]**1:11** Lit *not according to man* [h]**1:16** Lit *flesh and blood* [i]**1:18** Other mss read *Peter* [j]**1:20** Lit *Behold, before God*

along also. 2 I went up because of a revelation
and presented to them the gospel I preach
among the Gentiles—but privately to those
recognized ⌊as leaders⌋—so that I might not be
running, or have run, in vain. 3 But not even
Titus who was with me, though he was a
Greek, was compelled to be circumcised.
4 ⌊This issue arose⌋ because of false brothers
smuggled in, who came in secretly to spy on
our freedom that we have in Christ Jesus, in
order to enslave us. 5 But we did not yield in
submission to these people for even an hour,
so that the truth of the gospel would remain
for you.

6 But from those recognized as important
(what they really were makes no difference to
me; God does not show favoritism[a])—those
recognized as important added nothing to me.
7 On the contrary, they saw that I had been
entrusted with the gospel for the uncircumcised, just as Peter was for the circumcised.
8 For He who was at work with Peter in the
apostleship to the circumcised was also at work
with me among the Gentiles. 9 When James,
•Cephas, and John, recognized as pillars,
acknowledged the grace that had been given to
me, they gave the right hand of fellowship to
me and Barnabas, ⌊agreeing⌋ that we should go
to the Gentiles and they to the circumcised.
10 ⌊They asked⌋ only that we would remember
the poor, which I made every effort to do.

Freedom from the Law

11 But when Cephas[b] came to Antioch, I
opposed him to his face because he stood condemned.[c] 12 For he used to eat with the Gentiles before certain men came from James.
However, when they came, he withdrew and
separated himself, because he feared those
from the circumcision party. 13 Then the rest of
the Jews joined his hypocrisy, so that even
Barnabas was carried away by their hypocrisy.
14 But when I saw that they were deviating
from the truth of the gospel, I told Cephas[b] in
front of everyone, "If you, who are a Jew, live
like a Gentile and not like a Jew, how can you
compel Gentiles to live like Jews?"[d]

15 We are Jews by birth and not "Gentile
sinners"; 16 yet we know that no one is justified by the works of the law but by faith in Jesus
Christ.[e] And we have believed in Christ Jesus,
so that we might be justified by faith in Christ[f]
and not by the works of the law, because by the
works of the law no human being will[g] be justified. 17 But if, while seeking to be justified by
Christ, we ourselves are also found to be sinners, is Christ then a promoter[h] of sin? Absolutely not! 18 If I rebuild those things that I tore
down, I show myself to be a lawbreaker. 19 For
through the law I have died to the law, that I
might live to God. I have been crucified with
Christ; 20 and I no longer live, but Christ lives
in me. The life I now live in the flesh,[i] I live by
faith in the Son of God, who loved me and gave
Himself for me. 21 I do not set aside the grace
of God; for if righteousness comes through the
law, then Christ died for nothing.

Justification through Faith

3 You foolish Galatians! Who has hypno-
tized you,[j] before whose eyes Jesus
Christ was vividly portrayed[k] as crucified? 2 I
only want to learn this from you: Did you
receive the Spirit by the works of the law or
by hearing with faith?[l] 3 Are you so foolish?
After beginning with the Spirit, are you now
going to be made complete by the flesh?[m]
4 Did you suffer so much for nothing—if in
fact it was for nothing? 5 So then, does God[n]
supply you with the Spirit and work miracles
among you by the works of the law or by
hearing with faith?[l]

6 Just as Abraham **believed God, and it was
credited to him for righteousness,**[o] 7 so understand that those who have faith are Abraham's
sons. 8 Now the Scripture foresaw that God
would justify the Gentiles by faith and foretold
the good news to Abraham, saying, **All the
nations will be blessed in you.**[p] 9 So those
who have faith are blessed with Abraham, who
had faith.[q]

Law and Promise

10 For all who ⌊rely on⌋ the works of the
law are under a curse, because it is written:
**Cursed is everyone who does not continue
doing everything written in the book of the
law.**[r] 11 Now it is clear that no one is justified

[a]**2:6** Or *God is not a respecter of persons*; lit *God does not receive the face of man* [b]**2:11,14** Other mss read *Peter* [c]**2:11** Or *he was in the wrong* [d]**2:14** Some translations continue the quotation through v. 16 or v. 21. [e]**2:16** Or *by the faithfulness of Jesus Christ* [f]**2:16** Or *by the faithfulness of Christ* [g]**2:16** Lit *law all flesh will not* [h]**2:17** Or *servant* [i]**2:20** The physical body [j]**3:1** Other mss add *not to obey the truth* [k]**3:1** Other mss add *among you* [l]**3:2,5** Lit *by law works or faith hearing* or *hearing the message* [m]**3:3** By human effort [n]**3:5** Lit *He* [o]**3:6** Gn 15:6 [p]**3:8** Gn 12:3; 18:18 [q]**3:9** Or *with believing Abraham* [r]**3:10** Dt 27:26

before God by the law, because **the righteous
will live by faith.**[a] 12 But the law is not based
on faith; instead, **the one who does these
things will live by them.**[b] 13 Christ has
redeemed us from the curse of the law by
becoming a curse for us, because it is written:
Cursed is everyone who is hung on a tree.[c]
14 The purpose was that the blessing of Abraham would come to the Gentiles in Christ
Jesus, so that we could receive the promise of
the Spirit through faith.

15 Brothers, I'm using a human illustration.[d] No one sets aside even a human covenant that has been ratified, or makes additions
to it. 16 Now the promises were spoken to
Abraham and to his seed. He does not say
"and to seeds," as though referring to many,
but **and to your seed,**[e] referring to one, who
is Christ. 17 And I say this: the law, which
came 430 years later, does not revoke a covenant that was previously ratified by God,[f] so as
to cancel the promise. 18 For if the inheritance
is from the law, it is no longer from the promise; but God granted it to Abraham through
the promise.

The Purpose of the Law

19 Why the law then? It was added because
of transgressions until the Seed to whom the
promise was made would come. ⌊The law⌋ was
ordered through angels by means of a mediator.
20 Now a mediator is not for just one person,
but God is one. 21 Is the law therefore contrary
to God's promises? Absolutely not! For if a law
had been given that was able to give life, then
righteousness would certainly be by the law.
22 But the Scripture has imprisoned everything
under sin's power,[g] so that the promise by faith
in Jesus Christ might be given to those who
believe. 23 Before this faith came, we were con-
fined under the law, imprisoned until the coming faith was revealed. 24 The law, then, was
our guardian[h] until Christ, so that we could be
justified by faith. 25 But since that faith has
come, we are no longer under a guardian,[h]
26 for you are all sons of God through faith in
Christ Jesus.

Sons and Heirs

27 For as many of you as have been baptized
into Christ have put on Christ. 28 There is no
Jew or Greek, slave or free, male or female; for
you are all one in Christ Jesus. 29 And if you are
Christ's, then you are Abraham's seed, heirs
according to the promise.

4 1 Now I say
that as long as the heir is a child, he differs in no way from a slave, though he is the
owner of everything. 2 Instead, he is under
guardians and stewards until the time set by his
father. 3 In the same way we also, when we
were children, were in slavery under the elemental forces of the world. 4 But when the
completion of the time came, God sent His Son,
born of a woman, born under the law, 5 to
redeem those under the law, so that we might
receive adoption as sons. 6 And because you are
sons, God has sent the Spirit of His Son into
our[i] hearts, crying, "•*Abba*, Father!" 7 So you
are no longer a slave, but a son; and if a son,
then an heir through God.

Paul's Concern for the Galatians

8 But in the past, when you didn't know
God, you were enslaved to things[j] that by
nature are not gods. 9 But now, since you know
God, or rather have become known by God,
how can you turn back again to the weak and
bankrupt elemental forces? Do you want to be
enslaved to them all over again? 10 You observe
⌊special⌋ days, months, seasons, and years. 11 I
am fearful for you, that perhaps my labor for
you has been wasted.

12 I beg you, brothers: become like me, for I
also became like you. You have not wronged
me; 13 you know that previously I preached the
gospel to you in physical weakness, 14 and
though my physical condition was a trial for
you,[k] you did not despise or reject me. On the
contrary, you received me as an angel of God,
as Christ Jesus ⌊Himself⌋.

15 What happened to this blessedness of
yours? For I testify to you that, if possible, you
would have torn out your eyes and given them
to me. 16 Have I now become your enemy by
telling you the truth? 17 They[l] are enthusiastic
about you, but not for any good. Instead, they
want to isolate you so you will be enthusiastic
about them. 18 Now it is always good to be
enthusiastic about good—and not just when I
am with you. 19 My children, again I am in the

[a] **3:11** Hab 2:4 [b] **3:12** Lv 18:5 [c] **3:13** Dt 21:23 [d] **3:15** Lit *I speak according to man* [e] **3:16** Gn 12:7; 13:15; 17:8; 24:7
[f] **3:17** Other mss add *in Christ* [g] **3:22** Lit *under sin* [h] **3:24,25** The word translated *guardian* in vv. 24–25 is different from the word in Gl 4:2. In our culture, we do not have a slave who takes a child to and from school, protecting the child from harm or corruption. In Gk the word *paidogogos* described such a slave. This slave was not a teacher. [i] **4:6** Other mss read *your*
[j] **4:8** Or *beings* [k] **4:14** Other mss read *me* [l] **4:17** The false teachers

pains of childbirth for you until Christ is formed
in you. 20 I'd like to be with you right now and
change my tone of voice, because I don't know
what to do about you.

Sarah and Hagar: Two Covenants

21 Tell me, you who want to be under the
law, don't you hear the law? 22 For it is written
that Abraham had two sons, one by a slave and
the other by a free woman. 23 But the one by
the slave was born according to the flesh, while
the one by the free woman was born as the
result of a promise. 24 These things are illustra-
tions,[a] for the women represent the two covenants. One is from Mount Sinai and bears
children into slavery—this is Hagar. 25 Now
Hagar is Mount Sinai in Arabia and corresponds
to the present Jerusalem, for she is in slavery
with her children. 26 But the Jerusalem above
is free, and she is our mother. 27 For it is written:

> **Rejoice, O barren woman**
> **who does not give birth.**
> **Break forth and shout,**
> **you who are not in labor,**
> **for the children of the desolate**
> **are many,**
> **more numerous than those**
> **of the woman**
> **who has a husband.**[b]

28 Now you, brothers, like Isaac, are children
of promise. 29 But just as then the child born
according to the flesh persecuted the one born
according to the Spirit, so also now. 30 But
what does the Scripture say?

> **Throw out the slave and her son, for**
> **the son of the slave will never inherit**
> **with the son of the free woman.**[c]

31 Therefore, brothers, we are not children of
the slave but of the free woman.

Freedom of the Christian

5 Christ has liberated us into freedom.
Therefore stand firm and don't submit
again to a yoke of slavery. 2 Take note! I, Paul,
tell you that if you get circumcised, Christ will
not benefit you at all. 3 Again I testify to every
man who gets circumcised that he is obligated
to keep the entire law. 4 You who are trying to
be justified by the law are alienated from
Christ; you have fallen from grace! 5 For by the
Spirit we eagerly wait for the hope of righteousness from faith. 6 For in Christ Jesus
neither circumcision nor uncircumcision
accomplishes anything; what matters is faith
working through love.

7 You were running well. Who prevented
you from obeying the truth? 8 This persuasion
did not come from Him who called you. 9 A little yeast leavens the whole lump of dough.
10 In the Lord I have confidence in you that you
will not accept any other view. But whoever it
is who is troubling you will pay the penalty.
11 Now brothers, if I still preach circumcision,
why am I still persecuted? In that case the
offense of the cross has been abolished. 12 I
wish those who are disturbing you might also
get themselves castrated!

13 For you are called to freedom, brothers;
only don't use this freedom as an opportunity
for the flesh, but serve one another through
love. 14 For the entire law is fulfilled in one
statement: **Love your neighbor as yourself.**[d]
15 But if you bite and devour one another,
watch out, or you will be consumed by one
another.

The Spirit versus the Flesh

16 I say then, •walk by the Spirit and you
will not carry out the desire of the flesh. 17 For
the flesh desires what is against the Spirit, and
the Spirit desires what is against the flesh;
these are opposed to each other, so that you
don't do what you want. 18 But if you are led by
the Spirit, you are not under the law.

19 Now the works of the flesh are
obvious:[e f] sexual immorality, moral impurity, promiscuity, 20 idolatry, sorcery,
hatreds, strife, jealousy, outbursts of anger,
selfish ambitions, dissensions, factions,
21 envy,[g] drunkenness, carousing, and anything similar, about which I tell you in
advance—as I told you before—that those
who practice such things will not inherit the
kingdom of God.

22 But the fruit of the Spirit is love, joy,
peace, patience, kindness, goodness, faith,[h]
23 gentleness, self-control. Against such things
there is no law. 24 Now those who belong to
Christ Jesus have crucified the flesh with its
passions and desires. 25 If we live by the Spirit,
we must also follow the Spirit. 26 We must not
become conceited, provoking one another,
envying one another.

[a]**4:24** Typology or allegory [b]**4:27** Is 54:1 [c]**4:30** Gn 21:10 [d]**5:14** Lv 19:18 [e]**5:19** Other mss add *adultery* [f]**5:19** Lit *obvious, which are:* [g]**5:21** Other mss add *murders* [h]**5:22** Or *faithfulness*

Carry One Another's Burdens

6 Brothers, if someone is caught in any wrongdoing, you who are spiritual should restore such a person with a gentle spirit, watching out for yourselves so you won't be tempted also. 2 Carry one another's burdens; in this way you will fulfill the law of Christ. 3 For if anyone considers himself to be something when he is nothing, he is deceiving himself. 4 But each person should examine his own work, and then he will have a reason for boasting in himself alone, and not in respect to someone else. 5 For each person will have to carry his own load.

6 The one who is taught the message must share his goods with the teacher. 7 Don't be deceived: God is not mocked. For whatever a man sows he will also reap, 8 because the one who sows to his flesh will reap corruption from the flesh, but the one who sows to the Spirit will reap eternal life from the Spirit. 9 So we must not get tired of doing good, for we will reap at the proper time if we don't give up. 10 Therefore, as we have opportunity, we must work for the good of all, especially for those who belong to the household of faith.

Concluding Exhortation

11 Look at what large letters I have written to you in my own handwriting. 12 Those who want to make a good showing in the flesh are the ones who would compel you to be circumcised—but only to avoid being persecuted for the cross of Christ. 13 For even the circumcised don't keep the law themselves; however, they want you to be circumcised in order to boast about your flesh. 14 But as for me, I will never boast about anything except the cross of our Lord Jesus Christ, through whom[a] the world has been crucified to me, and I to the world. 15 For[b] both circumcision and uncircumcision mean nothing; ⌊what matters⌋ instead is a new creation. 16 May peace be on all those who follow this standard, and mercy also be on the Israel of God!

17 From now on, let no one cause me trouble, because I carry the marks of Jesus on my body. 18 Brothers, the grace of our Lord Jesus Christ be with your spirit. •Amen.

Ephesians

Greeting

1 Paul, an apostle of Christ Jesus by God's will:

To the saints and believers in Christ Jesus at Ephesus.[c]

2 Grace to you and peace from God our Father and the Lord Jesus Christ.

God's Rich Blessings

3 Blessed be the God and Father of our Lord Jesus Christ, who has blessed us with every spiritual blessing in the heavens, in Christ; 4 for He chose us in Him, before the foundation of the world, to be holy and blameless in His sight.[d] In love[e] 5 He predestined us to be adopted through Jesus Christ for Himself, according to His favor and will, 6 to the praise of His glorious grace that He favored us with in the Beloved.

7 In Him we have redemption through His blood, the forgiveness of our trespasses, according to the riches of His grace 8 that He lavished on us with all wisdom and understanding. 9 He made known to us the •mystery of His will, according to His good pleasure that He planned in Him 10 for the administration[f] of the days of fulfillment[g] —to bring everything together in the •Messiah, both things in heaven and things on earth in Him.

11 In Him we were also made His inheritance,[h] predestined according to the purpose of the One who works out everything in agreement with the decision of His will, 12 so that we who had already put our hope in the Messiah might bring praise to His glory.

13 In Him you also, when you heard the word of truth, the gospel of your salvation—in Him when you believed—were sealed with the

[a]**6:14** Or *which* [b]**6:15** Other mss add *in Christ Jesus* [c]**1:1** Other mss omit *at Ephesus* [d]**1:4** Vv. 3–14 are 1 sentence in Gk. [e]**1:4** Or *In His sight in love* [f]**1:10** Or *dispensation*; lit *house law* (Gk *oikonomia*) [g]**1:10** Lit *the fulfillment of times* [h]**1:11** Or *we also were chosen as an inheritance*, or *we also received an inheritance*

promised Holy Spirit. 14 He is the down payment of our inheritance, for the redemption of the possession,[a] to the praise of His glory.

Prayer for Spiritual Insight

15 This is why, since I heard about your faith in the Lord Jesus and your love for all the saints, 16 I never stop giving thanks for you as I remember you in my prayers. 17 ⌊I pray⌋ that the God of our Lord Jesus Christ, the glorious Father,[b] would give you a spirit of wisdom and revelation in the knowledge of Him. 18 ⌊I pray⌋ that the eyes of your heart may be enlightened so you may know what is the hope of His calling, what are the glorious riches of His inheritance among the saints, 19 and what is the immeasurable greatness of His power to us who believe, according to the working of His vast strength.

God's Power in Christ

20 He demonstrated ⌊this power⌋ in the Messiah by raising Him from the dead and seating Him at His right hand in the heavens—21 far above every ruler and authority, power and dominion, and every title given,[c] not only in this age but also in the one to come. 22 And **He put everything under His feet**[d] and appointed Him as head over everything for the church, 23 which is His body, the fullness of the One who fills all things in every way.

From Death to Life

2 And you were dead in your trespasses and sins 2 in which you previously •walked according to this worldly age, according to the ruler of the atmospheric domain,[e] the spirit now working in the disobedient.[f] 3 We too all previously lived among them in our fleshly desires, carrying out the inclinations of our flesh and thoughts, and by nature we were children under wrath, as the others were also. 4 But God, who is abundant in mercy, because of His great love that He had for us,[g] 5 made us alive with the •Messiah even though we were dead in trespasses. By grace you are saved! 6 He also raised us up with Him and seated us with Him in the heavens, in Christ Jesus, 7 so that in the coming ages He might display the immeasurable riches of His grace in ⌊His⌋ kindness to us in Christ Jesus. 8 For by grace you are saved through faith, and this is not from yourselves; it is God's gift— 9 not from works, so that no one can boast. 10 For we are His creation—created in Christ Jesus for good works, which God prepared ahead of time so that we should walk in them.

Unity in Christ

11 So then, remember that at one time you were Gentiles in the flesh—called "the uncircumcised" by those called "the circumcised," done by hand in the flesh. 12 At that time you were without the Messiah, excluded from the citizenship of Israel, and foreigners to the covenants of the promise, with no hope and without God in the world. 13 But now in Christ Jesus, you who were far away have been brought near by the blood of the Messiah. 14 For He is our peace, who made both groups one and tore down the dividing wall of hostility. In His flesh, 15 He did away with the law of the commandments in regulations, so that He might create in Himself one new man from the two, resulting in peace. 16 ⌊He did this so⌋ that He might reconcile both to God in one body through the cross and put the hostility to death by it.[h] 17 When ⌊Christ⌋ came, He proclaimed the good news of peace to you who were far away and peace to those who were near. 18 For through Him we both have access by one Spirit to the Father. 19 So then you are no longer foreigners and strangers, but fellow citizens with the saints, and members of God's household, 20 built on the foundation of the apostles and prophets, with Christ Jesus Himself as the cornerstone. 21 The whole building is being fitted together in Him and is growing into a holy sanctuary in the Lord, 22 in whom you also are being built together for God's dwelling in the Spirit.

Paul's Ministry to the Gentiles

3 For this reason, I, Paul, the prisoner of Christ Jesus on behalf of you Gentiles—2 you have heard, haven't you, about the administration of God's grace that He gave to me for you? 3 The •mystery was made known to me by revelation, as I have briefly written above. 4 By reading this you are able to understand my insight about the mystery of the •Messiah. 5 This was not made known to people[i] in other generations as it is now revealed

[a]**1:14** *the possession* could be either man's or God's [b]**1:17** Or *the Father of glory* [c]**1:21** Lit *every name named* [d]**1:22** Ps 8:6 [e]**2:2** Lit *ruler of the authority of the air* [f]**2:2** Lit *sons of disobedience* [g]**2:4** Lit *love with which He loved us* [h]**2:16** Or *death in Himself* [i]**3:5** Lit *to the sons of men*

Turn to page 92.

to His holy apostles and prophets by the Spirit: 6 the Gentiles are co-heirs, members of the same body, and partners of the promise in Christ Jesus through the gospel. 7 I was made a servant of this ⌊gospel⌋ by the gift of God's grace that was given to me by the working of His power.

8 This grace was given to me—the least of all the saints!—to proclaim to the Gentiles the incalculable riches of the Messiah, 9 and to shed light for all about the administration of the mystery hidden for ages in God who created all things. 10 This is so that God's multi-faceted wisdom may now be made known through the church to the rulers and authorities in the heavens. 11 This is according to the purpose of the ages, which He made in the Messiah, Jesus our Lord, 12 in whom we have boldness, access, and confidence through faith in Him.[a] 13 So then I ask you not to be discouraged over my afflictions on your behalf, for they are your glory.

Prayer for Spiritual Power

14 For this reason I bow my knees before the Father[b] 15 from whom every family in heaven and on earth is named. 16 ⌊I pray⌋ that He may grant you, according to the riches of His glory, to be strengthened with power through His Spirit in the inner man, 17 and that the Messiah may dwell in your hearts through faith. ⌊I pray that⌋ you, being rooted and firmly established in love, 18 may be able to comprehend with all the saints what is the length and width, height and depth ⌊of God's love⌋, 19 and to know the Messiah's love that surpasses knowledge, so you may be filled with all the fullness of God.

20 Now to Him who is able to do above and beyond all that we ask or think—according to the power that works in you— 21 to Him be glory in the church and in Christ Jesus to all generations, forever and ever. •Amen.

Unity and Diversity in the Body of Christ

4 I, therefore, the prisoner in the Lord, urge you to •walk worthy of the calling you have received, 2 with all humility and gentleness, with patience, accepting[c] one another in love, 3 diligently keeping the unity of the Spirit with the peace that binds ⌊us⌋. 4 There is one body and one Spirit, just as you were called to one hope[d] at your calling; 5 one Lord, one faith, one baptism, 6 one God and Father of all, who is above all and through all and in all.

7 Now grace was given to each one of us according to the measure of the •Messiah's gift. 8 For it says:

> **When He ascended on high,**
> **He took prisoners into captivity;[e]**
> **He gave gifts to people.[f]**

9 But what does "He ascended" mean except that He[g] descended to the lower parts of the earth?[h] 10 The One who descended is the same as the One who ascended far above all the heavens, that He might fill[i] all things. 11 And He personally gave some to be apostles, some prophets, some evangelists, some pastors and teachers, 12 for the training of the saints in the work of ministry, to build up the body of Christ, 13 until we all reach unity in the faith and in the knowledge of God's Son, ⌊growing⌋ into a mature man with a stature measured by Christ's fullness. 14 Then we will no longer be little children, tossed by the waves and blown around by every wind of teaching, by human cunning with cleverness in the techniques of deceit. 15 But speaking the truth in love, let us grow in every way into Him who is the head—Christ. 16 From Him the whole body, fitted and knit together by every supporting ligament, promotes the growth of the body for building up itself in love by the proper working of each individual part.

Living the New Life

17 Therefore, I say this and testify in the Lord: You should no longer walk as the Gentiles walk, in the futility of their thoughts. 18 They are darkened in their understanding, excluded from the life of God, because of the ignorance that is in them and because of the hardness of their hearts. 19 They became callous and gave themselves over to promiscuity for the practice of every kind of impurity with a desire for more and more.[j]

20 But that is not how you learned about the Messiah, 21 assuming you heard Him and were taught by Him, because the truth is in Jesus: 22 you took off[k] your former way of life, the old man that is corrupted by deceitful desires;

[a] **3:12** Or *through His faithfulness* [b] **3:14** Other mss add *of our Lord Jesus Christ* [c] **4:2** Or *tolerating* [d] **4:4** Lit *called in one hope* [e] **4:8** Or *He led the captives* [f] **4:8** Ps 68:18 [g] **4:9** Other mss add *first* [h] **4:9** Or *the lower parts, namely, the earth* [i] **4:10** Or *fulfill*; see Eph 1:23 [j] **4:19** Lit *with greediness* [k] **4:21–22** Or *Jesus. This means: take off* (as a command)

23 you are being renewed[a] in the spirit of your minds; 24 you put on[b] the new man, the one created according to God's ⌊likeness⌋ in righteousness and purity of the truth.

25 Since you put away lying, **Speak the truth, each one to his neighbor,**[c] because we are members of one another. 26 **Be angry and do not sin.**[d] Don't let the sun go down on your anger, 27 and don't give the Devil an opportunity. 28 The thief must no longer steal. Instead, he must do honest work with his own hands, so that he has something to share with anyone in need. 29 No rotten talk should come from your mouth, but only what is good for the building up of someone in need,[e] in order to give grace to those who hear. 30 And don't grieve God's Holy Spirit, who sealed you[f] for the day of redemption. 31 All bitterness, anger and wrath, insult and slander must be removed from you, along with all wickedness. 32 And be kind and compassionate to one another, forgiving one another, just as God also forgave you[g] in Christ.

5 Therefore, be imitators of God, as dearly loved children. 2 And walk in love, as the Messiah also loved us and gave Himself for us, a sacrificial and fragrant offering to God. 3 But sexual immorality and any impurity or greed should not even be heard of[h] among you, as is proper for saints. 4 And coarse and foolish talking or crude joking are not suitable, but rather giving thanks. 5 For know and recognize this: no sexually immoral or impure or greedy person, who is an idolater, has an inheritance in the kingdom of the Messiah and of God.

Light versus Darkness

6 Let no one deceive you with empty arguments, for because of these things God's wrath is coming on the disobedient.[i] 7 Therefore, do not become their partners. 8 For you were once darkness, but now ⌊you are⌋ light in the Lord. Walk as children of light— 9 for the fruit of the light[j] ⌊results⌋ in all goodness, righteousness, and truth— 10 discerning what is pleasing to the Lord. 11 Don't participate in the fruitless works of darkness, but instead, expose them. 12 For it is shameful even to mention what is done by them in secret. 13 Everything exposed by the light is made clear, 14 for what makes everything clear is light. Therefore it is said:

Get up, sleeper, and rise up
  from the dead,
and the Messiah will shine
  on you.[k]

Consistency in the Christian Life

15 Pay careful attention, then, to how you walk—not as unwise people but as wise— 16 making the most of the time,[l] because the days are evil. 17 So don't be foolish, but understand what the Lord's will is. 18 And don't get drunk with wine, which ⌊leads to⌋ reckless actions, but be filled with the Spirit:

19 speaking to one another in psalms,
  hymns, and spiritual songs,
singing and making music to the Lord
  in your heart,
20 giving thanks always
  for everything
to God the Father in the name
  of our Lord Jesus Christ,
21 submitting to one another in the fear
  of Christ.

Wives and Husbands

22 Wives, submit[m] to your own husbands as to the Lord, 23 for the husband is head of the wife as also Christ is head of the church. He is the Savior of the body. 24 Now as the church submits to Christ, so wives should ⌊submit⌋ to their husbands in everything. 25 Husbands, love your wives, just as also Christ loved the church and gave Himself for her, 26 to make her holy, cleansing[n] her in the washing of water by the word. 27 He did this to present the church to Himself in splendor, without spot or wrinkle or any such thing, but holy and blameless. 28 In the same way, husbands should love their wives as their own bodies. He who loves his wife loves himself. 29 For no one ever hates his own flesh, but provides and cares for it, just as Christ does for the church, 30 since we are members of His body.[o]

31 **For this reason a man will leave**
  his father and mother
and be joined to his wife,
and the two will become
  one flesh.[p]

[a]**4:22–23** Or *desires; renew* (as a command) [b]**4:23–24** Or *minds; and put on* (as a command) [c]**4:25** Zch 8:16 [d]**4:26** Ps 4:4 [e]**4:29** Lit *for the building up of the need* [f]**4:30** Or *Spirit, by whom you were sealed* [g]**4:32** Other mss read *us* [h]**5:3** Or *be named* [i]**5:6** Lit *sons of disobedience* [j]**5:9** Other mss read *fruit of the Spirit*; see Gl 5:22, but compare Eph 5:11–14 [k]**5:14** This poem may have been an early Christian hymn based on several passages in Isaiah; see Is 9:2; 26:19; 40:1; 51:17; 52:1; 60:1. [l]**5:16** Lit *buying back the time* [m]**5:22** Other mss omit *submit* [n]**5:26** Or *having cleansed* [o]**5:30** Other mss add *and of His flesh and of His bones* [p]**5:31** Gn 2:24

32 This •mystery is profound, but I am talking
about Christ and the church. 33 To sum up,
each one of you is to love his wife as himself,
and the wife is to respect her husband.

Children and Parents

6 Children, obey your parents in the
Lord, because this is right. 2 **Honor
your father and mother**—which is the first
commandment[a] with a promise— 3 **that it
may go well with you and that you may
have a long life in the land.**[b] [c] 4 And fathers,
don't stir up anger in your children, but bring
them up in the training and instruction of the
Lord.

Slaves and Masters

5 Slaves, obey your human[d] masters with
fear and trembling, in the sincerity of your
heart, as to Christ. 6 Don't ⌊work only⌋ while
being watched, in order to please men, but as
slaves of Christ, do God's will from your heart.[e]
7 Render service with a good attitude, as to the
Lord and not to men, 8 knowing that whatever
good each one does, slave or free, he will
receive this back from the Lord. 9 And masters,
treat them the same way, without threatening
them, because you know that both their and
your Master is in heaven, and there is no favoritism with Him.

Christian Warfare

10 Finally, be strengthened by the Lord and
by His vast strength. 11 Put on the full armor of
God so that you can stand against the tactics[f] of
the Devil. 12 For our battle is not against flesh
and blood, but against the rulers, against the
authorities, against the world powers of this
darkness, against the spiritual forces of evil in
the heavens. 13 This is why you must take up
the full armor of God, so that you may be able
to resist in the evil day, and having prepared
everything, to take your stand. 14 Stand, therefore,

with truth like a belt
  around your waist,
righteousness like armor
  on your chest,
15 and your feet sandaled
  with readiness for the gospel
  of peace.[g]
16 In every situation take the shield
  of faith,
and with it you will be able
  to extinguish
the flaming arrows
  of the evil one.
17 Take the helmet of salvation,
and the sword of the Spirit,
  which is God's word.

18 With every prayer and request, pray at all
times in the Spirit, and stay alert in this, with
all perseverance and intercession for all the
saints. 19 Pray also for me, that the message
may be given to me when I open my mouth to
make known with boldness the •mystery of
the gospel. 20 For this I am an ambassador in
chains. Pray that I might be bold enough in
Him to speak as I should.

Paul's Farewell

21 Tychicus, our dearly loved brother and
faithful servant[h] in the Lord, will tell you everything so that you also may know how I am and
what I'm doing. 22 I am sending him to you for
this very reason, to let you know how we are
and to encourage your hearts.
23 Peace to the brothers, and love with
faith, from God the Father and the Lord Jesus
Christ. 24 Grace be with all who have undying
love for our Lord Jesus Christ.[i] [j]

Philippians

Greeting

1 Paul and Timothy, slaves of Christ Jesus:
To all the saints in Christ Jesus who are in
Philippi, including the •overseers and deacons.
2 Grace to you and peace from God our
Father and the Lord Jesus Christ.

[a]**6:2** Or *is a preeminent commandment* [b]**6:3** Or *life on the earth* [c]**6:2–3** Ex 20:12 [d]**6:5** Lit *according to the flesh* [e]**6:6** Lit *from soul* [f]**6:11** Or *schemes*, or *tricks* [g]**6:15** Ready to go tell others about the gospel [h]**6:21** Or *deacon* [i]**6:24** Other mss add *Amen.* [j]**6:24** Lit *all who love our Lord Jesus Christ in incorruption*

Thanksgiving and Prayer

3 I give thanks to my God for every remembrance of you,[a] 4 always praying with joy for all
of you in my every prayer, 5 because of your
partnership in the gospel from the first day
until now. 6 I am sure of this, that He who
started a good work in you[b] will carry it on to
completion until the day of Christ Jesus. 7 It is
right for me to think this way about all of you,
because I have you in my heart,[c] and you are all
partners with me in grace, both in my imprisonment and in the defense and establishment
of the gospel. 8 For God is my witness, how I
deeply miss all of you with the affection of
Christ Jesus. 9 And I pray this: that your love
will keep on growing in knowledge and every
kind of discernment, 10 so that you can determine what really matters and can be pure and
blameless in[d] the day of Christ, 11 filled with
the fruit of righteousness that ⌊comes⌋ through
Jesus Christ, to the glory and praise of God.

Advance of the Gospel

12 Now I want you to know, brothers, that
what has happened to me has actually resulted
in the advancement of the gospel, 13 so that it
has become known throughout the whole imperial guard,[e] and to everyone else, that my imprisonment is for Christ.[f] 14 Most of the brothers in
the Lord have gained confidence from my
imprisonment and dare even more to speak the
message[g] fearlessly. 15 Some, to be sure, preach
Christ out of envy and strife, but others out of
good will.[h] 16 These do so out of love, knowing
that I am appointed for the defense of the gospel;
17 the others proclaim Christ out of rivalry, not
sincerely, seeking to cause ⌊me⌋ trouble in my
imprisonment.[i] 18 What does it matter? Just that
in every way, whether out of false motives or
true, Christ is proclaimed. And in this I rejoice.
Yes, and I will rejoice 19 because I know this will
lead to my deliverance[j] through your prayers
and help from the Spirit of Jesus Christ. 20 My
eager expectation and hope is that I will not be
ashamed about anything, but that now as
always, with all boldness, Christ will be highly
honored in my body, whether by life or by death.

Living Is Christ

21 For me, living is Christ and dying is gain.
22 Now if I live on in the flesh, this means fruitful work for me; and I don't know which one I
should choose. 23 I am pressured by both. I
have the desire to depart and be with Christ—
which is far better— 24 but to remain in the
flesh is more necessary for you. 25 Since I am
persuaded of this, I know that I will remain and
continue with all of you for your advancement
and joy in the faith, 26 so that, because of me,
your confidence may grow in Christ Jesus
when I come to you again.

27 Just one thing: live your life in a manner
worthy of the gospel of Christ. Then, whether
I come and see you or am absent, I will hear
about you that you are standing firm in one
spirit, with one mind,[k] working side by side for
the faith of the gospel, 28 not being frightened
in any way by your opponents. This is evidence
of their destruction, but of your deliverance—
and this is from God. 29 For it has been given to
you on Christ's behalf not only to believe in
Him, but also to suffer for Him, 30 having the
same struggle that you saw I had and now hear
about me.

Christian Humility

2 If then there is any encouragement in
Christ, if any consolation of love, if any
fellowship with the Spirit, if any affection and
mercy, 2 fulfill my joy by thinking the same way,
having the same love, sharing the same feelings,
focusing on one goal. 3 Do nothing out of rivalry
or conceit, but in humility consider others as
more important than yourselves. 4 Everyone
should look out not ⌊only⌋ for his own interests,
but also for the interests of others.

Christ's Humility and Exaltation

5 Make your own attitude that of Christ
Jesus,

6 who, existing in the form of God,
did not consider equality
with God
as something to be used
for His own advantage.[l]
7 Instead He emptied Himself
by assuming the form of a slave,
taking on the likeness of men.
And when He had come as a man
in His external form,

[a]**1:3** Or *for your every remembrance of me* [b]**1:6** Or *work among you* [c]**1:7** Or *because you have me in your heart* [d]**1:10** Or *until* [e]**1:13** Lit *praetorium,* a Lat word that can also refer to a military headquarters, to the governor's palace, or to Herod's palace [f]**1:13** Lit *in Christ* [g]**1:14** Other mss add *of God* [h]**1:15** The good will of men, or God's good will or favor [i]**1:17** Lit *sincerely, intending to raise tribulation to my bonds* [j]**1:19** Or *salvation,* or *vindication* [k]**1:27** Lit *soul* [l]**2:6** Or *to be grasped,* or *to be held on to*

8 He humbled Himself
by becoming obedient
to the point of death—even to death
on a cross.
9 For this reason God also
highly exalted Him
and gave Him the name that is above
every name,
10 so that at the name of Jesus
every knee should bow—
of those who are in heaven
and on earth and under the earth—
11 and every tongue should confess
that Jesus Christ is Lord,
to the glory of God
the Father.

Lights in the World

12 So then, my dear friends, just as you have
always obeyed, not only in my presence, but
now even more in my absence, work out your
own salvation with fear and trembling. 13 For it
is God who is working in you, ⌊enabling you⌋
both to will and to act for His good purpose.
14 Do everything without grumbling and arguing, 15 so that you may be blameless and pure,
children of God who are faultless in a crooked
and perverted generation, among whom you
shine like stars in the world. 16 Hold firmly[a] the
message of life. Then I can boast in the day of
Christ that I didn't run in vain or labor for nothing. 17 But even if I am poured out as a drink
offering on the sacrifice and service of your
faith, I am glad and rejoice with all of you. 18 In
the same way you also should rejoice and share
your joy with me.

Timothy and Epaphroditus

19 Now I hope in the Lord Jesus to send
Timothy to you soon so that I also may be
encouraged when I hear news about you.
20 For I have no one else like-minded who will
genuinely care about your interests; 21 all seek
their own interests, not those of Jesus Christ.
22 But you know his proven character, because
he has served with me in the gospel ministry
like a son with a father. 23 Therefore, I hope to
send him as soon as I see how things go with
me. 24 And I am convinced in the Lord that I
myself will also come quickly.
25 But I considered it necessary to send you
Epaphroditus—my brother, co-worker, and fellow soldier, as well as your messenger and minister to my need— 26 since he has been longing
for all of you and was distressed because you
heard that he was sick. 27 Indeed, he was so
sick that he nearly died. However, God had
mercy on him, and not only on him but also on
me, so that I would not have one grief on top of
another. 28 For this reason, I am very eager to
send him so that you may rejoice when you see
him again and I may be less anxious.
29 Therefore, welcome him in the Lord with all
joy and hold men like him in honor, 30 because
he came close to death for the work of Christ,
risking his life to make up what was lacking in
your ministry to me.

Knowing Christ

3 Finally, my brothers, rejoice in the Lord.
To write to you again about this is no
trouble for me and is a protection for you.
2 Watch out for "dogs,"[b] watch out for evil
workers, watch out for those who mutilate the
flesh. 3 For we are the circumcision, the ones
who serve by the Spirit of God, boast in Christ
Jesus, and do not put confidence in the flesh—
4 although I once had confidence in the flesh
too. If anyone else thinks he has grounds for
confidence in the flesh, I have more: 5 circumcised the eighth day; of the nation of Israel, of
the tribe of Benjamin, a Hebrew born of
Hebrews; as to the law, a •Pharisee; 6 as to
zeal, persecuting the church; as to the righteousness that is in the law, blameless.
7 But everything that was a gain to me, I
have considered to be a loss because of Christ.
8 More than that, I also consider everything to
be a loss in view of the surpassing value of
knowing Christ Jesus my Lord. Because of Him
I have suffered the loss of all things and consider them filth, so that I may gain Christ 9 and
be found in Him, not having a righteousness of
my own from the law, but one that is through
faith in Christ[c] —the righteousness from God
based on faith. 10 ⌊My goal⌋ is to know Him and
the power of His resurrection and the fellowship of His sufferings, being conformed to His
death, 11 assuming that I will somehow reach
the resurrection from among the dead.

Reaching Forward to God's Goal

12 Not that I have already reached ⌊the
goal⌋ or am already fully mature, but I make
every effort to take hold of it because I also
have been taken hold of by Christ Jesus.

[a]**2:16** Or *Offer,* or *Hold out* [b]**3:2** An expression of contempt for the unclean, those outside the people of God [c]**3:9** Or *through the faithfulness of Christ*

13 Brothers, I do not[a] consider myself to have
taken hold of it. But one thing I do: forgetting
what is behind and reaching forward to what
is ahead, 14 I pursue as my goal the prize
promised by God's heavenly[b] call in Christ
Jesus. 15 Therefore, all who are mature should
think this way. And if you think differently
about anything, God will reveal this to you
also. 16 In any case, we should live up to whatever ⌊truth⌋ we have attained. 17 Join in imitat-
ing me, brothers, and observe those who live
according to the example you have in us.
18 For I have often told you, and now say again
with tears, that many live as enemies of the
cross of Christ. 19 Their end is destruction;
their god is their stomach; their glory is in
their shame. They are focused on earthly
things, 20 but our citizenship is in heaven,
from which we also eagerly wait for a Savior,
the Lord Jesus Christ. 21 He will transform the
body of our humble condition into the likeness of His glorious body, by the power that
enables Him to subject everything to Himself.

Practical Counsel

4 So then, in this way, my dearly loved
brothers, my joy and crown, stand firm in
the Lord, dear friends. 2 I urge Euodia and I
urge Syntyche to agree in the Lord. 3 Yes, I also
ask you, true partner,[c] to help these women
who have contended for the gospel at my side,
along with Clement and the rest of my co-
workers whose names are in the book of life.
4 Rejoice in the Lord always. I will say it again:
Rejoice! 5 Let your graciousness be known to
everyone. The Lord is near. 6 Don't worry
about anything, but in everything, through
prayer and petition with thanksgiving, let your
requests be made known to God. 7 And the
peace of God, which surpasses every thought,
will guard your hearts and your minds in
Christ Jesus.
8 Finally brothers, whatever is true, whatever is honorable, whatever is just, whatever is
pure, whatever is lovely, whatever is com-
mendable—if there is any moral excellence
and if there is any praise—dwell on these
things. 9 Do what you have learned and
received and heard and seen in me, and the
God of peace will be with you.

Appreciation of Support

10 I rejoiced in the Lord greatly that now at
last you have renewed your care for me. You
were, in fact, concerned about me, but lacked
the opportunity ⌊to show it⌋. 11 I don't say this
out of need, for I have learned to be content in
whatever circumstances I am. 12 I know both
how to have a little, and I know how to have
a lot. In any and all circumstances I have
learned the secret ⌊of being content⌋—
whether well-fed or hungry, whether in abundance or in need. 13 I am able to do all things
through Him[d] who strengthens me. 14 Still,
you did well by sharing with me in my hardship.
15 And you, Philippians, know that in the
early days of the gospel, when I left Macedonia, no church shared with me in the matter of giving and receiving except you alone.
16 For even in Thessalonica you sent ⌊gifts⌋ for
my need several times. 17 Not that I seek the
gift, but I seek the fruit that is increasing to
your account. 18 But I have received everything in full, and I have an abundance. I am
fully supplied, having received from Epaphroditus what you provided—a fragrant offering,
a welcome sacrifice, pleasing to God. 19 And
my God will supply all your needs according to
His riches in glory in Christ Jesus. 20 Now to
our God and Father be glory forever and ever.
•Amen.

Final Greetings

21 Greet every saint in Christ Jesus. Those
brothers who are with me greet you. 22 All the
saints greet you, but especially those from Caesar's household. 23 The grace of the Lord Jesus
Christ be with your spirit.[e]

[a]**3:13** Other mss read *not yet* [b]**3:14** Or *upward* [c]**4:3** Or *true Syzygus*, possibly a person's name [d]**4:13** Other mss read *Christ* [e]**4:23** Other mss add *Amen.*

Colossians

Greeting

1 Paul, an apostle of Christ Jesus by God's
will, and Timothy our[a] brother:
2 To the saints and faithful brothers in
Christ in Colossae.
Grace to you and peace from God our
Father.[b]

Thanksgiving

3 We always thank God, the Father of our
Lord Jesus Christ, when we pray for you, 4 for
we have heard of your faith in Christ Jesus and
of the love you have for all the saints 5 because
of the hope reserved for you in heaven. You
have already heard about ⌊this hope⌋ in the
message of truth, the gospel 6 that has come to
you. It is bearing fruit and growing all over the
world, just as it has among you since the day
you heard it and recognized God's grace in the
truth.[c] 7 You learned this from Epaphras, our
much loved fellow slave. He is a faithful minister of the •Messiah on your[d] behalf, 8 and he
has told us about your love in the Spirit.

Prayer for Spiritual Growth

9 For this reason also, since the day we
heard this, we haven't stopped praying for you.
We are asking that you may be filled with the
knowledge of His will in all wisdom and spiritual understanding, 10 so that you may •walk
worthy of the Lord, fully pleasing ⌊to Him⌋,
bearing fruit in every good work and growing in
the knowledge of God. 11 May you be strengthened with all power, according to His glorious
might, for all endurance and patience, with joy
12 giving thanks to the Father, who has enabled
you[e] to share in the saints'[f] inheritance in the
light. 13 He has rescued us from the domain of
darkness and transferred us into the kingdom
of the Son He loves, 14 in whom we have
redemption,[g] the forgiveness of sins.

The Centrality of Christ

15 He is the image of the invisible God,
the firstborn over all creation;[h]
16 because by Him everything
was created,
in heaven and on earth, the visible
and the invisible,
whether thrones or dominions
or rulers or authorities—
all things have been created
through Him and for Him.
17 He is before all things, and by Him
all things hold together.
18 He is also the head of the body,
the church;
He is the beginning, the firstborn
from the dead,
so that He might come to have
first place in everything.
19 For God was pleased ⌊to have⌋
all His fullness dwell in Him,
20 and through Him to reconcile
everything to Himself
by making peace through the blood
of His cross[i] —
whether things on earth or things
in heaven.

21 And you were once alienated and hostile
in mind because of your evil actions. 22 But
now He has reconciled you by His physical
body[j] through His death, to present you holy,
faultless, and blameless before Him— 23 if
indeed you remain grounded and steadfast in
the faith, and are not shifted away from the
hope of the gospel that you heard. ⌊This gospel⌋
has been proclaimed in all creation under
heaven, and I, Paul, have become a minister of
it.

Paul's Ministry

24 Now I rejoice in my sufferings for you,
and I am completing in my flesh what is lacking
in Christ's afflictions for His body, that is, the
church. 25 I have become its minister, according to God's administration that was given to
me for you, to make God's message fully
known, 26 the •mystery hidden for ages and
generations but now revealed to His saints.
27 God wanted to make known to those among
the Gentiles the glorious wealth of this mystery, which is Christ in you, the hope of glory.
28 We proclaim Him, warning and teaching
everyone with all wisdom, so that we may

[a] **1:1** Lit *the* [b] **1:2** Other mss add *and the Lord Jesus Christ* [c] **1:6** Or *and truly recognized God's grace* [d] **1:7** Other mss read *our* [e] **1:12** Other mss read *us* [f] **1:12** Or *holy ones'* [g] **1:14** Other mss add *through His blood* [h] **1:15** The One who is preeminent over all creation [i] **1:20** Other mss add *through Him* [j] **1:22** His body of flesh on the cross

present everyone mature in Christ. 29 I labor for this, striving with His strength that works powerfully in me.

2 For I want you to know how great a struggle I have for you, for those in Laodicea, and for all who have not seen me in person. 2 ⌊I want⌋ their hearts to be encouraged and joined together in love, so that they may have all the riches of assured understanding, and have the knowledge of God's •mystery—Christ.[a] 3 In Him all the treasures of wisdom and knowledge are hidden.

Christ versus the Colossian Heresy

4 I am saying this so that no one will deceive you with persuasive arguments. 5 For I may be absent in body, but I am with you in spirit, rejoicing to see your good order and the strength of your faith in Christ.

6 Therefore as you have received Christ Jesus the Lord, •walk in Him, 7 rooted and built up in Him and established in the faith, just as you were taught, and overflowing with thankfulness.

8 Be careful that no one takes you captive through philosophy and empty deceit based on human tradition, based on the elemental forces of the world, and not based on Christ. 9 For in Him the entire fullness of God's nature[b] dwells bodily,[c] 10 and you have been filled by Him, who is the head over every ruler and authority. 11 In Him you were also circumcised with a circumcision not done with hands, by putting off the body of flesh, in the circumcision of the •Messiah. 12 Having been buried with Him in baptism, you were also raised with Him through faith in the working of God, who raised Him from the dead. 13 And when you were dead in trespasses and in the uncircumcision of your flesh, He made you alive with Him and forgave us all our trespasses. 14 He erased the certificate of debt, with its obligations, that was against us and opposed to us, and has taken it out of the way by nailing it to the cross. 15 He disarmed the rulers and authorities and disgraced them publicly; He triumphed over them by Him.[d]

16 Therefore don't let anyone judge you in regard to food and drink or in the matter of a festival or a new moon or a sabbath day.[e] 17 These are a shadow of what was to come; the substance is[f] the Messiah. 18 Let no one disqualify you,[g] insisting on ascetic practices and the worship of angels, claiming access to a visionary realm and inflated without cause by his fleshly mind. 19 He doesn't hold on to the head, from whom the whole body, nourished and held together by its ligaments and tendons, develops with growth from God.

20 If you died with Christ to the elemental forces of this world, why do you live as if you still belonged to the world? Why do you submit to regulations: 21 "Don't handle, don't taste, don't touch"? 22 All these ⌊regulations⌋ refer to what is destroyed by being used up; they are human commands and doctrines. 23 Although these have a reputation of wisdom by promoting ascetic practices, humility, and severe treatment of the body, they are not of any value against fleshly indulgence.

The Life of the New Man

3 So if you have been raised with the •Messiah, seek what is above, where the Messiah is, seated at the right hand of God. 2 Set your minds on what is above, not on what is on the earth. 3 For you have died, and your life is hidden with the Messiah in God. 4 When the Messiah, who is your[h] life, is revealed, then you also will be revealed with Him in glory.

5 Therefore, put to death whatever in you is worldly:[i] sexual immorality, impurity, lust, evil desire, and greed, which is idolatry. 6 Because of these, God's wrath comes on the disobedient,[j] 7 and you once •walked in these things when you were living in them. 8 But now you must also put away all the following: anger, wrath, malice, slander, and filthy language from your mouth. 9 Do not lie to one another, since you have put off the old man with his practices 10 and have put on the new man, who is being renewed in knowledge according to the image of his Creator. 11 Here there is not Greek and Jew, circumcision and uncircumcision, barbarian, Scythian,[k] slave and free; but Christ is all and in all.

The Christian Life

12 Therefore, God's chosen ones, holy and loved, put on heartfelt compassion, kindness,

[a] **2:2** Other mss read *mystery of God, both of the Father and of Christ*; other ms variations exist on this v. [b] **2:9** Or *the deity* [c] **2:9** Or *nature lives in a human body* [d] **2:15** Or *them through it*; that is, through the cross [e] **2:16** Or *or sabbaths* [f] **2:17** Or *substance belongs to* [g] **2:18** Or *no one cheat us out of your prize* [h] **3:4** Other mss read *our* [i] **3:5** Lit *death, the members on the earth* [j] **3:6** Other mss omit *on the disobedient* [k] **3:11** A term for a savage

humility, gentleness, and patience, 13 accepting one another and forgiving one another if
anyone has a complaint against another. Just
as the Lord has forgiven you, so also you must
⌊forgive⌋. 14 Above all, ⌊put on⌋ love—the perfect bond of unity. 15 And let the peace of the
Messiah, to which you were also called in one
body, control your hearts. Be thankful. 16 Let
the message about the Messiah dwell richly
among you, teaching and admonishing one
another in all wisdom, and singing psalms,
hymns, and spiritual songs, with gratitude in
your hearts to God. 17 And whatever you do,
in word or in deed, do everything in the name
of the Lord Jesus, giving thanks to God the
Father through Him.

Christ in Your Home

18 Wives, be submissive to your
husbands, as is fitting in the Lord.
19 Husbands, love your wives and don't
become bitter against them.
20 Children, obey your parents in
everything, for this is pleasing in
the Lord.
21 Fathers, do not exasperate your
children, so they won't become
discouraged.
22 Slaves, obey your human masters in
everything; don't work only while
being watched, in order to please
men, but ⌊work⌋ wholeheartedly,
fearing the Lord.
23 Whatever you do, do it enthusiasti-
cally,[a] as something done for the
Lord and not for men, 24 knowing
that you will receive the reward of
an inheritance from the Lord—you
serve the Lord Christ. 25 For the
wrongdoer will be paid back for
whatever wrong he has done, and
there is no favoritism.

4 Masters, supply your slaves with what
is right and fair, since you know
that you too have a Master in
heaven.

Speaking to God and Others

2 Devote yourselves to prayer; stay alert in it
with thanksgiving. 3 At the same time, pray
also for us that God may open a door to us for
the message, to speak the •mystery of the
•Messiah—for which I am in prison— 4 so that
I may reveal it as I am required to speak.
5 •Walk in wisdom toward outsiders, making
the most of the time. 6 Your speech should
always be gracious, seasoned with salt, so that
you may know how you should answer each
person.

Christian Greetings

7 Tychicus, a loved brother, a faithful servant, and a fellow slave in the Lord, will tell you
all the news about me. 8 I have sent him to you
for this very purpose, so that you may know
how we are,[b] and so that he may encourage
your hearts. 9 He is with Onesimus, a faithful
and loved brother, who is one of you. They will
tell you about everything here.
10 Aristarchus, my fellow prisoner, greets
you, as does Mark, Barnabas' cousin (concerning whom you have received instructions: if he
comes to you, welcome him), 11 and so does
Jesus who is called Justus. These alone of the
circumcision are my co-workers for the kingdom of God, and they have been a comfort to
me. 12 Epaphras, who is one of you, a slave of
Christ Jesus, greets you. He is always contend-
ing for you in his prayers, so that you can stand
mature and fully assured[c] in everything God
wills. 13 For I testify about him that he works
hard[d] for you, for those in Laodicea, and for
those in Hierapolis. 14 Luke, the loved physi-
cian, and Demas greet you. 15 Give my greetings to the brothers in Laodicea, and to
Nympha and the church in her house. 16 And
when this letter has been read among you,
have it read also in the church of the Laodic-
eans; and see that you also read the letter from
Laodicea. 17 And tell Archippus, "Pay attention
to the ministry you have received in the Lord,
so that you can accomplish it."
18 This greeting is in my own hand—Paul.
Remember my imprisonment. Grace be with
you.[e]

[a]**3:23** Lit *do it from the soul* [b]**4:8** Other mss read *that he may know how you are* [c]**4:12** Other mss read *and complete*
[d]**4:13** Other mss read *he has a great zeal* [e]**4:18** Other mss add *Amen.*

1 Thessalonians

Greeting

1 Paul, Silvanus,[a] and Timothy:
To the church of the Thessalonians in God the Father and the Lord Jesus Christ.
Grace to you and peace.[b]

Thanksgiving

2 We always thank God for all of you, remembering you constantly in our prayers. 3 We recall, in the presence of our God and Father, your work of faith, labor of love, and endurance of hope in our Lord Jesus Christ, 4 knowing your election, brothers loved by God. 5 For our gospel did not come to you in word only, but also in power, in the Holy Spirit, and with much assurance. You know what kind of men we were among you for your benefit, 6 and you became imitators of us and of the Lord when, in spite of severe persecution, you welcomed the message with the joy from the Holy Spirit. 7 As a result, you became an example to all the believers in Macedonia and Achaia. 8 For the Lord's message rang out from you, not only in Macedonia and Achaia, but in every place that your faith[c] in God has gone out, so we don't need to say anything. 9 For they themselves report about us what kind of reception we had from you: how you turned to God from idols to serve the living and true God, 10 and to wait for His Son from heaven, whom He raised from the dead—Jesus, who rescues us from the coming wrath.

Paul's Conduct

2 For you yourselves know, brothers, that our visit with you was not without result. 2 On the contrary, after we had previously suffered and been outrageously treated in Philippi, as you know, we were emboldened by our God to speak the gospel of God to you in spite of great opposition. 3 For our exhortation didn't come from error or impurity or an intent to deceive. 4 Instead, just as we have been approved by God to be entrusted with the gospel, so we speak, not to please men, but rather God, who examines our hearts. 5 For we never used flattering speech, as you know, or had greedy motives—God is our witness— 6 and we didn't seek glory from people, either from you or from others. 7 Although we could have been a burden as Christ's apostles, instead we were gentle[d] among you, as a nursing mother nurtures her own children. 8 We cared so much for you that we were pleased to share with you not only the gospel of God but also our own lives, because you had become dear to us. 9 For you remember our labor and hardship, brothers. Working night and day so that we would not burden any of you, we preached God's gospel to you. 10 You are witnesses, and so is God, of how devoutly, righteously, and blamelessly we conducted ourselves with you believers. 11 As you know, like a father with his own children, 12 we encouraged, comforted, and implored each one of you to •walk worthy of God, who calls you into His own kingdom and glory.

Reception and Opposition to the Message

13 Also, this is why we constantly thank God, because when you received the message about God that you heard from us, you welcomed it not as a human message, but as it truly is, the message of God, which also works effectively in you believers. 14 For you, brothers, became imitators of God's churches in Christ Jesus that are in Judea, since you have also suffered the same things from people of your own country, just as they did from the Jews. 15 They killed both the Lord Jesus and the prophets, and persecuted us; they displease God, and are hostile to everyone, 16 hindering us from speaking to the Gentiles so that they may be saved. As a result, they are always adding to the number of their sins, and wrath has overtaken them completely.[e]

Paul's Desire to See Them

17 But as for us, brothers, after we were forced to leave you for a short time (in person, not in heart), we greatly desired and made every effort to return and see you face to face. 18 So we wanted to come to you—even I, Paul, time and again—but Satan hindered us. 19 For who is our hope, or joy, or crown of

[a]**1:1** Or *Silas*; see Ac 15:22–32; 16:19–40; 17:1–16 [b]**1:1** Other mss add *from God our Father and the Lord Jesus Christ*
[c]**1:8** Or *in every place news of your faith* [d]**2:7** Other mss read *infants* [e]**2:16** Or *to the end*

boasting in the presence of our Lord Jesus at
His coming? Is it not you? 20 For you are our
glory and joy!

Anxiety in Athens

3 Therefore, when we could no longer
stand it, we thought it was better to be
left alone in Athens. 2 And we sent Timothy,
our brother and God's co-worker[a] in the gospel
of Christ, to strengthen and encourage you
concerning your faith, 3 so that no one will be
shaken by these persecutions. For you yourselves know that we are appointed to[b] this.
4 In fact, when we were with you, we told you
previously that we were going to suffer persecution, and as you know, it happened. 5 For
this reason, when I could no longer stand it, I
also sent to find out about your faith, fearing
that the tempter had tempted you and that our
labor might be for nothing.

Encouraged by Timothy

6 But now Timothy has come to us from you
and brought us good news about your faith and
love, and that you always have good memories
of us, wanting to see us, as we also want to see
you. 7 Therefore, brothers, in all our distress
and persecution, we were encouraged about
you through your faith. 8 For now we live, if
you stand firm in the Lord. 9 How can we thank
God for you in return for all the joy we experience because of you before our God, 10 as we
pray earnestly night and day to see you face to
face and to complete what is lacking in your
faith?

Prayer for the Church

11 Now may our God and Father Himself,
and our Lord Jesus, direct our way to you.
12 And may the Lord cause you to increase and
overflow with love for one another and for
everyone, just as we also do for you. 13 May He
make your hearts blameless in holiness before
our God and Father at the coming of our Lord
Jesus with all His saints. •Amen.[c]

The Call to Sanctification

4 Finally then, brothers, we ask and
encourage you in the Lord Jesus, that as
you have received from us how you must
•walk and please God—as you are doing[d] —do
so even more. 2 For you know what commands we gave you through the Lord Jesus.
3 For this is God's will, your sanctification:
that you abstain from sexual immorality, 4 so
that each of you knows how to possess his
own vessel[e] in sanctification and honor, 5 not
with lustful desires, like the Gentiles who
don't know God. 6 This means one must not
transgress against and defraud his brother in
this matter, because the Lord is an avenger of
all these offenses,[f] as we also previously told
and warned you. 7 For God has not called us to
impurity, but to sanctification. 8 Therefore,
the person who rejects this does not reject
man, but God, who also gives you His Holy
Spirit.

Loving and Working

9 About brotherly love: you don't need me
to write you because you yourselves are taught
by God to love one another. 10 In fact, you are
doing this toward all the brothers in the entire
region of Macedonia. But we encourage you,
brothers, to do so even more, 11 to seek to lead
a quiet life, to mind your own business,[g] and to
work with your own hands, as we commanded
you, 12 so that you may walk properly[h] in the
presence of outsiders[i] and not be dependent on
anyone.[j]

The Comfort of Christ's Coming

13 We do not want you to be uninformed,
brothers, concerning those who are •asleep, so
that you will not grieve like the rest, who have
no hope. 14 Since we believe that Jesus died
and rose again, in the same way God will bring
with Him those who have fallen asleep
through[k] Jesus.[l] 15 For we say this to you by a
revelation from the Lord:[m] We who are still
alive at the Lord's coming will certainly have no
advantage over[n] those who have fallen asleep.
16 For the Lord Himself will descend from
heaven with a shout,[o] with the archangel's
voice, and with the trumpet of God, and the
dead in Christ will rise first. 17 Then we who
are still alive will be caught up together with
them in the clouds to meet the Lord in the air;
and so we will always be with the Lord.
18 Therefore encourage[p] one another with
these words.

[a]**3:2** Other mss read *servant* [b]**3:3** Or *we are destined for* [c]**3:13** Other mss omit *Amen.* [d]**4:1** Lit *walking* [e]**4:4** Or *to control his own body,* or *to acquire his own wife* [f]**4:6** Lit *things* [g]**4:11** Lit *to practice one's own things* [h]**4:12** Or *may live respectably* [i]**4:12** Non-Christians [j]**4:12** Or *not need anything,* or *not be in need* [k]**4:14** Or *asleep in* [l]**4:14** *those who have fallen asleep through Jesus* = Christians who have died [m]**4:15** Or *a word of the Lord* [n]**4:15** Or *certainly not precede* [o]**4:16** Or *command* [p]**4:18** Or *comfort*

The Day of the Lord

5 About the times and the seasons: brothers, you do not need anything to be written to you. 2 For you yourselves know very
well that the Day of the Lord will come just
like a thief in the night. 3 When they say,
"Peace and security," then sudden destruction
comes on them, like labor pains on a pregnant
woman, and they will not escape. 4 But you,
brothers, are not in the dark, so that this day
would overtake you like a thief. 5 For you are
all sons of light and sons of the day. We're not
of the night or of darkness. 6 So then, we must
not sleep, like the rest, but we must stay
awake and be sober. 7 For those who sleep,
sleep at night, and those who get drunk are
drunk at night. 8 But since we are of the day,
we must be sober and put the armor of faith
and love on our chests, and put on a helmet of
the hope of salvation. 9 For God did not
appoint us to wrath, but to obtain salvation
through our Lord Jesus Christ, 10 who died for
us, so that whether we are awake or •asleep,
we will live together with Him. 11 Therefore
encourage one another and build each other
up as you are already doing.

Exhortations and Blessings

12 Now we ask you, brothers, to give recognition to those who labor among you and lead
you in the Lord and admonish you, 13 and to
esteem them very highly in love because of
their work. Be at peace among yourselves.
14 And we exhort you, brothers: warn those
who are lazy,[a] comfort the discouraged, help
the weak, be patient with everyone. 15 See to it
that no one repays evil for evil to anyone, but
always pursue what is good for one another and
for all.

16 Rejoice always!
17 Pray constantly.
18 Give thanks in everything,
for this is God's will for you
in Christ Jesus.
19 Don't stifle the Spirit.
20 Don't despise prophecies,
21 but test all things.
Hold on to what is good.
22 Stay away from every form
of evil.

23 Now may the God of peace Himself sanctify you completely. And may your spirit, soul,
and body be kept sound and blameless for the
coming of our Lord Jesus Christ. 24 He who
calls you is faithful, who also will do it.
25 Brothers, pray for us also. 26 Greet all the
brothers with a holy kiss. 27 I charge you by the
Lord that this letter be read to all the brothers.
28 May the grace of our Lord Jesus Christ be
with you!

2 Thessalonians

Greeting

1 Paul, Silvanus,[b] and Timothy:
To the church of the Thessalonians in
God our Father and the Lord Jesus Christ.
2 Grace to you and peace from God our
Father and the Lord Jesus Christ.

God's Judgment and Glory

3 We must always thank God for you, brothers, which is fitting, since your faith is flourishing, and the love of every one of you for one
another is increasing. 4 Therefore we ourselves
boast about you among God's churches—about
your endurance and faith in all the persecutions
and afflictions you endure. 5 It is a clear evidence of God's righteous judgment that you
will be counted worthy of God's kingdom, for
which you also are suffering, 6 since it is righteous for God to repay with affliction those who
afflict you, 7 and ⌊to reward⌋ with rest you who
are afflicted, along with us. ⌊This will take
place⌋ at the revelation of the Lord Jesus from
heaven with His powerful angels, 8 taking vengeance with flaming fire on those who don't
know God and on those who don't obey the
gospel of our Lord Jesus. 9 These will pay the
penalty of everlasting destruction, away from
the Lord's presence and from His glorious

[a]**5:14** Or *who are disorderly,* or *who are undisciplined* [b]**1:1** Or *Silas;* see Ac 15:22–32; 16:19–40; 17:1–16

strength, 10 in that day when He comes to be glorified by His saints and to be admired by all those who have believed, because our testimony among you was believed. 11 And in view of this, we always pray for you that our God will consider you worthy of His calling, and will, by His power, fulfill every desire for goodness and the work of faith, 12 so that the name of our Lord Jesus will be glorified by you, and you by Him, according to the grace of our God and the Lord Jesus Christ.

The Man of Lawlessness

2 Now concerning the coming of our Lord Jesus Christ and our being gathered to Him: we ask you, brothers, 2 not to be easily upset in mind or troubled, either by a spirit or by a message or by a letter as if from us, alleging that the Day of the Lord[a] has come. 3 Don't let anyone deceive you in any way. For ⌊that day⌋ will not come unless the apostasy[b] comes first and the man of lawlessness[c] is revealed, the son of destruction. 4 He opposes and exalts himself above every so-called god or object of worship, so that he sits[d] in God's sanctuary,[e] publicizing that he himself is God.

5 Don't you remember that when I was still with you I told you about this? 6 And you know what currently restrains ⌊him⌋, so that he will be revealed in his time. 7 For the •mystery of lawlessness is already at work; but the one now restraining will do so until he is out of the way, 8 and then the lawless one will be revealed. The Lord Jesus will destroy him with the breath of His mouth and will bring him to nothing with the brightness of His coming. 9 The coming ⌊of the lawless one⌋ is based on Satan's working, with all kinds of false miracles, signs, and wonders, 10 and with every unrighteous deception among those who are perishing. ⌊They perish⌋ because they did not accept the love of the truth in order to be saved. 11 For this reason God sends them a strong delusion so that they will believe what is false, 12 so that all will be condemned—those who did not believe the truth but enjoyed unrighteousness.

Stand Firm

13 But we must always thank God for you, brothers loved by the Lord, because from the beginning[f] God has chosen you for salvation through sanctification by the Spirit and through belief in the truth. 14 He called you to this through our gospel, so that you might obtain the glory of our Lord Jesus Christ. 15 Therefore, brothers, stand firm and hold to the traditions you were taught, either by our message or by our letter.

16 May our Lord Jesus Christ Himself and God our Father, who has loved us and given us eternal encouragement and good hope by grace, 17 encourage your hearts and strengthen you in every good work and word.

Pray for Us

3 Finally, pray for us, brothers, that the Lord's message may spread rapidly and be honored, just as it was with you, 2 and that we may be delivered from wicked and evil men, for not all have faith. 3 But the Lord is faithful; He will strengthen and guard you from the evil one. 4 We have confidence in the Lord about you, that you are doing and will do what we command. 5 May the Lord direct your hearts to God's love and Christ's endurance.

Warning against Irresponsible Behavior

6 Now we command you, brothers, in the name of our Lord Jesus Christ, to keep away from every brother who •walks irresponsibly and not according to the tradition received from us. 7 For you yourselves know how you must imitate us: we were not irresponsible among you; 8 we did not eat anyone's bread free of charge; instead, we labored and toiled, working night and day, so that we would not be a burden to any of you. 9 It is not that we don't have the right ⌊to support⌋, but we did it to make ourselves an example to you so that you would imitate us. 10 In fact, when we were with you, this is what we commanded you: "If anyone isn't willing to work, he should not eat." 11 For we hear that there are some among you who walk irresponsibly, not working at all, but interfering with the work ⌊of others⌋. 12 Now we command and exhort such people, by the Lord Jesus Christ, that quietly working, they may eat their own bread.[g] 13 Brothers, do not grow weary in doing good.

14 And if anyone does not obey our instruction in this letter, take note of that person; don't associate with him, so that he may be

[a]**2:2** Other mss read *Christ* [b]**2:3** Or *rebellion* [c]**2:3** Other mss read *man of sin* [d]**2:4** Other mss add *as God* [e]**2:4** Or *temple* [f]**2:13** Other mss read *because as a firstfruit* [g]**3:12** Or *food*

ashamed. 15 Yet don't treat him as an enemy, but warn him as a brother.

Final Greetings

16 May the Lord of peace Himself give you peace always in every way. The Lord be with all of you. 17 This greeting is in my own hand—Paul. This is a sign in every letter; this is how I write. 18 The grace of our Lord Jesus Christ be with all of you.

1 Timothy

Greeting

1 Paul, an apostle of Christ Jesus according to the command of God our Savior and of Christ Jesus, our hope:

2 To Timothy, my true child in the faith.

Grace, mercy, and peace from God the[a] Father and Christ Jesus our Lord.

False Doctrine and Misuse of the Law

3 As I urged you when I went to Macedonia, remain in Ephesus so that you may command certain people not to teach other doctrine 4 or to pay attention to myths and endless genealogies. These promote empty speculations rather than God's plan, which operates by faith. 5 Now the goal of our instruction is love from a pure heart, a good conscience, and a sincere faith. 6 Some have deviated from these and turned aside to fruitless discussion. 7 They want to be teachers of the law, although they don't understand what they are saying or what they are insisting on. 8 Now we know that the law is good, provided one uses it legitimately. 9 We know that the law is not meant for a righteous person, but for the lawless and rebellious, for the ungodly and sinful, for the unholy and irreverent, for those who kill their fathers and mothers, for murderers, 10 for the sexually immoral and homosexuals, for kidnappers, liars, perjurers, and for whatever else is contrary to the sound teaching 11 based on the glorious gospel of the blessed God that was entrusted to me.

Paul's Testimony

12 I give thanks to Christ Jesus our Lord, who has strengthened me, because He considered me faithful, appointing me to the ministry— 13 one who was formerly a blasphemer, a persecutor, and an arrogant man. Since it was out of ignorance that I had acted in unbelief, I received mercy, 14 and the grace of our Lord overflowed, along with the faith and love that are in Christ Jesus. 15 This saying is trustworthy and deserving of full acceptance: "Christ Jesus came into the world to save sinners"—and I am the worst of them. 16 But I received mercy because of this, so that in me, the worst ⌊of them⌋, Christ Jesus might demonstrate the utmost patience as an example to those who would believe in Him for eternal life. 17 Now to the King eternal, immortal, invisible, the only[b] God, be honor and glory forever and ever. •Amen.

Engage in Battle

18 Timothy, my child, I am giving you this instruction in keeping with the prophecies previously made about you, so that by them you may strongly engage in battle, 19 having faith and a good conscience. Some have rejected these and have suffered the shipwreck of their faith. 20 Hymenaeus and Alexander are among them, and I have delivered them to Satan, so that they may be taught not to blaspheme.

Instructions on Prayer

2 First of all, then, I urge that petitions, prayers, intercessions, and thanksgivings be made for everyone, 2 for kings and all those who are in authority, so that we may lead a tranquil and quiet life in all godliness and dignity. 3 This is good, and it pleases God our Savior, 4 who wants everyone to be saved and to come to the knowledge of the truth.

5 For there is one God
and one mediator between God
and man,
a man, Christ Jesus,

[a]1:2 Other mss read *our* [b]1:17 Other mss add *wise*

6 who gave Himself—a ransom for all,
a testimony at the proper time.

7 For this I was appointed a herald, an apostle (I am telling the truth;[a] I am not lying), and a teacher of the Gentiles in faith and truth.

Instructions to Men and Women

8 Therefore I want the men in every place
to pray, lifting up holy hands without anger or
argument. 9 Also, the women are to dress
themselves in modest clothing, with decency
and good sense; not with elaborate hairstyles,
gold, pearls, or expensive apparel, 10 but with
good works, as is proper for women who
affirm that they worship God. 11 A woman
should learn in silence with full submission.
12 I do not allow a woman to teach or to have
authority over a man; instead, she is to be
silent. 13 For Adam was created first, then
Eve. 14 And Adam was not deceived, but the
woman was deceived and transgressed. 15 But
she will be saved through childbearing, if she
continues[b] in faith, love, and holiness, with
good sense.

Qualifications of Church Leaders

3 This saying is trustworthy:[c] "If anyone
aspires to be an •overseer, he desires a
noble work." 2 An overseer, therefore, must be
above reproach, the husband of one wife, self-
controlled, sensible, respectable, hospitable,
an able teacher,[d] 3 not addicted to wine, not a
bully but gentle, not quarrelsome, not
greedy— 4 one who manages his own household competently, having his children under
control with all dignity. 5 (If anyone does not
know how to manage his own household, how
will he take care of God's church?) 6 He must
not be a new convert, or he might become
conceited and fall into the condemnation of
the Devil. 7 Furthermore, he must have a good
reputation among outsiders, so that he does
not fall into disgrace and the Devil's trap.

8 Deacons, likewise, should be worthy of
respect, not hypocritical, not drinking a lot of
wine, not greedy for money, 9 holding the
•mystery of the faith with a clear conscience.
10 And they must also be tested first; if they
prove blameless, then they can serve as deacons. 11 Wives, too, must be worthy of respect,
not slanderers, self-controlled, faithful in everything. 12 Deacons must be husbands of one
wife, managing their children and their own
households competently. 13 For those who
have served well as deacons acquire a good
standing for themselves, and great boldness in
the faith that is in Christ Jesus.

The Mystery of Godliness

14 I write these things to you, hoping to
come to you soon. 15 But if I should be delayed,
⌊I have written⌋ so that you will know how people ought to act in God's household, which is
the church of the living God, the pillar and
foundation of the truth. 16 And most certainly,
the mystery of godliness is great:

He[e] was manifested in the flesh,
justified in the Spirit,
seen by angels,
preached among the Gentiles,
believed on in the world,
taken up in glory.

Demonic Influence

4 Now the Spirit explicitly says that in the
latter times some will depart from the
faith, paying attention to deceitful spirits and
the teachings of demons, 2 through the
hypocrisy of liars whose consciences are
seared. 3 They forbid marriage and demand
abstinence from foods that God created to be
received with gratitude by those who believe
and know the truth. 4 For everything created
by God is good, and nothing should be
rejected if it is received with thanksgiving,
5 since it is sanctified by the word of God and
by prayer.

A Good Servant of Jesus Christ

6 If you point these things out to the brothers, you will be a good servant of Christ Jesus,
nourished by the words of the faith and of the
good teaching that you have followed. 7 But
have nothing to do with irreverent and silly
myths. Rather, train yourself in godliness,
8 for,

the training of the body has
a limited benefit,
but godliness is beneficial
in every way,
since it holds promise
for the present life
and also for the life to come.

[a] **2:7** Other mss add *in Christ* [b] **2:15** Lit *if they continue* [c] **3:1** *This saying is trustworthy* could refer to 1 Tm 2:15. [d] **3:2** Or *hospitable, skillful in teaching* [e] **3:16** Other mss read *God*

9 This saying is trustworthy and deserves full
acceptance. 10 In fact, we labor and strive[a] for
this, because we have put our hope in the living God, who is the Savior of everyone, especially of those who believe.

Instructions for Ministry

11 Command and teach these things. 12 No
one should despise your youth; instead, you
should be an example to the believers in
speech, in conduct, in love,[b] in faith, in purity.
13 Until I come, give your attention to public
reading, exhortation, and teaching. 14 Do not
neglect the gift that is in you; it was given to
you through prophecy, with the laying on of
hands by the council of elders. 15 Practice
these things; be committed to them, so that
your progress may be evident to all. 16 Be con-
scientious about yourself and your teaching;
persevere in these things, for by doing this
you will save both yourself and your hearers.

5 Do not rebuke an older man, but exhort
him as a father, younger men as brothers,
2 older women as mothers, and with all propri-
ety, the younger women as sisters.

The Support of Widows

3 Support[c] widows who are genuinely widows. 4 But if any widow has children or grandchildren, they should learn to practice their
religion toward their own family first and to
repay their parents, for this pleases God. 5 The
real widow, left all alone, has put her hope in
God and continues night and day in her petitions and prayers; 6 however, she who is self-
indulgent is dead even while she lives. 7 Command this, so that they won't be blamed. 8 Now
if anyone does not provide for his own relatives,
and especially for his household, he has denied
the faith and is worse than an unbeliever.

9 No widow should be placed on the official
support list[d] unless she is at least 60 years old,
has been the wife of one husband, 10 and is well
known for good works—that is, if she has
brought up children, shown hospitality, washed
the saints' feet, helped the afflicted, and
devoted herself to every good work. 11 But
refuse to enroll younger widows; for when they
are drawn away from Christ by desire, they
want to marry, 12 and will therefore receive
condemnation because they have renounced
their original pledge. 13 At the same time, they
also learn to be idle, going from house to house;
they are not only idle, but are also gossips and
busybodies, saying things they shouldn't say.
14 Therefore, I want younger women to marry,
have children, manage their households, and
give the adversary no opportunity to accuse us.
15 For some have already turned away to follow
Satan. 16 If any[e] believing woman has widows,
she should help them, and the church should
not be burdened, so that it can help those who
are genuinely widows.

Honoring the Elders

17 The elders who are good leaders should
be considered worthy of an ample honorarium,[f]
especially those who work hard at preaching
and teaching. 18 For the Scripture says:

> **You must not muzzle an ox**
> **that is threshing grain,**[g]
> **and,**
> The laborer is worthy
> of his wages.

19 Don't accept an accusation against an
elder unless it is supported by two or three
witnesses. 20 Publicly rebuke[h] those who sin,
so that the rest will also be afraid. 21 I solemnly charge you, before God and Christ
Jesus and the elect angels, to observe these
things without prejudice, doing nothing out of
favoritism. 22 Don't be too quick to lay hands
on[i] anyone, and don't share in the sins of others. Keep yourself pure. 23 Don't continue
drinking only water, but use a little wine
because of your stomach and your frequent ill-
nesses. 24 Some people's sins are evident,
going before them to judgment, but ⌊the sins⌋
of others follow them. 25 Likewise, good
works are obvious, and those that are not ⌊ob-
vious⌋ cannot remain hidden.

Honoring Masters

6 All who are under the yoke as slaves
must regard their own masters to be
worthy of all respect, so that God's name and
His teaching will not be blasphemed. 2 And
those who have believing masters should not
be disrespectful to them because they are
brothers, but should serve them better, since
those who benefit from their service are
believers and dearly loved.

[a]**4:10** Other mss read *and suffer reproach* [b]**4:12** Other mss add *in spirit* [c]**5:3** Lit *Honor* [d]**5:9** Lit *be enrolled* [e]**5:16** Other mss add *believing man or* [f]**5:17** Lit *of double honor,* or possibly *of respect and remuneration* [g]**5:18** Dt 25:4 [h]**5:20** Before the congregation [i]**5:22** To ordain

False Doctrine and Human Greed

Teach and encourage these things. 3 If anyone teaches other doctrine and does not agree with the sound teaching of our Lord Jesus Christ and with the teaching that promotes godliness, 4 he is conceited, understanding nothing, but having a sick interest in disputes and arguments over words. From these come envy, quarreling, slanders, evil suspicions, 5 and constant disagreement among men whose minds are depraved and deprived of the truth, who imagine that godliness[a] is a way to material gain.[b] 6 But godliness with contentment is a great gain.

7 For we brought nothing
into the world, and[c] we can take
nothing out.
8 But if we have food and clothing,[d]
we will be content with these.

9 But those who want to be rich fall into temptation, a trap, and many foolish and harmful desires, which plunge people into ruin and destruction. 10 For the love of money is a root[e] of all kinds of evil, and by craving it, some have wandered away from the faith and pierced themselves with many pains.

Compete for the Faith

11 Now you, man of God, run
from these things;
but pursue righteousness, godliness,
faith,
love, endurance, and gentleness.
12 Fight the good fight for the faith;
take hold of eternal life,
to which you were called
and have made a good confession
before many witnesses.

13 In the presence of God, who gives life to all, and before Christ Jesus, who gave a good confession before Pontius •Pilate, I charge you 14 to keep the commandment without spot or blame until the appearing of our Lord Jesus Christ, 15 which God[f] will bring about in His own time. ⌊He is⌋

the blessed and only Sovereign,
the King of kings,
and the Lord of lords,
16 the only One who has immortality,
dwelling in unapproachable light,
whom none of mankind has seen
or can see,
to whom be honor and eternal might.
•Amen.

Instructions to the Rich

17 Instruct those who are rich in the present age not to be arrogant or to set their hope on the uncertainty of wealth, but on God,[g] who richly provides us with all things to enjoy. 18 ⌊Instruct them⌋ to do good, to be rich in good works, to be generous, willing to share, 19 storing up for themselves a good foundation for the age to come, so that they may take hold of life that is real.

Guard the Heritage

20 Timothy, guard what has been entrusted to you, avoiding irreverent, empty speech and contradictions from the "knowledge" that falsely bears that name. 21 By professing it, some people have deviated from the faith.

Grace be with all of you.

2 Timothy

Greeting

1 Paul, an apostle of Christ Jesus by God's will, for the promise of life in Christ Jesus:

2 To Timothy, my dearly loved child.

Grace, mercy, and peace from God the Father and Christ Jesus our Lord.

Thanksgiving

3 I thank God, whom I serve with a clear conscience as my forefathers did, when I constantly remember you in my prayers night and day. 4 Remembering your tears, I long to see you so that I may be filled with

[a]**6:5** Referring to religion as a means of financial gain [b]**6:5** Other mss add *From such people withdraw yourself.* [c]**6:7** Other mss add *it is clear that* [d]**6:8** Or *food and shelter* [e]**6:10** Or *is the root* [f]**6:15** Lit *He* [g]**6:17** Other mss read *on the living God*

joy, 5 clearly recalling your sincere faith that
first lived in your grandmother Lois, then in
your mother Eunice, and that I am convinced
is in you also.
6 Therefore, I remind you to keep ablaze the
gift of God that is in you through the laying on
of my hands. 7 For God has not given us a spirit[a]
of fearfulness, but one of power, love, and
sound judgment.

Not Ashamed of the Gospel

8 So don't be ashamed of the testimony
about our Lord, or of me His prisoner. Instead,
share in suffering for the gospel, relying on the
power of God,

9 who has saved us and called us
with a holy calling,
not according to our works,
but according to His own purpose
and grace,
which was given to us
in Christ Jesus
before time began.
10 This has now been made evident
through the appearing of our Savior
Christ Jesus,
who has abolished death
and has brought life and immortality
to light through the gospel.

11 For this ⌊gospel⌋ I was appointed a herald,
apostle, and teacher,[b] 12 and that is why I suffer these things. But I am not ashamed,
because I know whom I have believed and am
persuaded that He is able to guard what has
been entrusted to me[c] until that day.

Be Loyal to the Faith

13 Hold on to the pattern of sound teaching
that you have heard from me, in the faith and
love that are in Christ Jesus. 14 Guard, through
the Holy Spirit who lives in us, that good thing
entrusted to you. 15 This you know: all those in
Asia have turned away from me, including
Phygelus and Hermogenes. 16 May the Lord
grant mercy to the household of Onesiphorus,
because he often refreshed me and was not
ashamed of my chains. 17 On the contrary,
when he was in Rome, he diligently searched
for me and found me. 18 May the Lord grant
that he obtain mercy from the Lord on that day.
And you know how much he ministered at
Ephesus.

Be Strong in Grace

2 You, therefore, my child, be strong in the
grace that is in Christ Jesus. 2 And what
you have heard from me in the presence of
many witnesses, commit to faithful men who
will be able to teach others also.
3 Share in suffering as a good soldier of
Christ Jesus. 4 To please the recruiter, no one
serving as a soldier gets entangled in the concerns of everyday life. 5 Also, if anyone competes as an athlete, he is not crowned unless he
competes according to the rules. 6 It is the
hardworking farmer who ought to be the first
to get a share of the crops. 7 Consider what I
say, for the Lord will give you understanding in
everything.
8 Keep in mind Jesus Christ, risen from
the dead, descended from David, according
to my gospel. 9 For this I suffer, to the point
of being bound like a criminal; but God's
message is not bound. 10 This is why I
endure all things for the elect: so that they
also may obtain salvation, which is in Christ
Jesus, with eternal glory. 11 This saying is
trustworthy:

For if we have died with Him,
we will also live with Him;
12 if we endure,
we will also reign with Him;
if we deny Him, He will also deny us;
13 if we are faithless, He remains faithful,
for He cannot deny Himself.

An Approved Worker

14 Remind them of these things, charging
them before God[d] not to fight about words;
this is in no way profitable and leads to the
ruin of the hearers. 15 Be diligent to present
yourself approved to God, a worker who
doesn't need to be ashamed, correctly teaching the word of truth. 16 But avoid irreverent, empty speech, for this will produce an
even greater measure of godlessness. 17 And
their word will spread like gangrene, among
whom are Hymenaeus and Philetus. 18 They
have deviated from the truth, saying that the
resurrection has already taken place, and are
overturning the faith of some. 19 Nevertheless, God's solid foundation stands firm, having this inscription:

The Lord knows those who are His,[e]
and

[a]**1:7** Or *Spirit* [b]**1:11** Other mss add *of the Gentiles* [c]**1:12** Or *guard what I have entrusted to Him*, or *guard my deposit*
[d]**2:14** Other mss read *before the Lord* [e]**2:19** Nm 16:5

Everyone who names the name
of the Lord
must turn away from unrighteousness.

20 Now in a large house there are not only
gold and silver bowls, but also those of wood
and earthenware, some for special[a] use, some
for ordinary. 21 So if anyone purifies himself
from these things, he will be a special[b] instrument, set apart, useful to the Master, prepared
for every good work.

22 Flee from youthful passions, and pursue
righteousness, faith, love, and peace, along with
those who call on the Lord from a pure heart.
23 But reject foolish and ignorant disputes,
knowing that they breed quarrels. 24 The Lord's
slave must not quarrel, but must be gentle to
everyone, able to teach,[c] and patient,
25 instructing his opponents with gentleness.
Perhaps God will grant them repentance to
know the truth. 26 Then they may come to their
senses and escape the Devil's trap, having been
captured by him to do his will.

Difficult Times Ahead

3 But know this: difficult times will come
in the last days. 2 For people will be lovers of self, lovers of money, boastful, proud,
blasphemers, disobedient to parents, ungrateful, unholy, 3 unloving, irreconcilable, slanderers, without self-control, brutal, without love
for what is good, 4 traitors, reckless, conceited,
lovers of pleasure rather than lovers of God,
5 holding to the form of religion but denying its
power. Avoid these people!

6 For among them are those who worm
their way into households and capture idle
women burdened down with sins, led along by
a variety of passions, 7 always learning and
never able to come to a knowledge of the truth.
8 Just as Jannes and Jambres resisted Moses, so
these also resist the truth, men who are corrupt
in mind, worthless in regard to the faith. 9 But
they will not make further progress, for their
lack of understanding will be clear to all, as
theirs[d] was also.

The Sacred Scriptures

10 But you have followed my teaching, conduct, purpose, faith, patience, love, and endurance, 11 along with the persecutions and
sufferings that came to me in Antioch, Iconium, and Lystra. What persecutions I
endured! Yet the Lord rescued me from them
all. 12 In fact, all those who want to live a godly
life in Christ Jesus will be persecuted. 13 Evil
people and imposters will become worse,
deceiving and being deceived. 14 But as for you,
continue in what you have learned and firmly
believed, knowing those from whom you
learned, 15 and that from childhood you have
known the sacred Scriptures, which are able to
instruct you for salvation through faith in Christ
Jesus. 16 All Scripture is inspired by God[e] and is
profitable for teaching, for rebuking, for cor-
recting for training in righteousness, 17 so that
the man of God may be complete, equipped for
every good work.

Fulfill Your Ministry

4 Before God and Christ Jesus, who is
going to judge the living and the dead,
and by His appearing and His kingdom, I solemnly charge you: 2 proclaim the message; per-
sist in it whether convenient or not; rebuke,
correct, and encourage with great patience and
teaching. 3 For the time will come when they
will not tolerate sound doctrine, but according
to their own desires, will accumulate teachers
for themselves because they have an itch to
hear something new.[f] 4 They will turn away
from hearing the truth and will turn aside to
myths. 5 But as for you, keep a clear head about
everything, endure hardship, do the work of an
evangelist, fulfill your ministry.

6 For I am already being poured out as a
drink offering, and the time for my departure
is close. 7 I have fought the good fight, I have
finished the race, I have kept the faith. 8 In
the future, there is reserved for me the crown
of righteousness, which the Lord, the righteous Judge, will give me on that day, and not
only to me, but to all those who have loved His
appearing.

Final Instructions

9 Make every effort to come to me soon,
10 for Demas has deserted me, because he
loved this present world, and has gone to Thessalonica. Crescens has gone to Galatia, Titus to
Dalmatia. 11 Only Luke is with me. Bring Mark
with you, for he is useful to me in the ministry.
12 I have sent Tychicus to Ephesus. 13 When
you come, bring the cloak I left in Troas with

[a]**2:20** Or *honorable* [b]**2:21** Or *an honorable* [c]**2:24** Or *everyone, skillful in teaching* [d]**3:9** Referring to Jannes and Jambres [e]**3:16** Lit *breathed out by God*; the Scripture is the product of God's Spirit working through men; see 2 Pt 1:20–21. [f]**4:3** Or *to hear what they want to hear*; lit *themselves, itching in the hearing*

Carpus, as well as the scrolls, especially the parchments. 14 Alexander the coppersmith did great harm to me. The Lord will repay him according to his works. 15 Watch out for him yourself, because he strongly opposed our words.

16 At my first defense, no one came to my assistance, but everyone deserted me. May it not be counted against them. 17 But the Lord stood with me and strengthened me, so that the proclamation might be fully made through me, and all the Gentiles might hear. So I was rescued from the lion's mouth. 18 The Lord will rescue me from every evil work and will bring me safely into His heavenly kingdom. To Him be the glory forever and ever! •Amen.

Benediction

19 Greet Prisca and Aquila, and the household of Onesiphorus. 20 Erastus has remained at Corinth; Trophimus I left sick at Miletus. 21 Make every effort to come before winter. Eubulus greets you, as do Pudens, Linus, Claudia, and all the brothers.

22 The Lord be with your spirit. Grace be with you!

Titus

Greeting

1 Paul, a slave of God, and an apostle of Jesus Christ for the faith of God's elect and the knowledge of the truth that leads[a] to godliness, 2 in the hope of eternal life that God, who cannot lie, promised before time began, 3 and has in His own time revealed His message in the proclamation that I was entrusted with by the command of God our Savior:

4 To Titus, my true child in our common faith.

Grace and peace from God the Father and Christ Jesus our Savior.

Titus' Ministry in Crete

5 The reason I left you in Crete was to set right what was left undone and, as I directed you, to appoint elders in every town: 6 someone who is blameless, the husband of one wife, having faithful[b] children not accused of wildness or rebellion. 7 For an •overseer, as God's manager, must be blameless, not arrogant, not quick tempered, not addicted to wine, not a bully, not greedy for money, 8 but hospitable, loving what is good, sensible, righteous, holy, self-controlled, 9 holding to the faithful message as taught, so that he will be able both to encourage with sound teaching and to refute those who contradict it.

10 For there are also many rebellious people, idle talkers and deceivers, especially those from Judaism.[c] 11 It is necessary to silence them; they overthrow whole households by teaching for dishonest gain what they should not. 12 One of their very own prophets said,

> Cretans are always liars, evil beasts,
> lazy gluttons.[d]

13 This testimony is true. So, rebuke them sharply, that they may be sound in the faith 14 and may not pay attention to Jewish myths and the commandments of men who reject the truth.

15 To the pure, everything is pure, but to those who are defiled and unbelieving nothing is pure; in fact, both their mind and conscience are defiled. 16 They profess to know God, but they deny Him by their works. They are detestable, disobedient, and disqualified for any good work.

Sound Teaching

2 But you must speak what is consistent with sound teaching. 2 Older men are to be self-controlled, worthy of respect, sensible, and sound in faith, love, and endurance. 3 In the same way, older women are to be reverent in behavior, not slanderers, not addicted to much wine. ⌊They are⌋ to teach what is good, 4 so that they may encourage the young women to love their husbands and children, 5 to be sensible, pure, good homemakers, and submissive to their husbands, so that God's message will not be slandered.

[a]**1:1** Or *corresponds* [b]**1:6** Or *believing* [c]**1:10** Lit *the circumcision* [d]**1:12** This saying is from the Cretan poet Epimenides (6th century B.C.).

6 Likewise, encourage the young men to be
sensible 7 about everything. Set an example of
good works yourself, with integrity and dignity[a]
in your teaching. 8 Your message is to be sound
beyond reproach, so that the opponent will be
ashamed, having nothing bad to say about us.
9 Slaves are to be submissive to their masters in everything, and to be well-pleasing, not
talking back 10 or stealing, but demonstrating
utter faithfulness, so that they may adorn the
teaching of God our Savior in everything.
11 For the grace of God has appeared, with
salvation[b] for all people, 12 instructing us to
deny godlessness and worldly lusts and to live
in a sensible, righteous, and godly way in the
present age, 13 while we wait for the blessed
hope and the appearing of the glory of our great
God and Savior, Jesus Christ. 14 He gave Himself for us to redeem us from all lawlessness and
to cleanse for Himself a special people, eager to
do good works.
15 Say these things, and encourage and
rebuke with all authority. Let no one disregard[c]
you.

The Importance of Good Works

3 Remind them to be submissive to rulers
and authorities, to obey, to be ready for
every good work, 2 to slander no one, to avoid
fighting, and to be kind, always showing gentleness to all people. 3 For we too were once
foolish, disobedient, deceived, captives of various passions and pleasures, living in malice
and envy, hateful, detesting one another.

4 But when the goodness and love
for man
appeared from God our Savior,
5 He saved us—
not by works of righteousness
that we had done,
but according to His mercy,
through the washing of regeneration
and renewal by the Holy Spirit.
6 This ⌊Spirit⌋ He poured out
on us abundantly
through Jesus Christ our Savior,
7 so that having been justified
by His grace,
we may become heirs with the hope
of eternal life.

8 This saying is trustworthy. I want you to
insist on these things, so that those who have
believed God might be careful to devote themselves to good works. These are good and profitable for everyone. 9 But avoid foolish debates,
genealogies, quarrels, and disputes about the
law, for they are unprofitable and worthless.
10 Reject a divisive person after a first and second warning, 11 knowing that such a person is
perverted and sins, being self-condemned.

Final Instructions and Closing

12 When I send Artemas to you, or Tychicus, make every effort to come to me in Nicop-
olis, for I have decided to spend the winter
there. 13 Diligently help Zenas the lawyer and
Apollos on their journey, so that they will lack
nothing.
14 And our people must also learn to devote
themselves to good works for cases of urgent
need, so that they will not be unfruitful. 15 All
those who are with me greet you. Greet those
who love us in the faith. Grace be with all of
you.

Philemon

Greeting

Paul, a prisoner of Christ Jesus, and Timothy, our brother:
To Philemon, our dear friend and co-
worker, 2 to Apphia our sister,[d] to Archippus
our fellow soldier, and to the church that meets
in your house.
3 Grace to you and peace from God our
Father and the Lord Jesus Christ.

Philemon's Love and Faith

4 I always thank my God when I mention you
in my prayers, 5 because I hear of your love and
faith toward[e] the Lord Jesus and for all the saints.

[a]2:7 Other mss add *incorruptibility* [b]2:11 Or *appeared, bringing salvation* [c]2:15 Or *despise* [d]2 Other mss read *our beloved* [e]5 Lit *faith that you have toward*

6 ⌊I pray⌋ that your participation in the faith may become effective through knowing every good thing that is in us[a] for ⌊the glory of⌋ Christ. 7 For I have great joy and encouragement from your love, because the hearts of the saints have been refreshed through you, brother.

An Appeal for Onesimus

8 For this reason, although I have great boldness in Christ to command you to do what is right, 9 I appeal, instead, on the basis of love. I, Paul, as an elderly man[b] and now also as a prisoner of Christ Jesus, 10 appeal to you for my child, whom I fathered[c] while in chains—Onesimus.[d] 11 Once he was useless to you, but now he is useful to both you and me. 12 I am sending him—a part of myself[e] —back to you.[f] 13 I wanted to keep him with me, so that in my imprisonment for the gospel he might serve me in your place. 14 But I didn't want to do anything without your consent, so that your good deed might not be out of obligation, but of your own free will. 15 For perhaps this is why he was separated ⌊from you⌋ for a brief time, so that you might get him back permanently, 16 no longer as a slave, but more than a slave—as a dearly loved brother. This is especially so to me, but even more to you, both in the flesh and in the Lord.[g]

17 So if you consider me a partner, accept him as you would me. 18 And if he has wronged you in any way, or owes you anything, charge that to my account. 19 I, Paul, write this with my own hand: I will repay it—not to mention to you that you owe me even your own self. 20 Yes, brother, may I have joy from you in the Lord; refresh my heart in Christ. 21 Since I am confident of your obedience, I am writing to you, knowing that you will do even more than I say. 22 But meanwhile, also prepare a guest room for me, for I hope that through your prayers I will be restored to you.

Final Greetings

23 Epaphras, my fellow prisoner in Christ Jesus, greets you, and so do 24 Mark, Aristarchus, Demas, and Luke, my co-workers.

25 The grace of the Lord[h] Jesus Christ be with your spirit.

Hebrews

The Nature of the Son

1 Long ago God spoke to the fathers by the prophets at different times and in different ways. 2 In these last days, He has spoken to us by ⌊His⌋ Son, whom He has appointed heir of all things and through whom He made the universe.[i] 3 He is the radiance[j] of His glory, the exact expression[k] of His nature, and He sustains all things by His powerful word. After making purification for sins,[l] He sat down at the right hand of the Majesty on high.[m] 4 So He became higher in rank than the angels, just as the name He inherited is superior to theirs.

The Son Superior to Angels

5 For to which of the angels did He ever say, **You are My Son; today I have become Your Father,**[n] [o] or again, **I will be His Father, and He will be My Son?**[p] 6 When He again brings His firstborn into the world,[q] He says, **And all God's angels must worship Him.**[r] 7 And about the angels He says:

> **He makes His angels winds,**[s]
> **and His servants**[t]
> **a fiery flame;**[u]

8 but about the Son:

> **Your throne, O God, is forever**
> **and ever,**
> **and the scepter of Your kingdom**
> **is a scepter of justice.**
> 9 **You have loved righteousness**
> **and hated lawlessness;**

[a] **6** Other mss read *in you* [b] **9** Or *an ambassador* [c] **10** Referring to the fact that Paul led him to Christ; see 1 Co 4:15 [d] **10** The name *Onesimus* in Gk means "useful." [e] **12** Lit *him—that is, my inward parts* [f] **12** Other mss read *him back. Receive him as a part of myself.* [g] **16** Both physically and spiritually [h] **25** Other mss read *our Lord* [i] **1:2** Lit *ages* [j] **1:3** Or *reflection* [k] **1:3** Or *representation, or copy, or reproduction* [l] **1:3** Other mss read *for our sins by Himself* [m] **1:3** Or *He sat down on high at the right hand of the Majesty* [n] **1:5** Or *have begotten You* [o] **1:5** Ps 2:7 [p] **1:5** 2 Sm 7:14; 1 Ch 17:13 [q] **1:6** Or *And again, when He brings His firstborn into the world* [r] **1:6** Dt 32:43 LXX; Ps 97:7 [s] **1:7** Or *spirits* [t] **1:7** Or *ministers* [u] **1:7** Ps 104:4

this is why God, Your God,
has anointed You,
rather than Your companions,[a] [b]
with the oil of joy.

10 And:

In the beginning, Lord,
You established the earth,
and the heavens are the works
of Your hands;
11 they will perish,
but You remain.
They will all wear out
like clothing;
12 You will roll them up
like a cloak,[c]
and they will be changed
like a robe.
But You are the same,
and Your years
will never end.[d]

13 Now to which of the angels has He ever
said:

Sit at My right hand
until I make Your enemies
Your footstool?[e] [f]

14 Are they not all ministering spirits sent out
to serve those who are going to inherit salvation?

Warning against Neglect

2 We must therefore pay even more attention to what we have heard, so that we
will not drift away. 2 For if the message spoken
through angels was legally binding,[g] and every
transgression and disobedience received a just
punishment, 3 how will we escape if we
neglect such a great salvation? It was first spoken by the Lord and was confirmed to us by
those who heard Him. 4 At the same time, God
also testified by signs and wonders, various
miracles, and distributions ⌊of gifts⌋ from the
Holy Spirit according to His will.

Jesus and Humanity

5 For He has not subjected to angels the
world to come that we are talking about. 6 But
one has somewhere testified:

What is man,
that You remember him,
or the son of man,
that You care for him?
7 You made him lower
than the angels
for a short time;
You crowned him with glory
and honor[h]
8 and subjected everything
under his feet.[i]

For in subjecting everything to him, He left
nothing not subject to him. As it is, we do not
yet see **everything subjected** to him. 9 But
we do see Jesus—**made lower than the
angels for a short time** so that by God's grace
He might taste death for everyone—crowned
with glory and honor because of the suffering
of death.

10 For it was fitting, in bringing many sons
to glory, that He, for whom and through whom
all things exist, should make the source[j] of their
salvation perfect through sufferings. 11 For the
One who sanctifies and those who are sanctified all have one Father.[k] That is why He is not
ashamed to call them brothers, 12 saying:

I will proclaim Your name
to My brothers;
I will sing hymns to You
in the congregation.[l]

13 Again, **I will trust in Him.**[m] And again,
**Here I am with the children God gave
Me.**[n]

14 Now since the children have flesh and
blood in common, He also shared in these, so
that through His death He might destroy the
one holding the power of death—that is, the
Devil— 15 and free those who were held in
slavery all their lives by the fear of death.
16 For it is clear that He does not reach out to
help angels, but to help Abraham's offspring.
17 Therefore He had to be like His brothers in
every way, so that He could become a merciful
and faithful high priest in service[o] to God, to
make propitiation[p] for the sins of the people.
18 For since He Himself was tested and has
suffered, He is able to help those who are
tested.

[a] **1:9** Or *associates* [b] **1:8–9** Ps 45:6–7 [c] **1:12** Other mss omit *like a cloak* [d] **1:10–12** Ps 102:25–27 [e] **1:13** Or *enemies a footstool for Your feet* [f] **1:13** Ps 110:1 [g] **2:2** Or *valid*, or *reliable* [h] **2:7** Other mss add *and set him over the works of your hands* [i] **2:6–8** Ps 8:5–7 LXX [j] **2:10** Or *pioneer*, or *leader* [k] **2:11** Or *father*, or *origin*, or *all are of one* [l] **2:12** Ps 22:22 [m] **2:13** Is 8:17 LXX; 12:2 LXX; 2 Sm 22:3 LXX [n] **2:13** Is 8:18 LXX [o] **2:17** Lit *things* [p] **2:17** The word *propitiation* has to do with the removal of divine wrath. Jesus' death is the means that turns God's wrath from the sinner; see 2 Co 5:21.

Our Apostle and High Priest

3 Therefore, holy brothers and companions
in a heavenly calling, consider Jesus, the
apostle and high priest of our confession; 2 He
was faithful to the One who appointed Him,
just as Moses was in all God's[a] household.
3 For Jesus[b] is considered worthy of more glory
than Moses, just as the builder has more honor
than the house. 4 Now every house is built by
someone, but the One who built everything is
God. 5 Moses was faithful as a servant in all
God's[a] household, as a testimony to what
would be said ⌊in the future⌋. 6 But Christ was
faithful as a Son over His household, whose
household we are if we hold on to the courage
and the confidence of our hope.[c]

Warning against Unbelief

7 Therefore, as the Holy Spirit says:

Today, if you hear His voice,
8 **do not harden your hearts**
as in the rebellion,
on the day of testing
in the desert,
9 **where your fathers tested Me,**
tried ⌊Me⌋,
and saw My works
10 **for 40 years.**
Therefore I was provoked
with this generation
and said, "They always go astray
in their hearts,
and they have not known
My ways."
11 **So I swore in My anger,**
"They will not enter My rest."[d]

12 Watch out, brothers, so that there won't be
in any of you an evil, unbelieving heart that
departs from the living God. 13 But encourage
each other daily, while it is still called **today,** so
that none of you is hardened by sin's deception. 14 For we have become companions of
the •Messiah if we hold firmly until the end
the reality[e] that we had at the start. 15 As it is
said:

Today, if you hear His voice,
do not harden your hearts
as in the rebellion.[f]

16 For who heard and rebelled? Wasn't it really
all who came out of Egypt under Moses?
17 And with whom was He "provoked for 40
years"? Was it not with those who sinned,
whose bodies fell in the desert? 18 And to
whom did He "swear that they would not
enter His rest," if not those who disobeyed?
19 So we see that they were unable to enter
because of unbelief.

The Promised Rest

4 Therefore, while the promise remains of
entering His rest, let us fear so that none
of you should miss it.[g] 2 For we also have
received the good news just as they did; but
the message they heard did not benefit them,
since they were not united with those who
heard it in faith[h] 3 (for we who have believed
enter the rest), in keeping with what[i] He has
said:

So I swore in My anger,
they will not enter My rest.[j]

And yet His works have been finished since
the foundation of the world, 4 for somewhere
He has spoken about the seventh day in this
way:

And on the seventh day
God rested from all His works.[k]

5 Again, in that passage ⌊He says⌋, **They will**
never enter My rest.[j] 6 Since it remains for
some to enter it, and those who formerly
received the good news did not enter because
of disobedience, 7 again, He specifies a certain
day—**today**—speaking through David after
such a long time, as previously stated:

Today if you hear His voice,
do not harden your hearts.[f]

8 For if Joshua had given them rest, He would
not have spoken later about another day. 9 A
Sabbath rest remains, therefore, for God's people. 10 For the person who has entered His rest
has rested from his own works, just as God did
from His. 11 Let us then make every effort to
enter that rest, so that no one will fall into the
same pattern of disobedience.
12 For the word of God is living and effective and sharper than any two-edged sword,
penetrating as far as to divide soul, spirit, joints,
and marrow; it is a judge of the ideas and
thoughts of the heart. 13 No creature is hidden
from Him, but all things are naked and exposed

[a]**3:2,5** Lit *His* [b]**3:3** Lit *He* [c]**3:6** Other mss add *firm to the end* [d]**3:7–11** Ps 95:7–11 [e]**3:14** Or *confidence* [f]**3:15; 4:7** Pss 95:7–8 [g]**4:1** Or *should seem to miss it* [h]**4:2** Other mss read *since it was not united by faith in those who heard* [i]**4:3** Or *rest), just as* [j]**4:3,5** Ps 95:11 [k]**4:4** Gn 2:2

to the eyes of Him to whom we must give an account.

Our Great High Priest

14 Therefore since we have a great high priest who has passed through the heavens—Jesus the Son of God—let us hold fast to the confession. 15 For we do not have a high priest who is unable to sympathize with our weaknesses, but One who has been tested in every way as we are, yet without sin. 16 Therefore let us approach the throne of grace with boldness, so that we may receive mercy and find grace to help us at the proper time.

The Messiah, a High Priest

5 For every high priest taken from men is appointed in service[a] to God for the people, to offer both gifts and sacrifices for sins. 2 He is able to deal gently with those who are ignorant and are going astray, since he himself is also subject to weakness. 3 Because of this, he must make a sin offering for himself as well as for the people. 4 No one takes this honor on himself; instead, a person is called by God, just as Aaron was. 5 In the same way, the •Messiah did not exalt Himself to become a high priest, but the One who said to Him, **You are My Son; today I have become Your Father,**[b] 6 also said in another passage, **You are a priest forever in the order of Melchizedek.**[c]

7 During His earthly life,[d] He offered prayers and appeals, with loud cries and tears, to the One who was able to save Him from death, and He was heard because of His reverence. 8 Though a Son, He learned obedience through what He suffered. 9 After He was perfected, He became the source of eternal salvation to all who obey Him, 10 and He was declared by God a high priest "in the order of Melchizedek."

The Problem of Immaturity

11 We have a great deal to say about this, and it's difficult to explain, since you have become slow to understand. 12 For though by this time you ought to be teachers, you need someone to teach you again the basic principles of God's revelation. You need milk, not solid food. 13 Now everyone who lives on milk is inexperienced with the message about righteousness, because he is an infant. 14 But solid food is for the mature—for those whose senses have been trained to distinguish between good and evil.

Warning against Regression

6 Therefore, leaving the elementary message about the •Messiah, let us go on to maturity, not laying again the foundation of repentance from dead works, faith in God, 2 teaching about ritual washings,[e] laying on of hands, the resurrection of the dead, and eternal judgment. 3 And we will do this if God permits.

4 For it is impossible to renew to repentance those who were once enlightened, who tasted the heavenly gift, became companions with the Holy Spirit, 5 tasted God's good word and the powers of the coming age, 6 and who have fallen away, because,[f] to their own harm, they are recrucifying the Son of God and holding Him up to contempt. 7 For ground that has drunk the rain that has often fallen on it, and that produces vegetation useful to those it is cultivated for, receives a blessing from God. 8 But if it produces thorns and thistles, it is worthless and about to be cursed, and will be burned at the end.

9 Even though we are speaking this way, dear friends, in your case we are confident of the better things connected with salvation. 10 For God is not unjust; He will not forget your work and the love[g] you showed for His name when you served the saints—and you continue to serve them. 11 Now we want each of you to demonstrate the same diligence for the final realization of your hope, 12 so that you won't become lazy, but imitators of those who inherit the promises through faith and perseverance.

Inheriting the Promise

13 For when God made a promise to Abraham, since He had no one greater to swear by, He swore by Himself:

14 **I will most certainly bless you,**
and I will greatly multiply you.[h]

15 And so, after waiting patiently, Abraham[i] obtained the promise. 16 For men swear by something greater than themselves, and for them a confirming oath ends every dispute. 17 Because God wanted to show His unchangeable purpose even more clearly to the heirs of

[a]**5:1** Lit *things* [b]**5:5** Ps 2:7 [c]**5:6** Ps 110:4; Gn 14:18–20 [d]**5:7** Lit *In the days of His flesh* [e]**6:2** Or *about baptisms* [f]**6:6** Or *while* [g]**6:10** Other mss read *labor of love* [h]**6:14** Gn 22:17 [i]**6:15** Lit *he*

the promise, He guaranteed it with an oath, 18 so that through two unchangeable things, in which it is impossible for God to lie, we who have fled for refuge might have strong encouragement to seize the hope set before us. 19 We have this ⌊hope⌋—like a sure and firm anchor of the soul—that enters the inner sanctuary behind the curtain. 20 Jesus has entered there on our behalf as a forerunner, because He has become a "high priest forever in the order of Melchizedek."

The Greatness of Melchizedek

7 For this Melchizedek—

King of Salem, priest of the Most High
God,
who met Abraham and blessed him
as he returned from defeating
the kings,
2 and Abraham gave him a tenth
of everything;
first, his name means
"king of righteousness,"
then also, "king of Salem,"
meaning "king of peace";
3 without father, mother, or genealogy,
having neither beginning of days
nor end of life,
but resembling the Son of God—

remains a priest forever.

4 Now consider how great this man was, to whom even Abraham the patriarch gave a tenth of the plunder! 5 The sons of Levi who receive the priestly office have a commandment according to the law to collect a tenth from the people—that is, from their brothers—though they have ⌊also⌋ descended from Abraham.[a] 6 But one without this[b] lineage collected tithes from Abraham and blessed the one who had the promises. 7 Without a doubt,[c] the inferior is blessed by the superior. 8 In the one case, men who will die receive tithes; but in the other case, ⌊Scripture⌋ testifies that he lives. 9 And in a sense Levi himself, who receives tithes, has paid tithes through Abraham, 10 for he was still within his forefather[d] when Melchizedek met him.

A Superior Priesthood

11 If, then, perfection came through the Levitical priesthood (for under it the people received the law), what further need was there for another priest to arise in the order of Melchizedek, and not to be described as being in the order of Aaron? 12 For when there is a change of the priesthood, there must be a change of law as well. 13 For the One about whom these things are said belonged to a different tribe, from which no one has served at the altar. 14 Now it is evident that our Lord came from Judah, and about that tribe Moses said nothing concerning priests.

15 And this becomes clearer if another priest like Melchizedek arises, 16 who doesn't become a ⌊priest⌋ based on a legal command concerning physical[e] descent but based on the power of an indestructible life. 17 For it has been testified:

**You are a priest forever in the order
of Melchizedek.**[f]

18 So the previous commandment is annulled because it was weak and unprofitable 19 (for the law perfected nothing), but a better hope is introduced, through which we draw near to God.

20 None of this ⌊happened⌋ without an oath. For others became priests without an oath, 21 but He with an oath made by the One who said to Him:

**The Lord has sworn,
and He will not change His mind,
You are a priest forever.**[f]

22 So Jesus has also become the guarantee of a better covenant.

23 Now many have become ⌊Levitical⌋ priests, since they are prevented by death from remaining in office. 24 But because He remains forever, He holds His priesthood permanently. 25 Therefore He is always able to save[g] those who come to God through Him, since He always lives to intercede for them.

26 For this is the kind of high priest we need: holy, innocent, undefiled, separated from sinners, and exalted above the heavens. 27 He doesn't need to offer sacrifices every day, as high priests do—first for their own sins, then for those of the people. He did this once for all when He offered Himself. 28 For the law appoints as high priests men who are weak, but the promise of the oath, which came after the law, ⌊appoints⌋ a Son, who has been perfected forever.

[a]**7:5** Lit *have come out of Abraham's loins* [b]**7:6** Lit *their* [c]**7:7** Or *Beyond any dispute* [d]**7:10** Lit *still in his father's loins* [e]**7:16** Or *fleshly* [f]**7:17,21** Ps 110:4 [g]**7:25** Or *He is able to save completely*

A Heavenly Priesthood

8 Now the main point of what is being said
is this: we have this kind of high priest,
who sat down at the right hand of the throne
of the Majesty in the heavens, 2 a minister of
the sanctuary and the true tabernacle, which
the Lord set up, and not man. 3 For every high
priest is appointed to offer gifts and sacrifices;
therefore it was necessary for this ⌊priest⌋ also
to have something to offer. 4 Now if He were
on earth, He wouldn't be a priest, since there
are those[a] offering the gifts prescribed by the
law. 5 These serve as a copy and shadow of the
heavenly things, as Moses was warned when
he was about to complete the tabernacle. For
He said, **Be careful that you make everything
according to the pattern that was shown to
you on the mountain.**[b] 6 But Jesus[c] has now
obtained a superior ministry, and to that
degree He is the mediator of a better covenant,
which has been legally enacted on better
promises.

A Superior Covenant

7 For if that first ⌊covenant⌋ had been faultless, no opportunity would have been sought
for a second one. 8 But finding fault with His
people,[d] He says:[e]

> **"Look, the days are coming,"**
> **says the Lord,**
> **"when I will make**
> **a new covenant**
> **with the house of Israel**
> **and with the house**
> **of Judah—**
> 9 **not like the covenant**
> **that I made with their fathers**
> **on the day I took them**
> **by their hand**
> **to lead them out of the land**
> **of Egypt.**
> **Because they did not continue**
> **in My covenant,**
> **I disregarded them,"**
> **says the Lord.**
> 10 **"But this is the covenant**
> **that I will make**
> **with the house of Israel**
> **after those days,"**
> **says the Lord:**
> **"I will put My laws**
> **into their minds,**
> **and I will write them**
> **on their hearts,**
> **and I will be their God,**
> **and they will be My people.**
> 11 **And each person will not teach**
> **his fellow citizen,**[f]
> **and each his brother, saying,**
> **'Know the Lord,'**
> **because they will all**
> **know Me,**
> **from the least to the greatest**
> **of them.**
> 12 **For I will be merciful**
> **to their wrongdoing,**
> **and I will never again remember**
> **their sins."**[g] [h]

13 By saying, **a new** ⌊**covenant**⌋, He has
declared that the first is old. And what is old
and aging is about to disappear.

Old Covenant Ministry

9 Now the first ⌊covenant⌋ also had regulations for ministry and an earthly sanctuary. 2 For a tabernacle was set up; and in the
first room, which is called "the holy place,"
were the lampstand, the table, and the presentation loaves. 3 Behind the second curtain, the
tabernacle was called "the holy of holies." 4 It
contained the gold altar of incense and the ark
of the covenant, covered with gold on all sides,
in which there was a gold jar containing the
manna, Aaron's rod that budded, and the tablets of the covenant. 5 The cherubim of glory
were above it overshadowing the mercy seat.
It is not possible to speak about these things in
detail right now.

6 These things having been set up this way,
the priests enter the first room repeatedly, performing their ministry. 7 But the high priest
alone enters the second room, and that only
once a year, and never without blood, which he
offers for himself and for the sins of the people
committed in ignorance. 8 The Holy Spirit was
making it clear that the way into the holy of
holies had not yet been disclosed while the first
tabernacle was still standing. 9 This is a symbol
for the present time, during which gifts and sacrifices are offered that cannot perfect the wor-
shiper's conscience. 10 They are physical
regulations and only deal with food, drink, and
various washings imposed until the time of restoration.

[a]**8:4** Other mss read *priests* [b]**8:5** Ex 25:40 [c]**8:6** Lit *He* [d]**8:8** Lit *with them* [e]**8:8** Other mss read *finding fault, He says to them* [f]**8:11** Other mss read *neighbor* [g]**8:12** Other mss add *and their lawless deeds* [h]**8:8–12** Jr 31:31–34

New Covenant Ministry

11 Now the •Messiah has appeared, high
priest of the good things that have come.[a] In
the greater and more perfect tabernacle not
made with hands (that is, not of this creation),
12 He entered the holy of holies once for all, not
by the blood of goats and calves, but by His own
blood, having obtained eternal redemption.
13 For if the blood of goats and bulls and the
ashes of a heifer sprinkling those who are
defiled, sanctify for the purification of the flesh,
14 how much more will the blood of the Messiah, who through the eternal Spirit offered
Himself without blemish to God, cleanse our[b]
consciences from dead works to serve the living God?

15 Therefore He is the mediator of a new
covenant,[c] so that those who are called might
receive the promise of the eternal inheritance,
because a death has taken place for redemption from the transgressions ⌊committed⌋
under the first covenant. 16 Where a will
exists, the death of the testator must be established. 17 For a will is valid only when people
die, since it is never in force while the testator
is living. 18 That is why even the first covenant was inaugurated with blood. 19 For when
every commandment had been proclaimed by
Moses to all the people according to the law,
he took the blood of calves and goats, along
with water, scarlet wool, and hyssop, and
sprinkled the scroll itself and all the people,
20 saying, **This is the blood of the covenant
that God has commanded for you.**[d] 21 In the
same way, he sprinkled the tabernacle and all
the vessels of worship with blood.
22 According to the law almost everything is
purified with blood, and without the shedding
of blood there is no forgiveness.

23 Therefore it was necessary for the copies
of the things in the heavens to be purified with
these ⌊sacrifices⌋, but the heavenly things themselves ⌊to be purified⌋ with better sacrifices
than these. 24 For the Messiah did not enter a
sanctuary made with hands (only a model[e] of
the true one) but into heaven itself, that He
might now appear in the presence of God for
us. 25 He did not do this to offer Himself many
times, as the high priest enters the sanctuary
yearly with the blood of another. 26 Otherwise,
He would have had to suffer many times since
the foundation of the world. But now He has
appeared one time, at the end of the ages, for
the removal of sin by the sacrifice of Himself.
27 And just as it is appointed for people to die
once—and after this, judgment— 28 so also the
Messiah, having been offered once to bear the
sins of many, will appear a second time, not to
bear sin, but[f] to bring salvation to those who
are waiting for Him.

The Perfect Sacrifice

10 Since the law has ⌊only⌋ a shadow of
the good things to come, and not the
actual form of those realities, it can never perfect the worshipers by the same sacrifices they
continually offer year after year. 2 Otherwise,
wouldn't they have stopped being offered,
since the worshipers, once purified, would no
longer have any consciousness of sins? 3 But in
the sacrifices[g] there is a reminder of sins every
year. 4 For it is impossible for the blood of bulls
and goats to take away sins.

5 Therefore, as He was coming into the
world, He said:

You did not want sacrifice
and offering,
but You prepared a body for Me.
6 **You did not delight**
in whole burnt offerings
and sin offerings.
7 **Then I said, "See, I have come—**
it is written about Me
in the volume of the scroll—
to do Your will, O God!"[h]

8 After He says above, **You did not desire or
delight in sacrifices and offerings, whole
burnt offerings and sin offerings,** (which are
offered according to the law), 9 He then says,
See, I have come to do Your will.[i] He takes
away the first to establish the second. 10 By this
will, we have been sanctified through the offering of the body of Jesus Christ once and for all.

11 Now every priest stands day after day
ministering and offering time after time the
same sacrifices, which can never take away
sins. 12 But this man, after offering one sacrifice
for sins forever, sat down at the right hand of
God. 13 He is now waiting until His enemies
are made His footstool. 14 For by one offering
He has perfected forever those who are sanctified. 15 The Holy Spirit also testifies to us about
this. For after He had said:

[a]**9:11** Other mss read *that are to come* [b]**9:14** Other mss read *your* [c]**9:15** The Gk word used here and in vv. 15–18 can be translated *covenant, will,* or *testament.* [d]**9:20** Ex 24:8 [e]**9:24** Or *antitype*, or *figure* [f]**9:28** Lit *time, apart from sin,* [g]**10:3** Lit *in them* [h]**10:5–7** Ps 40:6–8 [i]**10:9** Other mss add *O God*

16 **This is the covenant that I will make**
with them
after those days, says the Lord:
I will put My laws on their hearts,
and I will write them
on their minds,

17 ⌊He adds⌋:

I will never again remember
their sins and
their lawless acts.[a]

18 Now where there is forgiveness of these,
there is no longer an offering for sin.

Exhortations to Godliness

19 Therefore, brothers, since we have boldness to enter the sanctuary through the blood of
Jesus, 20 by the new and living way that He has
inaugurated for us, through the curtain (that is,
His flesh); 21 and since we have a great high
priest over the house of God, 22 let us draw
near with a true heart in full assurance of faith,
our hearts sprinkled ⌊clean⌋ from an evil conscience and our bodies washed in pure water.
23 Let us hold on to the confession of our hope
without wavering, for He who promised is
faithful. 24 And let us be concerned about one
another in order to promote love and good
works, 25 not staying away from our meetings,
as some habitually do, but encouraging each
other, and all the more as you see the day drawing near.

Warning against Willful Sin

26 For if we deliberately sin after receiving
the knowledge of the truth, there no longer
remains a sacrifice for sins, 27 but a terrifying
expectation of judgment, and the fury of a fire
about to consume the adversaries. 28 If anyone disregards Moses' law, he dies without
mercy, based on the testimony of two or three
witnesses. 29 How much worse punishment,
do you think one will deserve who has trampled on the Son of God, regarded as profane[b]
the blood of the covenant by which he was
sanctified, and insulted the Spirit of grace?
30 For we know the One who has said, **Ven-**
geance belongs to Me, I will repay,[c d] and
again, **The Lord will judge His people.**[e] 31 It
is a terrifying thing to fall into the hands of the
living God!

32 Remember the earlier days when, after
you had been enlightened, you endured a hard
struggle with sufferings. 33 Sometimes you
were publicly exposed to taunts and afflictions,
and at other times you were companions of
those who were treated that way. 34 For you
sympathized with the prisoners[f] and accepted
with joy the confiscation of your possessions,
knowing that you yourselves have a better and
enduring possession.[g] 35 So don't throw away
your confidence, which has a great reward.
36 For you need endurance, so that after you
have done God's will, you may receive what
was promised.

37 For in yet **a very little while,**
the Coming One will come
and not delay.
38 **But My righteous one**[h] **will live**
by faith;
and if he draws back,
My soul has no pleasure
in him.[i]

39 But we are not those who draw back and
are destroyed, but those who have faith and
obtain life.

Heroes of Faith

11 Now faith is the reality[j] of what is
hoped for, the proof[k] of what is not
seen. 2 For by it our ancestors were approved.
3 By faith we understand that the universe
was[l] created by the word[m] of God, so that what
is seen has been made from things that are not
visible.
4 By faith Abel offered to God a better sacrifice than Cain ⌊did⌋. By this he was approved as
a righteous man, because God approved his
gifts, and even though he is dead, he still speaks
through this.
5 By faith, Enoch was taken away so that he
did not experience death, and **he was not to be**
found because God took him away.[n] For prior
to his transformation he was approved, having
pleased God. 6 Now without faith it is impossible to please God, for the one who draws near
to Him must believe that He exists and rewards
those who seek Him.
7 By faith Noah, after being warned about
what was not yet seen, in reverence built an
ark to deliver his family. By this he condemned

[a]**10:16–17** Jr 31:33–34 [b]**10:29** Or *ordinary* [c]**10:30** Other mss add *says the Lord* [d]**10:30** Dt 32:35 [e]**10:30** Dt 32:36
[f]**10:34** Other mss read *sympathized with my imprisonment* [g]**10:34** Other mss add *in heaven* [h]**10:38** Other mss read *the righteous one* [i]**10:37–38** Is 26:20 LXX; Hab 2:3–4 [j]**11:1** Or *assurance* [k]**11:1** Or *conviction* [l]**11:3** Or *the worlds were,* or *the ages were* [m]**11:3** Or *voice,* or *utterance* [n]**11:5** Gn 5:21–24

the world and became an heir of the righteousness that comes by faith.
8 By faith Abraham, when he was called,
obeyed and went out to a place he was going to
receive as an inheritance; he went out, not
knowing where he was going. 9 By faith he
stayed as a foreigner in the land of promise, living in tents with Isaac and Jacob, co-heirs of the
same promise. 10 For he was looking forward to
the city that has foundations, whose architect
and builder is God.
11 By faith even Sarah herself, when she
was barren, received power to conceive offspring, even though she was past the age, since
she[a] considered that the One who had promised was faithful. 12 And therefore from one
man—in fact, from one as good as dead—came
offspring as numerous as the stars of heaven
and as innumerable as the grains of sand by the
seashore.
13 These all died in faith without having
received the promises, but they saw them from
a distance, greeted them, and confessed that
they were foreigners and temporary residents
on the earth. 14 Now those who say such things
make it clear that they are seeking a homeland.
15 If they had been remembering that land they
came from, they would have had opportunity to
return. 16 But they now aspire to a better
land—a heavenly one. Therefore God is not
ashamed to be called their God, for He has prepared a city for them.
17 By faith Abraham, when he was tested,
offered up Isaac; he who had received the
promises was offering up his unique son,
18 about whom it had been said, **In Isaac your
seed will be called.**[b] 19 He considered God to
be able even to raise someone from the dead,
from which he also got him back as an
illustration.[c]
20 By faith Isaac blessed Jacob and Esau concerning things to come. 21 By faith Jacob, when
he was dying, blessed each of the sons of
Joseph, and, **he worshiped, leaning on the top
of his staff.**[d] 22 By faith Joseph, as he was nearing the end of his life, mentioned the exodus of
the sons of Israel and gave instructions concerning his bones.
23 By faith Moses, after he was born, was
hidden by his parents for three months,
because they saw that the child was beautiful,
and they didn't fear the king's edict. 24 By faith
Moses, when he had grown up, refused to be
called the son of Pharaoh's daughter 25 and
chose to suffer with the people of God rather
than to enjoy the short-lived pleasure of sin.
26 For he considered reproach for the sake of
the •Messiah to be greater wealth than the
treasures of Egypt, since his attention was on
the reward.
27 By faith he left Egypt behind, not being
afraid of the king's anger, for he persevered, as
one who sees Him who is invisible. 28 By faith
he instituted the •Passover and the sprinkling
of the blood, so that the destroyer of the firstborn might not touch them. 29 By faith they
crossed the Red Sea as though they were on dry
land. When the Egyptians attempted to do this,
they were drowned.
30 By faith the walls of Jericho fell down
after being encircled for seven days. 31 By faith
Rahab the prostitute received the spies in peace
and didn't perish with those who disobeyed.
32 And what more can I say? Time is too
short for me to tell about Gideon, Barak,
Samson, Jephthah, of David and Samuel and
the prophets, 33 who by faith conquered
kingdoms, administered justice, obtained
promises, shut the mouths of lions,
34 quenched the raging of fire, escaped the
edge of the sword, gained strength after
being weak, became mighty in battle, and
put foreign armies to flight. 35 Women
received their dead raised to life again. Some
men were tortured, not accepting release, so
that they might gain a better resurrection,
36 and others experienced mockings and
scourgings, as well as bonds and imprisonment. 37 They were stoned,[e] they were
sawed in two, they died by the sword, they
wandered about in sheepskins, in goatskins,
destitute, afflicted, and mistreated. 38 The
world was not worthy of them. They wandered in deserts, mountains, caves, and holes
in the ground.
39 All these were approved through their
faith, but they did not receive what was promised, 40 since God had provided something better for us, so that they would not be made
perfect without us.

The Call to Endurance

12 Therefore since we also have such a
large cloud of witnesses surrounding

[a]**11:11** Or *By faith Abraham, even though he was past age—and Sarah herself was barren—received the ability to procreate since he* [b]**11:18** Gn 21:12 [c]**11:19** Or *foreshadowing*, or *parable*, or *type* [d]**11:21** Gn 47:31 [e]**11:37** Other mss add *they were tempted*

us, let us lay aside every weight and the sin
that so easily ensnares us, and run with endurance the race that lies before us, 2 keeping our
eyes on Jesus,[a] the source and perfecter[b] of our
faith, who for the joy that lay before Him[c]
endured a cross and despised the shame, and
has sat down at the right hand of God's throne.

Fatherly Discipline

3 For consider Him who endured such hostility from sinners against Himself, so that you
won't grow weary and lose heart. 4 In struggling against sin, you have not yet resisted to
the point of shedding your blood. 5 And you
have forgotten the exhortation that addresses
you as sons:

> **My son, do not take**
> **the Lord's discipline**
> **lightly,**
> **or faint when you are reproved**
> **by Him;**
> 6 **for the Lord disciplines the one**
> **He loves,**
> **and punishes every son**
> **whom He receives.**[d]

7 Endure it as discipline: God is dealing with
you as sons. For what son is there whom a
father does not discipline? 8 But if you are
without discipline—which all[e] receive[f] —then
you are illegitimate children and not sons.
9 Furthermore, we had natural fathers discipline us, and we respected them. Shouldn't we
submit even more to the Father of spirits and
live? 10 For they disciplined us for a short time
based on what seemed good to them, but He
does it for our benefit, so that we can share His
holiness. 11 No discipline seems enjoyable at
the time, but painful. Later on, however, it
yields the fruit of peace and righteousness to
those who have been trained by it.

12 Therefore strengthen your tired hands
and weakened knees, 13 and make straight
paths for your feet, so that what is lame may not
be dislocated,[g] but healed instead.

Warning against Rejecting God's Grace

14 Pursue peace with everyone, and holiness—without it no one will see the Lord.
15 See to it that no one falls short of the grace of
God and that no root of bitterness springs up,
causing trouble and by it, defiling many. 16 And
see that there isn't any immoral or irreverent
person like Esau, who sold his birthright in
exchange for one meal. 17 For you know that
later, when he wanted to inherit the blessing,
he was rejected because he didn't find any
opportunity for repentance, though he sought it
with tears.

18 For you have not come to what could be
touched, to a blazing fire, to darkness, gloom,
and storm, 19 to the blast of a trumpet, and the
sound of words. (Those who heard it begged
that not another word be spoken to them, 20 for
they could not bear what was commanded:
And if even an animal touches the mountain,
it must be stoned![h] 21 And the appearance was
so terrifying that Moses said, **I am terrified and**
trembling.[i]) 22 Instead, you have come to
Mount Zion, to the city of the living God (the
heavenly Jerusalem), to myriads of angels in festive gathering, 23 to the assembly of the firstborn whose names have been written[j] in
heaven, to God who is the judge of all, to the
spirits of righteous people made perfect, 24 to
Jesus (mediator of a new covenant), and to the
sprinkled blood, which says better things than
the ⌊blood⌋ of Abel.

25 See that you do not reject the One who
speaks; for if they did not escape when they
rejected Him who warned them on earth,
even less will we if we turn away from Him
who warns us from heaven. 26 His voice
shook the earth at that time, but now He has
promised, **Yet once more I will shake not**
only the earth but also heaven.[k] 27 Now this
expression, "Yet once more," indicates the
removal of what can be shaken—that is, created things—so that what is not shaken might
remain. 28 Therefore, since we are receiving a
kingdom that cannot be shaken, let us hold on
to grace.[l] By it, we may serve God acceptably,
with reverence and awe; 29 for our God is a
consuming fire.

Final Exhortations

13 Let brotherly love continue. 2 Don't
neglect to show hospitality, for by
doing this some have welcomed angels as
guests without knowing it. 3 Remember the
prisoners, as though you were in prison with
them, and the mistreated, as though you your-

[a]**12:2** Or *looking to Jesus* [b]**12:2** Or *the founder and completer* [c]**12:2** Or *who instead of the joy lying before Him*; that is, the joy of heaven [d]**12:6** Pr 3:11–12 [e]**12:8** In context *all* refers to Christians. [f]**12:8** Lit *discipline, of which all have become participants* [g]**12:13** Or *so that the lame will not be turned aside* [h]**12:20** Ex 19:12 [i]**12:21** Dt 9:19 [j]**12:23** Or *registered* [k]**12:26** Hg 2:6 [l]**12:28** Or *let us give thanks*, or *let us have grace*

selves were suffering bodily.[a] 4 Marriage must be respected by all, and the marriage bed kept undefiled, because God will judge immoral people and adulterers. 5 Your life should be free from the love of money. Be satisfied with what you have, for He Himself has said, **I will never leave you or forsake you.**[b] 6 Therefore, we may boldly say:

> **The Lord is my helper;**
> **I will not be afraid.**
> **What can man do to me?**[c]

7 Remember your leaders who have spoken God's word to you. As you carefully observe the outcome of their lives, imitate their faith. 8 Jesus Christ is the same yesterday, today, and forever. 9 Don't be led astray by various kinds of strange teachings; for it is good for the heart to be established by grace and not by foods, since those involved in them have not benefited. 10 We have an altar from which those who serve the tabernacle do not have a right to eat. 11 For the bodies of those animals whose blood is brought into the holy of holies by the high priest as a sin offering are burned outside the camp. 12 Therefore Jesus also suffered outside the gate, so that He might sanctify[d] the people by His own blood. 13 Let us then go to Him outside the camp, bearing His disgrace. 14 For here we do not have an enduring city; instead, we seek the one to come. 15 Therefore, through Him let us continually offer up to God a sacrifice of praise, that is, the fruit of our lips that confess His name. 16 Don't neglect to do good and to share, for God is pleased with such sacrifices. 17 Obey your leaders[e] and submit to them, for they keep watch over your souls as those who will give an account, so that they can do this with joy and not with grief, for that would be unprofitable for you. 18 Pray for us; for we are convinced that we have a clear conscience, wanting to conduct ourselves honorably in everything. 19 And I especially urge you to pray[f] that I may be restored to you very soon.

Benediction and Farewell

20 Now may the God of peace, who brought up from the dead our Lord Jesus—the great Shepherd of the sheep—with the blood of the everlasting covenant, 21 equip[g] you with all that is good to do His will, working in us what is pleasing in His sight, through Jesus Christ, to whom be glory forever and ever.[h] •Amen.

22 Brothers, I urge you to receive this word of exhortation, for I have written to you in few words. 23 Be aware that our brother Timothy has been released. If he comes soon enough, he will be with me when I see you. 24 Greet all your leaders and all the saints. Those who are from Italy greet you. 25 Grace be with all of you.

James

Greeting

1 James, a slave of God and of the Lord Jesus Christ:

To the 12 tribes in the Dispersion.

Greetings.

Trials and Maturity

2 Consider it a great joy, my brothers, whenever you experience various trials, 3 knowing that the testing of your faith produces endurance. 4 But endurance must do its complete work, so that you may be mature and complete, lacking nothing.

5 Now if any of you lacks wisdom, he should ask God, who gives to all generously and without criticizing, and it will be given to him. 6 But let him ask in faith without doubting. For the doubter is like the surging sea, driven and tossed by the wind. 7 That person should not expect to receive anything from the Lord. 8 An indecisive man is unstable in all his ways.

9 The brother of humble circumstances should boast in his exaltation; 10 but the one who is rich ⌊should boast⌋ in his humiliation, because he will pass away like a flower of the

[a] **13:3** Or *mistreated, since you are also in a body* [b] **13:5** Dt 31:6 [c] **13:6** Ps 118:6 [d] **13:12** Or *set apart*, or *consecrate* [e] **13:17** Or *rulers* [f] **13:19** Lit *to do this* [g] **13:21** Or *perfect* [h] **13:21** Other mss omit *and ever*

field. 11 For the sun rises with its scorching
heat and dries up the grass; its flower falls off,
and its beautiful appearance is destroyed. In the
same way, the rich man will wither away while
pursuing his activities.
12 Blessed is a man who endures trials,[a]
because when he passes the test he will receive
the crown of life that He[b] has promised to those
who love Him.
13 No one undergoing a trial should say, "I
am being tempted by God." For God is not
tempted by evil,[c] and He Himself doesn't tempt
anyone. 14 But each person is tempted when
he is drawn away and enticed by his own evil
desires. 15 Then after desire has conceived, it
gives birth to sin, and when sin is fully grown,
it gives birth to death.
16 Don't be deceived, my dearly loved
brothers. 17 Every generous act and every perfect gift is from above, coming down from the
Father of lights; with Him there is no variation
or shadow cast by turning. 18 By His own
choice, He gave us a new birth by the message
of truth[d] so that we would be the •firstfruits of
His creatures.

Hearing and Doing the Word

19 My dearly loved brothers, understand
this: everyone must be quick to hear, slow to
speak, and slow to anger, 20 for man's anger
does not accomplish God's righteousness.
21 Therefore, ridding yourselves of all moral
filth and evil excess, humbly receive the
implanted word, which is able to save you.[e]
22 But be doers of the word and not hearers only, deceiving yourselves. 23 Because if
anyone is a hearer of the word and not a doer,
he is like a man looking at his own face[f] in a
mirror; 24 for he looks at himself, goes away,
and right away forgets what kind of man he
was. 25 But the one who looks intently into
the perfect law of freedom and perseveres in
it, and is not a forgetful hearer but a doer who
acts—this person will be blessed in what he
does.
26 If anyone[g] thinks he is religious, without
controlling his tongue but deceiving his heart,
his religion is useless. 27 Pure and undefiled
religion before our[h] God and Father is this: to
look after orphans and widows in their distress
and to keep oneself unstained by the world.

The Sin of Favoritism

2 My brothers, hold your faith in our glorious Lord Jesus Christ without showing
favoritism. 2 For suppose a man comes into
your meeting wearing a gold ring, dressed in
fine clothes, and a poor man dressed in dirty
clothes also comes in. 3 If you look with favor
on the man wearing the fine clothes so that
you say, "Sit here in a good place," and yet you
say to the poor man, "Stand over there," or,
"Sit here on the floor by my footstool,"
4 haven't you discriminated among yourselves
and become judges with evil thoughts?
5 Listen, my dear brothers: Didn't God
choose the poor in this world to be rich in faith
and heirs of the kingdom that He has promised
to those who love Him? 6 Yet you dishonored
that poor man. Don't the rich oppress you and
drag you into the courts? 7 Don't they blaspheme the noble name that you bear?
8 If you really carry out the royal law prescribed in Scripture, **Love your neighbor as
yourself**,[i] you are doing well. 9 But if you show
favoritism, you commit sin and are convicted
by the law as transgressors. 10 For whoever
keeps the entire law, yet fails in one point, is
guilty of ⌊breaking it⌋ all. 11 For He who said,
Do not commit adultery,[j] also said, **Do not
murder**.[k] So if you do not commit adultery, but
you do murder, you are a lawbreaker.
12 Speak and act as those who will be judged
by the law of freedom. 13 For judgment is without mercy to the one who hasn't shown mercy.
Mercy triumphs over judgment.

Faith and Works

14 What good is it, my brothers, if someone
says he has faith, but does not have works? Can
his faith[l] save him?
15 If a brother or sister is without clothes
and lacks daily food, 16 and one of you says to
them, "Go in peace, keep warm, and eat well,"
but you don't give them what the body needs,
what good is it? 17 In the same way faith, if it
doesn't have works, is dead by itself.
18 But someone will say, "You have faith,
and I have works."[m] Show me your faith without works, and I will show you faith from my
works.[n] 19 You believe that God is one; you do
well. The demons also believe—and they shud-
der.

[a]**1:12** Lit *trial*, used as a collective [b]**1:12** Other mss read *that the Lord* [c]**1:13** Or *evil persons*, or *evil things* [d]**1:18** *message of truth* = the gospel [e]**1:21** Lit *save your souls* [f]**1:23** Lit *at the face of his birth* [g]**1:26** Other mss add *among you* [h]**1:27** Or *before the* [i]**2:8** Lv 19:18 [j]**2:11** Ex 20:14; Dt 5:18 [k]**2:11** Ex 20:13; Dt 5:17 [l]**2:14** Or *Can faith*, or *Can that faith*, or *Can such faith* [m]**2:18** The quotation may end here or after v. 18b or v. 19. [n]**2:18** Other mss read *Show me your faith from your works, and from my works I will show you my faith.*

20 Foolish man! Are you willing to learn that faith without works is useless? 21 Wasn't Abraham our father justified by works when he offered Isaac his son on the altar? 22 You see that faith was active together with his works, and by works, faith was perfected. 23 So the Scripture was fulfilled that says, **Abraham believed God, and it was credited to him for righteousness,**[a] and he was called God's friend. 24 You see that a man is justified by works and not by faith alone. 25 And in the same way, wasn't Rahab the prostitute also justified by works when she received the messengers and sent them out by a different route? 26 For just as the body without the spirit is dead, so also faith without works is dead.

Controlling the Tongue

3 Not many should become teachers, my brothers, knowing that we will receive a stricter judgment; 2 for we all stumble in many ways. If anyone does not stumble in what he says,[b] he is a mature man who is also able to control his whole body.[c]

3 Now when we put bits into the mouths of horses to make them obey us, we also guide the whole animal.[d] 4 And consider ships: though very large and driven by fierce winds, they are guided by a very small rudder wherever the will of the pilot directs. 5 So too, though the tongue is a small part ⌊of the body⌋, it boasts great things. Consider how large a forest a small fire ignites. 6 And the tongue is a fire. The tongue, a world of unrighteousness, is placed among the parts of our ⌊bodies⌋; it pollutes the whole body, sets the course of life on fire, and is set on fire by •hell.

7 For every creature—animal or bird, reptile or fish—is tamed and has been tamed by man, 8 but no man can tame the tongue. It is a restless evil, full of deadly poison. 9 With it we bless our[e] Lord and Father, and with it we curse men who are made in God's likeness. 10 Out of the same mouth come blessing and cursing. My brothers, these things should not be this way. 11 Does a spring pour out sweet and bitter water from the same opening? 12 Can a fig tree produce olives, my brothers, or a grapevine ⌊produce⌋ figs? Neither can a saltwater spring yield fresh water.

The Wisdom from Above

13 Who is wise and understanding among you? He should show his works by good conduct with wisdom's gentleness. 14 But if you have bitter envy and selfish ambition in your heart, don't brag and lie in defiance of the truth. 15 Such wisdom does not come down from above, but is earthly, sensual, demonic. 16 For where envy and selfish ambition exist, there is disorder and every kind of evil. 17 But the wisdom from above is first pure, then peace-loving, gentle, compliant, full of mercy and good fruits, without favoritism and hypocrisy. 18 And the fruit of righteousness is sown in peace by those who make peace.

Proud or Humble

4 What is the source of the wars and the fights among you? Don't they come from the cravings that are at war within you?[f] 2 You desire and do not have. You murder and covet and cannot obtain. You fight and war. You do not have because you do not ask. 3 You ask and don't receive because you ask wrongly, so that you may spend it on your desires for pleasure.

4 Adulteresses![g] Do you not know that friendship with the world is hostility toward God? So whoever wants to be the world's friend becomes God's enemy. 5 Or do you think it's without reason the Scripture says that the Spirit He has caused to live in us yearns jealously?[h]

6 But He gives greater grace. Therefore He says:

> **God resists the proud,**
> **but gives grace to the humble.**[i]

7 Therefore, submit to God. But resist the Devil, and he will flee from you. 8 Draw near to God, and He will draw near to you. Cleanse your hands, sinners, and purify your hearts, double-minded people! 9 Be miserable and mourn and weep. Your laughter must change to mourning and your joy to sorrow. 10 Humble yourselves before the Lord, and He will exalt you.

11 Don't criticize one another, brothers. He who criticizes a brother or judges his brother criticizes the law and judges the law. But if you judge the law, you are not a doer of the law but

[a]**2:23** Gn 15:6 [b]**3:2** Lit *in word* [c]**3:2** Lit *to bridle the whole body* [d]**3:3** Lit *whole body* [e]**3:9** Or *bless the* [f]**4:1** Lit *war in your members* [g]**4:4** Other mss read *Adulterers and adulteresses* [h]**4:5** Or *He who caused the Spirit to live in us yearns jealously,* or *the spirit He caused to live in us yearns jealously,* or *He jealously yearns for the Spirit He made to live in us* [i]**4:6** Pr 3:34

a judge. 12 There is one lawgiver and judge[a]
who is able to save and to destroy. But who are
you to judge your neighbor?

Our Will and His Will

13 Come now, you who say, "Today or
tomorrow we will travel to such and such a city
and spend a year there and do business and
make a profit." 14 You don't even know what
tomorrow will bring—what your life will be!
For you are a bit of smoke that appears for a little while, then vanishes.
15 Instead, you should say, "If the Lord
wills, we will live and do this or that." 16 But as
it is, you boast in your arrogance. All such
boasting is evil. 17 So, for the person who
knows to do good and doesn't do it, it is a sin.

Warning to the Rich

5 Come now, you rich people! Weep and
wail over the miseries that are coming on
you. 2 Your wealth is ruined: your clothes are
moth-eaten; 3 your silver and gold are cor-
roded, and their corrosion will be a witness
against you and will eat your flesh like fire. You
stored up treasure in the last days! 4 Look! The
pay that you withheld from the workers who
reaped your fields cries out, and the outcry of
the harvesters has reached the ears of the Lord
of •Hosts.[b] 5 You have lived luxuriously on the
land and have indulged yourselves. You have
fattened your hearts for[c] the day of slaughter.
6 You have condemned—you have mur-
dered—the righteous man; he does not resist
you.

Waiting for the Lord

7 Therefore, brothers, be patient until the
Lord's coming. See how the farmer waits for
the precious fruit of the earth and is patient
with it until it receives the early and the late
rains. 8 You also must be patient. Strengthen
your hearts, because the Lord's coming is near.
9 Brothers, do not complain about one
another, so that you will not be judged. Look,
the judge stands at the door!
10 Brothers, take the prophets who spoke in
the Lord's name as an example of suffering and
patience. 11 See, we count as blessed those
who have endured.[d] You have heard of Job's
endurance and have seen the outcome from the
Lord: the Lord is very compassionate and merciful.

Truthful Speech

12 Now above all, my brothers, do not
swear, either by heaven or by earth or with any
other oath. Your "yes" must be "yes," and your
"no" must be "no," so that you won't fall under
judgment.[e]

Effective Prayer

13 Is anyone among you suffering? He
should pray. Is anyone cheerful? He should sing
praises. 14 Is anyone among you sick? He
should call for the elders of the church, and
they should pray over him after anointing him
with olive oil in the name of the Lord. 15 The
prayer of faith will save the sick person, and the
Lord will raise him up; and if he has committed
sins, he will be forgiven. 16 Therefore, confess
your sins to one another and pray for one
another, so that you may be healed. The
intense prayer of the righteous is very powerful. 17 Elijah was a man with a nature like ours;
yet he prayed earnestly that it would not rain,
and for three years and six months it did not
rain on the land. 18 Then he prayed again, and
the sky gave rain and the land produced its
fruit.
19 My brothers, if any among you strays
from the truth, and someone turns him back,
20 he should know that whoever turns a sinner
from the error of his way will save his •life from
death and cover a multitude of sins.

1 Peter

Greeting

1 Peter, an apostle of Jesus Christ:
To the temporary residents of the Dispersion in the provinces of Pontus, Galatia,
Cappadocia, Asia, and Bithynia, chosen
2 according to the foreknowledge of God the

[a]**4:12** Other mss omit *and judge* [b]**5:4** Gk *Sabaoth*; this word is a transliteration of the Hb word for *Hosts*, or *Armies*. [c]**5:5** Or *hearts in* [d]**5:11** Or *have persevered* [e]**5:12** Other mss read *fall into hypocrisy*

Father and set apart by the Spirit for obedience
and ⌊for the⌋ sprinkling with the blood of Jesus
Christ.

May grace and peace be multiplied to you.

A Living Hope

3 Blessed be the God and Father of our Lord
Jesus Christ. According to His great mercy, He
has given us a new birth into a living hope
through the resurrection of Jesus Christ from
the dead, 4 and into an inheritance that is
imperishable, uncorrupted, and unfading, kept
in heaven for you, 5 who are being protected by
God's power through faith for a salvation that is
ready to be revealed in the last time. 6 You
rejoice in this,[a] though now for a short time you
have had to be distressed by various trials 7 so
that the genuineness of your faith—more valuable than gold, which perishes though refined
by fire—may result in[b] praise, glory, and honor
at the revelation of Jesus Christ. 8 You love
Him, though you have not seen Him. And
though not seeing Him now, you believe in
Him and rejoice with inexpressible and glorious joy, 9 because you are receiving the goal of
your[c] faith, the salvation of your souls.[d]

10 Concerning this salvation, the prophets
who prophesied about the grace that would
come to you searched and carefully investigated. 11 They inquired into what time or what
circumstances[e] the Spirit of Christ within them
was indicating when He testified in advance to
the messianic sufferings[f] and the glories that
would follow.[g] 12 It was revealed to them that
they were not serving themselves but you concerning things that have now been announced
to you through those who preached the gospel
to you by the Holy Spirit sent from heaven.
Angels desire to look into these things.

A Call to Holy Living

13 Therefore, get your minds ready for
action,[h] being self-disciplined, and set your
hope completely on the grace to be brought to
you at the revelation of Jesus Christ. 14 As obedient children, do not be conformed to the
desires of your former ignorance 15 but, as the
One who called you is holy, you also are to be
holy in all your conduct; 16 for it is written, **Be
holy, because I am holy.**[i]

17 And if you address as Father the One who
judges impartially based on each one's work,
you are to conduct yourselves in reverence during this time of temporary residence. 18 For you
know that you were redeemed from your
empty way of life inherited from the fathers,
not with perishable things, like silver or gold,
19 but with the precious blood of Christ, like
that of a lamb without defect or blemish. 20 He
was destined[j] before the foundation of the
world, but was revealed at the end of the times
for you 21 who through Him are believers in
God, who raised Him from the dead and gave
Him glory, so that your faith and hope are in
God.

22 By obedience to the truth,[k] having purified yourselves[l] for sincere love of the brothers,
love one another earnestly from a pure[m] heart,
23 since you have been born again—not of perishable seed but of imperishable—through the
living and enduring word of God. 24 For

All flesh is like grass,
and all its glory like a flower
of the grass.
The grass withers, and the flower
drops off,
25 **but the word of the Lord**
endures forever.[n]

And this is the word that was preached as the
gospel to you.

The Living Stone and a Holy People

2 So rid yourselves of all wickedness, all
deceit, hypocrisy, envy, and all slander.
2 Like newborn infants, desire the unadulter-
ated spiritual milk, so that you may grow by it
in ⌊your⌋ salvation,[o] 3 since **you have tasted
that the Lord is good.**[p] 4 Coming to Him, a living stone—rejected by men but chosen and
valuable to God— 5 you yourselves, as living
stones, are being built into a spiritual house for
a holy priesthood to offer spiritual sacrifices
acceptable to God through Jesus Christ. 6 For it
stands in Scripture:

Look! I lay a stone in Zion,
a chosen and valuable
cornerstone,
and the one who believes in Him
will never be put to shame![q] [r]

[a]**1:6** Or *In this (fact) rejoice* [b]**1:7** Lit *may be found for* [c]**1:9** Other mss read *our,* or they omit the possessive pronoun [d]**1:9** Or *your lives* [e]**1:11** Or *inquired about the person or time* [f]**1:11** Or *the sufferings of Christ* [g]**1:11** Lit *the glories after that* [h]**1:13** Lit *Therefore, gird the loins of your minds* [i]**1:16** Lv 11:44–45; 19:2; 20:7 [j]**1:20** Or *was chosen,* or *was known* [k]**1:22** Other mss add *through the Spirit* [l]**1:22** Or *purified your souls* [m]**1:22** Other mss omit *pure* [n]**1:24–25** Is 40:6–8 [o]**2:2** Other mss omit *in your salvation* [p]**2:3** Ps 34:8 [q]**2:6** Or *be disappointed* [r]**2:6** Is 28:16 LXX

7 So the honor is for you who believe; but for
the unbelieving,

The stone that the builders
rejected—
this One has become
the cornerstone,[a]

and

8 **A stone that causes men**
to stumble,[b]
and a rock that trips them up.[c] [d]

They stumble by disobeying the message; they
were destined for this.

9 But you are **a chosen race,**[e] [f]
a royal priesthood,[g]
a holy nation,[h] **a people**
for His possession,[i]
so that you may proclaim
the praises[j] [k]
of the One who called you
out of darkness
into His marvelous light.
10 Once you were not a people,
but now you are God's people;
you had not received mercy,
but now you have received mercy.

A Call to Good Works

11 Dear friends, I urge you as aliens and
temporary residents to abstain from fleshly
desires that war against you.[l] 12 Conduct yourselves honorably among the Gentiles,[m] so that
in a case where they speak against you as
those who do evil, they may, by observing
your good works, glorify God in a day of
visitation.[n]
13 Submit to every human institution
because of the Lord, whether to the Emperor[o]
as the supreme authority, 14 or to governors as
those sent out by him to punish those who do
evil and to praise those who do good. 15 For it
is God's will that you, by doing good, silence
the ignorance of foolish people. 16 As God's
slaves, ⌊live⌋ as free people, but don't use your
freedom as a way to conceal evil. 17 Honor
everyone. Love the brotherhood. Fear God.
Honor the Emperor.[o]

Submission of Slaves to Masters

18 Household slaves, submit yourselves to
your masters with all respect, not only to the
good and gentle but also to the cruel.[p] 19 For it
⌊brings⌋ favor[q] if, because of conscience toward
God,[r] someone endures grief from suffering
unjustly. 20 For what credit is there if you
endure when you sin and are beaten? But when
you do good and suffer, if you endure, it brings
favor with God.

21 For you were called to this,
because Christ also suffered for you,
leaving you an example,
so that you should follow in His steps.
22 He **did not commit sin,**
and no deceit was found
in His mouth;[s]
23 when reviled, He did not revile
in return;
when suffering, He did not threaten,
but committed Himself to the One
who judges justly.
24 He Himself bore our sins
in His body on the tree,
so that, having died to sins,
we might live for righteousness;
by **His wounding**
you have been healed.[t]
25 For you **were like sheep**
going astray,[u]
but you have now returned
to the shepherd and guardian[v]
of your souls.

Wives and Husbands

3 Wives, in the same way, submit yourselves to your own husbands so that,
even if some disobey the ⌊Christian⌋ message,
they may be won over[w] without a message by
the way their wives live, 2 when they observe
your pure, reverent lives. 3 Your beauty should
not consist of outward things ⌊like⌋ elaborate
hairstyles and the wearing of gold ornaments[x]
or fine clothes; 4 instead, ⌊it should consist of⌋
the hidden person of the heart with the imperishable quality of a gentle and quiet spirit,
which is very valuable in God's eyes. 5 For in
the past, the holy women who hoped in God

[a]**2:7** Ps 118:22 [b]**2:8** Or *a stone causing stumbling* [c]**2:8** Or *a rock to trip over* [d]**2:8** Is 8:14 [e]**2:9** Or *chosen generation*, or *chosen nation* [f]**2:9** Is 43:20 LXX; Dt 7:6; 10:15 [g]**2:9** Ex 19:6; 23:22 LXX; Is 61:6 [h]**2:9** Ex 19:6; 23:22 LXX [i]**2:9** Ex 19:5; 23:22 LXX; Dt 4:20; 7:6; Is 43:21 LXX [j]**2:9** Or *the mighty deeds* [k]**2:9** Is 42:12; 43:21 [l]**2:11** Lit *against the soul* [m]**2:12** Or *among the nations*, or *among the pagans* [n]**2:12** A day when God intervenes in human history, either in grace or in judgment [o]**2:13,17** Lit *king* [p]**2:18** Lit *crooked*, or *unscrupulous* [q]**2:19** Other mss add *with God* [r]**2:19** Other mss read *because of a good conscience* [s]**2:22** Is 53:9 [t]**2:24** Is 53:5 [u]**2:25** Is 53:6 [v]**2:25** Or *overseer* [w]**3:1** Lit *may be gained* [x]**3:3** Lit *and of putting around of gold items*

also beautified themselves in this way, submitting to their own husbands, 6 just as Sarah
obeyed Abraham, calling him lord. You have
become her children when you do good and
aren't frightened by anything alarming.
7 Husbands, in the same way, live with
your wives with understanding of their weaker
nature[a] yet showing them honor as co-heirs of
the grace of life, so that your prayers will not be
hindered.

Do No Evil

8 Now finally, all of you should be like-
minded and sympathetic, should love believers,[b]
and be compassionate and humble,[c] 9 not paying
back evil for evil or insult for insult but, on the
contrary, giving a blessing, since you were called
for this, so that you can inherit a blessing.

10 **For the one who wants to love life**
and to see good days
must keep his tongue
from evil
and his lips from speaking deceit,
11 **and he must turn away from evil**
and do good.
He must seek peace and pursue it,
12 **because the eyes of the Lord**
are on the righteous
and His ears are open
to their request.
But the face of the Lord is
against those who do evil.[d]

Undeserved Suffering

13 And who will harm[e] you if you are passionate for what is good?[f] 14 But even if you
should suffer for righteousness, you are blessed.
Do not fear what they fear or be disturbed,[g]
15 but set apart the •Messiah[h] as Lord in your
hearts, and always be ready to give a defense to
anyone who asks you for a reason[i] for the hope
that is in you. 16 However, do this with gentleness and respect, keeping your conscience
clear,[j] so that when you are accused,[k] those who
denounce your Christian life will be put to
shame. 17 For it is better to suffer for doing good,
if that should be God's will,[l] than for doing evil.

18 For Christ also suffered for sins
once for all,[m]
the righteous for the unrighteous,[n]
that He might bring you[o] to God,
after being put to death
in the fleshly realm[p]
but made alive in the spiritual realm.[q]

19 In that state[r] He also went and made a proclamation to the spirits in prisons[s] 20 who in the
past were disobedient, when God patiently
waited in the days of Noah while an ark was
being prepared; in it, a few—that is, eight
people[t] —were saved through water. 21 Baptism,
which corresponds to this, now saves you (not
the removal of the filth of the flesh, but the
pledge[u] of a good conscience toward God)
through the resurrection of Jesus Christ. 22 Now
that He has gone into heaven, He is at God's
right hand, with angels, authorities, and powers
subjected to Him.

Following Christ

4 Therefore, since Christ suffered[v] in the
flesh,[w] arm yourselves also with the
same resolve[x] —because the One who suffered in the flesh[w] has finished with sin[y] —
2 in order to live the remaining time in the
flesh,[w] no longer for human desires,[z] but for
God's will. 3 For there has already been
enough time spent in doing the will of the
pagans:[aa] carrying on in unrestrained behavior,
evil desires, drunkenness, orgies, carousing,
and lawless idolatry. 4 In regard to this, they
are surprised that you don't plunge with them
into the same flood[ab] of dissipation—and they
slander you. 5 They will give an account to the
One who stands ready to judge the living and
the dead. 6 For this reason the gospel was also
preached to ⌊those who are now⌋ dead, so that,
although they might be judged by men in the
fleshly realm,[p] they might live by God in the
spiritual realm.[ac]

[a]**3:7** Lit *understanding as the weaker vessel* [b]**3:8** Lit *brotherly-loving* [c]**3:8** Other mss read *courteous* [d]**3:10–12** Ps 34:12–16 [e]**3:13** Or *will mistreat*, or *will do evil to* [f]**3:13** Lit *you are zealots*, or *you are partisans for the good*, or *you are eager to do good* [g]**3:14** Is 8:12 [h]**3:15** Other mss read *set God* [i]**3:15** Or *who demands of you an accounting* [j]**3:16** Lit *good*; or *keeping a clear conscience* [k]**3:16** Other mss read *when they speak against you as evildoers* [l]**3:17** Lit *if the will of God should will* [m]**3:18** Other mss read *died for sins on our behalf*; other mss read *died for our sins*; other mss read *died for sins on your behalf* [n]**3:18** Or *the Righteous One in the place of the unrighteous many* [o]**3:18** Other mss read *us* [p]**3:18; 4:6** Or *in the flesh* [q]**3:18** Or *in the spirit*, or *in the Spirit* [r]**3:19** Or *In whom*, or *At that time*, or *In which* [s]**3:19** The *spirits in prison* are most likely fallen supernatural beings or angels; see 2 Pt 2:4; Jd 6. [t]**3:20** Lit *souls* [u]**3:21** Or *the appeal* [v]**4:1** Other mss read *suffered for us* [w]**4:1,2** *In the flesh* probably means "in human existence"; see 1 Pt 3:18. [x]**4:1** Or *perspective*, or *attitude* [y]**4:1** Or *the one who has suffered in the flesh has ceased from sin* [z]**4:2** Lit *for desires of human beings* [aa]**4:3** Or *Gentiles* [ab]**4:4** Lit *you don't run with them into the same pouring out* [ac]**4:6** Or *in the spirit*

End-Time Ethics

7 Now the end of all things is near; therefore, be clear-headed and disciplined for prayer.
8 Above all, keep your love for one another at
full strength, since **love covers a multitude of
sins.**[a] 9 Be hospitable to one another without
complaining. 10 Based on the gift they have
received, everyone should use it to serve others, as good managers of the varied grace of
God. 11 If anyone speaks, ⌊his speech should
be⌋ like the oracles of God; if anyone serves,
⌊his service should be⌋ from the strength God
provides, so that in everything God may be glorified through Jesus Christ. To Him belong the
glory and the power forever and ever. •Amen.

Christian Suffering

12 Dear friends, when the fiery ordeal[b]
arises among you to test you, don't be surprised by it, as if something unusual were
happening to you. 13 Instead, as you share in
the sufferings of the •Messiah rejoice, so that
you may also rejoice with great joy at the revelation of His glory. 14 If you are ridiculed for
the name of Christ, you are blessed, because
the Spirit of glory and of God rests on you.[c]
15 None of you, however, should suffer as a
murderer, a thief, an evildoer, or as a med-
dler.[d] 16 But if ⌊anyone suffers⌋ as a Christian,
he should not be ashamed, but should glorify
God with that name. 17 For the time has
come for judgment to begin with God's
household; and if it begins with us, what will
the outcome be for those who disobey the
gospel of God?

18 **And if the righteous is saved**
with difficulty,
what will become of the ungodly
and the sinner?[e]

19 So those who suffer according to God's will
should, in doing good, entrust themselves to a
faithful Creator.

About the Elders

5 Therefore, as a fellow elder and witness
to the sufferings of the •Messiah, and also
a participant in the glory about to be revealed,
I exhort the elders among you: 2 shepherd
God's flock among you, not overseeing[f] out of
compulsion but freely, according to God's
⌊will⌋;[g] not for the money but eagerly; 3 not
lording it over those entrusted to you, but
being examples to the flock. 4 And when the
chief Shepherd appears, you will receive the
unfading crown of glory.

5 Likewise, you younger men, be subject to
the elders. And all of you clothe yourselves
with[h] humility toward one another, because

God resists the proud,
but gives grace to the humble.[i]

6 Humble yourselves therefore under the
mighty hand of God, so that He may exalt you
in due time,[j] 7 casting all your care upon Him,
because He cares about you.

Conclusion

8 Be sober! Be on the alert! Your adversary
the Devil is prowling around like a roaring lion,
looking for anyone he can devour. 9 Resist him,
firm in the faith, knowing that the same sufferings are being experienced by your brothers in
the world.

10 Now the God of all grace, who called you
to His eternal glory in Christ Jesus, will personally[k] restore, establish, strengthen, and support
you after you have suffered a little.[l] 11 To Him
be the dominion[m] forever.[n] •Amen.

12 Through Silvanus,[o] whom I consider a
faithful brother, I have written briefly, encouraging you and testifying that this is the true
grace of God. Take your stand in it! 13 She who
is in Babylon, also chosen, sends you greetings,
as does Mark, my son. 14 Greet one another
with a kiss of love. Peace to all of you who are
in Christ.[p]

[a]**4:8** Pr 10:12 [b]**4:12** Lit *the burning* [c]**4:14** Other mss add *He is blasphemed because of them, but He is glorified because of you.* [d]**4:15** Or *as one who defrauds others* [e]**4:18** Pr 11:31 LXX [f]**5:2** Other mss omit *overseeing* [g]**5:2** Other mss omit *according to God's will* [h]**5:5** Lit *you tie around yourselves* [i]**5:5** Pr 3:34 LXX [j]**5:6** Lit *in time* [k]**5:10** Lit *Himself* [l]**5:10** Or *a little while, or to a small extent* [m]**5:11** Other mss read *dominion and glory*; other mss read *glory and dominion* [n]**5:11** Other mss read *forever and ever* [o]**5:12** Or *Silas*; Ac 15:22–32; 16:19–40; 17:1–16 [p]**5:14** Other mss read *Christ Jesus. Amen.*

2 Peter

Greeting

1 Simeon[a] Peter, a slave and an apostle of
Jesus Christ:
To those who have obtained a faith of equal
privilege with ours[b] through the righteousness
of our God and Savior Jesus Christ.
2 May grace and peace be multiplied to you
through the knowledge of God and of Jesus our
Lord.

Growth in the Faith

3 For His[c] divine power has given us everything required for life and godliness, through
the knowledge of Him who called us by[d] His
own glory and goodness. 4 By these He has
given us very great and precious promises, so
that through them you may share in the divine
nature, escaping the corruption that is in the
world because of evil desires. 5 For this very
reason, make every effort to supplement your
faith with goodness, goodness with knowledge, 6 knowledge with self-control, self-control with endurance, endurance with
godliness, 7 godliness with brotherly affection,
and brotherly affection with love. 8 For if
these qualities are yours and are increasing,
they will keep you from being useless or
unfruitful in the knowledge of our Lord Jesus
Christ. 9 The person who lacks these things is
blind and shortsighted, and has forgotten the
cleansing from his past sins. 10 Therefore,
brothers, make every effort to confirm your
calling and election, because if you do these
things you will never stumble. 11 For in this
way, entry into the eternal kingdom of our
Lord and Savior Jesus Christ will be richly supplied to you.
12 Therefore I will always remind you
about these things, even though you know
them and are established in the truth you
have. 13 I consider it right, as long as I am in
this tent,[e] to wake you up with a reminder,
14 knowing that I will soon lay aside my tent,
as our Lord Jesus Christ has also shown me.
15 And I will also make every effort that after
my departure[f] you may be able to recall these
things at any time.

The Trustworthy Prophetic Word

16 For we did not follow cleverly contrived
myths when we made known to you the power
and coming of our Lord Jesus Christ; instead,
we were eyewitnesses of His majesty. 17 For
when He received honor and glory from God
the Father, a voice came to Him from the
Majestic Glory:

> This is My beloved Son.[g]
> I take delight in Him![h]

18 And we heard this voice when it came from
heaven while we were with Him on the holy
mountain. 19 So we have the prophetic word
strongly confirmed. You will do well to pay
attention to it, as to a lamp shining in a dismal
place, until the day dawns and the morning
star arises in your hearts. 20 First of all, you
should know this: no prophecy of Scripture
comes from one's own interpretation, 21
because no prophecy ever came by the will of
man; instead, moved by the Holy Spirit, men
spoke from God.

The Judgment of False Teachers

2 But there were also false prophets
among the people, just as there will be
false teachers among you. They will secretly
bring in destructive heresies, even denying the
Master who bought them, and will bring swift
destruction on themselves. 2 Many will follow
their unrestrained ways, and because of them
the way of truth will be blasphemed. 3 In their
greed they will exploit you with deceptive
words. Their condemnation, ⌊pronounced⌋
long ago, is not idle, and their destruction does
not sleep.
4 For if God didn't spare the angels who
sinned, but threw them down into Tartarus[i]
and delivered them to be kept in chains[j] of
darkness until judgment; 5 and if He didn't
spare the ancient world, but protected Noah, a
preacher of righteousness, and seven others,[k]
when He brought a flood on the world of the
ungodly; 6 and if He reduced the cities of
Sodom and Gomorrah to ashes and condemned
them to ruin,[l] making them an example to

[a]**1:1** Simon [b]**1:1** Or *obtained a faith of the same kind as ours* [c]**1:3** Lit *As His* [d]**1:3** Or *to* [e]**1:13** A euphemism for Peter's body [f]**1:15** Or *my death* [g]**1:17** Other mss read *My Son, My Beloved* [h]**1:17** A reference to the transfiguration; see Mt 17:5 [i]**2:4** *Tartarus* is a Gk name for a subterranean place of divine punishment lower than Hades. [j]**2:4** Other mss read *in pits* [k]**2:5** Lit *righteousness, as the eighth* [l]**2:6** Other mss omit *to ruin*

those who were going to be ungodly;[a] 7 and if He rescued righteous Lot, distressed by the unrestrained behavior of the immoral 8 (for as he lived among them, that righteous man tormented himself day by day with the lawless deeds he saw and heard)— 9 then the Lord knows how to rescue the godly from trials and to keep the unrighteous under punishment until the day of judgment, 10 especially those who follow the polluting desires of the flesh and despise authority.

Bold, arrogant people! They do not tremble when they blaspheme the glorious ones; 11 however, angels, who are greater in might and power, do not bring a slanderous charge against them before the Lord.[b] 12 But these people, like irrational animals—creatures of instinct born to be caught and destroyed—speak blasphemies about things they don't understand, and in their destruction they too will be destroyed, 13 suffering harm as the payment for unrighteousness. They consider it a pleasure to carouse in the daytime. They are blots and blemishes, delighting in their deceptions[c] as they feast with you, 14 having eyes full of adultery and always looking for sin, seducing unstable people, and with hearts trained in greed. Accursed children! 15 By abandoning the straight path, they have gone astray and have followed the path of Balaam, the son of Bosor,[d] who loved the wages of unrighteousness, 16 but received a rebuke for his transgression: a speechless donkey spoke with a human voice and restrained the prophet's madness.

17 These people are springs without water, mists driven by a whirlwind. The gloom of darkness has been reserved for them. 18 For uttering bombastic, empty words, they seduce, by fleshly desires and debauchery, people who have barely escaped[e] from those who live in error. 19 They promise them freedom, but they themselves are slaves of corruption, since people are enslaved to whatever defeats them. 20 For if, having escaped the world's impurity through the knowledge of our Lord and Savior Jesus Christ, they are again entangled in these things and defeated, the last state is worse for them than the first. 21 For it would have been better for them not to have known the way of righteousness than, after knowing it, to turn back from the holy commandment delivered to them. 22 It has happened to them according to the true proverb: **A dog returns to its own vomit,**[f] and, "a sow, after washing itself, wallows in the mud."

The Day of the Lord

3 Dear friends, this is now the second letter I've written you; in both, I awaken your pure understanding with a reminder, 2 so that you can remember the words previously spoken by the holy prophets, and the commandment of our Lord and Savior ⌊given⌋ through your apostles. 3 First, be aware of this: scoffers will come in the last days to scoff, following their own lusts, 4 saying, "Where is the promise of His coming? For ever since the fathers fell •asleep, all things continue as they have been since the beginning of creation." 5 They willfully ignore this: long ago the heavens and the earth existed out of water and through water by the word of God. 6 Through these the world of that time perished when it was flooded by water. 7 But by the same word the present heavens and earth are held in store for fire, being kept until the day of judgment and destruction of ungodly men.

8 Dear friends, don't let this one thing escape you: with the Lord one day is like 1,000 years, and 1,000 years like one day. 9 The Lord does not delay His promise, as some understand delay, but is patient with you, not wanting any to perish, but all to come to repentance.

10 But the Day of the Lord will come like a thief;[g] on that ⌊day⌋ the heavens will pass away with a loud noise, the elements will burn and be dissolved, and the earth and the works on it will be disclosed.[h] 11 Since all these things are to be destroyed in this way, ⌊it is clear⌋ what sort of people you should be in holy conduct and godliness 12 as you wait for and earnestly desire the coming of the day of God, because of which the heavens will be on fire and be dissolved, and the elements will melt with the heat. 13 But based on His promise, we wait for new heavens and a new earth, where righteousness will dwell.

Conclusion

14 Therefore, dear friends, while you wait for these things, make every effort to be found in peace without spot or blemish before Him. 15 Also, regard the patience of our Lord as ⌊an

[a]**2:6** Other mss read *an example of what is going to happen to the ungodly* [b]**2:11** Other mss read *them from the Lord* [c]**2:13** Other mss read *delighting in the love feasts* [d]**2:15** Other mss read *Beor* [e]**2:18** Or *people who are barely escaping* [f]**2:22** Pr 26:11 [g]**3:10** Other mss add *in the night* [h]**3:10** Other mss read *will be burned up*

opportunity for salvation, just as our dear
brother Paul, according to the wisdom given to
him, has written to you. 16 He speaks about
these things in all his letters, in which there are
some matters that are hard to understand. The
untaught and unstable twist them to their own
destruction, as they also do with the rest of the
Scriptures.

17 Therefore, dear friends, since you have
been forewarned, be on your guard, so that
you are not led away by the error of the
immoral and fall from your own stability.
18 But grow in the grace and knowledge of our
Lord and Savior Jesus Christ. To Him be the
glory both now and to the day of eternity.[a]
•Amen.[b]

1 John

Prologue

1 What was from the beginning,
what we have heard,
what we have seen with our eyes,
what we have observed,
and have touched with our hands,
concerning the Word of life—
2 that life was revealed,
and we have seen it
and we testify and declare to you
the eternal life that was
with the Father
and was revealed to us—
3 what we have seen and heard
we also declare to you,
so that you may have fellowship
along with us;
and indeed our fellowship is
with the Father
and with His Son Jesus Christ.
4 We are writing these things[c]
so that our[d] joy may be complete.

Fellowship with God

5 Now this is the message we have heard
from Him and declare to you: God is light, and
there is absolutely no darkness in Him. 6 If we
say, "We have fellowship with Him," and
•walk in darkness, we are lying and are not
practicing[e] the truth. 7 But if we walk in the
light as He Himself is in the light, we have
fellowship with one another, and the blood of
Jesus His Son cleanses us from all sin. 8 If we
say, "We have no sin," we are deceiving ourselves, and the truth is not in us. 9 If we confess
our sins, He is faithful and righteous to forgive
us our sins and to cleanse us from all unrighteousness. 10 If we say, "We have not sinned,"
we make Him a liar, and His word is not in us.

2 My little children, I am writing you
these things so that you may not sin. But
if anyone does sin, we have an •advocate with
the Father—Jesus Christ the righteous One.
2 He Himself is the propitiation[f] for our sins,
and not only for ours, but also for those of the
whole world.

God's Commands

3 This is how we are sure that we have
come to know Him: by keeping His commands.
4 The one who says, "I have come to know
Him," without keeping His commands, is a liar,
and the truth is not in him. 5 But whoever
keeps His word, truly in him the love of God is
perfected.[g] This is how we know we are in
Him: 6 the one who says he remains in Him
should •walk just as He walked.

7 Dear friends, I am not writing you a new
command, but an old command that you have
had from the beginning. The old command is
the message you have heard. 8 Yet I am writing
you a new command, which is true in Him and
in you, because the darkness is passing away
and the true light is already shining.

9 The one who says he is in the light but
hates his brother is in the darkness until now.
10 The one who loves his brother remains in
the light, and there is no cause for stumbling in
him.[h] 11 But the one who hates his brother is
in the darkness, walks in the darkness, and
doesn't know where he's going, because the
darkness has blinded his eyes.

[a]**3:18** Or *now and forever* [b]**3:18** Other mss omit *Amen.* [c]**1:4** Other mss add *to you* [d]**1:4** Other mss read *your* [e]**1:6** Or *not living according to* [f]**2:2** The word *propitiation* has to do with the removal of divine wrath. Jesus' death is the means that turns God's wrath from the sinner; see 2 Co 5:21. [g]**2:5** Or *truly completed* [h]**2:10** Or *in it*

Turn to page 95.

Reasons for Writing

12 I am writing to you, little children,
because your sins have been forgiven
on account of His name.
13 I am writing to you, fathers,
because you have come to know
the One who is
from the beginning.
I am writing to you, young men,
because you have had victory
over the evil one.
14 I have written to you, children,
because you have come to know
the Father.
I have written to you, fathers,
because you have come to know
the One who is from the beginning.
I have written to you, young men,
because you are strong,
God's word remains in you,
and you have had victory
over the evil one.

A Warning about the World

15 Do not love the world or the things that
belong to[a] the world. If anyone loves the world,
love for the Father is not in him. 16 For everything that belongs to[b] the world—the lust of
the flesh, the lust of the eyes, and the pride in
one's lifestyle—is not from the Father, but is
from the world. 17 And the world with its lust
is passing away, but the one who does God's
will remains forever.

The Last Hour

18 Children, it is the last hour. And as you
have heard, "Antichrist is coming," even now
many antichrists have come. We know from
this that it is the last hour. 19 They went out
from us, but they did not belong to us; for if
they had belonged to us, they would have
remained with us. However, they went out so
that it might be made clear that none of them
belongs to us.

20 But you have an anointing from the Holy
One, and you all have knowledge.[c] 21 I have
not written to you because you don't know the
truth, but because you do know it, and because
no lie comes from the truth. 22 Who is the liar,
if not the one who denies that Jesus is the
•Messiah? He is the antichrist, the one who
denies the Father and the Son. 23 No one who
denies the Son can have the Father; he who
confesses the Son has the Father as well.

Remaining with God

24 What you have heard from the beginning
must remain in you. If what you have heard
from the beginning remains in you, then you
will remain in the Son and in the Father.
25 And this is the promise that He Himself
made to us: eternal life. 26 I have written these
things to you about those who are trying to
deceive you.

27 The anointing you received from Him
remains in you, and you don't need anyone to
teach you. Instead, His anointing teaches you
about all things, and is true and is not a lie; just
as it has taught you, remain in Him.

God's Children

28 So now, little children, remain in Him, so
that when He appears we may have boldness
and not be ashamed before Him at His coming.
29 If you know that He is righteous, you know
this as well: everyone who does what

3 is right has been born of Him. 1 Look at
how great a love[d] the Father has given us,
that we should be called God's children. And
we are! The reason the world does not know us
is that it didn't know Him. 2 Dear friends, we
are God's children now, and what we will be
has not yet been revealed. We know that when
He appears, we will be like Him, because we
will see Him as He is. 3 And everyone who has
this hope in Him purifies himself just as He is
pure.

4 Everyone who commits sin also breaks the
law;[e] sin is the breaking of law. 5 You know
that He was revealed so that He might take
away sins,[f] and there is no sin in Him.
6 Everyone who remains in Him does not sin;
everyone who sins has not seen Him or known
Him.

7 Little children, let no one deceive you!
The one who does what is right is righteous,
just as He is righteous. 8 The one who commits
sin is of the Devil, for the Devil has sinned from
the beginning. The Son of God was revealed for
this purpose: to destroy the Devil's works.
9 Everyone who has been born of God does not
sin, because His[g] seed remains in him; he is not
able to sin, because he has been born of God.
10 This is how God's children—and the Devil's
children—are made evident.

[a]2:15 Lit *things in* [b]2:15 Lit *that is in* [c]2:20 Other mss read *and you know all things* [d]3:1 Or *at what sort of love* [e]3:4 Or *also commits iniquity* [f]3:5 Other mss read *our sins* [g]3:9 God's

Love's Imperative

Whoever does not do what is right is not of God, especially the one who does not love his brother. 11 For this is the message you have heard from the beginning: we should love one another, 12 unlike Cain, who was of the evil one and murdered[a] his brother. And why did he murder him? Because his works were evil, and his brother's were righteous. 13 Do not be surprised, brothers, if the world hates you. 14 We know that we have passed from death to life because we love our brothers. The one who does not love remains in death. 15 Everyone who hates his brother is a murderer, and you know that no murderer has eternal life residing in him.

Love in Action

16 This is how we have come to know love: He laid down His life for us. We should also lay down our lives for our brothers. 17 If anyone has this world's goods and sees his brother in need but shuts off his compassion from him—how can God's love reside in him?

18 Little children, we must not love in word or speech, but in deed and truth; 19 that is how we will know we are of the truth, and will convince our hearts in His presence, 20 because if our hearts condemn us, God is greater than our hearts and knows all things.

21 Dear friends, if our hearts do not condemn ⌊us⌋ we have confidence before God, 22 and can receive whatever we ask from Him because we keep His commands and do what is pleasing in His sight. 23 Now this is His command: that we believe in the name of His Son Jesus Christ, and love one another as He commanded us. 24 The one who keeps His commands remains in Him, and He in him. And the way we know that He remains in us is from the Spirit He has given us.

The Spirit of Truth and the Spirit of Error

4 Dear friends, do not believe every spirit, but test the spirits to determine if they are from God, because many false prophets have gone out into the world.

2 This is how you know the Spirit of God: Every spirit who confesses that Jesus Christ has come in the flesh[b] is from God. 3 But every spirit who does not confess Jesus[c] is not from God. This is the spirit of the antichrist; you have heard that he is coming, and he is already in the world now.

4 You are from God, little children, and you have conquered them, because the One who is in you is greater than the one who is in the world. 5 They are from the world. Therefore what they say is from the world, and the world listens to them. 6 We are from God. Anyone who knows God listens to us; anyone who is not from God does not listen to us. From this we know the Spirit of truth and the spirit of deception.

Knowing God through Love

7 Dear friends, let us love one another, because love is from God, and everyone who loves has been born of God and knows God. 8 The one who does not love does not know God, because God is love. 9 God's love was revealed among us in this way:[d] God sent His •One and Only Son into the world so that we might live through Him. 10 Love consists in this: not that we loved God, but that He loved us and sent His Son to be the[e] propitiation[f] for our sins. 11 Dear friends, if God loved us in this way, we also must love one another. 12 No one has ever seen God.[g] If we love one another, God remains in[h] us and His love is perfected in us.

13 This is how we know that we remain in Him and He in us: He has given to us from His Spirit. 14 And we have seen and we testify that the Father has sent the Son as Savior of the world. 15 Whoever confesses[i] that Jesus is the Son of God—God remains in him and he in God. 16 And we have come to know and to believe the love that God has for us. God is love, and the one who remains in love remains in God, and God remains in him.

17 In this, love is perfected with us so that we may have confidence in the day of judgment; for we are as He is in this world. 18 There is no fear in love; instead, perfect love drives out fear, because fear involves punishment.[j] So the one who fears has not reached perfection in love. 19 We love[k] because He first loved us.

Keeping God's Commands

20 If anyone says, "I love God," yet hates his brother, he is a liar. For the person who does not love his brother whom he has seen cannot

[a]**3:12** Or *slaughtered* [b]**4:2** Or *confesses Jesus to be the Christ come in the flesh* [c]**4:3** Other mss read *confess that Jesus has come in the flesh* [d]**4:9** Or *revealed in us* [e]**4:10** Or *a* [f]**4:10** The word *propitiation* has to do with the removal of divine wrath. Jesus' death is the means that turns God's wrath from the sinner; see 2 Co 5:21. [g]**4:12** Since God is an infinite being, no one can see Him in His absolute essential nature; see Ex 33:18–23. [h]**4:12** Or *remains among* [i]**4:15** Or *acknowledges* [j]**4:18** Or *fear has its own punishment* or *torment* [k]**4:19** Other mss add *Him*

love God whom he has not seen.[a] 21 And we
have this command from Him: the one who
loves God must also love his brother.

5 Everyone who believes that Jesus is the
•Messiah has been born of God, and
everyone who loves the parent also loves his
child. 2 This is how we know that we love
God's children when we love God and obey[b]
His commands. 3 For this is what love for God
is: to keep His commands. Now His commands
are not a burden, 4 because whatever has been
born of God conquers the world. This is the
victory that has conquered the world: our
faith. 5 And who is the one who conquers the
world but the one who believes that Jesus is
the Son of God?

The Sureness of God's Testimony

6 Jesus Christ—He is the One who came by
water and blood; not by water only, but by
water and by blood. And the Spirit is the One
who testifies, because the Spirit is the truth.
7 For there are three that testify:[c] 8 the Spirit,
the water, and the blood—and these three are
in agreement. 9 If we accept the testimony of
men, God's testimony is greater, because it is
God's testimony that He has given about His
Son. 10 (The one who believes in the Son of
God has the testimony in himself. The one who
does not believe God has made Him a liar,
because he has not believed in the testimony
that God has given about His Son.) 11 And this
is the testimony: God has given us eternal life,
and this life is in His Son.

12 The one who has the Son has life. The
one who doesn't have the Son of God does not
have life. 13 I have written these things to you
who believe in the name of the Son of God, so
that you may know that you have eternal life.

Effective Prayer

14 Now this is the confidence we have
before Him: whenever we ask anything according to His will, He hears us. 15 And if we know
that He hears whatever we ask, we know that
we have what we have asked Him for.

16 If anyone sees his brother committing a
sin that does not bring death, he should ask,
and God[d] will give life to him—to those who
commit sin that doesn't bring death. There is
sin[e] that brings death. I am not saying he
should pray about that. 17 All unrighteousness
is sin, and there is sin that does not bring death.

Conclusion

18 We know that everyone who has been
born of God does not sin, but the One[f] who is
born of God keeps him,[g] [h] and the evil one does
not touch him.

19 We know that we are of God, and the
whole world is under the sway of the evil one.

20 And we know that the Son of God has
come and has given us understanding so that
we may know the true One.[i] We are in the true
One—that is, in His Son Jesus Christ. He is the
true God and eternal life.

21 Little children, guard yourselves from
idols.

2 John

Greeting

The Elder:[j]
To the elect lady[k] and her children, whom
I love in truth—and not only I, but also all who
have come to know the truth— 2 because of
the truth that remains in us and will be with us
forever.

3 Grace, mercy, and peace will be with us
from God the Father and from Jesus Christ, the
Son of the Father, in truth and love.

[a] **4:20** Other mss read *seen, how is he able to love . . . seen?* (as a question) [b] **5:2** Other mss read *keep* [c] **5:7–8** Other mss (the Lat Vg and a few late Gk mss) read *testify in heaven, the Father, the Word, and the Holy Spirit, and these three are One. 8 And there are three who bear witness on earth:* [d] **5:16** Lit *He* [e] **5:16** Or *is a sin* [f] **5:18** Jesus Christ [g] **5:18** Other mss read *himself* [h] **5:18** Or *the one who is born of God keeps himself* [i] **5:20** Other mss read *the true God* [j] **1** Or *Presbyter* [k] **1** Or *Kyria,* a proper name; probably a literary figure for a local church known to John; the *children* would be its members.

Truth and Deception

4 I was very glad to find some of your children •walking in truth, in keeping with a command we have received from the Father. 5 So
now I urge you, lady—not as if I were writing
you a new command, but one we have had
from the beginning—that we love one another.
6 And this is love: that we walk according to His
commands. This is the command as you have
heard it from the beginning: you must walk in
love.[a]
7 Many deceivers have gone out into the
world; they do not confess the coming of Jesus
Christ in the flesh.[b] This is the deceiver and
the antichrist. 8 Watch yourselves so that you
don't lose what we[c] have worked for, but you
may receive a full reward. 9 Anyone who does
not remain in the teaching about Christ, but
goes beyond it, does not have God. The one
who remains in that teaching, this one has
both the Father and the Son. 10 If anyone
comes to you and does not bring this teaching,
do not receive him into your home, and don't
say, "Welcome," to him; 11 for the one who
says, "Welcome," to him shares in his evil
works.

Farewell

12 Though I have many things to write to
you, I don't want to do so with paper and ink.
Instead, I hope to be with you and talk face to
face[d] so that our joy may be complete.
13 The children of your elect sister send you
greetings.

3 John

Greeting

The Elder:
To my dear friend[e] Gaius, whom I love in
truth.
2 Dear friend,[f] I pray that you may prosper
in every way and be in good health, just as
your soul prospers. 3 For I was very glad
when some brothers came and testified to your
⌊faithfulness⌋ to the truth—how you are •walk-
ing in the truth. 4 I have no greater joy than
this: to hear that my children are walking in the
truth.

Gaius Commended

5 Dear friend,[f] you are showing your faith[g]
by whatever you do for the brothers, and this
⌊you are doing⌋ for strangers; 6 they have testified to your love before the church. You will
do well to send them on their journey in a
manner worthy of God, 7 since they set out for
the sake of the name, accepting nothing from
pagans. 8 Therefore, we ought to support such
men, so that we can be co-workers with[h] the
truth.

Diotrephes and Demetrius

9 I wrote something to the church, but
Diotrephes, who loves to have first place
among them, does not receive us. 10 This is
why, if I come, I will remind him of the works
he is doing, slandering us with malicious
words. And he is not satisfied with that! He not
only refuses to welcome the brothers himself,
but he even stops those who want to do so and
expels them from the church.
11 Dear friend,[f] do not imitate what is evil,
but what is good. The one who does good is of
God; the one who does evil has not seen God.
12 Demetrius has a ⌊good⌋ testimony from
everyone, and from the truth itself. And we also
testify for him, and you know that our testimony is true.

Farewell

13 I have many things to write you, but I
don't want to write to you with pen and ink.
14 I hope to see you soon, and we will talk face
to face.[i]
Peace be with you. The friends send you
greetings. Greet the friends by name.

[a]6 Lit *in it* [b]7 Or *confess Jesus Christ as coming in the flesh* [c]8 Other mss read *you* [d]12 Lit *mouth to mouth* [e]1 Or *my beloved* [f]2,5,11 Or *Beloved* [g]5 Lit *are doing faith* [h]8 Or *co-workers for* [i]14 Lit *mouth to mouth*

Jude

Greeting

Jude, a slave of Jesus Christ, and a brother of
James:
To those who are the called, loved[a] by God
the Father and kept by Jesus Christ.
2 May mercy, peace, and love be multiplied
to you.

Jude's Purpose in Writing

3 Dear friends, although I was eager to write
you about our common salvation, I found it necessary to write and exhort you to contend for
the faith that was delivered to the saints once
for all. 4 For certain men, who were designated
for this judgment long ago, have come in by
stealth; they are ungodly, turning the grace of
our God into promiscuity and denying our only
Master and Lord, Jesus Christ.

Apostates: Past and Present

5 Now I want to remind you, though you
know all these things: the Lord, having first of
all[b] saved a people out of Egypt, later
destroyed those who did not believe; 6 and He
has kept, with eternal chains in darkness for
the judgment of the great day, angels who did
not keep their own position but deserted their
proper dwelling. 7 In the same way, Sodom
and Gomorrah and the cities around them
committed sexual immorality and practiced
perversions,[c] just as they did, and serve as an
example by undergoing the punishment of
eternal fire.
8 Nevertheless, these dreamers likewise
defile their flesh, despise authority, and blaspheme glorious beings. 9 Yet Michael the
archangel, when he was disputing with the
Devil in a debate about Moses' body, did not
dare bring an abusive condemnation against
him, but said, "The Lord rebuke you!" 10 But
these people blaspheme anything they don't
understand, and what they know by instinct,
like unreasoning animals—they destroy themselves with these things. 11 Woe to them! For
they have traveled in the way of Cain, have
abandoned themselves to the error of Balaam
for profit, and have perished in Korah's rebellion.

The Apostates' Doom

12 These are the ones who are like dangerous reefs[d] at your love feasts. They feast with
you, nurturing only themselves without fear.
They are waterless clouds carried along by
winds; trees in late autumn—fruitless, twice
dead, pulled out by the roots; 13 wild waves of
the sea, foaming up their shameful deeds; wandering stars for whom is reserved the blackness
of darkness forever!
14 And Enoch, in the seventh ⌊generation⌋
from Adam, prophesied about them:

Look! The Lord comes[e]
  with thousands of His holy ones
15 to execute judgment on all, and to
  convict them[f]
of all their ungodly deeds that they
  have done
  in an ungodly way,
and of all the harsh things
  ungodly sinners
have said against Him.

16 These people are discontented grumblers,
•walking according to their desires; their
mouths utter arrogant words, flattering people
for their own advantage.
17 But you, dear friends, remember the
words foretold by the apostles of our Lord Jesus
Christ; 18 they told you, "In the end time there
will be scoffers walking according to their own
ungodly desires." 19 These people create divisions and are merely natural, not having the
Spirit.

Exhortation and Benediction

20 But you, dear friends, building yourselves up in your most holy faith and praying
in the Holy Spirit, 21 keep yourselves in the
love of God, expecting the mercy of our Lord
Jesus Christ for eternal life. 22 Have mercy on
some who doubt; 23 save others by snatching
⌊them⌋ from the fire; on others have mercy in
fear, hating even the garment defiled by the
flesh.
24 Now to Him who is able to protect you
from stumbling and to make you stand in the
presence of His glory, blameless and with great

[a]1 Other mss read *sanctified* [b]5 Other mss place *first of all* after *remind you* [c]7 Lit *and went after other flesh* [d]12 Or *like spots* [e]14 Or *came* [f]15 Lit *convict all*

joy, 25 to the only God our Savior, through Jesus Christ our Lord,[a] be glory, majesty, power, and authority before all time,[b] now, and forever. •Amen.

Revelation

Prologue

1 The revelation of[c] Jesus Christ that God gave Him to show His •slaves what must quickly[d] take place. He sent it and signified it[e] through His angel to His slave John, 2 who testified to God's word and to the testimony[f] about Jesus Christ, in all he saw.[g] 3 Blessed is the one who reads and blessed are those who hear the words of this prophecy and keep[h] what is written in it, because the time is near!

4 John:

To the seven churches in the province of Asia.[i]

Grace and peace to you from[j] the One who is, who was, and who is coming; from the seven spirits[k] before His throne; 5 and from Jesus Christ, the faithful witness, the firstborn from the dead and the ruler of the kings of the earth.

To Him who loves us and has set us free[l] from our sins by His blood, 6 and made us a kingdom,[m] priests[n] to His God and Father—to Him be the glory and dominion forever and ever. •Amen.

7 **Look! He is coming with the clouds,**
and every eye will see Him,
including those who pierced[o]
Him.
And all the families of the earth[p] [q]
will mourn over Him.[r] [s]
This is certain. Amen.

8 "I am the •Alpha and the Omega," says the Lord God, "the One who is, who was, and who is coming, the Almighty."

John's Vision of the Risen Lord

9 I, John, your brother and partner in the tribulation, kingdom, and perseverance in Jesus, was on the island called Patmos because of God's word and the testimony about Jesus.[t] 10 I was in the Spirit[u] [v] on the Lord's day,[w] and I heard behind me a loud voice like a trumpet 11 saying, "Write on a scroll[x] what you see and send it to the seven churches: Ephesus, Smyrna, Pergamum, Thyatira, Sardis, Philadelphia, and Laodicea."

12 I turned to see the voice that was speaking to me. When I turned I saw seven gold lampstands, 13 and among the lampstands was One like the •Son of Man,[y] dressed in a long robe, and with a gold sash wrapped around His chest. 14 His head and hair were white like wool—white as snow, His eyes like a fiery flame, 15 His feet like fine bronze fired in a furnace, and His voice like the sound of cascading[z] waters. 16 In His right hand He had seven stars; from His mouth came a sharp two-edged sword; and His face was shining like the sun at midday.[aa]

17 When I saw Him, I fell at His feet like a dead man. He laid His right hand on me, and said, "Don't be afraid! I am the First and the Last, 18 and the Living One. I was dead, but look—I am alive forever and ever, and I hold the keys of death and •Hades. 19 Therefore write what you have seen, what is, and what will take place after this. 20 The secret[ab] of the seven stars you saw in My right hand, and of the seven gold lampstands, is this: the seven stars are the angels[ac] of the seven churches, and the seven lampstands[ad] are the seven churches.

[a] **25** Other mss omit *through Jesus Christ our Lord* [b] **25** Other mss omit *before all time* [c] **1:1** Or *Revelation of*, or *A revelation of* [d] **1:1** Or *soon* [e] **1:1** Made it known through symbols [f] **1:2** Or *witness* [g] **1:2** Lit *as many as he saw* [h] **1:3** Or *follow*, or *obey* [i] **1:4** Lit *churches in Asia*; that is, the Roman province that is now a part of modern Turkey [j] **1:4** Other mss add *God* [k] **1:4** Or *the sevenfold Spirit* [l] **1:5** Other mss read *has washed us* [m] **1:6** Other mss read *kings and* [n] **1:6** Or *made us into* (or *to be*) *a kingdom of priests*; see Ex 19:6 [o] **1:7** Or *impaled* [p] **1:7** Or *All the tribes of the land* [q] **1:7** Gn 12:3; 28:14; Zch 14:17 [r] **1:7** Or *will wail because of Him* [s] **1:7** Dn 7:13; Zch 12:10 [t] **1:9** Lit *the witness of Jesus* [u] **1:10** Lit *I became in the Spirit* or *in spirit* [v] **1:10** John was brought by God's Spirit into a realm of spiritual vision. [w] **1:10** Sunday [x] **1:11** Or *book* [y] **1:13** Or *like a son of man* [z] **1:15** Lit *many* [aa] **1:16** Lit *like the sun shines in its power* [ab] **1:20** Or *mystery* [ac] **1:20** Or *messengers* [ad] **1:20** Other mss add *that you saw*

The Letters to the Seven Churches

The Letter to Ephesus

2 "To the angel[a] of the church in Ephesus
write:
"The One who holds the seven stars in His
right hand and who walks among the seven
gold lampstands says: 2 I know your works,
your labor, and your endurance, and that you
cannot tolerate evil. You have tested those who
call themselves apostles and are not, and you
have found them to be liars. 3 You also possess
endurance and have tolerated ⌊many things⌋
because of My name, and have not grown
weary. 4 But I have this against you: you have
abandoned the love ⌊you had⌋ at first.
5 Remember then how far you have fallen;
repent, and do the works you did at first. Otherwise, I will come to you[b] and remove your
lampstand from its place—unless you repent.
6 Yet you do have this: you hate the practices of
the Nicolaitans, which I also hate.
7 "Anyone who has an ear should listen to
what the Spirit says to the churches. I will give
the victor the right to eat from the tree of life,
which is in[c] the paradise of God.

The Letter to Smyrna

8 "To the angel of the church in Smyrna
write:
"The First and the Last, the One who was
dead and came to life, says: 9 I know your[d] tribulation and poverty, yet you are rich. ⌊I know⌋
the slander of those who say they are Jews and
are not, but are a •synagogue of Satan. 10 Don't
be afraid of what you are about to suffer. Look,
the Devil is about to throw some of you into
prison to test you, and you will have tribulation
for 10 days. Be faithful until death, and I will
give you the crown[e] of life.
11 "Anyone who has an ear should listen to
what the Spirit says to the churches. The victor
will never be harmed by the second death.

The Letter to Pergamum

12 "To the angel of the church in Pergamum
write:
"The One who has the sharp, two-edged
sword says: 13 I know[f] where you live—where
Satan's throne is! And you are holding on to My
name and did not deny your faith in Me,[g] even
in the days of Antipas, My faithful witness, who
was killed among you, where Satan lives. 14 But
I have a few things against you. You have some
there who hold to the teaching of Balaam, who
taught Balak to place a stumbling block[h] in
front of the sons of Israel: to eat meat sacrificed
to idols and to commit sexual immorality.[i] 15 In
the same way, you also have those who hold to
the teaching of the Nicolaitans.[j] 16 Therefore
repent! Otherwise, I will come to you quickly
and fight against them with the sword of My
mouth.
17 "Anyone who has an ear should listen to
what the Spirit says to the churches. I will give
the victor some of the hidden manna.[k] I will
also give him a white stone, and on the stone a
new name is inscribed that no one knows
except the one who receives it.

The Letter to Thyatira

18 "To the angel of the church in Thyatira
write:
"The Son of God, the One whose eyes are
like a fiery flame, and whose feet are like fine
bronze says: 19 I know your works—your love,
faithfulness,[l] service, and endurance. Your last
works are greater than the first. 20 But I have
this against you: you tolerate the woman
Jezebel, who calls herself a prophetess, and
teaches and deceives My slaves to commit sexual immorality[i] and to eat meat sacrificed to
idols. 21 I gave her time to repent, but she does
not want to repent of her sexual immorality.[m]
22 Look! I will throw her into a sickbed, and
those who commit adultery with her into great
tribulation, unless they repent of her[n] practices. 23 I will kill her children with the
plague.[o] Then all the churches will know that I
am the One who examines minds[p] and hearts,
and I will give to each of you according to your
works. 24 I say to the rest of you in Thyatira,
who do not hold this teaching, who haven't
known the deep things[q] of Satan—as they
say—I do not put any other burden on you.
25 But hold on to what you have until I come.
26 The victor and the one who keeps My works
to the end: I will give him authority over the
nations—

[a]**2:1** Or *messenger* here and elsewhere [b]**2:5** Other mss add *quickly* [c]**2:7** Other mss read *in the midst of* [d]**2:9** Other mss add *works and* [e]**2:10** Or *wreath* [f]**2:13** Other mss add *your works and* [g]**2:13** Or *deny My faith* [h]**2:14** Or *to place a trap* [i]**2:14,20** Or *commit fornication* [j]**2:15** Other mss add *which I hate* [k]**2:17** Other mss add *to eat* [l]**2:19** Or *faith* [m]**2:21** Or *her fornication* [n]**2:22** Other mss read *their* [o]**2:23** Or *I will surely kill her children* [p]**2:23** Lit *kidneys* [q]**2:24** Or *the secret things*

27 **and He will shepherd[a] them**
with an iron scepter;
He will shatter them like pottery[b] —
just as I have received ⌊this⌋ from My Father.
28 I will also give him the morning star.
29 "Anyone who has an ear should listen to
what the Spirit says to the churches.

The Letter to Sardis

3 "To the angel of the church in Sardis
write:
"The One who has the seven spirits of God
and the seven stars says: I know your works;
you have a reputation[c] for being alive, but you
are dead. 2 Be alert and strengthen[d] what
remains, which is about to die, for I have not
found your works complete before My God.
3 Remember therefore what you have received
and heard; keep it, and repent. But if you are
not alert, I will come[e] like a thief, and you have
no idea at what hour I will come against you.[f]
4 But you have a few people[g] in Sardis who
have not defiled[h] their clothes, and they will
walk with Me in white, because they are worthy. 5 In the same way, the victor will be
dressed in white clothes, and I will never erase
his name from the book of life, but will
acknowledge his name before My Father and
before His angels.
6 "Anyone who has an ear should listen to
what the Spirit says to the churches.

The Letter to Philadelphia

7 "To the angel of the church in Philadelphia write:
"The Holy One, the True One, the One
who has the key of David, who opens and no
one will close, and closes and no one opens
says: 8 I know your works. Because you have
limited strength, have kept My word, and
have not denied My name, look, I have placed
before you an open door that no one is able to
close. 9 Take note! I will make those from the
•synagogue of Satan, who claim to be Jews
and are not, but are lying—note this—I will
make them come and bow down at your feet,
and they will know that I have loved you. 10
Because you have kept My command to
endure,[i] I will also keep you from the hour of
testing that is going to come over the whole
world to test those who live on the earth. 11 I
am coming quickly. Hold on to what you have,
so that no one takes your crown. 12 The victor: I will make him a pillar in the sanctuary of
My God, and he will never go out again. I will
write on him the name of My God, and the
name of the city of My God—the new Jerusalem, which comes down out of heaven from
My God—and My new name.
13 "Anyone who has an ear should listen to
what the Spirit says to the churches.

The Letter to Laodicea

14 "To the angel of the church in Laodicea
write:
"The •Amen, the faithful and true Witness, the Originator[j] of God's creation says:
15 I know your works, that you are neither
cold nor hot. I wish that you were cold or
hot. 16 So, because you are lukewarm, and
neither hot nor cold, I am going to vomit[k]
you out of My mouth. 17 Because you say,
'I'm rich; I have become wealthy, and need
nothing,' and you don't know that you are
wretched, pitiful, poor, blind, and naked, 18 I
advise you to buy from Me gold refined in the
fire so that you may be rich, and white
clothes so that you may be dressed and your
shameful nakedness not be exposed, and
ointment to spread on your eyes so that you
may see. 19 As many as I love, I rebuke and
discipline. So be committed[l] and repent.
20 Listen! I stand at the door and knock. If
anyone hears My voice and opens the door, I
will come in to him and have dinner with
him, and he with Me. 21 The victor: I will
give him the right to sit with Me on My
throne, just as I also won the victory and sat
down with My Father on His throne.
22 "Anyone who has an ear should listen to
what the Spirit says to the churches."

The Throne Room of Heaven

4 After this I looked, and there in heaven
was an open door. The first voice that I
had heard speaking to me like a trumpet said,
"Come up here, and I will show you what
must take place after this."
2 Immediately I was in the Spirit,[m] and
there in heaven a throne was set. One was
seated on the throne, 3 and the One seated[n]
looked like jasper[o] and carnelian[p] stone. A

[a]**2:27** Or *rule*; see 19:15 [b]**2:27** Ps 2:9 [c]**3:1** Lit *have a name* [d]**3:2** Other mss read *guard* [e]**3:3** Other mss add *upon you* [f]**3:3** Or *upon you* [g]**3:4** Lit *few names* [h]**3:4** Or *soiled* [i]**3:10** Lit *My word of endurance* [j]**3:14** Or *Ruler*, or *Source*, or *Beginning* [k]**3:16** Or *spit* [l]**3:19** Or *be zealous* [m]**4:2** Lit *I became in the Spirit* or *in spirit* [n]**4:3** Other mss omit *and the One seated* [o]**4:3** A precious stone [p]**4:3** A translucent red gem

rainbow that looked like an emerald surrounded the throne. 4 Around that throne were
24 thrones, and on the thrones sat 24 elders
dressed in white clothes, with gold crowns on
their heads. 5 From the throne came flashes of
lightning, rumblings, and thunder. Burning
before the throne were seven fiery torches,
which are the seven spirits of God. 6 Also
before the throne was something like a sea of
glass, similar to crystal. In the middle[a] and
around the throne were four living creatures
covered with eyes in front and in back. 7 The
first living creature was like a lion; the second
living creature was like a calf; the third living
creature had a face like a man; and the fourth
living creature was like a flying eagle. 8 Each of
the four living creatures had six wings; they
were covered with eyes around and inside. Day
and night they never stop,[b] saying:

Holy, holy, holy,[c]
Lord God, the Almighty,
who was, who is, and who is coming.

9 Whenever the living creatures give glory,
honor, and thanks to the One seated on the
throne, the One who lives forever and ever,
10 the 24 elders fall down before the One
seated on the throne, worship the One who
lives forever and ever, cast their crowns before
the throne, and say:

11 Our Lord and God,[d]
You are worthy to receive
glory and honor and power,
because You have created all things,
and because of Your will
they exist and were created.

The Lamb Takes the Scroll

5 Then I saw in the right hand of the One
seated on the throne a scroll with writing
on the inside and on the back, sealed with seven
seals. 2 I also saw a mighty angel proclaiming in
a loud voice, "Who is worthy to open the scroll
and break its seals?" 3 But no one in heaven or
on earth or under the earth was able to open the
scroll or even to look in it. 4 And I cried and
cried because no one was found worthy to open[e]
the scroll or even to look in it.
5 Then one of the elders said to me, "Stop
crying. Look! The Lion from the tribe of Judah,
the Root of David, has been victorious so that
He may open the scroll and[f] its seven seals."
6 Then I saw one like a slaughtered lamb standing between[g] the throne and the four living
creatures and among the elders. He had seven
horns and seven eyes, which are the seven spirits of God sent into all the earth. 7 He came and
took ⌊the scroll⌋[h] out of the right hand of the
One seated on the throne.

The Lamb Is Worthy

8 When He took the scroll, the four living
creatures and the 24 elders fell down before
the Lamb. Each one had a harp and gold bowls
filled with incense, which are the prayers of the
saints. 9 And they sang a new song:

You are worthy to take the scroll
and to open its seals;
because You were slaughtered,
and You redeemed[i] ⌊people⌋[j] for God
by Your blood
from every tribe and language
and people and nation.
10 You made them a kingdom[k]
and priests to our God,
and they will reign on the earth.

11 Then I looked, and heard the voice of
many angels around the throne, and also of the
living creatures, and of the elders. Their number was countless thousands, plus thousands of
thousands. 12 They said with a loud voice:

The Lamb who was slaughtered
is worthy
to receive power and riches
and wisdom and strength
and honor and glory and blessing!

13 I heard every creature in heaven, on earth,
under the earth, on the sea, and everything in
them say:

Blessing and honor and glory
and dominion
to the One seated on the throne,
and to the Lamb, forever and ever!

14 The four living creatures said, "•Amen,"
and the elders fell down and worshiped.

The First Seal on the Scroll

6 Then I saw[l] the Lamb open one of the
seven[m] seals, and I heard one of the four

[a]**4:6** Lit *In the middle of the throne* [b]**4:8** Or *they never rest* [c]**4:8** Other mss read *holy* 9 times [d]**4:11** Other mss add *the Holy One*; other mss read *O Lord* [e]**5:4** Other mss add *and read* [f]**5:5** Other mss add *loose* [g]**5:6** Or *standing in the middle of* [h]**5:7** Other mss include *the scroll* [i]**5:9** Or *purchased* [j]**5:9** Other mss read *us* [k]**5:10** Other mss read *them kings* [l]**6:1** Lit *saw when* [m]**6:1** Other mss omit *seven*

living creatures say with a voice like thunder, "Come!"[a b] 2 I looked, and there was a white horse. The horseman on it had a bow; a crown was given to him, and he went out as a victor to conquer.[c]

The Second Seal

3 When He opened the second seal, I heard the second living creature say, "Come!"[a b] 4 Then another horse went out, a fiery red one, and its horseman was empowered[d] to take peace from the earth, so that people would slaughter one another. And a large sword was given to him.

The Third Seal

5 When He opened the third seal, I heard the third living creature say, "Come!"[a b] And I looked, and there was a black horse. The horseman on it had a balance scale in his hand. 6 Then I heard something like a voice among the four living creatures say, "A quart of wheat for a •denarius, and three quarts of barley for a denarius—but do not harm the olive oil and the wine."

The Fourth Seal

7 When He opened the fourth seal, I heard the voice of the fourth living creature say, "Come!"[a b] 8 And I looked, and there was a pale green[e] horse. The horseman on it was named Death, and •Hades was following after him. Authority was given to them[f] over a fourth of the earth, to kill by the sword, by famine, by plague, and by the wild animals of the earth.

The Fifth Seal

9 When He opened the fifth seal, I saw under the altar the souls of those slaughtered because of God's word and the testimony they had.[g] 10 They cried out with a loud voice: "O Lord,[h] holy and true, how long until You judge and avenge our blood from those who live on the earth?" 11 So a white robe was given to each of them, and they were told to rest a little while longer until ⌊the number of⌋ their fellow slaves and their brothers, who were going to be killed just as they had been, would be completed.

The Sixth Seal

12 Then I saw Him open[i] the sixth seal. A violent earthquake occurred; the sun turned black like sackcloth made of goat hair; the entire moon[j] became like blood; 13 the stars[k] of heaven fell to the earth as a fig tree drops its unripe figs when shaken by a high wind; 14 the sky separated like a scroll being rolled up; and every mountain and island was moved from its place.

15 Then the kings of the earth, the nobles, the military commanders, the rich, the powerful, and every slave and free person hid in the caves and among the rocks of the mountains. 16 And they said to the mountains and to the rocks, "Fall on us and hide us from the face of the One seated on the throne and from the wrath of the Lamb, 17 because the great day of Their[l] wrath has come! And who is able to stand?"

The Sealed of Israel

7 After this I saw four angels standing at the four corners of the earth, restraining the four winds of the earth so that no wind could blow on the earth or on the sea or on any tree. 2 Then I saw another angel rise up from the east, who had the seal of the living God. He cried out in a loud voice to the four angels who were empowered[m] to harm the earth and the sea: 3 "Don't harm the earth or the sea or the trees until we seal the slaves of our God on their foreheads." 4 And I heard the number of those who were sealed:

144,000 sealed from every tribe
of the sons of Israel:
5 12,000 sealed from the tribe of Judah,
12,000[n] from the tribe of Reuben,
12,000 from the tribe of Gad,
6 12,000 from the tribe of Asher,
12,000 from the tribe of Naphtali,
12,000 from the tribe of Manasseh,
7 12,000 from the tribe of Simeon,
12,000 from the tribe of Levi,
12,000 from the tribe of Issachar,
8 12,000 from the tribe of Zebulun,
12,000 from the tribe of Joseph,
12,000 sealed from the tribe
of Benjamin.

[a]**6:1,3,5,7** Other mss add *and see* [b]**6:1,3,5,7** Or *Go!* [c]**6:2** Lit *went out conquering and in order to conquer* [d]**6:4** Or *was granted*; lit *was given* [e]**6:8** Or *a greenish gray* [f]**6:8** Other mss read *him* [g]**6:9** Other mss add *about the Lamb* [h]**6:10** Or *Master* [i]**6:12** Lit *I saw when He opened* [j]**6:12** Or *the full moon* [k]**6:13** Perhaps meteors [l]**6:17** Other mss read *His* [m]**7:2** Lit *angels to whom it was given* [n]**7:5–8** Other mss add *sealed* after each number

A Multitude from the Great Tribulation

9 After this I looked, and there was a vast
multitude from every nation, tribe, people, and
language, which no one could number, standing
before the throne and before the Lamb. They
were robed in white with palm branches in their
hands. 10 And they cried out in a loud voice:

Salvation belongs to our God,
who is seated on the throne,
and to the Lamb!

11 All the angels stood around the throne,
the elders, and the four living creatures, and
they fell on their faces before the throne and
worshiped God, 12 saying:

•Amen! Blessing and glory
and wisdom
and thanksgiving and honor
and power and strength,
be to our God forever and ever.
Amen.

13 Then one of the elders asked me, "Who
are these people robed in white, and where did
they come from?"
14 I said to him, "Sir,[a] you know."
Then he told me:

These are the ones coming out
of the great tribulation.
They washed their robes
and made them white
in the blood of the Lamb.
15 For this reason they are
before the throne of God,
and they serve Him day and night
in His sanctuary.
The One seated on the throne
will shelter[b] them:
16 no longer will they hunger; no longer
will they thirst;
no longer will the sun strike them,
or any heat.
17 Because the Lamb who is at the center
of the throne will shepherd them;
He will guide them to springs
of living waters,
and God will wipe away every tear
from their eyes.

The Seventh Seal

8 When He opened the seventh seal, there
was silence in heaven for about half an
hour. 2 Then I saw the seven angels who stand
in the presence of God; seven trumpets were
given to them. 3 Another angel, with a gold
incense burner, came and stood at the altar. He
was given a large amount of incense to offer
with the prayers of all the saints on the gold
altar in front of the throne. 4 The smoke of the
incense, with the prayers of the saints, went
up in the presence of God from the angel's
hand. 5 The angel took the incense burner,
filled it with fire from the altar, and hurled it to
the earth; there were thunders, rumblings,
lightnings, and an earthquake. 6 And the seven
angels who had the seven trumpets prepared
to blow them.

The First Trumpet

7 The first ⌊angel⌋[c] blew his trumpet, and
hail and fire, mixed with blood, were hurled to
the earth. So a third of the earth was burned
up, a third of the trees were burned up, and all
the green grass was burned up.

The Second Trumpet

8 The second angel blew his trumpet, and
something like a great mountain ablaze with
fire was hurled into the sea. So a third of the sea
became blood, 9 a third of the living creatures
in the sea died, and a third of the ships were
destroyed.

The Third Trumpet

10 The third angel blew his trumpet, and a
great star, blazing like a torch, fell from
heaven. It fell on a third of the rivers and
springs of water. 11 The name of the star is
Wormwood,[d] and a third of the waters
became wormwood. So, many of the people
died from the waters, because they had been
made bitter.

The Fourth Trumpet

12 The fourth angel blew his trumpet, and a
third of the sun was struck, a third of the moon,
and a third of the stars, so that a third of them
were darkened. A third of the day was without
light, and the night as well.
13 I looked, and I heard an eagle,[e] flying in
mid-heaven,[f] saying in a loud voice, "Woe!
Woe! Woe to those who live on the earth,
because of the remaining trumpet blasts that
the three angels are about to sound!"

[a]**7:14** Lit *My lord* [b]**7:15** Or *will spread His tent over* [c]**8:7** Other mss include *angel* [d]**8:11** *Wormwood* is absinthe, a bitter herb. [e]**8:13** Other mss read *angel* [f]**8:13** Very high

The Fifth Trumpet

9 The fifth angel blew his trumpet, and I
saw a star that had fallen from heaven to
earth. The key to the shaft of the •abyss was
given to him. 2 He opened the shaft of the
abyss, and smoke came up out of the shaft like
smoke from a great[a] furnace so that the sun
and the air were darkened by the smoke from
the shaft. 3 Then out of the smoke locusts
came to the earth, and power[b] was given to
them like the power that scorpions have on
the earth. 4 They were told not to harm the
grass of the earth, or any green plant, or any
tree, but only people who do not have God's
seal on their foreheads. 5 They were not permitted to kill them, but were to torment
⌊them⌋ for five months; their torment is like
the torment caused by a scorpion when it
strikes a man. 6 In those days people will seek
death and will not find it; they will long to die,
but death will flee from them.
7 The appearance of the locusts was like
horses equipped for battle. On their heads
were something like gold crowns; their faces
were like men's faces; 8 they had hair like
women's hair; their teeth were like lions'
teeth; 9 they had chests like iron breastplates;
the sound of their wings was like the sound of
chariots with many horses rushing into battle;
10 and they had tails with stingers, like scorpions, so that with their tails they had the power[b]
to harm people for five months. 11 They had as
their king[c] the angel of the abyss; his name in
Hebrew is Abaddon,[d] and in Greek he has the
name Apollyon.[e] 12 The first woe has passed.
There are still two more woes to come after
this.

The Sixth Trumpet

13 The sixth angel blew his trumpet. From
the four[f] horns of the gold altar that is before
God, I heard a voice 14 say to the sixth angel
who had the trumpet, "Release the four angels
bound at the great river Euphrates." 15 So the
four angels who were prepared for the hour,
day, month, and year were released to kill a
third of the human race. 16 The number of
mounted troops was 200 million;[g] I heard their
number. 17 This is how I saw the horses in my
vision: The horsemen had breastplates that
were fiery red, hyacinth blue, and sulfur yel-
low. The heads of the horses were like lions'
heads, and from their mouths came fire,
smoke, and sulfur. 18 A third of the human race
was killed by these three plagues—by the fire,
the smoke, and the sulfur that came from their
mouths. 19 For the power of the horses is in
their mouths and in their tails, because their
tails, like snakes, have heads, and they inflict
injury with them.
20 The rest of the people, who were not
killed by these plagues, did not repent of the
works of their hands to stop worshiping
demons and idols of gold, silver, bronze, stone,
and wood, which are not able to see, hear, or
walk. 21 And they did not repent of their murders, their sorceries,[h] their sexual immorality,
or their thefts.

The Mighty Angel and the Small Scroll

10 Then I saw another mighty angel coming down from heaven, surrounded by
a cloud, with a rainbow over his head.[i] His
face was like the sun, his legs[j] were like fiery
pillars, 2 and he had a little scroll opened in his
hand. He put his right foot on the sea, his left
on the land, 3 and he cried out with a loud
voice like a roaring lion. When he cried out,
the seven thunders spoke with their voices.
4 And when the seven thunders spoke, I was
about to write. Then I heard a voice from
heaven, saying, "Seal up what the seven thunders said, and do not write it down!"
5 Then the angel that I had seen standing on
the sea and on the land raised his right hand to
heaven. 6 He swore an oath by the One who
lives forever and ever, who created heaven and
what is in it, the earth and what is in it, and the
sea and what is in it: "There will no longer be
an interval of time,[k] 7 but in the days of the
sound of the seventh angel, when he will blow
his trumpet, then God's hidden plan[l] will be
completed, as He announced to His servants[m]
the prophets."
8 Now the voice that I heard from heaven
spoke to me again and said, "Go, take the scroll
that lies open in the hand of the angel who is
standing on the sea and on the land."
9 So I went to the angel and asked him to
give me the little scroll. He said to me, "Take
and eat it; it will be bitter in your stomach, but
it will be as sweet as honey in your mouth."

[a]**9:2** Other mss omit *great* [b]**9:3,10** Or *authority* [c]**9:11** Or *as king over them* [d]**9:11** Or *destruction* [e]**9:11** Or *destroyer* [f]**9:13** Other mss omit *four* [g]**9:16** Other mss read *100 million* [h]**9:21** Or *magic potions*, or *drugs*; Gk *pharmakon* [i]**10:1** Or *a halo on his head* [j]**10:1** Or *feet* [k]**10:6** Or *be a delay* [l]**10:7** Or *God's secret* or *mystery*, see Rv 1:20; 17:5,7 [m]**10:7** Or *slaves*

10 Then I took the little scroll from the
angel's hand and ate it. It was as sweet as honey
in my mouth, but when I ate it, my stomach
became bitter. 11 And I was told,[a] "You must
prophesy again about[b] many peoples, nations,
languages, and kings."

The Two Witnesses

11 Then I was given a measuring reed
like a rod,[c] with these words: "Go[d]
and measure God's sanctuary and the altar, and
⌊count⌋ those who worship there. 2 But
exclude the courtyard outside the sanctuary.
Don't measure it, because it is given to the
nations,[e] and they will trample the holy city
for 42 months. 3 I will empower[f] my two witnesses, and they will prophesy for 1,260 days,[g]
dressed in sackcloth."[h] 4 These are the two
olive trees and the two lampstands that stand
before the Lord[i] of the earth. 5 If anyone wants
to harm them, fire comes from their mouths
and consumes their enemies; if anyone wants
to harm them, he must be killed in this way.
6 These men have the power to close the sky
so that it does not rain during the days of their
prophecy. They also have power over the
waters to turn them into blood, and to strike
the earth with any plague whenever they
want.

The Witnesses Martyred

7 When they finish their testimony, the
beast[j] that comes up out of the •abyss will
make war with them, conquer them, and kill
them. 8 Their dead bodies[k] will lie in the
public square[l] of the great city, which is
called, prophetically,[m] Sodom and Egypt,
where also their Lord was crucified. 9 And
representatives from[n] the peoples, tribes,
languages, and nations will view their bodies
for three and a half days and not permit their
bodies to be put into a tomb. 10 Those who
live on the earth will gloat over them and celebrate and send gifts to one another, because
these two prophets tormented those who live
on the earth.

The Witnesses Resurrected

11 But after the three and a half days, the
breath[o] of life from God entered them, and they
stood on their feet. So great fear fell on those
who saw them. 12 Then they heard[p] a loud
voice from heaven saying to them, "Come up
here." They went up to heaven in a cloud,
while their enemies watched them. 13 At that
moment a violent earthquake took place, a
tenth of the city fell, and 7,000 people were
killed in the earthquake. The survivors were
terrified and gave glory to the God of heaven.
14 The second woe has passed. Take note: the
third woe is coming quickly!

The Seventh Trumpet

15 The seventh angel blew his trumpet, and
there were loud voices in heaven saying:

The kingdom of the world has become
  the ⌊kingdom⌋
of our Lord and of His •Messiah,
  and He will reign forever and ever!

16 The 24 elders, who were seated before God
on their thrones, fell on their faces and worshiped God, 17 saying:

We thank You, Lord God,
  the Almighty, who is and who was,[q]
because You have taken
  Your great power and have begun
  to reign.
18 The nations were angry,
  but Your wrath has come.
The time has come for the dead
  to be judged,
and to give the reward
  to Your servants the prophets,
to the saints, and to those who fear
  Your name, both small and great,
and the time has come to destroy
  those who destroy the earth.

19 God's sanctuary in heaven was opened, and
the ark of His covenant[r] appeared in His sanctuary. There were lightnings, rumblings, thunders, an earthquake,[s] and severe hail.

The Woman, the Child, and the Dragon

12 A great sign[t] appeared in heaven: a
woman clothed with the sun, with the
moon under her feet, and a crown of 12 stars
on her head. 2 She was pregnant and cried out
in labor and agony to give birth. 3 Then

[a]**10:11** Lit *And they said to me* [b]**10:11** Or *prophesy again against* [c]**11:1** Other mss add *and the angel stood up* [d]**11:1** Lit *Arise* [e]**11:2** Or *Gentiles* [f]**11:3** Lit *I will give to* [g]**11:3** Three and a half years of thirty-day months [h]**11:3** Mourning garment of coarse, often black, material [i]**11:4** Other mss read *God* [j]**11:7** Or *wild animal* [k]**11:8** Lit *Their corpse* [l]**11:8** Or *lie on the broad street* [m]**11:8** Or *spiritually,* or *symbolically* [n]**11:9** Lit *And from* [o]**11:11** Or *spirit* [p]**11:12** Other mss read *Then I heard* [q]**11:17** Other mss add *and who is to come* [r]**11:19** Other mss read *ark of the covenant of the Lord* [s]**11:19** Other mss omit *an earthquake* [t]**12:1** Or *great symbolic display,* see Rv 12:3

another sign[a] appeared in heaven: There was a great fiery red dragon having seven heads and 10 horns, and on his heads were seven diadems.[b] 4 His tail swept away a third of the stars in heaven and hurled them to the earth. And the dragon stood in front of the woman who was about to give birth, so that when she did give birth he might devour her child. 5 But she gave birth to a Son—a male who is going to shepherd[c] all nations with an iron scepter—and her child was caught up to God and to His throne. 6 The woman fled into the wilderness, where she had a place prepared by God, to be fed there[d] for 1,260 days.

The Dragon Thrown Out of Heaven

7 Then war broke out in heaven: Michael and his angels fought against the dragon. The dragon and his angels also fought, 8 but he could not prevail, and there was no place for them in heaven any longer. 9 So the great dragon was thrown out—the ancient serpent, who is called the Devil[e] and Satan,[f] the one who deceives the whole world. He was thrown to earth, and his angels with him.

10 Then I heard a loud voice in heaven say:

The salvation and the power
  and the kingdom of our God
and the authority of His •Messiah
  have now come,
because the accuser of our brothers
  has been thrown out:
the one who accuses them
  before our God day and night.
11 They conquered him by the blood
  of the Lamb
and by the word of their testimony,
for they did not love their lives
  in the face of death.
12 Therefore rejoice, O heavens,
  and you who dwell in them!
Woe to the earth and the sea,
for the Devil has come down to you
  with great fury,
because he knows he has a short time.

The Woman Persecuted

13 When the dragon saw that he had been thrown to earth, he persecuted the woman who gave birth to the male. 14 The woman was given two wings of a great eagle, so that she could fly from the serpent's presence to her place in the wilderness, where she was fed for a time, times, and half a time.[g] 15 From his mouth the serpent spewed water like a river after the woman, to sweep her away in a torrent. 16 But the earth helped the woman: the earth opened its mouth and swallowed up the river that the dragon had spewed from his mouth. 17 So the dragon was furious with the woman and left to wage war against the rest of her offspring[h]—those who keep the commandments of God and have the testimony about Jesus. 18 He[i] stood on the sand of the sea.[j]

The Beast from the Sea

13 And I saw a beast coming up out of the sea. He[k] had 10 horns and seven heads. On his horns were 10 diadems, and on his heads were blasphemous names.[l] 2 The beast I saw was like a leopard, his feet were like a bear's, and his mouth was like a lion's mouth. The dragon gave him his power, his throne, and great authority. 3 One of his heads appeared to be fatally wounded,[m] but his fatal wound was healed. The whole earth was amazed and followed the beast.[n] 4 They worshiped the dragon because he gave authority to the beast. And they worshiped the beast, saying, "Who is like the beast? Who is able to wage war against him?"

5 A mouth was given to him to speak boasts and blasphemies. He was also given authority to act[o] [p] for 42 months. 6 He began to speak[q] blasphemies against God: to blaspheme His name and His dwelling—those who dwell in heaven. 7 And he was permitted to wage war against the saints and to conquer them. He was also given authority over every tribe, people, language, and nation. 8 All those who live on the earth will worship him, everyone whose name was not written from the foundation of the world in the book[r] of life of the Lamb who was slaughtered.[s]

9 If anyone has an ear, he should listen:

10 If anyone is destined for captivity,

[a]**12:3** Or *another symbolic display* [b]**12:3** Or *crowns* [c]**12:5** Or *rule* [d]**12:6** Lit *God, that they might feed her there* [e]**12:9** Gk *diabolos*, meaning slanderer [f]**12:9** Hb word meaning adversary [g]**12:14** An expression occurring in Dn 7:25; 12:7 that means 3 ½ years or 42 months (Rv 11:2; 13:5) or 1,260 days (Rv 11:3) [h]**12:17** Or *seed* [i]**12:18** Other mss read *I*. "He" is apparently a reference to the dragon. [j]**12:18** Some translations put Rv 12:18 either in Rv 12:17 or Rv 13:1. [k]**13:1** The beasts in Rv 13:1,11 are customarily referred to as "he" or "him" rather than "it." The Gk word for a beast (*therion*) is grammatically neuter. [l]**13:1** Other mss read *heads was a blasphemous name* [m]**13:3** Lit *be slain to death* [n]**13:3** Lit *amazed after the beast* [o]**13:5** Other mss read *wage war* [p]**13:5** Or *to rule* [q]**13:6** Lit *He opened his mouth in* [r]**13:8** Or *scroll* [s]**13:8** Or *written in the book of life of the Lamb who was slaughtered from the foundation of the world*

into captivity he goes.
If anyone is to be killed[a] with a sword,
with a sword he will be killed.

Here is the endurance and the faith of the
saints.[b]

The Beast from the Earth

11 Then I saw another beast coming up out
of the earth; he had two horns like a lamb,[c] but
he sounded like a dragon. 12 He exercises all
the authority of the first beast on his behalf and
compels the earth and those who live on it to
worship the first beast, whose fatal wound was
healed. 13 He also performs great signs, even
causing fire to come down from heaven to earth
before people. 14 He deceives those who live
on the earth because of the signs that he is permitted to perform on behalf of the beast, telling
those who live on the earth to make an image[d]
of the beast who had the sword wound yet
lived. 15 He was permitted to give a spirit[e] to
the image of the beast, so that the image of the
beast could both speak and cause whoever
would not worship the image of the beast to be
killed. 16 And he requires everyone—small and
great, rich and poor, free and slave—to be
given a mark[f] on his[g] right hand or on his[g] forehead, 17 so that no one can buy or sell unless he
has the mark: the beast's name or the number
of his name.
18 Here is wisdom:[h] The one who has
understanding must calculate[i] the number of
the beast, because it is the number of a man.[j]
His number is 666.[k]

The Lamb and the 144,000

14 Then I looked, and there on Mount
Zion stood the Lamb, and with Him
were 144,000 who had His name and His
Father's name written on their foreheads. 2 I
heard a sound[l] from heaven like the sound of
cascading waters and like the rumbling of
loud thunder. The sound I heard was also like
harpists playing on their harps. 3 They sang[m]
a new song before the throne and before the
four living creatures and the elders, but no
one could learn the song except the 144,000
who had been redeemed[n] from the earth.
4 These are the ones not defiled with women,
for they have kept their virginity. These are
the ones who follow the Lamb wherever He
goes. They were redeemed[o n] from the
human race as the •firstfruits for God and the
Lamb. 5 No lie was found in their mouths;
they are blameless.

The Proclamation of Three Angels

6 Then I saw another angel flying in mid-
heaven, having the eternal gospel to announce
to the inhabitants of the earth—to every
nation, tribe, language, and people. 7 He spoke
with a loud voice: "Fear God and give Him
glory, because the hour of His judgment has
come. Worship the Maker of heaven and earth,
the sea and springs of water."
8 A second angel[p] followed, saying: "It has
fallen, Babylon the Great has fallen,[q] who made
all nations drink the wine of her sexual immorality,[r] which brings wrath."
9 And a third angel[s] followed them and
spoke with a loud voice: "If anyone worships
the beast and his image and receives a mark on
his forehead or on his hand, 10 he will also
drink the wine of God's wrath, which is mixed
full strength in the cup of His anger. He will be
tormented with fire and sulfur in the sight of
the holy angels and in the sight of the Lamb,
11 and the smoke of their torment will go up
forever and ever. There is no rest[t] day or night
for those who worship the beast and his image,
or anyone who receives the mark of his name.
12 Here is the endurance[u v] of the saints, who
keep the commandments of God and the faith
in Jesus."[w]
13 Then I heard a voice from heaven saying,
"Write: Blessed are the dead who die in the
Lord from now on."

"Yes," says the Spirit, "let them rest from
their labors, for their works follow them!"

Reaping the Earth's Harvest

14 Then I looked, and there was a white
cloud, and One like the Son of Man[x] was
seated on the cloud, with a gold crown on His
head and a sharp sickle in His hand. 15 Another
angel came out of the sanctuary, crying out in a

[a]**13:10** Other mss read *anyone kills* [b]**13:10** Or *This calls for the endurance and faith of the saints.* [c]**13:11** Or *ram* [d]**13:14** Or *statue;* or *likeness* [e]**13:15** Or *give breath,* or *give life* [f]**13:16** Or *stamp,* or *brand* [g]**13:16** Lit *their* [h]**13:18** Or *This calls for wisdom* [i]**13:18** Or *count,* or *figure out* [j]**13:18** Or *is a man's number,* or *is the number of a person* [k]**13:18** One Gk ms plus other ancient evidence read *616* [l]**14:2** Or *voice* [m]**14:3** Other mss add *as it were* [n]**14:3,4** Or *purchased* [o]**14:4** Other mss add *by Jesus* [p]**14:8** Lit *Another angel, a second* [q]**14:8** Other mss omit the second *has fallen* [r]**14:8** Or *wine of her passionate immorality* [s]**14:9** Lit *Another angel, a third* [t]**14:11** Lit *They have no rest* [u]**14:12** Or *This calls for the endurance of the saints* [v]**14:12** This is what the endurance of the saints means [w]**14:12** Or *and faith in Jesus,* or *their faith in,* or *faithfulness to Jesus* [x]**14:14** Or *like a son of man*

loud voice to the One who was seated on the
cloud, "Use your sickle and reap, for the time
to reap has come, since the harvest of the earth
is ripe." 16 So the One seated on the cloud
swung His sickle over the earth, and the earth
was harvested.
17 Then another angel who also had a
sharp sickle came out of the sanctuary in
heaven. 18 Yet another angel, who had
authority over fire, came from the altar, and
he called with a loud voice to the one who
had the sharp sickle, "Use your sharp sickle
and gather the clusters of grapes from earth's
vineyard, because its grapes have ripened."
19 So the angel swung his sickle toward earth
and gathered the grapes from earth's vineyard, and he threw them into the great winepress of God's wrath. 20 Then the press was
trampled outside the city, and blood flowed
out of the press up to the horses' bridles for
about 180 miles.[a]

Preparation for the Bowl Judgments

15 Then I saw another great and awe-
inspiring sign[b] in heaven: seven angels
with the seven last plagues, for with them,
God's wrath will be completed. 2 I also saw
something like a sea of glass mixed with fire,
and those who had won the victory from the
beast, his image,[c] and the number of his name,
were standing on the sea of glass with harps
from God.[d] 3 They sang the song of God's servant Moses, and the song of the Lamb:

Great and awe-inspiring are
    Your works, Lord God,
    the Almighty;
righteous and true are Your ways,
    King of the Nations.
4 Lord, who will not fear and glorify
    Your name?
Because You alone are holy,
because all the nations will come
    and worship before You,
because Your righteous acts
    have been revealed.

5 After this I looked, and the heavenly sanctuary—the tabernacle of testimony—was
opened. 6 Out of the sanctuary came the seven
angels with the seven plagues, dressed in clean,
bright linen, with gold sashes wrapped around
their chests. 7 One of the four living creatures
gave the seven angels seven gold bowls filled
with the wrath of God who lives forever and
ever. 8 Then the sanctuary was filled with
smoke from God's glory and from His power,
and no one could enter the sanctuary until the
seven plagues of the seven angels were completed.

The First Bowl

16 Then I heard a loud voice from the
sanctuary saying to the seven angels,
"Go and pour out the seven[e] bowls of God's
wrath on the earth." 2 The first went and
poured out his bowl on the earth, and severely
painful sores[f] broke out on the people who
had the mark of the beast and who worshiped
his image.

The Second Bowl

3 The second[g] poured out his bowl into the
sea. It turned to blood like a dead man's, and all
life[h] in the sea died.

The Third Bowl

4 The third[g] poured out his bowl into the
rivers and the springs of water, and they
became blood. 5 I heard the angel of the waters
say:

You are righteous, who is
    and who was, the Holy One,
for You have decided these things.
6 Because they poured out the blood
    of the saints and the prophets,
You also gave them blood to drink;
    they deserve it!

7 Then I heard someone from the altar say:

Yes, Lord God, the Almighty,
true and righteous are
    Your judgments.

The Fourth Bowl

8 The fourth[g] poured out his bowl on the
sun. He[i] was given the power[j] to burn people
with fire, 9 and people were burned by the
intense heat. So they blasphemed the name
of God who had the power[j] over these
plagues, and they did not repent and give
Him glory.

[a]**14:20** Lit *1,600 stadia* [b]**15:1** Or *and awesome symbolic display* [c]**15:2** Other mss add *his mark* [d]**15:2** Or *harps of God*; that is, harps belonging to the service of God [e]**16:1** Other mss omit *seven* [f]**16:2** Lit *and a severely painful sore* [g]**16:3,4,8** Other mss add *angel* [h]**16:3** Lit *and every soul of life* [i]**16:8** Or *It* [j]**16:8,9** Or *authority*

The Fifth Bowl

10 The fifth[a] poured out his bowl on the
throne of the beast, and his kingdom was
plunged into darkness. People[a] gnawed their
tongues from pain 11 and blasphemed the God
of heaven because of their pains and their
sores, yet they did not repent of their actions.

The Sixth Bowl

12 The sixth[a] poured out his bowl on the
great river Euphrates, and its water was dried
up to prepare the way for the kings from the
east. 13 Then I saw three unclean spirits like
frogs ⌊coming⌋ from the dragon's mouth, from
the beast's mouth, and from the mouth of the
false prophet. 14 For they are spirits of demons
performing signs, who travel to the kings of
the whole world to assemble them for the battle of the great day of God, the Almighty.

15 "Look, I am coming like a thief. Blessed is
the one who is alert and remains clothed[c] so that
he may not go naked, and they see his shame."

16 So they assembled them at the place
called in Hebrew Armagedon.[d] [e]

The Seventh Bowl

17 Then the seventh[a] poured out his bowl
into the air,[f] and a loud voice came out of the
sanctuary,[g] from the throne, saying, "It is
done!" 18 There were lightnings, rumblings,
and thunders. And a severe earthquake
occurred like no other since man has been on
the earth—so great was the quake. 19 The great
city split into three parts, and the cities of the
nations[h] fell. Babylon the Great was remembered in God's presence; He gave her the cup
filled with the wine of His fierce anger.
20 Every island fled, and the mountains disappeared.[i] 21 Enormous hailstones, each weigh-
ing about 100 pounds,[j] fell from heaven on the
people, and they[k] blasphemed God for the
plague of hail because that plague was
extremely severe.

The Woman and the Scarlet Beast

17 Then one of the seven angels who had
the seven bowls came and spoke with
me: "Come, I will show you the judgment of
the notorious prostitute[l] who sits on many[m]
waters. 2 The kings of the earth committed
sexual immorality with her, and those who live
on the earth became drunk on the wine of her
sexual immorality." 3 So he carried me away in
the Spirit[n] to a desert. I saw a woman sitting
on a scarlet beast that was covered[o] with blasphemous names, having seven heads and 10
horns. 4 The woman was dressed in purple
and scarlet, adorned with gold, precious
stones, and pearls. She had a gold cup in her
hand filled with everything vile and with the
impurities of her[p] prostitution. 5 On her forehead a cryptic name was written:

BABYLON THE GREAT
THE MOTHER OF
PROSTITUTES
AND OF THE VILE THINGS
OF THE EARTH

6 Then I saw that the woman was drunk on
the blood of the saints and on the blood of the
witnesses to Jesus. When I saw her, I was
utterly astounded.

The Meaning of the Woman and of the Beast

7 Then the angel said to me, "Why are you
astounded? I will tell you the secret meaning[q]
of the woman and of the beast, with the seven
heads and the 10 horns, that carries her. 8 The
beast that you saw was, and is not, and is about
to come up from the •abyss and go to destruction. Those who live on the earth whose names
were not written in the book of life from the
foundation of the world will be astounded
when they see the beast that was, and is not,
and will be present ⌊again⌋.

9 "Here is the mind with wisdom:[r] the
seven heads are seven mountains on which the
woman is seated. 10 They are also seven kings:[s]
five have fallen, one is, the other has not yet
come, and when he comes, he must remain for
a little while. 11 The beast that was and is not,
is himself the eighth, yet is of the seven and
goes to destruction. 12 The 10 horns you saw
are 10 kings who have not yet received a king-

[a]**16:10,12,17** Other mss add *angel* [b]**16:10** Lit *They* [c]**16:15** Or *and guards his clothes* [d]**16:16** Other mss read *Armageddon*; other mss read *Harmegedon*; other mss read *Mageddon*; other mss read *Magedon* [e]**16:16** Traditionally *the hill of Megiddo*, a great city that guarded the pass between the coast and the valley of Jezreel or Esdraelon; see Jdg 5:19; 2 Kg 9:27 [f]**16:17** Or *on the air* [g]**16:17** Other mss add *of heaven* [h]**16:19** Or *the Gentile cities* [i]**16:20** Lit *mountains were not found* [j]**16:21** Lit *about a talent*; talents varied in weight upwards from 75 pounds [k]**16:21** Lit *people* [l]**17:1** Traditionally, *the great whore* [m]**17:1** Or *by many* [n]**17:3** Or *in spirit* [o]**17:3** Lit *was filled* [p]**17:4** Other mss read *of earth's* [q]**17:7** Lit *the mystery* [r]**17:9** Or *This calls for the mind with wisdom* [s]**17:10** Some editors or translators put *They are also seven kings:* in v. 9.

dom, but they will receive authority as kings
with the beast for one hour. 13 These have one
purpose, and they give their power and authority to the beast. 14 These will make war against
the Lamb, but the Lamb will conquer them
because He is Lord of lords and King of kings.
Those with Him are called and elect and faithful."
15 He also said to me, "The waters you saw,
where the prostitute was seated, are peoples,
multitudes, nations, and languages. 16 The 10
horns you saw, and the beast, will hate the
prostitute. They will make her desolate and
naked, devour her flesh, and burn her up with
fire. 17 For God has put it into their hearts to
carry out His plan by having one purpose, and
to give their kingdom[a] to the beast until God's
words are accomplished. 18 And the woman
you saw is the great city that has an empire[b]
over the kings of the earth."

The Fall of Babylon the Great

18 After this I saw another angel with
great authority coming down from
heaven, and the earth was illuminated by his
splendor. 2 He cried in a mighty voice:

It has fallen,[c] Babylon the Great
  has fallen!
She has become a dwelling
  for demons,
a haunt[d] for every unclean spirit,
a haunt[d] for every unclean bird,
and a haunt[d] for every unclean
  and despicable beast.[e]
3 For all the nations have drunk[f]
the wine of her sexual immorality,
  which brings wrath.
The kings of the earth have committed
  sexual immorality with her,
and the merchants of the earth
  have grown wealthy
  from her excessive luxury.

4 Then I heard another voice from heaven:

Come out of her, My people,
so that you will not share in her sins,
or receive any of her plagues.
5 For her sins are piled up[g]
  to heaven,
and God has remembered her crimes.
6 Pay her back the way she also paid,
and double it according to her works.
In the cup in which she mixed,
mix a double portion for her.
7 As much as she glorified herself
  and lived luxuriously,
give her that much torment and grief.
Because she says in her heart,
  'I sit as queen;
I am not a widow,
  and I will never see grief,'
8 therefore her plagues will come
  in one day[h] —
death, and grief, and famine.
She will be burned up with fire,
because the Lord God who judges her
  is mighty.

The World Mourns Babylon's Fall

9 The kings of the earth who have committed sexual immorality and lived luxuriously
with her will weep and mourn over her when
they see the smoke of her burning. 10 They
stand far off in fear of her torment, saying:

Woe, woe, the great city,
Babylon, the mighty city!
For in a single hour[h]
your judgment has come.

11 The merchants of the earth will also weep
and mourn over her, because no one buys their
merchandise any longer— 12 merchandise of
gold, silver, precious stones, and pearls; fine fab-
rics of linen, purple, silk, and scarlet; all kinds of
fragrant wood products; objects of ivory; objects
of expensive wood, brass,[i] iron, and marble;
13 cinnamon, spice,[j] [k] incense, myrrh,[l] and
frankincense; wine, olive oil, fine wheat flour,
and grain; cattle and sheep; horses and carriages; and human bodies and souls.[m] [n]

14 The fruit you craved has left you.
All your splendid
  and glamorous things are gone;
they will never find them again.

15 The merchants of these things, who became
rich from her, will stand far off in fear of her
torment, weeping and mourning, 16 saying:

[a]**17:17** Or *sovereignty* [b]**17:18** Or *has sovereignty* or *rulership* [c]**18:2** Other mss omit *It has fallen* [d]**18:2** Or *prison* [e]**18:2** Other mss omit the words *and a haunt for every unclean beast.* The words *and despicable* then refer to the *bird* of the previous line. [f]**18:3** Other mss read *have collapsed*; other mss read *have fallen* [g]**18:5** Or *sins have reached up* [h]**18:8,10** Suddenly [i]**18:12** Or *bronze*, or *copper* [j]**18:13** Other mss omit *spice* [k]**18:13** Or *amomum*, an aromatic plant [l]**18:13** Or *perfume* [m]**18:13** Or *carriages; and slaves, namely, human beings* [n]**18:13** Slaves; "bodies" was the Gk way of referring to slaves; "souls of men" was the Hb way.

Woe, woe, the great city,
clothed in fine linen, purple,
and scarlet,
adorned with gold, precious stones,
and pearls;
17 because in a single hour[a]
such fabulous wealth
was destroyed!

And every shipmaster, seafarer, the sailors, and all who do business by sea, stood far
off 18 as they watched the smoke from her
burning and kept crying out: "Who is like the
great city?" 19 They threw dust on their
heads and kept crying out, weeping, and
mourning:

Woe, woe, the great city,
where all those who have ships
on the sea
became rich from her wealth;
because in a single hour[a]
she was destroyed.
20 Rejoice over her, heaven, and you
saints, apostles, and prophets,
because God has executed
your judgment on her![a]

The Finality of Babylon's Fall

21 Then a mighty angel picked up a stone
like a large millstone and threw it into the sea,
saying:

In this way, Babylon the great city
will be thrown down violently
and never be found again.
22 The sound of harpists, musicians,
flutists, and trumpeters
will never be heard in you again;
no craftsman of any trade
will ever be found in you again;
the sound of a mill
will never be heard in you again;
23 the light of a lamp will never shine
in you again;
and the voice of a groom and bride
will never be heard in you again.
⌊All this will happen⌋
because your merchants
were the nobility of the earth,
because all the nations were deceived
by your sorcery,[c]
24 and the blood of prophets and saints,
and all those slaughtered on earth,
was found in you.[d]

Heaven Exults over Babylon

19 After this I heard something like the
loud voice of a vast multitude in heav-
en, saying:

Hallelujah![e]
Salvation, glory, and power belong
to our God,
2 because His judgments are true[f]
and righteous,
because He has judged
the notorious prostitute
who corrupted the earth
with her sexual immorality;
and He has avenged the blood
of His servants that was
on her hands.

3 A second time they said:

Hallelujah![g]
Her smoke ascends forever and ever!

4 Then the 24 elders and the four living
creatures fell down and worshiped God, who is
seated on the throne, saying:

•Amen! Hallelujah![g]

5 A voice came from the throne, saying:

Praise our God,
all you His servants,
you who fear Him,
both small and great!

Marriage of the Lamb Announced

6 Then I heard something like the voice of a
vast multitude, like the sound of cascading
waters, and like the rumbling of loud thunder,
saying:

Hallelujah[g] —because our Lord God,
the Almighty,
has begun to reign!
7 Let us be glad, rejoice,
and give Him glory,
because the marriage of the Lamb
has come,
and His wife has prepared herself.
8 She was permitted to wear fine linen,
bright and pure.

[a]**18:17,19** Suddenly [b]**18:20** Or *God pronounced on her the judgment she passed on you*; see Rv 18:6 [c]**18:23** Ancient sorcery or witchcraft often used spells and drugs. Here the term may be non-literal, that is, Babylon drugged the nations with her beauty and power. [d]**18:24** Lit *in her* [e]**19:1** Lit *Praise Yahweh*; the Gk word is transliterated *hallelujah* from a Hb expression of praise and is used in many places in the OT, such as Ps 106:1. [f]**19:2** Valid; see Jn 8:16; 19:35 [g]**19:3,4,6** See note at Rv 19:1

For the fine linen represents the righteous acts
of the saints.
9 Then he[a] said to me, "Write: Blessed are
those invited to the marriage feast of the
Lamb!" He also said to me, "These words of
God are true." 10 Then I fell at his feet to worship him, but he said to me, "Don't do that! I
am a fellow •slave with you and your brothers
who have the testimony about[b] Jesus. Worship
God, because the testimony about[b] Jesus is the
spirit of prophecy."

The Rider on a White Horse

11 Then I saw heaven opened, and there
was a white horse! Its rider is called Faithful
and True, and in righteousness He judges and
makes war. 12 His eyes were like a fiery flame,
and on His head were many crowns. He had a
name written that no one knows except Himself. 13 He wore a robe stained with blood,[c] and
His name is called the Word of God. 14 The
armies that were in heaven followed Him on
white horses, wearing pure white linen.
15 From His mouth came a sharp[d] sword, so
that with it He might strike the nations. He will
shepherd[e] them with an iron scepter. He will
also trample the winepress of the fierce anger
of God, the Almighty. 16 And on His robe and
on His thigh He has a name written:

KING OF KINGS
AND LORD OF LORDS

The Beast and His Armies Defeated

17 Then I saw an angel standing in the sun,
and he cried out in a loud voice, saying to all
the birds flying in mid-heaven, "Come, gather
together for the great supper of God, 18 so that
you may eat the flesh of kings, the flesh of
commanders, the flesh of mighty men, the flesh
of horses and of their riders, and the flesh of
everyone, both free and •slave, small and
great."
19 Then I saw the beast, the kings of the
earth, and their armies gathered together to
wage war against the rider on the horse and
against His army. 20 But the beast was taken
prisoner, and along with him the false prophet,
who had performed signs on his authority,[f] by
which he deceived those who accepted the
mark of the beast and those who worshiped his
image. Both of them were thrown alive into the
lake of fire that burns with sulfur. 21 The rest
were killed with the sword that came from the
mouth of the rider on the horse, and all the
birds were filled with their flesh.

Satan Bound

20 Then I saw an angel coming down
from heaven with the key to the
•abyss and a great chain in his hand. 2 He
seized the dragon, that ancient serpent who is
the Devil and Satan,[g] and bound him for 1,000
years. 3 He threw him into the abyss, closed it,
and put a seal on it so that he would no longer
deceive the nations until the 1,000 years were
completed. After that, he must be released for
a short time.

The Saints Reign with the Messiah

4 Then I saw thrones, and people seated
on them who were given authority to judge.
⌊I⌋ also ⌊saw⌋ the souls of those who had been
beheaded[h] because of their testimony about
Jesus and because of God's word, who had
not worshiped the beast or his image, and
who had not accepted the mark on their foreheads or their hands. They came to life and
reigned with the •Messiah for 1,000 years.
5 The rest of the dead did not come to life
until the 1,000 years were completed. This is
the first resurrection. 6 Blessed and holy is
the one who shares in the first resurrection!
The second death has no power[i] over these,
but they will be priests of God and the Messiah, and they will reign with Him for 1,000
years.

Satanic Rebellion Crushed

7 When the 1,000 years are completed,
Satan will be released from his prison 8 and will
go out to deceive the nations at the four corners
of the earth, Gog and Magog, to gather them for
battle. Their number is like the sand of the sea.
9 They came up over the surface of the earth
and surrounded the encampment of the saints,
the beloved city. Then fire came down from
heaven[j] and consumed them. 10 The Devil who
deceived them was thrown into the lake of fire
and sulfur where the beast and the false
prophet are, and they will be tormented day
and night forever and ever.

[a] **19:9** Probably an angel; see Rv 17:1; 22:8–9 [b] **19:10** Or *testimony to* [c] **19:13** Or *a robe dipped in* [d] **19:15** Other mss add *double-edged* [e] **19:15** Or *rule* [f] **19:20** Lit *signs before him* [g] **20:2** Other mss add *who deceives the whole world* [h] **20:4** All who had given their lives for their faith in Christ [i] **20:6** Or *authority* [j] **20:9** Other mss add *from God*

The Great White Throne Judgment

11 Then I saw a great white throne and One
seated on it. Earth and heaven fled from His
presence, and no place was found for them. 12 I
also saw the dead, the great and the small,
standing before the throne, and books were
opened. Another book was opened, which is
the book of life, and the dead were judged
according to their works by what was written
in the books.
13 Then the sea gave up its dead, and Death
and •Hades gave up their dead; all[a] were
judged according to their works. 14 Death and
Hades were thrown into the lake of fire. This is
the second death, the lake of fire.[b] 15 And anyone not found written in the book of life was
thrown into the lake of fire.

The New Creation

21 Then I saw a new heaven and a new
earth, for the first heaven and the first
earth had passed away, and the sea existed no
longer. 2 I also saw the Holy City, new Jerusalem, coming down out of heaven from God,
prepared like a bride adorned for her husband.
3 Then I heard a loud voice from the
throne:[c]

> Look! God's dwelling[d] is
> with men,
> and He will live with them.
> They will be His people,
> and God Himself will be with them
> and be their God.[e]
> 4 He will wipe away every tear
> from their eyes.
> Death will exist no longer;
> grief, crying, and pain will exist
> no longer,
> because the previous things[f]
> have passed away.

5 Then the One seated on the throne said,
"Look! I am making everything new." He
also said, "Write, because these words[g] are
faithful and true." 6 And He said to me, "It is
done! I am the •Alpha and the Omega, the
Beginning and the End. I will give to the
thirsty from the spring of living water as a
gift. 7 The victor will inherit these things,
and I will be his God, and he will be My son.
8 But the cowards, unbelievers,[h] vile, murderers, sexually immoral, sorcerers, idolaters, and all liars—their share will be in the
lake that burns with fire and sulfur, which is
the second death."

The New Jerusalem

9 Then one of the seven angels, who had
held the seven bowls filled with the seven last
plagues, came and spoke with me: "Come, I
will show you the bride, the wife of the Lamb."
10 He then carried me away in the Spirit[i] to a
great and high mountain and showed me the
holy city, Jerusalem, coming down out of
heaven from God, 11 arrayed with God's glory.
Her radiance was like a very precious stone,
like a jasper stone, bright as crystal. 12 ⌊The
city⌋ had a massive high wall, with 12 gates.
Twelve angels were at the gates; ⌊on the gates⌋,
names were inscribed, the names of the 12
tribes of the sons of Israel. 13 There were three
gates on the east, three gates on the north,
three gates on the south, and three gates on the
west. 14 The city wall had 12 foundations, and
on them were the 12 names of the Lamb's 12
apostles.
15 The one who spoke with me had a gold
measuring rod to measure the city, its gates,
and its wall. 16 The city is laid out in a square;
its length and width are the same. He measured the city with the rod at 12,000 *stadia*.[j]
Its length, width, and height are equal.
17 Then he measured its wall, 144 •cubits
according to human measurement, which the
angel used. 18 The building material of its wall
was jasper, and the city was pure gold like
clear glass.
19 The foundations of the city wall were
adorned with every kind of precious stone:

> the first foundation jasper,
> the second sapphire,
> the third chalcedony,
> the fourth emerald,
> 20 the fifth sardonyx,
> the sixth carnelian,
> the seventh chrysolite,
> the eighth beryl,
> the ninth topaz,
> the tenth chrysoprase,
> the eleventh jacinth,
> the twelfth amethyst.

21 The 12 gates are 12 pearls; each individual
gate was made of a single pearl. The broad

[a]**20:13** Lit *each* [b]**20:14** Other mss omit *the lake of fire* [c]**21:3** Other mss read *from heaven* [d]**21:3** Or *tent*, or *tabernacle* [e]**21:3** Other mss omit *and be their God* [f]**21:4** Or *the first things* [g]**21:5** Other mss add *of God* [h]**21:8** Other mss add *the sinful* [i]**21:10** Or *in spirit* [j]**21:16** A *stadion* (sg) equals about 600 feet; the total is about 1,400 miles.

street[a] of the city was pure gold, like transparent glass.

22 I did not see a sanctuary in it, because the Lord God the Almighty and the Lamb are its sanctuary. 23 The city does not need the sun or the moon to shine on it, because God's glory illuminates it, and its lamp is the Lamb. 24 The nations[b] will walk in its light, and the kings of the earth will bring their glory into it.[c] 25 Each day its gates will never close because it will never be night there. 26 They will bring the glory and honor of the nations into it.[d] 27 Nothing profane will ever enter it: no one who does what is vile or false, but only those written in the Lamb's book of life.

The Source of Life

22 Then he showed me the river[e] of living water, sparkling like crystal, flowing from the throne of God and of the Lamb 2 down the middle of the broad street ⌊of the city⌋. On both sides of the river was the tree of life[f] bearing 12 kinds of fruit, producing its fruit every month. The leaves of the tree are for healing the nations, 3 and there will no longer be any curse. The throne of God and of the Lamb will be in the city,[g] and His servants will serve Him. 4 They will see His face, and His name will be on their foreheads. 5 Night will no longer exist, and people will not need lamplight or sunlight, because the Lord God will give them light. And they will reign forever and ever.

The Time Is Near

6 Then he said to me, "These words are faithful and true. And the Lord, the God of the spirits of the prophets,[h] has sent His angel to show His servants what must quickly take place."[i]

7 "Look, I am coming quickly! Blessed is the one who keeps the prophetic words of this book."

8 I, John, am the one who heard and saw these things. When I heard and saw them, I fell down to worship at the feet of the angel who had shown them to me. 9 But he said to me, "Don't do that! I am a fellow •slave with you, your brothers the prophets, and those who keep the words of this book. Worship God." 10 He also said to me, "Don't seal the prophetic words of this book, because the time is near. 11 Let the unrighteous go on in unrighteousness; let the filthy go on being made filthy; let the righteous go on in righteousness; and let the holy go on being made holy."

12 "Look! I am coming quickly, and My reward is with Me to repay each person according to what he has done. 13 I am the •Alpha and the Omega, the First and the Last, the Beginning and the End.

14 "Blessed are those who wash their robes,[j] so that they may have the right to the tree of life and may enter the city by the gates. 15 Outside are the dogs, the sorcerers, the sexually immoral, the murderers, the idolaters, and everyone who loves and practices lying.

16 "I, Jesus, have sent My angel to attest these things to you[k] for the churches. I am the Root and the Offspring of David, the Bright Morning Star."

17 Both the Spirit and the bride say, "Come!" Anyone who hears should say, "Come!" And the one who is thirsty should come. Whoever desires should take the living water as a gift.

18 I testify to everyone who hears the prophetic words of this book: If anyone adds to them, God will add to him the plagues that are written in this book. 19 And if anyone takes away from the words of this prophetic book, God will take away his share of the tree of life and the holy city, written in this book.

20 He who testifies about these things says, "Yes, I am coming quickly."

•Amen! Come, Lord Jesus!

21 The grace of the Lord Jesus[l] be with all the saints.[m] Amen.[n]

[a]**21:21** Or *The public square* [b]**21:24** Other mss add *of those who are saved* [c]**21:24** Other mss read *will bring to Him the nations' glory and honor* [d]**21:26** Other mss add *in order that they might go in* [e]**22:1** Other mss read *pure river* [f]**22:2** Or *was a tree of life*, or *was a tree that gives life* [g]**22:3** Lit *in it* [h]**22:6** Other mss read *God of the holy prophets* [i]**22:6** Or *soon* [j]**22:14** Other mss read *who keep His commandments* [k]**22:16** *you* (pl in Gk) [l]**22:21** Other mss add *Christ* [m]**22:21** Other mss omit *the saints* [n]**22:21** Other mss omit *Amen.*

Psalms and Proverbs

Psalms

BOOK I

(Psalms 1–41)

Psalm 1

The Two Ways

1 How happy is the man
who does not follow[a] the advice
of the wicked,
or take[b] the path of sinners,
or join a group[c] of mockers!
2 Instead, his delight is
in the LORD's instruction,
and he meditates on it day and night.
3 He is like a tree planted beside streams
of water[d]
that bears its fruit in season[e]
and whose leaf does not wither.
Whatever he does prospers.

4 The wicked are not like this;
instead, they are like chaff
that the wind blows away.
5 Therefore the wicked will not survive[b]
the judgment,
and sinners will not be
in the community of the righteous.

6 For the LORD watches over the way
of the righteous,
but the way of the wicked
leads to ruin.

Psalm 2

Coronation of the Son

1 Why do the nations rebel[f]
and the peoples plot in vain?
2 The kings of the earth
take their stand
and the rulers conspire together
against the LORD
and His Anointed One:[g]
3 "Let us tear off their chains
and free ourselves
from their restraints."[h]

4 The One enthroned[i] in heaven laughs;
the Lord ridicules them.
5 Then He speaks to them in His anger
and terrifies them in His wrath:
6 "I have consecrated My King[j]
on Zion, My holy mountain."
7 I will declare the LORD's decree:
He said to Me, "You are My Son;[k]
today I have become Your[l] Father.
8 Ask of Me,
and I will make the nations
Your[l] inheritance
and the ends of the earth
Your[l] possession.
9 You will break[m] them
with a rod of iron;
You[n] will shatter them like pottery."[o]

10 So now, kings, be wise;
receive instruction, you judges
of the earth.
11 Serve the LORD with reverential awe,
and rejoice with trembling.
12 Pay homage to[p] the Son, or He[q]
will be angry,
and you will perish in your rebellion,[r]
for His[s] anger may ignite
at any moment.
All those who take refuge in Him[t]
are happy.

Psalm 3

Confidence in Troubled Times

A psalm of David when he fled
from his son Absalom.

1 LORD, how my foes increase!
There are many who attack me.
2 Many say about me,
"There is no help for him in God."
•*Selah*

3 But You, LORD, are a shield around me,
my glory, and the One who lifts up
my head.
4 I cry aloud to the LORD,
and He answers me
from His holy mountain. *Selah*

5 I lie down and sleep;
I wake again because the LORD
sustains me.

[a]**1:1** Lit *not walk in* [b]**1:1,5** Lit *stand in* [c]**1:1** Or *or sit in the seat* [d]**1:3** Or *beside irrigation canals* [e]**1:3** Lit *in its season*
[f]**2:1** Or *conspire,* or *rage* [g]**2:2** Or *anointed one* [h]**2:3** Lit *and throw their ropes from us* [i]**2:4** Lit *who sits* [j]**2:6** Or *king*
[k]**2:7** Or *me, "You are My son* [l]**2:7,8** Or *your* [m]**2:9** LXX, Syr, Tg read *shepherd* [n]**2:9** Or *you* [o]**2:9** Lit *a potter's vessel*
[p]**2:12** Lit *Kiss* [q]**2:12** Or *son, otherwise he* [r]**2:12** Lit *perish way* [s]**2:12** Or *his* [t]**2:12** Or *him*

6 I am not afraid of the thousands
of people
who have taken their stand against me
on every side.

7 Rise up, LORD!
Save me, my God!
You strike all my enemies on the cheek;
You break the teeth of the wicked.
8 Salvation belongs to the LORD;
may Your blessing be on Your people.
Selah

Psalm 4
A Night Prayer

For the choir director:
with stringed instruments. A Davidic psalm.

1 Answer me when I call,
God, who vindicates me.[a]
You freed me from affliction;
be gracious to me and hear my prayer.

2 How long, exalted men, will my honor
be insulted?
⌊How long⌋ will you love
what is worthless
and pursue a lie? •*Selah*
3 Know that the LORD has set apart
the faithful for Himself;
the LORD will hear when I call to Him.
4 Be angry[b] and do not sin;
on your bed, reflect in your heart
and be still. *Selah*
5 Offer sacrifices in righteousness[c]
and trust in the LORD.

6 Many are saying, "Who can show us
anything good?"
Look on us with favor, LORD.

7 You have put more joy in my heart
than they have when their grain
and new wine abound.
8 I will both lie down and sleep
in peace,
for You alone, LORD, make me live
in safety.

Psalm 5
The Refuge of the Righteous

For the choir director: with the flutes.
A Davidic psalm.

1 Listen to my words, LORD;
consider my sighing.
2 Pay attention to the sound of my cry,
my King and my God,
for I pray to You.

3 At daybreak, LORD, You hear my voice;
at daybreak I plead my case to You
and watch expectantly.

4 For You are not a God who delights
in wickedness;
evil cannot lodge with You.
5 The boastful cannot stand
in Your presence;
You hate all evildoers.
6 You destroy those who tell lies;
the LORD abhors a man of bloodshed
and treachery.

7 But I enter Your house
by the abundance of Your faithful love;
I bow down toward
Your holy temple
in reverential awe of You.
8 LORD, lead me in Your righteousness,
because of my adversaries;[d]
make Your way straight before me.

9 For there is nothing reliable in what
they say;[e]
destruction is within them;
their throat is an open grave;
they flatter with their tongues.
10 Punish them, God;
let them fall by their own schemes.
Drive them out because of
their many crimes,
for they rebel against You.

11 But let all who take refuge in You
rejoice;
let them shout for joy forever.
May You shelter them,
and may those who love Your name
boast about You.
12 For You, LORD, bless
the righteous one;
You surround him with favor
like a shield.

Psalm 6
A Prayer for Mercy

For the choir director:
with stringed instruments,
according to •*Sheminith*. A Davidic psalm.

1 LORD, do not rebuke me in Your anger;

[a]**4:1** Or *God of my righteousness* [b]**4:4** Or *Tremble* [c]**4:5** Or *Offer right sacrifices*; lit *Sacrifice sacrifices of righteousness*
[d]**5:8** Or *of those who lie in wait for me* [e]**5:9** Lit *in his mouth*

do not discipline me in Your wrath.
2 Be gracious to me, LORD,
for I am weak;[a]
heal me, LORD, for my bones
are shaking;
3 my whole being is shaken
with terror.
And You, LORD—how long?

4 Turn, LORD! Rescue me;
save me because of
Your faithful love.
5 For there is no remembrance of You
in death;
who can thank You in •Sheol?

6 I am weary from my groaning;
with my tears I dampen my pillow[b]
and drench my bed every night.
7 My eyes are swollen from grief;
they[c] grow old because of all
my enemies.

8 Depart from me, all evildoers,
for the LORD has heard the sound
of my weeping.
9 The LORD has heard my plea
for help;
the LORD accepts my prayer.
10 All my enemies will be ashamed
and shake with terror;
they will turn back and suddenly
be disgraced.

Psalm 7

Prayer for Justice

A *Shiggaion*[d] of David, which he sang to the LORD concerning the words of •Cush,[e] a Benjaminite.

1 LORD my God, I seek refuge
in You;
save me from all my pursuers
and rescue me,
2 or they[f] will tear me like a lion,
ripping me apart, with no one
to rescue me.[g]
3 LORD my God, if I have done this,
if there is injustice on my hands,
4 if I have done harm to one at peace
with me
or have plundered[h] my adversary
without cause,
5 may an enemy pursue
and overtake me;
may he trample me to the ground
and leave my honor in the dust.
•Selah

6 Rise up, LORD, in Your anger;
lift Yourself up against the fury
of my adversaries;
awake for me;[i]
You have ordained[j] a judgment.
7 Let the assembly of peoples gather
around You;
take Your seat[k] on high over it.
8 The LORD judges the peoples;
vindicate me, LORD,
according to my righteousness
and my integrity.[l]

9 Let the evil of the wicked come
to an end,
but establish the righteous.
The One who examines the thoughts
and emotions[m]
is a righteous God.
10 My shield is with[n] God,
who saves the upright in heart.
11 God is a righteous judge,
and a God who executes justice
every day.

12 If anyone does not repent,
God[o] will sharpen His sword;
He has strung[p] His bow
and made it ready.
13 He has prepared His deadly weapons;
He tips His arrows with fire.

14 See, he is pregnant with evil,
conceives trouble, and gives birth
to deceit.
15 He dug a pit and hollowed it out,
but fell into the hole
he had made.
16 His trouble comes back
on his own head,
and his violence falls on the top
of his head.

17 I will thank the LORD
for His righteousness;
I will sing about the name
of the LORD, the •Most High.

[a]**6:2** Or *sick* [b]**6:6** Lit *bed* [c]**6:7** LXX, Aq, Sym, Jer read *I* [d]Perhaps a passionate song with rapid changes of rhythm, or a dirge [e]LXX, Aq, Sym, Theod, Jer read *of the Cushite* [f]**7:2** Lit *he* [g]**7:2** Lit *ripping, and without a rescuer* [h]**7:4** Or *me and have spared* [i]**7:6** LXX reads *awake, Lord my God* [j]**7:6** Or *me; ordain* [k]**7:7** MT reads *and return* [l]**7:8** Lit *integrity on me* [m]**7:9** Lit *examines hearts and kidneys* [n]**7:10** Lit *on* [o]**7:12** Lit *He* [p]**7:12** Lit *bent*; that is, bent the bow to string it

Psalm 8

God's Glory, Man's Dignity

For the choir director: on the •*Gittith*.
A Davidic psalm.

1 LORD, our Lord,
how magnificent is Your name
throughout the earth!

You have covered the heavens
with Your majesty.[a]
2 Because of Your adversaries,
You have established a stronghold[b]
from the mouths of children
and nursing infants,
to silence the enemy and the avenger.

3 When I observe Your heavens,
the work of Your fingers,
the moon and the stars,
which You set in place,
4 what is man that You remember him,
the son of man that You look
after him?
5 You made him little less than God[c d]
and crowned him with glory
and honor.
6 You made him lord over the works
of Your hands;
You put everything under his feet:[e]
7 all the sheep and oxen,
as well as animals in the wild,
8 birds of the sky,
and fish of the sea
passing through the currents
of the seas.

9 LORD, our Lord,
how magnificent is Your name
throughout the earth!

Psalm 9

Celebration of God's Justice

For the choir director:
according to *Muth-labben*.[f] A Davidic psalm.

1 I will thank the LORD with all my heart;
I will declare all
Your wonderful works.
2 I will rejoice and boast about You;
I will sing about Your name,
•Most High.

3 When my enemies retreat,
they stumble and perish before You.
4 For You have upheld my just cause;[g]
You are seated on Your throne
as a righteous judge.
5 You have rebuked the nations:
You have destroyed the wicked;
You have erased their name forever
and ever.
6 The enemy has come to eternal ruin;
You have uprooted the cities,
and the very memory of them
has perished.

7 But the LORD sits enthroned forever;
He has established His throne
for judgment.
8 He judges the world with righteousness;
He executes judgment on the peoples
with fairness.
9 The LORD is a refuge for the oppressed,
a refuge in times of trouble.
10 Those who know Your name
trust in You
because You have not abandoned
those who seek You, LORD.

11 Sing to the LORD, who dwells in Zion;
proclaim His deeds
among the peoples.
12 For the One who seeks an accounting
for bloodshed remembers them;
He does not forget the cry
of the afflicted.

13 Be gracious to me, LORD;
consider my affliction at the hands
of those who hate me.
Lift me up from the gates of death,
14 so that I may declare all Your praises.
I will rejoice in Your salvation
within the gates of Daughter Zion.[h]
15 The nations have fallen into the pit
they made;
their foot is caught in the net
they have concealed.
16 The LORD has revealed Himself;
He has executed justice,
striking down[i] the wicked[j]
by the work of their hands.
•Higgaion. •Selah

17 The wicked will return to •Sheol—
all the nations that forget God.
18 For the oppressed will not always
be forgotten;

[a]**8:1** Lit *earth, which has set Your splendor upon the heavens* [b]**8:2** LXX reads *established praise* [c]**8:5** LXX reads *angels* [d]**8:5** Or *gods*, or *a god*, or *heavenly beings*; Hb *Elohim* [e]**8:6** Or *authority* [f]Perhaps a musical term [g]**9:4** Lit *my justice and my cause* [h]**9:14** Jerusalem [i]**9:16** Or *justice, snaring* [j]**9:16** LXX, Aq, Syr, Tg read *justice, the wicked is trapped*

the hope of the afflicted[a]
will not perish forever.
19 Rise up, LORD! Do not let man prevail;
let the nations be judged
in Your presence.
20 Put terror in them, LORD;
let the nations know they are
only men. *Selah*

Psalm 10

1 LORD,[b] why do You stand so far away?
Why do You hide in times of trouble?
2 In arrogance the wicked
relentlessly pursue the afflicted;
let them be caught in the schemes
they have devised.

3 For the wicked one boasts about
his own cravings;
the one who is greedy curses[c]
and despises the LORD.
4 In all his scheming,
the wicked arrogantly thinks:[d]
"There is no accountability,
⌊since⌋ God does not exist."
5 His ways are always secure;[e]
Your lofty judgments are beyond
his sight;
he scoffs at all his adversaries.
6 He says to himself, "I will never
be moved—
from generation to generation
without calamity."
7 Cursing, deceit, and violence
fill his mouth;
trouble and malice are
under his tongue.
8 He waits in ambush near the villages;
he kills the innocent in secret places;
his eyes are on the lookout
for the helpless.
9 He lurks in secret like a lion in a thicket.
He lurks in order to seize the afflicted.
He seizes the afflicted and drags him
in his net.
10 He crouches and bends down;
the helpless fall because of
his strength.
11 He says to himself, "God has forgotten;
He hides His face and will never see."
12 Rise up, LORD God! Lift up Your hand.
Do not forget the afflicted.
13 Why has the wicked despised God?
He says to himself, "You will not
demand an account."
14 But You Yourself have seen trouble
and grief,
observing it in order to take the matter
into Your hands.
The helpless entrusts himself to You;
You are a helper of the fatherless.
15 Break the arm of the wicked
and evil person;
call his wickedness into account
until nothing remains of it.[f]
16 The LORD is King forever and ever;
the nations will perish
from His land.
17 LORD, You have heard the desire
of the humble;[g]
You will strengthen their hearts.
You will listen carefully,
18 doing justice for the fatherless
and the oppressed,
so that men of the earth
may terrify ⌊them⌋ no more.

Psalm 11
Refuge in the LORD

For the choir director. Davidic.

1 I have taken refuge in the LORD.
How can you say to me,
"Escape to the mountain like a bird![h]
2 For look, the wicked string the bow;
they put the[i] arrow
on the bowstring
to shoot from the shadows
at the upright in heart.
3 When the foundations are destroyed,
what can the righteous do?"

4 The LORD is in His holy temple;
the LORD's throne is in heaven.
His eyes watch;
He examines[j] •everyone.
5 The LORD examines the righteous
and the wicked.
He hates the lover of violence.
6 He will rain burning coals and sulfur[k]
on the wicked;

[a]**9:18** Alt Hb tradition reads *humble* [b]**10:1** A few Hb mss and LXX connect Pss 9–10. Together these 2 psalms form a partial •acrostic. [c]**10:3** Or *he blesses the greedy* [d]**10:4** Lit *wicked according to the height of his nose* [e]**10:5** Or *prosperous* [f]**10:15** Lit *account You do not find* [g]**10:17** Other Hb mss, LXX, Syr read *afflicted* [h]**11:1** LXX, Syr, Jer, Tg, MT reads *to your mountain, bird* [i]**11:2** Lit *their* [j]**11:4** Lit *His eyelids examine* [k]**11:6** Sym; MT reads *rain snares, fire*; the difference between the 2 Hb words is 1 letter

a scorching wind will be their portion.[a]
7 For the LORD is righteous; He loves
righteous deeds.
The upright will see His face.

Psalm 12
Oppression by the Wicked

For the choir director: according to •*Sheminith.* A Davidic psalm.

1 Help, LORD, for no
faithful one remains;
the loyal have disappeared
from the •human race.
2 They lie to one another;
they speak with flattering lips
and deceptive hearts.
3 May the LORD cut off all flattering lips
and the tongue that speaks boastfully.
4 They say, "Through our tongues
we have power;[b]
our lips are our own—who can be
our master?"

5 "Because of the oppression
of the afflicted
and the groaning of the poor,
I will now rise up," says the LORD.
"I will put in a safe place the one
who longs for it."

6 The words of the LORD
are pure words,
like silver refined
in an earthen furnace,
purified seven times.

7 You, LORD, will guard us;[c]
You will protect us[d]
from this generation forever.
8 The wicked wander[e] everywhere,
and what is worthless is exalted
by the human race.

Psalm 13
A Plea for Deliverance

For the choir director. A Davidic psalm.

1 LORD, how long will You continually
forget me?
How long will You hide Your face
from me?
2 How long will I store up
anxious concerns[f] within me,
agony in my mind every day?
How long will my enemy
dominate me?

3 Consider me and answer,
LORD, my God.
Restore brightness to my eyes;
otherwise, I will sleep in death,
4 my enemy will say,
"I have triumphed
over him,"
and my foes will rejoice
because I am shaken.

5 But I have trusted in
Your faithful love;
my heart will rejoice in
Your deliverance.
6 I will sing to the LORD
because He has treated
me generously.

Psalm 14
A Portrait of Sinners

For the choir director. Davidic.

1 The fool says in his heart,
"God does not exist."
They are corrupt; their actions
are revolting.
There is no one who does good.
2 The LORD looks down from heaven
on the •human race
to see if there is one who is wise,
one who seeks God.
3 All have turned away;
all alike have become corrupt.
There is no one who does good,
not even one.[g]

4 Will evildoers never understand?
They consume my people
as they consume bread;
they do not call on the LORD.

5 Then[h] they will be filled
with terror,
for God is with those
who are[i] righteous.
6 You ⌊sinners⌋ frustrate the plans
of the afflicted,
but the LORD is his refuge.

7 Oh, that Israel's deliverance
would come from Zion!

[a]**11:6** Lit *be the portion of their cup* [b]**12:4** Lit *That say, "By our tongues we are strengthened* [c]**12:7** Some Hb mss, LXX, Jer; other Hb mss read *them* [d]**12:7** Some Hb mss, LXX; other Hb mss read *him* [e]**12:8** Lit *walk about* [f]**13:2** Or *up counsels* [g]**14:3** Two Hb mss, some LXX mss add the material found in Rm 3:13–18 [h]**14:5** Or *There* [i]**14:5** Lit *with the generation of the*

When the LORD restores
His captive people,
Jacob will rejoice; Israel will be glad.[a]

Psalm 15

A Description of the Godly

A Davidic psalm.

1 LORD, who can dwell in Your tent?
Who can live on Your holy mountain?

2 The one who lives honestly,
practices righteousness,
and acknowledges the truth
in his heart—
3 who does not slander with his tongue,
who does not harm his friend
or discredit his neighbor,
4 who despises the one rejected
by the LORD,[b]
but honors those who •fear the LORD,
who keeps his word
whatever the cost,
5 who does not lend his money
at interest
or take a bribe against the innocent—
the one who does these things
will never be moved.

Psalm 16

Confidence in the LORD

A Davidic •*Miktam.*

1 Protect me, God, for I take refuge
in You.
2 I[c] said to the LORD, "You are my Lord;
I have no good besides You."[d]
3 As for the holy people who are
in the land,
they are the noble ones in whom is
all my delight.
4 The sorrows of those who take
another ⌊god⌋
for themselves multiply;
I will not pour out their drink offerings
of blood,
and I will not speak their names
with my lips.

5 LORD, You are my portion[e]
and my cup ⌊of blessing⌋;
You hold my future.
6 The boundary lines have fallen for me
in pleasant places;
indeed, I have a beautiful inheritance.
7 I will praise the LORD
who counsels me—
even at night my conscience
instructs me.
8 I keep the LORD in mind[f] always.
Because He is at my right hand,
I will not be shaken.

9 Therefore my heart is glad,
and my spirit rejoices;
my body also rests securely.
10 For You will not abandon me
to •Sheol;
You will not allow Your Faithful One
to see the •Pit.[g]
11 You reveal the path of life to me;
in Your presence is abundant joy;
in Your right hand are
eternal pleasures.

Psalm 17

A Prayer for Protection

A Davidic prayer.

1 LORD, hear a just cause;
pay attention to my cry;
listen to my prayer—
from lips free of deceit.
2 Let my vindication come from You,
⌊for⌋ You see what is right.
3 You have tested my heart;
You have visited by night;
You have tried me and found
nothing ⌊evil⌋;
I have determined that my mouth
will not sin.[h]
4 Concerning what people do:
by the word of Your lips[i]
I have avoided the ways of the violent.
5 My steps are on Your paths;
my feet have not slipped.

6 I call on You, God,
because You will answer me;
listen closely to me; hear what I say.
7 Display the wonders
of Your faithful love,
Savior of all who seek refuge
from those who rebel
against Your right hand.[j]

[a]**14:7** Or *let Jacob rejoice; let Israel be glad.* [b]**15:4** Lit *in his eyes the rejected is despised* [c]**16:2** Some Hb mss, LXX, Syr, Jer; other Hb mss read *You* [d]**16:2** Or *"Lord, my good; there is none besides You."* [e]**16:5** Or *allotted portion* [f]**16:8** Lit *front of me* [g]**16:10** LXX reads *see decay* [h]**17:3** Or *[evil]; my mouth will not sin* [i]**17:4** God's law [j]**17:7** Or *love, You who save with Your right hand those seeking refuge from adversaries*

8 Guard me as the apple of Your eye;[a]
hide me in the shadow of Your wings
9 from[b] the wicked
who treat me violently,[c]
my deadly enemies
who surround me.

10 They have become hardened;[d]
their mouths speak arrogantly.
11 They advance against me;[e]
now they surround me.
They are determined[f]
to throw ⌊me⌋ to the ground.
12 They are[g] like a lion eager to tear,
like a young lion lurking in ambush.

13 Rise up, LORD!
Confront him; bring him down.
With Your sword, save me
from the wicked.
14 With Your hand, LORD, ⌊save me⌋
from men,
from men of the world,
whose portion is in this life:
You fill their bellies with what
You have in store,
their sons are satisfied,
and they leave their surplus
to their children.

15 But I will see Your face
in righteousness;
when I awake, I will be satisfied
with Your presence.[h]

Psalm 18

Praise for Deliverance

For the choir director. Of the servant of the LORD, David, who spoke the words of this song to the LORD on the day the LORD rescued him from the hand of all his enemies and from the hand of Saul. He said:

1 I love You, LORD, my strength.
2 The LORD is my rock,
my fortress, and my deliverer,
my God, my mountain
where I seek refuge,
my shield and the •horn
of my salvation,
my stronghold.
3 I called to the LORD, who is
worthy of praise,
and I was saved from my enemies.

4 The ropes of death were wrapped
around me;
the torrents of destruction terrified me.
5 The ropes of •Sheol entangled me;
the snares of death confronted me.
6 I called to the LORD in my distress,
and I cried to my God for help.
From His temple He heard my voice,
and my cry to Him reached His ears.

7 Then the earth shook and quaked;
the foundations of the mountains
trembled;
they shook because He burned
with anger.
8 Smoke rose from His nostrils,
and consuming fire ⌊came⌋
from His mouth;
coals were set ablaze by it.[i]
9 He parted the heavens
and came down,
a dark cloud beneath His feet.
10 He rode on a cherub and flew,
soaring on the wings of the wind.
11 He made darkness His hiding place,
dark storm clouds His canopy
around Him.
12 From the radiance of His presence,
His clouds swept onward with hail
and blazing coals.
13 The LORD thundered from[j] heaven;
the •Most High projected His voice.[k]
14 He shot His arrows
and scattered them;
He hurled[l] lightning bolts
and routed them.
15 The depths of the sea became visible,
the foundations of the world
were exposed,
at Your rebuke, LORD,
at the blast of the breath
of Your nostrils.

16 He reached down from on high
and took hold of me;
He pulled me out of deep waters.
17 He rescued me
from my powerful enemy
and from those who hated me,
for they were too strong for me.
18 They confronted me in the day
of my distress,

[a]**17:8** Lit *as the pupil, the daughter of the eye* [b]**17:9** Lit *from the presence of* [c]**17:9** Or *who plunder me* [d]**17:10** Lit *have closed up their fat* [e]**17:11** Vg; one Hb ms, LXX read *They cast me out*; MT reads *Our steps* [f]**17:11** Lit *They set their eyes* [g]**17:12** Lit *He is* [h]**17:15** Lit *form* [i]**18:8** Or *ablaze from Him* [j]**18:13** Some Hb mss, LXX, Tg, Jer; other Hb mss read *in* [k]**18:13** Other Hb mss read *voice, with hail and fiery coals* [l]**18:14** Or *multiplied*

but the LORD was my support.
19 He brought me out to a wide-
open place;
He rescued me because He delighted
in me.

20 The LORD rewarded me
according to my righteousness;
He repaid me
according to the cleanness of my hands.
21 For I have kept the ways of the LORD
and have not turned from my God
to wickedness.
22 Indeed, I have kept all His ordinances
in mind[a]
and have not disregarded His statutes.
23 I was blameless toward Him
and kept myself from sinning.
24 So the LORD repaid me
according to my righteousness,
according to the cleanness
of my hands in His sight.

25 With the faithful
You prove Yourself faithful;
with the blameless man
You prove Yourself blameless;
26 with the pure
You prove Yourself pure,
but with the crooked
You prove Yourself shrewd.
27 For You rescue an afflicted people,
but You humble those
with haughty eyes.
28 LORD, You light my lamp;
my God illuminates my darkness.
29 With You I can attack a barrier,[b]
and with my God I can leap over
a wall.

30 God—His way is perfect;
the word of the LORD is pure.
He is a shield to all who take refuge
in Him.
31 For who is God besides the LORD?
And who is a rock? Only our God.
32 God—He clothes me with strength
and makes my way perfect.
33 He makes my feet like the feet
of a deer
and sets me securely on the heights.[c]
34 He trains my hands for war;
my arms can bend a bow of bronze.
35 You have given me the shield
of Your salvation;
Your right hand upholds me,
and Your humility exalts me.
36 You widen ⌊a place⌋ beneath me
for my steps,
and my ankles do not give way.

37 I pursue my enemies
and overtake them;
I do not turn back until they are
wiped out.
38 I crush them, and they cannot get up;
they fall beneath my feet.
39 You have clothed me with strength
for battle;
You subdue my adversaries beneath me.
40 You have made my enemies retreat
before me;[d]
I annihilate those who hate me.
41 They cry for help, but there is no one
to save ⌊them⌋—
⌊they cry⌋ to the LORD, but He does not
answer them.
42 I pulverize them like dust
before the wind;
I trample them[e] like mud in the streets.

43 You have freed me from the feuds
among the people;
You have appointed me the head
of nations;
a people I had not known serve me.
44 Foreigners submit to me grudgingly;
as soon as they hear,[f] they obey me.
45 Foreigners lose heart
and come trembling
from their fortifications.

46 The LORD lives—may my rock
be praised!
The God of my salvation is exalted.
47 God—He gives me vengeance
and subdues peoples under me.
48 He frees me from my enemies.
You exalt me above my adversaries;
You rescue me from violent men.
49 Therefore I will praise You, LORD,
among the nations;
I will sing about Your name.
50 He gives great victories to His king;
He shows loyalty to His anointed,
to David and his descendants forever.

[a]**18:22** Lit *Indeed, all His ordinances have been in front of me* [b]**18:29** Or *ridge* [c]**18:33** Or *on my high places* [d]**18:40** Or *You gave me the necks of my enemies* [e]**18:42** Some Hb mss, LXX, Syr, Tg; other Hb mss read *I poured them out* [f]**18:44** Lit *At the hearing of the ear*

Psalm 19

The Witness of Creation and Scripture

For the choir director. A Davidic psalm.

1 The heavens declare the glory of God,
and the sky[a] proclaims the work
of His hands.
2 Day after day they pour out speech;
night after night
they communicate knowledge.[b]
3 There is no speech; there are no words;
their voice is not heard.
4 Their message[c] has gone out to all
the earth,
and their words to the ends
of the inhabited world.

In the heavens[d] He has pitched a tent
for the sun.
5 It is like a groom coming from
the[e] bridal chamber;
it rejoices like an athlete
running a course.
6 It rises from one end of the heavens
and circles[f] to their other end;
nothing is hidden from its heat.

7 The instruction of the LORD is perfect,
reviving the soul;
the •testimony of the LORD
is trustworthy,
making the inexperienced wise.
8 The precepts of the LORD are right,
making the heart glad;
the commandment of the LORD
is radiant,
making the eyes light up.
9 The •fear of the LORD is pure,
enduring forever;
the ordinances of the LORD are reliable
and altogether righteous.
10 They are more desirable than gold—
than an abundance of pure gold;
and sweeter than honey—
than honey dripping from the comb.
11 In addition, Your servant is warned
by them;
there is great reward in keeping them.

12 Who perceives his unintentional sins?
Cleanse me from my hidden faults.
13 Moreover, keep Your servant
from willful sins;
do not let them rule over me.
Then I will be innocent,
and cleansed from blatant rebellion.
14 May the words of my mouth
and the meditation of my heart
be acceptable to You,
LORD, my rock and my Redeemer.

Psalm 20

Deliverance in Battle

For the choir director. A Davidic psalm.

1 May the LORD answer you in a day
of trouble;
may the name of Jacob's God
protect you.
2 May He send you help
from the sanctuary
and sustain you from Zion.
3 May He remember all your offerings
and accept your •burnt offering.•*Selah*

4 May He give you what
your heart desires
and fulfill your whole purpose.
5 Let us shout for joy at your victory
and lift the banner in the name
of our God.
May the LORD fulfill all your requests.

6 Now I know that the LORD
gives victory to His anointed;
He will answer him
from His holy heaven
with mighty victories
from[g] His right hand.
7 Some take pride in a chariot,
and others in horses,
but we take pride in the name
of the LORD our God.
8 They collapse and fall,
but we rise and stand firm.
9 LORD, give victory to the king!
May He[h] answer us on the day
that we call.

Psalm 21

The King's Victory

For the choir director. A Davidic psalm.

1 LORD, the king finds joy
in Your strength.
How greatly he rejoices
in Your victory!
2 You have given him his heart's desire

[a]**19:1** Or *expanse* [b]**19:2** Or *Day to day pours out speech, and night to night communicates knowledge* [c]**19:4** LXX, Sym, Syr, Vg; MT reads *line* [d]**19:4** Lit *In them* [e]**19:5** Lit *his* [f]**19:6** Lit *its circuit is* [g]**20:6** Other Hb mss, Aq, Sym, Jer, Syr read *with the victorious might of* [h]**20:9** Or *LORD, save. May the king*

and have not denied the request
of his lips. •*Selah*
3 For You meet him with rich blessings;
You place a crown of pure gold
on his head.
4 He asked You for life, and You gave it
to him—
length of days forever and ever.
5 His glory is great through Your victory;
You confer majesty and splendor
on him.
6 You give him blessings forever;
You cheer him with joy
in Your presence.
7 For the king relies on the LORD;
through the faithful love
of the •Most High
he is not shaken.

8 Your hand will capture
all your enemies;
your right hand will seize
those who hate you.
9 You will make them ⌊burn⌋
like a fiery furnace when you appear;
the LORD will engulf them
in His wrath,
and fire will devour them.
10 You will wipe their descendants
from the earth
and their offspring
from the •human race.
11 Though they intend to harm[a] you
and devise a wicked plan,
they will not prevail.
12 Instead, you will put them to flight
when you aim your bow[b]
at their faces.

13 Be exalted, LORD, in Your strength;
we will sing and praise Your might.

Psalm 22

From Suffering to Praise

For the choir director: according to "The Deer of the Dawn."[c] A Davidic psalm.

1 My God, my God, why have You
forsaken me?
⌊Why are You⌋ so far
from my deliverance
and from my words of groaning?[d]
2 My God, I cry by day, but You
do not answer,
by night, yet I have no rest.
3 But You are holy,
enthroned on the praises of Israel.
4 Our fathers trusted in You;
they trusted, and You rescued them.
5 They cried to You and were set free;
they trusted in You
and were not disgraced.

6 But I am a worm and not a man,
scorned by men and despised by people.
7 Everyone who sees me mocks me;
they sneer[e] and shake their heads:
8 "He relies on[f] the LORD;
let Him rescue him;
let the LORD[g] deliver him,
since He takes pleasure in him."

9 You took me from the womb,
making me secure
while at my mother's breast.
10 I was given over to You at birth;[h]
You have been my God
from my mother's womb.

11 Do not be far from me,
because distress is near
and there is no one to help.

12 Many bulls surround me;
strong ones of Bashan encircle me.
13 They open their mouths against me—
lions, mauling and roaring.
14 I am poured out like water,
and all my bones are disjointed;
my heart is like wax,
melting within me.
15 My strength is dried up like baked clay;
my tongue sticks to the roof
of my mouth.
You put me into the dust of death.
16 For dogs have surrounded me;
a gang of evildoers has closed in
on me;
they pierced[i] my hands and my feet.
17 I can count all my bones;
people[j] look and stare at me.
18 They divided my garments
among themselves,
and they cast lots for my clothing.

19 But You, LORD, don't be far away.
My strength, come quickly to help me.
20 Deliver my life from the sword,

[a]**21:11** Lit *they stretch out evil against* [b]**21:12** Lit *aim with your bowstrings* [c]Perhaps a musical term [d]**22:1** Or *My words of groaning are so far from delivering me* (as a statement) [e]**22:7** Lit *separate with the lip* [f]**22:8** Or *Rely on* [g]**22:8** Lit *let Him* [h]**22:10** Lit *was cast on You from the womb* [i]**22:16** Some Hb mss, LXX, Syr; other Hb mss read *me; like a lion* [j]**22:17** Lit *they*

my very life[a] from the power
of the dog.
21 Save me from the mouth
of the lion!
You have rescued[b] me
from the horns of the wild oxen.

22 I will proclaim Your name
to my brothers;
I will praise You in the congregation.
23 You who •fear the LORD, praise Him!
All you descendants of Jacob,
honor Him!
All you descendants of Israel,
revere Him!
24 For He has not despised or detested
the torment of the afflicted.
He did not hide His face from him,
but listened when he cried to Him
for help.

25 I will give praise[c]
in the great congregation
because of You;
I will fulfill my vows
before those who fear You.[d]
26 The humble[e] will eat
and be satisfied;
those who seek the LORD
will praise Him.
May your hearts live forever!

27 All the ends of the earth
will remember
and turn to the LORD.
All the families of the nations
will bow down before You,
28 for kingship belongs to the LORD;
He rules over the nations.
29 All who prosper on earth will eat
and bow down;
all those who go down
to the dust
will kneel before Him—
even the one who cannot preserve
his life.
30 Descendants will serve Him;
the next generation will be told
about the Lord.
31 They will come and tell a people
yet to be born
about His righteousness—
what He has done.

Psalm 23
The Good Shepherd

A Davidic psalm.

1 The LORD is my shepherd;
there is nothing I lack.
2 He lets me lie down in green pastures;
He leads me beside quiet waters.
3 He renews my life;
He leads me along the right paths[f]
for His name's sake.
4 Even when I go
through the darkest valley,[g]
I fear no danger,
for You are with me;
Your rod and Your staff[h] —
they comfort me.

5 You prepare a table before me
in the presence of my enemies;
You anoint my head with oil;
my cup overflows.
6 Only goodness and faithful love
will pursue me
all the days of my life,
and I will dwell in[i] the house
of the LORD
as long as I live.[j]

Psalm 24
The King of Glory

A Davidic psalm.

1 The earth and everything in it,
the world and its inhabitants,
belong to the LORD;
2 for He laid its foundation on the seas
and established it on the rivers.

3 Who may ascend the mountain
of the LORD?
Who may stand in His holy place?
4 The one who has clean hands
and a pure heart,
who has not set his mind[k] on
what is false,
and who has not sworn deceitfully.
5 He will receive blessing
from the LORD,
and righteousness from the God
of his salvation.
6 Such is the generation of those
who seek Him,

[a]**22:20** Lit *my only one* [b]**22:21** Lit *answered* [c]**22:25** Lit *my praise* [d]**22:25** Lit *Him* [e]**22:26** Or *poor*, or *afflicted* [f]**23:3** Or *me in paths of righteousness* [g]**23:4** Or *the valley of the shadow of death* [h]**23:4** A shepherd's rod and crook [i]**23:6** LXX, Sym, Syr, Tg, Vg, Jer; MT reads *will return to* [j]**23:6** Lit *LORD for length of days*; traditionally *LORD forever* [k]**24:4** Or *not lifted up his soul*

who seek the face of the God
of Jacob.[a] •*Selah*
7 Lift up your heads, you gates!
Rise up, ancient doors!
Then the King of glory will come in.
8 Who is this King of glory?
The LORD, strong and mighty,
the LORD, mighty in battle.
9 Lift up your heads, you gates!
Rise up, ancient doors!
Then the King of glory will come in.
10 Who is He, this King of glory?
The LORD of •Hosts,
He is the King of glory. *Selah*

Psalm 25

Dependence on the LORD

Davidic.

1 LORD,[b] I turn my hope to You.[c]
2 My God, I trust in You.
Do not let me be disgraced;
do not let my enemies gloat over me.
3 Not one person who waits for You
will be disgraced;
those who act treacherously
without cause
will be disgraced.

4 Make Your ways known to me, LORD;
teach me Your paths.
5 Guide me in Your truth and teach me,
for You are the God of my salvation;
I wait for You all day long.
6 Remember, LORD, Your compassion
and Your faithful love,
for they ⌊have existed⌋ from antiquity.[d]
7 Do not remember the sins of my youth
or my acts of rebellion;
in keeping with Your faithful love,
remember me
because of Your goodness, LORD.

8 The LORD is good and upright;
therefore He shows sinners the way.
9 He leads the humble in what is right
and teaches them His way.
10 All the LORD's ways ⌊show⌋
faithful love and truth
to those who keep His covenant
and decrees.
11 Because of Your name, LORD,
forgive my sin, for it is great.

12 Who is the person who •fears the LORD?
He will show him the way
he should choose.
13 He will live a good life,
and his descendants will inherit
the land.[e]
14 The secret counsel of the LORD
is for those who fear Him,
and He reveals His covenant to them.
15 My eyes are always on the LORD,
for He will pull my feet out of the net.

16 Turn to me and be gracious to me,
for I am alone and afflicted.
17 The distresses of my heart increase;[f]
bring me out of my sufferings.
18 Consider my affliction and trouble,
and take away all my sins.
19 Consider my enemies;
they are numerous,
and they hate me violently.
20 Guard me and deliver me;
do not let me be put to shame,
for I take refuge in You.
21 May integrity and uprightness keep me,
for I wait for You.

22 God, redeem Israel, from all
its distresses.

Psalm 26

Prayer for Vindication

Davidic.

1 Vindicate me, LORD,
because I have lived with integrity
and have trusted in the LORD
without wavering.
2 Test me, LORD, and try me;
examine my heart and mind.
3 For Your faithful love is before my eyes,
and I live by Your truth.

4 I do not sit with the worthless
or associate with hypocrites.
5 I hate a crowd of evildoers,
and I do not sit with the wicked.
6 I wash my hands[g] in innocence
and go around Your altar, LORD,
7 raising my voice in thanksgiving
and telling about
Your wonderful works.

8 LORD, I love the house
where You dwell,

[a]**24:6** Some Hb mss, LXX, Syr; other Hb mss read *seek Your face, Jacob* [b]**25:1** The lines of this poem form an • acrostic. [c]**25:1** Or *To You, LORD, I lift up my soul* [d]**25:6** Or *everlasting* [e]**25:13** Or *earth* [f]**25:17** Or *Relieve the distresses of my heart* [g]**26:6** A ritual or ceremonial washing to express innocence

the place where Your glory resides.
9 Do not destroy me along with sinners,
or my life along with men of bloodshed
10 in whose hands are evil schemes,
and whose right hands are filled
with bribes.

11 But I live with integrity;
redeem me and be gracious to me.
12 My foot stands on level ground;
I will praise the LORD
in the assemblies.

Psalm 27
My Stronghold

Davidic.

1 The LORD is my light
and my salvation—
whom should I fear?
The LORD is the stronghold of my life—
of whom should I be afraid?
2 When evildoers came against me
to devour my flesh,
my foes and my enemies stumbled
and fell.
3 Though an army deploy against me,
my heart is not afraid;
though war break out against me,
still I am confident.

4 I have asked one thing from the LORD;
it is what I desire:
to dwell in the house of the LORD
all the days of my life,
gazing on the beauty of the LORD
and seeking ⌊Him⌋ in His temple.
5 For He will conceal me in His shelter
in the day of adversity;
He will hide me under the cover
of His tent;
He will set me high on a rock.
6 Then my head will be high
above my enemies around me;
I will offer sacrifices in His tent
with shouts of joy.
I will sing and make music to the LORD.

7 LORD, hear my voice when I call;
be gracious to me and answer me.
8 In Your behalf my heart says,
"Seek My face."
LORD, I will seek Your face.
9 Do not hide Your face from me;
do not turn Your servant away
in anger.
You have been my help;
do not leave me or abandon me,
God of my salvation.
10 Even if my father and mother
abandon me,
the LORD cares for me.

11 Because of my adversaries,
show me Your way, LORD,
and lead me on a level path.
12 Do not give me over to the will
of my foes,
for false witnesses rise up against me,
breathing violence.

13 I am certain that I will see
the LORD's goodness
in the land of the living.
14 Wait for the LORD;
be courageous and let your heart
be strong.
Wait for the LORD.

Psalm 28
My Strength

Davidic.

1 LORD, I call to You;
my rock, do not be deaf to me.
If You remain silent to me,
I will be like those going down
to the •Pit.
2 Listen to the sound of my pleading
when I cry to You for help,
when I lift up my hands
toward Your holy sanctuary.

3 Do not drag me away with the wicked,
with the evildoers,
who speak in friendly ways
with their neighbors,
while malice is in their hearts.
4 Repay them according to what
they have done—
according to the evil of their deeds.
Repay them according to the work
of their hands;
give them back what they deserve.
5 Because they do not consider
what the LORD has done
or the work of His hands,
He will tear them down and not
rebuild them.

6 May the LORD be praised,
for He has heard the sound
of my pleading.
7 The LORD is my strength
and my shield;

my heart trusts in Him,
and I am helped.
Therefore my heart rejoices,
and I praise Him with my song.

8 The LORD is the strength
of His people;[a]
He is a stronghold of salvation
for His anointed.
9 Save Your people,
bless Your possession,
shepherd them, and carry
them forever.

Psalm 29

The Voice of the LORD

A Davidic psalm.

1 Give the LORD—
you heavenly beings[b] —
give the LORD glory and strength.
2 Give the LORD the glory due His name;
worship the LORD
in the splendor of ⌊His⌋ holiness.[c]
3 The voice of the LORD is
above the waters.
The God of glory thunders—
the LORD, above vast waters,
4 the voice of the LORD in power,
the voice of the LORD in splendor.
5 The voice of the LORD
breaks the cedars;
the LORD shatters the cedars
of Lebanon.
6 He makes Lebanon skip like a calf,
and Sirion,[d] like a young wild ox.
7 The voice of the LORD flashes
flames of fire.
8 The voice of the LORD shakes
the wilderness;
the LORD shakes the wilderness
of Kadesh.
9 The voice of the LORD makes the deer
give birth[e]
and strips the woodlands bare.

In His temple all cry, "Glory!"

10 The LORD sat enthroned at the flood;
the LORD sits enthroned, King forever.
11 The LORD gives His people strength;
the LORD blesses His people
with peace.

Psalm 30

Joy in the Morning

A psalm; a dedication song for the house. Davidic.

1 I will exalt You, LORD,
because You have lifted me up
and have not allowed my enemies
to triumph over me.
2 LORD my God,
I cried to You for help, and You healed
me.
3 LORD, You brought me up from •Sheol;
You spared me from among those
going down[f] to the •Pit.

4 Sing to the LORD, you His faithful ones,
and praise His holy name.
5 For His anger lasts only a moment,
but His favor, a lifetime.
Weeping may spend the night,
but there is joy in the morning.

6 When I was secure, I said,
"I will never be shaken."
7 LORD, when You showed Your favor,
You made me stand
like a strong mountain;
when You hid Your face, I was terrified.
8 LORD, I called to You;
I sought favor from my Lord:
9 "What gain is there in my death,
in my descending to the Pit?
Will the dust praise You?
Will it proclaim Your truth?
10 LORD, listen and be gracious to me;
LORD, be my helper."

11 You turned my lament into dancing;
You removed my •sackcloth
and clothed me with gladness,
12 so that I can sing to You and not
be silent.
LORD my God, I will praise
You forever.

Psalm 31

A Plea for Protection

For the choir director. A Davidic psalm.

1 LORD, I seek refuge in You;
let me never be disgraced.
Save me by Your righteousness.

[a]**28:8** Some Hb mss, LXX, Syr; other Hb mss read *strength for them* [b]**29:1** Or *you angels*, or *you sons of the mighty*; lit LORD *sons of [the] gods* [c]**29:2** Or *in holy attire*, or *in holy appearance* [d]**29:6** Mount Hermon; Dt 3:9 [e]**29:9** Or *the oaks shake* [f]**30:3** Some Hb mss, LXX, Theod, Orig, Syr; other Hb mss, Aq, Sym, Tg, Jer read *from going down*

2 Listen closely to me; rescue me quickly.
Be a rock of refuge for me,
a mountain fortress to save me.
3 For You are my rock and my fortress;
You lead and guide me
because of Your name.
4 You will free me from the net
that is secretly set for me,
for You are my refuge.
5 Into Your hand I entrust my spirit;
You redeem[a] me, LORD, God of truth.

6 I[b] hate those who are devoted
to worthless idols,
but I trust in the LORD.
7 I will rejoice and be glad
in Your faithful love
because You have seen my affliction.
You have known the troubles
of my life
8 and have not handed me over
to the enemy.
You have set my feet
in a spacious place.

9 Be gracious to me, LORD,
because I am in distress;
my eyes are worn out
from angry sorrow—
my whole being[c] as well.
10 Indeed, my life is consumed with grief,
and my years with groaning;
my strength has failed
because of my sinfulness,[d]
and my bones waste away.
11 I am ridiculed by all my adversaries
and even by my neighbors.
I am an object of dread
to my acquaintances;
those who see me in the street
run from me.
12 I am forgotten: gone from memory
like a dead person—
like broken pottery.
13 I have heard the gossip of many;
terror is on every side.
When they conspired against me,
they plotted to take my life.

14 But I trust in You, LORD;
I say, "You are my God."
15 The course of my life is in Your power;
deliver me from the power
of my enemies
and from my persecutors.
16 Show Your favor to Your servant;
save me by Your faithful love.
17 LORD, do not let me be disgraced
when I call on You.
Let the wicked be disgraced;
let them be silent[e] [f] in •Sheol.
18 Let lying lips be quieted;
they speak arrogantly
against the righteous
with pride and contempt.

19 How great is Your goodness
that You have stored up for those
who •fear You,
and accomplished in the sight
of •everyone
for those who take refuge in You.
20 You hide them in the protection
of Your presence;
You conceal them in a shelter[g]
from the schemes of men,
from quarrelsome tongues.
21 May the LORD be praised,
for He has wonderfully shown
His faithful love to me
in a city under siege.[h]
22 In my alarm I had said,
"I am cut off from Your sight."
But You heard the sound
of my pleading
when I cried to You for help.

23 Love the LORD, all His faithful ones.
The LORD protects the loyal,
but fully repays the arrogant.
24 Be strong and courageous,
all you who put your hope
in the LORD.

Psalm 32
The Joy of Forgiveness

Davidic. A •*Maskil.*

1 How happy is the one
whose transgression is forgiven,
whose sin is covered!
2 How happy is the man
the LORD does not charge with sin,
and in whose spirit is no deceit!

3 When I kept silent,[i] my bones
became brittle
from my groaning all day long.

[a]**31:5** Or *You have redeemed*, or *You will redeem*, or *spirit. Redeem* [b]**31:6** One Hb ms, LXX, Syr, Vg, Jer read *You* [c]**31:9** Lit *my soul and my belly* [d]**31:10** LXX, Syr, Sym read *affliction* [e]**31:17** LXX reads *brought down* [f]**31:17** Or *them perish* or *wail* [g]**31:20** Lit *canopy* [h]**31:21** Or *a fortified city* [i]**32:3** Probably a reference to a refusal to confess sin

4 For day and night Your hand
was heavy on me;
my strength was drained[a]
as in the summer's heat. •*Selah*
5 Then I acknowledged my sin to You
and did not conceal my iniquity.
I said,
"I will confess my transgressions
to the LORD,"
and You took away the guilt of my sin.
Selah

6 Therefore let everyone who is faithful
pray to You
at a time that You may be found.[b]
When great floodwaters come,
they will not reach him.
7 You are my hiding place;
You protect me from trouble.
You surround me with joyful shouts
of deliverance. *Selah*

8 I will instruct you and show you
the way to go;
with My eye on you, I will give counsel.
9 Do not be like a horse or mule,
without understanding,
that must be controlled with bit
and bridle,
or else it will not come near you.

10 Many pains come to the wicked,
but the one who trusts in the LORD
will have faithful love surrounding him.
11 Be glad in the LORD and rejoice,
you righteous ones;
shout for joy,
all you upright in heart.

Psalm 33

Praise to the Creator

1 Rejoice in the LORD, you righteous ones;
praise from the upright is beautiful.
2 Praise the LORD with the lyre;
make music to Him with a ten-
stringed harp.
3 Sing a new song to Him;
play skillfully on the strings,
with a joyful shout.

4 For the word of the LORD is right,
and all His work is trustworthy.
5 He loves righteousness and justice;
the earth is full of the LORD's
unfailing love.

6 The heavens were made by the word
of the LORD,
and all the stars, by the breath
of His mouth.
7 He gathers the waters of the sea
into a heap;[c]
He puts the depths into storehouses.
8 Let the whole earth tremble
before the LORD;
let all the inhabitants of the world
stand in awe of Him.
9 For He spoke, and it came into being;
He commanded, and it came
into existence.

10 The LORD frustrates the counsel
of the nations;
He thwarts the plans of the peoples.
11 The counsel of the LORD
stands forever,
the plans of His heart from generation
to generation.
12 Happy is the nation whose God is
the LORD—
the people He has chosen to be
His own possession!

13 The LORD looks down from heaven;
He observes everyone.
14 He gazes on all the inhabitants
of the earth
from His dwelling place.
15 He alone crafts their hearts;
He considers all their works.
16 A king is not saved by a large army;
a warrior will not be delivered
by great strength.
17 The horse is a false hope for safety;
it provides no escape by
its great power.

18 Now the eye of the LORD is on those
who •fear Him—
those who depend on
His faithful love
19 to deliver them from death
and to keep them alive in famine.

20 We wait for the LORD;
He is our help and shield.
21 For our hearts rejoice in Him,
because we trust in His holy name.
22 May Your faithful love rest on us,
LORD,
for we put our hope in You.

[a]**32:4** Hb obscure [b]**32:6** Lit *time of finding* [c]**33:7** LXX, Tg, Syr, Vg, Jer read *sea as in a bottle*

Psalm 34
The LORD Delivers the Righteous

Concerning David, when he pretended to be insane in the presence of Abimelech,[a] who drove him out, and he departed.

1 I[b] will praise the LORD at all times;
His praise will always be on my lips.
2 I will boast in the LORD;
the humble will hear and be glad.
3 Proclaim with me the LORD's greatness;
let us exalt His name together.

4 I sought the LORD,
and He answered me
and delivered me from all my fears.
5 Those who look to Him are[c] radiant
with joy;
their faces will never be ashamed.
6 This poor man cried, and the LORD
heard ⌊him⌋
and saved him from all his troubles.
7 The angel of the LORD encamps
around those who •fear Him,
and rescues them.

8 Taste and see that the LORD is good.
How happy is the man
who takes refuge in Him!
9 Fear the LORD, you His saints,
for those who fear Him lack nothing.
10 Young lions[d] lack food and go hungry,
but those who seek the LORD
will not lack any good thing.

11 Come, children, listen to me;
I will teach you the fear of the LORD.
12 Who is the man who delights in life,
loving a long life to enjoy what is good?
13 Keep your tongue from evil
and your lips from deceitful speech.
14 Turn away from evil and do
what is good;
seek peace and pursue it.

15 The eyes of the LORD are
on the righteous,
and His ears are open to their cry
for help.
16 The face of the LORD is set
against those who do what is evil,
to erase all memory of them
from the earth.
17 The righteous[e] cry out,
and the LORD hears,
and delivers them from all
their troubles.
18 The LORD is near the brokenhearted;
He saves those crushed in spirit.

19 Many adversities come to the one
who is righteous,
but the LORD delivers him
from them all.
20 He protects all his bones;
not one of them is broken.
21 Evil brings death to the sinner,
and those who hate the righteous
will be punished.
22 The LORD redeems the life
of His servants,
and all who take refuge in Him
will not be punished.

Psalm 35
Prayer for Victory

Davidic.

1 Oppose my opponents, LORD;
fight those who fight me.
2 Take Your shields—
large and small—
and come to my aid.
3 Draw the spear and javelin
against my pursuers,
and assure me: "I am
your deliverance."

4 Let those who seek to kill me
be disgraced and humiliated;
let those who plan to harm me
be turned back and ashamed.
5 Let them be like husks in the wind,
with the angel of the LORD
driving them away.
6 Let their way be dark and slippery,
with the angel of the LORD
pursuing them.
7 They hid their net for me
without cause;
they dug a pit for me without cause.
8 Let ruin come on him unexpectedly,
and let the net that he hid
ensnare him;
let him fall into it—to his ruin.

9 Then I will rejoice in the LORD;
I will delight in His deliverance.
10 My very bones will say,
"LORD, who is like You,

[a] A reference to Achish, king of Gath [b] **34:1** The lines of this poem form an •acrostic. [c] **34:5** Some Hb mss, LXX, Aq, Syr, Jer read *Look to Him and be* [d] **34:10** LXX, Syr, Vg read *The rich* [e] **34:17** Lit *They*

rescuing the poor from one too strong
for him,
the poor or the needy from one
who robs him?"

11 Malicious witnesses come forward;
they question me about things
I do not know.
12 They repay me evil for good,
making me desolate.
13 Yet when they were sick,
my clothing was •sackcloth;
I humbled myself with fasting,
and my prayer was genuine.[a]
14 I went about ⌊grieving⌋ as if
for my friend or brother;
I was bowed down with grief,
like one mourning a mother.
15 But when I stumbled, they gathered
in glee;
they gathered against me.
Assailants I did not know
tore at me and did not stop.
16 With godless mockery[b]
they gnashed their teeth at me.

17 Lord, how long will You look on?
Rescue my life from their ravages,
my very life[c] from the young lions.
18 I will praise You
in the great congregation;
I will exalt You among many people.
19 Do not let my deceitful enemies
rejoice over me;
do not let those who hate me
without cause
look at me maliciously.
20 For they do not speak
in friendly ways,
but contrive deceitful schemes[d]
against those who live peacefully
in the land.
21 They open their mouths wide
against me and say,
"Aha, aha! We saw it!"[e]
22 You saw it, LORD; do not be silent.
Lord, do not be far from me.
23 Wake up and rise to my defense,
to my cause, my God and my LORD!
24 Vindicate me, LORD, my God,
in keeping with Your righteousness,
and do not let them rejoice over me.
25 Do not let them say in their hearts,
"Aha! Just what we wanted."
Do not let them say,
"We have swallowed him up!"
26 Let those who rejoice
at my misfortune
be disgraced and humiliated;
let those who exalt themselves over me
be clothed with shame and reproach.

27 Let those who want my vindication
shout for joy and be glad;
let them continually say,
"The LORD be exalted,
who wants His servant's well-being."
28 And my tongue will proclaim
Your righteousness,
Your praise all day long.

Psalm 36

Human Wickedness and God's Love

For the choir director. ⌊A psalm⌋ of David,
the LORD's servant.

1 An oracle within my heart
concerning the transgression
of the wicked:
There is no dread of God
before his eyes,
2 for in his own eyes he flatters himself
⌊too much⌋
to discover and hate his sin.
3 The words of his mouth are malicious
and deceptive;
he has stopped acting wisely
and doing good.
4 Even on his bed he makes
malicious plans.
He sets himself on a path
that is not good
and does not reject evil.

5 LORD, Your faithful love ⌊reaches⌋
to heaven,
Your faithfulness to the skies.
6 Your righteousness is
like the highest mountain;
Your judgments, like the deepest sea.
LORD, You preserve man and beast.
7 God, Your faithful love is so valuable
that •people take refuge in the shadow
of Your wings.
8 They are filled from the abundance
of Your house;
You let them drink
from Your refreshing stream,
9 for with You is life's fountain.
In Your light we will see light.

[a]**35:13** Lit *prayer returned to my chest* [b]**35:16** Hb obscure [c]**35:17** Lit *my only one* [d]**35:20** Lit *but devise deceitful words*
[e]**35:21** Lit *Our eyes saw!*

10 Spread Your faithful love over those
who know You,
and Your righteousness
over the upright in heart.
11 Do not let the foot of the arrogant
come near me
or the hand of the wicked
drive me away.
12 There the evildoers fall;
they have been thrown down
and cannot rise.

Psalm 37

Instruction in Wisdom

Davidic.

1 Do[a] not be agitated by evildoers;
do not envy those who do wrong.
2 For they wither quickly like grass
and wilt like tender green plants.

3 Trust in the LORD and do what is good;
dwell in the land and live securely.[b]
4 Take delight in the LORD,
and He will give you
your heart's desires.

5 Commit your way to the LORD;
trust in Him, and He will act,
6 making your righteousness shine
like the dawn,
your justice like the noonday.

7 Be silent before the LORD and wait
expectantly for Him;
do not be agitated by one
who prospers in his way,
by the man who carries out evil plans.

8 Refrain from anger and give up
⌊your⌋ rage;
do not be agitated—it can only
bring harm.
9 For evildoers will be destroyed,
but those who put their hope
in the LORD
will inherit the land.[c]
10 A little while, and the wicked will be
no more;
though you look for him, he will not
be there.
11 But the humble will inherit the land[c]
and will enjoy abundant prosperity.

12 The wicked schemes
against the righteous
and gnashes his teeth at him.
13 The Lord laughs at him
because He sees that his day is coming.
14 The wicked have drawn the sword
and strung the[d] bow
to bring down the afflicted and needy
and to slaughter those whose way
is upright.
15 Their swords will enter
their own hearts,
and their bows will be broken.

16 Better the little that the righteous
man has
than the abundance of many
wicked people.
17 For the arms[e] of the wicked
will be broken,
but the LORD supports the righteous.

18 The LORD watches over the blameless
all their days,
and their inheritance will last forever.
19 They will not be disgraced in times
of adversity;
they will be satisfied in days of hunger.

20 But the wicked will perish;
the LORD's enemies, like the glory
of the pastures,
will fade away—
they will fade away like smoke.

21 The wicked borrows
and does not repay,
but the righteous is gracious
and giving.
22 Those who are blessed by Him
will inherit the land,[c]
but those cursed by Him
will be destroyed.

23 A man's steps are established
by the LORD,
and He takes pleasure in his way.
24 Though he falls, he will not
be overwhelmed,
because the LORD holds his hand.[f]
25 I have been young and now I am old,
yet I have not seen
the righteous abandoned
or his children begging bread.
26 He is always generous, always lending,
and his children are a blessing.

27 Turn away from evil and do
what is good,

[a]**37:1** The lines of this poem form an •acrostic. [b]**37:3** Or *and cultivate faithfulness* [c]**37:9,11,22** Or *earth* [d]**37:14** Lit *their* [e]**37:17** Or *power* [f]**37:24** Or *LORD supports with His hand*

and dwell there[a] forever.
28 For the LORD loves justice
and will not abandon His faithful ones.
They are kept safe forever,
but the children of the wicked
will be destroyed.
29 The righteous will inherit the land[b]
and dwell in it permanently.

30 The mouth of the righteous
utters wisdom;
his tongue speaks what is just.
31 The instruction of his God is
in his heart;
his steps do not falter.

32 The wicked lies in wait
for the righteous
and seeks to kill him;
33 the LORD will not leave him
in his hand[c]
or allow him to be condemned
when he is judged.

34 Wait for the LORD and keep His way,
and He will exalt you to inherit
the land.
You will watch when the wicked
are destroyed.

35 I have seen a wicked, violent man
well-rooted[d] like
a flourishing native tree.
36 Then I passed by and[e] noticed
he was gone;
I searched for him, but he could not
be found.

37 Watch the blameless and observe
the upright,
for the man of peace will have
a future.[f]
38 But transgressors will all
be eliminated;
the future[f] of the wicked
will be destroyed.

39 The salvation of the righteous is
from the LORD,
their refuge in a time of distress.
40 The LORD helps and delivers them;
He will deliver them from the wicked
and will save them
because they take refuge in Him.

Psalm 38

Prayer of a Suffering Sinner

A Davidic psalm for remembrance.

1 LORD, do not punish me
in Your anger
or discipline me in Your wrath.
2 For Your arrows have sunk into me,
and Your hand has pressed down
on me.

3 There is no soundness in my body
because of Your indignation;
there is no health in my bones
because of my sin.
4 For my sins have flooded
over my head;
they are a burden too heavy for me
to bear.
5 My wounds are foul and festering
because of my foolishness.
6 I am bent over and brought low;
all day long I go around in mourning.
7 For my loins are full of burning pain,
and there is no health in my body.
8 I am faint and severely crushed;
I groan because of the anguish
of my heart.

9 Lord, my every desire is known to[g]
You;
my sighing is not hidden from You.
10 My heart races, my strength
leaves me,
and even the light of my eyes
has faded.[h]
11 My loved ones and friends stand back
from my affliction,
and my relatives stand at a distance.
12 Those who seek my life set traps,
and those who want to harm me
threaten to destroy me;
they plot treachery all day long.

13 I am like a deaf person; I do not hear.
I am like a speechless person
who does not open his mouth.
14 I am like a man who does not hear
and has no arguments in his mouth.
15 I put my hope in You, LORD;
You will answer, Lord my God.
16 For I said, "Don't let them rejoice
over me—

[a]**37:27** Dwell in the land [b]**37:29** Or *earth* [c]**37:33** Or *power* [d]**37:35** Hb obscure [e]**37:36** DSS, LXX, Syr, Vg, Jer; MT reads *Then he passed away, and I* [f]**37:37,38** Or *posterity* [g]**38:9** Lit *is in front of* [h]**38:10** Or *and the light of my eyes—even that is not with me*

those who are arrogant toward me
when I stumble."
17 For I am about to fall,
and my pain is constantly with me.
18 So I confess my guilt;
I am anxious because of my sin.
19 But my enemies are vigorous
and powerful;[a]
many hate me for no reason.
20 Those who repay evil for good
attack me for pursuing good.

21 LORD, do not abandon me;
my God, do not be far from me.
22 Hurry to help me,
Lord, my Savior.

Psalm 39

The Fleeting Nature of Life

For the choir director, for Jeduthun. A Davidic psalm.

1 I said, "I will guard my ways
so that I may not sin with my tongue;
I will guard my mouth with a muzzle
as long as the wicked are
in my presence."
2 I was speechless and quiet;
I kept silent, even from
⌊speaking⌋ good,
and my pain intensified.
3 My heart grew hot within me;
as I mused, a fire burned.
I spoke with my tongue:

4 "LORD, reveal to me the end of my life
and the number of my days.
Let me know how transitory I am.
5 You, indeed, have made my days short
in length,
and my life span as nothing
in Your sight.
Yes, every mortal man is only a vapor.
•*Selah*

6 Certainly, man walks about
like a mere shadow.
Indeed, they frantically rush around
in vain,
gathering possessions
without knowing who will get them.

7 "Now, Lord, what do I wait for?
My hope is in You.
8 Deliver me from all my transgressions;
do not make me the taunt of fools.
9 I am speechless; I do not open
my mouth
because of what You have done.
10 Remove Your torment from me;
I fade away because of the force
of Your hand.
11 You discipline a man with punishment
for sin,
consuming like a moth
what is precious to him;
every man is a mere vapor. *Selah*

12 "Hear my prayer, LORD,
and listen to my cry for help;
do not be silent at my tears.
For I am a foreigner residing
with You,
a sojourner like all my fathers.
13 Turn Your angry gaze from me
so that I may be cheered up
before I die and am gone."

Psalm 40

Thanksgiving and a Cry for Help

For the choir director. A Davidic psalm.

1 I waited patiently for the LORD,
and He turned to me
and heard my cry for help.
2 He brought me up
from a desolate[b] pit,
out of the muddy clay,
and set my feet on a rock,
making my steps secure.
3 He put a new song in my mouth,
a hymn of praise to our God.
Many will see and fear,
and put their trust in the LORD.

4 How happy is the man
who has put his trust in the LORD
and has not turned to the proud
or to those who run after lies!
5 LORD my God, You have done
many things—
Your wonderful works and Your plans
for us;
none can compare with You.
If I were to report
and speak ⌊of them⌋,
they are more than can be told.

6 You do not delight in sacrifice
and offering;
You open my ears to listen.[c]

[a]**38:19** Or *numerous* [b]**40:2** Or *watery* [c]**40:6** Lit *You hollow out ears for me*

You do not ask for
a whole •burnt offering
or a •sin offering.
7 Then I said, "See, I have come;
it is written about me in the volume
of the scroll.
8 I delight to do Your will, my God;
Your instruction resides
within me."[a]

9 I proclaim righteousness
in the great assembly;
see, I do not keep my mouth closed[b]
—as You know, LORD.
10 I did not hide Your righteousness
in my heart;
I spoke about Your faithfulness
and salvation;
I did not conceal Your constant love
and truth
from the great assembly.

11 LORD, do not withhold
Your compassion from me;
Your constant love and truth
will always guard me.
12 For troubles without number
have surrounded me;
my sins have overtaken me;
I am unable to see.
They are more than the hairs
of my head,
and my courage leaves me.
13 LORD, be pleased to deliver me;
hurry to help me, LORD.

14 Let those who seek to take my life
be disgraced and confounded.
Let those who wish me harm
be driven back and humiliated.
15 Let those who say to me, "Aha, aha!"
be horrified because of their shame.

16 Let all who seek You rejoice
and be glad in You;
let those who love Your salvation
continually say,
"The LORD is great!"
17 I am afflicted and needy;
the Lord thinks of me.
You are my help and my deliverer;
my God, do not delay.

Psalm 41

Victory in spite of Betrayal

For the choir director. A Davidic psalm.

1 Happy is one who cares for the poor;
the LORD will save him in a day
of adversity.
2 The LORD will keep him
and preserve him;
he will be blessed in the land.
You will not give him over
to the desire of his enemies.
3 The LORD will sustain him
on his sickbed;
You will heal him on the bed
where he lies.

4 I said, "LORD, be gracious to me;
heal me, for I have sinned
against You."
5 My enemies speak maliciously
about me:
"When will he die and be forgotten?"
6 When one ⌊of them⌋ comes to visit,
he speaks deceitfully;
he stores up evil in his heart;
he goes out and talks.
7 All who hate me whisper together
about me;
they plan to harm me.
8 "Lethal poison has been poured
into him,
and he won't rise again from where
he lies!"
9 Even my friend[c] in whom I trusted,
one who ate my bread,
has lifted up his heel against me.

10 But You, LORD, be gracious to me
and raise me up;
then I will repay them.
11 By this I know that You delight in me:
my enemy does not shout in triumph
over me.
12 You supported me because of
my integrity
and set me in Your presence forever.

13 May the LORD, the God of Israel,
be praised
from everlasting to everlasting.
•Amen and amen.

[a]**40:8** Lit *instruction within my inner being* [b]**40:9** Lit *not restrain my lips* [c]**41:9** Lit *Even a man of my peace*

BOOK II

(Psalms 42–72)

Psalm 42

Longing for God

For the choir director.
A •*Maskil* of the sons of Korah.

1 As a deer longs for streams of water,
so I long for You, God.
2 I thirst for God, the living God.
When can I come and appear
before God?
3 My tears have been my food
day and night,
while all day long people say to me,
"Where is your God?"
4 I remember this as I pour out my heart:
how I walked with many,
leading the festive procession
to the house of God,
with joyful and thankful shouts.

5 Why am I so depressed?
Why this turmoil within me?
Put your hope in God, for I will
still praise Him,
my Savior and my God.
6 I[a] am deeply depressed;
therefore I remember You
from the land of Jordan
and the peaks of Hermon,
from Mount Mizar.
7 Deep calls to deep in the roar
of Your waterfalls;
all Your breakers and Your billows
have swept over me.
8 The LORD will send His faithful love
by day;
His song will be with me in the night—
a prayer to the God of my life.

9 I will say to God, my rock,
"Why have You forgotten me?
Why must I go about in sorrow
because of the enemy's oppression?"
10 My adversaries taunt me,
as if crushing my bones,
while all day long they say to me,
"Where is your God?"
11 Why am I so depressed?
Why this turmoil within me?
Put your hope in God, for I will
still praise Him,
my Savior and my God.

Psalm 43[b]

1 Vindicate me, God, and defend
my cause
against an ungodly nation;
rescue me from the deceitful
and unjust man.
2 For You are the God of my refuge.
Why have You rejected me?
Why must I go about in sorrow
because of the enemy's oppression?

3 Send Your light and Your truth;
let them lead me.
Let them bring me
to Your holy mountain,
to Your dwelling place.
4 Then I will come to the altar of God,
to God, my greatest joy.
I will praise You with the lyre,
God, my God.

5 Why am I so depressed?
Why this turmoil within me?
Put your hope in God, for I will
still praise Him,
my Savior and my God.

Psalm 44

Israel's Complaint

For the choir director.
A •*Maskil* of the sons of Korah.

1 God, we have heard with our ears—
our forefathers have told us—
the work You accomplished
in their days,
in days long ago:
2 to plant them,
You drove out the nations
with Your hand;
to settle them,
You crushed the peoples.
3 For they did not take the land
by their sword—
their arm did not bring them victory—
but by Your right hand, Your arm,
and the light of Your face,
for You were pleased with them.

4 You are my King, my God,
who ordains[c] victories for Jacob.
5 Through You we drive back our foes;
through Your name we trample
our enemies.
6 For I do not trust in my bow,

[a]**42:5–6** Some Hb mss, LXX, Syr; other Hb mss read *Him, the salvation of His presence.* [6]*My God, I* [b]**Ps 43** Many Hb mss connect Pss 42–43 [c]**44:4** LXX, Syr, Aq; MT reads *King, God; ordain*

and my sword does not
bring me victory.
7 But You give us victory over our foes
and let those who hate us
be disgraced.
8 We boast in God all day long;
we will praise Your name forever.
•*Selah*

9 But You have rejected
and humiliated us;
You do not march out with our armies.
10 You make us retreat from the foe,
and those who hate us
have taken plunder for themselves.
11 You hand us over to be eaten
like sheep
and scatter us among the nations.
12 You sell Your people for nothing;
You make no profit from selling them.
13 You make us an object of reproach
to our neighbors,
a source of mockery and ridicule
to those around us.
14 You make us a joke among the nations,
a laughingstock[a] among the peoples.
15 My disgrace is before me all day long,
and shame has covered my face,
16 because of the voice of the scorner
and reviler,
because of the enemy and avenger.

17 All this has happened to us,
but we have not forgotten You
or betrayed Your covenant.
18 Our hearts have not turned back;
our steps have not strayed
from Your path.
19 But You have crushed us in a haunt
of jackals
and have covered us
with deepest darkness.
20 If we had forgotten the name of our God
and spread out our hands
to a foreign god,
21 wouldn't God have found this out,
since He knows the secrets
of the heart?
22 Because of You we are slain all day long;
we are counted as sheep
to be slaughtered.

23 Wake up, LORD!
Why are You sleeping?
Get up! Don't reject us forever!
24 Why do You hide Yourself
and forget our affliction and oppression?
25 For we have sunk down to the dust;
our bodies cling to the ground.
26 Rise up! Help us!
Redeem us because of
Your faithful love.

Psalm 45

A Royal Wedding Song

For the choir director: according to "The Lilies."[b] A •*Maskil* of the sons of Korah. A love song.

1 My heart is moved by a noble theme
as I recite my verses to the king;
my tongue is the pen of a skillful writer.
2 You are the most handsome of •men;
grace flows from your lips.
Therefore God has blessed you forever.

3 Mighty warrior, strap your sword
at your side.
In your majesty and splendor—
4 in your splendor ride triumphantly
in the cause of truth, humility,
and justice.
May your right hand show your awe-
inspiring deeds.
5 Your arrows pierce the hearts
of the king's enemies;
the peoples fall under you.

6 Your throne, God, is[c] forever and ever;
the scepter of Your[d] kingdom is
a scepter of justice.
7 You love righteousness
and hate wickedness;
therefore God, your God,
has anointed you,
more than your companions,
with the oil of joy.
8 Myrrh, aloes, and cassia ⌊perfume⌋
all your garments;
from ivory palaces harps bring you joy.
9 Kings' daughters are
among your honored women;
the queen, adorned with gold
from Ophir,
stands at your right hand.

10 Listen, daughter, pay attention
and consider:
forget your people
and your father's house,
11 and the king will desire your beauty.
Bow down to him, for he is your lord.

[a]**44:14** Lit *shaking of the head* [b]Apparently a hymn tune; compare Pss 60; 69; 80 [c]**45:6** Or *Your divine throne is*, or *Your throne is God's* [d]**45:6** Or *your*

12 The daughter of Tyre,
the wealthy people,
will seek your favor with gifts.

13 In ⌊her chamber⌋, the royal daughter
is all glorious,
her clothing embroidered with gold.
14 In colorful garments she is led
to the king;
after her, the virgins, her companions,
are brought to you.
15 They are led in with gladness
and rejoicing;
they enter the king's palace.

16 Your sons will succeed your ancestors;
you will make them princes
throughout the land.
17 I will cause your name
to be remembered
for all generations;
therefore the peoples will praise you
forever and ever.

Psalm 46
God Our Refuge

For the choir director. A song of the sons of Korah. According to *Alamoth*.[a]

1 God is our refuge and strength,
a helper who is always found
in times of trouble.
2 Therefore we will not be afraid,
though the earth trembles
and the mountains topple
into the depths of the seas,
3 though its waters roar and foam
and the mountains quake
with its turmoil. •*Selah*

4 ⌊There is⌋ a river—
its streams delight the city of God,
the holy dwelling place
of the •Most High.
5 God is within her;
she will not be toppled.
God will help her
when the morning dawns.
6 Nations rage, kingdoms topple;
the earth melts when He lifts
His voice.
7 The LORD of •Hosts is with us;
the God of Jacob is our stronghold.
Selah

8 Come, see the works of the LORD,
who brings devastation on the earth.
9 He makes wars cease
throughout the earth.
He shatters bows and cuts spears
to pieces;
He burns up the chariots.[b]
10 "Stop ⌊your fighting⌋—and know
that I am God,
exalted among the nations,
exalted on the earth."
11 The LORD of Hosts is with us;
the God of Jacob is our stronghold.
Selah

Psalm 47
God Our King

For the choir director.
A psalm of the sons of Korah.

1 Clap your hands, all you peoples;
shout to God with a jubilant cry.
2 For the LORD •Most High is awe-inspiring,
a great King over all the earth.
3 He subdues peoples under us
and nations under our feet.
4 He chooses for us our inheritance—
the pride of Jacob, whom He loves.
•*Selah*

5 God ascends amid shouts of joy,
the LORD, amid the sound
of trumpets.
6 Sing praise to God, sing praise;
sing praise to our King, sing praise!
7 Sing a song of instruction,[c]
for God is King of all the earth.

8 God reigns over the nations;
God is seated on His holy throne.
9 The nobles of the peoples
have assembled
⌊with⌋ the people of the God
of Abraham.
For the leaders[d] of the earth
belong to God;
He is greatly exalted.

Psalm 48
Zion Exalted

A song. A psalm of the sons of Korah.

1 The LORD is great and is highly praised
in the city of our God.
His holy mountain, 2 rising splendidly,

[a] This notation may refer to a high pitch, perhaps a tune sung by soprano voices; the Hb word means "young women."
[b] **46:9** Lit *chariots with fire* [c] **47:7** Hb *a Maskil* [d] **47:9** Lit *shields*

is the joy of the whole earth.
Mount Zion on the slopes of the north
is the city of the great King.
3 God is known as a stronghold
in its citadels.

4 Look! The kings assembled;
they advanced together.
5 They looked, and froze with fear;
they fled in terror.
6 Trembling seized them there,
agony like that of a woman in labor,
7 as You wrecked the ships of Tarshish
with the east wind.

8 Just as we heard, so we have seen
in the city of the LORD of •Hosts,
in the city of our God;
God will establish it forever. *•Selah*

9 God, within Your temple,
we contemplate Your faithful love.
10 Your name, God, like Your praise,
reaches to the ends of the earth;
Your right hand is filled with justice.
11 Mount Zion is glad.
The towns[a] of Judah rejoice
because of Your judgments.

12 Go around Zion, encircle it;
count its towers,
13 note its ramparts; tour its citadels
so that you can tell
a future generation:
14 "This God, our God
forever and ever—
He will lead us eternally."[b]

Psalm 49

Misplaced Trust in Wealth

For the choir director. A psalm of the sons of Korah.

1 Hear this, all you peoples;
listen, all who inhabit the world,
2 both low and high,[c]
rich and poor together.
3 My mouth speaks wisdom;
my heart's meditation
⌊brings⌋ understanding.
4 I turn my ear to a proverb;
I explain my riddle with a lyre.

5 Why should I fear in times of trouble?
The iniquity of my foes surrounds me.
6 They trust in their wealth
and boast of their abundant riches.
7 Yet these cannot redeem a person[d]
or pay his ransom to God—
8 since the price of redeeming him is
too costly,
one should forever stop trying[e] —
9 so that he may live forever
and not see the •Pit.

10 For one can see that wise men die;
the foolish and the senseless also
pass away.
Then they leave their wealth to others.
11 Their graves are their eternal homes,[f]
their homes from generation
to generation,
though they have named estates
after themselves.
12 But despite ⌊his⌋ assets,[g]
man will not last;
he is like the animals that perish.

13 This is the way of those
who are arrogant,
and of their followers,
who approve of their words.[h] *•Selah*
14 Like sheep they are headed for •Sheol;
Death will shepherd them.
The upright will rule over them
in the morning,
and their form will waste away
in Sheol,
far from their lofty abode.
15 But God will redeem my life
from the power of Sheol,
for He will take me. *Selah*

16 Do not be afraid when a man gets rich,
when the wealth[i]
of his house increases.
17 For when he dies, he will take
nothing at all;
his wealth[i] will not follow him down.
18 Though he praises himself
during his lifetime—
and people praise you
when you do well for yourself—
19 he will go to the generation
of his fathers;
they will never see the light.
20 A man with valuable possessions[j]
but without understanding
is like the animals that perish.

[a]**48:11** Lit *daughters* [b]**48:14** Some Hb mss, LXX; other Hb mss read *over death* [c]**49:2** Lit *both sons of Adam and sons of man* [d]**49:7** Or *Certainly he cannot redeem himself*, or *Yet he cannot redeem a brother* [e]**49:8** Or *costly, it will cease forever* [f]**49:11** LXX, Syr, Tg; MT reads *Their inner thought is that their houses are eternal* [g]**49:12** Or *honor* [h]**49:13** Lit *and after them with their mouth they were pleased* [i]**49:16,17** Or *glory* [j]**49:20** Or *with honor*

Psalm 50
God as Judge

A psalm of •Asaph.

1 God, the LORD God[a] speaks;
He summons the earth from east
to west.[b]
2 From Zion, the perfection of beauty,
God appears in radiance.[c]
3 Our God is coming; He will not
be silent!
Devouring fire precedes Him,
and a storm rages around Him.
4 On high, He summons heaven
and earth
in order to judge His people.
5 "Gather My faithful ones to Me,
those who made a covenant with Me
by sacrifice."
6 The heavens proclaim
His righteousness,
for God is the judge. *•Selah*

7 "Listen, My people, and I will speak;
I will testify against you, Israel.
I am God, your God.
8 I do not rebuke you for your sacrifices
or for your •burnt offerings,
which are continually before Me.
9 I will not accept a bull
from your household
or male goats from your pens,
10 for every animal of the forest is Mine,
the cattle on a thousand hills.
11 I know every bird of the mountains,[d]
and the creatures of the field are Mine.
12 If I were hungry, I would not tell you,
for the world and everything in it
is Mine.
13 Do I eat the flesh of bulls
or drink the blood of goats?
14 Sacrifice a thank offering to God,
and pay your vows to the •Most High.
15 Call on Me in a day of trouble;
I will rescue you,
and you will honor Me."

16 But God says to the wicked:
"What right do you have to recite
My statutes
and to take My covenant on your lips?
17 You hate instruction
and turn your back on My words.[e]
18 When you see a thief,
you make friends with him,
and you associate with adulterers.
19 You unleash your mouth for evil
and harness your tongue for deceit.
20 You sit, maligning your brother,
slandering your mother's son.
21 You have done these things,
and I kept silent;
you thought I was just like you.
But I will rebuke you
and lay out the case before you.[f]
22 "Understand this, you who forget God,
or I will tear you apart,
and there will be no rescuer.
23 Whoever sacrifices a thank offering
honors Me,
and whoever orders his conduct,
I will show him the salvation of God."

Psalm 51
A Prayer for Restoration

For the choir director. A Davidic psalm, when Nathan the prophet came to him after he had gone to Bathsheba.

1 Be gracious to me, God,
according to Your faithful love;
according to Your abundant compassion,
blot out my rebellion.
2 Wash away my guilt,
and cleanse me from my sin.
3 For I am conscious of my rebellion,
and my sin is always before me.
4 Against You—You alone—
I have sinned
and done this evil in Your sight.
So You are right
when You pass sentence;
You are blameless when You judge.
5 Indeed, I was guilty ⌊when I⌋ was born;
I was sinful when my mother
conceived me.

6 Surely You desire integrity
in the inner self,
and You teach me wisdom
deep within.
7 Purify me with hyssop,
and I will be clean;
wash me, and I will be
whiter than snow.

[a]**50:1** Or *The Mighty One, God, the LORD*, or *The God of gods, the LORD* [b]**50:1** Lit *from the rising of the sun to its setting* [c]**50:2** Or *God shines forth* [d]**50:11** LXX, Syr, Tg read *heavens* [e]**50:17** Or *and cast My words behind you* [f]**50:21** Lit *out before your eyes*

8 Let me hear joy and gladness;
let the bones You have crushed rejoice.
9 Turn Your face away[a] from my sins
and blot out all my guilt.

10 God, create a clean heart for me
and renew a steadfast[b] spirit
within me.
11 Do not banish me from Your presence
or take Your Holy Spirit from me.
12 Restore the joy of Your salvation to me,
and give me a willing spirit.[c]
13 Then I will teach the rebellious
Your ways,
and sinners will return to You.

14 Save me from the guilt of bloodshed,
God,
the God of my salvation,
and my tongue will sing
of Your righteousness.
15 Lord, open my lips,
and my mouth will declare Your praise.
16 You do not want a sacrifice,
or I would give it;
You are not pleased
with a •burnt offering.
17 The sacrifice pleasing to God is[d]
a broken spirit.
God, You will not despise a broken
and humbled heart.

18 In Your good pleasure, cause Zion
to prosper;
build[e] the walls of Jerusalem.
19 Then You will delight
in righteous sacrifices,
whole burnt offerings;
then bulls will be offered on Your altar.

Psalm 52

God Judges the Proud

For the choir director. A Davidic •*Maskil.* When Doeg the Edomite went and reported to Saul, telling him, "David went to Ahimelech's house."

1 Why brag about evil, you hero!
God's faithful love is constant.
2 Like a sharpened razor,
your tongue devises destruction,
working treachery.
3 You love evil instead of good,
lying instead of speaking truthfully.
•*Selah*

4 You love any words that destroy,
you treacherous tongue!

5 This is why God will bring
you down forever.
He will take you, ripping you out of
your tent;
He will uproot you from the land
of the living. *Selah*
6 The righteous will look on with awe
and will ridicule him:
7 "Here is the man
who would not make God his refuge,
but trusted in the abundance
of his riches,
taking refuge
in his destructive behavior."[f]

8 But I am like
a flourishing olive tree
in the house of God;
I trust in God's faithful love
forever and ever.
9 I will praise You forever for what
You have done.
In the presence of Your faithful people,
I will put my hope in Your name,
for it is good.

Psalm 53

A Portrait of Sinners

For the choir director: on *Mahalath.*[g] A Davidic •*Maskil.*

1 The fool says in his heart,
"God does not exist."
They are corrupt, and they do
vile deeds.
There is no one who does good.
2 God looks down from heaven
on the •human race
to see if there is one who is wise
and who seeks God.
3 Everyone has turned aside;
they have all become corrupt.
There is no one who does good,
not even one.

4 Will evildoers never understand?
They consume My people
as they consume bread;
they do not call on God.
5 Then they will be filled with terror—
terror like no other—

[a]**51:9** Lit *Hide Your face* [b]**51:10** Or *right* [c]**51:12** Or *and sustain me with a noble spirit* [d]**51:17** Lit *The sacrifices of God are* [e]**51:18** Or *rebuild* [f]**52:7** Or *riches, and grew strong in his evil desire*; lit *his destruction* [g]Perhaps a song tune, a musical instrument, or a dance; may be related to Hb for "sickness"

because God will scatter
the bones of those who besiege you.
You will put them to shame,
for God has rejected them.

6 Oh, that Israel's deliverance
would come from Zion!
When God restores His captive people,
Jacob will rejoice; Israel will be glad.

Psalm 54

Prayer for Deliverance

For the choir director:
with stringed instruments. A Davidic •*Maskil*.
When the Ziphites went and said to Saul, "Is
David not hiding among us?"

1 God, save me by Your name,
and vindicate me by Your might!
2 God, hear my prayer;
listen to the words of my mouth.
3 For strangers rise up against me,
and violent men seek my life.
They have no regard for God.[a] •*Selah*

4 God is my helper;
the Lord is the sustainer of my life.[b]
5 He will repay my adversaries
for ⌊their⌋ evil.
Because of Your faithfulness,
annihilate them.

6 I will sacrifice a freewill offering
to You.
I will praise Your name, LORD,
because it is good.
7 For He has delivered me
from every trouble,
and my eye has looked down on
my enemies.

Psalm 55

Betrayal by a Friend

For the choir director:
with stringed instruments. A Davidic •*Maskil*.

1 God, listen to my prayer
and do not ignore[c] my plea for help.
2 Pay attention to me and answer me.
I am restless and in turmoil
with my complaint,
3 because of the enemy's voice,
because of the pressure[d] of the wicked.
For they bring down disaster on me[e]
and harass me in anger.

4 My heart shudders within me;
terrors of death sweep over me.
5 Fear and trembling grip me;
horror has overwhelmed me.
6 I said, "If only I had[f] wings like a dove!
I would fly away and find rest.
7 How far away I would flee;
I would stay in the wilderness. •*Selah*
8 I would hurry to my shelter
from the raging wind and the storm."

9 Lord, confuse[g] and confound
their speech,[h]
for I see violence and strife
in the city;
10 day and night they make the rounds
on its walls.
Crime and trouble are within it;
11 destruction is inside it;
oppression and deceit never leave
its marketplace.

12 Now, it is not an enemy
who insults me—
otherwise I could bear it;
it is not a foe who rises up against me—
otherwise I could hide from him.
13 But it is you, a man who is my peer,
my companion and good friend!
14 We used to have close fellowship;
we walked with the crowd
into the house of God.

15 Let death take them by surprise;
let them go down to •Sheol alive,
because evil is in their homes
and within them.
16 But I call to God,
and the LORD will save me.
17 I complain and groan morning, noon,
and night,
and He hears my voice.
18 Though many are against me,
He will redeem me
from my battle unharmed.
19 God, the One enthroned from long ago,
will hear, and will humiliate them
Selah
because they do not change
and do not •fear God.

20 He[i] acts violently
against those at peace with him;
he violates his covenant.

[a]**54:3** Lit *They do not set God before them* [b]**54:4** Or *is with those who sustain my life* [c]**55:1** Lit *hide Yourself from* [d]**55:3** Or *threat*, or *oppression* [e]**55:3** LXX, Syr, Sym; MT reads *they cause me to totter* [f]**55:6** Lit *"Who will give to me . . . dove?* (as a question) [g]**55:9** Or *destroy* [h]**55:9** Lit *and divide their tongue* [i]**55:20** The evil man

21 His buttery words are smooth,[a]
but war is in his heart.
His words are softer than oil,
but they are drawn swords.

22 Cast your burden on the LORD,
and He will support you;
He will never allow the righteous
to be shaken.

23 You, God, will bring them down
to the pit of destruction;
men of bloodshed and treachery
will not live out half their days.
But I will trust in You.

Psalm 56

A Call for God's Protection

For the choir director: according to "A Silent Dove Far Away."[b] A Davidic •*Miktam.* When the Philistines seized him in Gath.

1 Be gracious to me, God,
for man tramples me;
he fights and oppresses me all day
long.
2 My adversaries trample me all day,
for many arrogantly fight against me.[c]
3 When I am afraid,
I will trust in You.
4 In God, whose word I praise,
in God I trust; I will not fear.
What can man do to me?

5 They twist my words all day long;
all their thoughts are against me
for evil.
6 They stir up strife,[d] they lurk;
they watch my steps
while they wait to take my life.
7 Will they escape in spite of such sin?
God, bring down the nations in wrath.

8 You Yourself have recorded
my wanderings.[e]
Put my tears in Your bottle.
Are they not in Your records?
9 Then my enemies will retreat
on the day when I call.
This I know: God is for me.

10 In God, whose word I praise,
in the LORD, whose word I praise,
11 in God I trust; I will not fear.
What can man do to me?

12 I am obligated by vows[f] to You, God;
I will make my thank offerings to You.
13 For You delivered me from death,
even my feet from stumbling,
to walk before God in the light of life.

Psalm 57

Praise for God's Protection

For the choir director: "Do Not Destroy."[b] A Davidic •*Miktam.* When he fled before Saul into the cave.

1 Be gracious to me, God, be gracious
to me,
for I take refuge in You.
I will seek refuge in the shadow
of Your wings
until danger passes.
2 I call to God •Most High,
to God who fulfills ⌊His purpose⌋
for me.[g]
3 He reaches down from heaven
and saves me,
challenging the one who tramples me.
•*Selah*
God sends His faithful love and truth.
4 I am in the midst of lions;
I lie down with those
who devour •men.
Their teeth are spears and arrows;
their tongues are sharp swords.
5 God, be exalted above the heavens;
let Your glory be above the whole earth.
6 They prepared a net for my steps;
I was downcast.
They dug a pit ahead of me,
but they fell into it! *Selah*
7 My heart is confident, God, my heart
is confident.
I will sing; I will sing praises.
8 Wake up, my soul![h]
Wake up, harp and lyre!
I will wake up the dawn.
9 I will praise You, Lord,
among the peoples;
I will sing praises to You
among the nations.
10 For Your faithful love is as high as
the heavens;
Your faithfulness reaches to the clouds.
11 God, be exalted above the heavens;
let Your glory be over the whole earth.

[a]**55:21** Other Hb mss, Sym, Syr, Tg, Jer read *His speech is smoother than butter* [b]Possibly a song tune [c]**56:2** Or *many fight against me, O exalted One,* or *many fight against me from the heights* [d]**56:6** Or *They attack* [e]**56:8** Or *misery* [f]**56:12** Lit *Upon me the vows* [g]**57:2** Or *who avenges me* [h]**57:8** Lit *glory*

Psalm 58

A Cry against Injustice

For the choir director: "Do Not Destroy."[a]
A Davidic •*Miktam*.

1 Do you really speak righteously,
you mighty ones?[b]
Do you judge •people fairly?
2 No, you practice injustice
in your hearts;
with your hands
you weigh out violence in the land.

3 The wicked go astray from the womb;
liars err from birth.
4 They have venom like the venom
of a snake,
like the deaf cobra that stops up its ears,
5 that does not listen to the sound
of the charmers
who skillfully weave spells.

6 God, knock the teeth
out of their mouths;
LORD, tear out the young lions' fangs.
7 They will vanish like water
that flows by;
they will aim their useless arrows.[c] [d]
8 Like a slug that moves along in slime,
like a woman's miscarried ⌊child⌋,
they will not see the sun.

9 Before your pots can feel the heat
of the thorns—
whether green or burning—
He will sweep them away.[e]
10 The righteous will rejoice
when he sees the retribution;
he will wash his feet in the blood
of the wicked.
11 Then people will say,
"Yes, there is a reward
for the righteous!
There is a God who judges
on earth!"

Psalm 59

God Our Stronghold

For the choir director: "Do Not Destroy."[a]
A Davidic •*Miktam*. When Saul sent ⌊agents⌋ to
watch the house and kill him.

1 Deliver me from my enemies,
my God;
protect me from those who rise up
against me.
2 Deliver me from those
who practice sin,
and save me from men of bloodshed.
3 LORD, look! They set an ambush for me.
Powerful men attack me,
but not because of any sin or rebellion
of mine.
4 For no fault of mine,
they run and take up a position.
Awake to help me, and take notice.
5 You, LORD God of •Hosts,
God of Israel,
rise up to punish all the nations;
do not show grace
to any wicked traitors. •*Selah*

6 They return at evening,
snarling like dogs
and prowling around the city.
7 Look, they spew from their mouths—
sharp words from[f] their lips.
"For who," ⌊they say,⌋ "will hear?"
8 But You laugh at them, LORD;
You ridicule all the nations.
9 I will keep watch for You,
my[g] strength,
because God is my stronghold.
10 My faithful God[h] will come
to meet me;
God will let me look down on
my adversaries.

11 Do not kill them; otherwise,
my people will forget.
By Your power, make them
homeless wanderers
and bring them down,
Lord, our shield.
12 The sin of their mouths is the word
of their lips,
so let them be caught in their pride.
They utter curses and lies.
13 Consume ⌊them⌋ in rage;
consume ⌊them⌋ until they are gone.
Then they will know to the ends
of the earth
that God rules over Jacob. *Selah*

14 And they return at evening,
snarling like dogs
and prowling around the city.

[a]Possibly a song tune [b]**58:1** Or *Can you really speak righteousness in silence?* [c]**58:7** Or *their arrows as if they were circumcised*; Hb obscure [d]**58:7** Or *they wither like trampled grass* [e]**58:9** Or *thorns, He will sweep it away, whether raw or cooking*, or *thorns, He will sweep him away alive in fury* [f]**59:7** Lit *swords are on* [g]**59:9** Some Hb mss, LXX, Vg, Tg; other Hb mss read *his* [h]**59:10** Alt Hb traditions read *God in His faithful love*, or *My God, His faithful love*

15 They scavenge for food;
they growl if they are not satisfied.
16 But I will sing of Your strength
and will joyfully proclaim
Your faithful love in the morning.
For You have been a stronghold for me,
a refuge in my day of trouble.
17 To You, my strength, I sing praises,
because God is my stronghold—
my faithful God.

Psalm 60

Prayer in Difficult Times

For the choir director: according to "The Lily of Testimony."[a] A Davidic •*Miktam* for teaching. When he fought with Aram-naharaim and Aram-zobah, and Joab returned and struck Edom in the Valley of Salt, ⌊killing⌋ 12,000.

1 God, You have rejected us;
You have broken out[b] against us;
You have been angry. Restore us![c]
2 You have shaken the land
and split it open.
Heal its fissures, for it shudders.
3 You have made Your people
suffer hardship;
You have given us a wine to drink
that made us stagger.
4 You have given a signal flag to those
who •fear You,
so that they can flee
before the archers.[d] •*Selah*
5 Save with Your right hand,
and answer me,
so that those You love may be rescued.
6 God has spoken in His sanctuary:[e]
"I will triumph!
I will divide up Shechem.
I will apportion the Valley of Succoth.
7 Gilead is Mine, Manasseh is Mine,
and Ephraim is My helmet;
Judah is My scepter.
8 Moab is My washbasin;
on Edom I throw My sandal.
Over Philistia I shout in triumph."
9 Who will bring me to the fortified city?
Who will lead me to Edom?
10 Is it not You, God, who have
rejected us?
God, You do not march out
with our armies.
11 Give us aid against the foe,
for human help is worthless.
12 With God we will perform valiantly;
He will trample our foes.

Psalm 61

Security in God

For the choir director: on stringed instruments. Davidic.

1 God, hear my cry;
pay attention to my prayer.
2 I call to You from the ends of the earth
when my heart is without strength.
Lead me to a rock that is
high above me,
3 for You have been a refuge for me,
a strong tower in the face
of the enemy.
4 I will live in Your tent forever
and take refuge under the shelter
of Your wings. •*Selah*
5 God, You have heard my vows;
You have given a heritage
to those who fear Your name.
6 Add days to the king's life;
may his years span
many generations.
7 May he sit enthroned
before God forever;
appoint faithful love and truth
to guard him.
8 Then I will continually sing
of Your name,
fulfilling my vows day by day.

Psalm 62

Trust in God Alone

For the choir director: according to Jeduthun. A Davidic psalm.

1 I am at rest in God alone;
my salvation comes from Him.
2 He alone is my rock and my salvation,
my stronghold;
I will never be shaken.
3 How long will you threaten a man?
Will all of you attack[f]
as if he were a leaning wall
or a tottering stone fence?
4 They only plan to bring him down
from his high position.
They take pleasure in lying;

[a]Possibly a song tune [b]**60:1** Lit *have burst through* [c]**60:1** Or *Turn back to us* [d]**60:4** Or *can rally before the archers*, or *can rally because of the truth* [e]**60:6** Or *has promised by His holy nature* [f]**62:3** Other Hb mss read *you be struck down*

they bless with their mouths,
but they curse inwardly. •*Selah*

5 Rest in God alone, my soul,
for my hope comes from Him.
6 He alone is my rock and my salvation,
my stronghold; I will not be shaken.
7 My salvation and glory
depend on God;
my strong rock, my refuge, is in God.
8 Trust in Him at all times, you people;
pour out your hearts before Him.
God is our refuge. *Selah*

9 •Men are only a vapor;
exalted men, an illusion.
On a balance scale, they go up;
together they ⌊weigh⌋ less than a vapor.
10 Place no trust in oppression,
or false hope in robbery.
If wealth increases,
pay no attention to it.[a]

11 God has spoken once;
I have heard this twice:
strength belongs to God,
12 and faithful love belongs to You, LORD.
For You repay each according to
his works.

Psalm 63
Praise God Who Satisfies

A Davidic psalm. When he was in the Wilderness of Judah.

1 God, You are my God; I eagerly seek
You.
I thirst for You;
my body faints for You
in a land that is dry, desolate,
and without water.
2 So I gaze on You in the sanctuary
to see Your strength and Your glory.

3 My lips will glorify You
because Your faithful love is better
than life.
4 So I will praise You as long as I live;
at Your name, I will lift up my hands.
5 You satisfy me as with rich food;[b]
my mouth will praise You
with joyful lips.

6 When, on my bed, I think of You,
I meditate on You
during the night watches
7 because You are my help;
I will rejoice in the shadow
of Your wings.
8 I follow close to You;
Your right hand holds on to me.

9 But those who seek to destroy
my life
will go into the depths of the earth.
10 They will be given over to the power
of the sword;
they will become the jackals' prey.
11 But the king will rejoice in God;
all who swear by Him[c] will boast,
for the mouths of liars will be shut.

Psalm 64
Protection from Evildoers

For the choir director. A Davidic psalm.

1 God, hear my voice when I complain.
Protect my life from the terror
of the enemy.
2 Hide me from the scheming
of the wicked,
from the mob of evildoers,
3 who sharpen their tongues
like swords
and aim bitter words like arrows,
4 shooting from concealed places
at the innocent.
They shoot at him suddenly
and are not afraid.
5 They encourage each other
in an evil plan;[d e]
they talk about hiding traps and say,
"Who will see them?"[f]
6 They devise crimes ⌊and say,⌋
"We have perfected a secret plan."
The inner man and the heart
are mysterious.

7 But God will shoot them
with arrows;
suddenly, they will be wounded.
8 They will be made to stumble;
their own tongues work
against them.
All who see them will shake
their heads.
9 Then everyone will fear
and will tell about God's work,
for they will understand
what He has done.

[a]**62:10** Lit *increases, do not set heart* [b]**63:5** Lit *with fat and fatness* [c]**63:11** Or *him*, referring to the king; 1 Sm 17:55; 2 Sm 14:19 [d]**64:5** Lit *word*, or *thing* [e]**64:5** Or *They hold fast to an evil purpose*, or *They establish for themselves an evil purpose* [f]**64:5** Or *us*, or *it*

10 The righteous rejoice in the LORD
and take refuge in Him;
all the upright in heart offer praise.

Psalm 65
God's Care for the Earth

For the choir director. A Davidic psalm. A song.

1 Praise is rightfully Yours,[a]
God, in Zion;[b]
vows to You will be fulfilled.
2 All humanity will come to You,
the One who hears prayer.
3 Iniquities overwhelm me;
only You can •atone for[c]
our rebellions.
4 How happy is the one You choose
and bring near to live in Your courts!
We will be satisfied with the goodness
of Your house,
the holiness of Your temple.[d]
5 You answer us in righteousness,
with awe-inspiring works,
God of our salvation,
the hope of all the ends of the earth
and of the distant seas;
6 You establish the mountains
by Your[e] power,
robed with strength;
7 You silence the roar of the seas,
the roar of their waves,
and the tumult of the nations.
8 Those who live far away are awed
by Your signs;
You make east and west shout for joy.

9 You visit the earth
and water it abundantly,
enriching it greatly.
God's stream is filled with water,
for You prepare the earth[f] in this way,
providing ⌊people⌋ with grain.
10 You soften it with showers and bless
its growth,
soaking its furrows and leveling
its ridges.
11 You crown the year
with Your goodness;
Your ways overflow with plenty.[g]
12 The wilderness pastures overflow,
and the hills are robed with joy.
13 The pastures are clothed with flocks,
and the valleys covered with grain.
They shout in triumph; indeed,
they sing.

Psalm 66
Praise for God's Mighty Acts

For the choir director. A song. A psalm.

1 Shout joyfully to God, all the earth!
2 Sing the glory of His name;
make His praise glorious.
3 Say to God, "How awe-inspiring
are Your works!
Your enemies will cringe before You
because of Your great strength.
4 All the earth will worship You
and sing praise to You.
They will sing praise to Your name."
•Selah

5 Come and see the works of God;
His acts toward •mankind are awe-
inspiring.
6 He turned the sea into dry land,
and they crossed the river on foot.
There we rejoiced in Him.
7 He rules forever by His might;
He keeps His eye on the nations.
The rebellious should not
exalt themselves. *Selah*
8 Praise our God, you peoples;
let the sound of His praise be heard.
9 He keeps us alive[h]
and does not allow our feet to slip.

10 For You, God, tested us;
You refined us as silver is refined.
11 You lured us into a trap;
You placed burdens on our backs.
12 You let men ride over our heads;
we went through fire and water,
but You brought us out
to abundance.[i]

13 I will enter Your house
with •burnt offerings;
I will pay You my vows
14 that my lips promised
and my mouth spoke
during my distress.
15 I will offer You fattened sheep
as burnt offerings,
with the fragrant smoke of rams;
I will sacrifice oxen
with goats. *Selah*

[a]**65:1** Or *Praise is silence to You*, or *Praise awaits You* [b]**65:1** Jerusalem [c]**65:3** Or *can forgive*, or *can wipe out* [d]**65:4** Or *house, Your holy temple* [e]**65:6** Some LXX mss, Vg; MT reads *His* [f]**65:9** Lit *prepare it* [g]**65:11** Lit *ways drip with fat* [h]**66:9** Lit *He sets our soul in life* [i]**66:12** Or *a place of satisfaction*

16 Come and listen, all who •fear God,
and I will tell what He has done
for me.
17 I cried out to Him with my mouth,
and praise was on my tongue.
18 If I had been aware of malice
in my heart,
the Lord would not have listened.
19 However, God has listened;
He has paid attention to the sound
of my prayer.
20 May God be praised!
He has not turned away my prayer
or turned His faithful love
from me.

Psalm 67

All Will Praise God

For the choir director:
with stringed instruments. A psalm. A song.

1 May God be gracious to us and bless
us;
look on us with favor *•Selah*
2 so that Your way may be known
on earth,
Your salvation among all nations.

3 Let the peoples praise You, God;
let all the peoples praise You.
4 Let the nations rejoice and shout
for joy,
for You judge the peoples with fairness
and lead the nations on earth. *Selah*
5 Let the peoples praise You, God,
let all the peoples praise You.

6 The earth has produced its harvest;
God, our God, blesses us.
7 God will bless us,
and all the ends of the earth
will •fear Him.

Psalm 68

God's Majestic Power

For the choir director. A Davidic psalm. A song.

1 God arises. His enemies scatter,
and those who hate Him flee
from His presence.
2 As smoke is blown away,
so You blow ⌊them⌋ away.
As wax melts before the fire,
so the wicked are destroyed
before God.
3 But the righteous are glad;
they rejoice before God and celebrate
with joy.

4 Sing to God! Sing praises
to His name.
Exalt Him who rides on the clouds[a] —
His name is •Yahweh[b] —and rejoice
before Him.
5 A father of the fatherless
and a champion of widows
is God in His holy dwelling.
6 God provides homes for those
who are deserted.
He leads out the prisoners
to prosperity,[c]
but the rebellious live
in a scorched land.

7 God, when You went out
before Your people,
when You marched
through the desert, *•Selah*
8 the earth trembled, and the skies
poured down ⌊rain⌋
before God, the God of Sinai,[d]
before God, the God of Israel.
9 You, God, showered
abundant rain;
You revived Your inheritance
when it languished.
10 Your people settled in it;
by Your goodness You provided
for the poor, God.

11 The Lord gave the command;
a great company of women brought
the good news:
12 "The kings of the armies flee—
they flee!"
She who stays at home divides
the spoil.
13 While[e] you lie
among the sheepfolds,[f]
the wings of a dove are covered
with silver,
and its feathers with glistening gold.
14 When the •Almighty scattered kings
in the land,
it snowed on Zalmon.[g]
15 Mount Bashan is
God's towering mountain;
Mount Bashan is a mountain
of many peaks.

[a]**68:4** Or *rides through the desert* [b]**68:4** Lit *Yah* [c]**68:6** Or *prisoners with joyous music*; Hb uncertain [d]**68:8** Lit *God, this Sinai* [e]**68:13** Or *If* [f]**68:13** Or *campfires*, or *saddlebags*; Hb obscure [g]**68:14** Or *Black Mountain*

16 Why gaze with envy,
you mountain peaks,
at the mountain[a] God desired
for His dwelling?
The LORD will live ⌊there⌋ forever!
17 God's chariots are tens of thousands,
thousands and thousands;
the Lord is among them
in the sanctuary[b]
as He was at Sinai.
18 You ascended to the heights,
taking away captives;
You received gifts from[c] people,
even from the rebellious,
so that the LORD God might live ⌊there⌋.[d]
19 May the Lord be praised!
Day after day He bears our burdens;
God is our salvation. *Selah*
20 Our God is a God of salvation,
and escape from death belongs
to the Lord GOD.
21 Surely God crushes the heads
of His enemies,
the hairy head of one who goes on
in his guilty acts.
22 The Lord said, "I will bring ⌊them⌋ back
from Bashan;
I will bring ⌊them⌋ back
from the depths of the sea
23 so that your foot may wade[e] in blood
and your dogs' tongues may have
their share
from the enemies."
24 People have seen Your procession, God,
the procession of my God,
my King, in the sanctuary.[b]
25 Singers[f] lead the way,
with musicians following;
among them are young women
playing tambourines.
26 Praise God in the assemblies;
⌊praise⌋ the LORD from the fountain
of Israel.
27 There is Benjamin, the youngest,
leading them,
the rulers of Judah in their assembly,[g]
the rulers of Zebulun, the rulers
of Naphtali.

28 Your God has decreed your strength.
Show Your strength, God,
You who have acted on our behalf.
29 Because of Your temple at Jerusalem,
kings will bring tribute to You.
30 Rebuke the beast[h] in the reeds,
the herd of bulls with the calves
of the peoples.
Trample underfoot those with bars
of silver.[i]
Scatter the peoples who take pleasure
in war.
31 Ambassadors will come[j] from Egypt;
•Cush[k] will stretch out its hands[l]
to God.

32 Sing to God, you kingdoms
of the earth;
sing praise to the Lord, *Selah*
33 to Him who rides in the ancient,
highest heavens.
Look, He thunders
with His powerful voice!
34 Ascribe power to God.
His majesty is over Israel,
His power among the clouds.
35 God, You are awe-inspiring
in Your sanctuaries.
The God of Israel gives power
and strength to His people.
May God be praised!

Psalm 69

A Plea for Rescue

For the choir director: according to "The Lilies."[m] Davidic.

1 Save me, God,
for the water has risen to my neck.
2 I have sunk in deep mud, and there is
no footing;
I have come into deep waters,
and a flood sweeps over me.
3 I am weary from my crying;
my throat is parched.
My eyes fail, looking for my God.
4 Those who hate me without cause
are more numerous than the hairs
of my head;
my deceitful enemies, who would
destroy me,
are powerful.
Though I did not steal, I must repay.

[a]**68:16** Mount Zion [b]**68:17,24** Or *in holiness* [c]**68:18** Lit *among* [d]**68:18** Or *even those rebelling against the LORD God's living there*, or *even rebels are living with the LORD God*; Hb obscure [e]**68:23** LXX, Syr read *dip* [f]**68:25** Some Hb mss, LXX, Syr read *Officials* [g]**68:27** Hb obscure [h]**68:30** Probably Egypt [i]**68:30** Or *peoples, trampling on those who take pleasure in silver*, or *peoples, trampling on the bars of silver*, or *peoples, who trample each other for bars of silver* [j]**68:31** Or *They bring red cloth*, or *They bring bronze* [k]**68:31** Modern Sudan [l]**68:31** Probably with tribute or in submission [m]Apparently a hymn tune; compare Pss 45; 60; 80

5 God, You know my foolishness,
and my guilty acts are not hidden
from You.
6 Do not let those who put their hope
in You
be disgraced because of me,
Lord GOD of •Hosts;
do not let those who seek You
be humiliated because of me,
God of Israel.
7 For I have endured insults because of
You,
and shame has covered my face.
8 I have become a stranger
to my brothers
and a foreigner to my mother's sons
9 because zeal for Your house
has consumed me,
and the insults of those who insult You
have fallen on me.
10 I mourned and fasted,
but it brought me insults.
11 I wore •sackcloth as my clothing,
and I was a joke to them.
12 Those who sit at the city •gate
talk about me,
and drunkards make up songs about me.

13 But as for me, LORD,
my prayer to You is for a time of favor.
In Your abundant, faithful love, God,
answer me with Your sure salvation.
14 Rescue me from the miry mud;
don't let me sink.
Let me be rescued from those
who hate me,
and from the deep waters.
15 Don't let the floodwaters
sweep over me
or the deep swallow me up;
don't let the •Pit close its mouth
over me.
16 Answer me, LORD,
for Your faithful love is good;
in keeping with
Your great compassion,
turn to me.
17 Don't hide Your face from Your servant,
for I am in distress.
Answer me quickly!
18 Draw near to me and redeem me;
ransom me because of my enemies.

19 You know the insults I endure—
my shame and disgrace.
You are aware of all my adversaries.
20 Insults have broken my heart,
and I am in despair.
I waited for sympathy,
but there was none;
for comforters, but found no one.
21 Instead, they gave me gall[a]
for my food,
and for my thirst
they gave me vinegar to drink.

22 Let their table set before them be
a snare,
and let it be a trap for ⌊their⌋ allies.
23 Let their eyes grow too dim to see,
and let their loins continually shake.
24 Pour out Your rage on them,
and let Your burning anger
overtake them.
25 Make their fortification desolate;
may no one live in their tents.
26 For they persecute the one You struck
and talk about the pain of those
You wounded.
27 Add guilt to their guilt;
do not let them share
in Your righteousness.
28 Let them be erased from the book
of life
and not be recorded with the righteous.

29 But as for me—poor and in pain—
let Your salvation protect me, God.
30 I will praise God's name with song
and exalt Him with thanksgiving.
31 That will please the LORD more than
an ox,
more than a bull with horns
and hooves.
32 The humble will see it and rejoice.
You who seek God, take heart!
33 For the LORD listens to the needy
and does not despise
His own who are prisoners.

34 Let heaven and earth praise Him,
the seas and everything that moves
in them,
35 for God will save Zion
and build up[b] the cities of Judah.
They will live there and possess it.
36 The descendants of His servants
will inherit it,
and those who love His name will live
in it.

[a]**69:21** A bitter substance [b]**69:35** Or *and rebuild*

Psalm 70
A Call for Deliverance

For the choir director. Davidic.
To bring remembrance.

1 God, deliver me.
Hurry to help me, LORD!

2 Let those who seek my life
be disgraced and confounded;
let those who wish me harm
be driven back and humiliated.
3 Let those who say, "Aha, aha!"
retreat because of their shame.

4 Let all who seek You rejoice
and be glad in You;
let those who love Your salvation
continually say, "God is great!"
5 I am afflicted and needy;
hurry to me, God.
You are my help and my deliverer;
LORD, do not delay.

Psalm 71
God's Help in Old Age

1 LORD, I seek refuge in You;
never let me be disgraced.
2 In Your justice, rescue and deliver me;
listen closely to me and save me.
3 Be a rock of refuge for me,
where I can always go.
Give the command to save me,
for You are my rock and fortress.
4 Deliver me, my God, from the hand
of the wicked,
from the grasp of the unjust
and oppressive.
5 For You are my hope, Lord GOD,
my confidence from my youth.
6 I have leaned on You from birth;
You took me from my mother's womb.
My praise is always about You.
7 I have become an ominous sign
to many,
but You are my strong refuge.
8 My mouth is full of praise
and honor to You all day long.

9 Don't discard me in my old age:
as my strength fails,
do not abandon me.
10 For my enemies talk about me,
and those who spy on me
plot together,
11 saying, "God has abandoned him;
chase him and catch him,
for there is no one to rescue ⌊him⌋."
12 God, do not be far from me;
my God, hurry to help me.
13 May my adversaries be disgraced
and confounded;
may those who seek my harm
be covered with disgrace
and humiliation.
14 But I will hope continually
and will praise You more
and more.
15 My mouth will tell
about Your righteousness
and Your salvation all day long,
though I cannot sum them up.
16 I come because of the mighty acts
of the Lord GOD;
I will proclaim Your righteousness,
Yours alone.

17 God, You have taught me
from my youth,
and I still proclaim
Your wonderful works.
18 Even when I am old and gray,
God, do not abandon me.
Then I will[a] proclaim Your power
to ⌊another⌋ generation,
Your strength to all who are to come.
19 Your righteousness
reaches heaven, God,
You who have done great things;
God, who is like You?
20 You caused me to experience
many troubles and misfortunes,
but You will revive me again.
You will bring me up again,
even from the depths of the earth.
21 You will increase my honor
and comfort me once again.
22 Therefore, with a lute
I will praise You
for Your faithfulness, my God;
I will sing to You with a harp,
Holy One of Israel.
23 My lips will shout for joy
when I sing praise to You,
because You have redeemed me.
24 Therefore, my tongue will proclaim
Your righteousness all day long,
for those who seek my harm
will be disgraced and confounded.

[a]**71:18** Lit *me until I*

Psalm 72
A Prayer for the King

Solomonic.

1 God, give Your justice to the king
and Your righteousness
to the king's son.
2 He will judge Your people
with righteousness
and Your afflicted ones with justice.
3 May the mountains bring prosperity[a]
to the people,
and the hills, righteousness.
4 May he vindicate the afflicted
among the people,
help the poor,
and crush the oppressor.

5 May he continue[b]
while the sun endures,
and as long as the moon,
throughout all generations.
6 May he be like rain that falls
on the cut grass,
like spring showers that water
the earth.
7 May the righteous[c] flourish
in his days,
and prosperity[a] abound
until the moon is no more.

8 And may he rule from sea to sea
and from the Euphrates
to the ends of the earth.
9 May desert tribes kneel before him
and his enemies lick the dust.
10 May the kings of Tarshish
and the coasts and islands bring tribute,
the kings of Sheba and Seba offer gifts.
11 And let all kings bow down to him,
all nations serve him.

12 For he will rescue the poor
who cry out
and the afflicted who have no helper.
13 He will have pity on the poor
and helpless
and save the lives of the poor.
14 He will redeem them from oppression
and violence,
for their lives are precious[d]
in his sight.

15 May he live long!
May gold from Sheba be given to him.
May prayer be offered
for him continually,
and may he be blessed all day long.
16 May there be plenty of grain
in the land;
may it wave on the tops
of the mountains.
May its crops be like Lebanon.
May people flourish in the cities
like the grass of the field.
17 May his name endure forever;
as long as the sun shines,
may his fame increase.
May all nations be blessed by him
and call him blessed.

18 May the LORD God, the God of Israel,
be praised,
who alone does wonders.
19 May His glorious name
be praised forever;
the whole earth is filled with His glory.
•Amen and amen.
20 The prayers of David son of Jesse
are concluded.

BOOK III
(Psalms 73–89)

Psalm 73
God's Ways Vindicated

A psalm of •Asaph.

1 God is indeed good to Israel,
to the pure in heart.
2 But as for me, my feet almost slipped;
my steps nearly went astray.
3 For I envied the arrogant;
I saw the prosperity of the wicked.

4 They have an easy time until they die,[e]
and their bodies are well-fed.[f]
5 They are not in trouble like others;
they are not afflicted like most people.
6 Therefore, pride is their necklace,
and violence covers them
like a garment.
7 Their eyes bulge out from fatness;
the imaginations of their hearts
run wild.
8 They mock, and they speak maliciously;
they arrogantly threaten oppression.
9 They set their mouths against heaven,
and their tongues strut
across the earth.

[a]**72:3,7** Or *peace* [b]**72:5** LXX; MT reads *May they fear you* [c]**72:7** Some Hb mss, LXX, Syr, Jer read *May righteousness*
[d]**72:14** Or *valuable* [e]**73:4** Lit *For there are no pangs to their death* [f]**73:4** Lit *fat*

10 Therefore His people turn to them[a]
and drink in their overflowing waters.[b]
11 They say, "How can God know?
Does the •Most High
know everything?"
12 Look at them—the wicked!
They are always at ease,
and they increase their wealth.

13 Did I purify my heart
and wash my hands in innocence
for nothing?
14 For I am afflicted all day long,
and punished every morning.
15 If I had decided to say
these things ⌊aloud⌋,
I would have betrayed Your people.[c]
16 When I tried to understand all this,
it seemed hopeless[d]
17 until I entered God's sanctuary.
Then I understood their destiny.
18 Indeed You put them in slippery places;
You make them fall into ruin.
19 How suddenly they become
a desolation!
They come to an end, swept away
by terrors.
20 Like one waking from a dream,
Lord, when arising, You will despise
their image.

21 When I became embittered
and my innermost being[e]
was wounded,
22 I was a fool and didn't understand;
I was an unthinking animal toward You.
23 Yet I am always with You;
You hold my right hand.
24 You guide me with Your counsel,
and afterwards You will take me up
in glory.[f]
25 Whom do I have in heaven but You?
And I desire nothing on earth but You.
26 My flesh and my heart may fail,
but God is the strength[g] of my heart,
my portion forever.
27 Those far from You
will certainly perish;
You destroy all who are
unfaithful to You.
28 But as for me, God's presence is
my good.
I have made the Lord GOD my refuge,
so I can tell about all You do.

Psalm 74

Prayer for Israel

A •*Maskil* of •Asaph.

1 Why have You
rejected ⌊us⌋ forever, God?
Why does Your anger burn
against the sheep of Your pasture?
2 Remember Your congregation,
which You purchased long ago
and redeemed as the tribe
for Your own possession.
⌊Remember⌋ Mount Zion
where You dwell.
3 Make Your way[h]
to the everlasting ruins,
to all that the enemy has destroyed
in the sanctuary.
4 Your adversaries roared
in the meeting place
where You met with us.[i]
They set up their emblems as signs.
5 It was like men in a thicket of trees,
wielding axes,
6 then smashing all the carvings
with hatchets and picks.
7 They set Your sanctuary on fire;
they utterly[j] desecrated
the dwelling place of Your name.
8 They said in their hearts,
"Let us oppress them relentlessly."
They burned down every place
throughout the land
where God met with us.[k]
9 We don't see any signs for us.
There is no longer a prophet.
And none of us knows how long
this will last.
10 God, how long will the foe mock?
Will the enemy insult
Your name forever?
11 Why do You hold back Your hand?
Stretch out[l] Your right hand
and destroy ⌊them⌋!

12 God my king is from ancient times,
performing saving acts on the earth.
13 You divided the sea with Your strength;
You smashed the heads
of the sea monsters

[a]**73:10** Lit *turn here* [b]**73:10** Lit *and waters of fullness are drained by them* [c]**73:15** Lit *betrayed the generation of Your sons* [d]**73:16** Lit *it was trouble in my eyes* [e]**73:21** Lit *my kidneys* [f]**73:24** Or *will receive me with honor* [g]**73:26** Lit *rock* [h]**74:3** Lit *Lift up Your steps* [i]**74:4** Lit *in Your meeting place* [j]**74:7** Lit *they to the ground* [k]**74:8** Lit *every meeting place of God in the land* [l]**74:11** Lit *From Your bosom*

in the waters;
14 You crushed the heads of •Leviathan;
You fed him to the creatures
of the desert.
15 You opened up springs and streams;
You dried up ever-flowing rivers.
16 The day is Yours, also the night;
You established the moon and the sun.
17 You set all the boundaries of the earth;
You made summer and winter.

18 Remember this: the enemy
has mocked the LORD,
and a foolish people has insulted
Your name.
19 Do not give the life of Your dove
to beasts;[a]
do not forget the lives
of Your poor people forever.
20 Consider the covenant,
for the dark places of the land
are full of violence.
21 Do not let the oppressed turn away
in shame;
let the poor and needy
praise Your name.
22 Arise, God, defend Your cause!
Remember the insults
that fools bring against You
all day long.
23 Do not forget the clamor
of Your adversaries,
the tumult of Your opponents
that goes up constantly.

Psalm 75

God Judges the Wicked

For the choir director: "Do Not Destroy."[b]
A psalm of •Asaph. A song.

1 We give thanks to You, God;
we give thanks to You, for Your name
is near.
People tell about Your wonderful works.

2 "When I choose a time,
I will judge fairly.
3 When the earth and all
its inhabitants shake,
I am the One who steadies its pillars.
•Selah
4 I say to the boastful, 'Do not boast,'
and to the wicked, 'Do not lift up
your •horn.
5 Do not lift up your horn
against heaven
or speak arrogantly.' "

6 Exaltation does not come
from the east, the west, or the desert,
7 for God is the judge:
He brings down one
and exalts another.
8 For there is a cup in the LORD's hand,
full of wine blended with spices,
and He pours from it.
All the wicked of the earth will drink,
draining it to the dregs.

9 As for me, I will tell about Him forever;
I will sing praise to the God of Jacob.

10 "I will cut off all the horns
of the wicked,
but the horns of the righteous will be
lifted up."

Psalm 76

God, the Powerful Judge

For the choir director:
with stringed instruments. A psalm of •Asaph.
A song.

1 God is known in Judah;
His name is great in Israel.
2 His tent is in Salem,[c]
His dwelling place in Zion.
3 There He shatters the bow's
flaming arrows,
the shield, the sword,
and the weapons of war. *•Selah*

4 You are resplendent and majestic
⌊coming down⌋ from the mountains
of prey.
5 The brave-hearted
have been plundered;
they have slipped
into their ⌊final⌋ sleep.
None of the warriors was able to lift
a hand.
6 At Your rebuke, God of Jacob,
both chariot and horse lay still.

7 And You—You are to be •feared.[d]
When You are angry,
who can stand before You?
8 From heaven
You pronounced judgment.
The earth feared and grew quiet

[a]**74:19** One Hb ms, LXX, Syr read *Do not hand over to beasts a soul that praises You* [b]Apparently a tune for the psalm
[c]**76:2** Jerusalem [d]**76:7** Or *are awe-inspiring*

9 when God rose up to judge
and to save all the lowly of the earth.
Selah
10 Even human wrath will praise You;
You will clothe Yourself
with their remaining wrath.[a]
11 Make and keep your vows
to the LORD your God;
let all who are around Him
bring tribute
to the awe-inspiring One.[b]
12 He humbles the spirit of leaders;
He is feared by the kings of the earth.

Psalm 77

Confidence in a Time of Crisis

For the choir director: according to Jeduthun. Of •Asaph. A psalm.

1 I cry aloud to God,
aloud to God, and He will hear me.
2 In my day of trouble I sought the Lord.
My hands were lifted up all night long;
I refused to be comforted.
3 I think of God; I groan;
I meditate; my spirit becomes weak.
•Selah
4 You have kept me from closing
my eyes;
I am troubled and cannot speak.
5 I consider days of old,
years long past.
6 At night I remember my music;
I meditate in my heart,
and my spirit ponders.
7 "Will the Lord reject forever
and never again show favor?
8 Has His faithful love ceased forever?
Is ⌊His⌋ promise at an end
for all generations?
9 Has God forgotten to be gracious?
Has He in anger
withheld His compassion?" *Selah*
10 So I say, "It is my sorrow[c]
that the right hand of the •Most High
has changed."
11 I will remember the LORD's works;
yes, I will remember
Your ancient wonders.
12 I will reflect on all You have done
and meditate on Your actions.
13 God, Your way is holy.
What god is great like God?
14 You are the God who works wonders;
You revealed Your strength
among the peoples.
15 With power You redeemed Your people,
the descendants of Jacob and Joseph.
Selah
16 The waters saw You, God.
The waters saw You; they trembled.
Even the depths shook.
17 The clouds poured down water.
The storm clouds thundered;
Your arrows flashed back and forth.
18 The sound of Your thunder was
in the whirlwind;
lightning lit up the world.
The earth shook and quaked.
19 Your way went through the sea,
and Your path through
the great waters,
but Your footprints were unseen.
20 You led Your people like a flock
by the hand of Moses and Aaron.

Psalm 78

Lessons from Israel's Past

A •*Maskil* of •Asaph.

1 My people, hear my instruction;
listen to what I say.
2 I will declare wise sayings;
I will speak mysteries from the past—
3 things we have heard and known
and that our fathers have passed down
to us.
4 We must not hide them
from their children,
but must tell a future generation
the praises of the LORD,
His might, and the wonderful works
He has performed.
5 He established a •testimony in Jacob
and set up a law in Israel,
which He commanded our fathers
to teach to their children
6 so that a future generation—
children yet to be born—might know.
They were to rise and tell
their children
7 so that they might put their confidence
in God
and not forget God's works,
but keep His commandments.
8 Then they would not be
like their fathers,

[a]**76:10** Hb obscure [b]**76:11** Or *tribute with awe* [c]**77:10** Lit *"My piercing*

a stubborn and rebellious generation,
a generation whose heart
was not loyal
and whose spirit was not faithful
to God.

9 The Ephraimite archers turned back
on the day of battle.
10 They did not keep God's covenant
and refused to live by His law.
11 They forgot what He had done,
the wonderful works
He had shown them.
12 He worked wonders in the sight
of their fathers,
in the land of Egypt, the region
of Zoan.
13 He split the sea
and brought them across;
the water stood firm like a wall.
14 He led them with a cloud by day
and with a fiery light
throughout the night.
15 He split rocks in the wilderness
and gave them drink as abundant
as the depths.
16 He brought streams out of the stone
and made water flow down like rivers.

17 But they continued to sin against Him,
rebelling in the desert
against the •Most High.
18 They deliberately[a] tested God,
demanding the food they craved.
19 They spoke against God, saying,
"Is God able to provide food
in the wilderness?
20 Look! He struck the rock and water
gushed out;
torrents overflowed.
But can He also provide bread
or furnish meat for His people?"
21 Therefore, the LORD heard
and became furious;
then fire broke out against Jacob,
and anger flared up against Israel
22 because they did not believe God
or rely on His salvation.
23 He gave a command
to the clouds above
and opened the doors of heaven.
24 He rained manna for them to eat;
He gave them grain from heaven.
25 People[b] ate the bread of angels.[c]
He sent them an abundant supply
of food.
26 He made the east wind blow
in the skies
and drove the south wind
by His might.
27 He rained meat on them like dust,
and winged birds like the sand
of the seas.
28 He made ⌊them⌋ fall in His camp,
all around His tent.[d] [e]
29 They ate and were
completely satisfied,
for He gave them what they craved.
30 Before they had satisfied their desire,
while the food was still in their mouths,
31 God's anger flared up against them,
and He killed some of their best men.
He struck down Israel's choice
young men.

32 Despite all this, they kept sinning
and did not believe
His wonderful works.
33 He made their days end in futility,
their years in sudden disaster.
34 When He killed ⌊some of⌋ them,
⌊the rest⌋ began to seek Him;
they repented and searched for God.
35 They remembered that God was
their rock,
the Most High God, their Redeemer.
36 But they deceived Him
with their mouths,
they lied to Him with their tongues,
37 their hearts were insincere
toward Him,
and they were unfaithful
to His covenant.
38 Yet He was compassionate;
He •atoned for[f] ⌊their⌋ guilt
and did not destroy ⌊them⌋.
He often turned His anger aside
and did not unleash[g] all His wrath.
39 He remembered that they were
⌊only⌋ flesh,
a wind that passes
and does not return.

40 How often they rebelled against Him
in the wilderness
and grieved Him in the desert.
41 They constantly tested God
and provoked the Holy One of Israel.

[a]**78:18** Lit *in their heart* [b]**78:25** Lit *Man* [c]**78:25** Lit *mighty ones* [d]**78:28** LXX, Syr read *in their camp . . . their tents* [e]**78:28** Or *in its camp, all around its tents* [f]**78:38** Or *He wiped out*, or *He forgave* [g]**78:38** Or *stir up*

42 They did not remember
His power ⌊shown⌋
on the day He redeemed them
from the foe,
43 when He performed
His miraculous signs in Egypt
and His marvels in the region of Zoan.
44 He turned their rivers into blood,
and they could not drink
from their streams.
45 He sent among them swarms of flies,
which fed on them,
and frogs, which devastated them.
46 He gave their crops to the caterpillar
and the fruit of their labor to the locust.
47 He killed their vines with hail
and their sycamore-fig trees with a flood.
48 He handed over their livestock to hail
and their cattle to lightning bolts.
49 He sent His burning anger
against them:
fury, indignation, and calamity—
a band of deadly messengers.[a]
50 He cleared a path for His anger.
He did not spare them from death,
but delivered their lives to the plague.
51 He struck all the firstborn in Egypt,
the first progeny of the tents of Ham.[b]
52 He led His people out like sheep
and guided them like a flock
in the wilderness.
53 He led them safely,
and they were not afraid;
but the sea covered their enemies.
54 He brought them to His holy land,
to the mountain
His right hand acquired.
55 He drove out nations before them.
He apportioned their inheritance by lot
and settled the tribes of Israel
in their tents.

56 But they rebelliously tested
the Most High God,
for they did not keep His decrees.
57 They treacherously turned away
like their fathers;
they became warped like a faulty bow.
58 They enraged Him
with their •high places
and provoked His jealousy
with their carved images.
59 God heard and became furious;
He completely rejected Israel.
60 He abandoned the tabernacle
at Shiloh,
the tent where He resided
among men.[c]
61 He gave up His strength[d] to captivity
and His splendor to the hand of a foe.
62 He surrendered His people
to the sword
because He was enraged
with His heritage.
63 Fire consumed His chosen young men,
and His young women
had no wedding songs.[e]
64 His priests fell by the sword,
but the[f] widows could not lament.[g]
65 Then the Lord awoke as if from sleep,
like a warrior from the effects of wine.
66 He beat back His foes;
He gave them lasting shame.
67 He rejected the tent of Joseph
and did not choose the tribe
of Ephraim.
68 He chose instead the tribe of Judah,
Mount Zion, which He loved.
69 He built His sanctuary
like the heights,[h]
like the earth that
He established forever.
70 He chose David His servant
and took him from the sheepfolds;
71 He brought him from tending ewes
to be shepherd over His people Jacob—
over Israel, His inheritance.
72 He shepherded them
with a pure heart
and guided them
with his skillful hands.

Psalm 79

Faith amid Confusion

A psalm of •Asaph.

1 God, the nations have invaded
Your inheritance,
desecrated Your holy temple,
and turned Jerusalem into ruins.
2 They gave the corpses of Your servants
to the birds of the sky for food,
the flesh of Your godly ones
to the beasts of the earth.
3 They poured out their blood
like water all around Jerusalem,

[a]**78:49** Or *angels* [b]**78:51** Ham's descendants who settled in Egypt; Ps 105:23,27 [c]**78:60** Hb *adam* [d]**78:61** See Ps 132:8 where the ark of the covenant is the *ark of His strength.* [e]**78:63** Lit *virgins were not praised* [f]**78:64** Lit *His* [g]**78:64** War probably prevented customary funerals. [h]**78:69** Either the heights of heaven or the mountain heights

and there was no one to bury ⌊them⌋.
4 We have become an object of reproach
to our neighbors,
a source of mockery and ridicule
to those around us.

5 How long, LORD? Will You
be angry forever?
Will Your jealousy keep burning like fire?
6 Pour out Your wrath on the nations
that don't acknowledge You,
on the kingdoms that don't call on
Your name,
7 for they have devoured Jacob
and devastated his homeland.
8 Do not hold past sins[a] against us;
let Your compassion come to us quickly,
for we have become weak.

9 God of our salvation, help us—
for the glory of Your name.
Deliver us and •atone for[b] our sins,
because of Your name.
10 Why should the nations ask,
"Where is their God?"
Before our eyes,
let vengeance for the shed blood
of Your servants
be known among the nations.
11 Let the groans of the prisoners
reach You;
according to Your great power,
preserve those condemned to die.

12 Pay back sevenfold to our neighbors
the reproach they have hurled at You,
Lord.
13 Then we, Your people, the sheep
of Your pasture,
will thank You forever;
we will declare Your praise
to generation after generation.

Psalm 80

A Prayer for Restoration

For the choir director: according to "The Lilies."[c] A testimony of •Asaph. A psalm.

1 Listen, Shepherd of Israel,
who guides Joseph like a flock;
You who sit enthroned
⌊on⌋ the •cherubim,
rise up
2 at the head of Ephraim,
Benjamin, and Manasseh.[d]
Rally Your power and come to save us.
3 Restore us, God;
look ⌊on us⌋ with favor,
and we will be saved.

4 LORD God of •Hosts,
how long will You be angry
with Your people's prayers?
5 You fed them the bread of tears
and gave them a full measure[e]
of tears to drink.
6 You set us at strife with our neighbors;
our enemies make fun of us.
7 Restore us, God of Hosts;
look ⌊on us⌋ with favor, and we will be
saved.

8 You uprooted a vine from Egypt;
You drove out the nations
and planted it.
9 You cleared ⌊a place⌋ for it;
it took root and filled the land.
10 The mountains were covered
by its shade,
and the mighty cedars[f]
with its branches.
11 It sent out sprouts toward the Sea[g]
and shoots toward the River.[h]

12 Why have You broken down its walls
so that all who pass by pick its fruit?
13 The boar from the forest gnaws at it,
and creatures of the field feed on it.
14 Return, God of Hosts.
Look down from heaven and see;
take care of this vine,
15 the root[i] Your right hand has planted,
the shoot[j] that You made strong
for Yourself.
16 It was cut down and burned up;[k]
they[l] perish at the rebuke
of Your countenance.
17 Let Your hand be with the man
at Your right hand,
with the son of man
You have made strong for Yourself.
18 Then we will not turn away from You;
revive us, and we will call
on Your name.
19 Restore us, LORD God of Hosts;
look ⌊on us⌋ with favor, and we will
be saved.

[a]**79:8** Or *hold the sins of past generations* [b]**79:9** Or *and wipe out*, or *and forgive* [c]Possibly a hymn tune; compare Pss 45; 60; 69 [d]**80:2** See Nm 2:17–24 for the order of these names in the marching order of the camp of Israel. [e]**80:5** Lit *a one-third measure* [f]**80:10** Lit *the cedars of God* [g]**80:11** The Mediterranean [h]**80:11** The Euphrates [i]**80:15** Hb obscure [j]**80:15** Or *son* [k]**80:16** Lit *burned with fire* [l]**80:16** Or *may they*

Psalm 81
A Call to Obedience

For the choir director: on the •*Gittith*.
Of •Asaph.

1 Sing for joy to God our strength;
shout in triumph to the God of Jacob.
2 Lift up a song—play the tambourine,
the melodious lyre, and the harp.
3 Blow the horn during the new moon
and during the full moon,
on the day of our feast.[a]
4 For this is a statute for Israel,
a judgment of the God of Jacob.
5 He set it up as an ordinance for Joseph
when He went throughout[b] the land
of Egypt.

I heard an unfamiliar language:
6 "I relieved his shoulder
from the burden;
his hands were freed from ⌊carrying⌋
the basket.
7 You called out in distress,
and I rescued you;
I answered you from the thundercloud.
I tested you at the waters of Meribah.
•*Selah*
8 Listen, My people, and I will
admonish you.
Israel, if you would only listen to Me!
9 There must not be a strange god
among you;
you must not bow down
to a foreign god.
10 I am •Yahweh your God,
who brought you up from the land
of Egypt.
Open your mouth wide, and I will
fill it.

11 "But My people did not listen to Me;
Israel did not obey Me.
12 So I gave them over
to their stubborn hearts
to follow their own plans.
13 If only My people would listen to Me
and Israel would follow My ways,
14 I would quickly subdue their enemies
and turn My hand against their foes."
15 Those who hate the LORD
would pretend submission to Him;
their doom would last forever.
16 But He would feed Israel[c]
with the best wheat.
"I would satisfy you with honey
from the rock."

Psalm 82
A Plea for Righteous Judgment

A psalm of •Asaph.

1 God has taken His place
in the divine assembly;
He judges among the gods:[d]
2 "How long will you judge unjustly
and show partiality to the wicked?
•*Selah*
3 Provide justice for the needy
and the fatherless;
uphold the rights of the oppressed
and the destitute.
4 Rescue the poor and needy;
save them from the hand
of the wicked."

5 They do not know or understand;
they wander in darkness.
All the foundations of the earth
are shaken.

6 I said, "You are gods;
you are all sons of the •Most High.
7 However, you will die like men
and fall like any other ruler."

8 Rise up, God, judge the earth,
for all the nations belong to You.

Psalm 83
Prayer against Enemies

A song. A psalm of •Asaph.

1 God, do not keep silent.
Do not be deaf, God; do not be idle.
2 See how Your enemies
make an uproar;
those who hate You
have acted arrogantly.[e]
3 They devise clever schemes
against Your people;
they conspire against
Your treasured ones.
4 They say, "Come, let us wipe them out
as a nation
so that Israel's name will no longer
be remembered."
5 For they have conspired with one mind;
they form an alliance[f] against You—
6 the tents of Edom and the Ishmaelites,

[a]**81:3** Either Passover or Tabernacles [b]**81:5** LXX, Syr, Jer read *out of* [c]**81:16** Lit *him* [d]**82:1** Either heavenly beings or earthly rulers [e]**83:2** Lit *have lifted their head* [f]**83:5** Lit *they cut a covenant*

Moab and the Hagrites,
7 Gebal, Ammon, and Amalek,
Philistia with the inhabitants of Tyre.
8 Even Assyria has joined them;
they lend support[a] to the sons of Lot.[b]
•*Selah*

9 Deal with them as ⌊You did⌋
with Midian,
as ⌊You did⌋ with Sisera
and Jabin at the Kishon River.
10 They were destroyed at En-dor;
they became manure for the ground.
11 Make their nobles like Oreb and Zeeb,
and all their tribal leaders like Zebah
and Zalmunna,
12 who said, "Let us seize God's pastures
for ourselves."

13 Make them like tumbleweed, my God,
like straw before the wind.
14 As fire burns a forest,
as a flame blazes through mountains,
15 so pursue them with Your tempest
and terrify them with Your storm.
16 Cover their faces with shame
so that they will seek
Your name, LORD.
17 Let them be put to shame
and terrified forever;
let them perish in disgrace.
18 May they know that You alone—
whose name is •Yahweh—
are the •Most High over all the earth.

Psalm 84
Longing for God's House

For the choir director: on the •*Gittith*. A psalm of the sons of Korah.

1 How lovely is Your dwelling place,
LORD of •Hosts.
2 I long and yearn
for the courts of the LORD;
my heart and flesh cry out for[c]
the living God.

3 Even a sparrow finds a home,
and a swallow, a nest for herself
where she places her young—
near Your altars, LORD of Hosts,
my King and my God.
4 How happy are those who reside
in Your house,
who praise You continually.•*Selah*

5 Happy are the people whose strength
is in You,
whose hearts are set on pilgrimage.
6 As they pass through the Valley
of Baca,[d]
they make it a source of springwater;
even the autumn rain will cover it
with blessings.[e]
7 They go from strength to strength;
each appears before God in Zion.

8 LORD God of Hosts, hear my prayer;
listen, God of Jacob. *Selah*
9 Consider our shield,[f] God;
look on the face of Your anointed one.

10 Better a day in Your courts
than a thousand ⌊anywhere else⌋.
I would rather be at the door
of the house of my God
than to live in the tents of the wicked.
11 For the LORD God is a sun and shield.
The LORD gives grace and glory;
He does not withhold the good
from those who live with integrity.
12 LORD of Hosts,
happy is the person who trusts in You!

Psalm 85
Restoration of Favor

For the choir director. A psalm of the sons of Korah.

1 LORD, You showed favor to Your land;
You restored Jacob's prosperity.[g]
2 You took away Your people's guilt;
You covered all their sin. •*Selah*
3 You withdrew all Your fury;
You turned from Your burning anger.

4 Return to us, God of our salvation,
and abandon Your displeasure with us.
5 Will You be angry with us forever?
Will You prolong Your anger for all
generations?
6 Will You not revive us again
so that Your people may rejoice in You?
7 Show us Your faithful love, LORD,
and give us Your salvation.

8 I will listen to what God will say;
surely the LORD will declare peace
to His people, His godly ones,
and not let them go back
to foolish ways.

[a]**83:8** Lit *they are an arm* [b]**83:8** Moab and Edom [c]**84:2** Or *flesh shout for joy to* [d]**84:6** Or *Valley of Tears* [e]**84:6** Or *pools* [f]**84:9** The king [g]**85:1** Or *restored Jacob from captivity*

9 His salvation is very near
those who fear Him,
so that glory may dwell in our land.
10 Faithful love and truth
will join together;
righteousness and peace
will embrace.
11 Truth will spring up
from the earth,
and righteousness will look
down from heaven.
12 Also, the LORD will provide
what is good,
and our land will yield its crops.
13 Righteousness will go before Him
to prepare the way for His steps.

Psalm 86

Lament and Petition

A Davidic prayer.

1 Listen, LORD, and answer me,
for I am poor and needy.
2 Protect my life, for I am faithful.
You are my God; save Your servant
who trusts in You.
3 Be gracious to me, Lord,
for I call to You all day long.
4 Bring joy to Your servant's life,
since I set my hope on You, Lord.
5 For You, Lord, are kind and ready
to forgive,
abundant in faithful love to all who call
on You.
6 LORD, hear my prayer;
listen to my plea for mercy.
7 I call on You in the day
of my distress,
for You will answer me.
8 Lord, there is no one like You
among the gods,
and there are no works
like Yours.
9 All the nations You have made
will come and bow down
before You, Lord,
and will honor Your name.
10 For You are great
and perform wonders;
You alone are God.
11 Teach me Your way, LORD,
and I will live by Your truth.
Give me an undivided mind to fear
Your name.
12 I will praise You with all my heart,
Lord my God,
and will honor Your name forever.
13 For Your faithful love for me
is great,
and You deliver my life
from the depths of •Sheol.
14 God, arrogant people
have attacked me;
a gang of ruthless men seeks
my life.
They have no regard for You.
15 But You, Lord, are a compassionate
and gracious God,
slow to anger and abundant
in faithful love and truth.
16 Turn to me and be gracious to me.
Give Your strength to Your servant;
save the son of Your female servant.
17 Show me a sign of Your goodness;
my enemies will see and be put
to shame
because You, LORD, have helped
and comforted me.

Psalm 87

Zion, the City of God

A psalm of the sons of Korah. A song.

1 His foundation is
on the holy mountains.
2 The LORD loves the gates of Zion
more than all the dwellings
of Jacob.[a]
3 Glorious things are said about you,
city of God. *•Selah*
4 "I will mention those
who know Me:
•Rahab, Babylon, Philistia, Tyre,
and •Cush[b] —
each one was born there."
5 And it will be said of Zion,
"This one and that one were born
in her."
The •Most High Himself will establish
her.
6 When He registers the peoples,
the LORD will record,
"This one was born there." *Selah*
7 Singers and dancers alike ⌊will say⌋,
"All my springs are in you."

[a]**87:2** Places in Israel [b]**87:4** Modern Sudan

*Psalm 88

A Cry of Desperation

A song. A psalm of the sons of Korah. For the choir director: according to *Mahalath Leannoth*. A •*Maskil* of Heman the Ezrahite.

1 LORD, God of my salvation,
I cry out before You day and night.
2 May my prayer reach Your presence;
listen to my cry.

3 For I have had enough troubles,
and my life is near •Sheol.
4 I am counted among those going down
to the •Pit.
I am like a man without strength,
5 abandoned[a] among the dead.
I am like the slain lying in the grave,
whom You no longer remember,
and who are cut off from Your care.[b]
6 You have put me in the lowest part
of the Pit,
in the darkest places, in the depths.
7 Your wrath weighs heavily on me;
You have overwhelmed me with all
Your waves. •*Selah*
8 You have distanced my friends
from me;
You have made me repulsive to them.
I am shut in and cannot go out.
9 My eyes are worn out from crying.
LORD, I cry out to You all day long;
I spread out my hands to You.

10 Do You work wonders for the dead?
Do departed spirits rise up
to praise You? *Selah*
11 Will Your faithful love be declared
in the grave,
Your faithfulness in •Abaddon?
12 Will Your wonders be known
in the darkness,
or Your righteousness in the land
of oblivion?

13 But I call to You for help, LORD;
in the morning my prayer meets You.
14 LORD, why do You reject me?
Why do You hide Your face from me?
15 From my youth,
I have been afflicted and near death.
I suffer Your horrors; I am desperate.
16 Your wrath sweeps over me;
Your terrors destroy me.
17 They surround me like water
all day long;
they close in on me from every side.
18 You have distanced loved one
and neighbor from me;
darkness is my ⌊only⌋ friend.[c]

Psalm 89

Perplexity about God's Promises

A •*Maskil* of Ethan the Ezrahite.

1 I will sing about the LORD's
faithful love forever;
with my mouth
I will proclaim Your faithfulness
to all generations.
2 For I will declare,
"Faithful love is built up forever;
You establish Your faithfulness
in the heavens."

3 ⌊The LORD said,⌋
"I have made a covenant
with My chosen one;
I have sworn an oath to David
My servant:
4 'I will establish your offspring forever
and build up your throne
for all generations.' " •*Selah*

5 LORD, the heavens praise
Your wonders—
Your faithfulness also—
in the assembly of the holy ones.
6 For who in the skies can compare
with the LORD?
Who among the heavenly beings[d] is
like the LORD?
7 God is greatly feared in the council
of the holy ones,
more awe-inspiring than[e]
all who surround Him.
8 LORD God of •Hosts,
who is strong like You, LORD?
Your faithfulness surrounds You.
9 You rule the raging sea;
when its waves surge, You still them.
10 You crushed •Rahab like one
who is slain;
You scattered Your enemies
with Your powerful arm.
11 The heavens are Yours; the earth also
is Yours.
The world and everything in it—
You founded them.

[a]**88:5** Or *set free* [b]**88:5** Or *hand* [c]**88:18** Or *from me, my friends. Oh darkness!* [d]**89:6** Or *the angels*, or *the sons of the mighty* [e]**89:7** Or *ones, revered by*

12 North and south—You created them.
Tabor and Hermon shout for joy
at Your name.
13 You have a mighty arm;
Your hand is powerful;
Your right hand is lifted high.
14 Righteousness and justice are
the foundation
of Your throne;
faithful love and truth go before You.
15 Happy are the people who know
the joyful shout;
LORD, they walk in the light
of Your presence.
16 They rejoice in Your name all day long,
and they are exalted
by Your righteousness.
17 For You are their magnificent strength;
by Your favor our •horn is exalted.
18 Surely our shield[a]
belongs to the LORD,
our king to the Holy One of Israel.

19 You once spoke in a vision
to Your loyal ones
and said: "I have granted help
to a warrior;
I have exalted one chosen[b]
from the people.
20 I have found David My servant;
I have anointed him
with My sacred oil.
21 My hand will always be with him,
and My arm will strengthen him.
22 The enemy will not afflict[c] him;
no wicked man will oppress him.
23 I will crush his foes before him
and strike those who hate him.
24 My faithfulness and love will be
with him,
and through My name
his horn will be exalted.
25 I will extend his power to the sea
and his right hand to the rivers.
26 He will call to Me, 'You are my Father,
my God, the rock of my salvation.'
27 I will also make him My firstborn,
greatest of the kings of the earth.
28 I will always preserve My faithful love
for him,
and My covenant with him
will endure.
29 I will establish his line forever,
his throne as long as heaven lasts.[d]
30 If his sons forsake My instruction
and do not live by My ordinances,
31 if they dishonor My statutes
and do not keep My commandments,
32 then I will call their rebellion
to account with the rod,
their sin with blows.
33 But I will not withdraw
My faithful love from him
or betray My faithfulness.
34 I will not violate My covenant
or change what My lips have said.
35 Once and for all
I have sworn an oath by My holiness;
I will not lie to David.
36 His offspring will continue forever,
his throne like the sun before Me,
37 like the moon, established forever,
a faithful witness in the sky." *Selah*

38 But You have spurned
and rejected him;
You have become enraged
with Your anointed.
39 You have repudiated the covenant
with Your servant;
You have completely dishonored
his crown.[e]
40 You have broken down all his walls;
You have reduced his fortified cities
to ruins.
41 All who pass by plunder him;
he has become a joke to his neighbors.
42 You have lifted high the right hand
of his foes;
You have made all his enemies rejoice.
43 You have also turned back
his sharp sword
and have not let him stand in battle.
44 You have made his splendor[f] cease
and have overturned his throne.
45 You have shortened the days
of his youth;
You have covered him with shame.
Selah

46 How long, LORD? Will You hide
Yourself forever?
Will Your anger keep burning like fire?
47 Remember how short my life is.
Have You created •everyone
for nothing?
48 What man can live
and never see death?

[a]**89:18** The king [b]**89:19** Or *exalted a young man* [c]**89:22** Or *not exact tribute from* [d]**89:29** Lit *as days of heaven*
[e]**89:39** Lit *have dishonored his crown to the ground* [f]**89:44** Hb obscure

Who can save himself from the power
of •Sheol? *Selah*
49 Lord, where are the former acts
of Your faithful love
that You swore to David
in Your faithfulness?
50 Remember, Lord, the ridicule
against Your servants—
in my heart I carry ⌊abuse⌋ from all
the peoples—
51 how Your enemies
have ridiculed, LORD,
how they have ridiculed every step
of Your anointed.

52 May the LORD be praised forever.
•Amen and amen.

BOOK IV

(Psalms 90–106)

Psalm 90

Eternal God and Mortal Man

A prayer of Moses the man of God.

1 Lord, You have been our refuge[a]
in every generation.
2 Before the mountains were born,
before You gave birth to the earth
and the world,
from eternity to eternity, You are God.

3 You return mankind to the dust,
saying, "Return, descendants of Adam."
4 For in Your sight a thousand years
are like yesterday that passes by,
like a few hours of the night.
5 You end their life;[b] they sleep.
They are like grass that grows
in the morning—
6 in the morning it sprouts and grows;
by evening it withers and dries up.

7 For we are consumed by Your anger;
we are terrified by Your wrath.
8 You have set our unjust ways
before You,
our secret sins in the light
of Your presence.
9 For all our days ebb away
under Your wrath;
we end our years like a sigh.
10 Our lives last[c] seventy years
or, if we are strong, eighty years.
Even the best of them are[d] struggle
and sorrow;
indeed, they pass quickly and we
fly away.
11 Who understands the power
of Your anger?
Your wrath matches the fear
that is due You.
12 Teach us to number our days carefully
so that we may develop wisdom
in our hearts.[e]

13 LORD—how long?
Turn and have compassion
on Your servants.
14 Satisfy us in the morning
with Your faithful love
so that we may shout with joy
and be glad all our days.
15 Make us rejoice for as many days
as You have humbled us,
for as many years as
we have seen adversity.
16 Let Your work be seen
by Your servants,
and Your splendor by their children.
17 Let the favor of the Lord our God be
on us;
establish for us the work
of our hands—
establish the work of our hands!

Psalm 91

The Protection of the Most High

1 The one who lives under the protection
of the •Most High
dwells in the shadow
of the •Almighty.

2 I will say[f] to the LORD, "My refuge
and my fortress,
my God, in whom I trust."

3 He Himself will deliver you
from the hunter's net,
from the destructive plague.
4 He will cover you with His feathers;
you will take refuge under His wings.
His faithfulness will be
a protective shield.
5 You will not fear the terror
of the night,
the arrow that flies by day,

[a]**90:1** A few Hb mss, LXX; MT reads *dwelling place* [b]**90:5** Or *You overwhelm them*; Hb uncertain [c]**90:10** Lit *The days of our years in them* [d]**90:10** LXX, Tg, Syr, Vg read *Even their span is*; Hb obscure [e]**90:12** Or *develop a heart of wisdom* [f]**91:1–2** LXX, Syr, Jer read *Almighty, saying*, or *Almighty, he will say*

6 the plague that stalks in darkness,
or the pestilence that ravages
at noon.
7 Though a thousand fall at your side
and ten thousand at your right hand,
the pestilence will not reach you.
8 You will only see it with your eyes
and witness the punishment
of the wicked.

9 Because you have made the LORD—
my refuge,
the Most High—your dwelling place,
10 no harm will come to you;
no plague will come near your tent.
11 For He will give His angels orders
concerning you,
to protect you in all your ways.
12 They will support you
with their hands
so that you will not strike your foot
against a stone.
13 You will tread on the lion
and the cobra;
you will trample the young lion
and the serpent.

14 Because he is lovingly devoted to Me,
I will deliver him;
I will exalt him because he knows
My name.
15 When he calls out to Me,
I will answer him;
I will be with him in trouble.
I will rescue him and give him honor.
16 I will satisfy him with a long life
and show him My salvation.

Psalm 92

God's Love and Faithfulness

A psalm. A song for the Sabbath day.

1 It is good to praise the LORD,
to sing praise to Your name,
•Most High,
2 to declare Your faithful love
in the morning
and Your faithfulness at night,
3 with a ten-stringed harp
and the music of a lyre.

4 For You have made me rejoice, LORD,
by what You have done;
I will shout for joy
because of the works of Your hands.
5 How magnificent are Your works,
LORD,
how profound Your thoughts!
6 A stupid person does not know,
a fool does not understand this:
7 though the wicked sprout like grass
and all evildoers flourish,
they will be eternally destroyed.
8 But You, LORD, are exalted forever.
9 For indeed, LORD, Your enemies—
indeed, Your enemies will perish;
all evildoers will be scattered.
10 You have lifted up my •horn
like that of a wild ox;
I have been anointed[a] with oil.
11 My eyes look down on my enemies;
my ears hear evildoers
when they attack me.

12 The righteous thrive like a palm tree
and grow like a cedar tree in Lebanon.
13 Planted in the house of the LORD,
they thrive in the courtyards
of our God.
14 They will still bear fruit in old age,
healthy and green,
15 to declare: "The LORD is just;
He is my rock,
and there is no unrighteousness
in Him."

Psalm 93

God's Eternal Reign

1 The LORD reigns! He is robed
in majesty;
The LORD is robed,
enveloped in strength.
The world is firmly established;
it cannot be shaken.
2 Your throne has been established
from the beginning;[b]
You are from eternity.
3 The floods have lifted up, LORD,
the floods have lifted up their voice;
the floods lift up
their pounding waves.
4 Greater than the roar of many waters—
the mighty breakers of the sea—
the LORD on high is majestic.

5 LORD, Your testimonies
are completely reliable;
holiness is the beauty of[c] Your house
for all the days to come.

[a]**92:10** Syr reads *You have anointed me* [b]**93:2** Lit *from then* [c]**93:5** Or *holiness characterizes*

Psalm 94

The Just Judge

1 LORD, God of vengeance—
God of vengeance, appear.
2 Rise up, Judge of the earth;
repay the proud what they deserve.
3 LORD, how long will the wicked—
how long will the wicked gloat?

4 They pour out arrogant words;
all the evildoers boast.
5 LORD, they crush Your people;
they afflict Your heritage.
6 They kill the widow
and the foreigner
and murder the fatherless.
7 They say, "The LORD
doesn't see it.
The God of Jacob
doesn't pay attention."

8 Pay attention, you stupid people!
Fools, when will you be wise?
9 Can the One who shaped the ear
not hear,
the One who formed the eye not see?
10 The One who instructs nations,
the One who teaches
man knowledge—
does He not discipline?
11 The LORD knows man's thoughts;
they are meaningless.[a]

12 LORD, happy is the man You discipline
and teach from Your law
13 to give him relief from troubled times
until a pit is dug for the wicked.
14 The LORD will not forsake His people
or abandon His heritage,
15 for justice will again be righteous,
and all the upright in heart will follow[b]
it.

16 Who stands up for me
against the wicked?
Who takes a stand for me
against evildoers?
17 If the LORD had not been my help,
I would soon rest in the silence
⌊of death⌋.
18 If I say, "My foot is slipping,"
Your faithful love
will support me, LORD.
19 When I am filled with cares,
Your comfort brings me joy.

20 Can a corrupt throne—
one that creates trouble by law—
become Your ally?
21 They band together against the life
of the righteous
and condemn the innocent to death.
22 But the LORD is my refuge;
my God is the rock of my protection.
23 He will pay them back for their sins
and destroy them for their evil.
The LORD our God will destroy them.

Psalm 95

Worship and Warning

1 Come, let us shout joyfully
to the LORD,
shout triumphantly to the rock
of our salvation!
2 Let us enter His presence
with thanksgiving;
let us shout triumphantly to Him
in song.

3 For the LORD is a great God,
a great King above all gods.
4 The depths of the earth are
in His hand,
and the mountain peaks are His.
5 The sea is His; He made it.
His hands formed the dry land.

6 Come, let us worship
and bow down;
let us kneel before the LORD
our Maker.
7 For He is our God,
and we are the people
of His pasture,
the sheep under His care.[c]

Today, if you hear His voice:
8 "Do not harden your hearts
as at Meribah,
as on that day at Massah
in the wilderness
9 where your fathers tested Me;
they tried Me, though they had seen
what I did.
10 For 40 years I was disgusted
with that generation;
I said, 'They are a people whose hearts
go astray;
they do not know My ways.'
11 So I swore in My anger,
'They will not enter My rest.'"

[a]**94:11** Or *futile* [b]**94:15** Or *heart will support*; lit *heart after* [c]**95:7** Lit *sheep of His hand*

Psalm 96
King of the Earth

1 Sing a new song to the LORD;
sing to the LORD, all the earth.
2 Sing to the LORD, praise His name;
proclaim His salvation from day to day.
3 Declare His glory among the nations,
His wonderful works among all peoples.

4 For the LORD is great and is
highly praised;
He is feared above all gods.
5 For all the gods of the peoples are idols,
but the LORD made the heavens.
6 Splendor and majesty are before Him;
strength and beauty are in His sanctuary.

7 Ascribe to the LORD, you families
of the peoples,
ascribe to the LORD glory and strength.
8 Ascribe to the LORD the glory
of His name;
bring an offering and enter His courts.
9 Worship the LORD in the splendor
of ⌊His⌋ holiness;
tremble before Him, all the earth.

10 Say among the nations:
"The LORD reigns.
The world is firmly established;
it cannot be shaken.
He judges the peoples fairly."
11 Let the heavens be glad
and the earth rejoice;
let the sea and all that fills it resound.
12 Let the fields and everything
in them exult.
Then all the trees of the forest
will shout for joy
13 before the LORD, for He is coming—
for He is coming to judge the earth.
He will judge the world
with righteousness
and the peoples with His faithfulness.

Psalm 97
The Majestic King

1 The LORD reigns! Let the earth rejoice;
let the many coasts and islands be glad.

2 Clouds and thick darkness surround
Him;
righteousness and justice are
the foundation of His throne.
3 Fire goes before Him
and burns up His foes
on every side.
4 His lightning lights up the world;
the earth sees and trembles.
5 The mountains melt like wax
at the presence of the LORD—
at the presence of the Lord of all
the earth.

6 The heavens proclaim
His righteousness;
all the peoples see His glory.

7 All who serve carved images,
those who boast in idols, will be
put to shame.
All the gods[a] must worship Him.

8 Zion hears and is glad,
and the towns[b] of Judah rejoice
because of Your judgments, LORD.
9 For You, LORD,
are the •Most High over
all the earth;
You are exalted above all the gods.

10 You who love the LORD, hate evil!
He protects the lives of His godly ones;
He rescues them from the hand
of the wicked.
11 Light dawns[c] [d] for the righteous,
gladness for the upright in heart.
12 Be glad in the LORD,
you righteous ones,
and praise His holy name.[e]

Psalm 98
Praise the King

A psalm.

1 Sing a new song to the LORD,
for He has performed wonders;
His right hand and holy arm
have won Him victory.
2 The LORD has made His victory
known;
He has revealed His righteousness
in the sight of the nations.
3 He has remembered His love
and faithfulness to the house of Israel;
all the ends of the earth
have seen our God's victory.

4 Shout to the LORD, all the earth;
be jubilant, shout for joy, and sing.

[a]**97:7** LXX, Syr read *All His angels*; Heb 1:6 [b]**97:8** Lit *daughters* [c]**97:11** One Hb ms, LXX, other versions read *rises to shine*; Ps 112:4 [d]**97:11** Lit *Light is sown* [e]**97:12** Lit *praise the mention*, or *memory, of His holiness*

5 Sing to the LORD with the lyre,
with the lyre and melodious song.
6 With trumpets and the blast
of the ram's horn
shout triumphantly
in the presence of the LORD,
our King.

7 Let the sea and all that fills it,
the world and those who live in it,
resound.
8 Let the rivers clap their hands;
let the mountains shout together
for joy
9 before the LORD,
for He is coming to judge the earth.
He will judge the world righteously
and the peoples fairly.

Psalm 99
The King Is Holy

1 The LORD reigns! Let
the peoples tremble.
He is enthroned above the •cherubim.
Let the earth quake.
2 The LORD is great in Zion;
He is exalted above all the peoples.
3 Let them praise Your great
and awe-inspiring name.
He is holy.

4 The mighty King loves justice.
You have established fairness;
You have administered justice
and righteousness in Jacob.
5 Exalt the LORD our God;
bow in worship at His footstool.
He is holy.

6 Moses and Aaron were
among His priests;
Samuel also was among
those calling on His name.
They called to the LORD,
and He answered them.
7 He spoke to them in a pillar of cloud;
they kept His decrees and the statutes
He gave them.
8 LORD our God, You answered them.
You were a God who forgave them,
but punished[a] their misdeeds.[b]

9 Exalt the LORD our God;
bow in worship at His holy mountain,
for the LORD our God is holy.

Psalm 100
Be Thankful

A psalm of thanksgiving.

1 Shout triumphantly to the LORD,
all the earth.
2 Serve the LORD with gladness;
come before Him with joyful songs.
3 Acknowledge that the LORD is God.
He made us, and we are His[c] —
His people, the sheep of His pasture.
4 Enter His gates with thanksgiving
and His courts with praise.
Give thanks to Him and praise
His name.
5 For the LORD is good, and His love
is eternal;
His faithfulness endures
through all generations.

Psalm 101
A Vow of Integrity

A Davidic psalm.

1 I will sing of faithful love and justice;
I will sing praise to You, LORD.
2 I will pay attention to the way
of integrity.
When will You come to me?
I will live with integrity of heart
in my house.
3 I will not set anything godless
before my eyes.
I hate the doing of transgression;
it will not cling to me.
4 A devious heart will be far from me;
I will not be involved with[d] evil.

5 I will destroy anyone
who secretly slanders his neighbor;
I cannot tolerate anyone
with haughty eyes
or an arrogant heart.
6 My eyes ⌊favor⌋ the faithful of the land
so that they may sit down with me.
The one who follows the way
of integrity
may serve me.
7 No one who acts deceitfully
will live in my palace;
no one who tells lies
will remain in my presence.[e]
8 Every morning I will destroy
all the wicked of the land,

[a]**99:8** Lit *avenged* [b]**99:8** Or *but avenged misdeeds done against them* [c]**100:3** Alt Hb tradition, other Hb mss, LXX, Syr, Vg read *and not we ourselves* [d]**101:4** Lit *not know* [e]**101:7** Lit *in front of my eyes*

eliminating all evildoers
from the LORD's city.

Psalm 102
Affliction in Light of Eternity

A prayer of an afflicted person who is weak and pours out his lament before the LORD.

1 LORD, hear my prayer;
let my cry for help come before You.
2 Do not hide Your face from me
in my day of trouble.
Listen closely to me;
answer me quickly when I call.

3 For my days vanish like smoke,
and my bones burn like a furnace.
4 My heart is afflicted,
withered like grass;
I even forget to eat my food.
5 Because of the sound of my groaning,
my flesh sticks to my bones.
6 I am like a desert owl,[a]
like an owl among the ruins.
7 I stay awake;
I am like a solitary bird on a roof.
8 My enemies taunt me all day long;
they ridicule and curse me.
9 I eat ashes like bread
and mingle my drinks with tears
10 because of Your indignation and wrath;
for You have picked me up
and thrown me aside.
11 My days are like a lengthening shadow,
and I wither away like grass.

12 But You, LORD, are enthroned forever;
Your fame ⌊endures⌋ to all generations.
13 You will arise and have compassion
on Zion,
for it is time to show favor to her—
the appointed time has come.
14 For Your servants take delight
in its stones
and favor its dust.

15 Then the nations will fear the name
of the LORD,
and all the kings of the earth
Your glory,
16 for the LORD will rebuild Zion;
He will appear in His glory.
17 He will pay attention to the prayer
of the destitute
and will not despise their prayer.
18 This will be written
for a later generation,
and a newly created people will praise
the LORD:
19 He looked down from
His holy heights—
the LORD gazed out from heaven
to earth—
20 to hear a prisoner's groaning,
to set free those condemned to die,[b]
21 so that they might declare
the name of the LORD in Zion
and His praise in Jerusalem,
22 when peoples and kingdoms
are assembled
to serve the LORD.

23 He has broken my[c] strength
in midcourse;
He has shortened my days.
24 I say: "My God, do not take me
in the middle of my life![d]
Your years continue
through all generations.
25 Long ago You established the earth,
and the heavens are the work
of Your hands.
26 They will perish, but You will endure;
all of them will wear out like clothing.
You will change them like a garment,
and they will pass away.
27 But You are the same,
and Your years will never end.
28 Your servants' children
will dwell ⌊securely⌋,
and their offspring will be established
before You."

Psalm 103
The Forgiving God

Davidic.

1 My soul, praise the LORD,
and all that is within me, praise
His holy name.
2 My soul, praise the LORD,
and do not forget all His benefits.

3 He forgives all your sin;
He heals all your diseases.
4 He redeems your life from the •Pit;
He crowns you with faithful love
and compassion.
5 He satisfies you[e] with goodness;
your youth is renewed like the eagle.

[a]**102:6** Or *a pelican of the desert* [b]**102:20** Lit *free sons of death* [c]**102:23** Other Hb mss, LXX read *His* [d]**102:24** Lit *my days* [e]**103:5** Lit *satisfies your ornament*; Hb obscure

6 The LORD executes acts
of righteousness
and justice for all the oppressed.
7 He revealed His ways to Moses,
His deeds to the people of Israel.
8 The LORD is compassionate
and gracious,
slow to anger and full of faithful love.
9 He will not always accuse ⌊us⌋
or be angry forever.
10 He has not dealt with us as
our sins deserve
or repaid us according to our offenses.

11 For as high as the heavens are above
the earth,
so great is His faithful love
toward those who fear Him.
12 As far as the east is from the west,
so far has He removed
our transgressions from us.
13 As a father has compassion
on his children,
so the LORD has compassion on those
who fear Him.
14 For He knows what we are made of,
remembering that we are dust.

15 As for man, his days are like grass—
he blooms like a flower of the field;
16 when the wind passes over it,
it vanishes,
and its place is no longer known.[a]
17 But from eternity to eternity
the LORD's faithful love is toward
those who fear Him,
and His righteousness
toward the grandchildren
18 of those who keep His covenant,
who remember to observe
His instructions.
19 The LORD has established His throne
in heaven,
and His kingdom rules over all.

20 Praise the LORD,
⌊all⌋ His angels of great strength,
who do His word,
obedient to His command.
21 Praise the LORD, all His armies,
His servants who do His will.
22 Praise the LORD, all His works
in all the places where He rules.
My soul, praise the LORD!

Psalm 104
God the Creator

1 My soul, praise the LORD!
LORD my God, You are very great;
You are clothed with majesty
and splendor.
2 He wraps Himself in light as if it were
a robe,
spreading out the sky like a canopy,
3 laying the beams of His palace
on the waters ⌊above⌋,
making the clouds His chariot,
walking on the wings of the wind,
4 and making the winds
His messengers,[b]
flames of fire His servants.

5 He established the earth
on its foundations;
it will never be shaken.
6 You covered it with the deep
as if it were a garment;
the waters stood above the mountains.
7 At Your rebuke the waters fled;
at the sound of Your thunder
they hurried away—
8 mountains rose and valleys sank[c] —
to the place You established for them.
9 You set a boundary they cannot cross;
they will never cover the earth again.

10 He causes the springs to gush
into the valleys;
they flow between the mountains.
11 They supply water
for every wild beast;
the wild donkeys quench their thirst.
12 The birds of the sky live
beside ⌊the springs⌋;
they sing among the foliage.
13 He waters the mountains
from His palace;
the earth is satisfied by the fruit
of Your labor.

14 He causes grass to grow
for the livestock
and ⌊provides⌋ crops for man
to cultivate,
producing food from the earth,
15 wine that makes man's heart glad—
making his face shine with oil—
and bread that sustains man's heart.

[a]**103:16** Lit *place no longer knows it* [b]**104:4** Or *angels* [c]**104:7–8** Or *away. They flowed over the mountains and went down valleys*

16 The trees of the LORD flourish,[a]
the cedars of Lebanon that He planted.
17 There the birds make their nests;
the stork makes its home
in the pine trees.
18 The high mountains are
for the wild goats;
the cliffs are a refuge for hyraxes.

19 He made the moon to mark
the[b] seasons;
the sun knows when to set.
20 You bring darkness,
and it becomes night,
when all the forest animals stir.
21 The young lions roar for their prey
and seek their food from God.
22 The sun rises; they go back
and lie down in their dens.
23 Man goes out to his work
and to his labor until evening.

24 How countless are Your works, LORD!
In wisdom You have made them all;
the earth is full of Your creatures.[c]
25 Here is the sea, vast and wide,
teeming with creatures
beyond number—
living things both large and small.
26 There the ships move about,
and •Leviathan, which You formed
to play there.

27 All of them wait for You
to give them their food
at the right time.
28 When You give it to them,
they gather it;
when You open Your hand,
they are satisfied with good things.
29 When You hide Your face,
they are terrified;
when You take away their breath,
they die and return to the dust.
30 When You send Your breath,[d]
they are created,
and You renew the face of the earth.

31 May the glory of the LORD
endure forever;
may the LORD rejoice in His works.
32 He looks at the earth, and it trembles;
He touches the mountains,
and they pour out smoke.
33 I will sing to the LORD all my life;
I will sing praise to my God
while I live.
34 May my meditation be pleasing
to Him;
I will rejoice in the LORD.
35 May sinners vanish from the earth
and the wicked be no more.
My soul, praise the LORD!
•Hallelujah!

Psalm 105

God's Faithfulness to His People

1 Give thanks to the LORD, call on
His name;
proclaim His deeds among the peoples.
2 Sing to Him, sing praise to Him;
tell about all His wonderful works!
3 Honor His holy name;
let the hearts of those who seek
the LORD rejoice.
4 Search for the LORD and for His strength;
seek His face always.
5 Remember the wonderful works
He has done,
His wonders, and the judgments
He has pronounced,[e]
6 you offspring of Abraham His servant,
Jacob's descendants—His chosen ones.

7 He is the LORD our God;
His judgments ⌊govern⌋
the whole earth.
8 He forever remembers His covenant,
the promise He ordained
for a thousand generations—
9 ⌊the covenant⌋ He made with Abraham,
swore[f] to Isaac,
10 and confirmed to Jacob as a decree
and to Israel as an everlasting covenant:
11 "I will give the land of Canaan to you
as your inherited portion."

12 When they were few in number,
very few indeed,
and temporary residents in Canaan,
13 wandering from nation to nation
and from one kingdom to another,
14 He allowed no one to oppress them;
He rebuked kings on their behalf:
15 "Do not touch My anointed ones,
or harm My prophets."

16 He called down famine against the land
and destroyed the entire food supply.

[a]**104:16** Lit *are satisfied* [b]**104:19** Lit *moon for* [c]**104:24** Lit *possessions* [d]**104:30** Or *Spirit* [e]**105:5** Lit *judgments of His mouth* [f]**105:9** Lit *and His oath*

17 He had sent a man ahead of them—
Joseph, who was sold as a slave.
18 They hurt his feet with shackles;
his neck was put in an iron collar.
19 Until the time his prediction
came true,
the word of the LORD tested him.
20 The king sent ⌊for him⌋
and released him;
the ruler of peoples set him free.
21 He made him master of his household,
ruler over all his possessions—
22 binding[a] his officials at will
and instructing his elders.

23 Then Israel went to Egypt;
Jacob lived as a foreigner in the land
of Ham.[b]
24 The LORD[c] made His people
very fruitful;
He made them more numerous
than their foes,
25 whose hearts He turned to hate
His people
and to deal deceptively
with His servants.
26 He sent Moses His servant,
and Aaron, whom He had chosen.
27 They performed His miraculous signs
among them,
and wonders in the land of Ham.[b]
28 He sent darkness, and it became dark—
for did they[d] not defy His commands?
29 He turned their waters into blood
and caused their fish to die.
30 Their land was overrun with frogs,
even in their kings' chambers.
31 He spoke, and insects came—
gnats throughout their country.
32 He gave them hail for rain,
and lightning throughout their land.
33 He struck their vines and fig trees
and shattered the trees
of their territory.
34 He spoke and locusts came—
young locusts without number.
35 They devoured all the vegetation
in their land
and consumed the produce
of their soil.
36 He struck all the firstborn
in their land,
all their first progeny.
37 Then He brought Israel out with silver
and gold,
and no one among
His tribes stumbled.
38 Egypt was glad when they left,
for dread of Israel[e] had fallen on them.
39 He spread a cloud as a covering
and ⌊gave⌋ a fire to light up the night.
40 They asked, and He brought quail
and satisfied them with bread
from heaven.
41 He opened a rock, and water
gushed out;
it flowed like a stream in the desert.
42 For He remembered His holy promise
to Abraham His servant.
43 He brought His people out
with rejoicing,
His chosen ones with shouts of joy.
44 He gave them the lands of the nations,
and they inherited
what other peoples had worked for.

45 ⌊All this happened⌋
so that they might keep His statutes
and obey His laws.
•Hallelujah!

Psalm 106

Israel's Unfaithfulness to God

1 •Hallelujah!
Give thanks to the LORD,
for He is good;
His faithful love endures forever.
2 Who can declare the LORD's mighty acts
or proclaim all the praise due Him?
3 How happy are those
who uphold justice,
who practice righteousness at all times.

4 Remember me, LORD,
when You show favor to Your people.
Come to me with Your salvation
5 so that I may enjoy the prosperity
of Your chosen ones,
rejoice in the joy of Your nation,
and boast about Your heritage.

6 Both we and our fathers have sinned;
we have gone astray
and have acted wickedly.
7 Our fathers in Egypt did not grasp
⌊the significance of⌋
Your wonderful works

[a]**105:22** LXX, Syr, Vg read *teaching* [b]**105:23,27** Egypt [c]**105:24** Lit *He* [d]**105:28** LXX, Syr read *for they did . . .* (as a statement) [e]**105:38** Lit *them*

or remember Your many acts
of faithful love;
instead, they rebelled by the sea—
the •Red Sea.
8 Yet He saved them
because of His name,
to make His power known.
9 He rebuked the Red Sea,
and it dried up;
He led them through the depths
as through a desert.
10 He saved them from the hand
of the adversary;
He redeemed them from the hand
of the enemy.
11 Water covered their foes;
not one of them remained.
12 Then they believed His promises
and sang His praise.

13 They soon forgot His works
and would not wait for His counsel.
14 They were seized with craving
in the wilderness
and tested God in the desert.
15 He gave them what they asked for,
but sent a wasting disease among them.

16 In the camp they were envious of Moses
and of Aaron, the LORD's holy one.
17 The earth opened up
and swallowed Dathan;
it covered the assembly of Abiram.
18 Fire blazed throughout their assembly;
flames consumed the wicked.

19 At Horeb they made a calf
and worshiped the cast metal image.
20 They exchanged their glory[a]
for the image of a grass-eating ox.
21 They forgot God their Savior,
who did great things in Egypt,
22 wonderful works in the land of Ham,[b]
awe-inspiring deeds at the Red Sea.
23 So He said
He would have destroyed them—
if Moses His chosen one
had not stood before Him in the breach
to turn His wrath away
from destroying ⌊them⌋.

24 They despised the pleasant land
and did not believe His promise.
25 They grumbled in their tents
and did not listen to the LORD's voice.
26 So He raised His hand against them
⌊with an oath⌋
that He would make them fall
in the desert
27 and would disperse
their descendants[c]
among the nations,
scattering them throughout the lands.

28 They aligned themselves with •Baal
of Peor
and ate sacrifices offered
to lifeless gods.[d]
29 They provoked the LORD
with their deeds,
and a plague broke out against them.
30 But Phinehas stood up and intervened,
and the plague was stopped.
31 It was credited to him as righteousness
throughout all generations to come.

32 They angered ⌊the LORD⌋ at the waters
of Meribah,
and Moses suffered[e]
because of them;
33 for they embittered his spirit,[f]
and he spoke rashly with his lips.

34 They did not destroy the peoples
as the LORD had commanded them,
35 but mingled with the nations
and adopted their ways.
36 They served their idols,
which became a snare to them.
37 They sacrificed their sons
and daughters to demons.
38 They shed innocent blood—
the blood of their sons and daughters
whom they sacrificed to the idols
of Canaan;
so the land became polluted
with blood.
39 They defiled themselves
by their actions
and prostituted themselves
by their deeds.

40 Therefore the LORD's anger burned
against His people,
and He abhorred His own inheritance.
41 He handed them over to the nations;
those who hated them ruled them.
42 Their enemies oppressed them,

[a]**106:20** = God [b]**106:22** Egypt [c]**106:27** Syr; MT reads *would make their descendants fall* [d]**106:28** Lit *sacrifices for dead ones* [e]**106:32** Lit *and it was evil for Moses* [f]**106:33** Some Hb mss, LXX, Syr, Jer; other Hb mss read *they rebelled against His Spirit*

and they were subdued
under their power.
43 He rescued them many times,
but they continued
to rebel deliberately
and were beaten down by their sin.

44 When He heard their cry,
He took note of their distress,
45 remembered His covenant with them,
and relented according to
the abundance
of His faithful love.
46 He caused them to be pitied
before all their captors.

47 Save us, LORD our God,
and gather us from the nations,
so that we may give thanks
to Your holy name
and rejoice in Your praise.

48 May the LORD, the God of Israel,
be praised
from everlasting to everlasting.
Let all the people say, "•Amen!"
Hallelujah!

BOOK V

(Psalms 107–150)

Psalm 107

Thanksgiving for God's Deliverance

1 Give thanks to the LORD,
for He is good;
His faithful love endures forever.
2 Let the redeemed
of the LORD proclaim
that He has redeemed them
from the hand of the foe
3 and has gathered them
from the lands—
from the east and the west,
from the north and the south.

4 Some[a] wandered
in the desolate wilderness,
finding no way to a city
where they could live.
5 They were hungry and thirsty;
their spirits failed[b] within them.
6 Then they cried out to the LORD
in their trouble;
He rescued them from their distress.
7 He led them by the right path
to go to a city where they could live.
8 Let them give thanks to the LORD
for His faithful love
and His wonderful works
for the •human race.
9 For He has satisfied the thirsty
and filled the hungry with good things.

10 Others[a] sat in darkness and gloom[c]—
prisoners in cruel chains—
11 because they rebelled
against God's commands
and despised the counsel
of the •Most High.
12 He broke their spirits[d]
with hard labor;
they stumbled, and there was no one
to help.
13 Then they cried out to the LORD
in their trouble;
He saved them from their distress.
14 He brought them out of darkness
and gloom[c]
and broke their chains apart.
15 Let them give thanks to the LORD
for His faithful love
and His wonderful works
for the human race.
16 For He has broken down
the bronze gates
and cut through the iron bars.

17 Fools suffered affliction
because of their rebellious ways
and their sins.
18 They loathed all food
and came near the gates of death.
19 Then they cried out to the LORD
in their trouble;
He saved them from their distress.
20 He sent His word and healed them;
He rescued them from the •Pit.
21 Let them give thanks to the LORD
for His faithful love
and His wonderful works
for the human race.
22 Let them offer sacrifices
of thanksgiving
and announce His works with shouts
of joy.

23 Others[a] went to sea in ships,
conducting trade on the vast waters.
24 They saw the LORD's works,
His wonderful works in the deep.

[a]**107:4,10,23** Lit *They* [b]**107:5** Lit *their soul fainted* [c]**107:10,14** Or *the shadow of death* [d]**107:12** Lit *hearts*

25 He spoke and raised a tempest
that stirred up the waves of the sea.[a]
26 Rising up to the sky, sinking down
to the depths,
their courage[b] melting away
in anguish,
27 they reeled and staggered
like drunken men,
and all their skill was useless.
28 Then they cried out to the LORD
in their trouble,
and He brought them
out of their distress.
29 He stilled the storm to a murmur,
and the waves of the sea[c]
were hushed.
30 They rejoiced when the waves[d]
grew quiet.
Then He guided them to the harbor
they longed for.
31 Let them give thanks to the LORD
for His faithful love
and His wonderful works
for the human race.
32 Let them exalt Him in the assembly
of the people
and praise Him in the council
of the elders.

33 He turns rivers into desert,
springs of water into thirsty ground,
34 and fruitful land
into salty wasteland,
because of the wickedness
of its inhabitants.
35 He turns a desert into a pool of water,
dry land into springs of water.
36 He causes the hungry to settle there,
and they establish a city
where they can live.
37 They sow fields and plant vineyards
that yield a fruitful harvest.
38 He blesses them,
and they multiply greatly;
He does not let
their livestock decrease.

39 When they are diminished
and are humbled
by cruel oppression and sorrow,
40 He pours contempt on nobles
and makes them wander in trackless
wastelands.
41 But He lifts the needy out of
their suffering
and makes their families ⌊multiply⌋
like flocks.
42 The upright see it and rejoice,
and all injustice shuts its mouth.

43 Let whoever is wise pay attention
to these things
and consider[e] the LORD's acts
of faithful love.

Psalm 108
A Plea for Victory

A song. A Davidic psalm.

1 My heart is confident, God;[f]
I will sing; I will sing praises
with the whole of my being.[g]
2 Wake up, harp and lyre!
I will wake up the dawn.
3 I will praise You, LORD,
among the peoples;
I will sing praises to You
among the nations.
4 For Your faithful love is higher
than the heavens;
Your faithfulness reaches the clouds.
5 God, be exalted above the heavens;
let Your glory be over
the whole earth.
6 Save with Your right hand
and answer me
so that those You love may be rescued.

7 God has spoken in His sanctuary:[h]
"I will triumph!
I will divide up Shechem.
I will apportion the Valley of Succoth.
8 Gilead is Mine, Manasseh is Mine,
and Ephraim is My helmet;
Judah is My scepter.
9 Moab is My washbasin;
on Edom I throw My sandal.
Over Philistia I shout in triumph."

10 Who will bring me to the fortified city?
Who will lead me to Edom?
11 Have You not rejected us, God?
God, You do not march out
with our armies.
12 Give us aid against the foe,
for human help is worthless.
13 With God we will perform valiantly;
He will trample our foes.

[a]**107:25** Lit *of it* [b]**107:26** Lit *souls* [c]**107:29** Lit *of them* [d]**107:30** Lit *when they* [e]**107:43** Lit *and let them consider* [f]**108:1** Some Hb mss, LXX, Syr add *my heart is confident*; Ps 57:7 [g]**108:1** Lit *praises, even my glory* [h]**108:7** Or *has promised by His holy nature*

Psalm 109

Prayer against an Enemy

For the choir director. A Davidic psalm.

1 God of my praise, do not be silent.
2 For wicked and deceitful mouths open
against me;
they speak against me
with lying tongues.
3 They surround me
with hateful words
and attack me without cause.
4 In return for my love
they accuse me,
but I continue to pray.[a]
5 They repay me evil for good,
and hatred for my love.

6 Set a wicked person over him;
let an accuser[b] stand
at his right hand.
7 When he is judged, let him
be found guilty,
and let his prayer be counted as sin.
8 Let his days be few;
let another take over his position.
9 Let his children be fatherless
and his wife a widow.
10 Let his children wander as beggars,
searching ⌊for food⌋ far[c]
from their demolished homes.
11 Let a creditor seize all he has;
let strangers plunder what he has
worked for.
12 Let no one show him kindness,
and let no one be gracious
to his fatherless children.
13 Let the line of his descendants
be cut off;
let their name be blotted out
in the next generation.
14 Let his forefathers' guilt
be remembered before the LORD,
and do not let his mother's sin
be blotted out.
15 Let their sins[d] always remain
before the LORD,
and let Him cut off ⌊all⌋ memory
of them from the earth.

16 For he did not think to show kindness,
but pursued the wretched poor
and the brokenhearted
in order to put them to death.
17 He loved cursing—
let it fall on him;
he took no delight in blessing—
let it be far from him.
18 He wore cursing like his coat—
let it enter his body like water
and go into his bones like oil.
19 Let it be like a robe he wraps
around himself,
like a belt he always wears.
20 Let this be the LORD's payment
to my accusers,
to those who speak evil
against me.

21 But You, GOD my Lord,
deal ⌊kindly⌋ with me
because of Your name;
deliver me because of the goodness
of Your faithful love.
22 For I am poor and needy;
my heart is wounded within me.
23 I fade away
like a lengthening shadow;
I am shaken off like a locust.
24 My knees are weak from fasting,
and my body is emaciated.[e]
25 I have become an object of ridicule
to my accusers;[f]
when they see me, they shake
their heads ⌊in scorn⌋.

26 Help me, LORD my God;
save me according to
Your faithful love
27 so they may know that this is
Your hand
and that You, LORD, have done it.
28 Though they curse, You will bless.
When they rise up, they will be
put to shame,
but Your servant will rejoice.
29 My accusers will be clothed
with disgrace;
they will wear their shame
like a cloak.
30 I will fervently thank the LORD
with my mouth;
I will praise Him in the presence
of many.
31 For He stands at the right hand
of the needy,
to save him from those who would
condemn him.

[a]**109:4** Lit *but I, prayer* [b]**109:6** Or *adversary* [c]**109:10** LXX reads *beggars, driven far* [d]**109:15** Lit *Let them* [e]**109:24** Lit *denied from fat* [f]**109:25** Lit *to them*

Psalm 110
The Priestly King

A Davidic psalm.

1 The LORD declared to my Lord:
"Sit at My right hand
until I make Your enemies
Your footstool."
2 The LORD will extend
Your mighty scepter from Zion.
Rule[a] over Your surrounding[b] enemies.
3 Your people will volunteer
on Your day of battle.[c]
In holy splendor, from the womb
of the dawn,
the dew
of Your youth belongs to You.[d]
4 The LORD has sworn an oath
and will not take it back:
"Forever, You are a priest
like Melchizedek."

5 The Lord is at Your right hand;
He will crush kings on the day
of His anger.
6 He will judge the nations,
heaping up corpses;
He will crush leaders
over the entire world.
7 He will drink from the brook
by the road;
therefore, He will lift up His head.

Psalm 111
Praise for the LORD's Works

1 •Hallelujah![e]
I will praise the LORD with all my heart
in the assembly of the upright
and in the congregation.

2 The LORD's works are great,
studied by all who delight in them.
3 All that He does is splendid
and majestic;
His righteousness endures forever.
4 He has caused His wonderful works
to be remembered.
The LORD is gracious
and compassionate.
5 He has provided food for those
who fear Him;
He remembers His covenant forever.
6 He has shown His people the power
of His works
by giving them the inheritance
of the nations.
7 The works of His hands are truth
and justice;
all His instructions are trustworthy.
8 They are established forever and ever,
enacted in truth and uprightness.
9 He has sent redemption to His people.
He has ordained His covenant forever.
His name is holy and awe-inspiring.

10 The •fear of the LORD is the beginning
of wisdom;
all who follow His instructions[f] have
good insight.
His praise endures forever.

Psalm 112
The Traits of the Righteous

1 •Hallelujah![e]
Happy is the man who •fears
the LORD,
taking great delight
in His commandments.

2 His descendants will be powerful
in the land;
the generation of the upright
will be blessed.
3 Wealth and riches are in his house,
and his righteousness endures forever.
4 Light shines in the darkness
for the upright.
He is gracious, compassionate,
and righteous.
5 Good will come to a man
who lends generously
and conducts his business fairly.
6 He will never be shaken.
The righteous will be
remembered forever.
7 He will not fear bad news;
his heart is confident,
trusting in the LORD.
8 His heart is assured; he will not fear.
In the end he will look in triumph
on his foes.
9 He distributes freely to the poor;
his righteousness endures forever.
His •horn will be exalted in honor.

10 The wicked man will see ⌊it⌋
and be angry;
he will gnash his teeth in despair.

[a]**110:2** One Hb ms, LXX, Tg read *You will rule* [b]**110:2** Lit *Rule in the midst of Your* [c]**110:3** Lit *power* [d]**110:3** Hb obscure
[e]**111:1; 112:1** The lines of this poem form an •acrostic. [f]**111:10** Lit *follow them*

The desire of the wicked will come
to nothing.

Psalm 113

Praise to the Merciful God

1 •Hallelujah!
Give praise, servants of the LORD;
praise the name of the LORD.
2 Let the name of the LORD be praised
both now and forever.
3 From the rising of the sun
to its setting,
let the name of the LORD be praised.

4 The LORD is exalted above
all the nations,
His glory above the heavens.
5 Who is like the LORD our God—
the One enthroned on high,
6 who stoops down to look
on the heavens and the earth?
7 He raises the poor from the dust
and lifts the needy from the garbage pile
8 in order to seat them with nobles—
with the nobles of His people.
9 He gives the childless woman
a household,
⌊making her⌋ the joyful mother
of children.
Hallelujah!

Psalm 114

God's Deliverance of Israel

1 When Israel came out of Egypt—
the house of Jacob from a people
who spoke a foreign language—
2 Judah became His sanctuary,
Israel, His dominion.

3 The sea looked and fled;
the Jordan turned back.
4 The mountains skipped like rams,
the hills, like lambs.
5 Why was it, sea, that you fled?
Jordan, that you turned back?
6 Mountains, that you skipped like rams?
Hills, like lambs?

7 Tremble, earth, at the presence
of the Lord,
at the presence of the God of Jacob,
8 who turned the rock into a pool
of water,
the flint into a spring of water.

Psalm 115

Glory to God Alone

1 Not to us, LORD, not to us,
but to Your name give glory
because of Your faithful love,
because of Your truth.
2 Why should the nations say,
"Where is their God?"
3 Our God is in heaven
and does whatever He pleases.

4 Their idols are silver and gold,
made by human hands.
5 They have mouths, but cannot speak,
eyes, but cannot see.
6 They have ears, but cannot hear,
noses, but cannot smell.
7 They have hands, but cannot feel,
feet, but cannot walk.
They cannot make a sound
with their throats.
8 Those who make them are[a] just
like them,
as are all who trust in them.

9 Israel,[b] trust in the LORD!
He is their help and shield.
10 House of Aaron, trust in the LORD!
He is their help and shield.
11 You who •fear the LORD,
trust in the LORD!
He is their help and shield.
12 The LORD remembers us
and will bless ⌊us⌋.
He will bless the house of Israel;
He will bless the house of Aaron;
13 He will bless those who fear
the LORD—
small and great alike.

14 May the LORD add to ⌊your numbers⌋,
both yours and your children's.
15 May you be blessed by the LORD,
the Maker of heaven and earth.
16 The heavens are the LORD's,[c]
but the earth He has given
to the •human race.
17 It is not the dead who praise the LORD,
nor any of those descending
into the silence ⌊of death⌋.
18 But we will praise the LORD,
both now and forever.
•Hallelujah!

[a]**115:8** Or *May those who make them become* [b]**115:9** Other Hb mss, LXX, Syr read *House of Israel* [c]**115:16** Lit *LORD's heavens*

Psalm 116

Thanks to God for Deliverance

1 I love the LORD because He has heard
my appeal for mercy.
2 Because He has turned His ear to me,
I will call ⌊out to Him⌋ as long as I live.

3 The ropes of death were wrapped
around me,
and the torments of •Sheol
overcame me;
I encountered trouble and sorrow.
4 Then I called on the name
of the LORD:
"LORD, save me!"

5 The LORD is gracious and righteous;
our God is compassionate.
6 The LORD guards the inexperienced;
I was helpless, and He saved me.
7 Return to your rest, my soul,
for the LORD has been good to you.
8 For You, ⌊LORD,⌋ rescued me
from death,
my eyes from tears,
my feet from stumbling.
9 I will walk before the LORD
in the land of the living.
10 I believed, even when I said,
"I am severely afflicted."
11 In my alarm I said,
"Everyone is a liar."

12 How can I repay the LORD
all the good He has done for me?
13 I will take the cup of salvation
and worship[a] the LORD.
14 I will fulfill my vows to the LORD
in the presence of all His people.

15 The death of His faithful ones
is valuable in the LORD's sight.
16 LORD, I am indeed Your servant;
I am Your servant, the son
of Your female servant.
You have loosened my bonds.

17 I will offer You a sacrifice
of thanksgiving
and will worship[a] the LORD.
18 I will fulfill my vows to the LORD,
in the very presence of all His people,
19 in the courts of the LORD's house—
within you, Jerusalem.
•Hallelujah!

Psalm 117

Universal Call to Praise

1 Praise the LORD, all nations!
Glorify Him, all peoples!
2 For great is His faithful love to us;
the LORD's faithfulness
endures forever.
•Hallelujah!

Psalm 118

Thanksgiving for Victory

1 Give thanks to the LORD,
for He is good;
His faithful love endures forever.
2 Let Israel say,
"His faithful love endures forever."
3 Let the house of Aaron say,
"His faithful love endures forever."
4 Let those who fear the LORD say,
"His faithful love endures forever."

5 I called to the LORD in distress;
the LORD answered me
⌊and put me⌋ in a spacious place.[b]
6 The LORD is for me;
I will not be afraid.
What can man do to me?
7 With the LORD for me as my helper,
I will look in triumph on those
who hate me.

8 It is better to take refuge in the LORD
than to trust in man.
9 It is better to take refuge
in the LORD
than to trust in nobles.

10 All the nations surrounded me;
in the name of the LORD
I destroyed them.
11 They surrounded me, yes,
they surrounded me;
in the name of the LORD
I destroyed them.
12 They surrounded me like bees;
they were extinguished like a fire
among thorns;
in the name of the LORD
I destroyed them.
13 You[c] pushed me[d] hard to make me fall,
but the LORD helped me.
14 The LORD is my strength
and my song;
He has become my salvation.

[a]**116:13,17** Or *proclaim* or *invoke the name of*; lit *call on the name of* [b]**118:5** Or *answered me with freedom*
[c]**118:13** Perhaps the enemy [d]**118:13** LXX, Syr, Jer read *I was pushed*

15 There are shouts of joy and victory
in the tents of the righteous:
"The LORD's right hand strikes
with power!
16 The LORD's right hand is raised!
The LORD's right hand strikes
with power!"
17 I will not die, but I will live
and proclaim what the LORD has done.
18 The LORD disciplined me severely
but did not give me over to death.

19 Open the gates of righteousness
for me;
I will enter through them
and give thanks to the LORD.
20 This is the gate of the LORD;
the righteous will enter through it.
21 I will give thanks to You
because You have answered me
and have become my salvation.
22 The stone that the builders rejected
has become the cornerstone.
23 This came from the LORD;
it is wonderful in our eyes.
24 This is the day the LORD has made;
let us rejoice and be glad in it.

25 LORD, save us!
LORD, please grant us success!
26 Blessed is he who comes
in the name of the LORD.
From the house of the LORD
we bless you.
27 The LORD is God and has given us
light.
Bind the festival sacrifice with cords
to the horns of the altar.
28 You are my God, and I will give
You thanks.
⌊You are⌋ my God; I will exalt You.
29 Give thanks to the LORD,
for He is good;
His faithful love endures forever.

Psalm 119

Delight in God's Word

א *Alef*

1 How[a] happy are those whose way
is blameless,
who live according to the law
of the LORD!
2 Happy are those who keep His decrees
and seek Him with all their heart.
3 They do nothing wrong;
they follow His ways.
4 You have commanded
that Your precepts
be diligently kept.
5 If only my ways were committed
to keeping Your statutes!
6 Then I would not be ashamed
when I think about
all Your commands.
7 I will praise You with a sincere heart
when I learn
Your righteous judgments.
8 I will keep Your statutes;
never abandon me.

ב *Bet*

9 How can a young man keep his way
pure?
By keeping Your[b] word.
10 I have sought You with all my heart;
don't let me wander
from Your commands.
11 I have treasured Your word
in my heart
so that I may not sin against You.
12 LORD, may You be praised;
teach me Your statutes.
13 With my lips I proclaim
all the judgments from Your mouth.
14 I rejoice in the way ⌊revealed by⌋
Your decrees
as much as in all riches.
15 I will meditate on Your precepts
and think about Your ways.
16 I will delight in Your statutes;
I will not forget Your word.

ג *Gimel*

17 Deal generously with Your servant
so that I might live;
then I will keep Your word.
18 Open my eyes so that I may see
wonderful things in Your law.
19 I am a stranger on earth;
do not hide Your commands
from me.
20 I am continually overcome
by longing for Your judgments.
21 You rebuke the proud, the accursed,
who wander from Your commands.
22 Take insult and contempt away
from me,

[a] **119:1** The stanzas of this poem form an •acrostic. [b] **119:9** Or *keeping it according to Your*

for I have kept Your decrees.
23 Though princes sit together speaking
against me,
Your servant will think
about Your statutes;
24 Your decrees are my delight
and my counselors.

ד *Dalet*

25 My life is down in the dust;
give me life through Your word.
26 I told You about my life,
and You listened to me;
teach me Your statutes.
27 Help me understand
the meaning of Your precepts
so that I can meditate on Your wonders.
28 I am weary[a] from grief;
strengthen me through Your word.
29 Keep me from the way of deceit,
and graciously give me
Your instruction.
30 I have chosen the way of truth;
I have set Your ordinances ⌊before me⌋.
31 I cling to Your decrees;
LORD, do not put me to shame.
32 I pursue the way of Your commands,
for You broaden my understanding.[b]

ה *He*

33 Teach me, LORD, the meaning
of Your statutes,
and I will always keep them.[c]
34 Help me understand Your instruction,
and I will obey it
and follow it with all my heart.
35 Help me stay on the path
of Your commands,
for I take pleasure in it.
36 Turn my heart to Your decrees
and not to material gain.
37 Turn my eyes
from looking at what is worthless;
give me life in Your ways.[d]
38 Confirm what You said
to Your servant,
for it produces reverence for You.
39 Turn away the disgrace I dread;
indeed, Your judgments are good.
40 How I long for Your precepts!
Give me life through
Your righteousness.

ו *Vav*

41 Let Your faithful love
come to me, LORD,
Your salvation, as You promised.
42 Then I can answer the one
who taunts me,
for I trust in Your word.
43 Never take the word of truth
from my mouth,
for I hope in Your judgments.
44 I will always keep Your law,
forever and ever.
45 I will walk freely in an open place
because I seek Your precepts.
46 I will speak of Your decrees
before kings
and not be ashamed.
47 I delight in Your commands,
which I love.
48 I will lift up my hands
to Your commands,
which I love,
and will meditate on Your statutes.

ז *Zayin*

49 Remember ⌊Your⌋ word
to Your servant;
You have given me hope through it.
50 This is my comfort in my affliction:
Your promise has given me life.
51 The arrogant constantly ridicule me,
but I do not turn away
from Your instruction.
52 LORD, I remember Your judgments
from long ago
and find comfort.
53 Rage seizes me because of the wicked
who reject Your instruction.
54 Your statutes are ⌊the theme of⌋
my song
during my earthly life.[e]
55 I remember Your name
in the night, LORD,
and I keep Your law.
56 This is my ⌊practice⌋:
I obey Your precepts.

ח *Khet*

57 The LORD is my portion;[f]
I have promised to keep Your words.
58 I have sought Your favor with all
my heart;

[a]**119:28** Or *My soul weeps* [b]**119:32** Lit *You enlarge my heart* [c]**119:33** Or *will keep it as my reward* [d]**119:37** Other Hb mss, Tg read *word* [e]**119:54** Lit *song in the house of my sojourning* [f]**119:57** Lit *You are my portion, LORD*

be gracious to me according to
Your promise.
59 I thought about my ways
and turned my steps back
to Your decrees.
60 I hurried, not hesitating
to keep Your commands.
61 Though the ropes of the wicked
were wrapped around me,
I did not forget Your law.
62 I rise at midnight to thank You
for Your righteous judgments.
63 I am a friend to all who •fear You,
to those who keep Your precepts.
64 LORD, the earth is filled with
Your faithful love;
teach me Your statutes.

ט *Tet*

65 LORD, You have treated
Your servant well,
just as You promised.
66 Teach me good judgment
and discernment,
for I rely on Your commands.
67 Before I was afflicted I went astray,
but now I keep Your word.
68 You are good, and You do
what is good;
teach me Your statutes.
69 The arrogant have smeared me
with lies,
but I obey Your precepts with all
my heart.
70 Their hearts are hard and insensitive,
but I delight in Your instruction.
71 It was good for me to be afflicted
so that I could learn Your statutes.
72 Instruction from Your lips is better
for me
than thousands of gold and silver pieces.

י *Yod*

73 Your hands made me and formed me;
give me understanding
so that I can learn Your commands.
74 Those who fear You will see me
and rejoice,
for I put my hope in Your word.
75 I know, LORD, that Your judgments
are just
and that You have afflicted me fairly.
76 May Your faithful love comfort me,
as You promised Your servant.
77 May Your compassion come to me
so that I may live,
for Your instruction is my delight.
78 Let the arrogant be put to shame
for slandering me with lies;
I will meditate on Your precepts.
79 Let those who fear You,
those who know Your decrees,
turn to me.
80 May my heart be blameless
regarding Your statutes
so that I will not be put to shame.

כ *Kaf*

81 I long for Your salvation;
I put my hope in Your word.
82 My eyes grow weary
⌊looking⌋ for what You have promised;
I ask, "When will You comfort me?"
83 Though I have become like a wineskin
⌊dried⌋ by smoke,
I do not forget Your statutes.
84 How many days ⌊must⌋
Your servant ⌊wait⌋?
When will You execute judgment
on my persecutors?
85 The arrogant have dug pits for me;
they violate Your instruction.
86 All Your commands are true;
people persecute me with lies—
help me!
87 They almost ended my life on earth,
but I did not abandon Your precepts.
88 Give me life in accordance with
Your faithful love,
and I will obey the decree
You have spoken.

ל *Lamed*

89 LORD, Your word is forever;
it is firmly fixed in heaven.
90 Your faithfulness is for all generations;
You established the earth,
and it stands firm.
91 They stand today in accordance with
Your judgments,
for all things are Your servants.
92 If Your instruction had not been
my delight,
I would have died in my affliction.
93 I will never forget Your precepts,
for You have given me life through them.
94 I am Yours; save me,
for I have sought Your precepts.

95 The wicked hope to destroy me,
but I contemplate Your decrees.
96 I have seen a limit to all perfection,
but Your command is without limit.

מ *Mem*

97 How I love Your teaching!
It is my meditation all day long.
98 Your command makes me wiser
than my enemies,
for it is always with me.
99 I have more insight than
all my teachers
because Your decrees are
my meditation.
100 I understand more than the elders
because I obey Your precepts.
101 I have kept my feet
from every evil path
to follow Your word.
102 I have not turned from
Your judgments,
for You Yourself have
instructed me.
103 How sweet Your word is
to my taste—
⌊sweeter⌋ than honey to my mouth.
104 I gain understanding
from Your precepts;
therefore I hate every false way.

נ *Nun*

105 Your word is a lamp for my feet
and a light on my path.
106 I have solemnly sworn
to keep Your righteous judgments.
107 I am severely afflicted;
LORD, give me life
through Your word.
108 LORD, please accept
my willing offerings of praise,
and teach me Your judgments.
109 My life is constantly in danger,[a]
yet I do not forget Your instruction.
110 The wicked have set a trap for me,
but I have not wandered
from Your precepts.
111 I have Your decrees
as a heritage forever;
indeed, they are the joy of my heart.
112 I am resolved to obey Your statutes
to the very end.[b]

ס *Samek*

113 I hate the double-minded,
but I love Your instruction.
114 You are my shelter and my shield;
I put my hope in Your word.
115 Depart from me, you evil ones,
so that I may obey
my God's commands.
116 Sustain me as You promised,
and I will live;
do not let me be ashamed
of my hope.
117 Sustain me so that I can be safe
and be concerned with
Your statutes continually.
118 You reject all who stray
from Your statutes,
for their deceit is a lie.
119 You remove all the wicked on earth
as if they were[c] dross;
therefore, I love Your decrees.
120 I tremble[d] in awe of You;
I fear Your judgments.

ע *Ayin*

121 I have done what is just and right;
do not leave me to my oppressors.
122 Guarantee Your servant's well-being;
do not let the arrogant oppress me.
123 My eyes grow weary ⌊looking for⌋
Your salvation
and for Your righteous promise.
124 Deal with Your servant based on
Your faithful love;
teach me Your statutes.
125 I am Your servant;
give me understanding
so that I may know Your decrees.
126 It is time for the LORD to act,
⌊for⌋ they have broken Your law.
127 Since I love Your commandments
more than gold, even the purest gold,
128 I carefully follow[e] all Your precepts
and hate every false way.

פ *Pe*

129 Your decrees are wonderful;
therefore I obey them.
130 The revelation of Your words
brings light
and gives understanding
to the inexperienced.

[a]**119:109** Lit *in my hand* [b]**119:112** Or *statutes; the reward is eternal* [c]**119:119** Other Hb mss, DSS, LXX, Aq, Sym, Jer read *All the wicked of the earth You count as* [d]**119:120** Lit *My flesh shudders* [e]**119:128** Lit *I therefore follow carefully*

131 I pant with open mouth
because I long for Your commands.
132 Turn to me and be gracious to me,
as is ⌊Your⌋ practice toward those
who love Your name.
133 Make my steps steady
through Your promise;
don't let sin dominate me.
134 Redeem me from human oppression,
and I will keep Your precepts.
135 Show favor to Your servant,
and teach me Your statutes.
136 My eyes pour out streams of tears
because people do not follow
Your instruction.

צ *Tsade*

137 You are righteous, LORD,
and Your judgments are just.
138 The decrees You issue are righteous
and altogether trustworthy.
139 My anger overwhelms me
because my foes forget Your words.
140 Your word is completely pure,
and Your servant loves it.
141 I am insignificant and despised,
but I do not forget Your precepts.
142 Your righteousness is
an everlasting righteousness,
and Your instruction is true.
143 Trouble and distress have overtaken me,
but Your commands are my delight.
144 Your decrees are righteous forever.
Give me understanding,
and I will live.

ק *Qof*

145 I call with all my heart;
answer me, LORD.
I will obey Your statutes.
146 I call to You; save me,
and I will keep Your decrees.
147 I rise before dawn and cry out for help;
I put my hope in Your word.
148 I am awake through each watch
of the night
to meditate on Your promise.
149 In keeping with Your faithful love,
hear my voice.
LORD, give me life, in keeping with
Your justice.
150 Those who pursue evil plans[a]
come near;
they are far from Your instruction.
151 You are near, LORD,
and all Your commands are true.
152 Long ago I learned from Your decrees
that You have established
them forever.

ר *Resh*

153 Consider my affliction and rescue me,
for I have not forgotten
Your instruction.
154 Defend my cause, and redeem me;
give me life, as You promised.
155 Salvation is far from the wicked
because they do not seek
Your statutes.
156 Your compassions are many, LORD;
give me life, according to
Your judgments.
157 My persecutors and foes are many.
I have not turned from Your decrees.
158 I have seen the disloyal
and feel disgust
because they do not keep Your word.
159 Consider how I love Your precepts;
LORD, give me life, according to
Your faithful love.
160 The entirety of Your word is truth,
and all Your righteous judgments
endure forever.

שׂ *Sin*/ שׁ *Shin*

161 Princes have persecuted me
without cause,
but my heart fears ⌊only⌋ Your word.
162 I rejoice over Your promise
like one who finds vast treasure.
163 I hate and abhor falsehood,
⌊but⌋ I love Your instruction.
164 I praise You seven times a day
for Your righteous judgments.
165 Abundant peace belongs to those
who love Your instruction;
nothing makes them stumble.
166 LORD, I hope for Your salvation
and carry out Your commands.
167 I obey Your decrees
and love them greatly.
168 I obey Your precepts and decrees,
for all my ways are before You.

ת *Tav*

169 Let my cry reach You, LORD;

[a] **119:150** Some Hb mss, LXX, Sym, Jer read *who maliciously persecute me*

give me understanding according to
Your word.
170 Let my plea reach You;
rescue me according to
Your promise.
171 My lips pour out praise,
for You teach me Your statutes.
172 My tongue sings about Your promise,
for all Your commandments
are righteous.
173 May Your hand be ready
to help me,
for I have chosen Your precepts.
174 I long for Your salvation, LORD,
and Your instruction is my delight.
175 Let me live, and I will praise You;
may Your judgments help me.
176 I wander like a lost sheep;
seek Your servant,
for I do not forget Your commands.

Psalm 120

A Cry for Truth and Peace

A •song of ascents.

1 In my distress I called to the LORD,
and He answered me:
2 "LORD, deliver me from lying lips
and a deceitful tongue."

3 What will He give you,
and what will He do to you,
you deceitful tongue?
4 A warrior's sharp arrows,
with burning charcoal![a]
5 What misery that I have stayed
in Meshech,
that I have lived among the tents
of Kedar![b]
6 I have lived too long
with those who hate peace.
7 I am for peace; but when I speak,
they are for war.

Psalm 121

The LORD Our Protector

A •song of ascents.

1 I raise my eyes toward the mountains.
Where will my help come from?
2 My help comes from the LORD,
the Maker of heaven and earth.

3 He will not allow your foot to slip;
your Protector will not slumber.
4 Indeed, the Protector of Israel
does not slumber or sleep.

5 The LORD protects you;
the LORD is a shelter right
by your side.[c]
6 The sun will not strike you by day,
or the moon by night.

7 The LORD will protect you
from all harm;
He will protect your life.
8 The LORD will protect your coming
and going
both now and forever.

Psalm 122

A Prayer for Jerusalem

A Davidic •song of ascents.

1 I rejoiced with those who said to me,
"Let us go to the house of the LORD."
2 Our feet are standing
within your gates, Jerusalem—

3 Jerusalem, built as a city ⌊should be⌋,
solidly joined together,
4 where the tribes, the tribes
of the LORD, go up
to give thanks to the name
of the LORD.
(This is an ordinance for Israel.)
5 There, thrones for judgment
are placed,
thrones of the house of David.

6 Pray for the peace of Jerusalem:
"May those who love you prosper;
7 may there be peace within your walls,
prosperity within your fortresses."
8 Because of my brothers and friends,
I will say, "Peace be with you."
9 Because of the house of the LORD
our God,
I will seek your good.

Psalm 123

Looking for God's Favor

A •song of ascents.

1 I lift my eyes to You,
the One enthroned in heaven.
2 Like a servant's eyes
on His master's hand,
like a servant girl's eyes
on her mistress's hand,

[a]**120:4** Lit *with coals of the broom bush* [b]**120:5** *Meshech*: a people far to the north of Palestine; *Kedar*: a nomadic people of the desert to the southeast [c]**121:5** Lit *is your shelter at your right hand*

so our eyes are on the LORD our God
until He shows us favor.

3 Show us favor, LORD, show us favor,
for we've had more than enough contempt.
4 We've had more than enough
scorn from the arrogant
⌊and⌋ contempt from the proud.

Psalm 124
The LORD Is on Our Side

A Davidic •song of ascents.

1 If the LORD had not been
on our side—
let Israel say—
2 If the LORD had not been on our side
when men attacked us,
3 then they would have
swallowed us alive
in their burning anger against us.
4 Then the waters would have
engulfed us;
the torrent would have swept over us;
5 the raging waters would have swept
over us.

6 Praise the LORD,
who has not let us be ripped apart
by their teeth.
7 We have escaped like a bird
from the hunter's net;
the net is torn, and we have escaped.
8 Our help is in the name of the LORD,
the Maker of heaven and earth.

Psalm 125
Israel's Stability

A •song of ascents.

1 Those who trust in the LORD are
like Mount Zion.
It cannot be shaken;
it remains forever.
2 Jerusalem—the mountains
surround her.
And the LORD surrounds His people,
both now and forever.

3 The scepter of the wicked
will not remain
over the land allotted to the righteous,
so that the righteous will not apply
their hands to injustice.
4 Do what is good, LORD, to the good,
to those whose hearts are upright.
5 But as for those who turn aside
to crooked ways,
the LORD will banish them
with the evildoers.

Peace be with Israel.

Psalm 126
Zion's Restoration

A •song of ascents.

1 When the LORD restored the fortunes
of Zion,[a]
we were like those who dream.
2 Our mouths were filled
with laughter then,
and our tongues with shouts of joy.
Then they said among the nations,
"The LORD has done great things
for them."
3 The LORD had done great things for us;
we were joyful.

4 Restore our fortunes,[b] LORD,
like watercourses in the •Negev.[c]
5 Those who sow in tears
will reap with shouts of joy.
6 Though one goes along weeping,
carrying the bag of seed,
he will surely come back with shouts
of joy,
carrying his sheaves.

Psalm 127
The Blessing of the LORD

A Solomonic •song of ascents.

1 Unless the LORD builds a house,
its builders labor over it in vain;
unless the LORD watches over
a city,
the watchman stays alert in vain.
2 In vain you get up early
and stay up late,
eating food earned by hard work;
certainly He gives sleep to the one
He loves.[d]
3 Sons are indeed a heritage
from the LORD,
children, a reward.
4 Like arrows in the hand
of a warrior
are the sons born in one's youth.

[a]**126:1** Or *LORD returned those of Zion who had been captives* [b]**126:4** Or *Return our captives* [c]**126:4** Seasonal streams in the arid south country [d]**127:2** Or *work; He gives such things to His loved ones while [they] sleep*

5 Happy is the man who has filled
his quiver with them.
Such men will never be put
to shame
when they speak with ⌊their⌋ enemies
at the city •gate.

Psalm 128

Blessings for Those Who Fear God

A •song of ascents.

1 How happy is everyone who •fears
the LORD,
who walks in His ways!
2 You will surely eat
what your hands have worked for.
You will be happy,
and it will go well for you.
3 Your wife will be like a fruitful vine
within your house,
your sons, like young olive trees
around your table.
4 In this very way
the man who fears the LORD
will be blessed.

5 May the LORD bless you from Zion,
so that you will see the prosperity
of Jerusalem
all the days of your life,
6 and will see your children's children!

Peace be with Israel.

Psalm 129

Protection of the Oppressed

A •song of ascents.

1 Since my youth they have often
attacked me—
let Israel say—
2 Since my youth they have often
attacked me,
but they have not prevailed
against me.
3 Plowmen plowed over my back;
they made their furrows long.
4 The LORD is righteous;
He has cut the ropes
of the wicked.

5 Let all who hate Zion
be driven back in disgrace.
6 Let them be like grass
on the rooftops,
which withers before it grows up[a]
7 and can't even fill the hands
of the reaper
or the arms of the one
who binds sheaves.
8 Then none who pass by will say,
"May the LORD's blessing be
on you."

We bless you in the name
of the LORD.

Psalm 130

Awaiting Redemption

A •song of ascents.

1 Out of the depths I call to You, LORD!
2 Lord, listen to my voice;
let Your ears be attentive
to my cry for help.

3 LORD, if You considered sins,
Lord, who could stand?
4 But with You there is forgiveness,
so that You may be revered.

5 I wait for the LORD; I wait,
and put my hope in His word.
6 I ⌊wait⌋ for the Lord
more than watchmen
for the morning—
more than watchmen
for the morning.

7 Israel, put your hope in the LORD.
For there is faithful love
with the LORD,
and with Him is redemption
in abundance.
8 And He will redeem Israel
from all its sins.

Psalm 131

A Childlike Spirit

A Davidic •song of ascents.

1 LORD, my heart is not proud;
my eyes are not haughty.
I do not get involved with things
too great or too difficult for me.
2 Instead, I have calmed
and quieted myself
like a little weaned child
with its mother;
I am like a little child.

3 Israel, put your hope in the LORD,
both now and forever.

[a]129:6 Or *it can be pulled out*

Psalm 132
David and Zion Chosen

A •song of ascents.

1 LORD, remember David
and all the hardships he endured,
2 and how he swore an oath to the LORD,
making a vow to the Mighty One
of Jacob:
3 "I will not enter my house[a]
or get into my bed,[b]
4 I will not allow my eyes to sleep
or my eyelids to slumber
5 until I find a place for the LORD,
a dwelling for the Mighty One
of Jacob."

6 We heard of ⌊the ark⌋ in Ephrathah;[c]
we found it in the fields of Jaar.[d]
7 Let us go to His dwelling place;
let us worship at His footstool.
8 Arise, LORD, come to Your resting place,
You and the ark ⌊that shows⌋
Your strength.
9 May Your priests be clothed
with righteousness,
and may Your godly people shout
for joy.
10 Because of Your servant David,
do not reject Your anointed one.[e]

11 The LORD swore an oath to David,
a promise He will not abandon:
"I will set one of your descendants[f]
on your throne.
12 If your sons keep My covenant
and My decrees that I will teach them,
their sons will also sit
on your throne, forever."

13 For the LORD has chosen Zion;
He has desired it for His home:
14 "This is My resting place forever;
I will make My home here
because I have desired it.
15 I will abundantly bless its food;
I will satisfy its needy with bread.
16 I will clothe its priests with salvation,
and its godly people will shout for joy.
17 There I will make a •horn grow
for David;
I have prepared a lamp for
My anointed one.
18 I will clothe his enemies with shame,
but the crown he wears[g]
will be glorious."

Psalm 133
Living in Harmony

A Davidic •song of ascents.

1 How good and pleasant it is
when brothers can live together!
2 It is like fine oil on the head,
running down on the beard,
running down Aaron's beard,
on his robes.
3 It is like the dew of Hermon[h]
falling on the mountains of Zion.
For there the LORD has appointed
the blessing—
life forevermore.

Psalm 134
Call to Evening Worship

A •song of ascents.

1 Now praise the LORD,
all you servants of the LORD
who stand in the LORD's house
at night!
2 Lift up your hands in the holy place,
and praise the LORD!

3 May the LORD,
Maker of heaven and earth,
bless you from Zion.

Psalm 135
The LORD Is Great

1 •Hallelujah!
Praise the name of the LORD.
Give praise, you servants of the LORD
2 who stand in the house of the LORD,
in the courts of the house of our God.
3 Praise the LORD, for the LORD is good;
sing praise to His name,
for it is delightful.
4 For the LORD has chosen Jacob
for Himself,
Israel as His treasured possession.

5 For I know that the LORD is great;
our Lord is greater than all gods.
6 The LORD does whatever He pleases
in heaven and on earth,
in the seas and all the depths.

[a]**132:3** Lit *enter the tent of my house* [b]**132:3** Lit *into the couch of my bed* [c]**132:6** Bethlehem or the district around it; Gn 35:19 [d]**132:6** Kiriath-jearim; 1 Sm 7:1–2 [e]**132:10** The king [f]**132:11** Lit *set the fruit of your womb* [g]**132:18** Lit *but on him his crown* [h]**133:3** The tallest mountain in the region, noted for its abundant precipitation

7 He causes the clouds to rise
from the ends of the earth.
He makes lightning for the rain
and brings the wind
from His storehouses.

8 He struck down the firstborn of Egypt,
both people and animals.
9 He sent signs and wonders
against you, Egypt,
against Pharaoh and all his officials.
10 He struck down many nations
and slaughtered mighty kings:
11 Sihon king of the Amorites,
Og king of Bashan,
and all the kings of Canaan.
12 He gave their land as an inheritance,
an inheritance to His people Israel.

13 LORD, Your name ⌊endures⌋ forever,
Your reputation, LORD,
through all generations.
14 For the LORD will judge His people
and have compassion
on His servants.

15 The idols of the nations are of silver
and gold,
made by human hands.
16 They have mouths, but cannot speak,
eyes, but cannot see.
17 They have ears, but cannot hear;
indeed, there is no breath
in their mouths.
18 Those who make them are just
like them,
as are all who trust in them.

19 House of Israel, praise the LORD!
House of Aaron, praise the LORD!
20 House of Levi, praise the LORD!
You who revere the LORD,
praise the LORD!
21 May the LORD be praised
from Zion;
He dwells in Jerusalem.
Hallelujah!

Psalm 136

God's Love Is Eternal

1 Give thanks to the LORD,
for He is good.
His love is eternal.
2 Give thanks to the God of gods.
His love is eternal.
3 Give thanks to the Lord of lords.
His love is eternal.
4 He alone does great wonders.
His love is eternal.
5 He made the heavens skillfully.
His love is eternal.
6 He spread the land on the waters.
His love is eternal.
7 He made the great lights:
His love is eternal.
8 the sun to rule by day,
His love is eternal.
9 the moon and stars to rule by night.
His love is eternal.
10 He struck the firstborn
of the Egyptians
His love is eternal.
11 and brought Israel out from among
them
His love is eternal.
12 with a strong hand
and outstretched arm.
His love is eternal.
13 He divided the •Red Sea
His love is eternal.
14 and led Israel through,
His love is eternal.
15 but hurled Pharaoh and his army
into the Red Sea.
His love is eternal.
16 He led His people in the wilderness.
His love is eternal.
17 He struck down great kings
His love is eternal.
18 and slaughtered famous kings—
His love is eternal.
19 Sihon king of the Amorites
His love is eternal.
20 and Og king of Bashan—
His love is eternal.
21 and gave their land as an inheritance,
His love is eternal.
22 an inheritance to Israel His servant.
His love is eternal.
23 He remembered us
in our humiliation
His love is eternal.
24 and rescued us from our foes.
His love is eternal.
25 He gives food to every creature.
His love is eternal.
26 Give thanks to the God of heaven!
His love is eternal.

Psalm 137

Lament of the Exiles

1 By the rivers of Babylon—

there we sat down and wept
when we remembered Zion.
2 There we hung up our lyres
on the poplar trees,
3 for our captors there asked us
for songs,
and our tormentors, for rejoicing:
"Sing us one of the songs of Zion."

4 How can we sing the LORD's song
on foreign soil?
5 If I forget you, Jerusalem,
may my right hand forget ⌊its skill⌋.
6 May my tongue stick to the roof
of my mouth
if I do not remember you,
if I do not exalt Jerusalem
as my greatest joy!

7 Remember, LORD,
⌊what⌋ the Edomites said
that day[a] at Jerusalem:
"Destroy it! Destroy it
down to its foundations!"
8 Daughter Babylon,
doomed to destruction,
happy is the one who pays you back
what you have done to us.
9 Happy is he who takes your little ones
and dashes them against the rocks.

Psalm 138

A Thankful Heart

Davidic.

1 I will give You thanks
with all my heart;
I will sing Your praise
before the heavenly beings.[b]
2 I will bow down
toward Your holy temple
and give thanks to Your name
for Your constant love and faithfulness.
You have exalted Your name
and Your promise above
everything else.
3 On the day I called, You answered me;
You increased strength within me.[c]
4 All the kings on earth
will give You thanks, LORD,
when they hear
what You have promised.[d]
5 They will sing of the LORD's ways,
for the LORD's glory is great.
6 Though the LORD is exalted,
He takes note of the humble;
but He knows the haughty from afar.

7 If I walk in the thick of danger,
You will preserve my life
from the anger of my enemies.
You will extend Your hand;
Your right hand will save me.
8 The LORD will fulfill ⌊His purpose⌋
for me.
LORD, Your love is eternal;
do not abandon the work
of Your hands.

Psalm 139

The All-Knowing, Ever-Present God

For the choir director. A Davidic psalm.

1 LORD, You have searched me
and known me.
2 You know when I sit down and when
I stand up;
You understand my thoughts
from far away.
3 You observe my travels and my rest;
You are aware of all my ways.
4 Before a word is on my tongue,
You know all about it, LORD.
5 You have encircled me;
You have placed Your hand on me.
6 ⌊This⌋ extraordinary knowledge is
beyond me.
It is lofty; I am unable to ⌊reach⌋ it.

7 Where can I go to escape
Your Spirit?
Where can I flee
from Your presence?
8 If I go up to heaven, You are there;
if I make my bed in •Sheol,
You are there.
9 If I live at the eastern horizon
⌊or⌋ settle at the western limits,[e]
10 even there Your hand will lead me;
Your right hand will
hold on to me.
11 If I say, "Surely the darkness
will hide me,
and the light around me
will become night"—
12 even the darkness is not dark to You.
The night shines like the day;
darkness and light are alike to You.

[a]**137:7** The day Jerusalem fell to the Babylonians in 586 B.C. [b]**138:1** Or *the gods* (Jb 1:6; 2:1), or *before judges* or *kings* (Ps 82:1,6–7; Ex 21:6; 22:7–8); Hb *Elohim* [c]**138:3** Hb obscure [d]**138:4** Lit *hear the words of Your mouth* [e]**139:9** Lit *I take up the wings of the dawn; I dwell at the end of the sea*

13 For it was You who created
my inward parts;[a]
You knit me together
in my mother's womb.
14 I will praise You,
because I have been remarkably
and wonderfully made.[b] [c]
Your works are wonderful,
and I know ⌊this⌋ very well.
15 My bones were not hidden from You
when I was made in secret,
when I was formed in the depths
of the earth.
16 Your eyes saw me when
I was formless;
all ⌊my⌋ days were written
in Your book and planned
before a single one of them began.

17 God, how difficult[d] Your thoughts are
for me ⌊to comprehend⌋;
how vast their sum is!
18 If I counted them,
they would outnumber the grains
of sand;
when I wake up,[e] I am still with You.

19 God, if only You would kill the wicked—
you bloodthirsty men, stay away
from me—
20 who invoke You deceitfully.
Your enemies swear ⌊by You⌋ falsely.
21 LORD, don't I hate those who hate You,
and detest those who rebel
against You?
22 I hate them with extreme hatred;
I consider them my enemies.

23 Search me, God, and know my heart;
test me and know my concerns.
24 See if there is any offensive[f] way
in me;
lead me in the everlasting way.

Psalm 140

Prayer for Rescue

For the choir director. A Davidic psalm.

1 Rescue me, LORD, from evil men.
Keep me safe from violent men
2 who plan evil in their hearts.
They stir up wars all day long.
3 They make their tongues
as sharp as a snake's bite;
viper's venom is under their lips.
•Selah

4 Protect me, LORD,
from the clutches of the wicked.
Keep me safe from violent men
who plan to make me stumble.[g]
5 The proud hide a trap with ropes
for me;
they spread a net along the path
and set snares for me. *Selah*

6 I say to the LORD, "You are my God."
Listen, LORD, to my cry for help.
7 Lord GOD, my strong Savior,
You shield my head on the day of battle.
8 LORD, do not grant the desires
of the wicked;
do not let them achieve their goals.
⌊Otherwise,⌋ they will become proud.
Selah

9 As for the heads of those
who surround me,
let the trouble their lips cause
overwhelm ⌊them⌋.
10 Let hot coals fall on them.
Let them be thrown into the fire,
into the abyss, never again to rise.
11 Do not let a slanderer stay in the land.
Let evil relentlessly[c] hunt down
a violent man.

12 I[h] know that the LORD upholds
the just cause of the poor,
justice for the needy.
13 Surely the righteous will praise
Your name;
the upright will live in Your presence.

Psalm 141

Protection from Sin and Sinners

A Davidic psalm.

1 LORD, I call on You; hurry to ⌊help⌋ me.
Listen to my voice when I call on You.
2 May my prayer be set before You
as incense,
the raising of my hands
as the evening offering.

3 LORD, set up a guard for my mouth;
keep watch at the door of my lips.

[a] **139:13** Lit *my kidneys* [b] **139:14** DSS, some LXX mss, Syr, Jer read *because You are remarkable and wonderful*
[c] **139:14; 140:11** Hb obscure [d] **139:17** Or *precious* [e] **139:18** Other Hb mss read *I come to an end* [f] **139:24** Or *idolatrous*
[g] **140:4** Lit *to trip up my steps* [h] **140:12** Alt Hb tradition reads *You*

4 Do not let my heart turn
to any evil thing
or wickedly perform reckless acts
with men who commit sin.
Do not let me feast on their delicacies.
5 Let the righteous one strike me—
it is ⌊an act of⌋ faithful love;
let him rebuke me—
it is oil for my head;
let me[a] not refuse it.
Even now my prayer is against
the evil acts of the wicked.[b]
6 When their rulers[c] will be thrown off
the sides of a cliff,
the people[d] will listen to my words,
for they are pleasing.

7 As when one plows and breaks up
the soil,
⌊turning up rocks⌋,
so our[e] bones have been scattered
at the mouth of •Sheol.

8 But my eyes ⌊look⌋ to You, Lord GOD.
I seek refuge in You; do not let me die.[f]
9 Protect me from[g] the trap
they have set for me,
and from the snares of evildoers.
10 Let the wicked fall into their own nets,
while I pass ⌊safely⌋ by.

Psalm 142
A Cry of Distress

A Davidic •*Maskil.* When he was in the cave.
A prayer.

1 I cry aloud to the LORD;
I plead aloud to the LORD for mercy.
2 I pour out my complaint before Him;
I reveal my trouble to Him.
3 Although my spirit is weak within me,
You know my way.

Along this path I travel
they have hidden a trap for me.
4 Look to the right and see:[h]
no one stands up for me;
there is no refuge for me;
no one cares about me.

5 I cry to You, LORD;
I say, "You are my shelter,
my portion in the land of the living."
6 Listen to my cry,
for I am very weak.
Rescue me from those who pursue me,
for they are too strong for me.
7 Free me from prison
so that I can praise Your name.
The righteous will gather around me
because You deal generously with me.

Psalm 143
A Cry for Help

A Davidic psalm.

1 LORD, hear my prayer.
In Your faithfulness listen to my plea,
and in Your righteousness answer me.
2 Do not bring Your servant
into judgment,
for no one alive is righteous
in Your sight.

3 For the enemy has pursued me,
crushing me to the ground,
making me live in darkness
like those long dead.
4 My spirit is weak within me;
my heart is overcome with dismay.

5 I remember the days of old;
I meditate on all You have done;
I reflect on the work
of Your hands.
6 I spread out my hands to You;
I am like parched land before You.
•*Selah*

7 Answer me quickly, LORD;
my spirit fails.
Don't hide Your face from me,
or I will be like those
going down to the •Pit.
8 Let me experience
Your faithful love in the morning,
for I trust in You.
Reveal to me the way I should go,
because I long for You.
9 Rescue me from my enemies, LORD;
I come to You for protection.[i]
10 Teach me to do Your will,
for You are my God.
May Your gracious Spirit
lead me on level ground.

11 Because of Your name, •Yahweh,
let me live.

[a]**141:5** Lit *my head* [b]**141:5** Lit *of them* [c]**141:6** Or *judges* [d]**141:6** Lit *cliff, and they* [e]**141:7** DSS reads *my*; some LXX mss, Syr read *their* [f]**141:8** Or *not pour out my life* [g]**141:9** Lit *from the hands of* [h]**142:4** DSS, LXX, Syr, Vg, Tg read *I look to the right and I see* [i]**143:9** One Hb ms, LXX; MT reads *I cover myself to You*

In Your righteousness deliver me
from trouble,
12 and in Your faithful love
destroy my enemies.
Wipe out all those who attack me,
for I am Your servant.

Psalm 144

A King's Prayer

Davidic.

1 May the LORD my rock be praised,
who trains my hands for battle
and my fingers for warfare.
2 He is my faithful love
and my fortress,
my stronghold and my deliverer.
He is my shield, and I take refuge
in Him;
He subdues my people[a] under me.

3 LORD, what is man,
that You care for him,
the son of man, that You think of him?
4 Man is like a breath;
his days are like a passing shadow.

5 LORD, part Your heavens
and come down.
Touch the mountains,
and they will smoke.
6 Flash ⌊Your⌋ lightning and scatter
the foe;[b]
shoot Your arrows and rout them.
7 Reach down[c] from on high;
rescue me from deep water,
and set me free
from the grasp of foreigners
8 whose mouths speak lies,
whose right hands are deceptive.

9 God, I will sing a new song to You;
I will play on a ten-stringed harp
for You—
10 the One who gives victory to kings,
who frees His servant David
from the deadly sword.
11 Set me free and rescue me
from the grasp of foreigners
whose mouths speak lies,
whose right hands are deceptive.

12 Then our sons will be like plants
nurtured in their youth,
our daughters, like corner pillars
that are carved in the palace style.
13 Our storehouses will be full,
supplying all kinds of produce;
our flocks will increase by thousands
and tens of thousands in
our open fields.
14 Our cattle will be well fed.[d]
There will be no breach ⌊in the walls⌋,
no going ⌊into captivity⌋,[e]
and no cry of lament in
our public squares.
15 Happy are the people with
such ⌊blessings⌋.
Happy are the people whose God is
the LORD.

Psalm 145

Praising God's Greatness

A Davidic hymn.

1 I[f] exalt You, my God the King,
and praise Your name
forever and ever.
2 I will praise You every day;
I will honor Your name
forever and ever.

3 •Yahweh is great
and is highly praised;
His greatness is unsearchable.
4 One generation will declare
Your works to the next
and will proclaim Your mighty acts.
5 I[g] will speak of Your glorious splendor
and[h] Your wonderful works.
6 They will proclaim the power
of Your awe-inspiring works,
and I will declare Your greatness.[i]
7 They will give a testimony
of Your great goodness
and will joyfully sing
of Your righteousness.

8 The LORD is gracious
and compassionate,
slow to anger and great in faithful love.
9 The LORD is good to everyone;
His compassion ⌊rests⌋
on all He has made.
10 All You have made
will praise You, LORD;
the[j] godly will bless You.

[a]**144:2** Other Hb mss, DSS, Aq, Syr, Tg, Jer read *subdues peoples*; Ps 18:47; 2 Sm 22:48 [b]**144:6** Lit *scatter them* [c]**144:7** Lit *down Your hands* [d]**144:14** Or *will bear heavy loads*, or *will be pregnant* [e]**144:14** Or *be no plague, no miscarriage* [f]**145:1** The lines of this poem form an •acrostic. [g]**145:5** LXX, Syr read *They* [h]**145:5** LXX, Syr read *and they will tell of* [i]**145:6** Alt Hb tradition, Jer read *great deeds* [j]**145:10** Lit *Your*

11 They will speak of the glory
of Your kingdom
and will declare Your might,
12 informing ⌊all⌋ people[a]
of Your mighty acts
and of the glorious splendor
of Your[b] kingdom.
13 Your kingdom is
an everlasting kingdom;
Your rule is for all generations.
The LORD is faithful in all His words
and gracious in all His actions.[c]
14 The LORD helps all who fall;
He raises up all who are oppressed.[d]
15 All eyes look to You,
and You give them their food
in due time.
16 You open Your hand
and satisfy the desire
of every living thing.

17 The LORD is righteous in all His ways
and gracious in all His acts.
18 The LORD is near all who call out
to Him,
all who call out to Him with integrity.
19 He fulfills the desires of those
who •fear Him;
He hears their cry for help and saves
them.
20 The LORD guards all those
who love Him,
but He destroys all the wicked.
21 My mouth will declare
the LORD's praise;
let every living thing
praise His holy name forever and ever.

Psalm 146

The God of Compassion

1 •Hallelujah!
My soul, praise the LORD.
2 I will praise the LORD all my life;
I will sing to the LORD as long as I live.

3 Do not trust in nobles,
in man, who cannot save.
4 When his breath[e] leaves him,
he returns to the ground;
on that day his plans die.

5 Happy is the one whose help is
the God of Jacob,
whose hope is in the LORD his God,
6 the Maker of heaven and earth,
the sea and everything in them.
He remains faithful forever,
7 executing justice for the exploited
and giving food to the hungry.
The LORD frees prisoners.
8 The LORD opens ⌊the eyes of⌋ the blind.
The LORD raises up those
who are oppressed.[d]
The LORD loves the righteous.
9 The LORD protects foreigners
and helps the fatherless
and the widow,
but He frustrates the ways
of the wicked.

10 The LORD reigns forever;
Zion, your God ⌊reigns⌋
for all generations.
Hallelujah!

Psalm 147

God Restores Jerusalem

1 •Hallelujah!
How good it is to sing to our God,
for praise is pleasant and lovely.

2 The LORD rebuilds Jerusalem;
He gathers Israel's exiled people.
3 He heals the brokenhearted
and binds up their wounds.
4 He counts the number of the stars;
He gives names to all of them.
5 Our Lord is great, vast in power;
His understanding is infinite.[f]
6 The LORD helps the afflicted
but brings the wicked to the ground.

7 Sing to the LORD with thanksgiving;
play the lyre to our God,
8 who covers the sky with clouds,
prepares rain for the earth,
and causes grass to grow on the hills.
9 He provides the animals
with their food,
and the young ravens,
what they cry for.

10 He is not impressed by the strength
of a horse;
He does not value the power[g]
of a man.
11 The LORD values those who fear Him,

[a]**145:12** Lit *informing the sons of man* [b]**145:12** LXX, Syr, Jer; MT reads *His* [c]**145:13** One Hb ms, DSS, LXX, Syr; most Hb mss omit *The LORD is faithful in all His words and gracious in all His actions.* [d]**145:14; 146:8** Lit *bowed down* [e]**146:4** Or *spirit* [f]**147:5** Lit *understanding has no number* [g]**147:10** Lit *legs*

those who put their hope
in His faithful love.

12 Exalt the LORD, Jerusalem;
praise your God, Zion!
13 For He strengthens the bars
of your gates
and blesses your children within you.
14 He endows your territory
with prosperity;[a]
He satisfies you
with the finest wheat.

15 He sends His command
throughout the earth;
His word runs swiftly.
16 He spreads snow like wool;
He scatters frost like ashes;
17 He throws His hailstones like crumbs.
Who can withstand His cold?
18 He sends His word and melts them;
He unleashes His winds,[a]
and the waters flow.

19 He declares His word to Jacob,
His statutes and judgments to Israel.
20 He has not done this for any nation;
they do not know[c] ⌊His⌋ judgments.
Hallelujah!

Psalm 148

Creation's Praise of the LORD

1 •Hallelujah!
Praise the LORD from the heavens;
praise Him in the heights.
2 Praise Him, all His angels;
praise Him, all His •hosts.
3 Praise Him, sun and moon;
praise Him, all you shining stars.
4 Praise Him, highest heavens,
and you waters above the heavens.
5 Let them praise the name
of the LORD,
for He commanded,
and they were created.
6 He set them in position
forever and ever;
He gave an order that will never
pass away.

7 Praise the LORD from the earth,
all sea monsters and ocean depths,
8 lightning[d] and hail, snow and cloud,
powerful wind that executes
His command,
9 mountains and all hills,
fruit trees and all cedars,
10 wild animals and all cattle,
creatures that crawl and flying birds,
11 kings of the earth and all peoples,
princes and all judges of the earth,
12 young men as well as young women,
old and young together.
13 Let them praise the name
of the LORD,
for His name alone is exalted.
His majesty covers heaven and earth.
14 He has raised up a •horn
for His people,
praise from all His godly ones,
from the Israelites, the people
close to Him.
Hallelujah!

Psalm 149

Praise for God's Triumph

1 •Hallelujah!
Sing to the LORD a new song,
His praise in the assembly
of the godly.
2 Let Israel celebrate its Maker;
let the children of Zion rejoice
in their King.
3 Let them praise His name
with dancing
and make music to Him
with tambourine and lyre.
4 For the LORD takes pleasure
in His people;
He adorns the humble with salvation.
5 Let the godly celebrate
in triumphal glory;
let them shout for joy on their beds.

6 Let the exaltation of God be
in their mouths[e]
and a two-edged sword
in their hands,
7 inflicting vengeance on the nations
and punishment on the peoples,
8 binding their kings with chains
and their dignitaries
with iron shackles,
9 carrying out the judgment
decreed against them.
This honor is for
all His godly people.
Hallelujah!

[a]**147:14** Or *peace* [b]**147:18** Or *breath* [c]**147:20** DSS, LXX, Syr, Tg read *He has not made known to them* [d]**148:8** Or *fire*
[e]**149:6** Lit *throat*

Psalm 150
Praise the LORD

1 •Hallelujah!
Praise God in His sanctuary.
Praise Him in His mighty heavens.
2 Praise Him for His powerful acts;
praise Him for His abundant greatness.

3 Praise Him with trumpet blast;
praise Him with harp and lyre.
4 Praise Him with tambourine
and dance;
praise Him with flute and strings.
5 Praise Him with resounding cymbals;
praise Him with clashing cymbals.

6 Let everything that breathes
praise the LORD.
Hallelujah!

Proverbs

The Purpose of Proverbs

1 The proverbs of Solomonson of David,
king of Israel:
2 For gaining wisdom
and being instructed;
for understanding insightful sayings;
3 for receiving wise instruction
⌊in⌋ righteousness, justice,
and integrity;
4 for teaching shrewdness
to the inexperienced,[a]
knowledge and discretion
to a young man—
5 a wise man will listen and increase
his learning,
and a discerning man
will obtain guidance—
6 for understanding a proverb
or a parable,[b]
the words of the wise,
and their riddles.

7 The •fear of the LORD
is the beginning of knowledge;
fools despise wisdom and instruction.[c]

Avoid the Path of the Violent

8 Listen, my son,
to your father's instruction,
and don't reject
your mother's teaching,
9 for they will be a garland of grace
on your head
and a ⌊gold⌋ chain around your neck.
10 My son, if sinners entice you,
don't be persuaded.
11 If they say—"Come with us!
Let's set an ambush and kill someone.[d]
Let's attack some innocent person
just for fun![e]
12 Let's swallow them alive, like •Sheol,
still healthy as they go down
to the •Pit.
13 We'll find all kinds
of valuable property
and fill our houses with plunder.
14 Throw in your lot with us,
and we'll all share our money"[f] —
15 my son, don't travel that road
with them
or set foot on their path,
16 because their feet run toward trouble
and they hurry to commit murder.[g]
17 It is foolish to spread a net
where any bird can see it,
18 but they set an ambush
to kill themselves;[h]
they attack their own lives.
19 Such are the paths of all who pursue
gain dishonestly;
it takes the lives of those who profit
from it.[i]

Wisdom's Plea

20 Wisdom calls out in the street;
she raises her voice
in the public squares.
21 She cries out above[j] the commotion;

[a]**1:4** Or *simple, or gullible* [b]**1:6** Or *an enigma* [c]**1:7** This verse states the theme of Pr. [d]**1:11** Lit *Let's ambush for blood* [e]**1:11** Lit *person for no reason* [f]**1:14** Lit *us; one bag will be for all of us* [g]**1:16** Lit *to shed blood* [h]**1:18** Lit *they ambush for their blood* [i]**1:19** Lit *takes the life of its masters* [j]**1:21** Lit *at the head of*

she speaks at the entrance
of the city •gates:
22 "How long, foolish ones, will you
love ignorance?
⌊How long⌋ will ⌊you⌋ mockers
enjoy mocking
and ⌊you⌋ fools hate knowledge?
23 If you turn to my discipline,[a]
then I will pour out my spirit on you
and teach you my words.
24 Since I called out and you refused,
extended my hand and no one
paid attention,
25 since you neglected all my counsel
and did not accept my correction,
26 I, in turn, will laugh at your calamity.
I will mock when terror strikes you,
27 when terror strikes you like a storm
and your calamity comes
like a whirlwind,
when trouble and stress
overcome you.
28 Then they will call me,
but I won't answer;
they will search for me, but won't
find me.
29 Because they hated knowledge,
didn't choose to fear the LORD,
30 were not interested in my counsel,
and rejected all my correction,
31 they will eat the fruit of their way
and be glutted with their own schemes.
32 For the waywardness
of the inexperienced will kill them,
and the complacency of fools
will destroy them.
33 But whoever listens to me
will live securely
and be free from the fear of danger."

Wisdom's Worth

2 My son, if you accept my words
and store up my commands
within you,
2 listening closely[b] to wisdom
and directing your heart
to understanding;
3 furthermore, if you call out to insight
and lift your voice to understanding,
4 if you seek it like silver
and search for it like hidden treasure,
5 then you will understand the •fears
of the LORD
and discover the knowledge of God.
6 For the LORD gives wisdom;
from His mouth come knowledge
and understanding.
7 He stores up success[c] for the upright;
He is a shield for those who live
with integrity
8 so that He may guard the paths of justice
and protect the way
of His loyal followers.
9 Then you will understand righteousness, justice,
and integrity—every good path.
10 For wisdom will enter your mind,
and knowledge will delight your heart.
11 Discretion will watch over you,
and understanding will guard you,
12 rescuing you from the way of evil—
from the one who says
perverse things,
13 ⌊from⌋ those who abandon
the right paths
to walk in ways of darkness,
14 ⌊from⌋ those who enjoy doing evil
and celebrate perversity,
15 whose paths are crooked,
and whose ways are devious.
16 It will rescue you
from a forbidden woman,
from a stranger[d]
with her flattering talk,
17 who abandons the companion
of her youth
and forgets the covenant of her God;
18 for her house sinks down to death
and her ways to the land
of the departed spirits.
19 None return who go to her;
none reach the paths of life.
20 So follow the way of good people,
and keep to the paths of the righteous.
21 For the upright will inhabit the land,
and those of integrity will remain
in it;
22 but the wicked will be cut off
from the land,
and the treacherous uprooted from it.

Trust the LORD

3 My son, don't forget my teaching,
but let your heart keep my commands;
2 for they will bring you
many days, a full life,[e] and well-being.

[a]1:23 Lit *back to my reprimands* [b]2:2 Lit *you, stretching out your ear* [c]2:7 Or *resourcefulness* [d]2:16 Or *foreign woman*
[e]3:2 Lit *days, years of life*

3 Never let loyalty and faithfulness
leave you.
Tie them around your neck;
write them on the tablet of your heart.
4 Then you will find favor
and high regard
in the sight of God and man.

5 Trust in the LORD with all your heart,
and do not rely on
your own understanding;
6 think about Him in all your ways,
and He will guide you
on the right paths.
7 Don't consider yourself to be wise;
•fear the LORD and turn away
from evil.
8 This will be healing for your body[a]
and strengthening for your bones.
9 Honor the LORD with your possessions
and with the first produce
of your entire harvest;
10 then your barns will be
completely filled,
and your vats will overflow
with new wine.
11 Do not despise the LORD's instruction,
my son,
and do not loathe His discipline;
12 for the LORD disciplines the one
He loves,
just as a father, the son he delights in.

Wisdom Brings Happiness

13 Happy is a man who finds wisdom
and who acquires understanding,
14 for she is more profitable than silver,
and her revenue is better than gold.
15 She is more precious than jewels;
nothing you desire compares with her.
16 Long life[b] is in her right hand;
in her left, riches and honor.
17 Her ways are pleasant,
and all her paths, peaceful.
18 She is a tree of life to those
who embrace her,
and those who hold on to her
are happy.

19 The LORD founded the earth
by wisdom
and established the heavens
by understanding.
20 By His knowledge the watery depths
broke open,
and the clouds dripped with dew.

21 Maintain ⌊your⌋ competence
and discretion.
My son, don't lose sight of them.
22 They will be life for you[c]
and adornment[d] for your neck.
23 Then you will go safely on your way;
your foot will not stumble.
24 When you lie[e] down, you will not
be afraid;
you will lie down, and your sleep
will be pleasant.
25 Don't fear sudden danger
or the ruin of the wicked
when it comes,
26 for the LORD will be your confidence[f]
and will keep your foot from a snare.

Treat Others Fairly

27 When it is in your power,[g]
don't withhold good from the one
to whom it is due.
28 Don't say to your neighbor, "Go away!
Come back later.
I'll give it tomorrow"—
when it is there with you.
29 Don't plan any harm
against your neighbor,
for he trusts you and lives near you.
30 Don't accuse anyone without cause,
when he has done you no harm.
31 Don't envy a violent man
or choose any of his ways;
32 for the devious are detestable
to the LORD,
but He is a friend[h] to the upright.
33 The LORD's curse is on the household
of the wicked,
but He blesses the home
of the righteous;
34 He mocks those who mock,
but gives grace to the humble.
35 The wise will inherit honor,
but He holds up fools to dishonor.[i]

A Father's Example

4 Listen, ⌊my⌋ sons,
to a father's discipline,
and pay attention so that
you may gain understanding,

[a]**3:8** Lit *navel* [b]**3:16** Lit *Length of days* [c]**3:22** Or *be your throat;* Hb *nephesh* can mean *throat, soul,* or *life.* [d]**3:22** Or *grace* [e]**3:24** LXX reads *sit* [f]**3:26** Or *be at your side* [g]**3:27** Lit *in the power of your hands* [h]**3:32** Or *confidential counsel* [i]**3:35** Or *but haughty fools dishonor,* or *but fools exalt dishonor*

2 for I am giving you good instruction.
Don't abandon my teaching.
3 When I was a son with my father,
tender and precious to my mother,
4 he taught me and said:
"Your heart must hold on
to my words.
Keep my commands and live.
5 Get wisdom, get understanding;
don't forget or turn away
from the words of my mouth.
6 Don't abandon wisdom, and she will
watch over you;
love her, and she will guard you.
7 Wisdom is supreme—so get wisdom.
And whatever else you get,
get understanding.
8 Cherish her, and she will exalt you;
if you embrace her, she will
honor you.
9 She will place a garland of grace
on your head;
she will give you a crown of beauty."

Two Ways of Life

10 Listen, my son. Accept my words,
and you will live many years.
11 I am teaching you the way of wisdom;
I am guiding you on straight paths.
12 When you walk, your steps will not
be hindered;
when you run, you will not stumble.
13 Hold on to instruction; don't let go.
Guard it, for it is your life.
14 Don't set foot on the path
of the wicked;
don't proceed in the way of evil ones.
15 Avoid it; don't travel on it.
Turn away from it, and pass it by.
16 For they can't sleep
unless they have done what is evil;
they are robbed of sleep
unless they make someone stumble.
17 They eat the bread of wickedness
and drink the wine of violence.
18 The path of the righteous is
like the light of dawn,
shining brighter and brighter
until midday.
19 But the way of the wicked is
like the darkest gloom;
they don't know what makes
them stumble.

The Straight Path

20 My son, pay attention to my words;
listen closely to my sayings.
21 Don't lose sight of them;
keep them within your heart.
22 For they are life to those
who find them,
and health to one's whole body.
23 Guard your heart above all else,[a]
for it is the source of life.
24 Don't let your mouth
speak dishonestly,
and don't let your lips talk deviously.
25 Let your eyes look forward;
fix your gaze[b] straight ahead.
26 Carefully consider the path[c]
for your feet,
and all your ways will be established.
27 Don't turn to the right or to the left;
keep your feet away from evil.

Avoid Seduction

5 My son, pay attention to my wisdom;
listen closely[d] to my understanding
2 so that ⌊you⌋ may maintain discretion
and your lips safeguard knowledge.
3 Though the lips
of the forbidden woman drip honey
and her words are[e] smoother than oil,
4 in the end she's as bitter
as •wormwood
and as sharp as a double-edged sword.
5 Her feet go down to death;
her steps head straight for •Sheol.
6 She doesn't consider the path of life;
she doesn't know that her ways
are unstable.

7 So now, ⌊my⌋ sons, listen to me,
and don't turn away from the words
of my mouth.
8 Keep your way far from her.
Don't go near the door of her house.
9 Otherwise, you will give up
your vitality to others
and your years to someone cruel;
10 strangers will drain your resources,
and your earnings will end up
in a foreigner's house.
11 At the end of your life,
you will lament
when your physical body
has been consumed,

[a]**4:23** Or *heart with all diligence* [b]**4:25** Lit *eyelids* [c]**4:26** Or *Clear a path* [d]**5:1** Lit *wisdom; stretch out your ear* [e]**5:3** Lit *her palate is*

12 and you will say,
"How I hated discipline,
and how my heart despised correction.
13 I didn't obey my teachers
or listen closely[a] to my mentors.
14 I was on the verge of complete ruin
before the entire community."

Enjoy Marriage

15 Drink water from your own cistern,
water flowing from your own well.
16 Should your springs flow
in the streets,
streams of water in the public squares?
17 They should be for you alone
and not for you ⌊to share⌋
with strangers.
18 Let your fountain be blessed,
and take pleasure in the wife
of your youth.
19 A loving doe, a graceful fawn—
let her breasts always satisfy you;
be lost in her love forever.
20 Why, my son, would you
be infatuated
with a forbidden woman
or embrace the breast of a stranger?
21 For a man's ways are
before the LORD's eyes,
and He considers all his paths.
22 A wicked man's iniquities entrap him;
he is entangled in the ropes
of his own sin.
23 He will die because there is
no instruction,
and be lost because of
his great stupidity.

Financial Entanglements

6 My son, if you have put up security
for your neighbor[b]
or entered into an agreement
with[c] a stranger,[d]
2 you have been trapped by the words
of your lips[e]—
ensnared by the words
of your mouth.
3 Do this, then, my son,
and free yourself,
for you have put yourself
in your neighbor's power:
Go, humble yourself, and plead
with your neighbor.
4 Don't give sleep to your eyes
or slumber to your eyelids.
5 Escape like a gazelle from a hunter,[f]
like a bird from a fowler's trap.[f]

Laziness

6 Go to the ant, you slacker!
Observe its ways and become wise.
7 Without leader, administrator, or ruler,
8 it prepares its provisions in summer;
it gathers its food during harvest.
9 How long will you stay in bed,
you slacker?
When will you get up
from your sleep?
10 A little sleep, a little slumber,
a little folding of the arms to rest,
11 and your poverty will come like
a robber,
your need, like a bandit.

The Malicious Man

12 A worthless person, a wicked man,
who goes around
speaking dishonestly,
13 who winks his eyes, signals
with his feet,
and gestures with his fingers,
14 who plots evil with perversity
in his heart—
he stirs up trouble constantly.
15 Therefore calamity
will strike him suddenly;
he will be shattered instantly—
beyond recovery.

What the LORD Hates

16 Six things the LORD hates;
in fact, seven are detestable to Him:
17 arrogant eyes, a lying tongue,
hands that shed innocent blood,
18 a heart that plots wicked schemes,
feet eager to run to evil,
19 a lying witness who gives
false testimony,
and one who stirs up trouble
among brothers.

Warning against Adultery

20 My son, keep your father's command,
and don't reject
your mother's teaching.

[a]**5:13** Lit *or turn my ear* [b]**6:1** Or *friend* [c]**6:1** Lit *or shaken hands for* or *with* [d]**6:1** The Hb word for *stranger* can refer to a foreigner, an Israelite outside one's family, or simply to another person. [e]**6:2** Lit *mouth* [f]**6:5** Lit *hand*

21 Always bind them to your heart;
tie them around your neck.
22 When you walk here and there,
they will guide you;
when you lie down, they will
watch over you;
when you wake up, they will
talk to you.
23 For a commandment is a lamp,
teaching is a light,
and corrective instructions are the way
to life.
24 They will protect you
from an evil woman,[a]
from the flattering[b] tongue of a stranger.
25 Don't lust in your heart for her beauty
or let her captivate you
with her eyelashes.
26 For a prostitute's fee is only a loaf
of bread,[c]
but an adulteress[d] goes
after ⌊your⌋ very life.
27 Can a man embrace fire[e]
and his clothes not be burned?
28 Can a man walk on coals
without scorching his feet?
29 So it is with the one who sleeps with
another man's wife;
no one who touches her
will go unpunished.
30 People don't despise the thief
if he steals
to satisfy himself when he is hungry.
31 Still, if caught, he must pay
seven times as much;
he must give up all the wealth
in his house.
32 The one who commits adultery[f]
lacks sense;
whoever does so destroys himself.
33 He will get a beating[g] and dishonor,
and his disgrace will
never be removed.
34 For jealousy enrages a husband,
and he will show no mercy
when he takes revenge.
35 He will not be appeased by anything
or be persuaded by lavish gifts.

7 My son, obey my words,
and treasure my commands.
2 Keep my commands and live;
protect my teachings
as you would the pupil of your eye.
3 Tie them to your fingers;
write them on the tablet of your heart.
4 Say to wisdom, "You are my sister,"
and call understanding ⌊your⌋ relative.
5 She will keep you
from a forbidden woman,
a stranger with her flattering talk.

A Story of Seduction

6 At the window of my house
I looked through my lattice.
7 I saw among the inexperienced,[h]
I noticed among the youths,
a young man lacking sense.
8 Crossing the street near her corner,
he strolled down the road to her house
9 at twilight, in the evening,
in the dark of the night.
10 A woman came to meet him,
dressed like a prostitute,
having a hidden agenda.[i]
11 She is loud and defiant;
her feet do not stay at home.
12 Now in the street, now in the squares,
she lurks at every corner.
13 She grabs him and kisses him;
she brazenly says[j] to him,
14 "I've made •fellowship offerings;[k]
today I've fulfilled my vows.
15 So I came out to meet you,
to search for you, and I've found you.
16 I've spread coverings on my bed—
richly colored linen from Egypt.
17 I've perfumed my bed
with myrrh, aloes, and cinnamon.
18 Come, let's drink deeply of lovemaking
until morning.
Let's feast on each other's love!
19 My husband isn't home;
he went on a long journey.
20 He took a bag of money with him
and will come home at the time
of the full moon."
21 She seduces him
with her persistent pleading;
she lures with her flattering[l] talk.
22 He follows her impulsively

[a]**6:24** LXX reads *from a married woman* [b]**6:24** Lit *smooth* [c]**6:26** Or *On account of a prostitute, [one is left with] only a loaf of bread* [d]**6:26** Lit *but a wife of a man* [e]**6:27** Lit *man take fire to his bosom* [f]**6:32** Lit *commits adultery with a woman* [g]**6:33** Or *plague* [h]**7:7** Or *simple*, or *gullible*, or *naive* [i]**7:10** Or *prostitute, with a guarded heart* [j]**7:13** Lit *she makes her face strong and says* [k]**7:14** Meat from a fellowship offering had to be eaten on the day it was offered; therefore she is inviting him to a feast at her house. [l]**7:21** Lit *smooth*

like an ox going to the slaughter,
like a deer bounding toward a trap[a]
23 until an arrow pierces its[b] liver,
like a bird darting into a snare—
he doesn't know it will cost him
his life.

24 Now, ⌊my⌋ sons, listen to me,
and pay attention to the words
of my mouth.
25 Don't let your heart turn aside
to her ways;
don't stray onto her paths.
26 For she has brought many
down to death;
her victims are countless.[c]
27 Her house is the road to •Sheol,
descending to the chambers of death.

Wisdom's Appeal

8 Doesn't Wisdom call out?
Doesn't Understanding make her voice
heard?
2 At the heights overlooking the road,
at the crossroads, she takes her stand.
3 Beside the gates at the entry to[d]
the city,
at the main entrance, she cries out:
4 "People, I call out to you;
my cry is to mankind.
5 Learn to be shrewd,
you who are inexperienced;
develop common sense,
you who are foolish.
6 Listen, for I speak of noble things,
and what my lips say is right.
7 For my mouth tells the truth,
and wickedness is detestable
to my lips.
8 All the words of my mouth
are righteous;
none of them are deceptive
or perverse.
9 All of them are clear to the perceptive,
and right to those
who discover knowledge.
10 Accept my instruction instead of silver,
and knowledge rather than pure gold.
11 For wisdom is better
than precious stones,
and nothing desirable can compare
with it.

12 I, Wisdom, share a home
with shrewdness
and have knowledge and discretion.
13 To •fear the LORD is to hate evil.
I hate arrogant pride, evil conduct,
and perverse speech.
14 I possess good advice
and competence;[e]
I have understanding and strength.
15 It is by me that kings reign
and rulers enact just law;
16 by me, princes lead,
as do nobles ⌊and⌋ all righteous judges.[f]
17 I love those who love me,
and those who search for me find me.
18 With me are riches and honor,
lasting wealth and righteousness.
19 My fruit is better than solid gold,
and my harvest than pure silver.
20 I walk in the way of righteousness,
along the paths of justice,
21 giving wealth as an inheritance
to those who love me,
and filling their treasuries.

22 The LORD made[g] me
at the beginning of His creation,[h]
before His works of long ago.
23 I was formed before ancient times,
from the beginning,
before the earth began.
24 I was brought forth
when there were no watery depths
and no springs filled with water.
25 I was brought forth
before the mountains and hills
were established,
26 before He made the land, the fields,
or the first soil on earth.
27 I was there when He established
the heavens,
when He laid out the horizon
on the surface of the ocean,
28 when He placed the skies above,
when the fountains of the ocean
gushed forth,
29 when He set a limit for the sea
so that the waters would not violate
His command,
when He laid out the foundations
of the earth.
30 I was a skilled craftsman[i] beside Him.

[a]**7:22** Text emended; lit *like shackles for the discipline of a fool*; Hb obscure [b]**7:23** Or *his* [c]**7:26** Or *and powerful men are all her victims* [d]**8:3** Lit *the mouth of* [e]**8:14** Or *resourcefulness* [f]**8:16** Some Hb mss, LXX read *nobles who judge the earth* [g]**8:22** Or *possessed*, or *begot* [h]**8:22** Lit *way* [i]**8:30** Or *a confidante*, or *a child*

I was His[a] delight every day,
always rejoicing before Him.
31 I was rejoicing in His inhabited world,
delighting in the •human race.

32 And now, ⌊my⌋ sons, listen to me;
those who keep my ways are happy.
33 Listen to instruction and be wise;
don't ignore it.
34 Anyone who listens to me is happy,
watching at my doors every day,
waiting by the posts of my doorway.
35 For the one who finds me finds life
and obtains favor from the LORD,
36 but the one who sins against me
harms himself;
all who hate me love death."

Wisdom versus Foolishness

9 Wisdom has built her house;
she has carved out her seven pillars.
2 She has prepared her meat;
she has mixed her wine;
she has also set her table.
3 She has sent out her servants;
she calls out from the highest points
of the city:
4 "Whoever is inexperienced,
enter here!"
To the one who lacks sense, she says,
5 "Come, eat my bread,
and drink the wine I have mixed.
6 Leave inexperience behind,
and you will live;
pursue the way of understanding.
7 The one who corrects a mocker
will bring dishonor on himself;
the one who rebukes a wicked man
will get hurt.[b]
8 Don't rebuke a mocker, or he will
hate you;
rebuke a wise man, and he will
love you.
9 Instruct a wise man, and he will be
wiser still;
teach a righteous man, and he will
learn more.

10 The •fear of the LORD is the beginning
of wisdom,
and the knowledge of the Holy One
is understanding.
11 For by Wisdom your days
will be many,
and years will be added to your life.
12 If you are wise, you are wise
for your own benefit;
if you mock, you alone will bear
⌊the consequences⌋."
13 The woman Folly is rowdy;
she is gullible and knows nothing.
14 She sits by the doorway of her house,
on a seat at the highest point
of the city,
15 calling to those who pass by,
who go straight ahead on their paths:
16 "Whoever is inexperienced,
enter here!"
To the one who lacks sense, she says,
17 "Stolen water is sweet,
and bread ⌊eaten⌋ secretly is tasty!"
18 But he doesn't know
that the departed spirits
are there,
that her guests are in the depths
of •Sheol.

A Collection of Solomon's Proverbs

10 Solomon's proverbs:

A wise son brings joy to his father,
but a foolish son, heartache
to his mother.

2 Ill-gotten gains do not profit anyone,
but righteousness rescues from death.

3 The LORD will not let the righteous
go hungry,
but He denies the wicked
what they crave.

4 Idle hands make one poor,
but diligent hands bring riches.

5 The son who gathers during summer
is prudent;
the son who sleeps during harvest
is disgraceful.

6 Blessings are on the head
of the righteous,
but the mouth of the wicked
conceals violence.

7 The remembrance of the righteous is
a blessing,
but the name of the wicked will rot.

8 A wise heart accepts commands,
but foolish lips will be destroyed.

[a]**8:30** LXX; Hb omits *His* [b]**9:7** Lit *man his blemish*

9 The one who lives with integrity
lives securely,
but whoever perverts his ways will be
found out.

10 A sly wink of the eye causes grief,
and foolish lips will be destroyed.

11 The mouth of the righteous is
a fountain of life,
but the mouth of the wicked
conceals violence.

12 Hatred stirs up conflicts,
but love covers all offenses.

13 Wisdom is found on the lips
of the discerning,
but a rod is for the back of the one
who lacks sense.

14 The wise store up knowledge,
but the mouth of the fool
hastens destruction.

15 A rich man's wealth is
his fortified city;
the poverty of the poor is
their destruction.

16 The labor of the righteous leads to life;
the activity of the wicked leads to sin.

17 The one who follows instruction is
on the path to life,
but the one who rejects correction
goes astray.

18 The one who conceals hatred has
lying lips,
and whoever spreads slander is a fool.

19 When there are many words,
sin is unavoidable,
but the one who controls his lips
is wise.

20 The tongue of the righteous is
pure silver;
the heart of the wicked is
of little value.

21 The lips of the righteous feed many,
but fools die for lack of sense.

22 The LORD's blessing enriches,
and struggle adds nothing to it.[a]

23 As shameful conduct is pleasure
for a fool,
so wisdom is for a man
of understanding.

24 What the wicked dreads will come
to him,
but what the righteous desires
will be given to him.

25 When the whirlwind passes,
the wicked are no more,
but the righteous are secure forever.

26 Like vinegar to the teeth and smoke
to the eyes,
so the slacker is to the one
who sends him ⌊on an errand⌋.

27 The •fear of the LORD prolongs life,[b]
but the years of the wicked
are cut short.

28 The hope of the righteous is joy,
but the expectation of the wicked
comes to nothing.

29 The way of the LORD is a stronghold
for the honorable,
but destruction awaits the malicious.

30 The righteous will never be shaken,
but the wicked will not remain
on the earth.

31 The mouth of the righteous
produces wisdom,
but a perverse tongue will be cut out.

32 The lips of the righteous know
what is appropriate,
but the mouth of the wicked,
⌊only⌋ what is perverse.

11 Dishonest scales are detestable
to the LORD,
but an accurate weight is His delight.

2 When pride comes, disgrace follows,
but with humility comes wisdom.

3 The integrity of the upright
guides them,
but the perversity of the treacherous
destroys them.

4 Wealth is not profitable on a day
of wrath,
but righteousness rescues from death.

5 The righteousness of the blameless
clears his path,

[a]**10:22** Or *and He adds no trouble to it* [b]**10:27** Lit *LORD adds to days*

but the wicked person will fall
because of his wickedness.

6 The righteousness of the upright
rescues them,
but the treacherous are trapped
by their own desires.

7 When the wicked dies,
his expectation comes to nothing,
and hope placed in wealth[a] [b] vanishes.

8 The righteous is rescued from trouble;
in his place, the wicked goes in.

9 With his mouth the ungodly
destroys his neighbor,
but through knowledge the righteous
are rescued.

10 When the righteous thrive,
a city rejoices,
and when the wicked die, there is
joyful shouting.

11 A city is built up by the blessing
of the upright,
but it is torn down by the mouth
of the wicked.

12 Whoever shows contempt
for his neighbor lacks sense,
but a man with understanding
keeps silent.

13 A gossip goes around revealing
a secret,
but the trustworthy keeps
a confidence.

14 Without guidance, people fall,
but with many counselors
there is deliverance.

15 If someone puts up security
for a stranger,
he will suffer for it,
but the one who hates
such agreements is protected.

16 A gracious woman gains honor,
but violent[c] men gain ⌊only⌋ riches.

17 A kind man benefits himself,
but a cruel man brings disaster
on himself.

18 The wicked man earns
an empty wage,
but the one who sows righteousness,
a true reward.

19 Genuine righteousness ⌊leads⌋ to life,
but pursuing evil ⌊leads⌋ to death.

20 Those with twisted minds
are detestable to the LORD,
but those with blameless conduct are
His delight.

21 Be assured[d] that the wicked
will not go unpunished,
but the offspring of the righteous
will escape.

22 A beautiful woman who rejects
good sense
is like a gold ring in a pig's snout.

23 The desire of the righteous
⌊turns out⌋ well,
but the hope of the wicked
⌊leads to⌋ wrath.

24 One person gives freely,
yet gains more;
another withholds what is right,
only to become poor.

25 A generous person will be enriched,
and the one who gives a drink of
water
will receive water.

26 People will curse anyone
who hoards grain,
but a blessing will come to the one
who sells it.

27 The one who searches
for what is good finds favor,
but if someone looks for trouble,
it will come to him.

28 Anyone trusting in his riches will fall,
but the righteous will flourish
like foliage.

29 The one who brings ruin
on his household
will inherit the wind,
and a fool will be a slave
to someone whose heart is wise.

30 The fruit of the righteous is a tree
of life,
but violence[e] takes lives.

[a]**11:7** LXX reads *hope of the ungodly* [b]**11:7** Or *strength* [c]**11:16** Or *ruthless* [d]**11:21** Lit *Hand to hand* [e]**11:30** LXX, Syr; MT reads *but a wise one*

31 If the righteous will be repaid
on earth,
how much more the wicked
and sinful.

12 Whoever loves instruction
loves knowledge,
but one who hates correction
is stupid.

2 The good obtain favor from the LORD,
but He condemns a man
who schemes.

3 Man cannot be made secure
by wickedness,
but the root of the righteous
is immovable.

4 A capable wife[a] is
her husband's crown,
but a wife who causes shame
is like rottenness in his bones.

5 The thoughts of the righteous
⌊are⌋ just,
but guidance from the wicked
⌊leads to⌋ deceit.

6 The words of the wicked are
a deadly ambush,
but the speech of the upright
rescues them.

7 The wicked are overthrown
and perish,
but the house of the righteous
will stand.

8 A man is praised for his insight,
but a twisted mind is despised.

9 Better to be dishonored, yet have
a servant,
than to act important but have
no food.

10 A righteous man cares about
his animal's health,
but ⌊even⌋ the merciful acts
of the wicked are cruel.

11 The one who works his land will have
plenty of food,
but whoever chases fantasies
lacks sense.

12 The wicked desire
what evil men have,[b]
but the root of the righteous
produces ⌊fruit⌋.

13 An evil man is trapped
by ⌊his⌋ rebellious speech,
but the righteous escapes from trouble.

14 A man will be satisfied with good
by the words of his mouth,
and the work of a man's hands
will reward him.

15 A fool's way is right in his own eyes,
but whoever listens to counsel
is wise.

16 A fool's displeasure is known at once,
but whoever ignores an insult
is sensible.

17 Whoever speaks the truth declares
what is right,
but a false witness, deceit.

18 There is one who speaks rashly,
like a piercing sword;
but the tongue of the wise
⌊brings⌋ healing.

19 Truthful lips endure forever,
but a lying tongue, only a moment.

20 Deceit is in the hearts of those
who plot evil,
but those who promote peace have joy.

21 No disaster ⌊overcomes⌋ the righteous,
but the wicked are full of misery.

22 Lying lips are detestable to the LORD,
but faithful people are His delight.

23 A shrewd person conceals knowledge,
but a foolish heart publicizes stupidity.

24 The diligent hand will rule,
but laziness will lead to forced labor.

25 Anxiety in a man's heart
weighs it down,
but a good word cheers it up.

26 A righteous man is careful in dealing
with his neighbor,[c]
but the ways of wicked men
lead them astray.

27 A lazy man doesn't roast his game,
but to a diligent man, his wealth
is precious.

[a]**12:4** Or *A wife of quality,* or *A wife of good character* [b]**12:12** Or *desire a stronghold of evil* [c]**12:26** Or *man guides his neighbor*

28 There is life in the path
of righteousness,
but another path leads to death.[a]

13 A wise son ⌊hears his⌋
father's instruction,
but a mocker doesn't listen to rebuke.

2 From the words of his mouth,
a man will enjoy good things,
but treacherous people have
an appetite for violence.

3 The one who guards his mouth protects his life;
the one who opens his lips invites
his own ruin.

4 The slacker craves, yet has nothing,
but the diligent is fully satisfied.

5 The righteous hate lying,
but the wicked act disgustingly
and disgracefully.

6 Righteousness guards people
of integrity,[b]
but wickedness undermines
the sinner.

7 One man pretends to be rich
but has nothing;
another pretends to be poor but has
great wealth.

8 Riches are a ransom for a man's life,
but a poor man hears no threat.

9 The light of the righteous
shines brightly,
but the lamp of the wicked
is extinguished.

10 Arrogance leads to nothing
but strife,
but wisdom is gained by those
who take advice.

11 Wealth obtained by fraud will dwindle,
but whoever earns it through labor[c]
will multiply it.

12 Delayed hope makes the heart sick,
but fulfilled desire is a tree of life.

13 The one who has contempt
for instruction will pay the penalty,
but the one who respects a command
will be rewarded.

14 A wise man's instruction is a fountain
of life,
turning people away from the snares
of death.

15 Good sense wins favor,
but the way of the treacherous
never changes.[d]

16 Every sensible person
acts knowledgeably,
but a fool displays his stupidity.

17 A wicked messenger falls into trouble,
but a trustworthy courier
⌊brings⌋ healing.

18 Poverty and disgrace ⌊come to⌋ those
who ignore instruction,
but the one who accepts rebuke
will be honored.

19 Desire fulfilled is sweet to the taste,
but fools hate to turn from evil.

20 The one who walks with the wise
will become wise,
but a companion of fools
will suffer harm.

21 Disaster pursues sinners,
but good rewards the righteous.

22 A good man leaves an inheritance
to his[e] grandchildren,
but the sinner's wealth is stored up
for the righteous.

23 The field of the poor yields
abundant food,
but without justice, it is swept away.

24 The one who will not use the rod
hates his son,
but the one who loves him disciplines
him diligently.

25 A righteous man eats
until he is satisfied,
but the stomach of the wicked
is empty.

14 Every wise woman builds her house,
but a foolish one tears it down
with her own hands.

2 Whoever lives with integrity
•fears the LORD,
but the one who is devious in his ways
despises Him.

[a]12:28 Or *righteousness, and in its path there is no death* [b]13:6 Lit *guards integrity of way* [c]13:11 Lit *whoever gathers upon (his) hand* [d]13:15 LXX, Syr, Tg read *treacherous will perish* [e]13:22 Or *inheritance: his*

3 The proud speech of a fool ⌊brings⌋
a rod ⌊of discipline⌋,[a]
but the lips of the wise protect them.

4 Where there are no oxen, the feeding-trough is empty,[b]
but an abundant harvest ⌊comes⌋
through the strength of an ox.

5 An honest witness does not deceive,
but a dishonest witness utters lies.

6 A mocker seeks wisdom
and doesn't find it,
but knowledge ⌊comes⌋ easily
to the perceptive.

7 Stay away from a foolish man;
you will gain no knowledge
from his speech.

8 The sensible man's wisdom is
to consider his way,
but the stupidity of fools
deceives ⌊them⌋.

9 Fools mock at making restitution,[c]
but there is goodwill
among the upright.

10 The heart knows its own bitterness,
and no outsider shares in its joy.

11 The house of the wicked
will be destroyed,
but the tent of the upright will stand.[d]

12 There is a way that seems right
to a man,
but its end is the way[e] to death.

13 Even in laughter a heart may be sad,
and joy may end in grief.

14 The disloyal will get
what their conduct deserves,
and a good man,
what his ⌊deeds deserve⌋.

15 The inexperienced believe anything,
but the sensible watch[f] their steps.

16 A wise man is cautious and turns
from evil,
but a fool is easily angered
and is careless.[g]

17 A quick-tempered man acts foolishly,
and a man who schemes is hated.

18 The gullible inherit foolishness,
but the sensible are crowned
with knowledge.

19 The evil bow before those
who are good,
the wicked, at the gates
of the righteous.

20 A poor man is hated even
by his neighbor,
but there are many who love the rich.

21 The one who despises
his neighbor sins,
but whoever shows kindness
to the poor will be happy.

22 Don't those who plan evil go astray?
But those who plan good find loyalty
and faithfulness.

23 There is profit in all hard work,
but endless talk[h] leads only to poverty.

24 The crown of the wise is their wealth,
but the foolishness of fools
produces foolishness.

25 A truthful witness rescues lives,
but one who utters lies is deceitful.

26 In the fear of the LORD one has
strong confidence
and his children have a refuge.

27 The fear of the LORD is a fountain
of life,
turning people from the snares
of death.

28 A large population is a king's splendor,
but a shortage of people is
a ruler's devastation.

29 A patient person ⌊shows⌋ great understanding,
but a quick-tempered one
promotes foolishness.

30 A tranquil heart is life to the body,
but jealousy is rottenness to the bones.

31 The one who oppresses the poor
insults their Maker,
but one who is kind to the needy
honors Him.

32 The wicked are thrown down
by their own sin,

[a]**14:3** Or *In the mouth of a fool is a rod for his back*, if text is emended [b]**14:4** Or *clean* [c]**14:9** Or *at guilt offerings* [d]**14:11** Lit *flourish* [e]**14:12** Lit *ways* [f]**14:15** Lit *the prudent understand* [g]**14:16** Or *and falls* [h]**14:23** Lit *but word of lips*

but the righteous have a refuge
when they die.

33 Wisdom resides in the heart
of the discerning;
she is known[a] even among fools.

34 Righteousness exalts a nation,
but sin is a disgrace to any people.

35 A king favors a wise servant,
but his anger falls on a disgraceful one.

15 A gentle answer turns away anger,
but a harsh word stirs up wrath.

2 The tongue of the wise
makes knowledge attractive,
but the mouth of fools
blurts out foolishness.

3 The eyes of the LORD are everywhere,
observing the wicked and the good.

4 The tongue that heals is a tree of life,
but a devious tongue[b] breaks the spirit.

5 A fool despises his father's instruction,
but a person who heeds correction
is sensible.

6 The house of the righteous
has great wealth,
but trouble accompanies the income
of the wicked.

7 The lips of the wise
broadcast knowledge,
but not so the heart of fools.

8 The sacrifice of the wicked
is detestable to the LORD,
but the prayer of the upright is
His delight.

9 The LORD detests the way
of the wicked,
but He loves the one
who pursues righteousness.

10 Discipline is harsh for the one
who leaves the path;
the one who hates correction will die.

11 •Sheol and •Abaddon lie open
before the LORD—
how much more, human hearts.

12 A mocker doesn't love one
who corrects him;
he will not consult the wise.

13 A joyful heart makes a face cheerful,
but a sad heart ⌊produces⌋
a broken spirit.

14 A discerning mind seeks knowledge,
but the mouth of fools feeds
on foolishness.

15 All the days of the oppressed
are miserable,
but a cheerful heart has
a continual feast.

16 Better a little with the •fear
of the LORD
than great treasure with turmoil.

17 Better a meal of vegetables
where there is love
than a fattened calf with hatred.

18 A hot-tempered man stirs up conflict,
but a man slow to anger calms strife.

19 A slacker's way is like a thorny hedge,
but the path of the upright is
a highway.

20 A wise son brings joy to his father,
but a foolish one despises his mother.

21 Foolishness brings joy to one
without sense,
but a man with understanding walks
a straight path.

22 Plans fail when there is no counsel,
but with many advisers they succeed.

23 A man takes joy in giving an answer;[c]
and a timely word—how good that is!

24 For the discerning the path of life
leads upward,
so that he may avoid going down
to Sheol.

25 The LORD destroys the house
of the proud,
but He protects the widow's territory.

26 The LORD detests the plans
of an evil man,
but pleasant words are pure.

27 The one who profits dishonestly troubles his household,
but the one who hates bribes will live.

28 The mind of the righteous person
thinks before answering,

[a]**14:33** LXX reads *unknown* [b]**15:4** Lit *but crookedness in it* [c]**15:23** Lit *in an answer of his mouth*

but the mouth of the wicked blurts out
evil things.

29 The LORD is far from the wicked,
but He hears the prayer
of the righteous.

30 Bright eyes cheer the heart;
good news strengthens[a] the bones.

31 An ear that listens to life-giving rebukes
will be at home among the wise.

32 Anyone who ignores instruction
despises himself,
but whoever listens to correction
acquires good sense.[b]

33 The fear of the LORD is
wisdom's instruction,
and humility comes before honor.

16 The reflections of the heart
belong to man,
but the answer of the tongue is
from the LORD.

2 All a man's ways seem right
in his own eyes,
but the LORD weighs the motives.[c]

3 Commit your activities to the LORD
and your plans will be achieved.

4 The LORD has prepared everything
for His purpose—
even the wicked for the day
of disaster.

5 Everyone with a proud heart is detestable to the LORD;
be assured,[d] he will not
go unpunished.

6 Wickedness is •atoned for by loyalty
and faithfulness,
and one turns from evil by the •fear
of the LORD.

7 When a man's ways please the LORD,
He[e] makes even his enemies to be
at peace with him.

8 Better a little with righteousness
than great income with injustice.

9 A man's heart plans his way,
but the LORD determines his steps.

10 God's verdict is on the lips of a king;[f]
his mouth should not err in judgment.

11 Honest balances and scales are
the LORD's;
all the weights in the bag[g] are
His concern.

12 Wicked behavior[h] is detestable
to kings,
since a throne is established
through righteousness.

13 Righteous lips are a king's delight,
and he loves one
who speaks honestly.

14 A king's fury is a messenger of death,
but a wise man appeases it.

15 When a king's face lights up,
there is life;
his favor is like a cloud with spring rain.

16 Acquire wisdom—
how much better it is than gold!
And acquire understanding—
it is preferable to silver.

17 The highway of the upright avoids evil;
the one who guards his way protects
his life.

18 Pride comes before destruction,
and an arrogant spirit before a fall.

19 Better to be lowly of spirit
with the humble[i]
than to divide plunder with the proud.

20 The one who understands a matter
finds success,
and the one who trusts in the LORD
will be happy.

21 Anyone with a wise heart
is called discerning,
and pleasant speech[j]
increases learning.

22 Insight is a fountain of life
for its possessor,
but folly is the instruction of fools.

23 A wise heart instructs its mouth
and increases learning
with its speech.[k]

[a]**15:30** Lit *makes fat* [b]**15:32** Lit *acquires a heart* [c]**16:2** Lit *weighs spirits* [d]**16:5** Lit *hand to hand* [e]**16:7** Or *he* [f]**16:10** Or *A divination is on the lips of a king* [g]**16:11** Merchants kept the stones for their balance scales in a bag. [h]**16:12** Whether the wicked behavior is on the part of the king or someone else is ambiguous in Hb. [i]**16:19** Alt Hb tradition reads *afflicted* [j]**16:21** Lit *and sweetness of lips* [k]**16:23** Lit *learning upon his lips*

24 Pleasant words are a honeycomb:
sweet to the taste[a] and health
to the body.[b]
25 There is a way that seems right
to a man,
but in the end it is the way of death.
26 A worker's appetite works for him
because his hunger[c] urges him on.
27 A worthless man digs up evil,
and his speech is like a scorching fire.
28 A contrary man spreads conflict,
and a gossip separates friends.
29 A violent man lures his neighbor,
leading him in a way that is not good.
30 The one who narrows his eyes
is planning deceptions;
the one who compresses his lips
brings about evil.
31 Gray hair is a glorious crown;
it is found in the way of righteousness.
32 Patience is better than power,
and controlling one's temper,[d]
than capturing a city.
33 The lot is cast into the lap,
but its every decision is
from the LORD.

17 Better a dry crust with peace
than a house full of feasting with strife.
2 A wise servant will rule over
a disgraceful son
and share an inheritance
among brothers.
3 A crucible is for silver and a smelter
for gold,
but the LORD is a tester of hearts.
4 A wicked person listens to
malicious talk;[e]
a liar pays attention to
a destructive tongue.
5 The one who mocks the poor insults
his Maker,
and one who rejoices over disaster
will not go unpunished.
6 Grandchildren are the crown
of the elderly,
and the pride of sons is their fathers.
7 Excessive speech is not appropriate
on a fool's lips;
how much worse are lies for a ruler.
8 A bribe seems like a magic stone
to its owner;
wherever he turns, he succeeds.
9 Whoever conceals an offense
promotes love,
but whoever gossips about it
separates friends.
10 A rebuke cuts into a perceptive person
more than a hundred lashes into a fool.
11 An evil man seeks only rebellion;
a cruel messenger[f] will be sent
against him.
12 Better for a man to meet a bear robbed
of her cubs
than a fool in his foolishness.
13 If anyone returns evil for good,
evil will never depart from his house.
14 To start a conflict is to release a flood;
stop the dispute before it breaks out.
15 Acquitting the guilty and condemning
the just—
both are detestable to the LORD.
16 Why does a fool have money
in his hand
with no intention of buying wisdom?
17 A friend loves at all times,
and a brother is born for a difficult time.
18 One without sense enters
an agreement[g]
and puts up security for his friend.
19 One who loves to offend loves strife;
one who builds a high threshold
invites injury.
20 One with a twisted mind
will not succeed,
and one with deceitful speech will fall
into ruin.
21 A man fathers a fool
to his own sorrow;
the father of a fool has no joy.
22 A joyful heart is good medicine,
but a broken spirit dries up the bones.

[a]**16:24** Lit *throat* [b]**16:24** Lit *bones* [c]**16:26** Lit *mouth* [d]**16:32** Lit *and ruling over one's spirit* [e]**17:4** Lit *to lips of iniquity*
[f]**17:11** Or *a merciless angel*; Ps 78:49 [g]**17:18** Lit *sense shakes hands*

23 A wicked man secretly takes a bribe
to subvert the course of justice.

24 Wisdom is the focus of the perceptive,
but a fool's eyes roam to the ends
of the earth.

25 A foolish son is grief to his father
and bitterness to the one
who bore him.

26 It is certainly not good to fine
an innocent person,
or to beat a noble for his honesty.[a]

27 The intelligent person restrains
his words,
and one who keeps a cool head[b]
is a man of understanding.

28 Even a fool is considered wise
when he keeps silent,
discerning, when he seals his lips.

18 One who isolates himself pursues
⌊selfish⌋ desires;
he rebels against all sound judgment.

2 A fool does not delight
in understanding,
but only wants to show off
his opinions.[c]

3 When a wicked man comes,
shame does also,
and along with dishonor, disgrace.

4 The words of a man's mouth
are deep waters,
a flowing river, a fountain of wisdom.

5 It is not good to show partiality
to the guilty
by perverting the justice
due the innocent.

6 A fool's lips lead to strife,
and his mouth provokes a beating.

7 A fool's mouth is his devastation,
and his lips are a trap for his life.

8 A gossip's words are like choice food
that goes down
to one's innermost being.[d]

9 The one who is truly lazy in his work
is brother to a vandal.[e]

10 The name of the LORD is
a strong tower;
the righteous run to it
and are protected.[f]

11 A rich man's wealth is
his fortified city;
in his imagination it is like a high wall.

12 Before his downfall a man's heart
is proud,
but before honor comes humility.

13 The one who gives an answer
before he listens—
this is foolishness and disgrace
for him.

14 A man's spirit can endure sickness,
but who can survive a broken spirit?

15 The mind of the discerning
acquires knowledge,
and the ear of the wise seeks it.

16 A gift opens doors[g] for a man
and brings him before the great.

17 The first to state his case seems right
until another comes and cross-
examines him.

18 ⌊Casting⌋ the lot ends quarrels
and separates powerful opponents.

19 An offended brother is
⌊harder to reach⌋[h]
than a fortified city,
and quarrels are like the bars
of a fortress.

20 From the fruit of his mouth
a man's stomach is satisfied;
he is filled with the product of his lips.

21 Life and death are in the power
of the tongue,
and those who love it will eat its fruit.

22 A man who finds a wife finds
a good thing
and obtains favor from the LORD.

23 The poor man pleads,
but the rich one answers roughly.

24 A man with many friends
may be harmed,[i]
but there is a friend who stays closer
than a brother.

[a]**17:26** Or *noble unfairly* [b]**17:27** Lit *spirit* [c]**18:2** Lit *to uncover his heart* [d]**18:8** Lit *to the chambers of the belly* [e]**18:9** Lit *master of destruction* [f]**18:10** Lit *raised high* [g]**18:16** Lit *gift makes room* [h]**18:19** LXX, Syr, Tg, Vg read *is stronger* [i]**18:24** Some LXX mss, Syr, Tg, Vg read *friends must be friendly*

19 Better a poor man who walks
in integrity
than someone who has deceitful lips
and is a fool.

2 Even zeal is not good
without knowledge,
and the one who acts hastily[a] sins.

3 A man's own foolishness leads
him astray,
yet his heart rages
against the LORD.

4 Wealth attracts many friends,
but a poor man is separated
from his friend.

5 A false witness will not
go unpunished,
and one who utters lies
will not escape.

6 Many seek the favor of a ruler,
and everyone is a friend of one
who gives gifts.

7 All the brothers of a poor man
hate him;
how much more do his friends
keep their distance from him!
He may pursue ⌊them with⌋ words,
⌊but⌋ they are not ⌊there⌋.[b]

8 The one who acquires good sense[c]
loves himself;
one who safeguards understanding
finds success.

9 A false witness will not
go unpunished,
and one who utters lies perishes.

10 Luxury is not appropriate for a fool—
how much less for a slave to rule
over princes!

11 A person's insight gives
him patience,
and his virtue is to overlook
an offense.

12 A king's rage is like a lion's roar,
but his favor is like dew on the grass.

13 A foolish son is his father's ruin,
and a wife's nagging is
an endless dripping.

14 A house and wealth are inherited
from fathers,
but a sensible wife is from the LORD.

15 Laziness induces deep sleep,
and a lazy person will go hungry.

16 The one who keeps commands
preserves himself;
one who disregards[d] his ways will die.

17 Kindness to the poor is a loan
to the LORD,
and He will give a reward
to the lender.[e]

18 Discipline your son
while there is hope;
don't be intent on killing him.[f]

19 A person with great anger bears
the penalty;
if you rescue him, you'll have
to do it again.

20 Listen to counsel
and receive instruction
so that you may be wise in later life.[g]

21 Many plans are in a man's heart,
but the LORD's decree will prevail.

22 A man's desire should be loyalty
to the covenant;
better to be a poor man
than a perjurer.

23 The •fear of the LORD leads to life;
one will sleep at night[h] without danger.

24 The slacker buries his hand
in the bowl;
he doesn't even bring it back
to his mouth.

25 Strike a mocker,
and the inexperienced learn
a lesson;
rebuke the discerning,
and he gains knowledge.

26 The one who assaults his father
and evicts his mother
is a disgraceful and shameful son.

27 If you stop listening to instruction,
my son,
you will stray from the words
of knowledge.

[a]**19:2** Lit *who is hasty with feet* [b]**19:7** Hb uncertain in this line [c]**19:8** Lit *acquires a heart* [d]**19:16** Or *despises*, or *treats lightly* [e]**19:17** Lit *to him* [f]**19:18** Lit *don't lift up your soul to his death* [g]**19:20** Lit *in your end* [h]**19:23** Lit *will spend the night satisfied*

28 A worthless witness mocks justice,
and a wicked mouth swallows iniquity.

29 Judgments are prepared for mockers,
and beatings for the backs of fools.

20 Wine is a mocker, beer is a brawler,
and whoever staggers because of them
is not wise.

2 A king's terrible wrath is
like the roaring of a lion;
anyone who provokes him
endangers himself.

3 It is honorable for a man to resolve
a dispute,
but any fool can get himself
into a quarrel.

4 The slacker does not plow
during planting season;[a]
at harvest time he looks,[b] and there is
nothing.

5 Counsel in a man's heart is
deep water;
but a man of understanding
draws it up.

6 Many a man proclaims his own loyalty,
but who can find a trustworthy man?

7 The one who lives with integrity
is righteous;
his children[c] who come after him
will be happy.

8 A king sitting on a throne to judge
sifts out all evil with his eyes.

9 Who can say, "I have kept
my heart pure;
I am cleansed from my sin"?

10 Differing weights
and varying measures[d] —
both are detestable to the LORD.

11 Even a young man is known
by his actions—
by whether his behavior is pure
and upright.

12 The hearing ear and the seeing eye—
the LORD made them both.

13 Don't love sleep, or you will
become poor;
open your eyes, and you'll have
enough to eat.

14 "It's worthless, it's worthless!"
the buyer says,
but after he is on his way, he gloats.

15 There is gold and a multitude
of jewels,
but knowledgeable lips are
a rare treasure.

16 Take his garment,[e]
for he has put up security for a stranger;
get collateral if it is for foreigners.

17 Food gained by fraud is sweet
to a man,
but afterwards his mouth is full
of gravel.

18 Finalize plans through counsel,
and wage war with sound guidance.

19 The one who reveals secrets is
a constant gossip;
avoid someone with a big mouth.

20 Whoever curses his father
or mother—
his lamp will go out in deep darkness.

21 An inheritance gained prematurely
will not be blessed ultimately.

22 Don't say, "I will avenge this evil!"
Wait on the LORD, and He will
rescue you.

23 Differing weights[f] are detestable
to the LORD,
and dishonest scales are unfair.

24 A man's steps are determined
by the LORD,
so how can anyone understand
his own way?

25 It is a trap for anyone to dedicate
something rashly
and later to reconsider his vows.

26 A wise king separates out the wicked
and drives the threshing wheel
over them.

27 A person's breath is the lamp
of the LORD,
searching the innermost parts.[g]

[a]**20:4** Lit *plow in winter* [b]**20:4** Lit *inquires* [c]**20:7** Lit *sons* [d]**20:10** Lit *Stone and stone, measure and measure* [e]**20:16** A debtor's outer garment held as collateral; Dt 24:12–13,17; Jb 22:6 [f]**20:23** Lit *A stone and a stone* [g]**20:27** Lit *the chambers of the belly*

28 Loyalty and faithfulness deliver a king;
through loyalty he maintains
his throne.

29 The glory of young men is
their strength,
and the splendor of old men is
gray hair.

30 Lashes and wounds purge away evil,
and beatings cleanse
the innermost parts.[a]

21 A king's heart is a water channel
in the LORD's hand:
He directs it wherever He chooses.

2 All the ways of a man seem right
to him,
but the LORD evaluates the motives.

3 Doing what is righteous and just
is more acceptable to the LORD
than sacrifice.

4 The lamp[b] that guides the wicked—
haughty eyes and an arrogant heart—
is sin.

5 The plans of the diligent certainly lead
to profit,
but anyone who is reckless
only becomes poor.

6 Making a fortune
through a lying tongue
is a vanishing mist,[c] a pursuit
of death.[d] [e]

7 The violence of the wicked
sweeps them away
because they refuse to act justly.

8 A guilty man's conduct is crooked,
but the behavior of the innocent
is upright.

9 Better to live on the corner of a roof
than to share a house
with a nagging wife.

10 A wicked person desires evil;
he has no consideration[f]
for his neighbor.

11 When a mocker is punished,
the inexperienced become wiser;
when one teaches a wise man,
he acquires knowledge.

12 The Righteous One considers
the house of the wicked;
He brings the wicked to ruin.

13 The one who shuts his ears to the cry
of the poor
will himself also call out
and not be answered.

14 A secret gift soothes anger,
and a covert bribe,[g] fierce rage.

15 Justice executed is a joy
to the righteous
but a terror to those
who practice iniquity.

16 The man who strays from the way
of wisdom
will come to rest
in the assembly of the departed spirits.

17 The one who loves pleasure
will become a poor man;
whoever loves wine and oil will not
get rich.

18 The wicked are a ransom
for the righteous,
and the treacherous, for[h] the upright.

19 Better to live in a wilderness
than with a nagging and hot-
tempered wife.

20 Precious treasure and oil are
in the dwelling of the wise,
but a foolish man consumes them.[i]

21 The one who pursues righteousness
and faithful love
will find life, righteousness,
and honor.

22 The wise conquer a city of warriors
and bring down its mighty fortress.

23 The one who guards his mouth
and tongue
keeps himself out of trouble.

24 The proud and arrogant person,
named "Mocker,"
acts with excessive pride.

25 A slacker's craving will kill him
because his hands refuse to work.
26 He is filled with craving[j] all day long,

[a]**20:30** Lit *beatings the chambers of the belly* [b]**21:4** Some Hb mss, ancient versions read *tillage* [c]**21:6** Or *a breath blown away* [d]**21:6** Some Hb mss, LXX, Vg read *a snare of death* [e]**21:6** Lit *is vanity, ones seeking death* [f]**21:10** Or *favor* [g]**21:14** Lit *a bribe in the bosom* [h]**21:18** Or *in place of* [i]**21:20** Lit *it* [j]**21:26** Lit *He craves a craving*

but the righteous give and don't
hold back.

27 The sacrifice of a wicked person
is detestable—
how much more so
when he brings it
with ulterior motives!

28 A lying witness will perish,
but the one who listens
will speak successfully.

29 A wicked man puts on a bold face,
but the upright man considers his way.

30 No wisdom, no understanding,
and no counsel
⌊will prevail⌋ against the LORD.

31 A horse is prepared for the day
of battle,
but victory comes from the LORD.

22 A good name is to be chosen
over great wealth;
favor is better than silver and gold.

2 The rich and the poor have this
in common:[a]
the LORD made them both.[b]

3 A sensible person sees danger
and takes cover,
but the inexperienced keep going
and are punished.

4 The result of humility is •fear
of the LORD,
along with wealth, honor, and life.

5 There are thorns and snares
on the path of the crooked;
the one who guards himself stays
far from them.

6 Teach a youth about the way
he should go;
even when he is old he will not depart
from it.

7 The rich rule over the poor,
and the borrower is a slave
to the lender.

8 The one who sows injustice
will reap disaster,
and the rod of his fury
will be destroyed.

9 A generous person[c] will be blessed,
for he shares his food with the poor.

10 Drive out a mocker, and conflict
goes too;
then lawsuits and dishonor will cease.

11 The one who loves a pure heart
and gracious lips—the king is his friend.

12 The LORD's eyes keep watch
over knowledge,
but He overthrows the words
of the treacherous.

13 The slacker says, "There's a lion outside!
I'll be killed in the streets!"

14 The mouth of the forbidden woman is
a deep pit;
a man cursed by the LORD will fall
into it.

15 Foolishness is tangled up in the heart
of a youth;
the rod of discipline will drive it away
from him.

16 Oppressing the poor
to enrich oneself,
and giving to the rich—both lead
only to poverty.

Words of the Wise

17 Listen closely,[d] pay attention
to the words of the wise,
and apply your mind
to my knowledge.

18 For it is pleasing if you keep them
within you
and if[e] they are constantly
on your lips.

19 I have instructed you today—
even you—
so that your confidence may be
in the LORD.

20 Haven't I written for you thirty sayings[f]
about counsel and knowledge,

21 in order to teach you true
and reliable words,
so that you may give
a dependable report[g]
to those who sent you?

22 Don't rob a poor man
because he is poor,

[a]**22:2** Lit *poor meet* [b]**22:2** Lit *all* [c]**22:9** Lit *Good of eye* [d]**22:17** Lit *Stretch out your ear* [e]**22:18** Or *you; let them be*, or *you, so that* [f]**22:20** Text emended; one Hb tradition reads *you previously*; alt Hb tradition reads *you excellent things*; LXX, Syr, Vg read *you three times* [g]**22:21** Lit *give dependable words*

and don't crush the oppressed
at the •gate,
23 for the LORD will take up their case
and will plunder those
who plunder them.

24 Don't make friends
with an angry man,[a]
and don't be a companion of a hot-tempered man,
25 or you will learn his ways
and entangle yourself in a snare.

26 Don't be one of those
who enter agreements,[b]
who put up security for loans.
27 If you have no money to pay,
even your bed will be taken
from under you.

28 Don't move an ancient property line
that your fathers set up.

29 Do you see a man skilled in his work?
He will stand in the presence of kings.
He will not stand in the presence
of unknown men.

23 When you sit down to dine
with a ruler,
consider carefully what[c] is before you,
2 and stick a knife in your throat
if you have a big[d] appetite;
3 don't desire his choice food,
for that food is deceptive.

4 Don't wear yourself out to get rich;
stop giving your attention to it.
5 As soon as your eyes fly to it,
it disappears,
for it makes wings for itself
and flies like an eagle to the sky.

6 Don't eat a stingy person's bread,[e]
and don't desire his choice food,
7 for as he thinks within himself,
so he is.
"Eat and drink," he says to you,
but his heart is not with you.
8 You will vomit the little you've eaten
and waste your pleasant words.

9 Don't speak to[f] a fool,
for he will despise the insight
of your words.

10 Don't move an ancient property line,
and don't encroach on the fields
of the fatherless,
11 for their Redeemer is strong,
and He will take up their case
against you.

12 Apply yourself to instruction
and listen to words of knowledge.

13 Don't withhold correction
from a youth;
if you beat him with a rod,
he will not die.
14 Strike him with a rod,
and you will rescue his life
from •Sheol.

15 My son, if your heart is wise,
my heart will indeed rejoice.
16 My innermost being will cheer
when your lips say what is right.

17 Don't be jealous of sinners;
instead, always •fear the LORD.
18 For then you will have a future,
and your hope will never fade.

19 Listen, my son, and be wise;
keep your mind on the right course.
20 Don't associate with those who drink
too much wine,
or with those who gorge themselves
on meat.
21 For the drunkard and the glutton
will become poor,
and grogginess will clothe ⌊them⌋
in rags.

22 Listen to your father who gave you life,
and don't despise your mother
when[g] she is old.
23 Buy—and do not sell—truth,
wisdom, instruction,
and understanding.
24 The father of a righteous son
will rejoice greatly,
and one who fathers a wise son
will delight in him.
25 Let your father and mother have joy,
and let her who gave birth to you
rejoice.

26 My son, give me your heart,
and let your eyes observe my ways.
27 For a prostitute is a deep pit,

[a] **22:24** Lit *with a master of anger* [b] **22:26** Lit *who shakes hands* [c] **23:1** Or *who* [d] **23:2** Lit *you are the master of an* [e] **23:6** Lit *eat bread of an evil eye* [f] **23:9** Lit *in the ears of* [g] **23:22** Or *because*

and a forbidden woman is
a narrow well;
28 indeed, she sets an ambush
like a robber
and increases those among men
who are unfaithful.

29 Who has woe? Who has sorrow?
Who has conflicts?
Who has complaints?
Who has wounds for no reason?
Who has red eyes?
30 Those who linger over wine,
those who go looking for mixed wine.
31 Don't gaze at wine when it is red,
when it gleams in the cup
and goes down smoothly.
32 In the end it bites like a snake
and stings like a viper.
33 Your eyes will see strange things,
and you will say absurd things.[a]
34 You'll be like someone sleeping
out at sea
or lying down on the top
of a ship's mast.
35 "They struck me, but[b] I feel no pain!
They beat me, but I didn't know it!
When will I wake up?
I'll look for another ⌊drink⌋."

24 Don't envy evil men
or desire to be with them,
2 for their hearts plan violence,
and their words stir up trouble.

3 A house is built by wisdom,
and it is established by understanding;
4 by knowledge the rooms are filled
with every precious
and beautiful treasure.

5 A wise warrior is better
than a strong one,
and a man of knowledge than one
of strength;
6 for you should wage war
with sound guidance—
victory comes with many counselors.

7 Wisdom is inaccessible to[c] a fool;
he does not open his mouth
at the •gate.
8 The one who plots evil
will be called a schemer.
9 A foolish scheme is sin,
and a mocker is detestable to people.

10 If you do nothing in a difficult time,
your strength is limited.
11 Rescue those being taken off to death,
and save those stumbling
toward slaughter.
12 If you say, "But we didn't know
about this,"
won't He who weighs hearts
consider it?
Won't He who protects
your life know?
Won't He repay a person according to
his work?

13 Eat honey, my son, for it is good,
and the honeycomb is sweet
to your palate;
14 realize that wisdom is the same
for you.
If you find it, you will have a future,
and your hope will never fade.

15 Don't set an ambush, wicked man,
at the camp[d] of the righteous man;
don't destroy his dwelling.
16 Though a righteous man falls
seven times,
he will get up,
but the wicked will stumble into ruin.

17 Don't gloat when your enemy falls,
and don't let your heart rejoice
when he stumbles,
18 or the LORD will see, be displeased,
and turn His wrath away from him.

19 Don't worry because of evildoers,
and don't envy the wicked.
20 For the evil have no future;
the lamp of the wicked will be put out.

21 My son, •fear the LORD, as well as
the king,
and don't associate with rebels,[e]
22 for their destruction
will come suddenly;
who knows what disaster these two
can bring?

23 These ⌊sayings⌋ also
belong to the wise:
It is not good to show partiality
in judgment.
24 Whoever says to the guilty,
"You are innocent"—

[a]**23:33** Or *will speak perversities* or *inverted things* [b]**23:35** LXX, Syr, Tg, Vg read *me," you will say, "But* [c]**24:7** Lit *is too high for* [d]**24:15** A rural encampment or home not under the protection of a city [e]**24:21** Or *those given to change*

people will curse him, and tribes
will denounce him;
25 but it will go well with those
who convict the guilty,
and a generous blessing will come
to them.

26 He who gives an honest answer
gives a kiss on the lips.

27 Complete your outdoor work,
and prepare your field;
afterwards, build your house.

28 Don't testify against your neighbor
without cause.
Don't deceive with your lips.
29 Don't say, "I'll do to him what he did
to me;
I'll repay the man for what
he has done."

30 I went by the field of a slacker
and by the vineyard of a man
lacking sense.
31 Thistles had come up everywhere,
weeds covered the ground,
and the stone wall was ruined.
32 I saw, and took it to heart;
I looked, and received instruction:
33 a little sleep, a little slumber,
a little folding of the arms
to rest,
34 and your poverty will come
like a robber,
your need, like a bandit.

Hezekiah's Collection

25 These too are proverbs of Solomon,
which the men of Hezekiah,
king of Judah, copied.

2 It is the glory of God to conceal
a matter
and the glory of kings to investigate
a matter.
3 As the heaven is high and the earth
is deep,
so the hearts of kings cannot
be investigated.

4 Remove impurities from silver,
and a vessel will be produced[a]
for a silversmith.
5 Remove the wicked
from the king's presence,
and his throne will be established
in righteousness.

6 Don't brag about yourself
before the king,
and don't stand in the place
of the great;
7 for it is better for him to say to you,
"Come up here!"
than to demote you in plain view
of a noble.[b]

8 Don't take a matter to court hastily.
Otherwise, what will
you do afterwards
if your opponent[c] humiliates you?
9 Make your case with your opponent[c]
without revealing another's secret;
10 otherwise, the one who hears
will disgrace you,
and you'll never live it down.[d]

11 A word spoken at the right time
is like golden apples on a silver tray.[e]
12 A wise correction to a receptive ear
is like a gold ring or an ornament
of gold.

13 To those who send him,
a trustworthy messenger
is like the coolness of snow
on a harvest day;
he refreshes the life of his masters.

14 The man who boasts about a gift
that does not exist
is like clouds and wind without rain.
15 A ruler can be persuaded
through patience,
and a gentle tongue can break a bone.
16 If you find honey, eat only
what you need;
otherwise, you'll get sick from it
and vomit.
17 Seldom set foot
in your neighbor's house;
otherwise, he'll get sick of you
and hate you.

18 A man giving false testimony
against his neighbor
is like a club, a sword, or a sharp arrow.
19 Trusting an unreliable person in a time
of trouble
is like a rotten tooth or a faltering foot.

20 Singing songs to a troubled heart

[a]**25:4** Lit *will come out*; Ex 32:24 [b]**25:7** Lit *you before a noble whom your eyes see* [c]**25:8,9** Or *neighbor* [d]**25:10** Lit *and your evil report will not turn back* [e]**25:11** Or *like apples of gold in settings of silver*

is like taking off clothing on a cold day,
or like ⌊pouring⌋ vinegar on soda.[a]
21 If your enemy is hungry, give him food
to eat,
and if he is thirsty, give him water
to drink;
22 for you will heap coals on his head,
and the LORD will reward you.

23 The north wind produces rain,
and a backbiting tongue, angry looks.
24 Better to live on the corner of a roof
than in a house shared
with a nagging wife.
25 Good news from a distant land
is like cold water to a parched throat.[b]
26 A righteous person who yields
to the wicked
is like a muddied spring
or a polluted well.
27 It is not good to eat too much honey,
or to seek glory after glory.
28 A man who does not control his temper
is like a city whose wall
is broken down.

26 Like snow in summer and rain
at harvest,
honor is inappropriate for a fool.
2 Like a flitting sparrow
or a fluttering swallow,
an undeserved curse goes nowhere.
3 A whip for the horse, a bridle
for the donkey,
and a rod for the backs of fools.
4 Don't answer a fool according to
his foolishness,
or you'll be like him yourself.
5 Answer a fool according to
his foolishness,
or he'll become wise in his own eyes.
6 The one who sends a message
by a fool's hand
cuts off his own feet
and drinks violence.
7 A proverb in the mouth of a fool
is like lame legs that hang limp.
8 Giving honor to a fool
is like binding a stone in a sling.[c]
9 A proverb in the mouth of a fool
is like a stick with thorns,
brandished by[d] the hand
of a drunkard.
10 The one who hires a fool, or who hires
those passing by,
is like an archer
who wounds everyone.
11 As a dog returns to its vomit,
so a fool repeats his foolishness.
12 Do you see a man who is wise
in his own eyes?
There is more hope for a fool
than for him.

13 The slacker says, "There's a lion
in the road—
a lion in the public square!"
14 A door turns on its hinge,
and a slacker, on his bed.
15 The slacker buries his hand
in the bowl;
he is too weary to bring it to his mouth.
16 In his own eyes, a slacker is wiser
than seven men
who can answer sensibly.

17 A passerby who meddles in a quarrel
that's not his
is like one who grabs a dog
by the ears.
18 Like a madman who throws
flaming darts and deadly arrows,
19 so is the man who deceives
his neighbor
and says, "I was only joking!"

20 Without wood, fire goes out;
without a gossip, conflict dies down.
21 As charcoal for embers and wood
for fire,
so is a quarrelsome man
for kindling strife.
22 A gossip's words are like choice food
that goes down to
one's innermost being.[e]

23 Smooth[f] lips with an evil heart
are like glaze on an earthen vessel.
24 A hateful person disguises himself
with his speech
and harbors deceit within.
25 When he speaks graciously,
don't believe him,
for there are seven abominations
in his heart.
26 Though his hatred is concealed
by deception,

[a]**25:20** Lit *natron* or *sodium carbonate* [b]**25:25** Or *a weary person* [c]**26:8** A stone bound in a sling would not release and could harm the person using the sling. A modern equivalent is jamming a cork in a gun barrel. [d]**26:9** Lit *thorn that goes up into* [e]**26:22** Lit *to the chambers of the belly* [f]**26:23** LXX; MT reads *Burning*

his evil will be revealed
in the assembly.
27 The one who digs a pit will fall
into it,
and whoever rolls a stone—
it will come back on him.
28 A lying tongue hates those it crushes,
and a flattering mouth causes ruin.

27 Don't boast about tomorrow,
for you don't know what a day
might bring.

2 Let another praise you, and not
your own mouth—
a stranger, and not your own lips.

3 A stone is heavy and sand, a burden,
but aggravation from a fool
outweighs them both.

4 Fury is cruel, and anger is a flood,
but who can withstand jealousy?

5 Better an open reprimand
than concealed love.

6 The wounds of a friend
are trustworthy,
but the kisses of an enemy
are excessive.
7 A person who is full tramples
on a honeycomb,
but to a hungry person,
any bitter thing is sweet.

8 A man wandering from his home
is like a bird wandering from its nest.

9 Oil and incense bring joy
to the heart,
and the sweetness of a friend is better
than self-counsel.[a]
10 Don't abandon your friend
or your father's friend,
and don't go to your brother's house
in your time of calamity;
better a neighbor nearby
than a brother far away.

11 Be wise, my son, and bring my heart
joy,
so that I can answer anyone
who taunts me.

12 The sensible see danger
and take cover;
the foolish keep going
and are punished.

13 Take his garment,[b]
for he has put up security
for a stranger;
get collateral if it is for foreigners.[c]

14 If one blesses his neighbor
with a loud voice early
in the morning,
it will be counted as a curse to him.

15 An endless dripping on a rainy day
and a nagging wife are alike.
16 The one who controls her controls
the wind
and grasps oil with his right hand.

17 Iron sharpens iron,
and one man sharpens another.[d]
18 Whoever tends a fig tree will eat
its fruit,
and whoever looks after his master
will be honored.

19 As the water reflects the face,
so the heart reflects the person.

20 •Sheol and •Abaddon are
never satisfied,
and people's eyes are never satisfied.

21 Silver is ⌊tested⌋ in a crucible,
gold in a smelter,
and a man, by the praise he receives.[e]

22 Though you grind a fool
in a mortar with a pestle
along with grain,
you will not separate his foolishness
from him.
23 Know well the condition of your flock,
and pay attention to your herds,
24 for wealth is not forever;
not even a crown lasts for all time.
25 When hay is removed
and new growth appears
and the grain from the hills
is gathered in,
26 lambs will provide your clothing,
and goats, the price of a field;
27 there will be enough goat's milk
for your food—
food for your household
and nourishment for your servants.

[a]**27:9** LXX reads *heart, but the soul is torn up by affliction* [b]**27:13** A debtor's outer garment held as collateral; Dt 24:12–13; Am 2:8 [c]**27:13** Lit *a foreign woman* [d]**27:17** Lit *and a man sharpens his friend's face* [e]**27:21** Lit *The crucible for silver and the smelter for gold, and a man for a mouth of praise.*

28 The wicked flee when no one
is pursuing ⌊them⌋,
but the righteous are as bold as a lion.

2 When a land is in rebellion, it has
many rulers,
but with a discerning
and knowledgeable person,
it endures.

3 A destitute leader[a] who oppresses
the poor
is like a driving rain that leaves
no food.

4 Those who reject the law
praise the wicked,
but those who keep the law battle
against them.

5 Evil men do not understand justice,
but those who seek the LORD
understand everything.

6 Better a poor man who lives
with integrity
than a rich man who distorts right
and wrong.[b]

7 A discerning son keeps the law,
but a companion of gluttons humiliates
his father.

8 Whoever increases his wealth
through excessive interest
collects it for one who is kind
to the poor.

9 Anyone who turns his ear
away from hearing the law—
even his prayer is detestable.

10 The one who leads the upright
into an evil way
will fall into his own pit,
but the blameless will inherit
what is good.

11 A rich man is wise in his own eyes,
but a poor man who has discernment
sees through him.

12 When the righteous triumph,
there is great rejoicing,[c]
but when the wicked come to power,
people hide themselves.

13 The one who conceals his sins
will not prosper,
but whoever confesses
and renounces them
will find mercy.

14 Happy is the one who is always
reverent,
but one who hardens his heart falls
into trouble.

15 A wicked ruler over a helpless people
is like a roaring lion or a charging bear.

16 A leader who lacks understanding
is very oppressive,
but one who hates unjust gain
prolongs his life.

17 A man burdened by bloodguilt[d]
will be a fugitive until death.
Let no one help him.

18 The one who lives with integrity
will be helped,
but one who distorts right and wrong[e]
will suddenly fall.

19 The one who works his land
will have plenty of food,
but whoever chases fantasies
will have his fill of poverty.

20 A faithful man will have
many blessings,
but one in a hurry to get rich
will not go unpunished.

21 It is not good to show partiality—
yet a man may sin for a piece of bread.

22 A greedy man[f] is in a hurry for wealth;
he doesn't know that poverty
will come to him.

23 One who rebukes a person
will later find more favor
than one who flatters[g] with his tongue.

24 The one who robs his father or mother
and says, "That's no sin,"
is a companion to a man who destroys.

25 A greedy person provokes conflict,
but whoever trusts in the LORD
will prosper.

26 The one who trusts in himself[h] is
a fool,
but one who walks in wisdom
will be safe.

[a]**28:3** LXX reads *A wicked man* [b]**28:6** Lit *who twists two ways* [c]**28:12** Lit *glory* [d]**28:17** Lit *the blood of a person*
[e]**28:18** Lit *who is twisted regarding two ways* [f]**28:22** Lit *A man with an evil eye* [g]**28:23** Lit *is smooth* [h]**28:26** Lit *his heart*

27 The one who gives to the poor
will not be in need,
but one who turns his eyes away[a]
will receive many curses.

28 When the wicked come to power,
people hide,
but when they are destroyed,
the righteous flourish.

29 One who becomes stiff-necked,
after many reprimands
will be broken suddenly—
and without a remedy.

2 When the righteous flourish,
the people rejoice,
but when the wicked rule,
people groan.

3 A man who loves wisdom brings joy
to his father,
but one who consorts with prostitutes
destroys his wealth.

4 By justice a king brings stability
to a land,
but a man ⌊who demands⌋
"contributions"[b]
demolishes it.

5 A man who flatters[c] his neighbor
spreads a net for his feet.

6 An evil man is caught by sin,
but the righteous one sings and rejoices.

7 The righteous person knows
the rights[d] of the poor,
but the wicked one does not understand these concerns.

8 Mockers inflame a city,
but the wise turn away anger.

9 If a wise man goes to court with a fool,
there will be ranting and raving
but no resolution.[e]

10 Bloodthirsty men hate
an honest person,
but the upright care about him.[f]

11 A fool gives full vent to his anger,[g]
but a wise man holds it in check.

12 If a ruler listens to lies,
all his servants will be wicked.

13 The poor and the oppressor have this
in common:[h]
the LORD gives light to the eyes of both.

14 A king who judges the poor
with fairness—
his throne will be established forever.

15 A rod of correction imparts wisdom,
but a youth left to himself[i]
is a disgrace to his mother.

16 When the wicked increase,
rebellion increases,
but the righteous will see their downfall.

17 Discipline your son, and he will give
you comfort;
he will also give you delight.

18 Without revelation[j] people run wild,
but one who keeps the law
will be happy.

19 A servant cannot be disciplined
by words;
though he understands,
he doesn't respond.

20 Do you see a man who speaks too soon?
There is more hope for a fool
than for him.

21 A slave pampered from his youth
will become arrogant[k] later on.

22 An angry man stirs up conflict,
and a hot-tempered man[l]
increases rebellion.

23 A person's pride will humble him,
but a humble spirit will gain honor.

24 To be a thief's partner is to hate oneself;
he hears the curse but will not testify.[m]

25 The fear of man is a snare,
but the one who trusts in the LORD
is protected.[n]

26 Many seek a ruler's favor,
but a man receives justice
from the LORD.

27 An unjust man is detestable
to the righteous,
and one whose way is upright
is detestable to the wicked.

[a]**28:27** Lit *who shuts his eyes* [b]**29:4** The Hb word usually refers to offerings in worship. [c]**29:5** Lit *is smooth on* [d]**29:7** Lit *justice* [e]**29:9** Lit *rest* [f]**29:10** Or *person, and seek the life of the upright* [g]**29:11** Lit *spirit* [h]**29:13** Lit *oppressor meet* [i]**29:15** Lit *youth sent away*; Jb 39:5; Is 16:2 [j]**29:18** Lit *vision* [k]**29:21** Hb obscure [l]**29:22** Lit *a master of rage* [m]**29:24** When a call for witnesses was made public, anyone with information who did not submit his testimony was under a curse; Lv 5:1. [n]**29:25** Lit *raised high*

The Words of Agur

30 The words of Agur son of Jakeh.
The oracle.[a]
The man's oration to Ithiel, to Ithiel
and Ucal:[b]

2 I am the least intelligent of men,[c]
and I lack man's ability
to understand.
3 I have not gained wisdom,
and I have no knowledge
of the Holy One.
4 Who has gone up to heaven
and come down?
Who has gathered the wind
in His hands?
Who has bound up the waters
in a cloak?
Who has established all the ends
of the earth?
What is His name,
and what is the name of His Son—
if you know?
5 Every word of God is pure;[d]
He is a shield to those who take refuge
in Him.
6 Don't add to His words,
or He will rebuke you, and you will be
proved a liar.

7 Two things I ask of You;
don't deny them to me before I die:
8 Keep falsehood and deceitful words
far from me.
Give me neither poverty nor wealth;
feed me with the food I need.
9 Otherwise, I might have too much
and deny You, saying,
"Who is the LORD?"
or I might have nothing and steal,
profaning[e] the name of my God.

10 Don't slander a servant to his master,
or he will curse you, and you will
become guilty.

11 There is a generation that curses
its father
and does not bless its mother.
12 There is a generation that is pure
in its own eyes,
yet is not washed from its filth.
13 There is a generation—how haughty
its eyes
and pretentious its looks.[f]
14 There is a generation whose teeth
are swords,
whose fangs are knives,
devouring the oppressed from the land
and the needy from among mankind.

15 The leech has two daughters:
Give, Give.
Three things are never satisfied;
four never say, "Enough!":
16 •Sheol; a barren womb;
earth, which is never satisfied
with water;
and fire, which never says, "Enough!"

17 As for the eye that ridicules a father
and despises obedience to a mother,
may ravens of the valley pluck it out
and young vultures eat it.

18 Three things are beyond me;
four I can't understand:
19 the way of an eagle in the sky,
the way of a snake on a rock,
the way of a ship at sea,
and the way of a man
with a young woman.

20 This is the way of an adulteress:
she eats and wipes her mouth
and says, "I've done nothing wrong."

21 The earth trembles under three things;
it cannot bear up under four:
22 a servant when he becomes king,
a fool when he is stuffed with food,
23 an unloved woman when she marries,
and a serving girl when she ousts
her lady.

24 Four things on earth are small,
yet they are extremely wise:
25 the ants are not a strong people,
yet they store up their food
in the summer;
26 hyraxes are not a mighty people,
yet they make their homes in the cliffs;
27 locusts have no king,
yet all of them march in ranks;
28 a lizard[g] can be caught in your hands,
yet it lives in kings' palaces.

[a]**30:1** Or *The burden*, or *Jakeh from Massa*; Pr 31:1 [b]**30:1** Hb uncertain. Sometimes read with different word division as *oration: I am weary, God, I am weary, God, and I am exhausted*, or *oration: I am not God, I am not God, that I should prevail.* LXX reads *My son, fear my words and when you have received them repent. The man says these things to the believers in God, and I pause.* [c]**30:2** Lit *I am more stupid than a man* [d]**30:5** Lit *refined*, like metal [e]**30:9** Lit *grabbing* [f]**30:13** Lit *and its eyelids lifted up* [g]**30:28** Or *spider*

29 Three things are stately in their stride,
even four are stately in their walk:
30 a lion, which is mightiest among beasts
and doesn't retreat before anything,
31 a strutting rooster,[a] a goat,
and a king at the head of his army.[b]
32 If you have been foolish
by exalting yourself,
or if you've been scheming,
put your hand over your mouth.
33 For the churning of milk
produces butter,
and twisting a nose draws blood,
and stirring up anger produces strife.

The Words of Lemuel

31 The words of King Lemuel,
an oracle[c] that his mother taught him:

2 What ⌊should I say⌋, my son?
What, son of my womb?
What, son of my vows?
3 Don't spend your energy on women
or your efforts on those
who destroy kings.
4 It is not for kings, Lemuel,
it is not for kings to drink wine
or for rulers ⌊to desire⌋ beer.
5 Otherwise, they[d] will drink,
forget what is decreed,
and pervert justice for all
the oppressed.[e]
6 Give beer to one who is dying,
and wine to one whose life is bitter.
7 Let him drink so that he can forget
his poverty
and remember his trouble no more.
8 Speak up[f] for those who have no voice,[g]
for the justice of all
who are dispossessed.[h]
9 Speak up,[f] judge righteously,
and defend the cause of[i] the oppressed
and needy.

In Praise of a Capable Wife

10 Who can find a capable wife?[j]
She is far more precious than jewels.[k]
11 The heart of her husband trusts in her,
and he will not lack anything good.
12 She rewards him with good, not evil,
all the days of her life.
13 She selects wool and flax[l]
and works with willing hands.
14 She is like the merchant ships,
bringing her food from far away.
15 She rises while it is still night
and provides food for her household
and portions[m] for her servants.
16 She evaluates a field and buys it;
she plants a vineyard
with her earnings.[n]
17 She draws on her strength[o]
and reveals that her arms are strong.
18 She sees that her profits are good,
and her lamp never goes out at night.
19 She extends her hands
to the spinning staff,
and her hands hold the spindle.
20 Her hands reach[p] out to the poor,
and she extends her hands to the needy.
21 She is not afraid for her household
when it snows,
for all in her household
are doubly clothed.[q]
22 She makes her own bed coverings;
her clothing is fine linen and purple.
23 Her husband is known
at the city •gates,
where he sits among the elders
of the land.
24 She makes and sells linen garments;
she delivers belts[r] to the merchants.
25 Strength and honor are her clothing,
and she can laugh at the time to come.
26 She opens her mouth with wisdom,
and loving instruction[s] is
on her tongue.
27 She watches over the activities
of her household
and is never idle.[t]
28 Her sons rise up and call her blessed.
Her husband also praises her:
29 "Many women[u] are capable,
but you surpass them all!"
30 Charm is deceptive and beauty
is fleeting,
but a woman who •fears the LORD
will be praised.
31 Give her the reward of her labor,[v]
and let her works praise her
at the city gates.

[a]**30:31** Or *a greyhound* [b]**30:31** LXX reads *king haranguing his people* [c]**31:1** Or *of Lemuel, king of Massa* [d]**31:5** Lit *he* [e]**31:5** Lit *sons of affliction* [f]**31:8,9** Lit *Open your mouth* [g]**31:8** Lit *who are mute* [h]**31:8** Lit *all the sons of passing away* [i]**31:9** Lit *and justice for* [j]**31:10** Or *a wife of quality,* or *a wife of good character*; Ru 2:1; 3:11 [k]**31:10** Vv. 10–31 form an •acrostic in Hb. [l]**31:13** Plant from which linen is made [m]**31:15** Or *tasks* [n]**31:16** Or *vineyard by her own labors* [o]**31:17** Lit *She wraps strength around her like a belt* [p]**31:20** Lit *Her hand reaches* [q]**31:21** LXX, Vg; MT reads *are dressed in scarlet* [r]**31:24** Or *sashes* [s]**31:26** Or *and the teaching of kindness* [t]**31:27** Lit *and does not eat the bread of idleness* [u]**31:29** Lit *daughters* [v]**31:31** Lit *the fruit of her hands*

Holman CSB Bullet Notes

HCSB Bullet Notes are one of the unique features of the Holman Christian Standard Bible ®. These notes explain frequently used biblical words or terms. These "bullet" words (for example: •abyss) are normally marked with a bullet only on their first occurrence in a chapter of the biblical text. However, certain important or easily misunderstood terms, such as •Jews or •slaves, will have more than one bullet per chapter. Other frequently used words, like •gate, are marked with bullets only where the use of the word fits the definitions given below. A few words in footnotes, like •acrostic, also have a bullet.

Abaddon	Either the grave or the realm of the dead
Abba	The Aramaic word for "father"
abyss	The *bottomless pit* or *the depths* (of the sea); the prison for Satan and the demons
acrostic	A device in Hebrew poetry in which each verse begins with a successive letter of the Hebrew alphabet
advocate	(see "Counselor/advocate")
Almighty	(see "God Almighty")
Alpha and Omega	The first and last letters of the Greek alphabet; it is used to refer to God the Father in Rv 1:8 and 21:6, and to Jesus, God the Son, in Rv 22:13.
Amen	The transliteration of a Hebrew word signifying that something is certain, valid, truthful, or faithful; it is often used at the end of biblical songs, hymns, and prayers.
Asia	A Roman province that is now part of modern Turkey; it did not refer to the modern continent of Asia.
asleep	A term used in reference to those who have died
atone/ atonement	A theological term for God's provision to deal with human sin. In the OT, it primarily means purification. In some contexts forgiveness, pardon, expiation, propitiation, or reconciliation is included. The basis of atonement is substitutionary sacrifice offered in faith. The OT sacrifices were types and shadows of the great and final sacrifice of Jesus on the cross.
Baal	A fertility god who was the main god of the Canaanite religion and the god of rain and thunderstorms; also the Hebrew word meaning "lord," "master," "owner," or "husband"
Beelzebul	A term of slander, which was variously interpreted "lord of flies," "lord of dung," or "ruler of demons"; 2 Kg 1:2; Mk 3:22
burnt offering(s)	Or *holocaust*, an offering completely burned to ashes; it was used in connection with worship, seeking God's favor, expiating sin, or averting judgment.
cause the downfall of/ causes to sin	The Greek word *skandalizo* has a root meaning of "snare" or "trap," but has no real English counterpart.
centurion	A Roman officer who commanded about 100 soldiers
Cephas	The Aramaic word for *rock*; it is parallel to the Greek word *petros* from which the English name Peter is derived; Jn 1:42; 1 Co 1:12.
cherubim	A class of winged angels, associated with the throne of God, who function as guardians and who prevented Adam and Eve from returning to the garden of Eden
chief priest(s)	A group of Jewish temple officers that included the highpriest, captain of the temple, temple overseers, and treasurers

company/regiment Or *cohort*, a Roman military unit that numbered as many as 600 men

completely destroy (see "set apart for destruction/completely destroy")

Counselor/advocate The Greek word *parakletos* means one called alongside to help, counsel, or protect; it is used of the Holy Spirit in Jn and in 1 Jn.

cubit An OT measurement of distance that equaled about 18 inches

Cush/Cushite The lands of the Nile in southern Egypt, including Nubia and Northern Sudan; the people who lived in that region

Decapolis Originally a federation of 10 Gentile towns east of the Jordan River

denarius A small silver Roman coin, which was equal to a day's wage for a common laborer

divination An attempt to foresee future events or discover hidden knowledge by means of physical objects such as water, arrows, flying birds, or animal livers

engaged Jewish engagement was a binding agreement that could only be broken by divorce.

everyone/human race Literally, *sons of man* or *sons of Adam*

fear(s) God or the LORD/the fear of the LORD No single English word conveys every aspect of the word *fear* in this phrase. The meaning includes worshipful submission, reverential awe, and obedient respect to the covenant-keeping God of Israel.

firstfruits The agricultural products harvested first and given to God as an offering; also the first of more products to come

fellowship sacrifice(s) or offering(s) An animal offering was given to maintain and strengthen a person's relationship with God. It was not required as a remedy for impurity or sin but was an expression of thanksgiving for various blessings. An important function of this sacrifice was to provide meat for the priests and the participants in the sacrifice; it was also called the *peace offering* or the *sacrifice of well-being.*

gate(s) The center for community discussions, political meetings, and trying of court cases

Gittith Perhaps an instrument, musical term, tune from Gath, or song for the grape harvest

God Almighty The Hebrew word is *El Shaddai*; *El* = "God," but the meaning of *Shaddai* is disputed; traditionally it is translated "Almighty".

Hades The Greek word for the place of the dead; it corresponds to the Hebrew word *Sheol*.

Hallelujah! Or *Praise the LORD!;* it literally means *Praise Yah!* (a shortened form of *Yahweh*)

headquarters/palace The Latin word *Praetorium* was used by Greek writers for the residence of the Roman governor; it may also refer to military headquarters, the imperial court, or the emperor's guard.

Hebrew Or *Aramaic*; the translation of this word is debated since some claim Aramaic was commonly spoken in Palestine during NT times. More recently others claim that Hebrew was the spoken language.

hell/hellfire Greek *Gehenna*; Aramaic for Valley of Hinnom on the south side of Jerusalem; it was formerly a place of human sacrifice and in NT times a place for the burning of garbage; the place of final judgment for those rejecting Christ.

Herod	The name of the Idumean family ruling Palestine from 37 B.C. to A.D. 95; the main rulers from this family mentioned in the NT are:
Herod I	(37 B.C.–4 B.C.) also known as Herod the Great; built the great temple in Jerusalem and massacred the male babies in Bethlehem
Herod Antipas	(4 B.C.–A.D. 39) son of Herod the Great; ruled one-fourth of his father's kingdom (Galilee and Perea); killed John the Baptist and mocked Jesus
Agrippa I	(A.D. 37–44) grandson of Herod the Great; beheaded James the apostle and imprisoned Peter
Agrippa II	(A.D. 52–c. 95) great-grandson of Herod the Great; heard Paul's defense
Herodians	Political supporters of Herod the Great and his family
Higgaion	Perhaps a musical notation, a device denoting a pause in an instrumental interlude, or a murmuring harp tone
high place(s)	An ancient place of worship most often associated with pagan religions, usually built on an elevated location
horn	A symbol of power based on the strength of animal horns
Hosanna	A term of praise derived from the Hebrew word for *save*
Hosts/hosts	Military forces consisting of God's angels, sometimes including the sun, moon, and stars, and occasionally, Israel
human race	(see "everyone")
I assure you	This is a phrase used only by Jesus to testify to the certainty and importance of His words; in Mt, Mk and Lk it is literally *Amen, I say to you,* and in Jn it is literally *Amen, amen, I say to you.*
Jew(s)	In Jn the term *Jews* usually indicates those in Israel who were opposed to Jesus, particularly the Jewish authorities in Jerusalem who led the nation.
Leviathan	Or *twisting one*; a mythological sea serpent or dragon associated with the chaos at creation. Sometimes it is applied to an animal such as a crocodile.
life/soul	The Greek word *psyche* can be translated life or soul.
mankind	Literally *sons of man* or *sons of Adam*
Mary Magdalene	Or *Mary of Magdala*; Magdala was probably on the western shore of the Sea of Galilee, north of Tiberias.
Maskil	From a Hebrew word meaning *to be prudent or to have insight*; possibly a contemplative, instructive, or wisdom psalm
men	Literally *sons of man* or *sons of Adam*
mercy seat	Or *place of atonement*; the gold lid on the ark of the covenant, first used in the tabernacle and later in the temple
Messiah	Or *the Christ*; the Greek word *Christos* means "the anointed one".
Miktam	A musical term of uncertain meaning, possibly denoting a plaintive style
Most High	The Hebrew word is *Elyon.* It is often used with other names of God, such as *El (God)* or *Yahweh (LORD)*; it is used to refer to God as the supreme being.
Mount of Olives	A mountain east of Jerusalem, across the Kidron Valley
Mystery	Transliteration of the Greek word *mysterion*; a secret hidden in the past but now revealed
Nazarene	A person from Nazareth; growing up in Nazareth was an aspect of the Messiah's humble beginnings; Jn 1:46.

Negev	An arid region in the southern part of Israel; the Hebrew word means "south".
offend	(see "cause the downfall of/ cause to sin")
offspring/ seed	This term is used literally or metaphorically to refer to plants or grain, sowing or harvest, male reproductive seed, human children or physical descendants, and also to spiritual children or to Christ (Gl 3:16).
One and Only	Or *one of a kind*, or *incomparable*, or *only begotten*; the Greek word can refer to someone's only child such as in Lk 7:12; 8:42; 9:38. It can also refer to someone's special child as in Heb 11:17.
oracle	A prophetic speech of a threatening or menacing character, often against the nations
overseer(s)	Or *elder(s)*, or *bishop(s)*
palace	(see "headquarters/palace")
Passover	The Israelite festival celebrated on the fourteenth day of the first month in the early spring. It was a celebration of the deliverance of the Israelites from Egypt, commemorating the final plague on Egypt when the firstborn were killed.
people	Literally *sons of man* or *sons of Adam*
perverted men	(see "wicked men/perverted men")
Pharisee(s)	In Judaism a religious sect that followed the whole written and oral law
Pilate	Pontius Pilate was governor of the province of Judea A.D. 26–36.
Pit	Either the grave or the realm of the dead
proconsul	The chief Roman government official in a senatorial province who presided over Roman court hearings
proselyte	A person from another race or religion who went through a prescribed ritual to become a Jew
Rabbi	The Hebrew word *Rabbi* means *my great one*; it is used of a recognized teacher of the Scriptures.
Rahab	Or *boisterous one*, a mythological sea serpent or dragon defeated at the time of creation. Scripture sometimes uses the name metaphorically to describe Egypt.
Red Sea	Literally *Sea of Reeds*
regiment	(see "company/regiment")
sackcloth	Garment made of poor quality material and worn as a sign of grief and mourning
sacred bread	Literally *bread of presentation*; 12 loaves, representing the 12 tribes of Israel, put on the table in the holy place in the tabernacle, and later in the temple. The priests ate the previous week's loaves; Ex 25:30; 29:32; Lv 24:5-9.
Sadducee(s)	In Judaism a religious sect that followed primarily the first 5 books of the OT (Torah or Pentateuch)
Samaritan(s)	People of mixed, Gentile/ Jewish ancestry who lived between Galilee and Judea and were hated by the Jews
Sanhedrin	The supreme council of Judaism with 70 members, patterned after Moses' 70 elders
scribe(s)	A professional group in Judaism that copied the law of Moses and interpreted it, especially in legal cases
seed	(see "offspring/seed")
Selah	A Hebrew word whose meaning is uncertain; various interpretations include: (1) a musical notation, (2) a pause for silence, (3) a signal for worshipers to fall prostrate on the ground, (4) a term for the worshipers to call out, and (5) a word meaning "forever"

set apart for destruction/ completely destroy	In Canaan or its neighboring countries, this was the destruction during war of a city, its inhabitants, and their possessions, including livestock.
Sheminith	A musical term meaning instruments or on the *instrument of eight strings*
Sheol	A Hebrew word for either the grave or the realm of the dead
sin offering(s)	Or *purification offering*; the *sin offering* was the most important OT sacrifice for cleansing from impurities. It provided purification from sin and certain forms of ceremonial uncleanness.
slave	The strong Greek word *doulos* cannot be accurately translated in English by "servant" or "bond servant"; the HCSB translates this word as "slave," not out of insensitivity to the legitimate concerns of modern English speakers, but out of a commitment to accurately convey the brutal reality of the Roman empire's inhumane institution as well as the ownership called for by Christ.
Son of Man	The most frequent title Jesus used for Himself; Dn 7:13
song of ascents	Probably the songs pilgrims sang as they traveled the roads going up to worship in Jerusalem; Pss 120–134
soul	(see "life/soul")
stumble	(see "cause the downfall of/ cause to sin")
synagogue	A place where the Jewish people met for prayer, worship and teaching of the Scriptures
tabernacle	Or *tent*, or *shelter*; terms used for temporary housing
take offense	(see "cause the downfall of/ cause to sin")
tassel	Fringe put on the clothing of devout Jews to remind them to keep the law; Nm 15:37-41
temple complex	In the Jerusalem temple, the complex included the sanctuary (the holy place and the holy of holies), at least 4 courtyards (for priests, Jewish men, Jewish women, and Gentiles), numerous gates, and several covered walkways.
testimony	A reference to either the Mosaic law in general or to a specific section of the law, the Ten Commandments, which were written on stone tablets and placed in the ark of the covenant (also called the ark of the testimony)
Unleavened Bread	A seven-day festival celebrated in conjunction with the Passover; Ex 12:1-20
walk	A term often used in a figurative way to mean "way of life" or "behavior"
wicked men/ perverted men	Literally *sons of Belial*; the basic meaning of *Belial* in Hebrew is "worthless".
wise men	The Greek word is *magoi*; the English word "Magi" is based on a Persian word. They were eastern sages who observed the heavens for signs and omens.
woman	When used in direct address, "Woman" was not a term of disrespect but of honor.
world	The organized Satanic system that is opposed to God and hostile to Jesus and His followers. The non-Christian culture including governments, educational systems, and businesses
wormwood	A small shrub used as a medicinal herb, noted for its bitter taste
Yah	(see "Yahweh")
Yahweh	Or *The LORD*; the personal name of God in Hebrew; "Yah" is the shortened form of the name.

Hear It!
Believe It!
Connect It!

Accepting Jesus as your Savior is the most important decision you can make. What does the Bible say about becoming a Christian?

God loves you.

Love consists in this: not that we loved God, but that He loved us.

1 John 4:10

Sin separates you from God.

Sin is choosing your way instead of God's way.

Sin separates people from God.

For all have sinned and fall short of the glory of God.

Romans 3:23

Everyone sins—even people who have already become Christians.

But God will forgive you and help you obey Him if you ask.

If we confess our sins, He is faithful and righteous to forgive us our sins and to cleanse us from all unrighteousness.

1 John 1:9

God sent Jesus so you could have eternal life.

God sent Jesus so you would not have to die for your sin. Jesus died on the cross, He was buried, and He rose from the dead.

For God loved the world in this way: He gave His One and Only Son, so that everyone who believes in Him will not perish but have eternal life.

John 3:16

Want to know more?

Just remember the ABCs of Becoming a Christian. You can find them at the front of this Bible. Follow the directions at the bottom of that page to discover how to become a Christian.

God's Holy Spirit will help you know when you are ready to become a Christian. If it is time for you to become a Christian, pray a prayer like the one below.

Dear God,

I know I have sinned and that my sin separates me from You. I am sorry for my sin. Please forgive me. I believe Jesus died on the cross for me so my sin can be forgiven. I believe Jesus rose from the dead and is alive.

I ask Jesus to come into my life to be my Savior and Lord. I will obey You and live for You the rest of my life. Thank You for loving and saving me from my sin.

Amen.

Now you can be baptized to show others that you are a Christian, participate in the Lord's Supper to remember what Jesus did for you, and tell others that Jesus is your Savior and Lord.

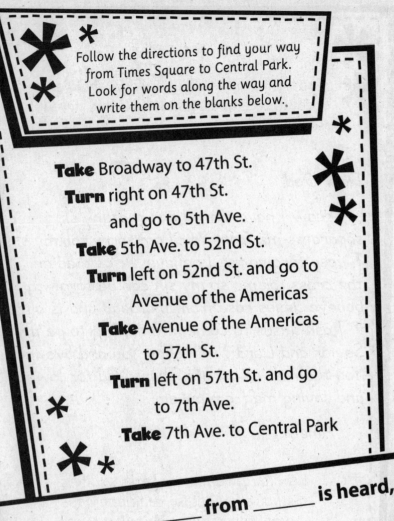

Follow the directions to find your way from Times Square to Central Park. Look for words along the way and write them on the blanks below.

Take Broadway to 47th St.

Turn right on 47th St. and go to 5th Ave.

Take 5th Ave. to 52nd St.

Turn left on 52nd St. and go to Avenue of the Americas

Take Avenue of the Americas to 57th St.

Turn left on 57th St. and go to 7th Ave.

Take 7th Ave. to Central Park

_____ _____ _____ from _____ is heard, _____ what ___ heard _____ _____ the _____ about _____.

Romans 10:17

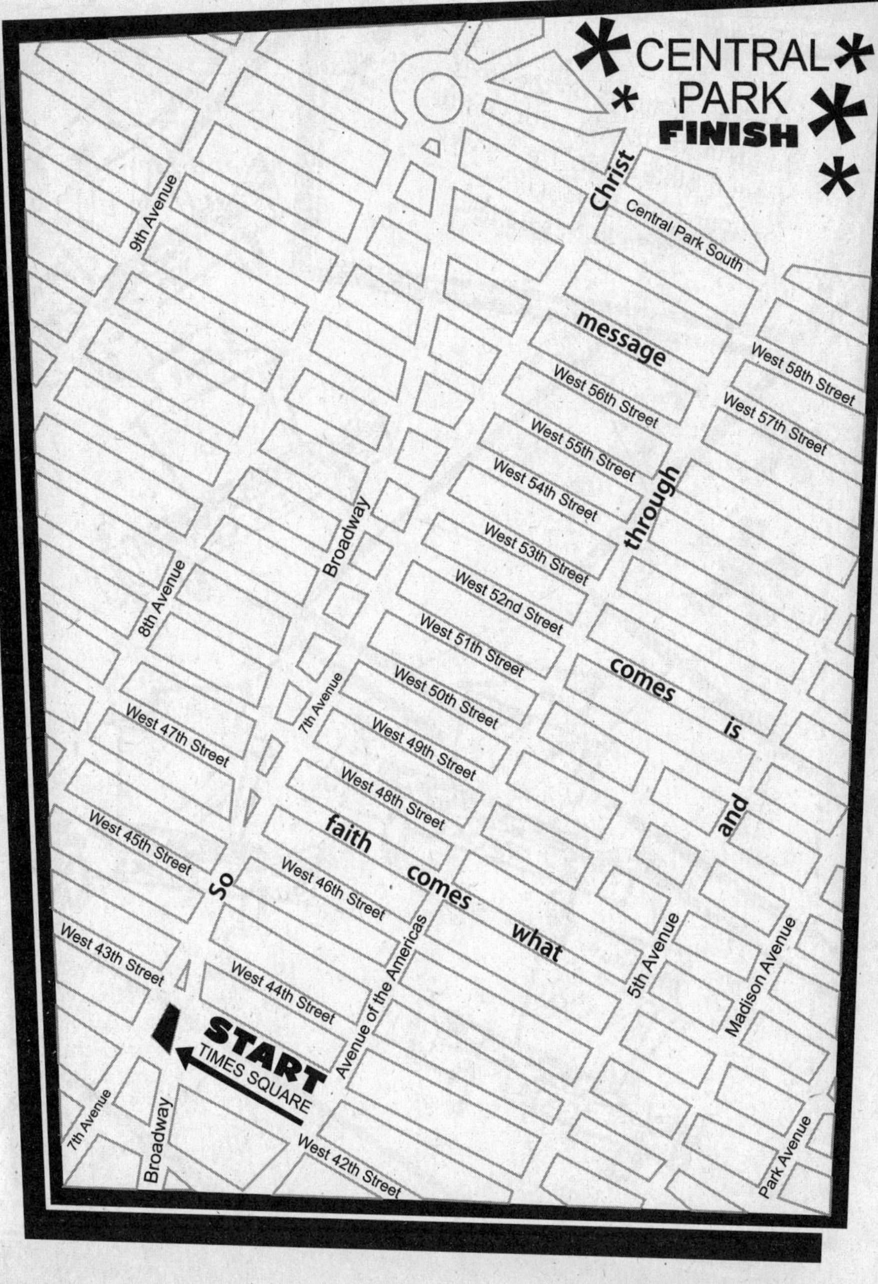
CENTRAL PARK
FINISH
Christ
Central Park South
message
West 58th Street
West 57th Street
West 56th Street
West 55th Street
West 54th Street
through
West 53th Street
West 52nd Street
West 51th Street
comes
is
West 50th Street
West 49th Street
and
West 48th Street
West 47th Street
faith
comes
what
So
West 45th Street
West 46th Street
West 44th Street
West 43th Street
West 42th Street
9th Avenue
8th Avenue
Broadway
7th Avenue
Avenue of the Americas
5th Avenue
Madison Avenue
Park Avenue
7th Avenue
Broadway
START
TIMES SQUARE

Use the numbers on the taxis to fill in the blanks with words from a Bible verse. Then check your work by looking up the verse in this Bible.

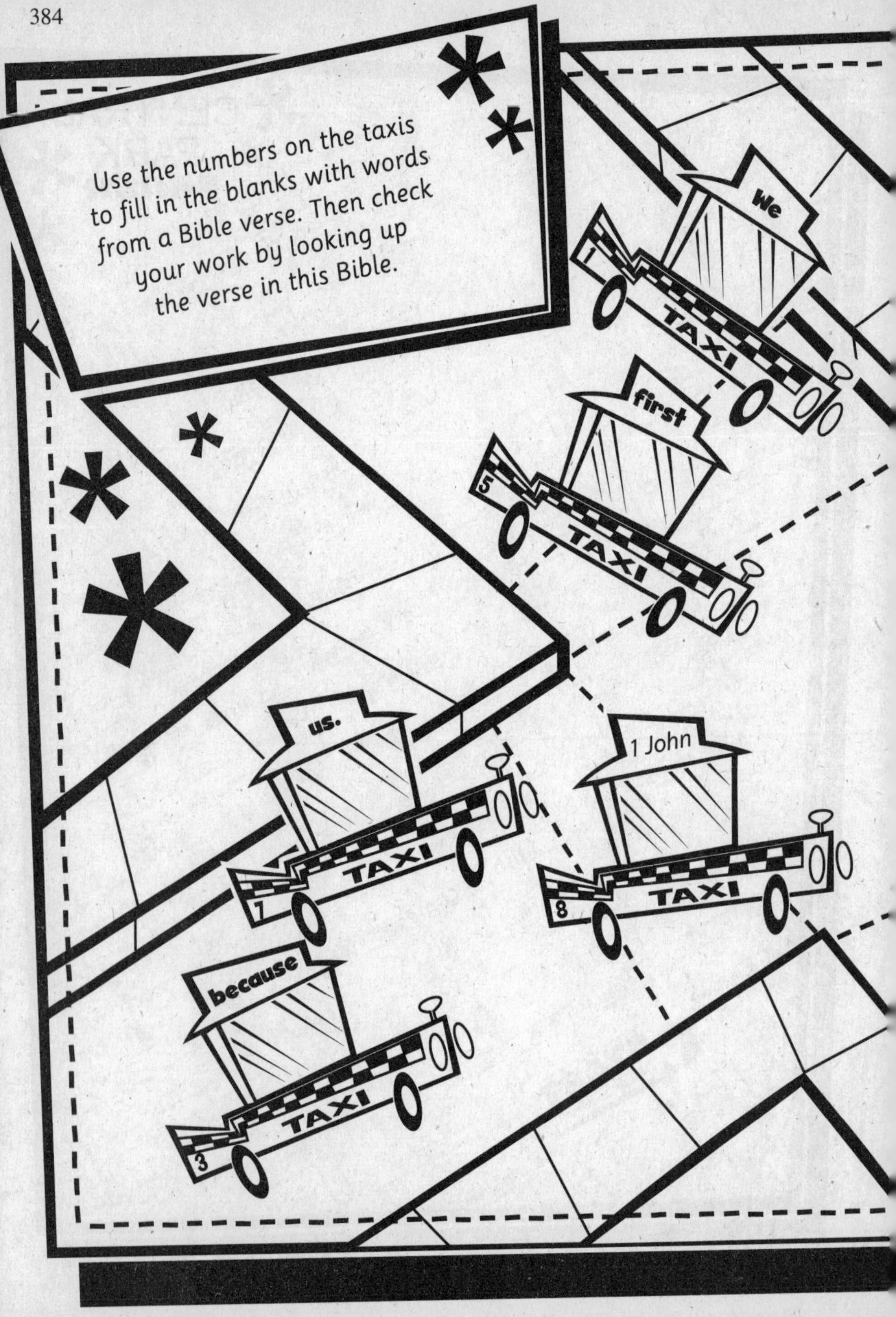

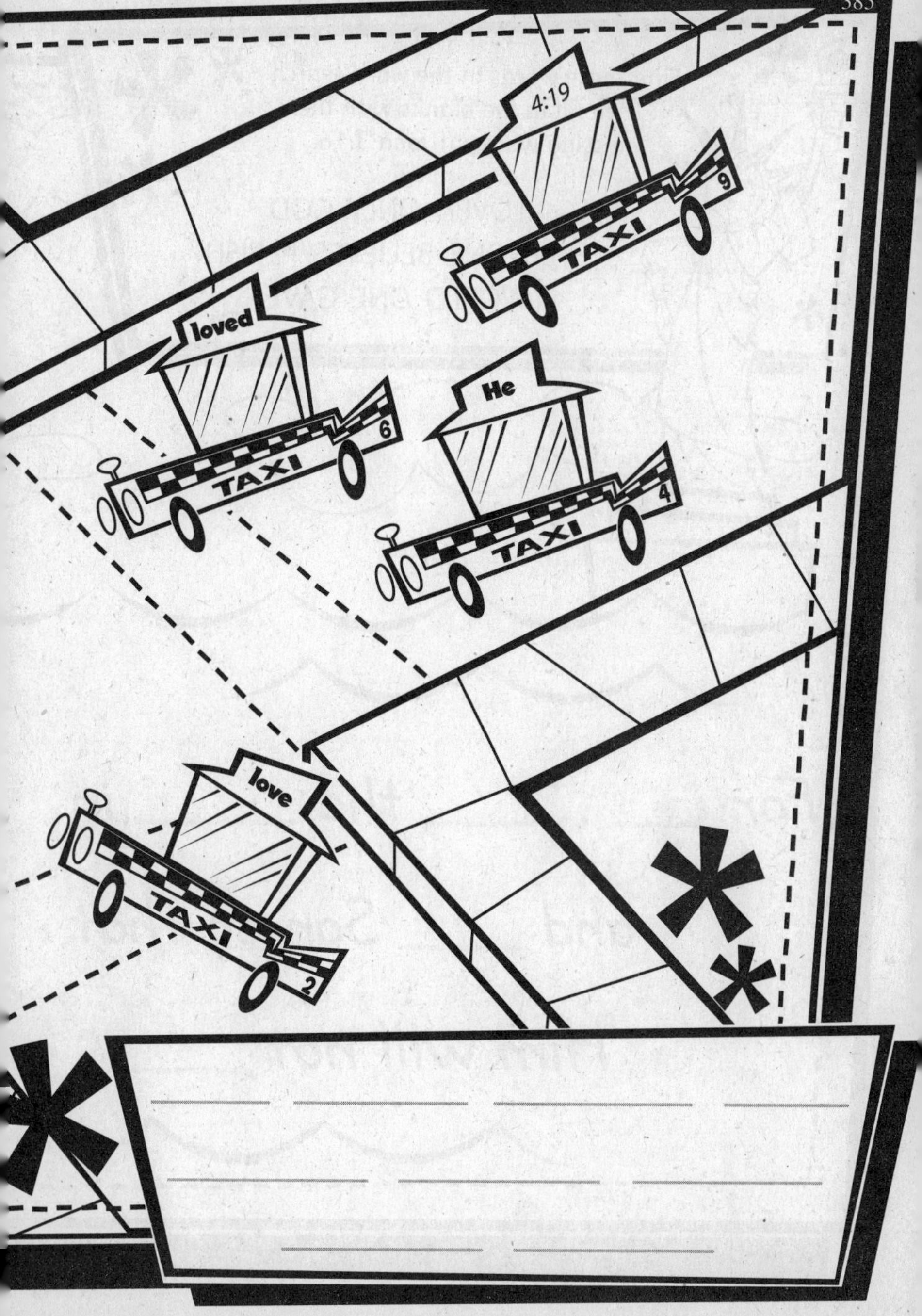
4:19
TAXI
9
loved
TAXI
6
He
TAXI
4
love
TAXI
2

Find these words in the word search.
Then fill in the blanks with the
missing words of John 3:16.

LOVED ONLY GOD
EVERYONE BELIEVES PERISH
WORLD ONE GAVE

For ____ ____ the ______ in

and ____ Son, so that

Him will not ______

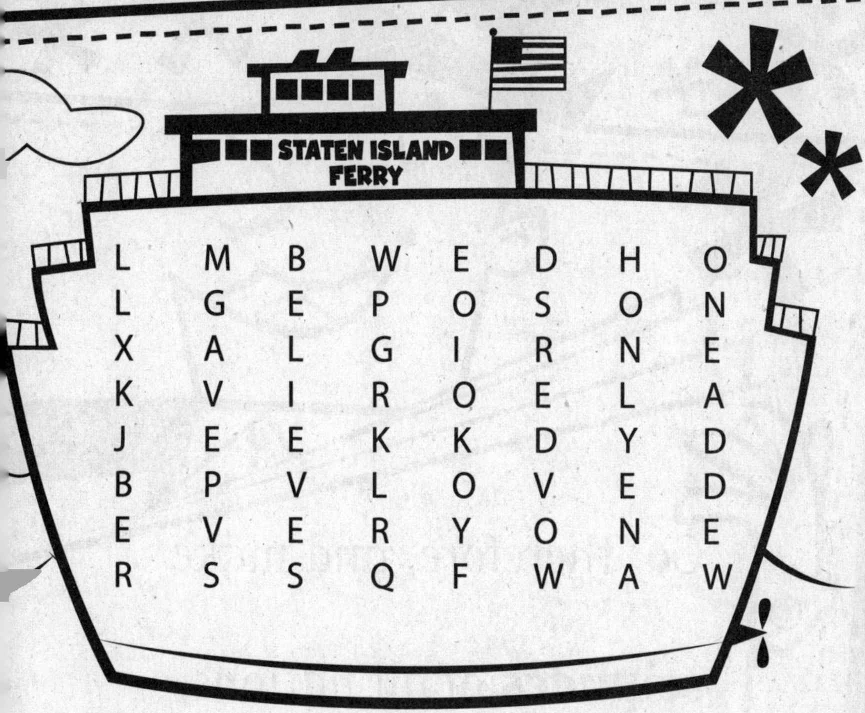

L	M	B	W	E	D	H	O
L	G	E	P	O	S	O	N
X	A	L	G	I	R	N	E
K	V	I	R	O	E	L	A
J	E	E	K	K	D	Y	D
B	P	V	L	O	V	E	D
E	V	E	R	Y	O	N	E
R	S	S	Q	F	W	A	W

this way: He ____ His ____

______ who ______ in

but have eternal life.

John 3:16

Go, therefore, and make
sciplides of all nations,
pitzgabin them in the name
of the **heFrat** and of the
Son and of the **Hylo Sirtip,**

Oops! Someone forgot to proofread the articles before the newspaper was printed. Can you correct the mistakes and complete this verse?

teaching them to **versebo** everything I have **mocdemand** you. And remember, I am with you **yaswal,** to the end of the age. *Matthew 28:19-20*

Look for hidden words as you walk through Central Park. Write the hidden words in the blanks provided. Then check your work by looking up the verse in this Bible.

must be
done
Your every
action
1 Corinthians
16:13-14
be brave and strong.
with love.
HOT
DOGS
TRASH

NOTES
NEW YORK
HOT DOGS
HOT
DOG